Fundamentals of

Financial accounting

The Willard J. Graham Series
in Accounting

Consulting Editor
ROBERT N. ANTHONY *Harvard University*

Fundamentals of Financial accounting

GLENN A. WELSCH
College of Business Administration
The University of Texas at Austin

and

ROBERT N. ANTHONY
Graduate School of Business Administration
Harvard University

Revised edition 1977

RICHARD D. IRWIN, INC. Homewood, Illinois 60430
Irwin-Dorsey Limited Georgetown, Ontario L7G 4B3

Revised Edition

First Printing, February 1977

ISBN 0-256-01907-X
Library of Congress Catalog Card No. 76-28891

Printed in the United States of America

To our wives,
Irma and Katherine

Preface

This Second Edition retains all of the features favorably commented upon by numerous faculty members who used the First Edition. It has been updated in all respects and approximately 80 percent of the assignment material has been replaced or revised. Additional problems contribute a measure of greater depth and analytical substance.

There has been some rearrangement of topics in certain chapters. In addition, the original Chapter 5 on revenue recognition, matching expenses with revenues, and information processing has been revised and divided into two separate chapters. The chapter on consolidated statements, originally Chapter 14, has been shifted to be the last chapter (Chapter 17) to provide more flexibility for those who desire to omit or de-emphasize it.

All of the teaching and student aids have been revised and retained. The Instructor's Manual has been revised and some additional evaluation materials added.

Many accounting instructors believe that it is sound pedagogy to divide the first course in accounting into two parts, the first semester or quarter focusing on financial accounting and the second on management accounting. Most texts, however, are not arranged so that such an approach is feasible with a single text.

This volume and its companion, *Fundamentals of Management Accounting,* are designed to overcome these problems. They provide material for a fully coordinated first course. As their titles indicate, this volume deals with the fundamentals of financial accounting, and its companion with the fundamentals of management accounting. Each volume can be used either for a one-semester or a one-quarter course. Both are designed to provide maximum flexibility for the instructor in the selection and order of materials for the classroom. They emphasize those aspects of accounting we believe essential for interpretation and use of accounting information. Mechanical and procedural details are minimized, while the conceptual, measurement, and communication aspects are emphasized.

This book is an introduction to financial accounting, which has as its primary subject the communication of relevant financial information to external parties. We strongly believe that a certain level of knowledge of the accounting model, the measurement processes involved, the data classifications, and terminology, is essential to the interpretation and effective use of financial statements and we have provided the necessary information in this volume. The key to sound use of financial statements is to understand what they do and do not say, the measurement approaches used, and the standards observed in their development. This is the case both for students who will continue their study of accounting and for those who will not. The materials are arranged to meet the requirements of a wide range of academic institutions and curricula.

This volume represents a significant departure from the traditional financial accounting textbook. A number of topics not traditionally covered in an elementary book have been included. In our judgment, much of the traditional material is essential; however, the recent thrusts and changes in financial accounting make it imperative that certain significant topics be accorded comprehensive treatment. This volume is unique because it avoids superficial treatment when it focuses on these new directions with special emphasis on concepts, rationale, measurement, and reporting. Certain traditional procedural topics are presented in appendixes should coverage of them be desired.

The primary features of the book and the instructional materials that accompany it are as follows:

At the outset the characteristics of the environment in which the accounting process operates is emphasized.

Accounting is viewed as an information processing model designed to enhance communication between the entity and the users of its financial reports.

The discussions emphasize concepts, standards, and generally accepted accounting principles as the rationale for the way certain things are done in accounting.

Throughout the chapters, the measurement approaches used in accounting and in reporting to decision makers are emphasized.

At the outset, the student is presented with a comprehensive description of the end products of the financial accounting process—the financial statements. Thus, the student learns what the reporting goals are before being introduced to the ways in which those goals are attained.

Throughout, the focus is on the corporation rather than on the sole proprietorship or the partnership. Actual case examples are utilized. As a consequence, income taxes, dividends, earnings per share, capital stock, the APB Opinions, and the FASB Statements are covered.

Relevant topics, not ordinarily treated in a first course, are discussed. These include cash flow, present value, consolidated statements, purchase versus pooling, statement of changes in financial position (both working capital and cash bases), compensating balances, price-level effects, and current value.

Some chapters are divided into *Parts* to provide flexibility in the selection of materials, and in making daily assignments that cover separable parts of the chapter.

One or more *Appendixes* follow some of the chapters. These appendixes focus on the clerical and mechanical aspects of the accounting process such as special journals, subsidiary ledgers, payrolls, and petty cash. Separation in appendixes facilitates their exclusion, or order of selection, without affecting the continuity of the course.

These features are of particular importance to nonaccounting majors since the first semester will be their only exposure to the fundamentals of financial accounting. For example, most of the external financial statements coming to the attention of the nonaccounting majors, both in school and in real life, will be consolidated statements. Similarly, an understanding of the effects of inflation on financial information is essential in these times to the interpretation of reported results.

The subject matter of the 17 chapters and 8 appendixes that comprise this volume has been arranged in what we believe to be a pedagogically sound sequence; nevertheless, considerable rearrangements can be made if the instructor so desires. Each chapter has a summary and almost all have a demonstration case, with a suggested solution. The purpose of the demonstration cases is to tie together the various subtopics discussed in the chapter. Following each chapter are study materials classified as (*a*) discussion questions, (*b*) short exercises (suitable for homework, class illustrations, and examinations), and (*c*) comprehensive problems and cases. Each of these groups of study materials is arranged to follow the topical sequence of the chapter.

In addition to the text itself, a wide selection of supplementary materials are available for students and for the instructor.

Answers to questions such as how much time should be spent on each chapter, how much homework should be required, and what materials should be omitted, depend on the objectives of the particular course, the time constraints, and the backgrounds of the students. This volume presents the maximum amount of material that can ordinarily be covered in a one-semester undergraduate course. Therefore, some choices usually must be made by the instructor. As mentioned above, we have arranged the topical materials to permit maximum flexibility in selecting among various options and in giving varying topical emphasis to fit practically all situations. Appendixes, parts of chapters, and even entire chapters may be omitted without adversely affecting the continuity of the course. The Instructor's Manual includes comments and suggestions that are particularly helpful in selecting among a number of possible options.

The list of students and faculty members to whom the authors feel a sense of gratitude for ideas and suggestions is too long to enumerate here. With respect to this volume, we are particularly grateful to the following individuals who devoted considerable time in discussions, reviewing parts of the manuscript, and testing materials:

Professors John Simon, Northern Illinois University; Phyllis Barker, Indiana State University; Bill Bailey, University of California at Los Angeles; Allen Bizzell, University of Texas; Gary Cunningham, Virginia Polytechnic Institute and State University; Lewis Davidson, University of North Carolina; Tom Harrison, University of Texas; Morley Lemon, University of Illinois; and Larry Tomassini, University of Texas; and to graduate students Roy Bukstein, Scott Ikenberry, Chuck Inman, Ronny Ross, Bob Sharp, Patti Smith, Beverly Spikes, and Dewey Ward. I especially wish to recognize the valuable editorial suggestions provided by Jacqueline Well and Kathy Anderson, graduate students at the University of Texas. The exceptional contribution of Margaret Whatley, MPA candidate, by way of critiques of subject matter, editorial suggestions, and organization of the essential tasks involved was appreciated.

Our thanks to the American Institute of Certified Public Accountants, American Accounting Association, and the authors identified by citations, for permission to quote from their publications and to Carborundum Company, Westinghouse Electric Corporation, and Clark Equipment Company for materials from their annual reports.

And, finally, sincere appreciation to I. L. Grimes, Jack Young, Bill Barnes, and the editors and staff at the Irwin Company who worked so diligently in putting the manuscript together. And perhaps the most important debt of gratitude is owed to Dick Irwin for suggesting and encouraging us to collaborate in developing these two volumes.

Suggestions and comments on the text and the related materials are solicited.

January 1977

GLENN A. WELSCH
ROBERT N. ANTHONY

Contents

1

Perspectives—the environment of accounting

PURPOSE OF THE CHAPTER

The objective of this book and its companion volume, *Fundamentals of Management Accounting,** is to develop your knowledge of, and your ability to use, accounting information. This volume, on **financial accounting,** focuses on the role of accounting information in the decision-making processes of parties external to the business; that is, owners, investors, potential investors, creditors, and the public at large. The second volume, on **management accounting,** focuses on the role of accounting information in the decision-making processes of managers with responsibilities inside the organization. Whether you ultimately become an owner, a manager, an investor, or a creditor, or even if your interest in an organization is only that of a concerned citizen, an understanding of accounting will significantly enhance your competence as a decision maker. As you study these two volumes you will develop an understanding of how accounting information influences resource-allocation decisions in all types of organizations: profit-making enterprises, nonprofit endeavors, governmental entities, and social programs. In practically all organizations, success depends in large part on the quality of the resource-allocation decisions that are made. Accounting information, in the broad sense, is used to aid in the decision-making process and to measure the results after the decisions are made and implemented.

---

* Robert N. Anthony and Glenn A. Welsch, *Fundamentals of Management Accounting* (Homewood, Ill.: Richard D. Irwin, Inc., 1977).

The purpose of this chapter is to present a broad perspective of accounting and the environment (i.e., the surroundings) in which it operates. We will focus on those features of the environment that bear directly on, and strongly influence, accounting. We also will seek to explain the basic role of accounting in the decision-making process and in the measurement of the financial results, irrespective of the particular type of endeavor.

A COMPLEX ENVIRONMENT

In many, perhaps most, aspects of life, we are associated with social, political, and economic organizations, such as businesses, churches, fraternal organizations, political parties, states, counties, schools, environmental groups (both public and private), chambers of commerce, and professional associations. Many of these organizations are complex and pose critical problems on which decisions must be made. The future quality of our society depends in large measure upon the collective decisions of the managers of organizations. These organizations are essential to the workings of a society; indeed, they constitute much of what we call "society." Although those organizations should be motivated primarily by service to the "public interest," it must be recognized that they are subject to manipulation by self-interests and, perhaps more importantly, that some of them constitute a drag on the society because they are inefficient, lack high purpose, and sometimes take actions that do not serve total society well.

Fundamental to a dynamic and successful society is the ability of each organization to measure and report its accomplishments, to undergo critical self-analysis, and, by means of sound decisions, to renew and grow so that the individual organization and societal objectives are best served. Essentially, society, and the various organizations that comprise it, thrives in direct proportion to the efficiency with which it allocates scarce resources: human talent, materials, services, and capital. To accomplish these broad goals, organizations and persons interested in specific organizations need information about the resources that the organization controls and how resources are generated and used. Accounting information is designed to meet these needs.

A monetary system provides one way for the measurement and communication of the flow of resources in and out of an organization. In a monetary system, the unit of exchange (dollars in our case) is the common denominator of measurement, the medium of exchange, and a store of value. Thus, it provides a basis for expressing, in large measure, the available resources and the resource flows of both the society as a whole and of the various organizations that comprise it. Accounting is directly concerned with measuring and reporting available resources and their flow. It provides monetary measurement of inputs (resources received) and outputs (goods produced and services rendered), and, as a consequence, it measures the efficiency of organizational performance. It also measures the available resources held and the claims against those resources.

Accounting measures the resources and resource flows of organizations within a society in terms of the monetary unit of that society. Thus, accounting uses the monetary system of each country within which it operates. This is one of the critical problems in accounting—the conversion of financial amounts from one monetary system to another monetary system in measuring resources and resource flows for multinational activities. Since accounting measures and reports financial resources in terms of the society's monetary unit, it is based on what is called the **unit-of-measure assumption.** The common denominator or yardstick used for accounting measurements in the United States is the dollar; the assumption is that the dollar is a useful measuring unit.[1]

ACCOUNTING DEFINED

Accounting focuses on the **measurement** and **reporting,** in monetary terms, of the flows of resources into (inflows) and out of (outflows) an organization, of the resources controlled by the organization, and of the claims against those resources. In doing this, accounting collects, processes, evaluates, and reports certain information. In addition, accounting involves broad judgmental and interpretative roles in the reporting and use of financial results. Accounting also measures, in monetary terms, the efficiency with which an organization uses the scarce resources available to it for carrying out its objectives.

Accounting serves those that use the information it provides in three, related ways:

1. Accounting provides information that is helpful in making decisions. Most important decisions, irrespective of the type of endeavor involved, are based, in part, upon complex financial or monetary considerations. **Accounting provides an important information base and a particular analytical orientation that help the decision maker assess the potential financial implications and potentials of various alternatives that are being considered.** The primary role of accounting, then, is to aid decision making.

2. Accounting reports the results of past decisions. Once decisions are made and implementation starts, critical and often subtle financial effects generally happen. These financial effects often are critical to the success of the endeavor. Thus, they must be continuously measured and

---

[1] The exchange unit (dollars) changes in purchasing power due to the effects of inflation and deflation; simply, the dollar does not always command the same amount of *real* goods. Since the dollar is the common denominator (the yard-stick) in the accounting process, as we shall see in Chapter 16, a special and complex problem is posed by inflation and deflation.

reported so that the decision maker can be appropriately informed of continuing and new problems, and of successes, over time. **Accounting provides a continuing measurement of the financial effects of a series of decisions already made, the results of which are communicated to the decision maker by means of periodic financial statements.**

3. **Accounting keeps track of a wide range of items to meet the scorekeeping and safeguarding responsibilities imposed on all organizations.** These include: how much cash is available for use; how much customers owe the company; what debts are owed by the organization; what items are owned, such as machinery and office equipment; and inventory levels.

We have said that accounting measures the resources and resource flows of an organization. Each such organization is called an **entity** for accounting purposes. In order to measure resources and resource flows, a careful identification of the entity must be made.

One of the essentials of any measurement process is a precise definition of specifically what is to be measured. Examples of specific things to be measured are the population of California, the rainfall in Michigan, the voter registrations in New York, or the bank deposits in Texas (each for a stipulated time). Similarly, in the measurement of resources and resource flows, accounting requires precise definition of the **specific entity** for which monetary or financial data are to be collected, measured, and reported. When a specific entity is carefully defined, such as the Adams Company, it is often referred to as an **accounting entity.** The whole nation is a specific entity, so is each business unit, and so are individual persons. In any measurement scheme, the definition of that which is to be measured often involves difficult problems. For example, in measuring the population of California should the amount include service personnel? college students? jail inmates? long-term visitors? hotel guests? Similarly, in defining an accounting entity, there are important problems to be resolved. For example, if we are to account for, say, the Adams Company, it is defined as a separate and specific accounting entity. The accounting entity has a specialized definition that is known as the **separate-entity assumption.**[2] The separate-entity assumption holds that for accounting measurement purposes, the particular entity being accounted for is carefully distinguished from all other similar and related entities and persons. Under this assumption, an accounting entity is held to be separate and distinct from its owner(s). A business is viewed as *owning the resources* (i.e., *assets*) used by it and as *owing the claims* (or *debts*) against those assets. The assets, debts, and activities of the business are kept completely separate, for measurement purposes, from those of the owners and other entities. For example, in the case of the Adams Company, the

[2] A list of the fundamental assumptions and principles underlying accounting is given on page 32.

personal activities of the owners are not included in the accounting measurements of the business itself.

TYPES OF BUSINESS ENTITIES

This book will focus primarily on accounting for business entities. There are three main types of business entities. Since they will be referred to often throughout this volume, their primary characteristics are explained below.

Sole proprietorship—a business owned by one person. This type of business entity is common in the fields of services, retailing, and farming. Generally, the owner is also the manager. Legally, the business and the owner are not separate entities—they are one and the same. However, accounting views the business as a separate entity to be distinguished from its owner.

Partnership—an unincorporated business owned by two or more persons known as partners. The agreements between the owners are set forth in a partnership contract. The contract specifies such matters as division of profits each period and distribution of resources when the business is terminated. As in the case of a sole proprietorship, a partnership is not legally separate from its owners. Legally, each partner is responsible for the debts of the business (i.e., each partner usually has what is called unlimited liability); however, accounting views the partners' personal activities as separate from the activities of the partnership.

Corporation—a business incorporated under the laws of a particular state, and the owners are known as shareholders or stockholders. Ownership is represented by shares of capital stock that can be freely bought and sold. When a proper application is filed by the organizers, the state issues a charter, which gives the corporation the right to operate legally as an entity, separate and apart from its owners. The owners enjoy what is called "limited liability"; that is, they are liable for the debts of the corporation only to the extent of their investment. The charter specifies the types and amounts of capital stock that can be issued. Most states require a minimum of two or three shareholders and a minimum amount of resources to be contributed at the time of organization. The shareholders elect a board of directors, which in turn employs managers and exercises general supervision of the corporation.[3] Accounting focuses on the corporation, not on the directors and managers as individuals.

In respect to economic importance, the corporation is the dominant form of business organization in the United States. The advantages of the corporate form include limited liability for the stockholders, con-

[3] There are a number of specialized types of entities that we do not discuss, such as joint ventures, mutual funds, cooperatives, investment trusts, and syndicates. Consideration of these is beyond the scope of this book.

tinuity of life, ease in transferring ownership (stock), and opportunities to raise large amounts of money by selling shares to a large number of people. Because of these advantages, most large and medium-sized businesses (and many small ones) are organized as corporations. We shall emphasize, therefore, this form of business. Nevertheless, the accounting concepts, standards, and measurement procedures apply generally to the other types of business.

ACCOUNTING AND ECONOMICS IN COMBINATION

Economics has been defined as the study of how people and society end up choosing, with or without the use of money, to employ scarce productive resources that could have alternative uses to produce various commodities and distribute them for consumption, now or in the future, among various people and groups in society.[4] This definition suggests a relationship to the definition of accounting. Like economics, accounting has a conceptual foundation. It focuses on the collection, measurement, and communication of information on the flows of scarce resources of specific entities. Accounting generally is viewed as also encompassing the **financial planning process** (discussed in *Fundamentals of Management Accounting*), which focuses on the planning and projection of **future** flows of scarce resources. Thus, accounting collects data and measures, interprets, and reports on those human activities that are the focus of economics. Economics basically attempts to *explain* economic relationships primarily on a conceptual level, whereas accounting attempts to *measure* the economic relationships primarily on a practical level. However, accounting measurements must be made as consistent as is feasible with economic concepts. Accounting must deal with the complex problems of measuring, in a practical way, the monetary effect of exchange transactions (i.e., resource inflows and outflows), the resources held, and the claims against those resources for each entity. Throughout these two volumes many of the theoretical and practical issues that arise in the measurement process will be discussed from the accounting viewpoint.

THE USE OF ACCOUNTING INFORMATION IN THE DECISION-MAKING PROCESS

We have said that your role as a future decision maker is significant, whether you become a manager, investor, professional person, owner of a business, or simply an interested citizen. Decision makers use various approaches for selecting one alternative from among a set of alternative

[4] Paul A. Samuelson, *Economics*, 9th ed. (New York: McGraw-Hill Book Co., 1975).

solutions to a given problem. Selection of the preferred alternative constitutes the basic decision. In the process of reaching decisions, the decision maker is concerned about the future since a decision cannot change the past; however, the effective decision maker does not neglect the past. Knowledge and interpretation of what has happened in the past aid in making decisions since history may shed considerable light on what the future is likely to hold. Thus, one of the fundamental inputs to decision making is dependable and relevant historical data. A large portion of historical data that are relevant to business decisions are expressed in monetary terms. They include costs (i.e., resources expended), revenues (i.e., resources earned), assets (i.e., things owned), liabilities (i.e., amounts owed), and owners' equity (i.e., total assets less total liabilities of the entity). Thus, accounting provides an important **information base** for decision making. The information provided by accounting must be understandable to the decision maker in order to preclude unwarranted interpretations in the decision-making process. This is a primary reason why measurements in accounting must adhere to certain standards and concepts.

On page 3, three ways in which accounting serves decision makers were outlined briefly. At this point we will reemphasize that the measurement and information reporting encompassed in the accounting process is essential to effective control and sound decision making by those individuals directly concerned with, and interested in, the endeavor.

Most entities, such as a business, a hospital, or a program to educate the disadvantaged, carry on their activities over an extended period of time, during which resources are committed and used with the expectation that desirable outputs will result in the form of goods and services. During the period of continuing activity, those involved in the organization, be they owners, sponsors, or managers, must have information about the continuing amounts of resources committed, resources used, resources on hand, and outputs (goods and services); and this information must be periodically reported, interpreted, and evaluated. The accounting process is designed to provide a continuing flow of such information to all interested parties. The **financial statements** constitute the primary means of communicating the relevant information on a continuing basis.

The management, sponsors, and owners of each organization need a constant and periodic flow of accounting information in their decision-making activities. In order to meet this need on a continuing basis, there must be a **cycle of information flow** and uses in the organization. This cycle is diagramed in Exhibit 1–1.

Now, let's see examples of how the flow of accounting information may aid decision makers in three different kinds of entities. We will consider a business, a hospital, and a community educational program for a disadvantaged group.

EXHIBIT 1–1
Accounting information in a decision and implementation cycle

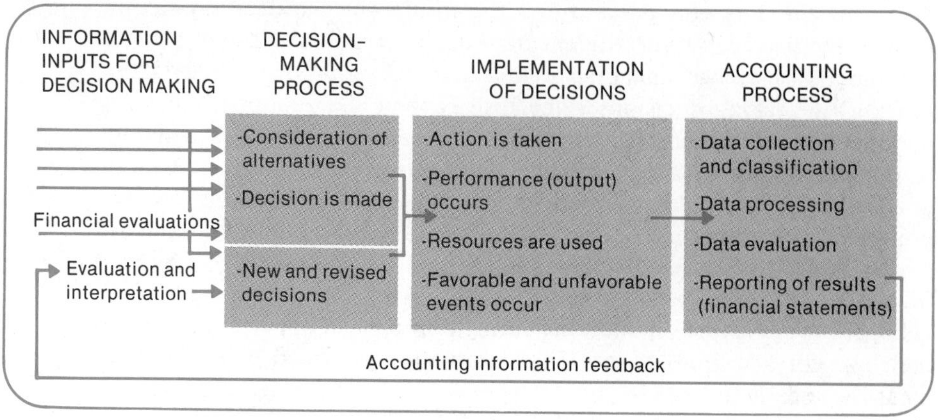

A business. First, the objectives of the business are formulated by the organizers. Initially, the owners provide the funds, which often are supplemented by funds provided by creditors. These funds then are used to acquire machinery, inventory, services, and other resources. As the business operates, additional resources are generated from the sale of goods and services. Many other things happen, most of which involve either the inflow or outflow of resources. The manager of the business needs information, on a continuing basis, that tells about the status of the resources. The manager wants to know such things as sources and amounts of funds, revenues (sales and services sold), expenses, how much is invested in inventory, what is the cash situation, how much is being spent for research and development, and how much money is being spent in the sales efforts.

The interested parties need answers to questions such as these for two fundamental reasons. First, accounting information in response to these and similar questions may aid importantly in making decisions about the entity to improve its effectiveness and efficiency. Second, accounting information tells the interested parties what the score was during the immediate past periods. This scorekeeping is important to the control and evaluation of performance. In Exhibit 1–1, **financial evaluations** are shown as one of the **information inputs** to the decision-making process. The exhibit also depicts the accounting process. Throughout this process, data such as that cited above are collected, measured, and reported. Through the reporting phase, the accounting information is communicated as an aid in making new decisions and in revising prior decisions.

Now, consider a shareholder (an owner) who has a substantial amount of funds invested in the business but has little opportunity to directly influence the management. Such an owner must decide whether to (1) retain the ownership interest, (2) expand or contract it, or (3) dispose of it completely. The shareholder also is interested in decisions that will lead to expansion of the business and raise its level of efficiency. As a consequence of these concerns, the owner would want to know such things as the trend of sales, the level of expenses, the amount invested in various assets (such as inventory and machinery), the debts of the business, and the cash balances. In other words, the investors would be very interested in knowing how the **management** is allocating the scarce resources provided them by the owners and the creditors. This information would be basic to taking one of the three actions listed above, or to guide the management. The financial reports provided on a continuing basis by the accounting process have as their primary objective the furnishing of information bearing on these questions. The accounting information thus provided should flow into the decision-making process of the owners in the ways depicted in Exhibit 1–1.

A hospital. Assume you are on the board of governors of a local hospital and, as a consequence, share the responsibility for the basic decisions and guidelines for its continued operation at an efficient level. Similar to the owner of a business, you have a wide variety of questions concerning its revenues, expenses, funds tied up in buildings and equipment, cost of charity services, and so on, that are in the scorekeeping category. You also are concerned with whether enough resources are being allocated to such activities as emergency care, sanitation, and nursing services. Before any sound decisions in these areas can be made for the future, you must have information about the past and current allocation of resources to them and what the output (quality and quantity of benefits) was. Thus, as a sponsor, you have many information needs that are important to your decisions for the future.

Now, consider the manager of the hospital. The manager needs accounting information about the operations of the hospital similar to that discussed above for the manager of a business, and for the same reasons. Typically, the manager will need more *detailed* accounting information than the sponsor. In any event, whether one is a sponsor or manager of the hospital, financial measurement and the reporting results should be continuing inputs to the decision-making processes.

An educational program for a disadvantaged group. As with the business and the hospital, there are both sponsors and managers of the program. They are vitally concerned with its resource needs and uses, the level of operational efficiency, and the extent to which the entity is attaining the goals set out for it. In addition to the all-important dedication and efforts of those carrying out the day-to-day activities, the financial problems and related decisions command the major attention of both the sponsors and the management—how resources are being committed, how they are being allocated, are they being allocated to the most critical phases of the program, are they being used efficiently, what additional resources are needed? These are indicative of the wide range of accounting information that is needed to make sound decisions and to direct the effort in a responsible way. The accounting process, if adequately designed for the situation, can provide, through the medium of continuing financial statements, information responses to many of these questions. The sponsors and the management, if they have a reasonable understanding of the financial considerations, can utilize the financial statements as important inputs to their decision-making process.

In summary, irrespective of the type of endeavor or the position of the decision maker, the need for a continuous flow of accounting information is useful to the decision maker. The flow of accounting information in the decision-making/implementation cycle, as depicted in Exhibit 1–1, is needed in all types of endeavors.

HISTORICAL PERSPECTIVES

Accounting is as old as the exchange processes (whether barter or monetary) that gradually developed with civilization. The earliest written records, including the Scriptures, contain references to what is now called accounting.

Accounting evolved in response to the economic needs of society. Prior to the 15th century it apparently followed no well-defined pattern except that it developed in answer to specific governing and trading needs of the era. The first known treatment of the subject of accounting was written in 1494, two years after the discovery of America. An Italian monk and mathematician, Fr. Luca Paciolo, described an approach that had been developed by the Italian merchants of the time to account for their activities as owner-managers of business ventures. Paciolo laid down the foundations of the basic "accounting model" that is used to this day. As economic activity moved from the feudal system to agriculture and then to the Industrial Revolution, accounting adapted to the evolving needs. As business units became more complex and broader in scope, accounting evolved in response to the increased planning and control responsibilities of management. As governments increased in size and became more centralized, accounting was developed to meet the increased responsibilities.

In the 17th and 18th centuries, the Industrial Revolution in England provided the impetus for the development of new approaches in accounting. The impetus was particularly in the direction of management accounting and the accumulation of data concerning the cost of manufacturing each product. In the latter half of the 19th century, English accountants, small in numbers but large in competence, appeared on the American scene. By 1900, the lead in accounting developments, provided earlier by the English, began to shift to America. Since the turn of the century, spearheaded by the accounting profession in the United States, accounting has experienced dynamic, and sometimes controversial, growth.

IMPORTANT GROUPS

At the present time, four important groups in the United States predominate in the development of financial accounting concepts and practice. A general knowledge of their respective historical and continuing roles is important to your understanding of accounting. The groups are: the American Institute of Certified Public Accountants; the Financial Accounting Standards Board; the U.S. Securities and Exchange Commission; and the American Accounting Association. The past and present roles of each group will be briefly reviewed.

American Institute of Certified Public Accountants (AICPA). This institute was organized a few years prior to the turn of the century by a group of accountants engaged in public and industrial accounting. Membership is limited to certified public accountants (see pages 13 and 14). In terms of direct impact on financial accounting practice, the AICPA has been the strongest force in accounting in recent decades. It carries on a wide-ranging program encompassing professional development, publications (including the magazine *Journal of Accountancy*), and the development and communication of accounting standards and procedures. During the approximate period 1930 to 1950, the AICPA's Committee on Accounting Procedure issued a number of Accounting Research Bulletins (ARBs) that enunciated certain *recommended* financial accounting principles and procedures. These recommendations were followed by much, but by no means all, of the accounting profession. In the realization of a developing need for increased effort and more adherence to prescribed accounting guidelines, in 1959 the AICPA organized the Accounting Principles Board (APB) to replace the former committee. The APB issued 31 numbered *Opinions* during its existence from 1959 through 1973. Basically, accountants are **required** to follow the provisions of the *Opinions*. The *Opinions* dealt with many of the tough issues of financial accounting; and as a consequence, many of them were highly controversial. Throughout this volume you will encounter a few references to the ARBs and numerous references to APB *Opinions*.

Financial Accounting Standards Board (FASB). This organization began operating June 1, 1973. It is appropriate to review its background. Accounting is a complex and frequently controversial professional activity. The intensity of the controversies in recent years is indicated by the fact that a wide range of interested individuals and groups (frequently representing special interests) have committed significant amounts of resources and time in attempting to influence the setting of accounting concepts and standards. The controversy on occasion entered the political arena, which is generally viewed as an inappropriate forum in which to establish sound accounting concepts and standards. Accounting issues increasingly have been important in litigation in the courts.

As you study accounting you will realize that the economic results reported by financial accounting, such as asset valuations, net income, and earnings per share, may have impacts on the economy, on the capital markets (including the stock market), and on many major decisions of individuals, groups, and entities. You also may appreciate how the selection of a particular financial accounting approach frequently has a significant impact on the financial results reported through the accounting process (such as net income and earnings per share). In the light of these issues, the AICPA in 1972 decided to reassess the approaches to establishing financial accounting concepts and standards. As a consequence of this reassessment, the APB was discontinued and in its place the Financial Accounting Standards Board was established. The seven FASB members are appointed by an independent board of trustees and serve on a full-time basis. The trustees are appointed by the AICPA. The FASB was organized to be independent. It has as its sole function the establishment and improvement of accounting concepts and standards. The accounting profession, through the FASB, intends to keep the standards-setting function in the private sector rather than by laws and governmental agencies.

Securities and Exchange Commission (SEC). This government regulatory agency operates under authority granted by the Securities Acts of 1933 and 1934. The acts gave the SEC authority to prescribe accounting guidelines for the financial reports required to be submitted by corporations that sell their securities in interstate commerce (i.e., registered companies). This includes all sizable corporations. The SEC requires these corporations to submit periodic reports, which are maintained in the files of the commission as a matter of public record. From the beginning, the SEC, as a matter of policy, generally followed the accounting concepts, standards, and procedures established by the AICPA committees. The SEC publishes "Regulation S-X," which prescribes the special guidelines to be followed by registered companies in preparing the financial reports submitted in conformance with the Securities Acts. Throughout its existence the SEC has exerted a significant impact on accounting. Its staff has worked closely with the accounting profession on the evolution and improvement of accounting standards.

American Accounting Association (AAA). This association was organized during the World War I period by a group of college accounting professors. The association sponsors and encourages the improvement of accounting teaching and accounting research (primarily on a theoretical plane), and publishes a magazine, *The Accounting Review.* Its committees issue reports that, coupled with the research activities of individual academicians, continue to exert a pervasive influence on the development of accounting theory and standards.

JUDGMENT IN ACCOUNTING

Financial accounting concepts and standards have been developed and articulated to increase the reliability and relevance of accounting measurements and reporting. Since accounting is man-made and must evolve to meet changing needs, it has a limited number of "provable" approaches. As you study accounting you will appreciate that it requires much professional judgment in application on the part of the accountant in order to capture the economic essence of transactions. Thus, accounting is intellectually stimulating; it is not a cut-and-dried subject. Rather, it is one that calls upon your intelligence, analytical ability, creativity, and judgment. Since accounting is a communication process involving an audience (users) of a wide diversity of knowledge, interest, and capabilities, it will call upon your ability as a communicator. The language encompasses concisely written phrases and symbols used to convey information about the resource flows measured for specific organizations.

THE ACCOUNTING PROFESSION

In the period since 1900, accountancy has attained the stature of a profession similar to law, medicine, engineering, and architecture. As with all recognized professions, it is subject to licensing, observes a code of professional ethics, requires a high level of professional competence, is dedicated to service to the public, requires a high level of academic study, and rests on a "common body of knowledge." The accountant, in addition to meeting specified academic requirements, may be licensed by the state to be a **certified public accountant,** or **CPA.** This designation was first established in 1894. The primary objective was the attainment of high standards of professional competence. It is granted under the law only upon completion of requirements specified by statute. Although the CPA requirements vary somewhat between states, generally they include a college degree with a major in accounting; good character; from one to five years specified experience; and successful completion of a three-day examination. The CPA examination, scheduled in each state simultaneously on a semiannual basis, is prepared by the American Institute of Certified Public Accountants and covers accounting theory, auditing, business law, and accounting practice.

As is common with physicians, engineers, lawyers, and architects, accountants (including CPAs) commonly are engaged in professional practice or are employed by businesses, government entities, nonprofit organizations, and so on.

Practice of public accounting

A CPA, practicing public accounting, is one who offers professional services to the public for a fee, as does the lawyer and physician. In this posture the accountant is appropriately known as an **independent CPA** because certain responsibilities also extend to the general public (third parties) rather than being limited to the specific business or other entity that pays for the services. The independent CPA is not an employee of the clients. This concept of independence from the client is an aspect that is unique to the accounting profession. The consequences of this aspect are not so widely understood as perhaps they should be. For example, the lawyer and the physician, in case of malpractice or incompetence, generally are subject to potential liability (lawsuits) that may extend only to the client or patient involved (and the family). In contrast, the independent CPA, in case of malpractice or negligence in the audit function, is subject to potential liability that may extend to all parties (whether known to the CPA or not) that have suffered loss or failed to make a profit through reliance on financial statements "approved" by the CPA.

While a single individual may practice public accounting, usually two or more individuals organize an accounting firm in the form of a partnership (in some states incorporation is permitted). Firms vary in size from a one-person office, to regional firms, to the "big-eight" firms, which have hundreds of offices located around the world. Nearly all accounting firms render three types of services: auditing, management advisory services, and tax services.

Auditing. An important function performed by the CPA in public practice is the **audit** or **attest function.** Its purpose is to lend credibility to the financial reports; that is, to assure that they are dependable. Primarily this function involves an examination of the financial reports prepared by the management in order to assure that they are in conformance with generally accepted accounting concepts and standards. In carrying out this function the independent CPA examines the underlying transactions, including the collection, classification, and assembly of the financial data incorporated in the financial reports. In performing these tasks, established professional standards must be maintained and the information reported must conform to "generally accepted accounting principles" appropriate for the entity involved. Additionally, the CPA is responsible for verifying that the financial reports "fairly present" the resource inflows and outflows and the financial position of the entity. The magnitude of these responsibilities may be appreciated when it is realized that the number of transactions involved in a major enterprise such as General Motors runs into the billions each year. The CPA, of course, does not examine each one of these transactions; rather, professional approaches are used to ascertain that they were properly measured and reported.

Occasionally, the auditor may encounter attempts, for example, to increase reported profit by omitting certain expenses or to overstate financial position by omitting certain debts. There are many intentional and unintentional potentialities for preparing misleading financial reports. The audit function performed by an independent CPA is the best protection available to the public in this respect. Many investors have learned the hazards of making investments in enterprises that do not have their financial reports examined by an independent CPA.

Management advisory services. Many independent CPA firms also offer advisory or consulting services. These services generally are accounting based and encompass such activities as the design and installation of accounting, data processing, profit-planning, and control (i.e., budget) systems; financial advice; forecasting; inventory controls; cost-effectiveness studies; and operational analyses. This facet of public practice is experiencing a rapid growth.

Tax services. CPAs in public practice usually are involved in rendering income tax services to their clients. This includes tax planning as a part of the decision-making process and determination of the income tax liability (by means of the annual tax return). The increasing complexity of state and federal tax laws, particularly income tax laws, demands a high level of competence.

The CPA's involvement in **tax planning** often is quite significant. Virtually every major business decision carries with it significant tax impacts; so much so, in fact, that tax-planning considerations frequently govern the decision. To illustrate the significance of tax effects in a simple way, assume two taxpayers, each of whom desires to borrow $100,000, and a going (i.e., actual) interest rate of 8 percent per year. Assume that taxpayer A has an average tax rate of 30 percent, whereas taxpayer B has a 50 percent rate. Let's evaluate the annual **net** or **effective interest cost** of each. The effective interest cost is the net cost of borrowing. It is the actual interest, less the reduction in income taxes resulting from including the interest cost on the income tax return as a deduction. To continue the illustration:

	Taxpayer A	*Taxpayer B*
Actual annual interest to be paid ($100,000 × 8%)................	$8,000	$8,000
Less: Tax saving:		
A ($8,000 × 30%)	2,400	
B ($8,000 × 50%)..		4,000
Net or effective after-tax interest cost	$5,600	$4,000
Net or effective after-tax interest rate:		
A ($5,600 ÷ $100,000)	5.6%	
B ($4,000 ÷ $100,000)...		4.0%

The tax savings is due to the fact that the $8,000 interest paid is a deductible expense on the income tax return of each party. Since this would reduce taxable income by $8,000, it would serve to reduce the amount of income taxes to be paid, the amount of which would depend upon the tax rate of the person or entity.

Often a critical decision is whether to raise needed funds by borrowing or by selling and issuing additional capital stock. The decision model must focus on determining the relative "cost" of each alternative. The cost of debt, net of tax, may turn out to be materially less than the cost of equity (i.e., funds provided by owners) since interest paid is deductible but dividends paid are not deductible for income tax purposes.

To illustrate the tax-savings effect on profits, assume AB Corporation needs $100,000 for expansion purposes. The funds needed can be borrowed from a local financial institution at 10 percent annual interest. The management is concerned about the high interest rate. Assuming the average income tax rate for the company is 40 percent, the effect on profits may be analyzed as follows:

	No borrowing	*Borrowing*	*Difference (cost of borrowing)*
Profits before interest and income taxes (assumed)	$75,000	$75,000	
Less: Interest expense	-0-	10,000	$10,000
Profit subject to income tax	75,000	65,000	
Less: Income tax expense (40%)	30,000	26,000	4,000
Profit after income taxes	$45,000	$39,000	$ 6,000

The net interest cost is as follows:

	Amount	*Percent*
Actual annual interest paid to lender	$10,000	10
Less: Tax savings ($10,000 × 40%)	4,000	4
Net or effective interest cost	$ 6,000	6

Employment by organizations

Many accountants, including CPAs and CMAs (Chartered Management Accountants), are employed by profit-making and nonprofit organizations. A company or other organization, depending upon its size and complexity, may employ from one up to hundreds of accountants. In the business enterprise, the chief financial officer, usually a vice president or controller, is a member of the management team. This responsibility generally entails a wide range of management, financial, and accounting duties. Exhibit 1–2 shows a typical organizational arrangement of the **financial function** in a business enterprise. In the business entity, accountants typically are engaged in a wide variety of activities, such as

EXHIBIT 1–2
Typical organization of the financial function

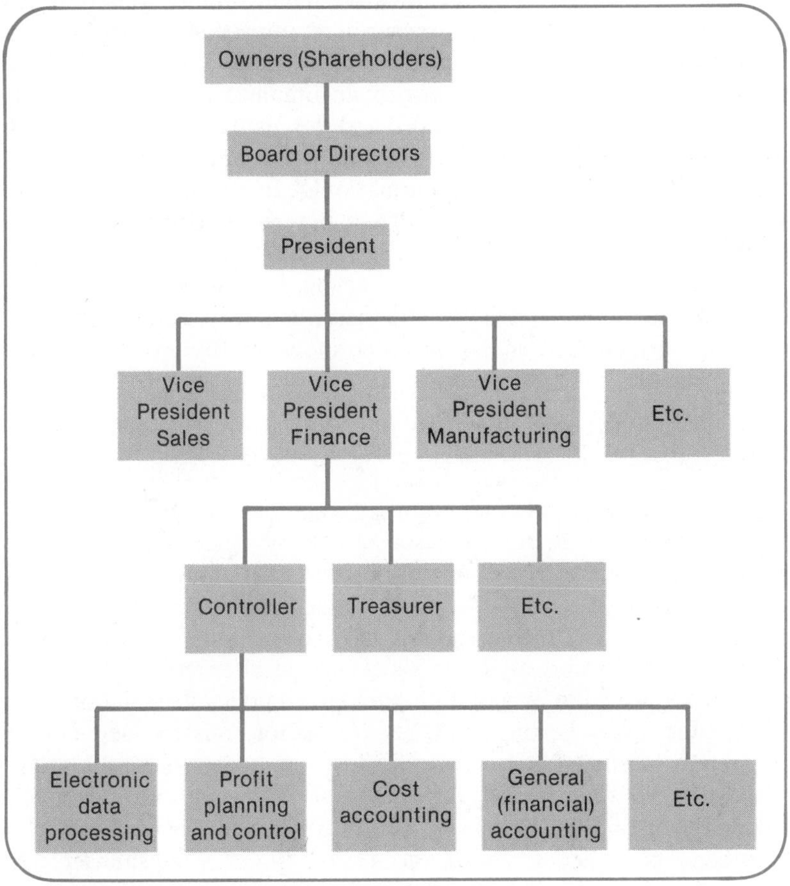

general management, general accounting, cost accounting, profit planning and control (i.e., budgeting), internal auditing, and electronic data processing. A common pattern in recent years has been the selection of a "financial expert" as the chief executive or president of the company. One primary function of the accountants in organizations is to provide data that are useful for managerial decision making and for controlling operations. In addition, the functions of external reporting, tax planning, control of assets, and a host of related responsibilities normally are performed by accountants in industry. The role of accountants within organizations is emphasized in *Fundamentals of Management Accounting* of this series.

Employment in the public sector

The vast and complex operations of governmental units, from the local to the international level, create a great need for accountants. Accountants employed in the public sector perform similar functions to those performed by their counterparts in private organizations. Additionally, the General Accounting Office (GAO) and the regulatory agencies, such as the Securities and Exchange Commission, Interstate Commerce Commission (ICC), Federal Power Commission (FPC), and Federal Communications Commission (FCC), utilize the services of accountants in carrying out their regulatory duties.

Finally, accountants are involved in varying capacities in the evolving programs of pollution control, health care, minority enterprises, and other socially oriented programs, whether sponsored by private industry or by government.

SOCIAL AND ECONOMIC SIGNIFICANCE OF ACCOUNTING

The broad areas of public-policy formulation and the ranking of national priorities are important issues to many citizens. Even casual knowledge tells us that the financial implications of public-policy formulation are important considerations. Accounting information assists policy makers to bring the financial complexities into focus for study, evaluation, and selection of the more favorable alternatives. First and foremost, the financial information that underlies policy formulation must have credibility; that is, the financial information must be dependable. The independent audit function provided by the accounting profession, coupled with the expertise of the accountant in sorting out relevant financial analyses and relationships, helps to meet this need. Similarly, the credibility of financial reports on business units is indispensable in the conduct of the business, the administration of the taxation process, and the protection of the broad public interest. Inefficiencies, errors, and selfish interests would cause the whole system to break down if these reports were not reliable. In the federal government, the General Accounting Office was established to audit and report to the Congress on the administration of public funds. Regulatory bodies such as the SEC and the ICC were established by law to protect the public interest. These and similar agencies, in good measure, rely upon audited financial reports in carrying out their statutory missions.

The growth of business organizations in size, particularly publicly held corporations, has brought pressure from stockholders, potential investors, creditors, governmental agencies, and the public at large, for increased financial disclosure. The public's right to know more about organizations that directly and indirectly affect them (whether or not they are shareholders) is being increasingly recognized as essential. An open society is one that has a high degree of freedom at the individual level and typically evidences an effective commitment to measuring the quality of life attained. These characteristics make it essential that the members of that society be provided adequate, understandable, and dependable financial information from the major institutions that comprise it. Voters are asked to decide upon revenue raising proposals, allocations of resources to many sources, and other questions. All of these decisions should be based upon adequate financial knowledge. Labor negotiations, environmental programs, economic opportunity programs, foreign aid, and education programs are but a few of the difficult problem areas important to all citizens that, for enlightened decision making, require extensive use of accounting information.

SOME MISCONCEPTIONS

Some people naively confuse a bookkeeper with an accountant and bookkeeping with accounting. In effect they confuse one of the minor parts with the whole of accounting. It is tantamount to comparing the simple administration of first aid with the complex practice of medicine by the physician. Bookkeeping is the routine and clerical side of accounting and requires only minimal knowledge of the accounting model. A bookkeeper records the repetitive and uncomplicated transactions in most businesses and may maintain the simple records of a very small business. In contrast, the accountant is a professional competent in the design of information systems, analysis of complex economic events, interpretative and analytical processes, reporting, financial advising, and management consulting.

Another prevalent misconception is that all of the financial affairs of an entity are subject to precise and accurate measurement and that the results of accounting, as reflected in the financial statements, are absolute facts. For example, that accounting numbers are influenced by estimates in many respects will be illustrated in subsequent chapters. Many people believe that accounting should measure and report the value of the entity, but accounting does not attempt to do this. In order to understand financial statements and to interpret them wisely for use in decision making, the user must be aware of their limitations as well as their usefulness. One should understand what they do and do not attempt to accomplish.

As a student of accounting you must be wary of these misconceptions.

To adequately understand financial statements and to be able to interpret the "figures" wisely, you must have a certain level of knowledge of the concepts and standards and the measurement procedures used in the accounting process. You must learn what accounting "is really like" and appreciate the reasons why certain things are done the way they are. This level of knowledge cannot be gained simply by reading a list of the "principles" and a list of the misconceptions. Neither can a generalized discussion of the subject matter suffice. A certain amount of involvement, primarily problem solving as used in mathematics courses, is essential in any study of accounting focused on the needs of the user. Therefore, we provide problems aimed at the desirable knowledge level for the user of financial statements.

ORGANIZATION OF CHAPTERS

The chapters in this volume have been divided into parts primarily to provide reasonable study units; however, this also provides your instructor with flexibility in priority selection of materials consistent with the time available. The strictly procedural aspects of accounting are presented in appendixes to the chapters to further provide flexibility to your instructor in attaining the knowledge level desired consistent with time constraints and course objectives.

DEMONSTRATION CASE FOR SELF-STUDY

This introductory case is presented to start you thinking, in monetary terms, of some of the resource inflows and outflows of a business. It deals with measuring and reporting certain accounting information for an individual involved in a simple business situation. The discussions in the chapter will not help you much with the monetary amounts or the format of the report. See what you can do with the case before studying the recommended solution that follows the case.

John's Bread Company

John Rath entered college in September 1967 with $600 he had saved during high school by working as a "bag boy" in a local grocery, plus $400 obtained on a loan from a local business executive, "payable at no interest until after you graduate and get a job." Unfortunately, John could expect no parental help. He realized that before the end of the year he would have to get a job sufficient to pay the full cost of his college education above the $1,000 cash on hand. The college was in a relatively small town, and employment opportunities for students were limited. At the end of the first semester John had not located a job. Eventually he did come up with an idea that he thought might be profitable. While working back home in the grocery, he had observed that "day-old" bread always sold out at a reduced price. He surveyed the grocery stores in the college town and found that they were serviced by a chain bakery from a distant town and that none of them sold day-old bread. He purchased an old sedan for $150 cash (including the registration fees), drove to another town (75 miles away), and located a local bakery that would provide him day-old bread at a reasonable price. Thereupon, he loaded the trunk and back seat with bread at a cost of $30 and returned. The first two stores he contacted took the entire load at a price of $50 and indicated a desire to obtain the same amount each Tuesday and Friday. John took one half of his remaining cash of $300 and set it aside in a separate bank account for the bread business. Within the month John was making one round trip every Monday and Thursday to supply the four grocery stores he had lined up. Not counting his time and the cost of operating his car, John earned $20 on the bread for each trip. His car averaged 15 miles per gallon of gasoline (regular at $0.30 per gallon). Each of the 28 trips made during the spring semester required 1 quart of oil ($0.50 per quart). During the semester he spent $42 for repairs, license, and insurance. All transactions were cash. At the end of the spring semester John ended up as follows: grade point average, 3.1; tires and motor worn out; an increase in his bank balance; income taxes owed equal to 20 percent of profit (assumed for illustrative purposes only), and the belief that he could expand his business to include more grocery stores. A fellow student offered him $500 for the business—"lock, stock, and barrel." Instead of selling, John decided to expand during the summer. The first step was to analyze the potential demand and the resources that would be needed. He immediately decided that he should acquire a used pickup truck (he located one he liked, priced at $1,250, less a $50 trade-in on his old car) since it would enable him to triple the amount of bread he could handle. He estimated that this amount would saturate the market. He estimated 12 miles per gallon of gas for the pickup; service, license, repairs, and insurance for one year of $150; and a value for the pickup after one year of $800. He then approached a local banker for a $900 loan to purchase the pickup, the loan to be payable at the end of 12 months (interest rate 7 percent). The banker was agreeable on the condition that John would develop for him a "profit report that would show for the spring semester just ended his sales, expenses, and profit for the bread operation." John was enthusiastic and, although he had never studied accounting, proceeded to prepare the report for the banker the next day.

Required:

Prepare the report for the banker. Include any comments that you consider relevant.

Solution:

JOHN'S BREAD COMPANY
Financial Report for the Banker
Spring Semester, 1968

Sales, Expenses, and Profit:			
Sales of bread (2 trips × 14 weeks × \$50)			\$1,400
Less cost of the bread (2 trips × 14 weeks × \$30)			840
Gross			560
Less expenses:			
Gasoline (2 trips× 150 miles × 14 weeks = 4,200 miles; 4,200 miles/15 = 280 gallons @ \$0.30)		\$ 84	
Oil (28 quarts @ \$0.50)		14	
Repairs, license, and insurance		42	
Automobile:*			
Cost at start	\$150		
Trade-in value at end	50		
Cost of using the automobile		100	
Total Expenses (excluding taxes)			240
Profit subject to income taxes			320
Income taxes (\$320 × 20%)			64
Profit for the semester (excluding John's time)			\$ 256

* This is the cost of using the automobile itself for the semester. This cost was occasioned by "wear-and-tear" through use for the semester. The \$100 expense for use is frequently called ***depreciation.*** A later chapter will explain more precisely the nature of depreciation as a cost of using equipment and similar items that have a limited life. The amounts given in this case relate to the period when these events took place.

Epilogue: At the end of five years, John left college with a degree (including much more knowledge of accounting) and, having sold the business, with \$11,000 cash in his pocket.

SUMMARY

Accounting interfaces with practically all aspects of the environment: social, economic, and political. Any open society is a complex one that is characterized by organizations—businesses, political parties, governmental entities, churches, social institutions, and private groups and associations. Each organization, whether local or international in scope, is an accounting entity. The essence of accounting is the measurement and reporting of financial information for an accounting entity. The measurement and reporting of the inflows and outflows of scarce resources and the financial position of each accounting entity is essential to (1) effective management of each such organization and (2) the understanding and evaluation of it by interested outside parties. Measurement of the financial characteristics of each such organization is essential because each of us is an important decision maker, both in respect to our individual interests and as a concerned citizen in the broader sense. Our decision-making potential is enhanced if we understand the financial impacts of alternative solutions to particular problems.

IMPORTANT TERMS

Unit-of-measure assumption
Accounting
Accounting entity
Separate-entity assumption
Sole proprietorship
Partnership
Corporation
Independent CPA
Auditing
Management advisory services
Tax services
Net or effective interest cost
Bookkeeping

QUESTIONS FOR DISCUSSION

1. Any open society is characterized by social, political, and economic organizations. Why is it essential that their accomplishments (or lack of accomplishments) be measured and reported?
2. Each entity, such as a church, welfare organization, or business, in a progressive society is involved in the allocation of scarce resources. These frequently are expressed (measured) in terms of the monetary unit. How is accounting information used in the allocation of resources in such entities?
3. In general, how does an interpretative knowledge of the resources held and the resource flows of an organization aid in decision making for the organization?
4. What is meant by an accounting entity?
5. Briefly distinguish between a sole proprietorship, a partnership, and a corporation.
6. In general, why is a knowledge of the financial implications of public-policy questions important to a concerned citizen? Where would you expect to find data concerning these implications?
7. What is the primary focus of accounting, irrespective of the type of entity?
8. Explain your general concept of the decision-making process. Refer to Exhibit 1–1.
9. Explain what is meant by the designation CPA.
10. Distinguish, in general terms, between the practice of public accounting and employment as an accountant in private organizations and in the public sector.
11. The independent CPA firm normally renders three services: auditing, management advisory, and tax. Briefly explain each.

12. In general, what are the duties of a controller in a business?
13. Distinguish between accounting and bookkeeping.
14. Explain the unit-of-measure assumption as applied in accounting.
15. Explain the separate-entity assumption as applied in accounting.

EXERCISES*

E1–1. Weston Retailers, Incorporated, owns and operates six department stores located in five different cities. The corporate charter, granted by the state, authorized 100,000 shares of common stock (par value $20 per share). The bylaws provide for the annual election of a board of directors numbering ten individuals, three of whom must be outside directors. In addition to the president, the officers will include three vice presidents: finance, merchandising, and promotion. In the finance function there will be a controller and a treasurer.

Required:

a. Prepare an organization chart for Weston Retailers and include a recommendation of the responsibilities of the controller.
b. Who elects the board of directors?
c. What are outside directors? Do you agree this is a good idea? Why?

(Hint: Use your present knowledge of a department store and your own opinions.)

E1–2. Assume you are the owner of "The College Shop," which specializes in items of special interest to college students. At the end of January 1978 you find that (for January only):

a. Sales, per the cash register tapes, totaled $60,000, plus one sale on credit (a special case) of $400.
b. With the help of a friend (who had majored in accounting) you determined that the goods sold during January had cost you $26,000 when they were purchased.
c. During the month, according to the checkbook, you paid $30,000 for salaries, utilities, supplies, advertising, and other expenses; however, you have not yet paid the $350 monthly rent on the store (including the fixtures).

On the basis of the data given, what was the amount of profit for January (disregard income taxes)? Show computations. (Hint: A convenient form to use would have the following major side captions: revenue from sales, expenses, and difference – profit before income taxes.)

E1–3. Dow Company, Inc., a small service organization, prepared the following report for the month of January:

---

* These exercises go beyond the chapter. They are designed to challenge your analytical capabilities.

Services, Expenses, and Profit

Services:		
Cash services (per cash register)	$35,000	
Credit services (per charge tickets; not collected by end of January)	25,000	$60,000
Expenses:		
Salaries and wages (paid by check)	29,000	
Salary for January not yet paid	800	
Supplies (taken from stock, purchased for cash in December)	2,000	
Estimated cost of wear and tear on used delivery truck for the month (depreciation)	100	
Other expenses (paid by check)	8,100	40,000
Difference—pretax profit		20,000
Estimated income taxes (to be paid next quarter)		6,000
Profit for January		$14,000

Required:

a. You have been asked by the owner (who knows very little about the financial side of business) to compute the "amount of cash that was generated in January by operations."

You decided to prepare a report for the owner with the following major side captions: cash inflows (collections), cash outflows (payments), and difference—net increase (or decrease) in cash. (Hint: There was a cash decrease; that is, a negative cash flow.)

b. See if you can reconcile the "difference—net increase (or decrease) in cash" you computed in (*a*) with the profit for January.

E1–4. Duke Corporation was organized by five individuals on January 1, 19A. At the end of 19A, the following financial data are available:

Total revenues	$40,000
Total expenses (excluding income taxes)	30,000
Cash balance	12,000
Receivables from customers (all considered collectible)	6,000
Inventory of merchandise (by inventory count at cost)	25,000
Payables owed to suppliers for merchandise purchased from them (will be paid during January 19B)	7,000

Assume a 22 percent tax rate on the profits of this corporation; the income taxes will be paid during the first quarter of 19B.

Required:

a. What was the amount of profit, after income taxes, for 19A?

b. Compute the "net worth" of the business (usually called owners' equity) at December 31, 19A.

(Hint: Liabilities total $9,200.)

PROBLEMS

P1–1. Assume you are the major shareholder of a small store, Campus Corner, Inc., that sells clothes for young people (specializing in the college crowd). The corporation has an average tax rate of 40 percent. The store is considering adding a department that will entail an outlay of \$20,000 cash, 75 percent of which will have to be obtained from outside the business.

Required:

a. Assuming the amount needed is borrowed for one year at 8½ percent interest per year, what would be the net or effective interest cost (1) in dollars and (2) as an effective after-tax rate of interest? Show computations.

b. Would you recommend "debt" or "equity" as the source? Explain.

P1–2. Upon graduation from high school, Jack Kane immediately accepted a job as a plumber's helper for a large local plumbing company. After three years of hard work, Jack received a plumber's license, whereupon he decided to go into business for himself. He had saved \$5,000 which he decided to invest in the business. His first step was to transfer this amount from his savings account to a business bank account for "Kane Plumbing Company, Incorporated." His lawyer had advised him to start as a corporation. He then purchased, for cash, a used panel truck for \$1,500 and \$800 worth of tools; rented limited space in a small building; inserted an ad in the local paper; and opened the doors on October 1, 1977. Immediately, Jack found himself very busy and, after one month, employed a helper. Although he knew practically nothing about the financial side of the business, he realized from his prior experience that a number of reports were required and that costs and collections had to be controlled carefully. Accordingly, at the end of the year, prompted in part by concern about his income tax situation (previously he only had to report his salary), he recognized the need for financial statements. At his urging, his wife undertook "to develop some financial statements for the business." With the help of a friend, on December 31, 1977, she gathered the following data for the three months just ended: Deposits in the bank account of collections for plumbing services were \$12,500. The following checks written: plumber's helper, \$1,000; payroll taxes paid, \$45; supplies purchased and used on jobs, \$6,000; oil, gas, and maintenance on truck, \$700; insurance, \$150; rent, \$200; utilities and telephone, \$150; and miscellaneous expenses, \$400 (including advertising). In addition, there were uncollected bills to customers for plumbing services amounting to \$1,400, and the rent for December amounting to \$150 had not been paid. The income tax rate on this corporation may be assumed to be 22 percent. Also assume that the "wear and tear on the truck and tools due to use during the three months" was estimated by Jack to be \$120.

Required:

a. Prepare a "profit" report for Kane Plumbing for the three months. Use the following main captions: revenues from services, expenses, difference—profit subject to income taxes, income taxes, and profit. (Hint: Revenues totaled $13,900.)

b. Do you visualize that Jack may have a potential need for one or more additional financial reports for 1977 and thereafter? Explain.

P1–3. During the summer, between her junior and senior years, Randy Walker was faced with the need to earn sufficient funds for the coming academic year. Unable to obtain a job with reasonable remuneration, she decided to try the lawn-care business for three months. After a survey of the potential, Randy acquired an old pickup truck on June 1 for $500. On each door she painted "Randy's Lawn Service, Ph. XX." Additionally, she spent $200 for mowers, trimmers, and so forth. To acquire these items she borrowed $1,000 cash on a note (endorsed by a friend) at 10 percent interest per annum, payable at the end of the three months (ending August 31).

At the end of the summer Randy realized that she had "done a lot of work and her bank account looked good," which prompted her to become concerned about how much profit her business had earned.

A review of her check stubs showed the following: Deposits in the bank of collections from customers were $5,800. The following checks written: gas, oil, and lubrication, $480; pickup repairs, $85; repair of mowers, $60; miscellaneous supplies used, $80; helpers, $1,500; payroll taxes, $75; payment for assistance in preparing payroll tax forms, $50; insurance, $120; telephone, $30; and $1,025 to pay off the note plus interest (on August 31). A notebook kept in the pickup, plus some unpaid bills, and so forth, reflected that customers still owed her $600 for lawn services rendered and that she owed $100 for gas and oil (credit card charges) and income taxes (estimated tax rate 20 percent). She estimated that the "wear and tear" for use of the truck and the other equipment for three months amounted to $150.

Required:

a. Prepare a "profit" report for Randy's Lawn Service covering the three months June, July, and August. Use the following main captions: revenues from services, expenses, difference—profit subject to income taxes, income taxes, and profit. (Hint: Total expenses excluding income taxes amounted to $2,755.)

b. Do you visualize a potential need for one or more additional financial reports for this company for 19A and thereafter? Explain.

P1–4. Assume you are president of Joy Retailers, Incorporated. At the end of the first year (December 31, 19A) of operations the following financial data are available for the company:

Cash	$ 13,100
Receivables from customers (all considered collectible)	15,000
Inventory of merchandise (based on physical count and priced at cost)	70,000
Equipment owned, at cost (at year-end, the estimated value to the business for future use was 90% of cost)	10,000
Note payable, one year (9% annual interest), owed to the bank (dated July 1, 19A)	20,000

Interest on the note through December 31, 19A (due to be paid to the bank on June 30, 19B)	900
Salary payable for 19A (on December 19A, this was owed to an employee who was away because of an emergency; will return around January 10, 19B, at which time the payment will be made)	1,100
Total sales revenue	100,000
Expenses paid, including the cost of the merchandise sold (excluding income taxes at a 30% rate; the taxes will be paid during the first quarter of 19B)	70,000

Required (*show computations*):

a. Compute the amount of profit after income taxes.

b. Compute the "net worth" of the business (generally called owners' equity) at December 31, 19A.

(Hint: Total liabilities amount to $30,100.)

2

Communication of accounting information

PURPOSE OF THE CHAPTER

In this chapter we consider the fundamentals of financial statements, which are the primary end products of the accounting process. Knowledge of what the financial statements are intended to communicate will enable you to understand better the concepts and measurement procedures that underlie the accounting process that generates them. Accounting is an **information system,** and the financial statements constitute an important communication medium.

The focus of the chapter will be on the communication of financial information about profit-making business entities. Some of the problems encountered in the measurement and classification of resources will be introduced. Finally, we will be interested in what financial statements say and will begin to learn some accounting terminology.

It is important to keep in mind as you study this chapter that we will focus on the purposes and nature of financial statements—not on how the amounts were derived. Since financial statements are a means of communication, we will consider briefly this broad area first.

COMMUNICATION OF ACCOUNTING INFORMATION

Communication consists of a flow of information from one party to one or more other parties. For communication to be effective, the recipient must understand what the sender intends to convey. In the process of communication there are obviously great problems in understanding precisely the words, symbols, and sounds used. Accounting comprises an **information system** that is designed to convey relevant financial information. First, accounting seeks to communicate with the **users** of the financial information—owners, potential investors, creditors, and other decision makers. Second, to the extent feasible, accounting aims to focus on the primary **types of decisions** that require financial information. Finally, accounting, on the basis of these two determinations, attempts to **report** the kinds of financial information needed in the decision-making process. Fundamentally, managers, owners, potential investors, creditors, and other decision makers, as a basis for assessing the present and future potentials of a business, want answers to three important questions: (1) What has been the performance of the business? (For example, how much profit has it earned?) (2) How does the business stand financially at the present time? (For example, what are its resources and how much does it owe?) (3) What are its future potentials? The financial statements discussed in this chapter are primary means of communication, developed by the accountant, that respond in part to questions (1) and (2). Although they are not directly responsive to the third question, they provide an important starting point in assessing the future.

Before looking at the financial statements, we should consider communication in general. As we make decisions of varying sorts, we must rely upon certain information that often is unique to each type of decision. Often, we must make decisions without adequate information. Either the needed information is not available to us or the cost and time entailed in developing it is prohibitive when compared to its potential benefits.[1] The nature and form in which information is "packaged" and communicated sometimes affects the decision. For example, some individuals are more influenced by graphic than by quantitative presentations; others find narrative preferable to tabular expression; some prefer summaries rather than details; and still others object to technical presentations of any sort.

Financial information and the means of communicating it frequently have strong and pervasive **behavioral impacts**[2] upon decision makers. The behavioral impacts of accounting extend to both positive and negative motivations of people. The frequency, form, and quality of one's communications with others are often important to motivations.

---

[1] This suggests the concept of *benefit-cost analysis;* that is, a comparison of the cost of a particular course of action, compared with the economic benefits or advantages derived from that course of action.

[2] A behavioral impact is an individual's response to external forces. An individual may be motivated toward or away from certain courses of action by information or observations that come to his attention. For example, one may be motivated to purchase a large automobile rather than a small one for reasons of prestige. However, a financial report showing the relative costs of operating the two automobiles may motivate the individual to purchase the small automobile. Thus, the report exerted a significant behavioral impact on the decision maker.

The terminology and symbols of accounting were devised over a long period of time in the search for ways to communicate financial information effectively. As is common with other professions, such as law and medicine, the terminology and symbols of accounting are somewhat technical. Accounting has developed in direct response to the needs of people. As a consequence, it is continuously evolving new concepts, terminology, procedures, and means of communication. In these two volumes, one of our considerations will be the terminology of accounting.

ACCOUNTING: AN INFORMATION SYSTEM

Accounting records the detailed financial history of the entity and, from that information, derives the financial statements. Thus, the **accounting process** involves the accumulation, analysis, measurement, interpretation, classification, and summarization of the results of each of the many business transactions that affected the entity during the year. After this processing, accounting then transmits or projects messages to potential decision makers. The messages are in the form of financial statements, and the decision makers are the users. Accounting generally does not generate the basic information (raw financial data); rather, the raw financial data results from the day-to-day transactions initiated, participated in, and completed by the employees of the enterprise. The accounting system includes procedures for collecting these data; and as an *information system,* the accounting process is designed to record these data and capture the **economic essence** of each transaction.[3]

An accounting system should be designed to classify financial information on a basis suitable for decision-making purposes and to process the tremendous quantities of data efficiently and accurately. The information system must be designed to report the results periodically, in a realistic and concise format that is comprehensible to users who generally have only a limited technical knowledge of accounting. The information system also must be designed to accommodate the special and complex needs of the internal management of the entity on a continuing basis. These internal needs extend primarily to the planning and control responsibilities of the managers of the enterprise; they are discussed in *Fundamentals of Management Accounting.*

The accountant has the primary responsibility for developing an accounting information system that is essential for most entities, whether operating on a profit or nonprofit basis. In designing an information system, the accountant must consider the factors of (1) cost, (2) benefit, (3) timeliness (i.e., reports must be rendered early), and (4) requirements of various outside influences, such as governmental regulatory agencies

[3] The accounting information system should be viewed as a part of the overall information system that necessarily operates in all entities.

(examples are the Securities and Exchange Commission and the Internal Revenue Service).

Now, we are ready to consider the fundamentals of **external financial statements** prepared for owners, potential investors, creditors, and other interested parties.

FUNDAMENTALS UNDERLYING ACCOUNTING

In Chapter 1 we briefly discussed the roles of the American Institute of Certified Public Accountants (AICPA), the Financial Accounting Standards Board (FASB), the Securities and Exchange Commission (SEC), and the American Accounting Association (AAA). Although the efforts of these and other organizations were significant, much of the evolution in accounting was initiated by industry and by firms of practicing accountants. As a result of all these forces, certain assumptions, concepts, principles, and standards evolved that today constitute the **fundamentals underlying accounting.** These fundamentals are man-made. They are continually being changed to meet the evolving needs of society and to keep financial measurement and reporting relevant to current trends

EXHIBIT 2–1

Fundamentals underlying accounting

Basic assumptions, principles, and procedures*	Text reference: Chapter	Text reference: Page
1. *Underlying assumptions:*		
a. Separate-entity assumption.	1	4
b. Continuity assumption.	2	39
c. Unit-of-measure assumption.	1	3
d. Time-period assumption.	5	141
2. *Underlying principles:*		
a. Revenue principle.	2	35
b. Cost principle.	2	38
c. Matching principle.	5	144
d. Objectivity principle.	2	38
e. Consistency principle.	8	285
f. Full-disclosure principle.	3	76
g. Exception or modifying principle.	9	323
(1) Materiality.		
(2) Conservatism.		
(3) Industry peculiarities.		
3. *Practices and procedures:*		
a. Those related to income and asset measurement.	Illustrated and discussed throughout the chapters to follow.	
b. Those related to the reporting of accounting results.		
c. Those not related to asset or income measurement or to the reporting of accounting results.		

* A similar tabulation including a brief explanation is presented in Exhibit 16–1.

and problems. They change primarily because of the research efforts of accountants and the activities of the above-named organizations.

The accounting profession has not agreed upon a single listing of the fundamentals underlying accounting; therefore, throughout the literature of accounting you will find variation in terminology and definition. For purposes of this book we will use the list given in Exhibit 2–1. At this point, we will simply list these fundamentals for your convenience in future reference. We have also listed the chapter and page numbers where each fundamental is *first* introduced. Throughout the discussions we often return to these fundamentals in order to explain the rationale for a particular accounting approach.

EXTERNAL FINANCIAL STATEMENTS

A primary objective of the accounting process is the development of financial statements that communicate relevant information to decision makers. An understanding of financial statements at the outset places you in an excellent position to interpret them and to understand how the accounting process operates. The three primary financial statements for a profit-making entity for **external reporting** to owners, potential investors, creditors, and other decision makers are the—

1. Income statement (more descriptively, statement of revenues, expenses, and profit).
2. Balance sheet (more descriptively, statement of assets, liabilities, and owners' equity).
3. Statement of changes in financial position (more descriptively, statement of working capital, or cash inflows and outflows).

These three statements summarize the financial activities of the business entity for each specific period of time. They can be produced at any time (such as end of the year, quarter, or month) and can apply to any time span (such as ten years, one year, one quarter, or one month). The heading of each statement contains a very specific statement of the **time dimensions** of the report. Although these three reports relate to each other, for convenience, at this point in your study, they will be considered separately. We will first illustrate them for a simple business situation; the next chapter discusses and illustrates a more complex situation.

The income statement

The income statement is designed to report the profit performance of a business entity for a specific period of time, such as a year, quarter, or month. Profit, or net income, represents the difference between revenues and expenses for the specified period. An income statement presents the **results of operations;** that is, it reports, for a specific period of time, the items that comprise the total revenue and the total expense and the resulting net income.

Exhibit 2–2 presents the income statement for the first year of operations of Business Aids, Incorporated, an enterprise that renders professional secretarial, reproduction, and mailing services for a fee. Business Aids was organized by three individuals as a corporation. Each owner (who is called a shareholder or stockholder) received 1,000 shares of capital stock as evidence of ownership. The heading of the statement specifically identifies the name of the entity, the title of the report, and the period of time over which the reported net income was earned. Note that the date encompasses a period of time—in this case, one year. There are three major captions: *revenues, expenses,* and *net income.* The detail presented under each caption is intended to be sufficient to meet the needs of decision makers interested in Business Aids, Incorporated. This latter point is significant because the composition and the detail of a financial statement vary, depending on the characteristics of the business entity and the needs of the users.

EXHIBIT 2–2

BUSINESS AIDS, INCORPORATED	←Name of entity	HEADING
Income Statement	←Title of report	
For the Year Ended December 31, 1977	←Time	
Revenues:		
Stenographic revenue	$30,000	
Printing revenue	20,000	
Mailing revenue	13,000	
Total Revenues		$63,000
Expenses:		
Salaries expense	30,750	
Payroll tax expense	1,100	
Rent expense for office space	2,400	
Rental payments for copier	6,600	
Utilities expense	400	
Advertising expense	960	
Supplies used expense	115	
Interest expense	75	
Depreciation expense on office equipment	600	
Total Expenses		43,000
Pretax income		20,000
Income tax expense ($20,000 × 20%)		4,000
Net Income		$16,000
Earnings per share ($16,000 ÷ 3,000 shares)		$ 5.33

Revenues. Revenues are inflows of cash and other items of value received for goods sold or services rendered. Although some of the revenue inflows are cash, others may include rights, such as receivables that ensue from extending credit to customers, or property received from a customer who is paying for a service with merchandise from the customer's own shelves. Typical sources of revenue, in addition to those illustrated for Business Aids, are sales of merchandise, commissions earned, rent revenue, dividends received on capital stock owned, and interest revenue.[4] Revenue is expressed in dollars as the bargained price agreed on by the two parties to the transaction. One of the fundamentals listed in Exhibit 2–1 is called the **revenue principle;** it is also called the *realization principle.* This principle governs the accounting for revenue. The revenue principle (1) incorporates a definition of revenue, as above; (2) states that revenue should be recognized[5] in the period when the sale is made (i.e., when ownership passes) or when the services are rendered which is not necessarily the same as the period when the related cash is collected; and (3) specifies that revenues should be measured as the cash received plus the cash equivalent (i.e., the fair-market value) of any other items received. The revenue principle is discussed in more detail in Chapter 5.

Expenses. Expenses represent outflows of resources, or the incurring of a debt, for goods and services used by an entity to earn revenues. Expenses may require the immediate payment of cash or, in the case of credit, the payment of cash some time after the expense is incurred. In some cases cash is paid *before* the expense is incurred, as in the case of the payment of office rent in *advance of occupancy.* For accounting purposes, an expense is recognized in the period in which it is incurred which is not necessarily the same as the period in which the cash is paid. **The period an expense is deemed to be incurred is the period in which the goods are used or the services are received.**

An expense may represent the cost of using equipment or buildings that were acquired and are being held for use in operating the business rather than for sale. Such items often have a high initial cost at the date of acquisition and, through use, are worn out over an extended period of time known as their **useful life.** As they are used in operating the business, a portion of their initial cost becomes an expense. This kind of expense is known as **depreciation.** For example, on January 1, 1977, Business Aids purchased office equipment for its own use at a cost of $6,000. It was estimated that the office equipment would have a useful life of ten years. Therefore, the **depreciation expense** each year for using the equipment is measured as $6,000 ÷ 10 years = $600. The income statement for 1977

---

[4] Revenue sometimes is called "income," such as rent income, interest income, and royalty income, but this practice leads to confusion. *Income should always refer to the difference between revenue and expense.*

[5] Recognized, as used in this context, means that the amount involved should be accounted for (i.e., recorded in the accounting system) at the specified time.

(Exhibit 2–2) reports this amount as an expense.[6] The interest expense was on a \$1,000, 9% note payable outstanding for 10 months ($\$1,000 \times 9\% \times {}^{10}/_{12} = \$75$).

Since a corporation must pay a 20 percent tax rate on the first \$25,000, a 22 percent on the next \$25,000 of income earned each year, and a 48 percent rate for income above that amount, Business Aids incurred an income tax expense of \$4,000.[7] Income tax expense may be listed along with the other expenses; however, Business Aids prefers to report it separately as illustrated, so that both pretax and after-tax income is shown.

Net income. Net income is the excess of total revenues over total expenses. If the total expenses exceed the total revenues, a **net loss** is reported. When revenues and expenses are equal for the period, the business is said to have operated at **breakeven.**

Earnings per share. The amount of earnings per share (EPS) is reported immediately below net income if the business is organized as a corporation. EPS is derived by dividing net income by the number of shares of common stock outstanding. Since Business Aids had 3,000 shares of stock outstanding (i.e., 1,000 shares were owned by each of the three shareholders) and a net income of \$16,000, EPS was computed as $\$16,000 \div 3,000 \text{ shares} = \$5.33$ per share for the year. Especially in recent years, EPS has been accorded an extensive amount of attention by security analysts and others. As a consequence, the accounting profession has come to accept it as an important information input for investors. Specific accounting guidelines were developed by the APB in *Opinion No. 15* for computing and reporting EPS in both simple and complex situations.

It is frequently said that the income statement is the most important of the three financial reports since it is designed to communicate to the user the detailed **results of operations** of the business for a specific period of time. **The accounting model for the income statement is:**

Revenues − Expenses = Net Income (i.e., R − E = NI)

The amount of net income represents a net increase in resources that flowed into the business entity during the period.

---

[6] Accounting for depreciation is discussed in detail in Chapter 10. In respect to expense recognition, see the matching principle, Chapter 5, for a detailed discussion.

[7] Corporations, except those that qualify under Subchapter S of the Internal Revenue Code, are required to pay income taxes. Sole proprietorships and partnerships, as business entities, and Subchapter S corporations are not subject to income taxes. In these situations, the owner, or owners, must report the income of the entity on their own income tax returns. For illustrative and problem purposes an average rate is used herein to simplify the arithmetic.

The balance sheet

The purpose of the balance sheet is to report the **financial position** of a business at a particular **point** in time. Financial position refers to the amount of resources (i.e., assets) and the liabilities of the business on a specific date. As a consequence, this statement is frequently called the statement of financial position. A more descriptive title would be the

EXHIBIT 2–3

BUSINESS AIDS, INCORPORATED
Balance Sheet
At December 31, 1977

Assets			*Liabilities*		
Cash		$13,600	Accounts payable	$ 900	
Accounts receivable		13,000	Income taxes payable	1,100	
Land		20,000	Note payable, short term, 9%	1,000	
Office equipment	$6,000		Total Liabilities		$ 3,000
Less: Accumulated depreciation	600	5,400			
			Shareholders' Equity		
			Contributed Capital:		
			Capital stock (3,000 shares, par value $10 per share)	$30,000	
			Contributed capital in excess of par	3,000	
			Retained earnings	16,000	
			Total Shareholders' Equity		49,000
Total Assets		$52,000	Total Liabilities and Shareholders' Equity		$52,000

statement of assets, liabilities, and owners' equity, since these are the three major captions on the statement.[8]

Exhibit 2–3 presents the balance sheet at the end of the first year of operations for Business Aids, Incorporated. Observe that the heading specifically identifies the name of the entity, the title of the report, and the specific date of the statement. Note the specific point in time—in this case, December 31, 1977—is clearly stated on the balance sheet. This contrasts with the dating on the income statement, which indicates a

[8] The designation "balance sheet" is unfortunate since it is not descriptive in any sense. It implies that the central fact is that it balances arithmetically, although this is actually an incidental feature. Because of the widespread use of the term, it will be used in this book.

period of time (such as one year). Below the heading the **Assets** are listed on the left and the **Liabilities** and **Owners' Equity** on the right. The result is that the two sides "balance" because the **accounting model for the balance sheet is:**[9]

Assets = Liabilities + Owners' Equity (i.e., A = L + OE)

As is the case with any equation, its elements may be transposed. For example, the model frequently is expressed to reflect the fact that owners' equity is a residual (i.e., the difference between the assets and liabilities of the entity), viz:

Assets − Liabilities = Owners' Equity (i.e., A − L = OE)

The accounting model is a basic building block in the total accounting process.[10] We will now define and discuss each of the three variables in this model.

Assets. Fundamentally, assets are the resources owned by the entity. They may be tangible (physical in character), such as land, buildings, and machinery, or intangible (characterized by legal claims or rights), such as amounts due from customers (a legal claim called accounts receivable) and patents (a protected right). In short, assets are the things of value, whether physical or not, owned by the entity.[11]

Observe in the balance sheet that each of the assets listed has an assigned dollar amount. The prevailing accounting view is that assets should generally be *measured* on the basis of the *total cost incurred in their acquisition.* In accounting, this is known as the **cost principle** (listed in Exhibit 2–1). To illustrate, the balance sheet for Business Aids reports "Land, $20,000"; this is the amount of resources that was paid for the land when it was acquired. It may well be that because of market changes, the fair-market value of the land at December 31, 1977 (date of the balance sheet), was actually $35,000. Nevertheless, under the cost principle, the report would reflect the land at its original acquisition cost. It follows that the balance sheet does not necessarily show the current fair-market value of the assets listed.

It is appropriate to inquire why accountants do not change the measurement of the assets for each subsequent balance sheet to reflect the then fair-market value or price. This is not done because of the **objectivity**

---

[9] Owners' equity for a corporation generally is called shareholders' or stockholders' equity. Alternative formats for the balance sheet are discussed later.

[10] The model also may be expressed as: Assets = Equities. Equities is used to denote (1) liabilities or creditors' equity, which represent claims of creditors; and (2) owners' equity, which represents claims of the owners.

[11] Assets also include prepaid expenses and deferred charges, since these generally represent valid rights or claims for goods and services paid for in advance. These kinds of assets are considered in later chapters.

principle listed in Exhibit 2–1. This principle holds that accounting must be carried out on an objective and factual basis. There are four important reasons why fair-market values are not used.

Because of the objectivity principle:

1. Extensive estimates are required—To restate asset measurements at each balance sheet date would require that estimates (usually costly appraisals) be made of the current market value of each asset.
2. Lack of objectivity in estimates—Accurate estimates for many assets would be difficult to determine since they would be subject to wide ranges of judgment. Accounting must be objective and factual. At acquisition, a buyer and a seller, each driving for the best bargain, establish a factual valuation of cost. Such "bargained costs" are an objective and factual measure of the value of the asset when acquired.
3. Manipulation of estimates—Estimated fair-market values have the potential to be deliberately misstated by the statement maker to make the asset amounts look more favorable than is the case.

Because of the continuity assumption:

4. Assets not acquired for sale—Many assets are acquired for use by the entity and not for resale.

The financial statements of a business are prepared on the assumption that it is a continuing enterprise; that is, a going concern. This is known as the **continuity assumption** in accounting (see Exhibit 2–1). The underlying assumption is that the business will not be sold or liquidated in the near future but will continue to carry on its operational objectives independently. Consequently, a building having an estimated useful life of 50 years would be depreciated over that long period on the assumption that the business will continue operations indefinitely.

The measurement of assets is one of the most complex and controversial issues in accounting; we shall explore it further in subsequent chapters.

Note particularly how the asset "Office equipment" is reported on the balance sheet. Recall from page 35 that this equipment cost $6,000 when it was acquired by Business Aids. Also, it was estimated that the equipment would have a ten-year useful life; thus, depreciation expense was calculated to be $600 per year. On the balance sheet, assets that depreciate, such as this one, are reported at cost in accordance with the cost principle. From the cost of the asset, a deduction is made for the *accumulated* depreciation from the date of acquisition to the balance sheet date. Thus, the equipment would be reported on the balance sheets at December 31, 1977, and December 31, 1978, as follows (explanatory detail added):

	December 31			
	1977		1978	
Office equipment (cost at acquisition)................	$6,000		$6,000	
Less: Accumulated depreciation				
(1 year × $600)...	600			
(2 years × $600).......................................			1,200	
Carrying, or book, value (at end of one year)......		$5,400		
(at end of two years).....				$4,800

Because of the importance of the market value (or replacement cost) of assets to statement users and because of continued inflation there is an increasing interest in disclosure (in footnotes to the statements) of these values as well as original cost. These issues are discussed in Chapter 16.

Liabilities. Liabilities are debts or obligations owed by the entity to the creditors. They arise as a result of the purchase of goods or services from others on credit and through cash borrowings to finance the business. If a business fails to pay its creditors, the law may accord the creditors the right to force the sale of assets sufficient to meet their claims.[12]

Business entities frequently borrow money on a **note payable.** In this case, a liability known as notes payable is created. A note payable, which may be short term or long term, generally specifies a definite maturity or repayment date and the rate or amount of interest charged by the lender. Also, many businesses purchase goods and services on open account that does not involve a note, thus creating a liability known as **accounts payable.** Income taxes frequently are paid, at least in part, several months after the end of the year. As a consequence, a liability to the government, **income taxes payable,** must be reported until the taxes are fully paid. You may observe in Exhibit 2–3 that Business Aids listed three liabilities and the amount of each. In respect to amounts, liabilities present few measurement problems since most liabilities are reported at the amount of the debt established by the parties to the transaction.

Owners' equity. The accounting model (page 38) shows owners' equity to be equal to the total assets minus the total liabilities of the business. Thus, the owners' equity is a **residual interest** or claim of the owners to the assets because creditor claims legally come first. Owners' equity sometimes is called net worth, capital, or proprietorship. However the preferable designations are for a sole proprietorship, owner's equity; for a partnership, partners' equity; and for a corporation, shareholders' or stockholders' equity. Owners' equity in a business derives from two sources: (1) contributed capital, which is the investment of cash or other assets in the business by the owner or owners; and (2) retained earnings, which are the accumulated profits of the business less the losses and with-

[12] In case of dissolution or sale of all the assets of a business, legally the creditors must be paid first; any remainder goes to the owners.

drawals. When the owners receive cash or other assets from the business through withdrawals (defined later), the total amount of owners' equity is reduced. When the business incurs a loss, owners' equity also is reduced.

In Exhibit 2–3, the shareholders' equity section reports the following:

1. Contributed capital—The three shareholders invested a total of \$33,000 in the business and received 3,000 shares of capital stock having a par value of \$10 per share (par value will be discussed in Chapter 13). They invested \$11 per share, or \$1 above par value. The 3,000 shares issued are reported at their par value (3,000 × \$10) as "Capital stock"; and the remainder, often called a premium (3,000 shares × \$1 = \$3,000), is reported as "Contributed capital in excess of par value."[13]
2. Retained earnings—The accumulated earnings less all dividends paid to shareholders since formation of the corporation is reported as "Retained earnings." During the first year the business earned \$16,000, as shown on the income statement (Exhibit 2–2). This amount is reported on the balance sheet for Business Aids at this date as retained earnings since no dividends had been paid to the shareholders.
3. Total shareholders' equity is the sum of the investment (\$33,000) plus the retained earnings (\$16,000) = \$49,000. This amount may be verified: Assets (\$52,000) − Liabilities (\$3,000) = Shareholders' Equity (\$49,000).

If, by contrast, a cash dividend of \$6,000 had been paid to the three shareholders, the balance sheet would have reflected cash of \$7,600 (\$13,600 − \$6,000) and retained earnings of \$10,000 (\$16,000 − \$6,000).

The form of organization utilized for Business Aids was a corporation. If the business were a sole proprietorship or a partnership, the "Owners' Equity" classification on the balance sheet would appear somewhat differently. Owners' equity for both a sole proprietorship and a partnership is illustrated below, utilizing the amounts for Business Aids from Exhibit 2–3.

Owners' Equity for a Sole Proprietorship

Owner's Equity:	
R. Nalle, capital	\$49,000

*Owners' Equity for a Partnership**

Partners' Equity:	
J. Doe, capital	16,333
R. Moe, capital	16,333
S. Roe, capital	16,334
Total Partners' Equity	\$49,000

* This assumes that each partner invested \$11,000 and that the income of \$16,000 was divided equally among them.

[13] Par value has a legal meaning that is discussed in Chapter 13.

Corporations may be required by law to maintain a distinction between contributed capital and retained earnings, as reflected in Exhibit 2–3. This is because the amount of dividends paid to shareholders normally cannot exceed the amount of retained earnings. In a partnership, the capital of each partner usually is increased by that partner's share of the net income and decreased by that partner's withdrawals of assets from the business. In a sole proprietorship, earnings are added to the proprietor's original invested capital and withdrawals are deducted.

Statement of changes in financial position

In recent years the **financing activities** of businesses have become increasingly complex. The business entity of today requires substantial funds for operations and expansion. These funds come from three sources: (1) owner investment, (2) borrowings, and (3) internally by earning a profit or selling noncash assets. In recognition of the need by users of financial statements for information concerning the investing and financing activities of the business, the APB issued *Opinion No. 19* in March 1971. This *Opinion* requires a **statement of changes in financial position**[14] to accompany the income statement and the balance sheet.

The objective of the statement of changes in financial position is to communicate to the user information about the inflows and outflows of cash (or, alternatively, working capital, defined later). Exhibit 2–4 presents a statement of changes in financial position for Business Aids. At this point you need not be concerned about the derivation of the amounts. Rather, your attention is called to the two basic classifications: cash generated (inflows of cash) and cash applied (outflows of cash). The difference between them represents the increase, or decrease, in cash during the period. Since investors and creditors often think in terms of present and potential future cash flows, this statement provides an important information input to the decision-making process. The accounting model for this statement is:

Cash Inflows − Cash Outflows = Change in Cash

Note: The statement, rather than being prepared on a cash basis, often if prepared on a working capital basis (discussed later).

The statement of changes in financial position is derived from an analysis of the balance sheet and the income statement. For example, total revenue reported on Exhibit 2–2 (the income statement) of $63,000, less $13,000 of the revenue (mailing) extended on credit, equals $50,000, reported as the cash inflow from revenue on Exhibit 2–4. Similarly, total expenses of $47,000 (including income tax expense), shown on

[14] This statement is an outgrowth of an earlier "statement of sources and applications of funds," which was optional.

EXHIBIT 2–4

BUSINESS AIDS, INCORPORATED
Statement of Changes in Financial Position—Cash Basis
For the Year Ended December 31, 1977

Cash Generated (inflows):		
From operations:		
From revenue	$50,000	
Less: Cash used for expenses	44,400	
Cash generated from operations		$ 5,600
From other sources:		
Investment by owners (stock issued)	33,000	
Loan—note payable	1,000	
Cash generated from other sources		34,000
Total Cash Generated during the Year (inflows)		39,600
Cash Applied (outflows):		
To purchase office equipment	6,000	
To purchase land	20,000	
Total Cash Applied during the Year (outflows)		26,000
Change—increase in cash during the year		$13,600

Exhibit 2–2, less the **noncash expenses** of $600 for depreciation, $900 for accounts payable, and $1,100 for income taxes payable, equals the $44,400 reported on Exhibit 2–4 as the cash used for expenses. Detailed discussion of the statement of changes in financial position is deferred to Chapter 15 because it requires special procedures that are best understood after your knowledge of accounting is substantial.

ACCRUAL BASIS ACCOUNTING

In the definition of revenue on page 35, we stated that revenue is recognized when **earned** rather than when the resulting cash is collected. Similarly, in defining expenses, we stated that an expense is recognized when **incurred** rather than when the required cash is paid. These definitions reflect the **accrual basis** of accounting, as contrasted with the cash basis. Frequently, revenue may be *earned* long before the cash is collected. For example, assume an appliance company sold a refrigerator for $300 on November 1, 1977, for a $100 down payment with the balance payable later, on May 1, 1978. Under the accrual basis, the $300 sale would be recognized in 1977. In other situations, cash may be collected before the revenue is earned. For example, a publishing company often receives cash for subscriptions before the magazines or newspapers are delivered. In this situation the revenue from the subscriptions would be recognized as the magazines are delivered rather than when the cash subscription price was collected. Similarly, expenses may be *incurred* before or after the cash payment date. For example, assume a plumbing firm completed a service job for the company in December 1977 and cash payment is to be made in February 1978. Under the accrual basis, the expense should be recognized in 1977 rather than in 1978. Or, expenses may be **prepaid;** that is, the cash is paid *before* the expense is incurred. For example, a company may choose to pay in advance a three-year premium of $300 for insurance on a building. The insurance expense would be $100 for each of the three years since the expense is *incurred* as the time covered by the policy passes.

The accrual basis is used in accounting so that revenues and expenses will be recognized in the period in which the activities occurred that caused those revenues and expenses. Cash inflows and outflows reflect **financing activities,** whereas revenues and expenses recognized on the accrual basis reflect the results of **operating activities.**

DEMONSTRATION CASE FOR SELF-STUDY

ABC Corporation

(Try to resolve the case before studying the suggested solution that follows it.)

ABC Corporation was organized by three investors on January 1, 1977. On that date, as initial, or start-up, cash, each investor bought 2,000 shares of capital stock (par $10 per share) and paid $12 per share in cash. In addition, the corporation borrowed $40,000 cash from a local bank, giving a three-year note payable. The note was dated January 1, 1977, and called for 8 percent interest per year. The interest is payable each December 31; and the maturity, or due date, of the note is December 31, 1979. Operations were started immediately.

On December 31, 1977, it was determined that the net income of ABC Company for the first year was $21,000, after deducting interest expense and income tax expense. On that date, each shareholder was paid a cash dividend of $2 per share.

Required:

1. What were the sources and amounts of cash to start the business?
2. Prepare the shareholders' equity section of the balance sheet for ABC Corporation at December 31, 1977.

Solution:

ABC CORPORATION

1. Sources and amounts of initial cash:

From owners (6,000 shares of stock at $12 per share)	$ 72,000
From creditors (note payable, 8% interest, 36 months to maturity)	40,000
Total Start-up Cash	$112,000

2. Partial balance sheet at December 31, 1977:

Shareholders' Equity

Capital stock (6,000 shares, par $10 per share)	$ 60,000
Contributed capital in excess of par value	12,000
Total Contributed Capital	72,000
Retained earnings (see Note *a*)	9,000
Total Shareholders' Equity	$ 81,000

Notes:

a. Computation of retained earnings:

Starting balance, January 1, 1977	$ -0-
Add net income for 1977	21,000
Total	21,000
Deduct dividends paid during 1977 (6,000 shares × $2)	12,000
Ending balance, December 31, 1977	$ 9,000

b. The $40,000 note payable will be reported on the balance sheet under the liability caption. The $3,200 interest paid will be reported on the income statement under the expense caption.

SUMMARY

The focus of this chapter was on the communication of accounting information to external users as a basis for their decision making. Your attention was directed primarily to profit-making entities, or business enterprises. The chapter explained and illustrated the basic features of the three required **external** financial reports—the income statement, the balance sheet, and the statement of changes in financial position.

The income statement, as a statement of operations, reports revenues, expenses, and the net income for a stated **period** of time. Earnings per share (EPS), which expressed the relationship between net income and the number of shares of common stock, was illustrated.

The balance sheet, as a statement of financial position, reports dollar amounts for the assets, liabilities, and owners' equity at a specific **point** in time.

The statement of changes in financial position, as a statement of the inflows and outflows of funds, reports those flows for a specific **period** of time.

The fundamental accounting model **Assets = Liabilities + Owners' Equity** was introduced as the foundation for the balance sheet and the accounting process in general. The distinction between the accrual basis and the cash basis was explained. The financial statements for a small company were illustrated. In the next chapter we will move one step forward and look at a more complex situation and, at the same time, add more concepts to your knowledge about the characteristics of the financial statements for a business entity.

A list of the broad fundamentals underlying accounting was given in Exhibit 2–1. Of those listed, the following have been defined and illustrated up to this point:

Designation	*Underlying fundamentals*
Unit-of-measure assumption	Measurement in accounting predominately is in terms of the monetary exchange unit. The dollar is the common denominator—the yardstick—for measurement in the accounting process.
Separate-entity assumption	For accounting purposes the entity must be specifically defined; a business is assumed to be separate and apart from its owners and other parties.
Revenue principle	Revenue should be given accounting recognition only when it is earned; that is, when a sale of goods is made or a service is rendered.
Cost principle	Assets acquired should be accounted for at the bargained cost when acquired and are subsequently carried at that cost.
Continuity assumption	Unless there is evidence to the contrary, accounting assumes that the business entity is not being sold or liquidated; that it will continue indefinitely as a "going concern" to carry out its intended operational objectives.
Objectivity principle	Accounting measures and reports the financial effects of transactions on an objective, factual, and verifiable basis. Insofar as possible, only objectively determined measurements are used.

IMPORTANT TERMS

Information system
Communication
Accounting process
External financial statements
Income statement
Revenues
Expenses
Depreciation expense
Net income
Earnings per share (EPS)
Balance sheet
Assets
Liabilities
Owners' equity
Unit-of-measure assumption
Separate-entity assumption
Revenue principle
Cost principle
Objectivity principle
Continuity assumption
Statement of changes in financial position
Accrual basis

QUESTIONS FOR DISCUSSION

1. Financial statements are the end products of the accounting process. Explain.
2. Generally, how would you define communication?
3. The accounting process generates financial reports for both "internal" and "external" audiences. Identify some of the groups in each audience.
4. Explain why accounting may be viewed as an information system.

5. Complete the following:

	Name of statement		*A more descriptive name*
a.	Income statement	*a.*	______________
b.	Balance sheet	*b.*	______________
c.	Statement of changes in financial position	*c.*	______________

6. What information should be included in the heading of each of the three required financial statements?
7. Explain why the income statement and the statement of changes in financial position are dated "For the Year Ended December 31, 19XX," whereas the balance sheet is dated "At December 31, 19XX."
8. Explain the revenue principle.
9. Briefly define revenue and expenses.
10. Briefly define the following: net income, net loss, and breakeven.
11. What are the purposes of (*a*) the income statement, (*b*) the balance sheet, and (*c*) the statement of changes in financial position?
12. Explain the accounting model for the income statement. What are the three major items reported on the income statement?
13. Explain the accounting model for the balance sheet. Define the three major components reported on the balance sheet.
14. Explain the accounting model for the statement of changes in financial position. Explain the three major components reported on the statement.
15. Why is owners' equity frequently referred to as a residual interest?
16. What are the two primary sources of owners' equity in a business?
17. What are appropriate titles for owners' equity for (*a*) a sole proprietorship, (*b*) a partnership, and (*c*) a corporation?

EXERCISES

E2–1. Walkin Grocery, Incorporated, has been in operation for six years. The 1977 annual financial statements are to be prepared for the shareholders and for submission to the bank as support for a line of credit. You have been requested to draft an appropriate heading and list of major captions for each of the three external reports that should be prepared.

E2–2. Kyle Realty, Incorporated, has been operating for five years and is owned by three investors. S. T. Kyle owns 60 percent of the outstanding stock of 9,000 shares and is the managing executive in charge. On December 31, 1977, the following financial items for the year were determined: commissions earned and collected in cash, $150,000, plus $20,000 uncollected; rental service fees earned and collected, $20,000; salaries expense paid, $60,000; commissions expense paid, $45,000; payroll taxes paid, $4,000; rent paid, $2,200 (not including December rent yet to be paid); utilities expense paid, $700; promotion and advertising paid, $6,400; and miscellaneous expenses paid, $300. There were no other unpaid expenses at December 31. Kyle Realty rents office space for its own use but owns the furniture therein. The furniture cost $5,000 when acquired and has an estimated life of ten years. The average corporate income tax rate is 30 percent. Also, during the year, the company paid the owners "out of profits" cash dividends amounting to $10,000. You have been requested to prepare an income statement for 1977. (Hint: EPS is $5.50.)

E2–3. Jan's is a retail store that specializes in ladies' clothes. The company uses its own store furniture, and the store space is rented. The following information is available at the end of the year, December 31, 1977:

Item	*Cost when acquired*	*Date acquired*	*Estimated useful life*
Furniture	$31,500	Jan. 1, 1974	7 years

Required:

a. Compute the depreciation expense for the year ended December 31, 1977. Show your computations.

b. Compute the total accumulated depreciation on the furniture to December 31, 1977.

c. What is the book or carrying value of the furniture at December 31, 1977?

E2–4. The University Bookstore was organized as a partnership by James Nash and Roy Opel; each contributed $25,000 cash to start the business. The store completed its first year of operations on December 31, 1977. On that date the following financial items were determined: cash on hand and in the bank, $32,000; due from customers from sales of books, $6,090; store and office equipment, purchased January 1, 1977, for $40,000 (estimated useful life ten years); amounts owed to publishers for books purchased, $6,000; and a note payable, 9 percent, one year, dated July 1, 1977, to a local bank for $2,000. The partners divided the annual profit of $16,000 equally, although none of it was withdrawn since they "needed it for growth of the store." You have been requested to prepare a balance sheet for the bookstore at December 31, 1977. (Hint: Total liabilities amounted to $8,090.)

E2–5. Macon Corporation is preparing a balance sheet at the end of 1977. The following amounts have been determined: retained earnings amount at the start of 1977 was $42,000; cash dividends paid to stockholders at the end of 1977 amounted to $30,000; and net income (after income taxes) for 1977 amounted to $24,000. Compute the amount of retained earnings at the end of 1977.

E2–6. Rice Manufacturing Corporation is preparing the annual financial report for shareholders. A statement of changes in financial position—cash basis must be prepared. The following data on cash flows were developed for the year ended December 31, 1977: cash inflow from operating revenues, $270,000; cash expended for operating expenses,

$190,000; sale of unissued Rice stock for cash, $30,000; cash dividends paid to shareholders during the year, $20,000; and payments on long-term notes payable, $40,000. During the year, three used machines were sold for $10,000 cash and $45,000 cash was expended for two new machines. The machines are used in the factory.

Required:

Prepare a statement of changes in financial position—cash basis for 1977. Follow the format illustrated in the chapter.

E2–7. On June 1, 1977, Rand Corporation prepared a balance sheet just prior to going out of business. The balance sheet totals reflected the following:

Assets (no cash)	$100,000
Liabilities	60,000
Stockholders' equity	40,000

Shortly thereafter, all of the assets were sold for cash.

Required:

a. How would the balance sheet appear immediately after the sale of the assets for cash for each separate case?

	Cash received for the assets	*Balances immediately after sale*		
		Assets	*Liabilities*	*Stockholders' equity*
Case A	$110,000	$____	$____	$____
Case B	100,000	____	____	____
Case C	90,000	____	____	____

b. How should the cash be distributed in each separate case?

	To creditors	*To stockholders*	*Total*
Case A	$____	$____	$____
Case B	____	____	____
Case C	____	____	____

PROBLEMS

P2–1. Aztec Rental Company was organized as a corporation in January 1977 by five investors. Each investor paid in $12,000 cash and received 200 shares of $50 par value stock. Immediately thereafter, the company obtained a $15,000 loan from a local bank. Rental equipment costing $52,000 was purchased for cash, and operations began. Careful records were maintained during the year. As a consequence, the following correct amounts were available at the end of December 1977:

Rental fees collected	$72,000	Cash on hand and in bank	$25,150
Rental fees uncollected	3,000	Rental equipment (cost)	52,000
Repair fees collected	10,000	Land for future building site	14,000
Salaries and wages paid	30,000	Other assets	8,000
Payroll taxes paid	800	Rent payable (December)	200
Repair parts purchased and used	700	Income taxes payable	1,400*
Rent paid (11 months)	2,200	Notes payable, long term	15,000
December rent not yet paid	200	Capital stock	50,000
Utilities paid	400	Cash dividends paid	10,000
Advertising expenditures paid	2,400	Accounts receivable	3,000
Insurance premiums paid for 1977	100	Accumulated depreciation	10,000
Miscellaneous expenses paid	1,500	Contributed capital in excess of par	10,000
Depreciation for the year on rental equipment	10,000		
Maintenance costs paid	200		
Income tax rate (average rate)	30%		

* Part of the income taxes was paid during the year.

Required:

You have been requested to use the above data to prepare an income statement and a balance sheet at the end of 1977. (Hint: The balance sheet total is $92,150.)

P2–2. Western Realty Company was organized early in 1973 as a corporation by four investors, each of whom invested $5,000 cash. The company has been moderately successful, despite the fact that internal financial controls are inadequate. Although financial reports have been prepared each year (primarily in response to income tax requirements), sound accounting practice has not been followed. As a consequence, the financial performance of the company was only vaguely known by the four shareholders. Recently, one of the shareholders, with the agreement of the others, sold his shares to a local CPA (not in public practice). The new shareholder was amazed when handed the report below, which was prepared by a secretary for the last meeting of the board of directors. The CPA could tell at a glance that the reported profit was wrong and quickly observed that there was no interest expense shown on a $10,000, 9 percent note payable that had been outstanding throughout the year. Also, no recognition had been given to office equipment that was purchased on January 1, 1977, at a cost of $14,000 and having an estimated five-year useful life.

WESTERN REALTY
Profit Statement
December 31, 1977

Commissions earned (all collected)	$130,000
Property management revenue (exclusive of $1,200 not collected)	8,000
Total	138,000
Salaries paid	32,000
Commissions paid	38,000
Payroll taxes paid	2,300
Office supplies expense	120
Rent paid	2,400
Utilities paid	500
Advertising (excluding the December bill for advertising of $4,000 not yet paid)	28,000
Miscellaneous expenses	400
Total	103,720
Profit for the year	$ 34,280

EPS: $34,280 ÷ 1,000 shares = $34.28.

Required:

You have been asked to redraft the income statement, including corrections. Assume an average income tax rate of 30 percent. (Hint: The correct EPS is $19.446.)

P2–3. At December 31, 1977, Big J Corporation had been in operation for one year. At the date of organization, each of the ten investors paid in $10,000 cash and each received 100 shares of capital stock. Due to a need for more capital, on January 1, 1977, the corporation also borrowed $90,000, at 8 percent interest per year, on a note from a local bank. Interest on the note was payable each December 31 and the loan matures December 31, 1980. On December 31, 1977, the income statement and the balance sheet (summarized) were as follows:

Income Statement
For the Year Ended December 31, 1977

Total revenue	$70,000
Total expenses	44,360
Pretax income	25,640
Income tax expense ($25,640 × 30%)	7,692
Net Income	$17,948

Balance Sheet
At December 31, 1977

Assets		*Liabilities*	
Cash	$ 22,231	Income taxes payable	$ 1,923*
Remaining assets	187,640	Notes payable, long term	90,000
		Stockholders' Equity	
		Capital stock (1,000 shares)	100,000
		Retained earnings	17,948
Total Assets	$209,871	Total Liabilities and Owners' Equity	$209,871

* Three fourths of the income taxes was paid during the year on a quarterly basis.

An independent CPA has audited the above amounts. The CPA found that the bookkeeper had neglected to include two transactions that occurred on December 31, 1977:

1. Payment of a cash dividend of $7.50 per share to each shareholder.
2. Cash payment of interest for one year on the long-term note payable owed to the bank.

Required:

Other than for these two transactions, the amounts were correct. Recast the income statement and the balance sheet to include the effects of these two transactions. Assume a 30 percent tax rate. (Hint: The balance sheet total is $195,171.)

P2–4. At the end of 1977, Foster Corporation prepared the following annual income statement and balance sheet:

Income Statement
For the Year Ended December 31, 1977

Revenues	$280,000
Expenses	248,000
Income before taxes	32,000
Income taxes (average rate, 30%)	9,600
Net Income	$ 22,400

Balance Sheet
At December 31, 1977

Assets

Cash		$ 18,000
Accounts receivable		22,000
Inventory		76,800
Fixtures	$25,000	
Less: Accumulated depreciation	7,000	18,000
Total Assets		$134,800

Liabilities

Accounts payable		$ 8,000
Income taxes payable (one half unpaid)		4,800
Notes payable, 9% (due June 30, 1978)		20,000
Total Liabilities		32,800
Shareholders' Equity		
Common stock, par $10, 5,000 shares	$50,000	
Contributed capital in excess of par	10,000	
Retained earnings	42,000	
Total Shareholders' Equity		102,000
Total Liabilities and Shareholders' Equity		$134,800

An independent audit of the above statements and underlying records revealed the following:

1. Depreciation expense included in total expense was $2,000 for 1977; it should have been $2,500.
2. A tentative order was received from a customer on December 31, 1977, for goods having a selling price of $10,000 and was included in sales revenue and accounts receivable. The goods were on hand (in inventory), and it is likely a sale may not materialize; the customer will decide by January 20, 1978. This should not have been recognized as a sale in 1977.

Required:

Other than these two items, the amounts were correct. Recast the two statements to take into account the depreciation error and the incorrect recognition of the tentative order. Show computations and assume an average income tax rate of 30 percent. (Hint: Revised EPS is $3.01.)

P2–5. ABC Furniture Store was organized at the start of 1977 with an investment of $90,000. At the end of the year, it was determined that net income after income taxes amounted to $15,000. During the year, the owners had not withdrawn any cash. You have been requested to develop the owners' equity section of the December 31, 1977, balance sheet under each of three different cases as follows:

Case A – Assume a sole proprietorship (owner A. B. Cole).

Case B – Assume a three-way partnership (Ames, Byron, and Cole) whereby each partner invested the same amount of cash at the start and net income is divided one third to each.

Case C – Assume a corporation whereby 3,000 shares were issued to each of three shareholders at $10 par value per share.

P2–6. In January 1977, Boston Stores, Incorporated, purchased a building at a cost of $200,000 and immediately put it to use as an expansion of the main store. It was determined that $40,000 of the purchase price applied to the land on which the building was located and the remainder applied to the building. At the end of the year, the management felt that the fair-market value of the property had increased "by about 10 percent." A local real estate agent, thinking a good deal might be lined up, indicated that "perhaps $240,000 could be gotten for the property." Although the company had no intention of selling the property, there were discussions to the effect that the property should be "listed on the balance sheet at $240,000, and certainly no less than $220,000." You have been asked for a definite statement, with reasoning, as to the correct accounting measurement to be shown, separately for the building and the land on the balance sheets at December 31, 1977, and 1978. Assume a 20-year estimated useful life for the building. In your response show the following:

Assets	*1977*	*1978*
Building		
Less: Accumulated depreciation		
Land		

Explain the basis for the amounts you show for each item. (Hint: Land is not subject to depreciation since it is not "used up" over time.)

P2–7. Stanford Corporation owns the following items of equipment and fixtures used in operating the business:

Item	*Date acquired*	*Cost when acquired*	*Estimated useful life*
Store fixtures	Jan. 1, 1974	$30,000	10 years
Delivery auto (panel)	Jan. 1, 1975	3,600	4 years
Office equipment	July 1, 1976	4,000	10 years
Land	Jan. 1, 1977	10,000	Indefinite – not subject to depreciation

Required:

a. You have been asked to compute depreciation expense for 1977 for each of the above assets (show your computations).

b. What would be the book or carrying value of each item on the balance sheet at December 31, 1977?

c. Can you think of any factors that might be missing that would affect the computation of depreciation? Explain.

3

Content of financial statements

PURPOSE OF THE CHAPTER

The preceding chapter introduced the concepts underlying the income statement, balance sheet, and statement of changes in financial position. In this chapter we turn our attention to appropriate *subclassifications* of the information presented in these statements. Classification is employed to enhance communication and the usefulness of the information presented. In addition, we will introduce **ratio analysis,** which often is helpful in the interpretation of financial statements. In the course of the discussions in this chapter, first we will illustrate the financial statements for a medium-sized enterprise. We will then discuss a more complicated set of financial statements for a large business.

In this chapter you should concentrate on understanding the nature of the classifications and the presentation of accounting information in the financial statements rather than on how the amounts shown are accumulated. At this time in your study of accounting, we do not anticipate that you will absorb all aspects of the financial statements that are presented; however, you should comprehend the primary features of each statement. You also should appreciate the importance of the end product of the accounting process—the financial statements—and be able to maintain perspective in the chapters to follow when studying the details of information processing, measurement, and reporting in terms of the accounting model. As you study the subsequent chapters, you should return frequently to this one for reference points and further study. Also, the exhibits will be helpful as a guide in solving some of the assigned problems in subsequent chapters.

CLASSIFICATION OF ITEMS ON THE FINANCIAL STATEMENTS

In order to assist the user of financial statements, some standardization of classifications has evolved. As a basis for discussion of these classifications, this section presents the financial statements for Diamond's, Incorporated, a large department store that has been in business for over 40 years. When these classifications are included on the statements, they are sometimes referred to as **classified financial statements.** Classified financial statements vary in terminology and arrangement from those for Business Aids, given in Chapter 2. These differences reflect the fact that financial statements are tailored to the **needs of users,** depending on the type of company and the nature of the industry.

The income statement

Exhibit 3–1 presents an income statement for Diamond's.[1] It follows the basic concept that: **Revenues − Expenses = Net Income.** Therefore, Exhibit 3–1, stripped of the detailed items, shows the following subclassifications:

Revenues

Expenses:
- Cost of goods sold
- Operating expenses
- Financial expenses
- Income tax expense

Income before extraordinary items
- Extraordinary gains and losses

Net income

Earnings per share

We will discuss the meaning of each of these classifications.

Revenues. The revenue of a business that sells services is called service revenue. The total revenue of a business that sells products or mer-

[1] The income statement discussed and illustrated in this section sometimes is referred to as a *multiple-step* income statement since it shows several groupings of data and after each group (or step) shows a difference. Each such difference is appropriately labeled, such as gross margin on sales. In contrast, a single-step income statement would be similar to that illustrated in Chapter 2, Exhibit 2–2, since only two major categories (revenues and expenses) were shown and there were no "step" differences. Many published income statements follow the single-step format. The classifications illustrated for Diamond's are used frequently; however, they are not mandatory.

EXHIBIT 3–1

DIAMOND'S, INCORPORATED
Income Statement
For the Year Ended December 31, 1977

Gross sales revenue		$3,620,000	
Less: Sales returns and allowances		5,000	
Net sales revenue			$3,615,000
Less: Cost of goods sold			2,416,000
Gross margin on sales			1,199,000
Operating Expenses:			
Selling Expenses:			
Sales salaries	$409,000		
Advertising and promotion	200,000		
Depreciation, store equipment	15,000		
Insurance	18,000		
Taxes (excluding income tax expense)	3,200		
Warranty expense	3,000		
Amortization of trademarks	2,000		
Miscellaneous	9,800		
Total Selling Expenses		660,000	
General and Administrative Expenses:			
Administrative salaries	179,000		
Office supplies used	8,100		
Estimated losses on doubtful accounts	3,600		
Depreciation, office equipment	1,000		
Insurance	2,000		
Taxes (excluding income tax expense)	400		
Miscellaneous	1,900		
Total General and Administrative Expenses		196,000	
Total Operating Expenses			856,000
Income from operations			343,000
Financial Expenses and Revenues:			
Interest expense		56,000	
Revenue from investments and funds		13,000	
Net Financial Expense			43,000
Pretax income			300,000
Income tax on operations			138,000
Income before extraordinary items			162,000
Extraordinary Items:			
Gain on sale of land held for appreciation*		51,000	
Less: Income tax on the gain		13,000	38,000
Net Income			$ 200,000
Earnings per share of common stock:			
Income before extraordinary items			$ 9.13
Extraordinary items			2.54
Net Income			$11.67

* We have assumed that this transaction met the two criteria for an extraordinary item.

chandise is called **sales revenue.** Merchandise sold and later returned by the customer represents **returned sales** and reduces revenue. Similarly, allowances granted to customers, say for a defect in the goods purchased from the store, reduces revenue. Therefore, **gross sales** for the period must be reduced by these two amounts in order to derive the correct net revenue amount, or **net sales,** for the period.

Expenses. An income statement may be designed to reflect several classifications of expenses. These classifications tend to vary, depending upon the type of business. For a merchandising business, which is one that sells goods manufactured by others, the usual classifications of expenses are:

1. Cost of goods sold. This expense reflects the amount that was incurred for the merchandise (or goods) that was sold during the period. For example, Diamond's sold goods during the period, at selling price, amounting to $3,615,000 net. This merchandise, when purchased by Diamond's, cost $2,416,000. The difference between these two amounts is known as the **gross margin on sales** (formerly called gross profit on sales). For Diamond's, the gross margin was $1,199,000. The gross margin indicates the markup on all of the goods sold during the period. To illustrate, the average markup *on cost* for Diamond's was $1,199,000 ÷ $2,416,000 = 49.6 percent; and *on selling price,* it was $1,199,000 ÷ $3,615,000 = 33.2 percent.

2. Operating expenses. These are the usual expenses that were incurred in operating the business during the period. Often they are subclassified further, as reflected in Exhibit 3–1, between **selling expenses** and **general and administrative expenses.** *Selling expenses* comprise all amounts incurred during the period in performing the sales activities. *General and administrative expenses* include the overall business expenses, such as the president's salary and the expenses of operating the accounting department.

3. Financial expenses. These are the expenses incurred as a result of borrowing money or for credit extended to the company. The cost of credit usually is referred to as **interest expense.** Since interest on debt is a financing expense rather than an operating expense, it is set out in a separate category from cost of goods sold and operating expenses.

Some businesses also collect interest for credit they have extended to others and receive interest revenue (discussed in a later chapter). When the amount of interest revenue is not substantial, instead of reporting it under the revenue caption, it is sometimes offset against interest expense as shown on Exhibit 3–1. When interest revenue is under the revenue classification, "gross margin" cannot be reported because that concept is disturbed. For this reason, and the desire to report both financial expenses and financial revenue under one caption, companies often report these as shown in Exhibit 3–1.

Extraordinary items. This special classification is used to report nonoperating gains and losses. Since these items are (1) **unusual in nature** and (2) **occur infrequently,** they are set out separately to aid the user in evaluating the profit performance of the business. To include them in the usual, regularly recurring revenue or expense categories would lead the user to believe they are normal and will occur again in the future. Observe in Exhibit 3–1 that when there are **extraordinary items,** income amounts will be shown immediately before and immediately after the extraordinary items.[2]

Income tax expense. This is the amount of income taxes incurred for the period. The amount of income subject to tax is defined by the Internal Revenue Code and often does not agree with the "accounting" income amount shown on the income statement. Detailed consideration of income taxes is beyond the scope of this book. However, we will use simplified tax rates and computations of income taxes to demonstrate appropriate reporting of the income tax expense and income taxes payable.

In Exhibit 3–1, observe that total income tax expense is \$138,000 + \$13,000 = \$151,000. When there are extraordinary items, income tax expense must be reported in two parts:

1. Income taxes based on normal operations is reported above the caption "Income before extraordinary items" (\$138,000 in Exhibit 3–1).
2. Income taxes based on the extraordinary items is reported with those items (\$13,000 in Exhibit 3–1).

Income amounts. Observe that three separate "income" amounts are reported: pretax income (an optional step amount), income before extraordinary items (required when there are extraordinary items) and, net income. Income before extraordinary items is the difference between "ordinary" revenues and expenses. Net income is always the last item (it is a difference) in the body of the income statement; as a result it is often called the "bottomline figure." It is after extraordinary items and has no qualifications—**it is the difference between total revenues and total expenses** (including extraordinary items).

Earnings per share. A corporation is required to show earnings-per-share amounts on the income statement for income before extraordi-

[2] APB *Opinion No. 30* requires that the following format be used at the bottom of the income statement when there are extraordinary items:

Income before extraordinary items.
Extraordinary items (net of any related income tax).
Net income.

nary items and for net income.[3] In Chapter 2, the computation of earnings per share was briefly discussed and illustrated. In that chapter, Business Aids, Incorporated, reported only one EPS amount since there were no extraordinary items. In contrast, Diamond's reported three EPS amounts since there was an extraordinary item.[4]

The balance sheet

In order to assist users, the assets, liabilities, and owners' equity are classified on the balance sheet into useful categories of similar items. The following classifications commonly are used.

Balance Sheet

Assets	*Liabilities*
Current assets	Current liabilities
Long-term investments and funds	Long-term liabilities
Fixed (or operational) assets	
Intangible assets	*Owners' Equity*
Deferred charges	Contributed capital
Other assets	Retained earnings

Exhibit 3–2 presents a balance sheet for Diamond's, Incorporated. This reports items under each of the *three major* categories—assets, liabilities, and owners' equity. These major categories were defined in Chapter 2. Exhibit 2–3 (Business Aids) presented a balance sheet in **account form;** that is, with assets on the left and liabilities and owners' equity on the right. In contrast, Exhibit 3–2 (Diamond's) presents a balance sheet in **statement or report form,** which reports the major captions in a vertical relationship. Both formats are widely used.

Current assets. Under this classification are listed cash and other resources that are expected to be realized in cash or sold or consumed

---

[3] APB *Opinion No. 15* requires that the two EPS amounts be reported; viz, (1) on income before extraordinary items and (2) on net income. However, many companies also report an EPS amount for the extraordinary category as shown on Exhibit 3–1.

[4] Earnings-per-share amounts are computed only for **common** stock outstanding. At this point in your study you need not be concerned about the computation of EPS amounts when both common and preferred stock are outstanding. This will be discussed later. However, for those interested, the amounts on Exhibit 3–1 were computed as follows:

Income before extraordinary items:	
($162,000 − $25,000, the dividend claim of the preferred) ÷ 15,000 shares =	$ 9.13
Extraordinary gain:	
$38,000 ÷ 15,000 shares =	2.54
Net income:	
($200,000 − $25,000) ÷ 15,000 shares =	$11.67

either within one year from the date of the balance sheet or during the **normal operating cycle** of the business, whichever is longer. The normal operating cycle tends to vary for each business because it is the average time required for the cycle—cash to cash. For a merchandising company it may be graphically presented as in Exhibit 3–3.

Current assets generally are listed on the balance sheet in order of decreasing liquidity. **Liquidity** refers to the average period of time required to convert a noncash resource to cash. In addition to cash, current assets include short-term or temporary investments, accounts receivable, inventories, and prepaid expenses. **Prepaid expenses** are goods or services paid in advance of their use, such as a two-year insurance premium and office supplies purchased some time before their actual use. When used, they become expenses. Since resources were expended to attain the goods or services prior to their actual usage and they will be used in the near future, they are classified on the balance sheet as current assets until used. To illustrate, assume a two-year insurance premium of $600 was paid on January 1, 1977. At the end of 1977, one half of the insurance period would have expired. Therefore, *insurance expense* for 1977 would be $300 and the remaining $300 would be reported on the balance sheet as a current asset because the company still has insurance coverage due for one more year. Similarly, in 1978, insurance expense would be $300 and there would be no prepaid insurance on this policy at December 31, 1978.

Creditors that have loaned money to the company on a short-term basis look primarily to current assets for payment when the amounts are due. Thus, a banker making a decision to grant short-term credit to a business is particularly interested in the amounts of accounts receivable, inventory, and other current assets.

Short-term investments in the marketable securities of another company are shown under current assets because by definition they are held only temporarily and will be converted to cash for use in the business through sale within the next year or next operating cycle. If a longer period is anticipated, investments must be reported under the caption "Long-term investments and funds."

Long-term investments and funds. The second classification of assets reports the investments the company intends to hold for the long run (more than one year). Long-term or permanent investments include such items as the stocks and bonds of other companies that have been purchased as investments, investments in real estate, and so on. This classification also includes cash set aside in special funds (such as a savings account) for use in the future for a specified purpose. The sinking fund to pay bonds reported in Exhibit 3–2 represents cash set aside for a special purpose. Eventually this fund will be expended to retire the bonds

EXHIBIT 3–2

DIAMOND'S, INCORPORATED
Balance Sheet
At December 31, 1977

Assets

Current Assets:			
Cash		$ 150,000	
Short-term investments		40,000	
Accounts receivable	$425,000		
Less: Allowance for doubtful accounts	15,000	410,000	
Notes receivable		20,000	
Merchandise inventory		1,510,000	
Office supplies inventory		1,000	
Prepaid insurance		4,000	
Total Current Assets			$2,135,000
Long-Term Investments and Funds:			
Stock of X Corporation		10,000	
Sinking fund to pay bonds		200,000	
Total Long-Term Investments and Funds			210,000
Fixed Assets:			
Store equipment	150,000		
Less: Accumulated depreciation	50,000	100,000	
Office equipment	16,000		
Less: Accumulated depreciation	4,000	12,000	
Total Fixed Assets			112,000
Intangible Assets:			
Trademarks			50,000
Other Assets:			
Land acquired for future store site			18,000
Total Assets			$2,525,000

Liabilities

Current Liabilities:		
Accounts payable	$ 180,000	
Notes payable	100,000	
Wages payable	16,000	
Income taxes payable	30,000	
Estimated warranty obligations	24,000	
Total Current Liabilities		$ 350,000
Long-Term Liabilities:		
Bank notes payable (maturity 1979)	100,000	
Bonds payable (7%, maturity 1987)	500,000	
Total Long-Term Liabilities		600,000
Total Liabilities		950,000

EXHIBIT 3–2 (*continued*)

Stockholders' Equity

Contributed Capital:		
Preferred stock, 5%, cumulative, 5,000 shares outstanding, par $100	500,000	
Common stock, 15,000 shares outstanding, nopar	750,000	
Contributed capital in excess of par, preferred stock	50,000	
Total Contributed Capital	1,300,000	
Retained earnings (see statement of retained earnings below)	275,000	
Total Stockholders' Equity		1,575,000
Total Liabilities and Stockholders' Equity		$2,525,000

DIAMOND'S, INCORPORATED
Statement of Retained Earnings
For the Year Ended December 31, 1977

Beginning balance, retained earnings, January 1, 1977	$220,000
Add net income for 1977	200,000
Total	420,000
Less dividends paid during 1977	145,000
Ending balance, retained earnings, December 31, 1977	$275,000

EXHIBIT 3–3
Operating cycle

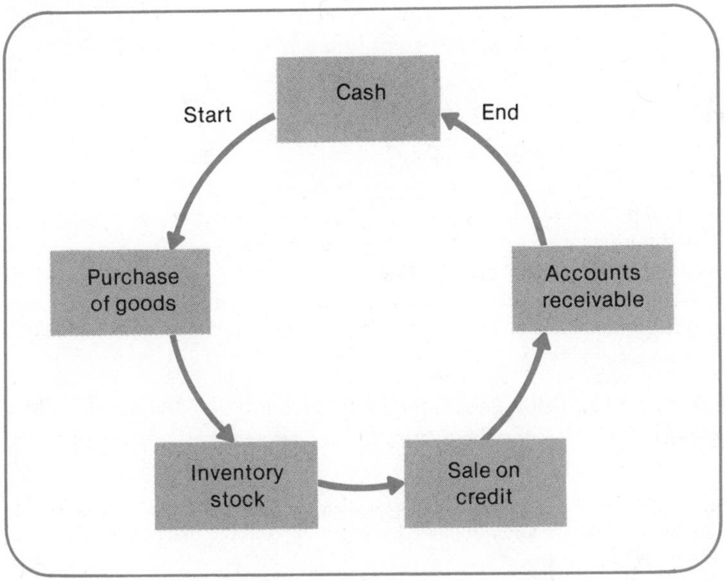

payable reported under "Long-Term Liabilities."[5] While the fund is in existence, it will earn interest revenue that will be reflected on the income statement as revenue from investments and funds (see Exhibit 3–1).

Fixed assets. This subcategory frequently is called "Operational Assets" or "Property, Plant, and Equipment." It includes those assets having physical substance (i.e., they are tangible) that were acquired for use in **operating the business** rather than for resale as inventory items or as an investment. Typically, they include buildings owned; land on which the buildings reside; and equipment, tools, and furniture and fixtures used in operating the business. They are long-lived and are used in the production and/or sale of other assets or services. Fixed assets, with the exception of land, are depreciated over time as they are used. Since their productive usefulness decreases as they are used, their initial cost is apportioned to expense over their estimated useful life. This apportionment of cost over their useful life is known as **depreciation.** Land is not depreciated because it does not wear out as do machinery, buildings, and so forth. The amount of depreciation computed for each period is reported on the income statement as an expense, and the cumulative amount of depreciation expense for all past periods since acquisition is deducted on the balance sheet from the cost of the asset to derive "book or carrying value." To illustrate, for Diamond's, the depreciation for office equipment was determined and reported as follows:

1. Income statement (Exhibit 3–1)—Depreciation expense for 1977, $1,000. This was computed as follows:

$$\frac{\text{Cost of the Equipment}}{\text{Estimated Useful Life}} = \frac{\$16{,}000}{16 \text{ Years}}$$
$$= \$1{,}000 \text{ Depreciation Expense (Each Year)}$$

2. Balance sheet (Exhibit 3–2)—The amounts shown for office equipment represent the following:

Office equipment, cost when acquired on January 1, 1974	$16,000
Accumulated depreciation expense from January 1, 1974 to December 31, 1977 ($1,000 × 4 years)	4,000
Difference—book value; amount of equipment cost not yet allocated to depreciation expense	$12,000

The difference, $12,000, generally is referred to as the **book value,** or **carrying value,** of the office equipment. At the end of the 16th year,

[5] The term "sinking fund," although widely used in accounting, is not descriptive. It simply refers to a cash fund set aside to pay a long-term debt at the maturity or due date.

the book value of the office equipment will be zero. Depreciation is discussed in detail in Chapter 10.

Intangible assets. This classification includes those assets having **no physical existence** (i.e., they are intangible) and having a long life. Their value is derived from the rights and privileges that are incident upon ownership. Examples are patents, trademarks, copyrights, franchises, and goodwill. Intangible assets generally are not acquired for resale but rather are used by the business as a part of operations. Thus, in this respect, they are akin to fixed assets. Intangible assets are discussed in detail in Chapter 10.

Deferred charges. This is a classification for long-term **prepayments** for goods and services that are expected to contribute to the generation of revenue in the future. They are the same as prepaid expenses (defined above), except that the prepayment is for more than one year. For example, the prepayment of a five-year insurance premium of $500 on January 1, 19A, theoretically would be reported as follows at December 31, 19A:

Income Statement:	
Insurance expense for 19A	$100
Balance Sheet:	
Prepaid expense	100
Deferred charge	300

When the amounts are relatively small (i.e., not material), the $400 prepayment is often reported as a prepaid expense.

Other assets. Some businesses own assets that do not reasonably fit into one of the preceding classifications. Thus, a miscellaneous category called **other assets** may be needed. For example, operational or fixed assets retired from service and being held for disposal would be reported under this category.

Current liabilities. This is the first category of liabilities and it reports the short-term debts. It encompasses those debts to be paid out of the current assets that will be converted to cash. Thus, current liabilities are expected to be paid within the coming year or within the normal operating cycle of the business, whichever is longer. The normal operating cycle was defined on page 62. Examples of current liabilities are short-term notes payable, amounts payable to creditors for goods and services purchased (called accounts payable), wages payable, income taxes payable, payroll taxes payable, interest payable, and revenue collected but not yet earned (discussed in Chapter 5).

At this point we can conveniently define a widely used concept—that of **working capital**—*which is the difference between total current assets and total current liabilities.* Thus, Diamond's working capital at December 31, 1977, was \$2,135,000 – \$350,000 = \$1,785,000. The significance of this amount will be discussed in later chapters; however, we may note that it is a measure of the liquidity of the business and its ability to meet its short-term debts.

Long-term liabilities. This is the caption that reports the long-term debts; that is, those not classified as current liabilities.

Owners' equity. Owners' equity represents the residual claim of the owners. This claim is the sum of the shareholders' investments plus the accumulated earnings of the company less the accumulated dividends paid. Exhibit 3–2 reports these two categories of stockholders' equity. These two categories are intended to report the **sources** of owners' equity. Each class of capital stock is reported separately. Diamond's balance sheet shows two classes of capital stock:[6] (1) preferred stock, 5,000 shares outstanding; and (2) common stock, 15,000 shares outstanding.

The amount labeled "Contributed capital in excess of par, preferred stock" shows that the preferred stock initially was sold at an average of \$10 per share above the par value of \$100 per share since the "excess" was \$10 × 5,000 shares = \$50,000. The par value is reported as one amount, and the excess is reported separately. The sum of the two amounts represents the amount contributed by the stockholders when the stock was sold initially. The amount of owners' equity does not represent what the residual claim is worth in terms of current market value; it is the "book value" of the claim.

Statement of retained earnings

Below the balance sheet for Diamond's (Exhibit 3–2), a supplementary statement is presented with the title **"statement of retained earnings."** This statement, although optional, generally is presented to provide "full disclosure." It explains the increases and decreases in retained earnings during the period. The statement starts with the balance in retained earnings at the beginning of the period. To that balance, net income for the year is added and dividends paid during the year are deducted. The result is the balance of retained earnings at the end of the period. After a number of years of operations, retained earnings becomes one of the primary sources of stockholders' equity in most corporations.

---

[6] Preferred stock is so designated because it has certain specified preferences over the common stock. In this particular case the preferred stock is reported as having two preferences: (1) a dividend preference of 5 percent—this means that dividends on the preferred stock must be paid each year equivalent to 5 percent of the par value per share of the preferred before any dividends can be paid on the common stock; and (2) a cumulative preference—this means that should dividends equivalent to 5 percent not be paid on the preferred stock for any year, the amount not paid will cumulate and must be paid in subsequent years before any dividends can be paid on the common stock. Capital stock is discussed in detail in Chapter 13.

The statement of retained earnings is a connecting link between the income statement and the balance sheet. In accounting for a sole proprietorship or partnership, this statement is not used.

Statement of changes in financial position

The purpose of this statement was discussed in Chapter 2. Basically, it reports the inflows and outflows of cash (or working capital) during the period. Exhibit 3–4 presents a statement of changes in financial position for Diamond's. Since much of the terminology on financial statements is optional to the preparer, you will observe some differences between the illustrations in Chapter 2 and in this chapter. Subclassification of the sources of cash (cash generated) as between operations, extraordinary items, and other sources was prescribed in APB *Opinion No. 19* in order to enhance the usefulness of the statement.

Diamond's statement is typical in that most of the cash generated during the year came from operations. Of the $271,700 cash generated, $228,700 or 84 percent, came from this one source.[7]

For instructional purposes, the statements of changes in financial position illustrated in Chapter 2 and in this chapter were based on **cash flow.** Many accountants prefer to base it on **working capital.** Either approach is permitted by APB *Opinion No. 19.* The choice between one that emphasizes working capital flows and one that emphasizes cash depends on the circumstances in the particular company. The statement of changes in financial position is discussed further in Chapter 15.

A MORE COMPLICATED SET OF FINANCIAL STATEMENTS

Up to this point you have studied two simplified sets of financial statements, stripped of much of the surrounding features. To complete this overview of financial statements for a business, we present a set of **published** financial statements for a well-known company, Carborundum Company. Corporations such as this one are said to "publish" their annual report because it is printed and distributed to each shareholder and to others upon request. Companies selling their stock on the exchanges (and some others) distribute such annual reports. The published annual report typically includes a number of features in addition to the financial statements, such as the president's letter to the shareholders, a list of the principal officers of the company, promotional data on the company's products (including pictures), and other information deemed to be of interest.

---

[7] To avoid misunderstanding—the land was sold for $56,000 cash, as shown in Exhibit 3–4; it cost $5,000; the resulting pretax extraordinary gain of $51,000 was reported on the income statement, Exhibit 3–1.

EXHIBIT 3–4

DIAMOND'S, INCORPORATED
Statement of Changes in Financial Position—Cash Basis
For the Year Ended December 31, 1977

Sources of Cash:			
From operations:			
Sales revenue		$3,615,000	
Revenue from investments		13,000	
		3,628,000	
Adjustments for noncash revenue (deduction)		5,000*[a]	
Cash inflow from sales and investments		3,623,000	
Expenses and cost of goods sold	$3,466,000*[b]		
Adjustments for noncash expenses deduction	(71,700)*[c]		
Cash outflow for expenses		3,394,300	
Net cash inflow from operations and investments			228,700
From extraordinary items (net of income taxes): Disposal of land ($56,000–$13,000)			43,000
Total Cash Generated			271,700
Uses of Cash:			
To pay dividends:			
On preferred stock		25,000	
On common stock		120,000	
To purchase land for future store site		18,000	
Total Cash Applied			163,000
Increase in cash during the year			$108,700

* At this point in your study, there is no need to be concerned with the derivation of these amounts; however, they may be reconciled as follows:

[a] The adjustment of $5,000 to revenue was due to an increase in accounts receivable of that amount during the period.

[b] Expenses from Exhibit 3–1:

Cost of goods sold	$2,416,000
Expenses	856,000
Interest expense	56,000
Income tax expense	138,000
Total Expenses	$3,466,000

[c] Noncash expenses from Exhibit 3–1:

Depreciation expense, store equipment	$15,000
Amortization of trademarks	2,000
Estimated losses on doubtful accounts	3,600
Depreciation expense, office equipment	1,000
Subtotal	21,600
Net change in accruals, deferrals, and accounts payable (data not given herein)	50,100
Total	$71,700

The following components from the 1975 annual report of The Carborundum Company, Inc., are included in Exhibit 3–5 for your study:[8]

1. Consolidated statement of income.
2. Consolidated statement of shareholders' equity.
3. Consolidated balance sheet.
4. Consolidated statement of changes in financial position (cash basis).
5. Report of independent accountants.
6. Summary of accounting policies.
7. Selected notes to the financial statements.

As recommended by the APB, **comparative** amounts are presented. That is, amounts for each item are reported for the current year and the preceding year.

There are a number of items reported on these statements you will not understand at this point in your study; however, you should understand a good portion of them. A good number of them will be discussed in subsequent chapters.

Income statement. The statement of income is dated "Year Ended December 31–." This means that the company uses a **fiscal year** the same as the calendar year. The fiscal year for a business also is referred to as the natural business year since it ends when the business normally is at its lowest level of activity. The period selected by the business for its usual operating purposes also is used for accounting. It often is referred to as the **accounting period** as well as the fiscal year.

Statement of shareholders' equity. This statement is included to tie together the income statement and balance sheet and to provide details concerning owners' equity. It partially implements the full-disclosure principle.

Balance sheet. This statement is dated "December 31,–" and follows closely the classifications discussed previously.

Statement of changes in financial position. This statement is dated the same as the income statement and is prepared on a cash basis.

Report of independent accountants. The independent CPA, as the outside auditor, is required to express an **opinion** on the financial statements or to state that an opinion cannot be expressed. The accountants' report on the statements of Carborundum Company, in the first paragraph, states the scope of the examination performed. In the second paragraph, the independent CPA has stated that in "our opinion, the consolidated state-

[8] The statements are labeled "Consolidated Statements." These two words indicate that Carborundum, as the parent company, owns over 50 percent of the outstanding voting stock of one or more other companies. This ownership gives the parent company a *controlling interest,* and the other companies are designated as subsidiaries. To prepare the statements on a *consolidated basis,* the financial statements of the subsidiaries are added on a line-by-line basis to those of the parent company. This subject is discussed further in Chapter 17.

EXHIBIT 3–5

Carborundum Company

Consolidated Statement of Income

(in thousands of dollars)

Year Ended December 31	1975		1974	
Sales	$563,064	100.0%	$556,848	100.0%
Cost of products sold	371,506	66.0	371,201	66.7
Gross margin	191,558	34.0	185,647	33.3
Selling, administrative and general expenses	125,233	22.2	122,724	22.0
Research and development expense	6,616	1.2	8,602	1.5
	131,849	23.4	131,326	23.5
Operating income	59,709	10.6	54,321	9.8
Other income (expense)				
Interest expense	(5,754)	(1.0)	(4,397)	(0.8)
Foreign currency exchange adjustments	(3,889)	(0.7)	386	0.1
Interest income	3,561	0.6	1,848	0.3
Equity in net income of partly owned companies	987	0.2	1,777	0.3
Other expense	(1,203)	(0.2)	(1,578)	(0.3)
Total other income (expense)	(6,298)	(1.1)	(1,964)	(0.4)
Income before taxes on income	53,411	9.5	52,357	9.4
Taxes on income	26,224	4.7	25,655	4.6
Net income	$ 27,187	4.8%	$ 26,702	4.8%
Net income per average outstanding common share	$ 7.00		$ 6.88	
Dividends per share	$ 1.70		$ 1.65	

Consolidated Statement of Shareholders' Equity

(in thousands of dollars)

1974	Common stock	Capital in excess of par value	Retained earnings	Total[1]
Balances at beginning of year	$ 11,734	$ 20,358	$172,585	$204,677
Net income			26,702	26,702
Dividends on common stock			(6,256)	(6,256)
Balances at end of year	11,734	20,358	193,031	225,123
1975				
Net income			27,187	27,187
Dividends on common stock			(6,599)	(6,599)
Stock options exercised – 2,050 shares	6	83		89
Common stock issued for acquired company – 60,009 shares	180	2,682		2,862
Balances at end of year	$ 11,920	$ 23,123	$213,619	$248,662

[1]*Before deducting cost of common stock held in treasury of $595.*

The 1975 Financial Review is an integral part of this statement.

EXHIBIT 3–5 (continued)

Consolidated Balance Sheet

(in thousands of dollars)

Assets — December 31	1975	1974
Current Assets		
Cash, including interest bearing deposits of $15,167 and $8,675, respectively	$ 16,111	$ 11,723
Marketable securities at cost and accrued interest, which approximates market	64,153	5,010
Accounts receivable, less allowance for losses of $2,980 and $3,780, respectively	97,079	112,905
Inventories	90,817	108,383
Deferred income tax benefits	9,737	9,394
Prepaid expenses	8,614	2,265
Total Current Assets	286,511	249,680
Investments and Other Assets		
Investments in and advances to associated companies and the non-consolidated subsidiary	14,208	12,996
Patents and processes	2,226	2,019
Goodwill	10,512	8,358
Other assets	5,413	5,512
Total Investments and Other Assets	32,359	28,885
Properties, Plants and Equipment, at Cost		
Land	4,965	4,420
Buildings	89,474	85,614
Machinery and equipment	200,743	185,587
Construction in progress	19,743	14,027
	314,925	289,648
Less depreciation and amortization	163,078	151,782
Total Properties, Plants and Equipment, net	151,847	137,866
Total Assets	$470,717	$416,431

Liabilities and Shareholders' Equity — December 31	1975	1974
Current Liabilities		
Notes payable to banks	$ 5,298	$ 13,364
Current portion of long-term debt	3,503	1,398
Accounts payable	41,649	42,367
Salaries and wages	14,682	17,425
Taxes on income	19,281	21,063
Interest, taxes and other liabilities	31,373	29,016
Total Current Liabilities	115,786	124,633
Long-Term Debt and Other Liabilities		
Long-term debt	74,181	36,990
Other liabilities	14,534	15,362
Total Long-Term Debt and Other Liabilities	88,715	52,352
Deferred Taxes on Income	18,149	14,918
Shareholders' Equity		
Preferred stock, par value $10 a share; 2,500,000 shares authorized but unissued		
Common stock, par value $3 a share; authorized 10,000,000 shares; issued 3,973,281 and 3,911,222 shares, respectively	11,920	11,734
Capital in excess of par value	23,123	20,358
Retained earnings	213,619	193,031
	248,662	225,123
Less common stock held in treasury, at cost—30,150 shares	595	595
Total Shareholders' Equity	248,067	224,528
Total Liabilities and Shareholders' Equity	$470,717	$416,431

EXHIBIT 3–5 (*continued*)

Consolidated Statement of Changes in Financial Position

(in thousands of dollars)

Year Ended December 31	1975	1974
Operations		
Sources of cash:		
Net income	$ 27,187	$ 26,702
Depreciation and amortization	13,491	11,954
Deferred income taxes	2,888	561
Equity in undistributed net (income) loss of partly owned companies	152	(1,136)
Net income adjusted for items not providing or using cash	43,718	38,081
Decrease in accounts receivable	15,826	–
Decrease in inventories	17,566	–
Increase in accounts payable	–	11,121
Increase in other current liabilities	694	14,561
Increase in other long-term liabilities	–	2,485
Total sources from operations	77,804	66,248
Uses of cash:		
Increase in accounts receivable	–	27,918
Increase in inventories	–	27,270
Increase in other current assets	6,349	947
Decrease in accounts payable	718	–
Decrease in other long-term liabilities	828	–
Total uses for operations	7,895	56,135
Cash provided from operations	69,909	10,113
Investment and shareholders' activities		
Sources of cash:		
Disposals of properties, plants and equipment	1,429	1,891
Sale of common stock under option plans	89	–
Total sources from investment and shareholders' activities	1,518	1,891
Uses of cash:		
Additions to properties, plants and equipment	28,901	31,123
Cash dividends paid	6,599	6,256
Increase in investments and other assets	3,626	1,265
Total uses for investment and shareholders' activities	39,126	38,644
Cash used for investment and shareholders' activities	(37,608)	(36,753)
Financing activities		
Sources of cash:		
Long-term borrowings	43,575	327
Increase in notes payable and current portion of long-term debt	–	9,517
Total sources from financing activities	43,575	9,844
Uses of cash:		
Repayments of long-term borrowings	6,384	2,623
Decrease in notes payable and current portion of long-term debt	5,961	–
Total uses for financing activities	12,345	2,623
Cash provided from financing activities	31,230	7,221
Increase (decrease) in cash and marketable securities	$ 63,531	$ (19,419)

The 1975 Financial Review is an integral part of this statement.

EXHIBIT 3–5 (*continued*)

Report of Independent Accountants

To the Shareholders' of The Carborundum Company:

We have examined the consolidated balance sheet of The Carborundum Company as of December 31, 1975 and 1974 and the related consolidated statements of income, of shareholders' equity and of changes in financial position for the years then ended. Our examinations were made in accordance with generally accepted auditing standards and accordingly included such tests of the accounting records and such other auditing procedures as we considered necessary in the circumstances.

In 1975 the Financial Accounting Standards Board issued Statement No. 8 "Accounting for the Translation of Foreign Currency Transactions and Foreign Currency Financial Statements" which is effective in 1976 and will require retroactive application. The effect of the provisions of this Statement on the consolidated financial statements for 1975 and 1974 as estimated by the Company is described on page 29.

In our opinion, the consolidated financial statements examined by us present fairly the financial position of The Carborundum Company and its subsidiaries at December 31, 1975 and 1974, the results of their operations and the changes in financial position for the years then ended, in conformity with generally accepted accounting principles consistently applied.

Buffalo, New York
February 18, 1976 Price Waterhouse & Co.

Summary of Significant Accounting Policies

The more important accounting practices and policies employed in the preparation of the consolidated financial statements are summarized below.

The consolidated financial statements include the accounts of the Company and all of its majority-owned subsidiaries except one in Argentina, excluded because of unsettled economic conditions and currency exchange restrictions.

Investments in corporate joint ventures where Carborundum ownership is from 20% to 50% are carried at cost plus equity in their undistributed net income. Investments in companies less than 20% owned and the non-consolidated subsidiary are carried at cost. Income from these investments is recorded when received.

The Company applies the current-noncurrent method for translation of accounts of foreign subsidiaries. Under this method all non-current assets, principally properties, plants and equipment, and related depreciation accounts are translated based upon rates of exchange which were in effect when these assets were acquired. Other asset and liability accounts are translated at the exchange rate prevailing at the end of the year. Income and expenses other than depreciation are translated at exchange rates prevailing during the year at each month-end. Foreign exchange translation credit adjustments attributable to unstable currency exchange conditions are deferred in a reserve for foreign currency exchange and are utilized to offset foreign exchange losses. Losses in excess of such reserve are charged to income as incurred. Anticipated losses as well as realized gains and losses on foreign exchange contracts are recognized currently.

Inventories are stated at the lower of cost or market. The cost of substantially all domestic inventories is determined on the last-in, first-out (LIFO) method of accounting. The cost of the remaining inventories is determined on the first-in, first-out (FIFO) method.

Patents and processes obtained in connection with acquisitions are carried at cost less accumulated amortization which is charged to income over their estimated economic lives. Costs applicable to development of patents and processes by the Company, as well as all other research and development costs, are charged to operations as incurred.

Goodwill represents the excess of acquisition cost over net assets of acquired companies at date of acquisition and is being amortized over 40 years on a straight-line basis.

Expenditures for properties, plants and equipment are capitalized and depreciated over the estimated useful lives of the assets principally on the straight-line method. When properties are retired or otherwise disposed of, their cost and related accumulated depreciation are removed from the accounts and any resulting gain or loss is recognized in income. Maintenance and repairs are charged to income as incurred, and renewals and betterments are capitalized.

Deferred income taxes are provided on amounts resulting from differences in depreciation methods and provisions for certain expenses and losses that enter into the determination of income for reporting purposes in different time periods from those for tax purposes.

Investment tax credits arising from acquisitions of qualified property, utilized to reduce federal taxes on income, are not material in amount and are reflected in net income on a flow-through basis.

EXHIBIT 3–5 (*continued*)

Summary of Significant Accounting Policies Continued

Income taxes have not been provided on the undistributed income of subsidiaries and corporate joint ventures because of the availability of offsetting foreign income tax credits, and because such undistributed income is expected to be reinvested indefinitely in such subsidiaries or other corporate ventures.

Costs related to formal pension plans are accrued and funded annually. Costs of all principal pension plans are actuarially determined and include amounts for current service and both amortization of and interest on unfunded prior service. Payments made to certain retired employees not under specific plans are charged to expense when paid.

Provision is made for product performance guarantees for pollution control and other manufactured capital equipment.

Notes to the Financial Statements (Selected)

Sales and Earnings

Sales in 1975 established a record for the fourteenth consecutive year. Consolidated worldwide sales reached $563.1 million, an increase of $6.3 million, or 1.1%, over 1974.

Net income of $27.2 million, or $7.00 per share, was also a record for the Company and exceeded 1974 earnings of $26.7 million by 1.8%.

During 1975, the Company acquired the net assets of several companies in the United States, which acquisitions were accounted for under the purchase method. Sales and net income of these companies are not material to the consolidated results of operations.

Working Capital

The Company's financial position continues to be strong. Net working capital amounted to $170.7 million, which is $45.7 million or 36.5% higher than 1974. This increase is principally attributable to the sale of $40 million of debentures during the year. Current assets of $286.5 million at year-end are 2.5 times current liabilities of $115.8 million.

Inventories of $34.7 million at December 31, 1975, and $42.0 million at December 31, 1974, were determined on the last-in, first-out (LIFO) method of accounting. The remaining inventories are stated on the first-in, first-out (FIFO) method.

During 1975, inventory quantities were reduced. This reduction resulted in a liquidation of LIFO inventory quantities carried at lower costs prevailing in prior years as compared with the cost of 1975 purchases, the effect of which increased net income by approximately $2.1 million or $.55 per share.

The classification of inventory as to components is not shown because Carborundum and its subsidiaries constitute an integrated industry wherein the finished products of one company or division may be used as a raw material by another or may be sold to customers.

Net losses from foreign currency exchange adjustments in 1975 amounted to $6.5 million of which $3.9 million was charged to income and the balance was charged against amounts previously provided. In 1974, exchange adjustment losses of $0.2 million were charged against amounts previously provided and net realized exchange adjustment gains of $0.4 million were reflected in income. At December 31, 1975 and December 31, 1974, the Company held foreign currency exchange contracts aggregating $32.8 million and $33.7 million respectively. Of the total exchange contracts held, $10.2 million were covered by hedge contracts at December 31, 1975 and the balance was covered in January, 1976. Included in foreign currency exchange adjustments for 1975 are net losses of $2.0 million relating to foreign currency exchange contracts.

In 1975 the Financial Accounting Standards Board issued Statement No. 8 "Accounting for the Translation of Foreign Currency Transactions and Foreign Currency Financial Statements". Under the provisions of this Statement, which is effective in 1976 and will

EXHIBIT 3–5 (*concluded*)

require retroactive application, the Company will be required to adopt the temporal method for translation of the accounts of foreign subsidiaries and to record in income currently foreign exchange translation adjustments as well as gains or losses attributable to foreign currency exchange contracts.

The estimated effect of the retroactive application of this Statement would increase reported net income for 1975 by $0.3 million or $.07 per share and reduce reported net income for 1974 by $4.1 million or $1.07 per share. The estimated cumulative effect on net income for the five years ending December 31, 1975 would be a reduction of $.14 per share. It is estimated that the retroactive application of the Statement would not have a material effect on the balance sheets at December 31, 1975 and 1974.

At December 31, 1975, short-term borrowings amounted to $5.3 million as compared to $13.4 million at the end of 1974. Interest rates on the amounts outstanding at the end of 1975 generally range from 6¼% to 12½%. The maximum short-term borrowings outstanding at any month-end during the year were $11.0 million. At December 31, 1975, the Company had available $60.3 million in unused lines of short-term credit. Compensating bank balances required under the terms of short-term financing arrangements were not material at December 31, 1975.

Total Assets, Capital Additions, and Depreciation

Total assets at December 31, 1975 amounted to $470.7 million, an increase of 13% over 1974. Additions to properties, plants and equipment totaled $28.9 million versus $31.1 million in 1974. Depreciation and amortization amounted to $13.5 million in 1975 and $12.0 million in 1974.

Income Taxes

A comparative summary of income taxes provided in the consolidated statement of income appears at right.

Other Long-Term Liabilities

Included in this caption are the deferred portion of management incentive compensation, liabilities of foreign subsidiaries for pensions, and minority interest in consolidated subsidiaries.

The Company has several long-term noncancelable leases in effect at December 31, 1975 for office and plant facilities. The annual rentals under such leases are not material.

Shareholders' Equity

Shareholders' equity at December 31, 1975, was $248.1 million, an increase of $23.5 million from 1974. Shareholders' equity per common share increased to $62.91 per share from $57.85 per share at the end of 1974. Net income as a percent of average shareholders' equity was 11.5% compared to 12.5% in 1974. Cash dividends paid per common share totaled $1.70 per share in 1975, compared with $1.65 per share in 1974.

At December 31, 1975, there were 100,000 shares of authorized and unissued common stock reserved for issuance under The Carborundum Savings Plan and 399,337 shares under the stock option plans.

Under the most restrictive terms of loan agreements at December 31, 1975, $77.6 million of consolidated retained earnings were unrestricted for the payment of cash dividends. Retained earnings include amounts transferred to statutory reserves by certain foreign subsidiaries.

(in thousands of dollars)

Year Ended December 31	1975	1974
Currently payable		
Federal	$ 7,539	$12,796
Foreign	14,969	10,528
State	2,305	1,886
	24,813	25,210
Deferred to future years (reduction)		
Federal	1,379	(2,020)
Foreign	(133)	2,847
State	165	(382)
	1,411	445
Total taxes on income	$26,224	$25,655

ments examined by us present fairly the financial position (i.e., the balance sheet), the results of their operations (i.e., the income statement), and the changes in financial position (i.e., the statement of changes in financial position) in conformity with generally accepted accounting principles." The key words are "present fairly" and "generally accepted accounting principles." If the statements do not meet these standards, the independent CPA must explain why an unqualified opinion cannot be expressed. Since the accountants' opinion relates to the "fairness" of the financial statement in its entirety, the opinion is viewed as a necessary part of the financial report.

Summary of accounting policies. Because of its importance, this section is required by APB *Opinion No. 22.* Its purpose is to explain the accounting policies followed by the company. This information significantly aids the user in interpreting the amounts reported. Observe that this company explained its accounting policies in respect to 12 different items.

Full disclosure. One of the broad fundamentals underlying accounting, listed in Exhibit 2–1, is the principle of full disclosure. This relates directly to the financial statements. It specifies that there should be complete and understandable reporting on the financial statements of all **significant information** relating to the economic affairs of the entity. To meet the requirements of this principle, the quantitative expressions in the financial statements frequently require narrative and detailed elaboration. As a consequence, practically all published financial statements will include a section often called "Notes to the Financial Statements." The notes are considered to be an integral part of the financial statements and are important to understanding and interpreting the amounts reported. To illustrate typical notes, six were selected from the Carborundum statements (see Exhibit 3–5, pages 74–75).

INTERPRETATIVE OR PROPORTIONAL RELATIONSHIPS

When using financial statements the decision maker often may gain further insight into the amounts if one or more **proportional relationships** are computed. A proportional relationship is based on *two* selected amounts from the financial statements that are related in a meaningful way. One, known as the **base amount,** is divided into the other to express the proportional relationship between the two. The result may be expressed as a ratio, a percent, or, sometimes, as a dollar amount. To illustrate, assume we are interpreting the income statement of hypothetical Company X. Assume there are two amounts of particular significance to our problem at hand. They are: (1) net sales, $300,000; and (2) net income, $45,000. Clearly, these two amounts are related in a relevant way. To analyze one aspect of their relationship, we can apply the concept of proportional analysis. We will use net sales as the base amount. Therefore, the computation would be:

$$\frac{\text{Net Income}}{\text{Net Sales}} = \frac{\$45{,}000}{\$300{,}000} = 0.15$$

The computed result can be expressed in any of the following ways: (1) as a ratio—net income was 0.15 of net sales; (2) as a percent—net income was 15 percent of net sales; or (3) as a dollar amount—for each $1 of net sales there was $0.15 net income. The relationship just computed is known as the **profit margin** since it is the relationship between profit and sales for the period.[9]

The concept of **earnings per share (EPS),** already illustrated, is another widely used relationship. EPS reflects a relevant relationship between income and the number of shares of common stock outstanding.

The concept of **return on investment (ROI)** is still another relationship especially useful to decision makers. It is particularly significant since it expresses the relationship between **profit** and **investment.** The income statement provides the income amount and the balance sheet provides the investment amount.

The concept of return on investment is frequently applied by almost everyone in one way or another. To illustrate, suppose you invested $1,000 on January 1, 1977, and at the end of the year you got back $1,200. Disregarding income taxes, you may say that you earned $200 during the year on your investment. Based on these amounts, what would be your ROI (i.e., your return on investment)? You may calculate that your return for the year was $200 ÷ $1,000 = 20 percent on the investment. Similarly, the return on investment for a business for a specific period of time may be computed as follows:

$$\frac{\text{Net Income}}{\text{Investment (Owners' Equity)}} = \text{Return on Investment}$$

The return on investment earned by Diamond's for 1977 would be computed as follows:[10]

$$\frac{\$162{,}000 \text{ (from Exhibit 3–1)}}{\$1{,}575{,}000 \text{ (from Exhibit 3–2)}} = 10.29 \text{ Percent}$$

---

[9] In computing the profit margin when there are extraordinary items, income before extraordinary items rather than net income generally should be used to avoid the distortion caused by the unusual and infrequently recurring items.

[10] Depending upon the nature of the problem and the preference of the decision maker, the income amount may be either (1) income before extraordinary items or (2) net income. Similarly, investment may be either (1) owners' equity or (2) total equity (i.e., liabilities plus owners' equity). When total equity is used, interest expense (net of tax) should be added back to income (see Chapter 16).

These three examples are sufficient at this point to introduce the concept of proportional analysis as applied to the interpretation of financial statements. In the chapters to follow, several more particularly useful relationships will be introduced and illustrated. Finally, in Chapter 16 the concept will be revisited and discussed in more detail.

Although a proportional relationship may be expressed as a ratio, a percent, or a dollar amount, the concept often is loosely referred to as **ratio analysis.**

FINANCIAL STATEMENTS RELATED TO THE DECISION PROCESS

Throughout the preceding pages, we have emphasized the point of view of the decision maker; that is, the user of the financial reports. In making decisions of various kinds, one must assess future prospects and probable future outcomes. Decision making deals with the future rather than with the past; therefore, the decision maker must make projections. Recent past events and trends generally provide the background for most projections if they are to be realistic. The financial statements provide valuable information concerning past transactions and their economic effects on the business. In making many decisions relating to a business entity, the decision maker must carefully interpret and evaluate the various financial factors. In addition, the decision maker must bring to bear his or her knowledge of such factors as technological constraints, environmental influences, and competitive forces in making certain decisions relating to the business. The following case is presented to demonstrate how accounting information may be important in decision making.

Jane Smith, individual. It was five years after Jane Smith received her B.A. in history at State University. During that time, Jane worked for a local business, first in sales and now as the general office manager. Since Jane did not take any business courses at State, her increasing responsibilities made it desirable that she enroll in several business courses in night school for the last three years. During the five years since her graduation, Jane saved approximately 10 percent of her salary, which she deposited in a savings account. The potential impact of inflation on this type of investment concerned Jane. A co-worker gave her a tip: "Purchase some of the stock of the X Corporation, which recently went public. The price is down now and I was told confidentially that it would double in the next two to three years based on their expected EPS trend." Since the X Corporation was in a distant state, Jane was unable to get much information about the management of the company. As to products, she was told that "the company is in the automotive parts manufacturing business." Jane was about ready to invest her savings of $4,000 in the stock when a friend suggested that she should "analyze the financial statements of the company for several years running before taking the big jump." Accordingly, Jane wrote the company and received the annual financial reports for the past three years. In discussing these statements with a friend, who was an accountant, they discovered several disconcerting facts. Among them were the following:

1. The cash position, taking into account borrowings, had steadily deteriorated.
2. The money tied up in inventory had increased at a greater rate than sales, suggesting the possibility of inadequate controls by the management.
3. The plant and equipment was largely depreciated, indicating it to be old and perhaps inefficient. Large outlays might be required in the near future for replacement.
4. The working capital ratio was low, compared with the industry average (as reported by Dun & Bradstreet, a New York-based firm that publishes such averages).
5. There appeared to be excessive debt in relation to owners' equity.
6. The EPS amounts were as follows:

	Last year	*1st year prior*	*2d year prior*
On income before extraordinary items	$1.60	$1.80	$1.80
On net income	4.50	3.00	2.00

   Examination of the income statement indicated that the dramatic increase in EPS on net income was due to sales of some land the company had owned for many years. The land had been acquired at a very low price and, when sold, brought premium prices. Jane realized that these unusual gains would not be repeated.
7. The notes revealed that the company had been sued for a large sum of money for negligence related to a serious accident in the plant. The case was pending.

On the basis of the above and some other information inputs to her decision process, Jane decided against making the investment. Subsequently, Jane learned that the business had encountered severe financial difficulties.

SUMMARY

In this chapter, you encountered the commonly used subclassifications of financial information on the income statement, balance sheet, and statement of changes in financial position. You learned some of the interpretative approaches used by the decision makers when relying on financial reports. You also learned to expect variations in the terminology and format of financial reports.

Financial reports of an existing company were presented to reinforce your understanding and for reference as you study the accounting process in the chapters to follow. The knowledge of financial statements, gained in Chapter 2 and in this chapter, should assure that in studying the details and complexities of accounting, you can maintain a broad view of accounting and keep in mind the nature of the end product—the financial statements. We reemphasize this point because, not infrequently, students soon become immersed in details and lose the broad perspective of the end results—the financial statements and their use.

We looked at a case where financial information exerted a significant impact on the decision maker. We will continue to focus on decision making because the overriding objective of accounting, as we have said, is to contribute to sound and realistic decisions.

In this chapter, we defined another of the broad fundamentals underlying accounting as listed in Exhibit 2–1, viz:

> Full-disclosure principle—There must be complete and understandable reporting on the financial statements of all significant economic information relating to the entity that may influence decisions. Notes to the financial statements generally are necessary to meet the full-disclosure principle, especially in respect to unusual transactions and circumstances.

In the next chapter your attention will be turned to the accounting process that collects and reports the financial data of an entity.

IMPORTANT TERMS

Cost of goods sold
Gross margin on sales
Operating expenses
Financial expenses
Extraordinary items
Income tax expense
Current assets
Normal operating cycle
Prepaid expenses
Long-term investments and funds
Fixed assets
Book value
Intangible assets
Deferred charges
Other assets
Current liabilities
Long-term liabilities
Statement of retained earnings
Fiscal year
Accountants' opinion
Full disclosure
Profit margin
Return on investment (ROI)

QUESTIONS FOR DISCUSSION

1. What is the primary purpose of subclassification of the information presented on financial statements?
2. What is gross margin? Why is it that the income statement for a service business does not include this specific item?

3. What are the two primary subclassifications of operating expenses reported on the income statement of a retail store?
4. Explain the subclassification "Financial expenses and revenues" on the income statement.
5. What are extraordinary items? Why should they be reported separately on the income statement?
6. Explain EPS. What EPS amounts should be reported on the income statement?
7. Briefly explain how income tax expense is reported on the income statement when there are extraordinary items.
8. Briefly define (*a*) current assets, (*b*) current liabilities, and (*c*) working capital.
9. What is a prepaid expense?
10. Distinguish between a prepaid expense and a deferred charge.
11. On a balance sheet, investments may be reported under either (*a*) current assets or (*b*) long-term investments and funds. Explain.
12. In respect to fixed assets, as reported on the balance sheet, briefly explain (*a*) cost, (*b*) accumulated depreciation, (*c*) book value, and (*d*) carrying value.
13. Briefly explain the two major subclassifications of owners' equity for a corporation.
14. What is meant by a comparative financial statement? Why are comparative financial statements desirable?
15. Briefly, what does the independent auditors' report encompass?
16. What is proportional analysis? Why is it often useful in interpreting financial statements?
17. Explain the full-disclosure principle.

EXERCISES

E3–1. Quality Department Store averages a 20 percent markup on net sales. During 1977, gross sales amounted to $309,000 and return sales were $9,000. You are requested to prepare the annual income statement from sales through gross margin on net sales. Show your computations.

E3–2. Mark Tire Company is developing the annual financial statements for 1977. The following amounts have been determined to be correct: sales, $260,000; selling expenses, $34,000; interest expense, $1,000; administrative expenses, $20,000; extraordinary loss, $4,000; sales returns and allowances, $3,000; cost of goods sold, $140,000; and interest revenue, $200.

Prepare a classified income statement for 1977. Assume 20,000 shares of common stock outstanding during the year and an average income tax rate on all items of 30 percent. (Hint: EPS on net income is $2.04 per share.)

E3–3. Bright Jewelers is developing the annual financial statements for 1977. The following amounts have been determined to be correct at December 31, 1977: cash, $20,000; accounts receivable, $12,000; merchandise inventory, $160,000; prepaid insurance, $600; investment in stock of Z Corporation (long term), $10,000; store equipment, $32,000; used store equipment held for disposal, $7,000; allowance for doubtful accounts, $800; accumulated depreciation, store equipment, $9,000; accounts payable, $27,000; long-term notes payable, $40,000; income taxes payable, $5,000; retained earnings, $49,800; and common stock, 100,000 shares outstanding, par $1 per share (originally sold at $1.10 per share).

You have been requested to prepare a classified balance sheet at December 31, 1977. (Hint: The balance sheet total is $231,800.)

E3–4. Tasty Bakery is developing the annual financial statements for 1977. The following cash-flow data have been determined to be correct for the year: sales revenue (including $12,000 not collected), $300,000; expenses, $270,000 (including $21,000 of noncash items); cash received from sale of used machine, $1,000; cash received for extraordinary item, $900; cash borrowed on a five-year note payable, $10,000; cash disbursement for dividends, $12,000; cash expenditure to purchase two new delivery trucks, $9,900; and cash paid on $5,000 mortgage payable. You have been requested to prepare a statement of changes in financial position on the cash basis for 1977. (Hint: Cash increased $24,000.)

E3–5. Blue Corporation has just completed the 1977 income statement (there were no extraordinary items), except for the EPS computations. Net income has been determined to be $145,000. Common stock outstanding during the year was 40,000 shares, and preferred stock (5 percent, $10 par value) outstanding was 10,000 shares. Compute the EPS amount for the income statement. (Hint: First subtract the preferred dividends of $100,000 × 5% = $5,000.)

E3–6. MK Corporation (common stock, 2,000 shares outstanding) is preparing the income statement for 1977. The pretax operating income has been determined to be $80,000, and there was a $20,000 pretax loss on storm damages to one of the plants properly classified as an extraordinary item. Total income tax expense has been correctly determined to be $24,000 on the basis of a 40 percent tax rate on operations and on the storm loss. You have been requested to complete the income statement starting with pretax operating income. (Hint: EPS on income before extraordinary items was $24.)

E3–7. The following is a list of major classifications and subclassifications on the balance sheet. Indicate, by numbering them in the order in which they normally appear on a balance sheet.

______ Current liabilities	______ Fixed assets
______ Liabilities	______ Current assets
______ Owners' equity	______ Retained earnings
______ Long-term liabilities	______ Contributed capital

_____ Long-term investments and funds
_____ Intangible assets
_____ Assets
_____ Other assets

E3–8. Berger, Incorporated, was organized in 1968 by ten investors. Each investor paid in $6,300 cash and received 600 shares of $10 par-value common stock. In 1973, to raise more capital, Berger, Incorporated, issued 2,000 shares of 5 percent preferred, nonparticipating, cumulative stock, par $20 per share, and received $45,000 in cash for it. On December 31, 1977, retained earnings amounted to $75,000. Prepare the stockholders' equity section of the balance sheet at December 31, 1977.

E3–9. Redy Manufacturing Company is preparing the annual financial statements at December 31, 1977. The company has acquired two investments:

a. Common stock of M Corporation, 1,000 shares purchased for $75,000 during 1970. M Corporation is a supplier of parts to Redy; therefore, the latter "intends to hold the stock indefinitely." The shares acquired represented 2 percent of the total shares outstanding. M stock was selling at $75 at the end of 1977.

b. Common stock of N Corporation purchased 500 shares at a cost of $40 per share on August 15, 1977. Redy made this investment to "temporarily use some idle cash that probably will be needed next year." N stock was selling at $44 at the end of 1977.

You have been requested to illustrate and explain the basis for the classification and amount that should be reported for each investment on the 1977 balance sheet of Redy.

E3–10. Dryden Company is preparing the balance sheet at December 31, 1977. The following assets are to be entered thereon:

1. Building, purchased 15 years ago (counting 1977); original cost, $120,000 estimated useful life 20 years from date of purchase.
2. Land, purchased 15 years ago (counting 1977); original cost, $9,000.

Required:

a. You are requested to show how the two items should be included on the balance sheet.

b. What amount of depreciation expense should be reported on the 1977 income statement?

E3–11. Super Retailers, on July 1, 1977, paid $3,600 cash for a two-year insurance premium. The premium was for a new insurance policy covering all of the assets owned. It is now December 31, 1977, and you are asked to respond to the following questions (show your computations):

a. How much should be reported for *insurance expense* on the income statement for year ended December 31, 1977?

b. What amount of *prepaid insurance* should be reported on the December 31, 1977, balance sheet?

E3–12. This exercise is designed to aid in your understanding of the contents of published financial statements and to observe differences in form and terminology. You are to refer to the financial statements of Carborundum Company presented in this chapter and respond to the following:

a. Income statement:
1. What title is used?
2. Is it a comparative statement? Explain.
3. Are there any extraordinary items?
4. What were the profit margins. Explain the 34 percent amount reported for 1975.
5. Did EPS increase?
6. What was the average income tax rate for 1975?

b. Consolidated statement of shareholders' equity
7. What amount was carried to the balance sheet?
8. What was the amount carried from the income statement?
9. What was the amount of dividends each year?

c. Balance sheet:
10. What was the amount of working capital at the end of each year?
11. Was accumulated depreciation reported on the balance sheet?
12. How many shares of each kind of stock were issued?

d. Statement of changes in financial position
13. Was this statement prepared on a working capital basis or on a cash basis?
14. What was the largest source of cash?
15. What was the largest use of cash?

e. Accountants' report:
16. Did the independent CPA believe that the statements "present fairly" the results of operations and financial position? Were there any exceptions on this point?

f. Summary of accounting policies:
17. How many accounting policies were explained?
18. What is the primary method of depreciation used by the company?

g. Notes to the financial statements:
19. For how many years has there been a continuing increase in sales?
20. Is the working capital position stronger or weaker in 1975?
21. Was there a gain or loss in 1975 on foreign currency translation?
22. What was the range of interest rates in 1975?
23. What was the amount of depreciation each year?

PROBLEMS

P3–1. Modern Supply, Inc., is developing the annual financial statements for 1977. The information given below has been verified as correct. There are 10,000 shares of common stock outstanding. Note that in some instances only totals are provided in order to shorten the solution.

Financial Information, 1977

Income Statement

Sales		$263,000
Selling expenses		42,000
Interest expense		1,000
Administrative expense		23,300
Return sales		3,000
Cost of goods sold		138,000
Extraordinary loss		2,000
Income tax expense on operations (40%)	$22,400	
Tax savings on extraordinary loss (40%)	800	21,600
Revenue from dividends on stock investment, K Corp.		300

Balance Sheet

Cash	$ 23,700
Accounts receivable	18,900
Allowance for doubtful accounts	500
Accounts payable	32,000
Retained earnings	107,500
Merchandise inventory	155,000
Investment in stock of K Corp. (long term)	4,000
Income taxes payable	5,000
Accumulated depreciation	16,600
Store equipment	70,000
Used equipment held for disposal	16,000
Common stock, par $10 per share	100,000
Long-term notes payable	10,000
Contributed capital in excess of par	16,000

Required:

a. On the basis of the listed data, prepare a classified income statement and a balance sheet for the year ended December 31, 1977.

b. Compute the profit margin and return on shareholders' equity. Evaluate each ratio.

(Hint: EPS on net income is $3.24.)

P3–2. Although Baker's Retail Store has been operating for only four years, the sales volume increase each year has been excellent; apparently it was occasioned by the location, a friendly atmosphere in the store, and a large stock for customer selection. Despite this appearance of success, the company has continually experienced a severe cash shortage, and a recent analysis by a consultant revealed significant inventory overstocking in numerous lines. Baker's Retail Store was organized as a corporation by Samuel Baker (now president) and four additional investors. Each owner invested $41,000 cash and received 400 shares of common stock (par value $100 per share). Although Sam Baker is recognized as an excellent retailer, he exhibits very little interest in the financial reports. At a recent meeting of the board of directors, the inadequacy of the financial reports was raised. The board voted to engage an independent CPA "to examine the accounting system, submit audited financial statements, analyze the financial situation, and make appropriate recommendations to the Board." The independent CPA has just been handed the following reports prepared for the last board meeting by the "store bookkeeper" (to simplify this case, assume that all of the figures are correct; also, only representative amounts have been included):

BAKER'S RETAIL STORE
Profit Statement
December 31, 1977

Revenues:		
Sales for the year	$572,000	
Interest collected on charge accounts	1,000	
Dividends received on stock of Y Corporation	200	$573,200
Costs and Expenses:		
Salaries, sales	66,500	
Salaries, administrative	36,000	
Depreciation, office equipment	1,200	
Depreciation, store equipment	6,000	
Store rent	18,000	
Office supplies used	800	
Store supplies used	1,900	
Cost of goods sold for the year	340,000	
Bad debt losses (estimated)	300	
Promotion costs	60,000	
Interest on debts	5,000	
Loss on fire damage (extraordinary loss)	1,200	
Insurance and taxes (two-thirds selling and one-third administrative)	6,000	
Miscellaneous expenses, sales	2,000	
Miscellaneous expenses, administrative	700	
Sales returns	8,000	
Income taxes on operations $8,000, less tax saving on fire loss $400; net taxes	7,600	561,200
Profit		$ 12,000

Balance Sheet

Assets		*Liabilities*	
Cash	$ 13,500	Accounts payable	$ 20,000
Accounts receivable (offset for allowance for bad debts $500)	23,500	Notes payable, short term	10,000
Merchandise inventory (at cost)	269,200	Notes payable, long term	80,000
Office supplies inventory	300	Rent due (for December 1977)	1,500
Store supplies inventory	1,600	Income taxes owed	4,600
Prepaid insurance	1,200	*Capital*	
Stock investment in Y Corporation	5,000	Stock, par $100, 2,000 shares	200,000
Store equipment (offset for accumulated depreciation, $25,600)	36,800	Excess paid over par	5,000
Office equipment (offset for accumulated depreciation, $6,000)	6,000	Retained earnings	36,000
	$357,100		$357,100

Required:

a. Prepare a classified income statement and a balance sheet.

b. Compute return on investment (owners' equity) and profit margin. Evaluate each ratio.

(Hint: EPS on income before extraordinary items is $6.40.)

P3–3. Small Company, a successful local automobile repair shop, is preparing the 1977 financial statements. On January 1, 1977, the company acquired a substantial quantity of new shop equipment (and related tools) for use in its testing and repair operations. The equipment involved a cash expenditure of $9,000. On the basis of past experience, the owner estimated the useful life of the new equipment to be five years, at which time it would sell for approximately 20 percent of the original cost.

Your advice is requested on two questions: (*a*) How much should be reported on the 1977 income statement for depreciation expense? (*b*) How should the new equipment be reported on the December 31, 1977 balance sheet? Show your computations and explanations.

(Hint: Residual value is represented by the 20 percent and should not be depreciated since it will be recovered at the time of disposal.)

P3–4. You are considering making a $20,000 investment in the common stock of either X Corporation or Y Corporation. The companies operate in different industries, and their managements have followed different financing policies. In reviewing the latest financial statements you observe the following data:

	X Corporation		Y Corporation	
From the balance sheets:				
Total assets		$240,000		$240,000
Total liabilities		100,000		10,000
Shares outstanding		5,000		10,000
From the income statements:				
Revenues		$ 93,800		$ 93,800
Expenses:				
Interest expense (rate 8%)	$ 8,000		$ 800	
Income tax expense (rate 40%)	24,000		24,000	
Remaining expenses	25,800	57,800	33,000	57,800
Net Income		$ 36,000		$ 36,000

From these amounts you observe that the two companies have (1) the same total amount of assets ($240,000), (2) the same amount of revenues ($93,800), and (3) the same net income ($36,000). However, as part of your analysis, you decide to compare the following: profit margin, return on stockholders' investment (owners' equity), and the aftertax, or net, interest rate.

Required:

a. Compute the above amounts for each company based on owners' equity. Show computations.

b. Which company would you select for the investment? Explain the basis for your choice.

(Hint: Refer to Chapter 2.)

P3–5. You are considering investing $50,000 in either A Corporation or B Corporation. Both companies have been operating in the same industry for a number of years. Your decision model calls for an evaluation and interpretation of the financial statements for the last five years; however, you have obtained the statements for last year only. Those statements provided the following data:

	A Corporation	*B Corporation*
Sales	$500,000	$700,000
Gross margin on sales	210,000	301,000
Income before extraordinary items	50,000	49,000
Net income	20,000	63,000
Total assets	300,000	400,000
Total liabilities (average interest rate 8%)	100,000	100,000
Owners' equity (total)	200,000	300,000
Shares outstanding	10,000	30,000
Income tax rate (average)	40%	40%

Required:

a. Based upon the above data (aside from other factors), what analytical steps would you suggest? Provide computations for each suggestion.

b. On the basis of your analytical results only, which company appears preferable as the investment choice? Explain why.

(Hint: Refer to Chapter 2.)

P3–6. The financial statements at the end of the fiscal year for Olsen Corporation are summarized below at June 30, 1977:

Income Statement

Sales	$800,000
Cost of goods sold	460,000
Gross margin on sales	340,000
Operating expenses and income taxes	292,000
Income before extraordinary items	48,000
Extraordinary gain (net of income taxes)	60,000
Net Income	$108,000

Balance Sheet

Current assets	$ 98,000
Investments	90,000
Fixed assets	330,000
Other assets	70,000
Total Assets	$588,000
Current liabilities	$ 98,000
Long-term liabilities	40,000
Total Liabilities	138,000
Capital stock, 8,000 shares	400,000
Contributed capital in excess of par	3,000
Retained earnings	47,000
Total Stockholders' Equity	450,000
Total Liabilities and Stockholders' Equity	$588,000

Required:

Several important investment decisions are under consideration by a large shareholder. Among the analytical data needed are certain financial ratios. Accordingly, assume you have decided to compute the following ratios:

Profit margin:

1. Profit margin based on net income.
2. Profit margin based on income before extraordinary items.

Return on investment:

3. Return on investment based on net income and total stockholders' equity.
4. Return on investment based on income before extraordinary items and total stockholders' equity.

Earnings per share:

5. Earnings per share based on net income.
6. Earnings per share based on income before extraordinary items.

For each of the three categories select those that you would deem most important and explain the basis for your choice.

P3–7. This problem is designed to aid you in understanding the content of published financial statements and to observe differences in form and terminology.

You are to refer to the financial statements of Carborundum Company presented in this chapter and respond to the following:

a. Income statement:

1. Is this a comparative statement? Explain.
2. Is this a consolidated statement? Explain.
3. Are there any extraordinary items?
4. What is the percent of income tax expense to pretax income?
5. What were the profit margins?
6. How many EPS amounts were reported?

b. Statement of shareholders' equity:

7. What amount was carried from the income statement?
8. What amount was carried to the balance sheet?
9. What caused retained earnings to change during 1975?

c. Balance sheet:

10. What was the working capital at the end of 1975?
11. How can one determine the amount of accumulated depreciation for each period?
12. Were there any unpaid income taxes at the end of 1975? How does this compare with income tax expense for 1975?
13. What percent of total assets was "provided" by shareholders by the end of 1975?
14. How many classes of capital stock have been issued? Did the stock sell at par?
15. At the end of 1975, what percent of stockholders' equity was represented by prior earnings retained in the business?

d. Statement of changes in financial position:
16. Can you tell from the heading whether it is based on working capital or on a cash basis?
17. How much cash was provided by operations each year?
18. In which year did cash increase by the greater amount?
19. In 1975, what item generated the largest amount of cash? What item used the largest amount of cash?
20. In which year did the company expend the most cash to retire long-term debt.

e. Accountants' report:
21. Who were the independent CPA's?
22. May this particular "accountants' report" presumably increase the reliability of the financial statements? Explain why.

f. Summary of accounting policies:
23. How many accounting policies are explained?
24. How are the inventories stated?
25. Over how many years is the goodwill being amortized?
26. Were there any investment tax credits?

g. Notes to the financial statements:
27. What was the percentage increase of 1975 sales over 1974 sales?
28. What was the percentage increase in working capital during 1975?
29. How much were the net losses from foreign currency translation in 1975?
30. What was the percentage increase in total assets during 1975?
31. What amount of retained earnings was restricted from dividends at the end of 1975?

4

Transaction analysis

PURPOSE OF THE CHAPTER

We have considered the objectives of financial accounting and studied the end product—the financial statements. We now turn our attention to the accounting process; the way in which the ongoing transactions are recorded, analyzed, and classified in a form suitable for generating the periodic financial statements. In this chapter we will learn the fundamentals of the accounting model and the analysis of transactions to determine and capture quantitatively their economic impacts on that model. We will focus on **transaction analysis** and **information processing.**

PART ONE: TRANSACTION ANALYSIS AND THE ACCOUNTING MODEL

NATURE OF TRANSACTIONS

Accounting focuses on certain events that have an economic impact on the entity. Those particular events are recorded in the accounting process and are generally referred to as **transactions.** This is a broad view of transactions and includes (1) those events that involve an exchange of resources (assets) and/or obligations (liabilities) between the business (i.e., the accounting entity) and one or more parties other than the entity; and (2) certain events (or economic occurrences) that are not between the entity and one or more parties but yet have a direct and measurable effect on the accounting entity.[1] Examples of the first category of transactions include the purchase of a machine, the sale of merchandise, the borrowing of cash, and the investment in the business by the owners. Examples of the second category of transactions include a casualty loss (such as a flood loss), depreciation of a fixed asset (as a result of use), and the "using up" of prepaid insurance. Throughout this book the word "transaction" will be used in the broad sense to include both types of events.

Most transactions are evidenced by an original business document of some sort; in the case of a sale on credit, a charge ticket is prepared and, in the case of a purchase of goods, an invoice is received. In certain other transactions, such as a cash sale, there may be no document other than the cash register tape. The documents that underlie, or support, transactions are usually called **source documents.** The important requirement, from the accounting point of view, is that there must be some procedure that will capture the raw economic data on each **transaction as it occurs.** Once this has been done, the data processing characteristics of the accounting model move the economic impact of each transaction from initial recording on to its final place—the periodic financial statements.

The fundamental feature of most transactions with external parties is that the business entity both gives up something and receives something in return. For example, in the case of a sale of merchandise for cash, the entity gives up resources (the goods sold) and receives in return another resource (cash). In the case of a credit sale of merchandise, the resource received at the time of sale is an account receivable (an asset). Later, another transaction occurs when the account receivable is collected; here, the resource relinquished is the receivable and the resource received is cash. As another example, in the purchase of an asset (either merchandise for resale or a truck purchased for use in the business), the entity acquires the asset and gives up cash, or, in the case of a credit purchase, incurs a liability. In the case of a credit purchase, another transaction occurs later when the debt is paid. At that time, the entity gives up a resource (cash) and "receives" satisfaction of the debt. The sale or purchase of services can be analyzed in the same way. Thus, transactions have a **dual economic effect** on the accounting entity. We will return to this dual effect when we consider the accounting model in the next section of this chapter.

THE FUNDAMENTAL ACCOUNTING MODEL

The fundamental accounting model expresses in algebraic format the status of the assets, debts, and owners' claims of an accounting

---

[1] A narrow definition of a transaction limits it to the first category; that is, events between the entity and one or more parties other than the entity. This definition is useful in certain circumstances and is conceptually correct. However, since accounting recognizes a number of events that are not transactions in the strict sense, we will use the term in the broader sense to simplify our terminology.

entity at any specific point in time. In Chapter 2 you learned the fundamental accounting model when you studied the balance sheet (the position statement), viz:

Assets = Liabilities + Owners' Equity

You also learned that owners' equity is (1) increased by investments (i.e., contributions) by the owners; (2) decreased by withdrawals by owners (such as dividends); (3) increased by revenues; and (4) decreased by expenses.[2] Thus, we can expand the fundamental accounting model as follows:

Assets = Liabilities + Owners' Equity

Increased by:	*Decreased by:*
Investments	**Withdrawals**
Revenues	**Expenses**

This model, since it is a broad economic description of an accounting entity, accommodates the *recording* of each transaction that directly affects the enterprise. The **dual economic effect** of each transaction is recorded in terms of this expanded accounting model. The dual effect is captured by the accounting process, whether the processing system is handwritten, mechanized, or computerized.

To illustrate how specific transactions are analyzed and how the dual effect is recorded in terms of the fundamental accounting model, let's take a simple but realistic situation. Throughout the example you should particularly note that (1) each transaction is recorded separately; (2) in recording each transaction the integrity of the accounting model is maintained (that is, assets will always equal liabilities plus owners' equity); and (3) the **dual effect,** as discussed in the preceding section, is recorded for each separate transaction.

The accounting model illustrated

B. Bass and three friends started a dry cleaning business on January 1, 1977, by investing a total of $10,000 cash from their personal savings accounts. Each investor was issued 100 shares of capital stock. Remember that the accounting entity, Bass Cleaners, Incorporated, is to be distinguished from the four investors. Exhibit 4–1 lists a series of transactions for the year 1977 and illustrates the dual effect of each transaction on the accounting model for the business. It also provides the information for developing the income statement and balance sheet shown in Exhibit 4–2. On the balance sheet, since this is a corporation, owners' equity is represented by the two sources: contributed capital and re-

[2] Owners' equity frequently is referred to as equity capital and, sometimes, net worth. The latter term is not recommended because it implies that owners' equity on the balance sheet states what the owners' claim is actually worth, which is not the case.

EXHIBIT 4–1

BASS CLEANERS, INCORPORATED
Transaction Analysis

Transactions	Assets		=	Liabilities		+	Stockholders' Equity	
a. Bass Cleaners received $10,000 cash invested by owners; 400 shares ($25 par value) of stock issued	Cash	+ $10,000					Capital stock (400 shares)	+ $10,000
b. Borrowed $5,000 cash on 8% note payable	Cash	+ 5,000		Note payable	+ $5,000			
c. Purchased delivery truck for cash at cost of $3,000	Cash	− 3,000						
	Delivery truck	+ 3,000						
d. Cleaning revenue collected in cash, $30,000	Cash	+ 30,000					Cleaning revenue	+ 30,000
e. Cleaning revenue earned, but the bill is not yet collected, $4,000	Accounts receivable	+ 4,000					Cleaning revenue	+ 4,000
f. Operating expenses paid in cash, $20,000	Cash	− 20,000					Operating expenses	− 20,000
g. Operating expenses incurred but not yet paid, $2,000				Accounts payable	+ 2,000		Operating expenses	− 2,000
h. Paid 8% interest on the $5,000 note payable, (*b*) above, with cash ($5,000 × 8% = $400)	Cash	− 400					Interest expense	− 400
i. Depreciation expense for one year on truck ($3,000 ÷ 5 years = $600)	Truck	− 600					Operating expenses, depreciation	− 600
j. Cash dividend of $1,500 paid to shareholders	Cash	− 1,500					Dividends paid (retained earnings)	− 1,500
k. Collected $1,000 cash on accounts receivable in (*e*)	Cash	+ 1,000						
	Accounts receivable	− 1,000						
l. Paid $500 cash on accounts payable in (*g*)	Cash	− 500		Accounts payable	− 500			
Totals (end of accounting period)	Total Assets	$26,000	=	Total Liabilities	$6,500	+	Total Stockholders' Equity	$19,500

EXHIBIT 4–2

BASS CLEANERS, INCORPORATED
Income Statement
For the Year Ended December 31, 1977

Cleaning revenue		$34,000
Operating expenses	$22,600	
Interest expense	400	23,000
Net Income		$11,000

Note: To simplify the illustration, income taxes are disregarded.

BASS CLEANERS, INCORPORATED
Balance Sheet
At December 31, 1977

Assets		
Cash		$20,600
Accounts receivable		3,000
Delivery truck	$ 3,000	
Less: Accumulated depreciation	600	2,400
Total Assets		$26,000
Liabilities		
Notes payable	5,000	
Accounts payable	1,500	
Total Liabilities		$ 6,500
Stockholders' Equity		
Contributed capital:		
Capital stock (400 shares)	10,000	
Retained earnings (net income, $11,000 minus dividends paid, $1,500)	9,500	
Total Stockholders' Equity		19,500
Total Liabilities and Stockholders' Equity		$26,000

tained earnings. Retained earnings represents the accumulated earnings of the corporation to date, less all dividends paid to date. This aspect of the balance sheet was explained and illustrated in Chapter 2 (pages 40–42) and in Chapter 3 (pages 66–67).[3]

From this simple situation you can view the broad perspective of the **accounting process.** Transactions occur that create raw economic data. Each transaction is subjected to **transaction analysis** and then each is recorded in terms of its **dual effect** on the fundamental accounting model. Finally, the financial statements at the end of the period are constructed from data accumulated in the accounting model.

This example, as reflected in Exhibits 4–1 and 4–2, indicates two

[3] If Bass Cleaners were a sole proprietorship or a partnership instead of a corporation, owners' equity would be shown as "Capital, owners' name" for each owner (see page 41).

primary data processing problems: (1) An efficient method is needed for keeping track of the **amounts** of each kind of asset (cash, accounts receivable, equipment, inventory, etc.); each kind of liability (notes payable, accounts payable, bonds payable, etc.); and each category of owners' equity (capital stock, dividends paid, revenues, and expenses). (2) A systematic method is needed for recording the **increases and decreases** in assets, liabilities, and owners' equity.

The account. These two data processing problems led early accountants to develop a series of **accounts.** A separate account is used for each

EXHIBIT 4-3

Ledger account (T-account form)

Cash

Left or Debit Side		*Right or Credit Side*	101
(Increases)		(Decreases)	
Investment by owners	10,000	To purchase truck	3,000
Loan from bank	5,000	Operating expenses	20,000
Cleaning revenue	30,000	Interest expense	400
Collections on accounts		Dividends paid	1,500
receivable	1,000	Payment on accounts payable	500

kind of asset, liability, and owners' equity. **An account is simply a standardized arrangement for recording data by categories.** Thus, in most accounting systems, you will find separate accounts, individually labeled, for each asset, such as cash, inventory, accounts receivable, equipment, land; for each liability, such as accounts payable, notes payable, taxes payable, and for each element of owners' equity, such as capital stock, sales revenue, service revenue, and various kinds of expenses. It is useful to think of an account as having two sides: the **left** or **debit** side and the **right** or **credit** side. The increases are recorded on one side and the decreases on the other side.[4] For example, the Cash account for Bass Cleaners may appear as in Exhibit 4-3.

Since the left or debit side of the Cash account (Exhibit 4-3) sums to \$46,000 and the right or credit side sums to \$25,400, the balance of cash is the difference: \$46,000 − \$25,400 = \$20,600. This is the amount of cash on hand at the end of the period, and this amount is the source of the balance sheet amount for cash reported in Exhibit 4-2. When the total

[4] Historically, and continuing to the present, accountants always refer to the left side as the debit side and to the right side as the credit side. For accounting purposes, the terms debit and credit have no other meanings. The words "to debit" and "to credit" should not be confused with "increase" or "decrease" as will become clear in the next few paragraphs. Contrary to what some people think, there is no implication of "goodness" attached to credits or "badness" attached to debits (or vice versa).

EXHIBIT 4–4
Ledger account (account form)

Account Title *Cash* Account Number *101*

Date	Explanation	F	Debit	Credit	Balance
Jan. 1	Investments	1	10,000		10,000
3	Borrowing	3	5,000		15,000
6	Truck purchased	3		3,000	12,000
7	Cleaning revenue	4	30,000		42,000
8	Operating expenses	4		20,000	22,000
10	Interest expense	5		400	21,600
15	Payments to owners	7		1,500	20,100
16	Collections on receivables	8	1,000		21,100
17	Payments on accounts payable	8		500	20,600

amount on the decrease side of the Cash account is larger than the total amount on the increase side, a cash deficit is indicated.

To facilitate the processing of accounting data, whether handwritten, mechanized, or computerized, each account generally is assigned an identification number for ready reference. For example, the Cash account may be assigned an identification code number such as 101. Although the above "T-account" format often is used for instructional convenience, a standard account format often used in manually maintained systems is shown in Exhibit 4–4.[5] Although rearranged, in effect it still has the debit side and credit side feature.

Recording increases and decreases in the accounts. In respect to the need for an efficient method of recording increases and decreases, a systematic and algebraically consistent accounting for each increase and decrease in assets, liabilities, and owners' equity is provided by the fundamental accounting model. This is a significant characteristic of the accounting model. Recall from Chapter 1 that in 1494 a mathematician

[5] Handwritten or manually maintained accounts in the formats shown here generally are used only in small businesses. Highly mechanized and computerized systems retain the concept of the account but not this format. T-accounts are primarily useful for instructional purposes.

(Paciolo) first described the fundamental accounting model used today. Perceiving the problem, and after designing the T-account (as illustrated above for cash), Paciolo applied an algebraic concept that has proven to be of great significance in decreasing errors made in carrying out the accounting process. The fundamental accounting model, **Assets = Liabilities + Owners' Equity,** itself is an algebraic model that balances and can be rearranged mathematically. Paciolo added another algebraic balance feature to it to accommodate the recording of increases and decreases in each account. Let's see how it was done.

Paciolo perceived that having designed the T-account with two sides in order to reflect increases and decreases, he could add still another algebraic **balancing feature** by simply *reversing* the position in the account of the "increases" and "decreases" on the *opposite sides* of the equal sign. To illustrate the point, he could have designed the system as follows:

Assets		**= Liabilities**		**+ Owners' Equity**	
Debit	*Credit*	*Debit*	*Credit*	*Debit*	*Credit*
+	−	+	−	+	−

Instead, in order to introduce a second algebraic balance feature, he designed the system used to this day with the "+" and "−" *in reverse order* on the opposite sides of the equal sign as follows:

Assets		**= Liabilities**		**+ Owners' Equity**	
Debit	*Credit*	*Debit*	*Credit*	*Debit*	*Credit*
+	−	−	+	−	+

The addition of this algebraic concept resulted in the second "balancing" feature; that is, **debits always equal credits.** Thus, the system used for recording increases and decreases in the accounts may be conveniently tabulated as follows:

	Increases	*Decreases*
Assets....................................	Debit	Credit
Liabilities................................	Credit	Debit
Owners' equity	Credit	Debit

Another way to view the debits = credits feature is in terms of the algebraic relationship: "The signs reverse on opposite sides of the equal sign."

It follows that for each transaction, and for all transactions, the debit amounts will always equal the credit amounts. To summarize, the two balancing features of the fundamental accounting model are:

1. **Assets = Liabilities + Owners' Equity**
2. **Debits = Credits**

Debit and credit for revenue and expenses. Owners' equity is increased by credits and decreased by debits. Revenues increase owners' equity; therefore they are recorded as credits. Expenses decrease in owners' equity; therefore they are recorded as debits. In other words, the debit/credit relationship for owners' equity accounts is applied to revenues and expenses as follows:[6]

Revenues are recorded as credits.
Expenses are recorded as debits.

TRANSACTION ANALYSIS

Transaction analysis is a term frequently used to describe the process of studying each transaction to determine its dual effect on the entity in terms of the accounting model. In transaction analysis a careful distinction is made between the cash basis and the accrual basis viewpoints. In Chapter 2, pages 43 and 44, the distinction between *cash basis accounting* and *accrual basis accounting* was discussed. The concept of **accrual accounting** requires that revenues and expenses be measured and reported in the accounting period in which they occur rather than when the related cash is received or paid. To illustrate, assume a sale of merchandise for $1,000 in 1977. In the case of a cash sale, there is one transaction to be recognized. In 1977, cash is increased by $1,000 and sales revenue of $1,000 has been earned. In this situation, sales revenue is measured at the same time that the cash is collected since they occur at the same time. Now, assume instead that it was a credit sale in 1977 and that the cash will be collected in 1978. In this situation, there would be two separate transactions to be given accounting recognition: (1) In 1977 the sales revenue and a receivable from the customer is recognized when the sale is consummated. (2) Later, in 1978 when the cash is collected on the receivable, a transaction must be recognized that would increase cash and decrease the receivable.

Now, let's see how each transaction is subjected to transaction analysis to determine (1) the dual economic effect on the entity and (2) how that dual effect is recorded in the accounts (i.e., in the fundamental accounting model).

Recall that for each transaction recorded, the **two separate balances** must be maintained, viz: (1) Assets = Liabilities + Owners' Equity and (2) Debits = Credits. Bass Cleaners, Incorporated, will be used to demonstrate, on the next few pages, the transaction analysis and the recording process. You should analyze each transaction (listed on page 94) and trace the manner in which the dual effect is recorded in the accounting

[6] To "charge an account" is a frequently used expression meaning to *debit* an account. Thus, the word "debit" is used as both a verb and a noun.

model by using T-accounts (rather than simple plus and minus as on page 94). The transactions are entered below in T-accounts and are keyed with letters for ready reference.

a. Received $10,000 cash invested by the four owners and issued 400 shares of capital stock (par value $25 per share).

Cash (asset)

	Debit		*Credit*
(*a*)	10,000		

Capital Stock (owners' equity)

	Debit		*Credit*
		(*a*)	10,000

Transaction analysis—The transaction increased the company's cash by $10,000, which was recorded in the Cash account as a debit (increase); liabilities were unaffected; owners' equity was increased by $10,000, which was recorded in the Capital Stock account as a credit (increase). Thus, the entry meets the test of both equations: assets equal liabilities plus owners' equity and debits equal credits.

b. Borrowed $5,000 cash from the bank on an 8 percent note payable.

Cash (asset)

	Debit		*Credit*
(*a*)	10,000		
(*b*)	5,000		

Notes Payable (liability)

	Debit		*Credit*
		(*b*)	5,000

Transaction analysis—The transaction increased the cash by $5,000, which was recorded in the Cash account as a debit (increase); liabilities were increased by $5,000, which is recorded in Notes Payable as a credit (increase); and owners' equity was unchanged. The entry meets the test of both equations.

c. Purchased a delivery truck for cash at a cost of $3,000.

Delivery Truck (asset)

	Debit		*Credit*
(*c*)	3,000		

Cash (asset)

	Debit		*Credit*
(*a*)	10,000	(*c*)	3,000
(*b*)	5,000		

Transaction analysis—The transaction increased the asset, delivery truck, by $3,000, which was recorded in that account as a debit (increase); the cash decreased by $3,000, which was recorded in the Cash account as a credit (decrease). Liabilities and owners' equity were not affected. The entry meets the test of both equations.

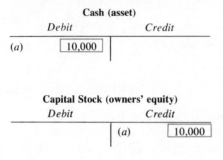

d. Cleaning revenue collected in cash, $30,000.

Cash (asset)

	Debit		*Credit*
(*a*)	10,000	(*c*)	3,000
(*b*)	5,000		
(*d*)	30,000		

Cleaning Revenue (owners' equity)

	Debit		*Credit*
		(*d*)	30,000

Transaction analysis—The transaction increased cash by $30,000, which was recorded in the asset account Cash as a debit (increase); liabilities were unaffected; owners' equity was increased by $30,000 as a result of the earning of revenue. Owners' equity was credited (increased) by $30,000. A separate account, "Cleaning Revenue," is used to keep track of this revenue. The entry meets the test of both equations.

e. Cleaning revenue earned, but the cash is not yet collected, $4,000.

Accounts Receivable (asset)

	Debit		*Credit*
(*e*)	4,000		

Cleaning Revenue (owners' equity)

	Debit		*Credit*
		(*d*)	30,000
		(*e*)	4,000

Transaction analysis—The transaction increased the company's asset, Accounts Receivable, by $4,000, which was recorded as a debit (increase) to that account; liabilities were unaffected; and owner's equity was increased by $4,000 as a result of earning revenue. Owners' equity was credited (increased) by $4,000. A separate account, "Cleaning Revenue," is used to keep track of this revenue. The entry meets the test of both equations.

f. Expenses paid in cash, $20,000.

Cash (asset)

	Debit		*Credit*
(*a*)	10,000	(*c*)	3,000
(*b*)	5,000	(*f*)	20,000
(*d*)	30,000		

Operating Expenses (owners' equity)

	Debit		*Credit*
(*f*)	20,000		

Transaction analysis—The transaction decreased the cash by $20,000, which was recorded in the Cash account as a credit (decrease); liabilities were unaffected; owners' equity was decreased by $20,000 as a result of paying expenses. Owners' equity was debited (decreased) for $20,000. A separate account, "Operating Expenses," is used to keep track of this expense. The entry meets the test of both equations.

g. Expenses incurred but not yet paid, $2,000.

Accounts Payable (liability)

	Debit		*Credit*
		(*g*)	2,000

Transaction analysis—This transaction increased the company's liabilities by $2,000, which was recorded as a credit (increase) to Accounts Payable; assets

Operating Expenses (owners' equity)

	Debit		*Credit*
(*f*)	20,000		
(*g*)	[2,000]		

were unaffected; owners' equity was decreased by $2,000. A separate account, "Operating Expenses," is used to keep track of this expense. The entry meets the test of both equations.

h. Paid cash for interest on note payable in (*b*) ($5,000 × 8% = $400).

Cash (asset)

	Debit		*Credit*
(*a*)	10,000	(*c*)	3,000
(*b*)	5,000	(*f*)	20,000
(*d*)	30,000	(*h*)	[400]

Interest Expense (owners' equity)

	Debit		*Credit*
(*h*)	[400]		

Transaction analysis – This transaction decreased the cash by $400, which was recorded as a credit (decrease) in the Cash account; the amount of the liability ($5,000) was unchanged; however, owners' equity was decreased by the amount of the interest ($400) since the payment of interest (but not principal of the note) represents an expense. Owners' equity was debited (decreased) for $400. A separate account, "Interest Expense," is used to keep track of this type of expense. This entry meets the test of both equations.

i. Depreciation expense for one year on the delivery truck computed ($3,000 ÷ 5 years = $600).

Operating Expenses (owners' equity)

	Debit		Credit
(*f*)	20,000		
(*g*)	2,000		
(*i*)	[600]		

Delivery Truck (asset)

	Debit		*Credit*
(*c*)	3,000		

Accumulated Depreciation, Delivery Truck (negative asset)

	Debit		*Credit*
		(*i*)	[600]

Transaction analysis – This transaction is caused by the internal utilization of an asset owned for operating purposes. The use gives rise to depreciation expense. Owners' equity was debited (decreased) to record the fact that an expense was incurred, the debit was recorded in a separate account, "Operating Expenses," established to keep track of this type of expense. Asset (delivery truck) was decreased due to the fact that a "part of the cost of the asset was used up in operations." Instead of crediting the asset account "Delivery Truck" directly, a related **negative or contra asset** account, "Accumulated Depreciation, Delivery Truck," is credited so that the depreciated amounts can be kept separately. This will be explained in detail in Chapter 10. This entry meets the test of both equations.

j. Paid $1,500 cash dividend to the stockholders.

Cash (asset)

	Debit		*Credit*
(*a*)	10,000	(*c*)	3,000
(*b*)	5,000	(*f*)	20,000
(*d*)	30,000	(*h*)	400
		(*j*)	1,500

Dividends Paid (negative owners' equity)

	Debit		*Credit*
(*j*)	1,500		

Transaction analysis – This transaction decreased the company's cash by $1,500, which was recorded in the Cash account as a credit (decrease); liabilities were unaffected; owners' equity was decreased by $1,500 as a result of the resources (cash) paid out of the business to the stockholders. Owners' equity was debited (decreased) by $1,500. A separate account, "Dividends Paid," sometimes is used to keep track of this decrease in owners' equity. Dividends are not an expense; rather they are a "distribution of profits" to the owners. This entry meets the test of both equations.

k. Collected $1,000 cash on accounts receivable in (*e*).

Cash (asset)

	Debit		*Credit*
(*a*)	10,000	(*c*)	3,000
(*b*)	5,000	(*f*)	20,000
(*d*)	30,000	(*h*)	400
(*k*)	1,000	(*j*)	1,500

Accounts Receivable (asset)

	Debit		*Credit*
(*e*)	4,000	(*k*)	1,000

Transaction analysis – This transaction increased the cash by $1,000, which was recorded as a debit (increase) in the Cash account; an asset (Accounts Receivable) was credited (decreased) by the same amount; liabilities and owners' equity were unaffected since there was simply a change in two assets but no change in total assets. This entry meets the test of both equations.

l. Paid $500 cash on accounts payable in (*g*).

Cash (asset)

	Debit		*Credit*
(*a*)	10,000	(*e*)	3,000
(*b*)	5,000	(*f*)	20,000
(*d*)	30,000	(*h*)	400
(*k*)	1,000	(*j*)	1,500
		(*l*)	500

Accounts Payable (liability)

	Debit		*Credit*
(*l*)	500	(*g*)	2,000

Transaction analysis – This transaction decreased the cash by $500, which was recorded as a credit (decrease) in the Cash account; liabilities (Accounts Payable) were decreased (debited) for $500; owners' equity was unaffected since there were no revenue or expense involved in this transaction, merely the payment of a debt. This entry meets the test of both equations.

Observe that each transaction affects a minimum of two separate accounts.

Now we may summarize the fundamental accounting model and the mechanics of the debt-credit concept in T-account format as follows, where + means increase and − means decrease:

Assets		**= Liabilities**		**+ Owners' Equity**	
Debit	*Credit*	*Debit*	*Credit*	*Debit*	*Credit*
+	−	−	+	−	+

Revenue (increase in owners' equity)	
Debit	*Credit*
	(To record)

Expenses (decrease in owners' equity)	
Debit	*Credit*
(To record)	

Note particularly that an increase in **revenue** (a credit) represents an **increase** in owners' equity and an increase in **expense** (a debit) represents a **decrease** in owners' equity. When a revenue is earned, the resources of the business are increased and, because of the dual effect, owners' equity is increased by the same amount. In contrast, when an expense is incurred, the resources of the business are decreased and, because of the dual effect, the owners' equity is decreased by the same amount.

PART TWO: THE FUNDAMENTALS OF INFORMATION PROCESSING

The accounting information-processing cycle is repeated each period. It involves a series of **sequential steps** starting with the initial transaction, and extending through the basic accounting records and finally to the required financial statements: income statement, balance sheet, and statement of changes in financial position. In this Part, we will consider the primary sequential steps in the information cycle in the order in which they are usually accomplished, viz: (1) raw data collection, (2) transaction analysis, (3) recording transactions in the **journal,** (4) transferring data from the journal to the **ledger,** (5) preparing a **trial balance,** and (6) preparing the required financial statements.

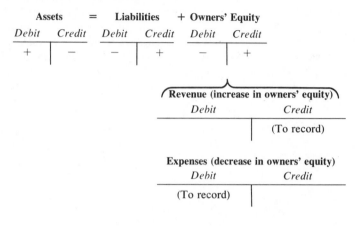

RAW DATA COLLECTION

The initial step in an accounting information-processing cycle is the collection of economic data on each transaction affecting the entity. Such economic data must be collected continuously as transactions occur. Transactions involving external parties usually generate documents that provide essential data. Examples are sales invoices, cash register tapes, purchase invoices, and signed receipts. Documentation must be generated internally for certain economic effects such as depreciation and the using up of office supplies. It is important to realize that most of the raw data (and the supporting documents) entered into an accounting system are not generated by the accounting function but by the various **operating** functions of the business. Since the quality of the outputs of an information-processing system are largely determined by the quality (and timeliness) of the inputs of raw data based on transactions, a carefully designed and controlled data collection system is necessary. Thus the initial data collection procedure constitutes an integral and important subsystem of an accounting information-processing system.

TRANSACTION ANALYSIS

This step in an information-processing system was discussed above (page 99). Recall that it is a mental process having as its objective determination of the economic effects on the entity of each transaction in terms of the basic accounting model: Assets = Liabilities + Owners' Equity. When transaction analysis is completed on a transaction, the economic effects are then **formally** entered in the accounting system.

THE JOURNAL

The economic effect of each transaction immediately after transaction analysis is **formally** entered in the accounting system in a record known as the **journal.**

In a simple situation one could record the transactions of a business entity directly in the separate accounts as was done for Bass Cleaners. However, in more complex situations, it is essential, as each transaction is analyzed, that its dual economic effect on the accounting model (i.e., the resultant entry) be recorded in one place in **chronological order** (i.e., in order of date). The accounting record designed for this particular purpose is known as the **journal.** Typically, the dual effects are first recorded therein and then are later transferred, or **posted,** to the appropriate accounts in the T-accounts as illustrated for Bass Cleaners.

The journal contains a chronological listing of the entries for each of the transactions. The format of the entry in the journal for each transaction is designed so that the dual effects on the accounting model and the debit and credit features are physically linked. For example, transaction (*a*) for Bass Cleaners would appear in the journal in the following format (note the debit is listed first and the credit is indented):

		Debit	*Credit*
(Date)	Cash	10,000	
	Capital stock		10,000
	To record investment of cash by owners.		

The physical linking of the dual effects of each transaction in the journal is in contrast to the separate accounts, where each entry is physically separated between two or more accounts. For example, you will recall that the dual effect of the above entry for Bass Cleaners would appear in the separate accounts as follows:

Cash				Capital Stock	
(Date)	10,000			(Date)	10,000

The chronological listing in the journal serves a useful purpose. For example, if at later date, one desires to trace an entry, knowledge of the approximate date of the entry may be helpful in locating it in the journal but not in the individual accounts. Similarly, one would have to examine two or more accounts (cards, sheets, etc.) to review the complete effects of a particular transaction. In contrast, the journal not only would facilitate the search but would provide the dual economic effects (in one place) and would indicate what separate records to refer to.

To facilitate your understanding, let's see how the journal might appear in a manually maintained system. The first three transactions for Bass Cleaners have been entered in a typical journal shown in Exhibit 4–5. Recording the transactions in this manner is known as **journalizing.** In respect to the **journal entries,** you should observe in particular that (1) each transaction and event is first recorded in the journal with a separate entry; (2) each entry is dated, and entries are recorded in chronological order; (3) for each transaction the debits (accounts and amounts) are entered first, the credits follow and are indented; and (4) as a consequence, the effects on the accounting model and the debits and credits are linked in one entry. These features, since they provide an "audit or tracing trail," facilitate subsequent examination of past transactions, and in the location of errors, and simplify subsequent accounting (as will be demonstrated later). Because it is the place of first recording of each transaction, the journal sometimes is referred to as a **book of original entry.** In contrast, the ledger is referred to as a **book of final entry.**

EXHIBIT 4–5

Journal

Page 1

Date	Account Titles and Explanation	Folio	Debit	Credit
Jan. 1	Cash	101	10,000	
	Capital stock	301		10,000
	Investment of cash by owners			
Jan. 3	Cash	101	5,000	
	Note payable	202		5,000
	Borrowed cash on 8% note			
Jan. 6	Delivery Truck	111	3,000	
	Cash	101		3,000
	Purchased delivery			
	truck for use in			
	the business.			

THE LEDGER

In the preceding illustration for Bass Cleaners (page 100) a separate account was maintained for each kind of asset, liability, and owners' equity. From this it is apparent that an accounting system typically will contain a large number of such accounts. Collectively, the accounts are known as the **ledger.** The ledger may be organized in numerous ways. Handwritten accounting systems may use a loose-leaf ledger—one page for each account. In the case of "machine accounting," a card ledger generally is used and there is a separate machine card for each account. In the case of a computerized accounting system, the ledger is maintained on magnetic tape or similar electronic storage devices, but there are still separate accounts as in the other systems (each account is identified by an assigned number).

Exhibit 4–6 shows the ledger for Bass Cleaners in T-account form.

EXHIBIT 4–6

BASS CLEANERS, INCORPORATED
LEDGER

ASSETS = LIABILITIES + OWNERS' EQUITY

ASSETS

Cash

(*a*)	10,000	(*c*)	3,000
(*b*)	5,000	(*f*)	20,000
(*d*)	30,000	(*h*)	400
(*k*)	1,000	(*j*)	1,500
		(*l*)	500

(Net debit balance, $20,600)

Accounts Receivable

(*e*)	4,000	(*k*)	1,000

(Net debit balance, $3,000)

Delivery Truck

(*c*)	3,000		

Accumulated Depreciation, Delivery Truck*

		(*i*)	600

LIABILITIES

Notes Payable

		(*b*)	5,000

Accounts Payable

(*l*)	500	(*g*)	2,000

(Net credit balance, $1,500)

OWNERS' EQUITY

Capital Stock

		(*a*)	10,000

Dividends Paid†

(*j*)	1,500		

Cleaning Revenue

		(*d*)	30,000
		(*e*)	4,000

(Net credit balance, $34,000)

Operating Expenses

(*f*)	20,000		
(*g*)	2,000		
(*i*)	600		

(Net credit balance, $22,600)

Interest Expense

(*h*)	400		

Totals 26,000 = 6,500 + 19,500

* Accumulated depreciation is a negative, or contra, asset account. For further explanation see Chapter 10.

† Dividends Paid represents a decrease in owners' equity since it shows the amount that was paid out as dividends to the stockholders. For further explanation see Chapter 13.

The accounting model, Assets = Liabilities + Owners' Equity, given at the top of this exhibit, and the totals at the bottom are shown only for your convenience in study; they would not appear in an actual ledger.

POSTING TO THE LEDGER

In the preceding section we stated that the data for each entry recorded in the journal are transferred, or *posted,* to the appropriate accounts in the ledger. In a business using a manual system, one may expect the entity to record the transactions in the journal each day and the posting (to the ledger) to occur less frequently, say every few days. Of course, the timing of these **information-processing activities** varies with the size and complexity of the entity.

In posting, the debits and credits reflected in the journal entries, are transferred directly as debits and credits to the indicated accounts in the ledger. In both the journal (Exhibit 4–5) and ledger (as in the Cash account, Exhibit 4–4), you can observe that there is a **"folio"** column, which is included to provide a numerical cross-reference between the journal and the ledger (this is often said "to provide an audit trail"). For example, the journal shown in Exhibit 4–5 shows a folio number of 101 for Cash, which indicates the account in the ledger to which that amount was posted. You will recall that this is the account number assigned to cash in Exhibit 4–4. Similarly, if you look at the ledger account for Cash, as shown in Exhibit 4–4, you will see on the first line of the account a folio number of 1, indicating that the particular amount posted came from page 1 of the journal. Folio numbers are entered during the posting process; therefore they also indicate whether posting has been accomplished. Transferring amounts from the journal to the ledger is called *posting*. Since the data ends up in the *ledger,* it is sometimes referred to as the *book of final entry.*

THE TRIAL BALANCE

At the end of the accounting period, as a matter of convenience, a **trial balance** is prepared from the ledger. A trial balance is simply a listing, in ledger-account order, of the ledger accounts and their respective net debit or credit balances. The net balance shown for each account is

EXHIBIT 4–7

BASS CLEANERS, INCORPORATED
Trial Balance
December 31, 1977

Account Titles	*Balance* Debit	Credit
Cash	$20,600	
Accounts receivable	3,000	
Delivery truck	3,000	
Accumulated depreciation, delivery truck		$ 600
Notes payable		5,000
Accounts payable		1,500
Capital stock (400 shares)		10,000
Dividends paid	1,500	
Cleaning revenues		34,000
Operating expenses	22,600	
Interest expense	400	
Totals	$51,100	$51,100

the difference between the total of the debits and the total of the credits in each ledger account.

Exhibit 4–7 shows the trial balance for Bass Cleaners at December 31, 1977. Basically, the trial balance provides two convenience factors: (1) the equality of debits and credits is easily checked; and (2) data are provided in a convenient form for construction of the income statement, balance sheet, and statement of changes in financial position.

FINANCIAL STATEMENTS

At the end of the accounting period (1) all transactions for the period will have been analyzed and entered in the journal by order of date, (2) all amounts in the journal will have been posted (transferred) to the ledger accounts, and (3) a trial balance will have been prepared from the ledger.

The next phase is completion of the three required financial statements as illustrated in the two prior chapters. The trial balance provides the basic data needed to prepare the financial statements at the end of the period.

DEMONSTRATION CASE—THE INFORMATION PROCESSING SYSTEM

La Paloma Apartments, Incorporated

This case illustrates the information-processing cycle. (Try to solve it before studying the suggested solution that follows.)

We have selected this case of a small business to demonstrate the complete accounting *information-processing cycle* from the initial capture of the raw economic data to the financial statements developed at the end of the period. Only representative and summary transactions have been selected in order to keep the length of the case within reason. You should study each step in the solution carefully since it reviews the concepts, principles, and procedures introduced in the chapters to this point.

On January 3, 1974, M. Hall and P. Garza formed a corporation to build and operate an apartment complex to be called La Paloma. At the start, each invested $40,000 cash and received 3,000 shares of $10 par value stock. Therefore, at that date the following entry was recorded in the accounts:

January 3, 1974:

Cash	80,000	
Capital stock, par $10 (6,000 shares)		60,000
Contributed capital in excess of par		20,000

Shortly thereafter, land was acquired for $30,000 and a construction contract was signed with a builder. The first apartments were rented on July 1, 1975. The owners decided to use a *fiscal year* (rather than the calendar year) for business purposes—July 1 through June 30. It is now June 30, 1977 and the occupancy rate during the year has been over 96 percent due to the quality of the apartments and the excellent management by Hall and Garza.

Since this is the second year of operations, certain accounts in the ledger will have balances carried over from June 30, 1976. Below you will find a complete list of the ledger accounts that will be needed for this case, with the balances carried over from the previous fiscal year. Ledger account (folio) numbers are provided at the left.

LA PALOMA APARTMENTS
Ledger Balances
July 1, 1976

		Balance	
Account No.	*Account Titles*	*Debit*	*Credit*
101	Cash	$ 5,000	
103	Accounts receivable (or rent receivable)		
105	Supplies inventory	2,000	
112	Prepaid insurance		
121	Land (apartment site)	30,000	
122	La Paloma apartment building	200,000	
123	Accumulated depreciation, apartment building		$ 10,000
125	Furniture and fixtures	60,000	
126	Accumulated depreciation, furniture and fixtures		12,000
131	Land for future apartment site		
201	Accounts payable		6,000
202	Property taxes payable		
203	Income taxes payable		
204	Mortgage payable, 8% (apartment building)		179,000
205	Note payable, long term		
301	Capital stock (par $10, 6,000 shares)		60,000
302	Contributed capital in excess of par		20,000
303	Retained earnings (accumulated earnings to June 30, 1976)		10,000
401	Rent revenue		
521	Utilities and telephone expense		
522	Apartment maintenance expense		
523	Salary and wage expense		
524	Insurance expense		
525	Property tax expense		
526	Depreciation expense		
527	Miscellaneous expenses		
531	Interest expense		
532	Income tax expense		
	Totals	$297,000	$297,000

Typical transactions (most of them summarized) for the 12-month fiscal period—July 1, 1976, through June 30, 1977—are listed below. To facilitate tracing, instead of a date, we will use the letter notation to the left of each transaction.

a. On November 1, 1976, paid $3,000 cash for a two-year insurance premium covering the building and contents and liability.

b. Rental revenue earned: collected in cash, $90,000; uncollected, $1,800.

c. Paid accounts payable (amounts owed from last year for expenses), $6,000.

d. Purchased a tract of land, at a cost of $35,000, as a planned site for another apartment complex to be constructed in "about three years." Cash amounting to $5,000 was paid and a long-term note payable (8 percent interest per annum, interest payable each six months) was signed for the balance.

e. Operating expenses incurred and paid in cash were:

Utilities and telephone expense	$26,000
Apartment maintenance expense	1,200
Salary and wage expense	3,000

f. At the end of the fiscal year (June 30, 1977) the following bills for expenses incurred had not been recorded or paid: June telephone bill, $40; and miscellaneous expenses, $1,100.

g. Paid interest for six months on the long-term note at 8 percent per annum. (Refer to item [*d*].)

h. An inventory count at the end of the fiscal period, June 30, 1977, showed remaining supplies on hand amounting to $400. Supplies used are considered a miscellaneous expense.

i. By the end of the fiscal period, June 30, 1977, one third (8 months out of 24 months) of the prepaid insurance premium of $3,000 paid in transaction (*a*) had expired.

j. Depreciation expense for the year was based on an estimated useful life of 20 years for the apartment and 5 years for the furniture and fixtures.

k. The property taxes for the year ending June 30, 1977, in the amount of $1,700 have not yet been recorded or paid.

l. Cash payment on the mortgage on the apartment was:

On principal	$ 8,000
Interest	10,700
Total Paid	$18,700

m. Income tax expense for the year ending June 30, 1977, was computed to be $4,900. This obligation will be paid in the next period.

Required:

Complete the accounting information-processing cycle by solving each of the following:

1. Set up a ledger with T-accounts that includes all of the accounts listed above; include the account numbers as given. Enter the July 1, 1976, balances in each account in this manner:

Cash		101
Balance	5,000	

2. Analyze, then journalize (i.e., enter in the journal), each transaction listed above for the period July 1, 1976, through June 30, 1977. Number the journal pages consecutively.
3. Post all entries from the journal to the ledger; utilize the folio columns.
4. Prepare a trial balance at June 30, 1977.
5. Prepare a classified income statement for the fiscal year ending June 30, 1977.
6. Prepare a classified balance sheet at June 30, 1977.

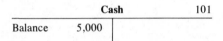

Suggested Solution:

Requirement 2:

JOURNAL

Page 1

Date 1976–77	Account Titles and Explanation	F	Debit	Credit
a.	Prepaid insurance	112	3,000	
	Cash	101		3,000
	Paid insurance premium for two years in advance.			
	(Explanatory note—An asset account, Prepaid Insurance, is debited because a future service, insurance coverage, has been paid for in advance.)			
b.	Cash	101	90,000	
	Accounts receivable (or rent receivable)	103	1,800	
	Rent revenue	401		91,800
	To record rent revenues earned for the year, of which $1,800 has not yet been collected.			
c.	Accounts payable	201	6,000	
	Cash	101		6,000
	Paid obligations carried over from previous year.			
d.	Land for future apartment site	131	35,000	
	Cash	101		5,000
	Note payable, long term	205		30,000
	Purchased land as a site for future apartment complex. (This is a second tract of land acquired; the present apartment building was constructed on the first tract.)			
e.	Utilities and telephone expense	521	26,000	
	Apartment maintenance expense	522	1,200	
	Salary and wage expense	523	3,000	
	Cash	101		30,200
	Paid expenses.			
f.	Utilities and telephone expense	521	40	
	Miscellaneous expenses	527	1,100	
	Accounts payable	201		1,140
	Expenses incurred but not yet paid.			

JOURNAL Page 2

Date 1976–77	Account Titles and Explanation	F	Debit	Credit
g.	Interest expense	531	1,200	
	Cash	101		1,200
	Paid six months' interest on long-term note ($30,000 × 8% × 6/12 = $1,200).			
h.	Miscellaneous expenses	527	1,600	
	Supplies inventory	105		1,600
	To record as expense supplies used from inventory during the year. (Explanatory note – Supplies are bought in advance of use; hence, at that time they are recorded as an asset, Supplies Inventory. As the supplies are used from inventory, the asset thus used becomes an expense. Refer to Office Supplies account – [$2,000 − $400 = $1,600].)			
i.	Insurance expense	524	1,000	
	Prepaid insurance	112		1,000
	To record as an expense the cost of the insurance that expired ($3,000 × 8/24 = $1,000).			
j.	Depreciation expense	526	22,000	
	Accumulated depreciation, apartment building	123		10,000
	Accumulated depreciation, furniture and fixtures	126		12,000
	Depreciation expense for one year. Computation: Apartment: $200,000 ÷ 20 years = $10,000 Furniture and fixtures: $60,000 ÷ 5 years = $12,000			
k.	Property tax expense	525	1,700	
	Property taxes payable	202		1,700
	Property taxes for the year not yet paid.			
l.	Mortgage payable	204	8,000	
	Interest expense	531	10,700	
	Cash	101		18,700
	Payments on principal of mortgage payable plus interest expense.			
m.	Income tax expense	532	4,900	
	Income taxes payable	203		4,900

Requirements 1 and 3:

LEDGER

Cash 101

Date	F	Amount	Date	F	Amount
Balance		5,000	(*a*)	1	3,000
(*b*)	1	90,000	(*c*)	1	6,000
			(*d*)	1	5,000
			(*e*)	1	30,200
			(*g*)	2	1,200
			(*l*)	2	18,700

(Net debit balance, $30,900)

Accounts Receivable 103

(*b*)	1	1,800			

Supplies Inventory 105

Balance		2,000	(*h*)	2	1,600

Prepaid Insurance 112

(*a*)	1	3,000	(*i*)	2	1,000

Land (Apartment Site) 121

Balance		30,000			

La Paloma Apartment Building 122

Balance		200,000			

Accumulated Depreciation, Apartment Building 123

			Balance		10,000
			(*j*)	2	10,000

Furniture and Fixtures 125

Date	F	Amount	Date	F	Amount
Balance		60,000			

Accumulated Depreciation, Furniture and Fixtures 126

			Balance		12,000
			(*j*)	2	12,000

Land for Future Apartment Site 131

(*d*)	1	35,000			

Accounts Payable 201

(*c*)	1	6,000	Balance		6,000
			(*f*)	1	1,140

Property Taxes Payable 202

			(*k*)	2	1,700

Income Taxes Payable 203

			(*m*)	2	4,900

Mortgage Payable (apartment building) 204

(*l*)	2	8,000	Balance		179,000

Note Payable, Long term 205

Date	F	Amount	Date	F	Amount
			(*d*)	1	30,000

Capital Stock 301

Date	F	Amount	Date	F	Amount
			Balance		60,000

Contributed Capital in Excess of Par 302

Date	F	Amount	Date	F	Amount
			Balance		20,000

Retained Earnings 303

Date	F	Amount	Date	F	Amount
			Balance		10,000

Rent Revenue 401

Date	F	Amount	Date	F	Amount
			(*b*)	1	91,800

Utilities and Telephone Expense 521

Date	F	Amount	Date	F	Amount
(*e*)	1	26,000			
(*f*)	1	40			

Apartment Maintenance Expense 522

Date	F	Amount	Date	F	Amount
(*e*)	1	1,200			

Salary and Wage Expense 523

Date	F	Amount	Date	F	Amount
(*e*)	1	3,000			

Insurance Expense 524

Date	F	Amount	Date	F	Amount
(*i*)	2	1,000			

Property Tax Expense 525

Date	F	Amount	Date	F	Amount
(*k*)	2	1,700			

Depreciation Expense 526

Date	F	Amount	Date	F	Amount
(*j*)	2	22,000			

Miscellaneous Expenses 527

Date	F	Amount	Date	F	Amount
(*f*)	1	1,100			
(*h*)	2	1,600			

Interest Expense 531

Date	F	Amount	Date	F	Amount
(*g*)	2	1,200			
(*l*)	2	10,700			

Income Tax Expense 532

Date	F	Amount	Date	F	Amount
(*m*)	2	4,900			

Requirement 4:

LA PALOMA APARTMENTS
Trial Balance
June 30, 1977

Account No.	Account Titles	Balance Debit	Balance Credit
101	Cash	$ 30,900	
103	Accounts receivable	1,800	
105	Supplies inventory	400	
112	Prepaid insurance (16 months)	2,000	
121	Land (apartment site)	30,000	
122	La Paloma apartment building	200,000	
123	Accumulated depreciation, apartment building		$ 20,000
125	Furniture and fixtures	60,000	
126	Accumulated depreciation, furniture and fixtures		24,000
131	Land for future apartment site	35,000	
201	Accounts payable		1,140
202	Property taxes payable		1,700
203	Income taxes payable		4,900
204	Mortgage payable (apartment building)		171,000
205	Note payable, long term		30,000
301	Capital stock (par $10, 6,000 shares)		60,000
302	Contributed capital in excess of par		20,000
303	Retained earnings (accumulated earnings to June 30, 1976)		10,000
401	Rent revenue		91,800
521	Utilities and telephone expense	26,040	
522	Apartment maintenance expense	1,200	
523	Salary and wage expense	3,000	
524	Insurance expense	1,000	
525	Property tax expense	1,700	
526	Depreciation expense	22,000	
527	Miscellaneous expenses	2,700	
531	Interest expense	11,900	
532	Income tax expense	4,900	
	Totals	$434,540	$434,540

Requirement 5:

Income Statement
For the Year Ended June 30, 1977

Revenue:		
Rent revenue		$91,800*
Operating Expenses:		
Utilities and telephone expense	$26,040	
Apartment maintenance expense	1,200	
Salary and wage expense	3,000	
Insurance expense	1,000	
Property tax expense	1,700	
Depreciation expense	22,000	
Miscellaneous expense	2,700	
Total Operating Expenses		57,640
Income from apartment operations		34,160
Financial expense:		
Interest expense		11,900
Pretax net income		22,260
Income tax expense		4,900
Net Income		$17,360

Earnings per share: $17,360 ÷ 6,000 shares = $2.89

* Notes:

a. These amounts were taken directly from Requirement 4, the trial balance.

b. Since no products are sold by this business, gross margin cannot be reported.

Requirement 6:

LA PALOMA APARTMENTS
Balance Sheet
At June 30, 1977

Assets

Current Assets:			
Cash		$ 30,900*	
Accounts receivable		1,800	
Supplies inventory		400	
Prepaid insurance		2,000	
Total Current Assets			$ 35,100
Fixed Assets:			
Land, apartment site		30,000	
La Paloma apartment building	$200,000		
Less: Accumulated depreciation, building	20,000	180,000	
Furniture and fixtures	60,000		
Less: Accumulated depreciation, furniture and fixtures	24,000	36,000	
Total Fixed Assets			246,000
Other Assets:			
Land acquired for future apartment site†			35,000
Total Assets			$316,100

Liabilities

Current Liabilities:		
Accounts payable	$ 1,140	
Property taxes payable	1,700	
Income taxes payable	4,900	
Total Current Liabilities		$ 7,740
Long-Term Liabilities:		
Mortgage payable	171,000	
Note payable, long term	30,000	
Total Long-Term Liabilities		201,000
Total Liabilities		208,740

Stockholders' Equity

Contributed Capital:		
Capital stock, par $10 (6,000 shares)	60,000	
Contributed capital in excess of par	20,000	
Total Contributed Capital	80,000	
Retained earnings (beginning balance $10,000 + net income $17,360)	27,360	
Total Stockholders' Equity		107,360
Total Liabilities and Stockholders' Equity		$316,100

* These amounts were taken directly from Requirement 4, the trial balance.

† Classified as "other" rather than "fixed" because this land is not currently being used for operating purposes.

SUMMARY

In this chapter we focused on the fundamental accounting model and the accounting information-processing system; they are outlined for study purposes in Exhibit 4–8. We discussed the nature of transactions that provide the raw economic data for input into the accounting information system. We learned that the fundamental accounting model—Assets = Liabilities + Owners' Equity—provides the basic framework for transaction analysis. The accounting model provides for recording the

EXHIBIT 4–8
The sequential accounting information-processing system

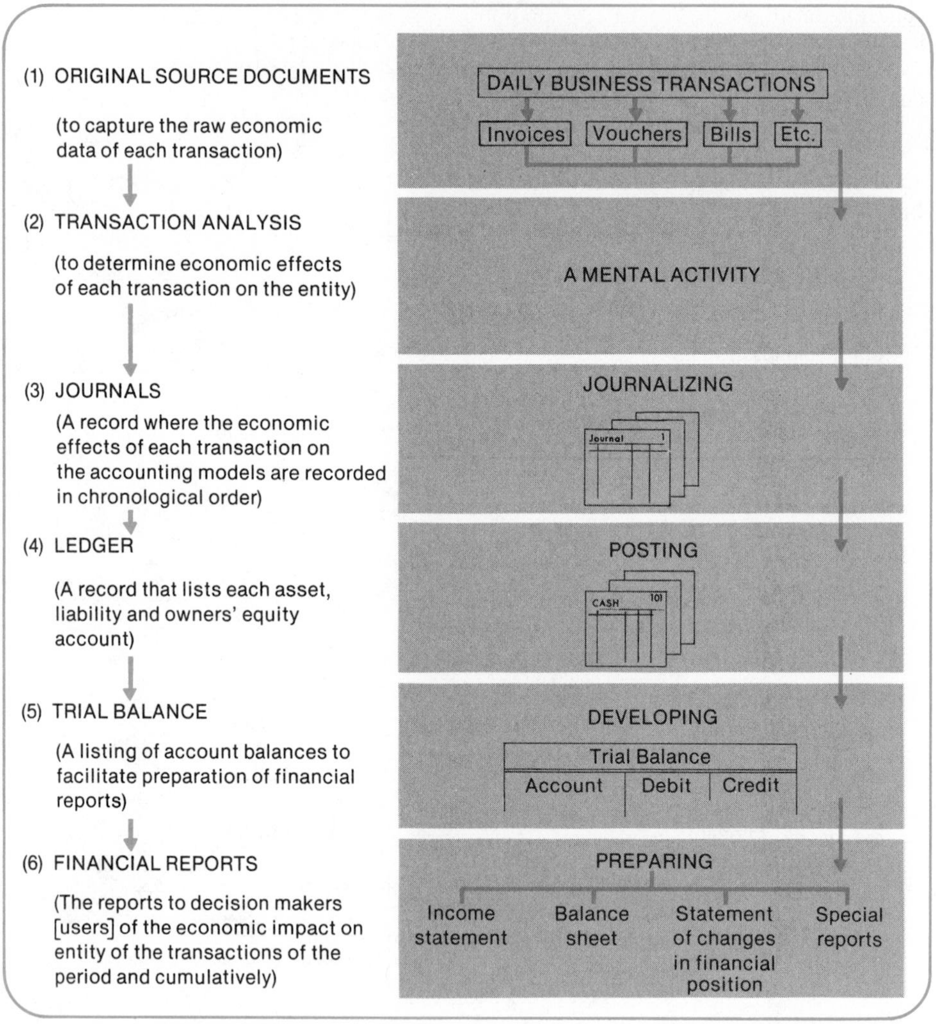

dual effect of each transaction. It encompasses two balancing features, the conditions of which must be met with respect to each transaction and event recorded, viz: (1) assets equals liabilities plus owners' equity and (2) debits equal credits. After analysis, the transactions are recorded (journalized) first in the journal, the resultant dual effect (i.e., the amounts debited and credited) then is posted to the ledger. The ledger reflects a separate account for each kind of asset, liability, and owners' equity. Normally, asset accounts will have debit balances, whereas liability accounts will have credit balances. Owners' equity accounts normally will show credits for the capital stock and retained earnings accounts—expenses will show debit balances, and revenues will show credit balances. The information-processing system, as a consequence, generates the data needed to develop the periodic financial statements: the income statement, balance sheet, and statement of changes in financial position.

The discussions in this chapter establish the basis for the accounting information-processing cycle for a business entity. It represents a cycle because it is repeated each accounting period (usually one year). The sequential steps in the information-processing cycle may be outlined as follows:

Step 1. Raw data collection—Economic data are collected for each transaction at the time of occurrence. Sales invoices, charge tickets, freight bills, notes, signed receipts, and so on, are source documents used in this step.

Step 2. Transaction analysis—Each transaction undergoes transaction analysis to determine how it affects the fundamental accounting model: Assets = Liabilities + Owners' Equity.

Step 3. Journalizing—Each transaction is recorded *chronologically* in the journal, which indicates the date, accounts to be debited and credited, amounts, and an explanation.

Step 4. Posting—Each amount entered in the journal is transferred, or posted, to the appropriate account in the ledger.

Step 5. Trial balance—At the end of the accounting period the balance in each account (i.e., the net debit or credit balance) in the ledger is determined. The balance of each ledger account then is listed on a trial balance. The equality of debits and credits is checked.

Step 6. Financial statements—The information on the trial balance is utilized to develop the periodic financial statements composed of the income statement, balance sheet, and statement of changes in financial position.

As we progress in our study, additions to and elaborations of this information-processing cycle will be introduced.

IMPORTANT TERMS

Transactions
Fundamental accounting model
Account
Debit
Credit
Transaction analysis
Journal
Journalizing
Posting
Ledger
Trial balance

QUESTIONS FOR DISCUSSION

1. Define a business transaction. Why does accounting focus on the individual business transaction?
2. Accounting focuses on certain events. What is meant by "certain events"?
3. Give the fundamental accounting model and briefly explain each variable included in it, including revenues, expenses, and investments and withdrawals by owners.
4. Explain why revenues increase and expenses decrease owners' equity.
5. What is the meaning of "to debit" and "to credit"?
6. Complete the following matrix by entering either debit or credit in each cell.

Item	Increases	Decreases
Assets		
Liabilities		
Owners' equity		
Revenues		
Expenses		

7. Complete the following matrix by entering either increase or decrease in each cell.

Item	Debit	Credit
Assets		
Liabilities		
Owners' equity		
Revenues		
Expenses		

8. Define the ledger. What purpose does it serve?
9. Define the journal. What purpose does it serve?
10. What is a trial balance? What purpose does it serve?
11. Distinguish between a book of original entry and a book of final entry.

12. Distinguish between journalizing and posting.
13. Outline the information-processing cycle for a business entity.
14. What does the term "audit trail" imply?
15. Define a fiscal period as used in accounting.

EXERCISES

E4–1. Tate Service Company has just been organized by Paula Tate, the sole owner. The following transactions have been completed:

a. Tate invested $25,000 cash in the business.
b. Equipment for use in the business was purchased at a cost of $3,500; one half was paid in cash and the balance is due in six months.
c. Service fees were earned amounting to $34,000, of which $6,000 was on credit.
d. Operating expenses incurred amounted to $23,000, of which $3,000 was on credit.
e. Cash was collected for $3,000 of the service fees performed on credit in (*c*) above.
f. Paid cash, $2,000, on the operating expenses that were on credit in (*d*) above.

Required:

Set up a format similar to the following and enter thereon each of the above transactions. Transaction (*a*) is entered as an example.

Transactions	Assets	=	Liabilities	+	Owner's Equity
a. Investment of cash in the business	Cash +$25,000				Capital, P. Tate + $25,000

Also determine the total amounts for assets, liabilities, and owner's equity after entry (*f*).

E4–2. Elgin Service Company completed the following transactions during the current accounting period:

a. Service fees earned amounted to $28,000, of which $25,000 was collected in cash.
b. Operating expenses incurred amounted to $20,000, of which $16,000 was paid in cash.
c. Bought two machines for operating purposes at the start of the year at a cost of $1,000 each; paid cash.
d. One of the machines was destroyed by fire one week after purchase; it was uninsured. The event to be considered is the fire. (Hint: Set up a fire loss expense account.)
e. The other machine has an estimated useful life to Elgin of four years. The event to be considered is the depreciation of the equipment since it was used for one year in rendering services.

Required:

Set up appropriate T-accounts and enter in them the dual effects on the accounting model of each of the above transactions. Key the amounts to the letters (*a*) through (*e*). Number the accounts consecutively starting with 101 for Cash.

E4–3. The following T-accounts for Blye Service Company, owned by T. Blye, reflect five different transactions (entries). You are requested to prepare a journal entry for each transaction and write a complete description of each transaction.

Cash

(*a*)	10,000	(*c*)	7,000
(*b*)	13,000	(*e*)	1,000
(*d*)	2,000		

Accounts Payable

(*e*)	1,000	(*c*)	2,000

Capital, T. Blye

		(*a*)	10,000

Accounts Receivable

(*b*)	3,000	(*d*)	2,000

Service Revenue Earned

		(*b*)	16,000

Operating Expenses Incurred

(*c*)	9,000		

E4–4. On January 1, 1977, Nancy Boyd and Donna Nance organized the B&N Service Company as a partnership. The transactions of the company for the first 45 days are stated below. You are requested to analyze each transaction and enter it in a journal similar to the one illustrated in Exhibit 4–5.

1977

Jan. 1 Cash invested by the partners was Boyd, $30,000; and Nance, $10,000.

3 Paid monthly rent, $300.

15 Purchased equipment for use in the business costing $12,000; paid one third down and signed a 9 percent note payable for the balance. Monthly payments (24) comprised of part principal and part interest are to be paid on the note.

30 Paid cash for operating expenses amounting to $10,000; in addition, operating expenses of $2,000 were incurred on credit.

30 Service fees earned amounted to $20,000, of which $15,000 was collected and the balance was on credit.

Feb. 10 Collected $1,500 on account for service fees previously performed which were on credit.

12 Paid $1,000 on the operating expenses previously incurred on credit.

15 Paid $365 on the equipment note, including $60 interest expense.

E4–5. Stern Air Conditioning Service Company, Incorporated, has been operating for three years. A. T. Stern, the majority shareholder, has built it up from a one-person organization to an operation requiring ten people. Few records have been maintained; however, Stern now realizes the need for a complete accounting system. The size and complexity of the business is partially indicated by the following selected transactions for 1977:

1977

Jan. 15 Purchased three new service trucks at $4,000 each; paid one half down and signed a one-year note for the 9 percent balance. Twelve monthly payments, including interest, are to be made on the note.

31 Service revenue earned in January amounted to $34,000, which included $3,000 on credit (due in 90 days).

Feb. 5 Dividends amounting to $1,000 paid in cash to the shareholders. (Hint: This decreases owners' equity.)

6 Operating expenses incurred in January amounted to $28,000, which included $4,000 on credit (payable in 60 days).

15 Paid $525 on the truck note, which included $45 interest.

Apr. 15 Paid 1976 taxes on business property, $120; this amount was recorded in 1976 as a liability (property taxes payable).

May 1 Collected $2,400 of the services extended on credit in January.

Required:

a. Journalize the above transactions in a form similar to that illustrated in Exhibit 4–5. Number the journal pages consecutively, starting with 51.

b. Post to T-accounts in the ledger; utilize the folio columns and enter dates. Number the ledger accounts consecutively, starting with 101 for the Cash account. As you post, keep in mind that there would be prior amounts carried over from 1976 in some of the ledger accounts.

E4–6. Dunn Service Company is in a situation where a considerable amount of credit is typical. For some time after it was first organized by A. D. Dunn, the only records maintained were for cash receipts and cash payments. Dunn states that "I watched my cash balance to see how I was doing; if cash went up I assumed a profit, and, to the contrary, if cash went down I assumed a loss." As the company expanded and became involved in more credit, Dunn realized that "I must look at the revenue earned and the expenses incurred on an accrual basis, as well as just the cash situation." Illustrative of the current situation is the following information for Dunn Company for the month of January 1977:

Service Revenues:	
Cash collected for services performed in January 1977..........	$36,000
Services performed in January 1977 on credit	4,000
Operating Expenses:	
Cash paid for expenses incurred in January 1977	17,000
Expenses incurred in January 1977 on credit........................	25,000

Note: Since is this a sole proprietorship, the business will report no income taxes.

Required:

a. Prepare a special statement on a cash basis to reflect cash inflows, cash outflows, and the change in cash occasioned by the above summarized transactions.

b. Prepare an income statement (accrual basis) to show computation of revenues earned, expenses incurred, and the differences (i.e., net income or loss).

c. Explain why the cash and accrual results were different.
d. Basically, what does this suggest as to the inappropriateness of cash amounts in reflecting profit performance for January?

E4–7. AB Partnership has been operating for one year, 1977. The two partners agreed to divide profits two thirds to Partner A and one third to Partner B. Neither partner understands accounting and financial reports. Although they kept no accounting records, they have agreed that the following amounts for 1977 are "OK with us":

Revenues:	
Collected in cash	$70,000
Not collected by end of 1977	25,000
Expenses:	
Paid in cash	60,000
Not paid by end of 1977	11,000

Required:

The partners have requested your advice in "splitting up the profit for 1977." Accordingly, you decide to do the following:

a. Prepare an income statement on an accrual basis that shows revenues, expenses, and the difference, net income (or loss). There will be no income taxes for the entity since this is a partnership.
b. Prepare a special statement on cash basis that shows cash inflows, cash outflows, and the difference, net increase (decrease) in cash.
c. Compute your recommendation for the division of profits for 1977.
d. Explain the basis for your recommendations.
e. Write an explanation for the partners of why the accrual and cash basis results are different.

E4–8. The bookkeeper of Best Company, a sole proprietorship, prepared the following trial balance at December 31, 1977:

Account Titles	*Debit*	*Credit*
Notes receivable	$ 4,000	
Supplies inventory		$ 200
Accounts payable	800	
Land	16,000	
Capital, Best		20,000
Cash	7,000	
Interest revenue	200	
Notes payable, long term		5,000
Operating expenses	19,000	
Interest expense		800
Other assets	9,583	
Service revenues		30,583
Total	$56,583	$56,583

The independent CPA (auditor) casually inspected the trial balance and concluded there were several errors on it. You have been requested to draft a correct trial balance. (Hint: All of the amounts are correct.)

PROBLEMS

P4–1. Listed below are the ledger accounts of the BB Rental Company, Incorporated.

a. Cash.
b. Accounts receivable.
c. Common stock.
d. Bonds payable.
e. Rental revenues earned.
f. Prepaid insurance premiums.
g. Interest revenue.
h. Investments, long term.
i. Interest expense.
j. Machinery and equipment.
k. Patents.
l. Income tax expense.
m. Property taxes payable.
n. Loss on sale of fixed assets.
o. Land, plant site (in use).
p. Contributed capital in excess of par.
q. Supplies inventory.
r. Notes payable, short term.
s. Retained earnings.
t. Short-term investments.
u. Other assets.
v. Operating expenses.
w. Income taxes payable.
x. Gain on sale of fixed assets.
y. Land for future plant site.
z. Revenue from investments.
aa. Wages payable.
bb. Accumulated depreciation.
cc. Merchandise inventory.

Complete a tabulation similar to the following (enter two check marks for each item):

	Type of account			*Normal balance*	
Item	*Asset*	*Liability*	*Owners' equity (including revenues and expenses)*	*Debit*	*Credit*

P4–2. Listed below are a series of accounts for Quality Service Company, Incorporated, which has been operating for three years. The accounts are numbered for identification. Below the accounts are a series of transactions. For each transaction indicate the account(s) to be debited and credited by entering the appropriate account number(s) to the right.

1. Cash.
2. Accounts receivable.
3. Supplies inventory.
4. Prepaid insurance.
5. Equipment.
6. Accumulated depreciation, equipment.
7. Patents.
8. Accounts payable.
9. Notes payable.
10. Wages payable.
11. Income taxes payable.
12. Capital stock, par $10
13. Contributed capital in excess of par value.
14. Service revenues earned.
15. Operating expenses.
16. Income tax expense.
17. Interest expense.
18. None of the above (explain).

Transactions	Debit	Credit
a. Example—Investment by shareholders to start the business; cash was received for stock in excess of the par value.	1	12,13
b. Purchased equipment for use in business; paid one half cash and gave note payable for balance.		
c. Paid cash for salaries and wages.		
d. Collected cash for services performed this period.		
e. Collected cash for services performed last period.		
f. Performed services this period on credit.		
g. Paid operating expenses incurred this period.		
h. Paid cash for operating expenses incurred last period.		
i. Incurred operating expenses this period, to be paid next period.		
j. Purchased supplies for inventory; paid cash.		
k. Used some of the supplies from inventory for operations.		
l. Purchased a patent; paid cash.		
m. Made a payment on the equipment note (*b*) above; the payment was in part on principal and in part interest thereon.		
n. Collected cash on accounts receivable for services previously performed.		
o. Paid cash on accounts payable for expenses previously incurred.		
p. Paid three fourths of the income tax expense for the year; the balance to be paid next period.		
q. On last day of current period, paid in cash an insurance premium covering the next two years.		

P4–3. Box Home Repair Service was started two years ago by M. E. Box as sole owner. By the end of the second year, three "crews" were operating and Box felt that the business was a success. Although prices charged were high, the customers appeared pleased in view of the quality of the work done and the efficiency with which repairs were completed. The following account balances were reflected by the ledger on January 1, 1977:

Account No.	Account Titles	Debit	Credit
101	Cash	$ 6,450	
105	Accounts receivable	3,700	
110	Building supplies inventory (for use on repair jobs)	1,500	
120	Trucks	15,000	
121	Accumulated depreciation on trucks		$ 6,000
200	Accounts payable		3,000
205	Note payable, short term		5,000
210	Wages payable		150
220	Note payable, long term		10,000
300	Capital, M. E. Box		2,500
400	Service revenue		
501	Operating expenses		
502	Depreciation expense		
503	Interest expense		
	Totals	$26,650	$26,650

During 1977 the following transactions occurred:

a. Paid the $150 wages payable carried over from 1976.
b. Purchased, for cash, additional building supplies for future use, $1,100 (debit the Building Supplies Inventory account).
c. Purchased an additional truck for $4,500 cash.
d. Collected $2,800 cash on the accounts receivable.
e. Paid off the $5,000 short-term note, plus six months' interest at 8 percent per annum.
f. Box invested an additional $5,000 cash in the business.
g. Repair fees earned in 1977, $82,000 which included $7,000 earned in 1977 but uncollected.
h. Paid operating expenses of $55,000 cash. Additional operating expenses of $4,000 were incurred; the cash will be paid for these in 1978.
i. According to an inventory count of the building supplies at December 31, 1977, unused supplies amounted to $1,100. (Hint: Supplies used should be debited to operating expenses: supplies used = amount on hand at start + additional purchased − ending inventory.)
j. Depreciation on the three trucks was computed on the basis of an estimated useful life of five years. The new truck will not be depreciated in 1977 since it was acquired near the end of the year.
k. Paid $6,000 on the long-term note, plus 8 percent interest on the $10,000 for one year.
l. Paid $5,000 on accounts payable.

Required:

1. Set up the ledger accounts listed above and enter the beginning balances; label these as "Balance."
2. Analyze each transaction, then enter it directly in the ledger accounts (you will not need additional accounts). Key your entries with the letter designation (in place of a date).
3. Prepare a trial balance at December 31, 1977. (Hint: Trial balance total, $104,500.)
4. Prepare an income statement. Since this is a sole proprietorship, the entity will pay no income taxes.

P4–4. Quality Stenographic and Mailing Service, Incorporated, was organized by three individuals during January 1977. Each investor paid in $5,000 cash and each received 400 shares of $10 par value stock. During 1977 the transactions listed below occurred. The letters at the left of each item will serve as the date notation.

a. Received the $15,000 investment by the organizers.
b. Purchased office equipment costing $6,000; paid cash.
c. Paid $400 cash for a two-year insurance premium on the office equipment.
d. Purchased a panel delivery truck at a cost of $4,000; paid $3,000 down and signed a $1,000, 90-day, 8 percent, interest-bearing note payable for the balance.

e. Purchased office supplies for cash to be used in the stenographic and mailing operations, $2,000. The supplies are for future use. (Therefore, debit Office Supplies Inventory.)

f. Revenues earned during the year were:

	Cash	*On credit*
Stenographic fees..............	$45,000	$6,000
Mailing fees	8,000	1,000

g. Operating expenses incurred during the year were:

Cash............................	$26,000
On credit	14,000

h. Paid the $1,000 note on the panel truck. Cash paid out was for the principal plus the interest for 90 days.

i. Purchased land for a future building site at a cost of $20,000; paid cash.

j. Depreciation on the truck for 1977 was computed on the basis of a five-year useful life; on the office equipment, useful life of ten years was assumed (compute full year depreciation on each).

k. By December 31, 1977, insurance for one year had expired. Prepaid Insurance should be decreased, and an expense recorded.

l. An inventory of the office supplies reflected $300 on hand at December 31, 1977. Supplies Inventory should be reduced, and an expense recognized.

Required:

1. Analyze and prepare a journal entry for each transaction listed. Use a form similar to Exhibit 4–5 and include an explanation for each transaction.
2. Prepare an income statement that reports total revenues, total expenses, pretax income, income taxes (assume an average 30 percent corporate tax rate), and net income. (Hint: Net income is $11,690.)
3. What is the ending balance in cash? Show computations. Why is it different than net income?

P4–5. Rapid Delivery Service was organized as a corporation on June 1, 1976. The management decided that the fiscal year for the company would be June 1 to May 31. The following transactions were selected from the first year for case purposes; for convenience, use the letter identification to the left as the date notation.

a. Cash invested was $15,000, and 1,000 shares of $10 par value capital stock was issued.

b. Three new delivery vehicles were purchased at a total cost of

$12,000. One half was paid in cash, and at 8 percent note payable was signed for the balance.

c. Operating supplies costing $450 were purchased for cash. These supplies were placed in operating supplies inventory and will be used gradually.

d. Delivery revenues earned amounted to $80,000, of which $11,000 was yet uncollected.

e. Operating expenses incurred amounted to $54,000, of which $8,000 was not yet paid in cash.

f. Paid cash for a two-year insurance premium in advance to insure the delivery equipment, $600.

g. Collected $9,000 on the credit extended for delivery services (item [*d*] above).

h. Paid $7,000 on the obligations for operating expenses (item [*e*] above).

i. An inventory count showed that two thirds of the operating supplies purchased ([*c*] above) had been used by May 31, 1977.

j. Paid $1,000 on the principal of the note given on the delivery vehicles ([*b*] above), plus six months' interest on $6,000.

k. Computed depreciation on the delivery vehicles for one year (up to May 31, 1977), assuming a five-year useful life.

l. On May 31, 1977, insurance for one year had expired.

Required:

1. Set up a journal similar to Exhibit 4–5, then journalize each item.
2. Post the journal entries to the ledger accounts as follows:

Account No.	*Account Titles*	*Account No.*	*Account Titles*
101	Cash	301	Common stock
102	Accounts receivable	302	Contributed capital in excess of par
103	Office supplies inventory		
104	Prepaid inserts	303	Retained earnings
105	Delivery vehicles	401	Delivery revenue
106	Accumulated depreciation, delivery vehicles	501	Operating expense
		502	Interest expense
201	Accounts payable	503	Depreciation expense
202	Note payable		

3. Prepare a trial balance at May 31, 1977. (Hint: The trial balance totals are $103,400.)
4. Compute the ending cash balance and pretax income. How much do they differ? Why do they differ?

P4–6. The ledger accounts for Roe Real Estate Agency, a corporation (organized three years previously) provided the annual trial balance shown below at March 31, 1977 (the end of the annual fiscal period).

Trial Balance
At March 31, 1977

Account Titles	*Debit*	*Credit*
Cash	$33,000	
Accounts receivable	48,900	
Office supplies inventory	200	
Automobiles (company cars)	6,000	
Accumulated depreciation, automobiles		$ 4,000
Office equipment	2,000	
Accumulated depreciation, office equipment		1,000
Accounts payable		2,000
Income taxes payable		
Salaries and commissions payable		1,000
Notes payable, long term		20,000
Capital stock (par $10, 3,000 shares)		30,000
Contributed capital in excess of par		3,000
Retained earnings (on April 1, 1976)		5,000
Dividends paid during the fiscal year	10,000	
Sales commissions earned		70,000
Management fees earned		6,000
Operating expenses (detail omitted to conserve time)	40,000	
Depreciation expense (on autos and office equipment)	500	
Interest expense	1,400	
Income tax expense		
Totals	$142,000	$142,000

Required:

a. Prepare a classified, multiple-step income statement for the year ending March 31, 1977. The above trial balance does not include income taxes. Assume an average corporate tax rate of 40 percent and that the income tax will be paid later. (Hint: EPS is $6.82.)

b. Prepare a classified balance sheet at March 31, 1977. (Hint: Refer to Chapter 3 for examples of classified statements.)

P4–7. Able, Baker, and Cain organized ABC Realty as a corporation to conduct a real estate and rental management business. Each contributed $20,000 cash and received 1,500 shares of stock (par value $10 per share). They commenced business on January 1, 1977. The transactions listed below are representative of those during the year. We have selected only a few of the actual transactions for case purposes. Also assume that these transactions comprise all of the transactions for the year. This case demonstrates the information processing cycle from the capture of raw economic data to the final output—the financial statements. Use the numbers at the left as the date notation.

1. Receipt of $60,000 cash invested by shareholders and issuance of 4,500 shares of stock. See the list of accounts given below.
2. Purchase of office equipment costing $6,000; paid one-third cash and charged the balance (one third due in three months, remainder due in six months). Credit Accounts Payable for the amount not paid in cash.

3. Purchased land for future office site at a cost of $20,000; paid cash.
4. Paid office rent in cash, 11 months at $200 per month. Beginning with this transaction, set up separate accounts for each type of expense.
5. Sold nine properties and collected sales commissions of $56,000. Set up an account "Realty Commissions Revenue."
6. Paid salaries and commissions to salespersons amounting to $52,000 and miscellaneous expenses amounting to $1,000.
7. Collected rental management fees, $20,000. Set up an account "Rental Management Revenue."
8. Paid utilities, $1,400.
9. Paid auto rental fees (auto rented for use in business), $2,400.
10. Paid for advertising, $7,500.
11. At year end, the December rent had not been paid.
12. The estimated life of the office equipment was ten years; assume use for the full year in 1977.
13. Additional commissions earned during 1977 on sale of real estate amounted to $64,000 of which $14,000 was uncollected at year-end.
14. Paid the installment on the office equipment (see 2 above).
15. Assume an average corporate income tax rate of 40 percent; the tax expense will be paid in 1978.

Required:

a. Analyze, then journalize, each of the above entries in chronological order. Number the journal pages consecutively, starting with 1.

b. Post each transaction from the journal to the ledger; use T-accounts as follows:

Account No.	*Account Titles*	*Account No.*	*Account Titles*
101	Cash	401	Realty commission revenue
102	Accounts receivable	402	Rental management revenue
103	Office equipment	501	Rent expense
104	Accumulated depreciation, office equipment	502	Salary and commission expense
105	Land for future office site	503	Miscellaneous expense
201	Accounts payable	504	Utilities expense
202	Income taxes payable	505	Auto rental expense
301	Capital stock	506	Advertising expense
302	Contributed capital in excess of par	507	Depreciation expense
		508	Income tax expense

Use folio cross-references when posting.

c. Prepare a trial balance from the ledger; check the equality of debits and credits. (Hint: Trial balance total is $231,800.)

d. Use the data on the trial balance to prepare a classified income statement and balance sheet. Refer to Chapter 3 for examples of classified statements. Because of its complexity, we will defer preparing a statement of changes in financial position until a later chapter. (Hint: EPS, $9.69.)

P4–8. Ace Moving and Storage Company was organized four years ago as a partnership by O. Snow and R. P. Dean; they share profits equally. Each contributed $20,000 cash initially; and since that time, a good portion of the profits have been left in the business for growth. Ace owns a large warehouse and 11 hauling vans. At the beginning, very few financial records were maintained; however, they now have one person who devotes full time to records and reports. Some disagreements with the Internal Revenue Service and tentative discussions of the possibility of changing to a corporation prompted Snow and Dean to approach an independent CPA for advice. As a consequence, the first audit was performed for 1976. For purposes of this case, we will utilize only representative accounts and transactions in order to minimize the time requirements. Assume that the accounts for Ace showed the following balance on January 1, 1977 (the fiscal and calendar years agree):

Account No.	*Account Titles*	*Debit*	*Credit*
101	Cash	$ 21,500	
103	Accounts receivable	15,000	
110	Supplies inventory	2,500	
112	Prepaid insurance		
131	Land (on which warehouse is located)	10,000	
133	Warehouse	80,000	
134	Accumulated depreciation, warehouse		$ 16,000
135	Moving vans	75,000	
136	Accumulated depreciation, moving vans		30,000
151	Land for future office building		
201	Accounts payable		10,000
210	Notes payable, long term (8%)		30,000
301	Capital, O. Snow		55,000
302	Withdrawals during the year, O. Snow		
305	Capital, R. P. Dean		63,000
306	Withdrawals during the year, R. P. Dean		
401	Trucking revenues		
402	Storage revenues		
501	Operating expenses		
502	Depreciation expense		
505	Interest expense		
	Totals	$204,000	$204,000

Representative transactions for 1977 follow (use the letter notation at the left for dating purposes):

a. Purchased land for future office building at a cost of $13,000; paid cash.

b. Revenues earned:

	Cash	Credit
Trucking	$220,000	$40,000
Storage	30,000	2,000

c. Paid $1,600 cash for a two-year insurance premium covering trucks, warehouse, and so on (assume this payment was made on January 2, 1977).

d. Purchased additional supplies for use in operations for cash, $1,600; these supplies are to be used as needed. Debit account 110.

e. At end of 1977 paid $10,000 on the principal of the long-term note payable, plus 8 percent interest on the $30,000 for 12 months.

f. Operating expenses incurred:

Cash	$195,000
On credit	23,000

g. Collections on accounts receivable (for trucking and storage services on credit), $38,000 (see [*b*] above).

h. Payments on accounts payable (expenses and services previously incurred on credit), $20,000 cash.

i. Withdrawals of cash by partners for personal use: Snow, $12,000; and Dean, $11,000. Debit accounts 302 and 306.

j. A full year's depreciation expense for 1977 was computed on the basis of the following useful lives: warehouse, 20 years; and moving vans, 5 years.

k. On December 31, 1977, an inventory showed supplies remaining on hand (unused) amounting to $1,800. Reduce Supplies Inventory and recognize an expense.

l. On December 31, 1977, insurance for one year had expired (see item [*c*] above).

Required:

1. Set up T-accounts for each account listed above (the above list includes all of the accounts needed) and enter therein the balances given in the following manner:

Cash			101
Balance	21,500		

2. Set up a journal similar to Exhibit 4–5 and enter each of the transactions. Use the letter designation for dating and include short explanations. Number the journal pages consecutively starting with 1.
3. Post each transaction entered in the journal to the ledger; complete the folio columns in both the journal and ledger.
4. Prepare a trial balance from the ledger accounts at December 31, 1977. (Hint: The trial balance total is $508,000.)
5. Prepare a classified income statement and balance sheet. See Chapter 3 for examples of classified statements. Since this is a partnership, the entity will have no income taxes. Show the fol-

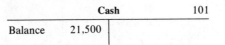

lowing detail on the balance sheet for the owner's equity of each partner:

Capital, name, January 1, 1977	$xx	
Add: Share of net income for 1977	xx	
Total	xx	
Less: Withdrawals during 1977	xx	
Capital, name, December 31, 1977		$xx

(Hint: Net income is $49,500, and the balance sheet totals $177,500.)

P4–9. PU Partnership was organized by the two owners in January 1977. It is now February 1978 and the partners are having difficulty in dividing the partnership profits for 1977. According to oral agreement between them, P is to get two thirds and U one third of the profits each year. The partners failed to set up an adequate accounting system; neither one has any knowledge of accounting or financial statements.

The following revenue and expense data for 1977 has been agreed on as being correct:

Revenues:	
Cash collected during 1977	$90,000
Credit basis and not collected by end of 1977	30,000
Expenses:	
Incurred and paid in cash during 1977	60,000
Incurred but not paid by end of 1977	15,000
Cash withdrawn by partners during 1977 for personal use:	
Partner P	6,000
Partner U	5,000

Note: Since this is a partnership, no income taxes will be paid by the entity.

Partner P feels that he should get $24,000 of the remaining profits and U $10,000. In contrast, partner U feels that P has $14,000 coming and he has $5,000.

Required:

You have been asked to help resolve this argument. You realize that computations of each partner must be analyzed and then a recommendation made. Accordingly, the following computations are required:

a. Prepare a summarized income statement on the accrual basis. (Hint: The cash withdrawn for personal use does not represent expense; rather it is a withdrawal of profit in advance.) Compute the division of profits on the accrual basis. Which partner used this basis?

b. Try to determine how the other partner derived the suggested division of profits.

c. Which partner was correct? Explain.

P4–10. (Note: This is a special case to test your analytical skills.) Simon Lavoie, a local attorney, decided to sell his practice and retire. He has had discussions with an attorney from another state who desires to relocate. The discussions have entered the complex stage of agreeing on a price. Among the important factors have been the financial statements on Lavoie's practice. Lavoie's secretary, under his direction, maintained the records. Each year they developed a "Statement of Profits" on a cash basis from the incomplete records maintained, and no balance sheet was prepared. Upon request, Lavoie provided the other attorney with the following statement of profits for 1977 prepared by his secretary:

S. LAVOIE
Statement of Profits
1977

Legal fees collected		$62,000
Expenses Paid:		
Rent for office space	$ 3,900	
Utilities	360	
Telephone	2,900	
Office salaries	19,000	
Office supplies	900	
Miscellaneous expenses	1,600	
Total Expenses		28,660
Profit for the year		$33,340

Upon agreement of the parties, you have been asked to "look into the financial figures for 1977." The other attorney appeared to question the figures, especially since they "appear to be on a 100 percent cash basis." Your investigations have revealed the following additional data at December 31, 1977:

a. Of the legal fees collected in 1977, $18,000 was for services performed prior to 1977.

b. At the end of 1977, legal fees of $7,000 that were performed during the year were uncollected.

c. Office equipment owned and used by Lavoie cost $3,000 and had an estimated useful life of ten years.

d. An inventory of office supplies reflected $200 worth of items purchased during the year that were still on hand. Also the records for 1976 indicate that the supplies on hand at the end of that year were approximately $125.

e. At the end of 1977 a secretary, whose salary is $7,200 per year, had not been paid for December because of a long trip that extended to January 15, 1978.

f. The phone bill for December 1977, amounting to $300, was not paid until January 11, 1978.

g. The office rent paid of $3,900 was for 13 months (it included the rent for January 1978).

Required:

On the basis of the above information, prepare an income statement for 1977 on an accrual basis. Show your computations for any amounts changed from those in the statement prepared by Lavoie's secretary.

5

Matching of expenses with revenue each period

PURPOSE OF THE CHAPTER

Net income is one of the more significant single amounts developed through the accounting process. In this chapter we will focus on several critical issues involved in the measurement of net income. We will examine some of the complications posed when the lifespan of a business is divided into a series of equal time periods, such as one year. We will consider the problem of realistically identifying revenues within the selected time period and then identifying the expenses that were incurred in order to generate the revenues for that period.

RELATIONSHIPS AMONG FINANCIAL STATEMENTS

In the preceding chapters the three periodic financial statements required for external reporting were discussed; however, the relationships among them were considered only indirectly. In Chapter 3 we stated that the three statements, plus the accompanying notes and the auditors' opinion, should be viewed as a single reporting package for the selected time period. In order to understand the overall financial aspects of a business, and in many decision-making situations, the entire reporting package generally is needed. Exhibit 5–1 presents the basic relationships among the three financial statements for a fiscal year—January 1 through December 31, 1977. In this exhibit you can visualize the starting point as the financial position as reported in the balance sheet at the end of the *prior* year and the ending point as the financial position reflected in the

EXHIBIT 5–1

Interrelationships in financial statements

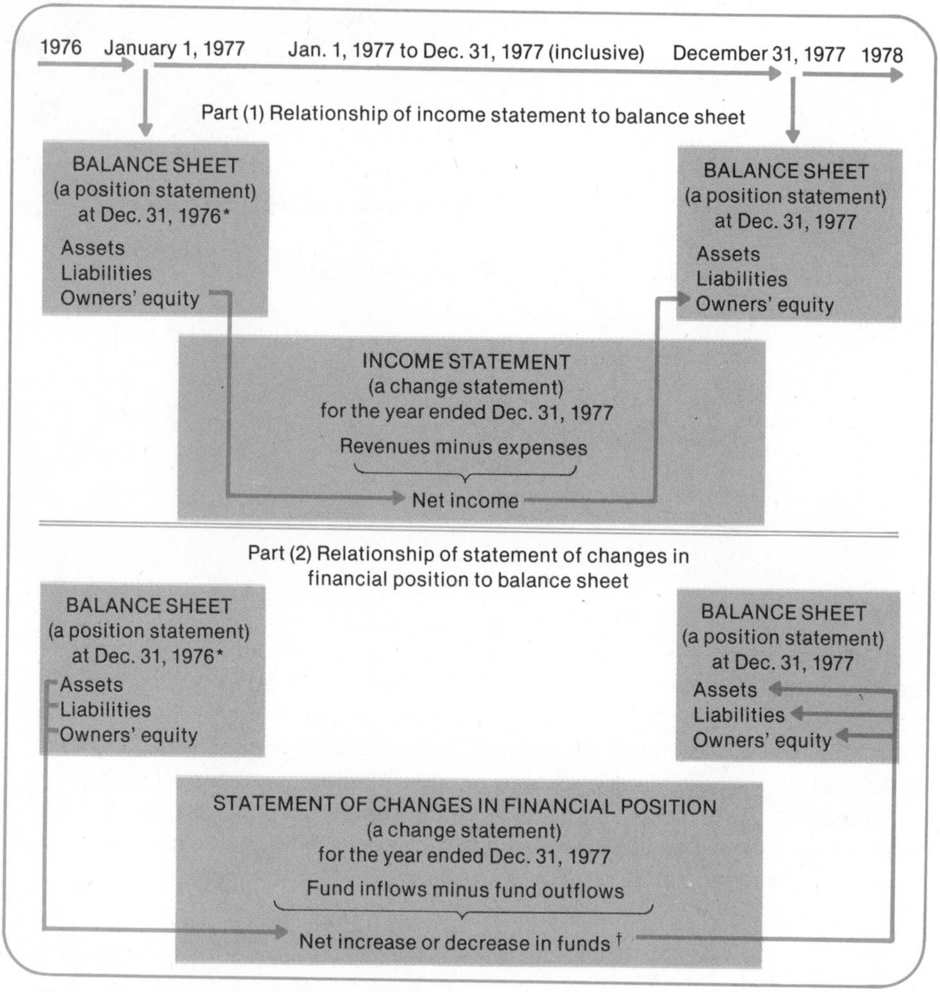

* This also is the balance sheet at the beginning of 1977.

† For this statement, funds are measured as either cash or working capital.

balance sheet at the end of the current year. The changes in financial position between the starting and ending points are communicated to the users by two different change statements:

1. Income statement—The income statement reports changes in owners' equity during the period as a result of operations. Net income increases owners' equity, and this is graphically shown in Exhibit 5–1, Part (1). The detailed amounts of revenue, expense, and extraordinary items that caused this change in owners' equity (or financial position) during the period are reported on the income statement for the period.

Therefore, the income statement reports detailed information to explain **one major category of changes** in financial position during the selected time period; that is, those resulting "from operations."

2. Statement of changes in financial position—This statement is designed to report, or explain, all the **causes** of changes in financial position (i.e., assets, liabilities, and contributed capital) during the period that result from the financing activities (funds inflows) and investing activities (funds outflows). It explains how funds (measured as cash or working capital) were generated and used by the entity during the selected time period.

TIME-PERIOD ASSUMPTION

Each financial statement should include in its heading a specific statement as to the **time dimension** of the report (see Chapter 2, page 32). Exhibit 5–1 reemphasizes the fact that the time dimension of the balance sheet is **at a specific date** (such as "At December 31, 19XX). The two "change" statements cover **a specified period of time** (such as, "For the Year Ended December 31, 19XX).

The lifespan of most business entities is indefinite. Society in general "lives by the calendar." This fact requires that the lifespan of an entity be divided into a series of short time periods, such as one year, for many measurement purposes, including financial reporting. The business community assumes that the activities of a business can be divided into a series of equal time periods. This is the **time-period assumption** (see Exhibit 2–1), and it is fundamental to the accounting process and financial reporting.

Because annual periods tend to be dominant throughout our society, the accounting period generally is viewed as being 12 consecutive months. As a consequence, we focus on the **annual** financial statements. Many firms use a year that corresponds to the natural cycle of the business, such as July 1 through June 30, rather than to the calendar year. A business (or accounting) year that does not correspond to the calendar year is known as a **fiscal year.** In addition to the annual financial statements, many businesses also prepare and publish quarterly reports for external parties. These usually are called **interim reports.** Monthly financial statements frequently are prepared; however, they are exclusively for **internal management** purposes. In the paragraphs to follow you will see that dividing the lifespan of a business into short periods of time often poses complex measurement and reporting problems.

PERIODIC RECOGNITION OF REVENUES AND EXPENSES

Dividing the lifespan of a business into short time periods, such as a year, for measurement purposes often poses complex accounting problems because some transactions **start in one accounting period and are,** in effect, **concluded in a subsequent period.** A **revenue** transaction may start in one accounting period and, in effect, conclude in a subsequent period. For example, the collection by a magazine publisher of a three-year subscription price in one accounting period requires that a fair share of the total revenue be assigned to each of the three periods as it is earned by delivery of the magazines.

Similarly, an expense transaction may start in one period and, in effect, conclude in a later period. For example, the prepayment of a two-year insurance premium occurs in one accounting period, yet each of the two periods covered by the insurance must be assigned a fair share of insurance expense.

Earning revenues through sales and services and the incurring of expenses necessary to generate those revenues is a **continuous process.** Since some transactions cover an extended period of time between their initiation and final completion and financial reports must be made for a specific time period, such as a month, quarter, or year, there must be a careful **cutoff** between the selected time periods so that the revenues and expenses for each such period can be accurately measured.

Frequently, it is difficult to identify a specific revenue and/or expense with a particular accounting period. In response to this problem, the **revenue principle** and the **matching principle** were evolved as two of the broad fundamentals underlying accounting (see Exhibit 2–1, page 32). These two principles focus on the measurement of net income for each period. *The revenue principle takes a timing precedence over the matching principle in the measurement process.* First, the revenue earned for the period from the sales of goods and services is measured; next, the matching principle is applied to measure the expenses incurred in generating that revenue. To reemphasize, for accounting measurement purposes, the revenue and matching principles require a careful cutoff of revenues and expenses at the end of each accounting period.

The revenue principle. The revenue principle was defined in Chapter 2 (page 35). This principle holds that revenue should be measured in the period in which it is earned, or realized. In identifying revenues with a specific period for measurement purposes, one must look to *when* the various transactions occurred rather than to the period in which the cash inflows occurred. The income statement for each particular period must report all of the revenue earned, or realized, in the period but must not report any revenue earned in a prior or following period.

The general guideline is that revenue is earned when a sales transaction is made (consummated) or when services are rendered. In the case of sales or services for cash, this guideline is easy to apply; however, in the case of credit sales or services, problems often arise. Sales or services made on the "normal" **short-term** credit basis follow the general rule, irrespective of whether there is a down payment. In contrast, sales and services made on a long-term credit basis, and with little or no down payment, pose the question of the **risk** that complete payment will not be made ultimately (a repossession may occur). For such situations, the accounting profession has developed exceptions to the general guideline. For example, in the case of land development companies, a practice is to sell undeveloped land for a down payment of around 5 percent with a 10- to 30-year payout period. For this particular industry, a current guideline is that sales revenue cannot be recognized until the period in which the cash payment reaches at least 10 percent. (There are some related accounting complexities in this industry that are beyond the scope of this book.)

Many companies sell large items of merchandise (such as a television set) on the **installment plan.** The usual provisions of an installment plan are: (1) a relatively small down payment is required; (2) the payment period is long and calls for monthly payments on principal plus interest; (3) the seller retains conditional title to the goods until full payment is made; and (4) bad debt losses cannot be reasonably estimated. These provisions, in combination, mean that there is a relatively high risk of reclaims of the merchandise because of nonpayment. The installment method of accounting has been developed to meet this unusual situation. Under this method the revenue is recognized as the **cash is collected.** As a consequence, this method is close to cash-basis accounting.

Another difficult problem arises in respect to long-term construction contracts. For example, assume a building contractor signs a contract to build a large plant at a cost of $3,500,000 and the construction period is three years, starting January 1, 19A. Now, assume further that the cost of the plant is estimated to be approximately $3,200,000 to the contractor; that is, an estimated profit of approximately $300,000. The question is: Should the profit be reported as earned (1) in 19C or (2) allocated on a fair basis to each of the three years? One method, called the **completed-contract method,** is a conservative approach in that no revenue is recognized until profit (the estimated $300,000) can be measured with certainty; that is, in 19C, the period of final completion. In contrast, the allocation method permits the recognition of revenue on the basis of estimates (usually based on the ratio of actual costs incurred during the period to total costs for the project) covering the three-year period. Thus, a portion of the estimated $300,000 would be recognized as revenue each year. The allocation method generally is called the **percentage-of-completion method.** At the present time a contractor is permitted to select either method. Many accountants believe that this choice between two accounting alternatives for the same set of facts is not sound. They believe that the profit should be allocated to each of the three periods based upon percentage of completion of the building by years (generally estimated by the architects). Of course, other accountants prefer the completed-contract method. Lack of agreement as to the best measurement approach primarily is the reason for the approval of alternatives. There are a number of other areas of accounting where measurement alternatives are permitted for the same set of facts. The accounting profession is striving to eliminate such alternative accounting choices.

The matching principle. Expenses were defined in Chapter 2 (page 35). The matching principle focuses on the measurement of expenses and the matching of them with the periodic revenues generated during the period. *The matching principle holds that all of the expenses incurred in generating revenue should be identified, or matched, with the revenue generated, period by period.*

In measuring and matching expenses with revenue, one must look to the **purpose** for which the expenses were incurred. If the purpose was to generate revenue, as is the usual case, the expenses should be identified with the period in which that revenue was recognized as earned. In this way the expenses are matched with the revenues of each period so that net income for each period is correctly measured. Expenses incurred in generating the revenue earned for the period must be reported in that period. Resources expended in one period to generate revenues in other periods must be apportioned to those other periods.

ADJUSTING ENTRIES

Application of the revenue and matching principles often requires special accounting entries at the end of the accounting period so that a strict cutoff of revenues and expenses between accounting periods is attained for measurement purposes. These special entries generally are called **adjusting entries** because they result in the adjustment of some account balances at the end of the accounting period. There are four general types of transactions that often cause adjusting entries:

Revenues (revenue principle applied):

1. *Recorded revenue* includes a collection of cash in full before the total revenue is earned; therefore, the total revenue must be apportioned between the current and one or more future accounting periods. Example: Rent revenue collected in advance of the period in which occupancy will occur. Revenue recognition must be *deferred* and identified with the period of occupancy.
2. *Unrecorded revenue* is revenue not yet recorded but that was earned in the current period although the cash is to be collected in a subsequent period. Example: Rent revenue earned due to occupancy during the current period but collection is to occur next period. Although the cash is not yet collected, the amount of revenue earned must be recorded in the current period.

Expenses (matching principle applied):

3. *Recorded cost* includes a payment of cash in full before the total expense is incurred in generating revenue; therefore, the total prepaid

amount must be apportioned between the current and one or more future accounting periods in which the related revenue is recognized as earned. Examples are:

a. The cost of a two-year insurance premium paid in advance and recorded as a prepaid expense. The prepaid cost must be apportioned, as insurance expense, over the current and future accounting periods covered by the insurance.

b. The cost of a machine having an estimated five-year useful life and recorded as an asset. The cost of the machine must be apportioned to each of the five years as depreciation expense because this is the time over which the machine helped generate revenue.

c. The cost of items purchased in advance of use, such as supplies, and recorded as an asset (supplies inventory). The cost must be apportioned as an expense over the periods in which the supplies are actually used in generating revenue.

4. *Unrecorded expense* is an expense that was incurred (and used in the generation of current revenue) but is not yet paid or recorded by the end of the current accounting period. Unrecorded expense must be identified with the current period to be matched with current revenue. Examples are:

   a. Wages earned by employees in the current period but not yet paid or recorded by the end of the current accounting period. Such wages must be recorded as an expense in the current period because that is when the services were received and used in generating revenue. Unpaid wages are often called *accrued wages.*

   b. Taxes incurred and not yet recorded in the current period and will not be paid until the next period.

   c. Interest cost, not yet recorded, on money borrowed during the current period and the cash payment of interest to be made in a later period.

At the end of each accounting period, after the regular entries are completed, the accountant must make a careful check of the records and supporting documents to determine whether or not there are any situations such as those listed above for which **adjusting entries** should be made. One or more such entries invariably will be required at the end of each accounting period. If any adjusting entries are overlooked, revenue for the period may be measured incorrectly and expenses may not be matched with revenues generated during the period. In either instance, the result would be incorrect measurement of amounts on both the income statement and the balance sheet.

Adjusting entries are not unusual. They require no additional competence, only a knowledge of the actual facts in respect to each item. In Chapters 3 and 4, the illustrations, exercises, and problems include several adjusting entries (depreciation expense, prepaid insurance, supplies used, and accrued or unpaid wages) routinely made without special identification or concern.

Observe that adjusting entries have two distinct characteristics: (1) they apportion revenue or expense between the current and one or more future periods and (2) they are recorded at the end of the accounting period.

The two technical terms "accrued" (or to accrue) and "deferred" (or to defer) frequently are used in accounting. A straightforward and practical definitional statement for our purposes is: Accrued, in the case of expenses, means not yet paid; and in the case of revenues, not yet collected. Deferred, in the case of expenses means paid in advance (prepaid); and in the case of revenues, collected in advance (precollected).

Item	*Brief definition*
1. Deferred revenue	A revenue collected, but not yet earned
2. Accrued revenue	A revenue earned, but not yet collected
3. Deferred expense	An expense paid, but not yet incurred
4. Accrued expense	An expense incurred, but not yet paid

ADJUSTING ENTRIES ILLUSTRATED

Several examples of each of the four general types of adjusting entries were cited above. In this section we will examine each of the examples, analyze them, and give the **adjusting entry** that should be made at the end of the period. These illustrations will serve to increase your understanding of the application of the accounting model and the measurement of periodic revenues and expenses. Throughout the examples to follow, we will refer to High-Rise Apartments and will assume that the **current** annual accounting period ends December 31, 1977.

Recorded revenue apportioned between accounting periods

Some businesses collect cash in advance of earning revenue from the sale of services or goods. In such situations the revenue must be apportioned to the period in which the services are rendered or the sale is consummated in accordance with the revenue principle (see page 142). This type of situation requires an adjusting entry at the end of the period to recognize (1) the correct amount of revenue for the current period and (2) an obligation in the future to provide the related goods or services. We will analyze one such situation for High-Rise Apartments that occurs because a few tenants pay their rent on the 15th of each month. (Note: Each entry is letter coded for reference in the illustrations to follow.)

Rent revenue collected in advance. On December 15, 1977, two tenants paid rent for the period December 15, 1977, to January 15, 1978, in the amount of $1,200. The sequence of entries would be:

Entry at date of collection of rent, December 15, 1977:

Cash	1,200	
Rent revenue		1,200
To record one month's rent for the period December 15, 1977, to January 15, 1978.		

Observe that the $1,200 cash collected included rent revenue for one-half month in 1977 and rent collected in advance for one-half month for 1978. As a consequence for 1977, the rent revenue was $600 and rent collected in advance was $600. The latter amount is a liability for High-Rise Apartments because there is a future obligation to provide occupancy for one-half month in 1978.

a. Adjusting entry at end of 1977:

Rent revenue	600	
Rent collected in advance		600
To adjust the accounts for revenue collected in advance as of the end of the current period.		

The adjusting entry serves two measurement purposes: (1) to apportion rent revenue for one-half month to 1977 for matching purposes, and (2) to record the obligation to furnish future occupancy to the lessee for one-half month in 1978.[1]

Unrecorded revenue

On occasion, at the end of the current period, there may be revenue that has been **earned** (in accordance with the revenue principle) but not yet recorded. Unrecorded revenue must be given accounting recognition in the period in which it was earned. This is accomplished by making an adjusting entry at the end of the current period to recognize (1) a receivable and (2) the revenue earned. We will analyze a typical situation for High-Rise Apartments.

Rent revenue unrecorded. On December 31, 1977, the manager of High-Rise Apartments, upon checking the rental records, found that two tenants had not paid their December rent amounting to $400. The sequence of entries would be:

b. Adjusting entry at December 31, 1977:

Rent revenue receivable	400	
Rent revenue		400
To record rent revenue earned in 1977 but not collected by year-end.		

[1] Observe that the entry at collection date, December 15, 1977, could have been recorded in a way that would preclude the need for an adjusting entry later, viz:

Cash	1,200	
Rent revenue		600
Rent collected in advance		600

Entry at date of collection in January 1978:

Cash	400	
Rent revenue receivable		400
To record collection of receivable for 1977 rent revenue.		

The adjusting entry at the end of 1977 served two measurement purposes: (1) to record rent revenue earned and (2) to record a receivable (an asset) for occupancy provided in 1977. Rent revenue receivable would be reported on the December 31, 1977, balance sheet as a current asset.

Recorded costs apportioned between accounting periods

A company frequently must make an expenditure of cash or incur a liability for assets or services that will help generate revenue in the current period and one or more future accounting periods. When such a transaction occurs, an **asset** is increased (debited). As the future periods pass, the asset cost is apportioned to *expense* so that there is a matching of expense with revenue for each of the periods affected. For High-Rise Apartments we will analyze three such transactions that occurred in 1977.

Prepaid insurance. On January 1, 1977, High-Rise paid in advance a two-year insurance premium of $2,400 on an apartment building. The sequence of entries for this deferred or **prepaid expense** would be:

Entry on date of payment, January 1, 1977:

Prepaid insurance	2,400	
Cash		2,400
To record payment of a two-year premium.		

c. Adjusting entry at end of current period, December 31, 1977:

Insurance expense	1,200	
Prepaid insurance		1,200
To record insurance expense for 12 months ($2,400 × 12/24).		

The latter entry would be repeated at the end of 1978. The adjusting entry serves two measurement purposes: (1) it apportions insurance expense to the current period for **matching** purposes, and (2) it adjusts (reduces) the Prepaid Insurance account to the correct asset amount for the unexpired insurance at the end of 1977. That is, at the end of 1977 the company was still entitled to one year of insurance protection and hence had an asset amounting to $1,200.

Depreciation. On January 1, 1976, a contractor completed an apartment building for High-Rise. The contract price of $360,000 was paid in cash. The building has an estimated useful life of 30 years and an estimated $60,000 *residual value* at the end of the 30 years. The sequence of entries would be:

Entry on date of purchase, January 1, 1976:

Apartment building	360,000	
Cash		360,000

d. Adjusting entry at end of current period, December 31, 1977:

Depreciation expense	10,000	
Accumulated depreciation, building		10,000
To record depreciation expense for one year.		

The adjusting entry would be repeated at the end of each year over the life of the building. The **estimated** amount expected to be recovered when the asset is finally sold or disposed of is known as the **residual value** (sometimes it is called scrap value). For computing depreciation, the cost of the asset must be reduced by the residual value. The difference – $360,000 – $60,000 = $300,000 – is the amount to be depreciated over the estimated useful life. Thus, the annual depreciation expense on the apartment building would be ($360,000 − $60,000) ÷ 30 years = $10,000.[2] The residual value of $60,000 is deducted since it is expected to be recovered at the end of the useful life. Again, the adjusting entry serves two measurement purposes: (1) it apportions a part of the cost of the building to expense for the current period for matching purposes, and (2) it adjusts (reduces) the amount of the asset to represent the unexpired cost of the asset. The credit to "Accumulated Depreciation, Building" could have been made directly to the building account with the same effect; however, it is desirable, for reporting purposes, to keep the balance of the asset account "Apartment Building" at original cost. This is accomplished by setting up a **contra,** or **offset,** account entitled "Accumulated Depreciation, Building." You will recall from Chapters 3 and 4 that on the balance sheet the building would be shown on one line at cost with a deduction on the next line for accumulated depreciation (see Exhibit 3–2).

Supplies inventory. On March 1, 1977, maintenance supplies were purchased at a cost of $600. At the date of purchase they were placed in the supply room inventory to be used as needed on a day-to-day basis. Since no accounting entry is made during the period when supplies of this type are used, an inventory of supplies remaining on hand at the end of the period is taken. At the end of 1977, an inventory of the supply room indicated that $200 of the supplies remained on hand; therefore, $400 must have been used in 1977 (assuming no beginning inventory). The sequence of entries would be:

---

[2] This example assumes straight-line depreciation; that is, an equal amount of depreciation expense is apportioned to each period. Other methods of depreciation will be discussed in Chapter 10.

Date of purchase, March 1, 1977:

Inventory of maintenance supplies	600	
Cash		600
To record purchase of supplies inventory.		

e. Adjusting entry at end of current period, December 31, 1977:

Maintenance expense	400	
Inventory of maintenance supplies		400
To record the amount of supplies used from inventory ($600 – $200).		

The adjusting entry serves two measurement purposes: (1) to apportion expense to 1977 for matching purposes, and (2) to adjust (reduce) the asset account Inventory to the cost of the supplies on hand carried over at the end of the period.

Unrecorded expenses

Most expenses are incurred and paid for during the same period; however, at the end of the period there usually are some expenses that have been **incurred** (i.e., the benefit realized) but not recorded (usually because payment has not been made). These unpaid unrecorded expenses frequently are referred to as **accrued expenses.** We will analyze three different transactions for High-Rise Apartments that started in 1977 and, in effect, continued to affect one or more future accounting periods.

Salary expense. On December 31, 1977, the manager of High-Rise was on a trip and due to return January 10, 1978. As a consequence, the manager's December salary of $600 was not paid or recorded by December 31, 1977. The sequence of entries for the accrued salary expense (disregard payroll taxes at this time) would be:

f. Adjusting entry at end of current period, December 31, 1977:

Salary expense	600	
Salaries payable (or accrued salaries payable)		600
To record salary expense and the liability for December salary not yet paid.		

At date of payment next period, January 10, 1978:

Salaries payable	600	
Cash		600
To record payment of a December 1977 salary.		

The adjusting entry serves two measurement purposes: (1) to record an expense incurred in 1977, and (2) to record the liability for the salary owed at the end of 1977.

Property tax expense. On December 30, 1977, a tax bill amounting to $4,700 was received from the city for 1977 property taxes. The taxes are due on February 15, 1978; hence they were unpaid and unrecorded at the end of 1977. The sequence of entries would be:

g. Adjusting entry at end of current period, December 31, 1977:[3]

Property tax expense	4,700	
Property taxes payable		4,700

To record 1977 property taxes incurred and the related liability.

The adjusting entry serves the same two measurement purposes enumerated above for salaries. When the taxes are paid, Cash will be credited and Property Taxes Payable debited for $4,700.

Interest expense. On November 1, 1977, the business borrowed $30,000 cash from a local bank on a 90-day note with an annual interest rate of 8 percent. The principal plus interest is due in three months. The sequence of entries is:

At date of loan, November 1, 1977:

Cash	30,000	
Note payable, short term		30,000

To record a three-month, 8 percent loan from the bank.

h. Adjusting entry at end of current period, December 31, 1977:

Interest expense	400	
Interest payable (or accrued interest payable)		400

To record accrued interest expense for two months on note payable ($30,000 × 8% × 2/12 = $400).

At date of payment of loan principal and interest, January 31, 1978:

Note payable, short term	30,000	
Interest payable (per adjusting entry)	400	
Interest expense (1978 – $30,000 × 8% × 1/12)	200	
Cash		30,600

To record payment of note and interest at maturity date.

At the end of 1977 the note payable is a liability of the business. Since the note has been outstanding for two months up to December 31, 1977, in addition to the liability for the principal, there also is a liability for **accrued interest** for two months. This liability exists because interest legally accrues with the **passage of time,** notwithstanding the fact that the interest is payable in cash at the maturity date of the note. The adjusting

[3] This is an example of a situation where there may or may not be an adjusting entry. For example, assume the tax bill was received on December 5, 1977. At that date a *current entry* may have been made identical to the adjusting entry given above. Obviously, under these circumstances, an adjusting entry at December 31, 1977, would not be needed.

entry accomplishes two measurement purposes: (1) to record interest expense incurred in 1977 for matching with 1977 revenue, and (2) to record a liability for the interest accrued at the end of 1977. The balance sheet at December 31, 1977, will report two liabilities in respect to this note: one for the principal amount ($30,000) and one for the interest liability ($400).

Recording adjusting entries. The above examples demonstrate that adjusting entries involve application of the measurement process in that at the end of the accounting period they usually require an analysis to apportion revenue and expense between the current and one or more future periods.

Failure to include adjustments will cause both the income statement and balance sheet to be incorrect. It is important to remember that an adjusting entry, when needed, results from a transaction that started in one period and, in effect, continues to one or more subsequent periods. This means that an analysis to determine whether an adjusting entry is needed, and if so, how should it be made, must be based on the sequence of events covering the periods affected. Demonstration Case B at the end of the chapter illustrates how the situation affects the adjusting entries.

Adjusting entries are made in the journal (dated the last day of the period) immediately after all of the regular transactions are recorded. They are then posted to the ledger in the usual way. This is necessary because they are full-fledged economic events in substance and their effects must be processed through the accounting information system and into the financial statements. These procedures are illustrated in the next chapter.

In some instances, it is difficult to draw a distinct line between regular and adjusting entries. There are no reasons for the distinction, other than the two listed immediately above. The important point is that adjusting entries (as well as many other entries) are necessary to appropriately measure periodic revenues and to match expenses with the revenues generated during the period.

DEMONSTRATION CASE A: FOR SELF-STUDY

(Try to resolve this case before studying the suggested solution that follows.)

New Service Corporation is owned by three stockholders and has been in operation for one year. Cash flow and expenses are critical problems. Recordkeeping has been kept at a minimum to keep expenses low. One secretary performs both the secretarial and recordkeeping functions. Because of a loan made to the corporation, the bank has requested an income statement and balance sheet. Accordingly, the secretary prepared the following (summarized for case purposes):

Income Statement
For the Year Ended December 31, 1977

Revenues:	
Service revenue	$60,000
Expenses:	
Salaries and wages	(46,200)
Utilities	(1,800)
Miscellaneous expenses	(1,000)
Net Income	$11,000

Balance Sheet
At December 31, 1977

Assets	
Cash	$ 4,000
Accounts receivable	17,000
Supplies inventory	8,000
Equipment	40,000
Other assets	16,000
Total Assets	$85,000
Liabilities	
Accounts payable	$ 9,000
Income taxes payable	
Note payable, one year, 9%	10,000
Stockholders' Equity	
Capital stock, par $10	50,000
Contributed capital in excess of par	5,000
Retained earnings	11,000
Total Liabilities and Stockholders' Equity	$85,000

After reading the two statements, the bank requested that a CPA examine them. The CPA found that the secretary did not include the following (i.e., the adjusting entries):

a. Supplies inventory on hand at December 31 amounted to $3,000.
b. Depreciation for 19A. The equipment was acquired during January 19A; estimated useful life, ten years; and no residual value.
c. The note payable was dated August 1, 19A, and the principal plus interest are payable at the end of one year.
d. Income taxes; assume an average tax rate of 22 percent.

Required:

1. Recast the above statements to incorporate the additional data.
2. Prepare the adjusting entries (in journal form) for the additional data at December 31, 19A.

Suggested Solution:

Requirement 1:

Income Statement
For the Year Ended December 31, 1977

	Amounts Reported	Effects of Adjusting Entries	Corrected Amounts
Revenue:			
Service revenue	$60,000		$60,000
Expenses:			
Salaries and wages	46,200		46,200
Utilities	1,800		1,800
Supplies expense		(*a*) + 5,000	5,000
Depreciation expense		(*b*) + 4,000	4,000
Interest expense		(*c*) + 375	375
Miscellaneous expense	1,000		1,000
Total Expense	49,000		58,375
Pretax income	$11,000		1,625
Income tax expense ($1,625 × 22%)		(*d*) + 358	358
Net Income			$ 1,267

Balance Sheet
At December 31, 1977

	Amounts Reported	Effects of Adjusting Entries	Corrected Amounts
Assets			
Cash	$ 4,000		$ 4,000
Accounts receivable	17,000		17,000
Supplies inventory	8,000	(*a*) − 5,000	3,000
Equipment	40,000		40,000
Accumulated depreciation		(*b*) − 4,000	(4,000)
Other assets	16,000		16,000
Total Assets	$85,000		$76,000
Liabilities			
Accounts payable	$ 9,000		$ 9,000
Income taxes payable		(*d*) + 358	358
Interest payable		(*c*) + 375	375
Note payable, one year, 9%	10,000		10,000
Total Liabilities	19,000		19,733
Stockholders' Equity			
Capital stock, par $10	50,000		50,000
Contributed capital in excess of par	5,000		5,000
Retained earnings	11,000	−11,000 + 1,267	1,267
Total Liabilities and Stockholders' Equity	$85,000		$76,000

Requirement 2:

Adjusting entries at December 31, 1977:

a. Supplies expense	5,000	
Supplies inventory		5,000

To reduce supplies inventory to the amount on hand December 31, 1977, $3,000 and to record supplies expense, $5,000.

b. Depreciation expense	4,000	
Accumulated depreciation		4,000

Depreciation for one year, $40,000 ÷ 10 years = $4,000.

c. Interest expense	375	
Interest payable		375

To record interest expense and the interest accrued (a liability) from August 1 to December 31, 1977 ($10,000 × 9% × 5/12 = $375).

d. Income tax expense	358	
Income taxes payable		358

To record income tax expense and the liability for unpaid tax as computed on the income statement.

DEMONSTRATION CASE B: FOR SELF-STUDY

(Try to resolve this case before studying the suggested solution that follows.)

This case is presented to illustrate why and how adjusting entries are directly influenced by the manner in which the *initial entry* (affecting two or more accounting periods) was made (see page 144). To determine whether an adjusting entry is needed, and if so, how it should be made, requires a careful analysis of the situation.

General situation: On July 1, 19A, Company K paid a two-year insurance premium amounting to $1,200. The annual accounting period ends on December 31.

Required:

1. How much of the premium should be reported as expense in the 19A, 19B, and 19C income statements?
2. What is the amount of prepaid insurance on December 31, 19A? How should this amount be reported on the 19A financial statements?
3. Company K could have recorded the $1,200 payment on July 1, 19A, in one of three ways as follows:

Case A:

Prepaid insurance	1,200	
Cash		1,200

Case B:

Insurance expense	1,200	
Cash		1,200

Case C:

Prepaid insurance	900	
Insurance expense	300	
Cash		1,200

For each case, give the appropriate adjusting entry (in journal form) at December 31, 19A. If no adjusting entry is required, explain why.

Suggested Solution:

Requirement 1:

Insurance expense: 19A – $1,200 × 6/24 = $300
19B – $1,200 × 12/24 = 600
19C – $1,200 × 6/24 = 300

Requirement 2:

Prepaid insurance on December 31, 19A – $1,200 × 18/24 = $900. This amount should be reported on the balance sheet at December 31, 19A, as a current asset. Theoretical strictness suggests that $300 of the $900 should be reported as a deferred charge; however, this is not done in practice because the effect is not material in this case.

Requirement 3:

Adjusting entry at December 31, 19A:

JOURNAL / **LEDGER**

Case A:

Insurance expense	300	
Prepaid insurance		300

To reduce prepaid insurance to $900 and to record insurance expense for 19A, $300.

Prepaid Insurance

Initial entry	1,200	Adj. entry	300

Insurance Expense

Adj. entry	300		

Case B:

Prepaid insurance	900	
Insurance expense		900

To record prepaid insurance at the end of 19A, $900 and to reduce insurance expense to $300 for 19A.

Insurance Expense

Initial entry	1,200	Adj. entry	900

Prepaid Insurance

Adj. entry	900		

Case C:

No adjusting entry is needed at December 31, 19A, because the correct amounts for both prepaid insurance at December 31, 19A, $900 and insurance expense for 19A, $300 were recorded on the transaction date, July 1, 19A.

Prepaid Insurance

Initial entry	900	

Insurance Expense

Initial entry	300	

SUMMARY

This chapter focused on the revenue and matching principles. Matching expenses with revenue for the period is critical because the lifespan of an enterprise, although indefinite in length, must be divided into a series of short time periods (usually one year) for periodic performance measurements. Primary among those measurements are the economic effects as reported in periodic financial statements.

In the measurement of net income, the **revenue principle** holds that revenues earned in the period through sale of goods or performance of services must be identified, measured, and reported for that period. The **matching principle** holds that the expenses incurred in generating those revenues must be identified, measured, and matched with revenues earned in the period to determine periodic net income. To implement the matching principle, certain transactions and events that extend from the current period to one or more future accounting periods must be analyzed at the end of the accounting period to apportion their expense effects to the future periods when they assist in the generation of revenues. The apportionment of some revenues and expenses require the use of adjusting entries. Adjusting entries follow the same concepts and procedures as entries for the usual transactions except that they are made at the end of the accounting period. At the end of the accounting period they are first entered in the journal and then are posted to the ledger in the same manner as other entries.

IMPORTANT TERMS

Time-period assumption	**Deferred revenue**
Interim reports	**Accrued revenue**
Revenue principle	**Deferred expense**
Matching principle	**Accrued expense**
Adjusting entries	**Contra or offset account**

QUESTIONS FOR DISCUSSION

1. Identify the two *change* statements and briefly explain why they are so designated.

2. Explain the time-period assumption.
3. What is an interim report?
4. What is the "natural business year"? How does it relate to accounting?
5. What revenue and expense recognition problems are caused by the time-period assumption?
6. Explain the revenue principle and the matching principle.
7. Contrast the completed contract method with the percentage-of-completion method of recognizing revenues.
8. What are adjusting entries? Why are they necessary?
9. What are the two distinct characteristics of adjusting entries?
10. Briefly define each of the following: accrued expense, accrued revenue, deferred expense, and deferred revenue.
11. In general, what two purposes are served by an adjusting entry for revenues?
12. In general, what two purposes are served by an adjusting entry for expenses?
13. AB Company collected $600 rent for the period December 15, 19A, to January 15, 19B. The $600 was credited to Rent Revenue Collected in Advance on December 15, 19A. Give the adjusting entry required on December 31, 19A (end of the accounting period).
14. Explain "estimated residual value." Why is it important in measuring depreciation expense?
15. Explain why adjusting entries are entered in the journal on the last day of the period and are then posted to the ledger.

EXERCISES

E5–1. Super Construction Company, Incorporated, specializes in major commercial construction. In April 19A, the company signed a contract to build a large warehouse. The contract price was $900,000, and the estimated construction cost was $720,000. Construction was started on June 1, 19A, and completed March 31, 19B. Actual construction costs were: 19A, $600,000; 19B, $130,000.

Required:

a. Complete the following tabulation for each separate case. Assume income recognition under percentage of completion is allocated on the basis of actual costs incurred to total estimated costs.

		Pretax income to be recognized	
Case	*Method*	*19A*	*19B*
A	Completed contract	$	$
B	Percentage completion		

b. Which method would you recommend for Super? Explain the basis for your choice.

E5–2. Day's Department Store is in the process of completing the accounting process for the year just ended, December 31, 1977. The current entries have been journalized and posted. The following data in respect to adjusting entries are available:

a. The Office supplies inventory at January 1, 1977, was $110. Office supplies purchased and debited to Office Supplies Inventory during the year amounted to $360. The year-end inventory showed $80 worth of supplies remained on hand.

b. Wages earned during December 1977 but unpaid and unrecorded at December 31, 1977, amounted to $1,100. (The last payroll was December 28, and the next payroll will be January 6, 1978.)

c. Three fourths of the basement of the store is rented to another merchant, J. B. Smith, who sells compatible, but not competitive, merchandise. On November 1, 1977, the store collected six months' rent in advance from Smith amounting to $3,600, which was credited in full to Rent Revenue when collected.

d. The rest of the basement is rented to Spears Specialty, at $300 per month, payable monthly. On December 31, 1977, the rent for November and December 1977 had not yet been collected nor recorded. Collection is expected January 10, 1978.

Required:

Give the adjusting entry for each situation that should be entered in the records at December 31, 1977.

E5–3. The information-processing cycle for the fiscal year ended December 31, 1977, has been completed for all of the current entries by Red Retailers, a men's store. Additional information from the records and related documents revealed the following:

a. Delivery equipment costing $19,000 was being used by the store. Estimates in respect to equipment were: (1) useful life six years and (2) residual value at the end of six years' use, $1,000. Assume depreciation for a full year for 1977.

b. On July 1, 1977, a two-year insurance premium amounting to $1,000 was paid in cash and debited to Prepaid Insurance.

c. Red rents one half of the building occupied by the store to another merchant, Brand Ladies Shop. The rent of $400 per month is payable six months in advance, each September 1 and March 1. The rent collection on September 1, 1977, was credited in full to Rent Revenue.

d. Red operates an alteration shop to meet its own needs. In addition, the shop does alterations for Brand. At the end of December 31, 1977, Brand had not paid for alterations completed amounting to $450; this amount has not been recorded as Alteration Shop Revenue.

Required:

Give the adjusting entry for each situation that should be entered in the records at December 31, 1977.

E5–4. Wiley Company, on August 1, 1977, in order to meet a cash shortage, obtained a $8,000, 9 percent loan from a local bank. The principal, plus interest, was payable at the end of 12 months. The annual accounting period for Wiley ends on December 31, 1977.

Required:

a. Give the journal entry on date of the loan, August 1, 1977.
b. Give the adjusting entry required on December 31, 1977.
c. Give the journal entry on date of payment, July 31, 1978.

E5–5. On April 1, 1977, Royce Corporation received a $12,000, 10 percent note from a customer in settlement of a $12,000 open account receivable. According to the terms, the principal of the note, plus the interest, was payable at the end of 12 months. The annual accounting period for Royce ends on December 31, 1977.

Required:

a. Give the journal entry for receipt of the note on April 1, 1977.
b. Give the adjusting entry required on December 31, 1977.
c. Give the journal entry on date of collection, March 30, 1978.

E5–6. Stokes Company is in the process of making adjusting entries for the year ended December 31, 1977. In developing information for the adjusting entries, we learned that on September 1, 1977, a two-year insurance premium of $1,800 was paid.

Required:

a. What amount should be reported on the 1977 income statement for insurance expense?
b. What amount should be reported on the December 31, 1977, balance sheet for prepaid insurance?
c. Give the adjusting entry at December 31, 1977, under each of two cases:

Case 1 – Assume that when the premium was paid on September 1, 1977, the bookkeeper debited the full amount to Prepaid Insurance.

Case 2 – Assume that when the premium was paid September 1, 1977, the bookkeeper debited Insurance Expense for the full amount.

(Hint: In Case 2 be sure you end with the same amount in the Prepaid Insurance account as in Case 1.)

E5–7. Taylor Manufacturing Company uses a large amount of shipping supplies, which are purchased in large volume, stored, and used as needed. At December 31, 1977, in collecting information as a basis for making the adjusting entries, the following data relating to shipping supplies were obtained from the records and supporting documents:

Shipping supplies on hand, January 1, 1977	$ 1,000
Purchases of shipping supplies during 1977	13,000
Shipping supplies on hand, per inventory, December 31, 1977	4,000

Required:

a. What amount should be reported on the 1977 income statement for shipping supplies expense?

b. What amount should be reported on the December 31, 1977, balance sheet for shipping supplies inventory?

c. Give the adjusting entry at December 31, 1977, assuming the purchases of shipping supplies were debited in full to Shipping Supplies Inventory ($13,000).

d. What adjusting entry would you make assuming the bookkeeper debited Shipping Supplies Expense for the $13,000 supplies? (Hint: In solving (*c*) and (*d*), be sure that each solution ends up with the same amount remaining in the Shipping Supplies Inventory account.)

E5–8. On December 31, 1977, Ralston Company prepared an income statement and balance sheet and failed to take into account three adjusting entries. The income statement, prepared on this basis, reflected a pretax income of $14,000. The balance sheet reflected total assets, $75,000; total liabilities, $25,000; and owners' equity, $50,000. The data for the three adjusting entries were:

1. Depreciation for the full year on equipment that cost $32,000; estimated useful life, ten years; and residual value, $2,000.
2. Wages amounting to $9,000 for the last three days of December 1977 not paid and not recorded (the next payroll will be on January 10, 1978).
3. Rent revenue of $600 was collected on December 10, 1977, on some office space for the period December 10, 1977, to January 9, 1978. The $600 was credited to rent revenue when collected.

Required:

Complete the following tabulation (indicate deductions with parentheses):

Item	*Pretax income*	*Assets*	*Liabilities*	*Owners' equity*
Balances reported	$14,000	$75,000	$25,000	$50,000
1. Effects of depreciation	______	______	______	______
2. Effects of wages	______	______	______	______
3. Effects of rent revenue	______	______	______	______
Correct balances	______	______	______	______

E5–9. On December 15, 1977, the bookkeeper for Tobin Company prepared the income statement and balance sheet given to the left below (summarized) but neglected to consider three of the adjusting entries.

	As prepared	Effects of adjusting entries	Corrected amounts
Income Statement:			
Revenues	$92,000	______	______
Expenses	(81,000)	______	______
Income tax expense		______	______
Income	$11,000		______
Balance Sheet:			
Assets			
Cash	$17,000	______	______
Accounts receivable	16,000	______	______
Rent receivable		______	______
Equipment*	40,000	______	______
Accumulated depreciation	(8,000)	______	______
	$65,000		______

* Acquired January 1, 1975; 10-year life, no residual value.

	As prepared	Effects of adjusting entries	Corrected amounts
Liabilities			
Accounts payable	$10,000	______	______
Income taxes payable		______	______
Owners' Equity			
Capital stock	40,000	______	______
Retained earnings	15,000	______	______
	$65,000		______

Data on the three adjusting entries:

1. Depreciation on the equipment not recorded for 1977.
2. Rent revenue of $800 for December 1977 not yet collected.
3. Income taxes for 1977 not paid or recorded; assume an average rate of 22 percent.

Required:

a. Prepare the three adjusting entries (in journal form) that were omitted.

b. Complete the two columns to the right above.

PROBLEMS

P5–1. The following information was provided by the records and related documents of Rancho Apartments (a corporation) at the end of the annual fiscal period, December 31, 1977:

Revenue:

1. Rental revenue collected in cash during 1977 for occupancy in 1977 (credited to Rent Revenue)	$97,000
2. Rental revenue earned for occupancy in December 1977 but not collected until 1978	8,000
3. In December 1977, collected rent revenue in advance for January 1978; that is, rent collected in advance	6,000

Salary expense:		
4.	Cash payment made in January 1977 for salaries incurred (earned) in December 1976	3,000
5.	Salaries incurred and paid during 1977 (debited to Salary Expense)	18,000
6.	Salaries earned by employees during December 1977 but not to be paid until January 1978	2,000
7.	Cash advance to employees in December 1977 for salaries to be earned in January 1978	4,000
Supplies used:		
8.	Supplies purchased for cash during 1977 (debited to Supplies Inventory when purchased)	6,000
9.	Supplies on hand (Supplies Inventory) on December 31, 1977	1,500
10.	Supplies on hand (Supplies Inventory) on January 1, 1977	2,000

Required:

What amount should be shown on the 1977 income statement for: (1) rent revenue; (2) salary expense; and (3) supplies expense? Show computations.

P5–2. Speedy Transportation Company (a corporation) is now in the process of completing the information-processing cycle for the accounting year ended December 31, 1977. The adjusting entries are now to be prepared for entry into the accounting system. The following data that must be considered have been developed from the records and related documents:

1. On September 1, 1977, a three-year insurance premium on equipment was paid amounting to $720 which was debited in full to Prepaid Insurance on that date.
2. During 1977, office supplies amounting to $1,400 were purchased for cash and debited in full to Supplies Inventory. At the end of 1977, an inventory of supplies remaining showed $200. There was no inventory of supplies on hand at January 1, 1977.
3. On December 31, 1977, the B&R Garage completed repairs on a truck at a cost of $450; the amount is not yet recorded and is payable by January 30, 1978.
4. In December 1977, a tax bill on equipment for 1977 amounting to $700 was received from the city. The taxes are due February 15, 1978, and have not been recorded.
5. On December 31, 1977, Speedy completed a hauling contract for an out-of-state company. The bill was for $3,500 payable within 30 days. No entry has been made for this transaction.
6. On July 1, 1977, Speedy purchased a new hauling van at a cash cost of $8,600. The estimated useful life of the van was five years, with an estimated residual value at that time of $600. Compute depreciation for six months in 1977.
7. On October 1, 1977, Speedy borrowed $6,000 from the local bank on a one-year, 10 percent note payable. The principal plus interest is payable at the end of 12 months.

Required:

a. Give in journal entry form, the adjusting entry required on December 31, 1977, related to each of the above transactions. Give a brief explanation with each entry.

b. By how much would pretax income be in error if the above adjusting entries were omitted? Explain.

P5–3. This case, taken from the experiences of May's Department Store (a corporation), has been selected to give you an opportunity to test your analytical ability in transaction analysis and in developing the adjusting entries where there are both notes receivable and notes payable. The annual fiscal period ends on December 31, 1977. Each of the two situations otherwise are independent.

Situation A—May's has arranged a line of credit whereby a local bank will provide them cash for short-term working capital needs. Repayment will vary from 60 to 90 days. Occasionally, the company also borrows a substantial amount on a long-term basis. On October 1, 1977, the corporation borrowed $42,000 on a one-year, 8 percent note. The principal plus interest are payable at the end of 12 months.

Situation B—May's sells approximately 42 percent of their goods on credit; accounts are due at the end of the month in which the sale is made. From time to time, special efforts must be made to collect an account. J. Doe was such a case. Doe owed the store $1,200 on an account that they have been unable to collect. Finally, on November 1, 1977, Doe gave them a 10 percent note for the $1,200 coupled with a mortgage on two personal automobiles. The note was for two years. At the end of the first full year, Doe agreed to pay one half of the principal ($600) plus interest on the amount of principal outstanding during the year. Final payment of principal and interest was due at the end of the second year.

Required:

a. What amount should be shown on May's income statement for 1977 for (1) interest expense and (2) interest revenue?

b. What items and amount(s) should be shown on the balance sheet at December 31, 1977?

c. Give the adjusting journal entry required for each situation at December 31, 1977. Show your computations.

d. What would be the amount of error in pretax income if the two adjusting entries were omitted? Explain.

P5–4. Modern Service Company is in the process of completing the information-processing cycle at the end of the annual accounting year, December 31, 1977. Below are listed the balances for each account at December 31, 1977 (*a*) before the adjusting entries for 1977 and (*b*) after the adjusting entries for 1977.

	Account balance, December 31, 1977			
	Before adjusting entries		*After adjusting entries*	
	Debit	*Credit*	*Debit*	*Credit*
a. Cash	$ 8,000		$ 8,000	
b. Service revenue receivable			400	
c. Prepaid insurance	300		200	
d. Fixed assets	120,200		120,200	
e. Accumulated depreciation, equipment		$ 21,500		$ 25,000
f. Income taxes payable				5,500
g. Capital stock		70,000		70,000
h. Retained earnings, January 1, 1977		14,000		14,000
i. Service revenue earned		60,000		60,400
j. Salary expense	37,000		37,000	
k. Depreciation expense			3,500	
l. Insurance expense			100	
m. Income tax expense			5,500	
	$165,500	$165,500	$174,900	$174,900

Required:

a. By comparing the amounts before and after the adjusting entries, reconstruct the four adjusting entries that were made for 1977. Provide a brief explanation of each.

b. Compute the amount of income assuming: (1) it is based on the preadjusted amounts and (2) it is based on the adjusted amounts. Which income amount is correct? Explain why.

P5–5. You are in the process of developing the adjusting entries for Box Service Company at December 31, 1977. Three items are of special concern. Data at hand concerning the three items are:

Cash inflows and outflows:	
Prepaid insurance—cash spent during 1977	$ 600
Interest expense—cash spent during 1977	700
Service revenue—cash collected during 1977	6,700

	Dec. 31, 1976	*Dec. 31, 1977*
Balance sheet amounts:		
Prepaid insurance (asset—debit)	$100	$400
Interest payable (liability—credit)	300	200
Unearned service revenue (liability—credit)	300	500

Required:

How much should be reported on the 1977 income statement for (show computations):

1. Insurance expense?
2. Interest expense?
3. Service revenue earned?

P5–6. Morris Transportation Company, a corporation, has been in operation since January 1, 1977. It is now December 31, 1977, the end of the annual accounting period. The company has not done well financially during the first year, although hauling revenue has been fairly good. The three stockholders manage the company, and they have not given much attention to recordkeeping. In view of a serious cash shortage, they asked a local bank for a $10,000 loan. The bank requested a complete financial statement. The statements below were prepared by a clerk and were then given to the bank.

MORRIS TRANSPORTATION COMPANY
December 31, 1977

Income Statement

Hauling revenue	$90,000
Expenses:	
Salaries	20,000
Maintenance	15,000
Other expenses	25,000
Total Expenses	60,000
Net Income	$30,000

Balance Sheet

Assets	
Cash	$ 1,000
Receivables	4,000
Inventory of maintenance supplies	5,000
Equipment	30,000
Other assets	37,000
Total Assets	$77,000
Liabilities	
Accounts payable	$ 7,000
Capital	
Capital stock	40,000
Retained earnings	30,000
Total Liabilities and Capital	$77,000

After briefly reviewing the statements and "looking into the situation," the bank requested that the statements be redone (with some expert help) to "incorporate depreciation, accruals, inventory counts, income taxes, and so on." As a consequence of a review of the records and supporting documents, the following additional information was developed:

a. The inventory of maintenance supplies should be $2,000, instead of the $5,000 shown on December 31, 1977. (Hint: Increase Maintenance Expense.)
b. Prepaid insurance at December 31, 1977, amounted to $1,000. The insurance premium had been debited to Other Expenses in full when paid.
c. The equipment cost $30,000 when purchased January 1, 1977, and has an estimated useful life of five years (no residual value).
d. Unpaid salaries at December 31, 1977, amounted to $1,500.
e. Unearned hauling revenue at December 31, 1977, amounted to

$3,000. This had been credited to Hauling Revenue when the cash was collected earlier.

f. Assume an income tax rate of 20 percent.

Required:

1. Give the six adjusting entries (in journal form) required by the above additional information for December 31, 1977.
2. Recast the above statements after taking into account the adjusting entries. You do not need to use subclassifications on the statements.

 Suggested form for the solution:

Items	Amounts reported	Changes Plus	Minus	Correct amounts
(List here each item from the two statements)	*inventory* *prepaid and*	+ 1000	− 3000	2000 26000 others

NI 17,500

(Hint: Correct balance sheet total is $69,000.)

3. Compute the amount of the error in (*a*) net income and (*b*) total assets due to the omission of the adjusting entries. Draft a brief non-technical report for the bank explaining causes of the differences.

P5–7. Small Company (a corporation) is completing the information-processing cycle for the annual accounting period that ended on December 31, 1977. All of the current entries for 1977 were correctly entered in the accounting system. A list of all of the ledger accounts and their respective balances (i.e., an unadjusted trial balance) was prepared immediately after the last current entry was journalized and posted.

The accountant was away for the next few days. During this time, a new assistant to the president requested that the bookkeeper prepare an income statement and balance sheet immediately "for our use" despite a suggestion by the bookkeeper that "the adjustments have to be determined by the accountant." Consequently, the following statements (summarized for case purposes) were prepared forthwith by the bookkeeper and given to the assistant.

Income Statement
For the Year Ended December 31, 1977

Revenues:

Sales	$240,000
Service	50,000
Total	290,000

Expenses:

Cost of goods sold	150,000
Salaries and wages	65,000
Utilities	18,000
Other expenses	7,000
Total	240,000
Net Income	$ 50,000

Balance Sheet
At December 31, 1977

Assets	
Cash	$ 23,000
Accounts receivable	61,000
Inventory	130,000
Prepaid insurance	6,000
Equipment*	100,000
Accumulated depreciation, equipment	(30,000)
Other assets	10,000
Total Assets	$300,000
Liabilities	
Accounts payable	$ 41,000
Income taxes payable	
Notes payable, one year, 9%	20,000
Stockholders' Equity	
Capital stock, par $10	150,000
Contributed capital in excess of par	15,000
Retained earnings	74,000
Total Liabilities and Stockholders' Equity	$300,000

* Acquired January 1, 1974; estimated 10-year life and no residual value.

After returning, the accountant immediately prepared another set of statements "that are correct to go upstairs" by including the following data:

a. The inventory at the end of December 1977 should have been $120,000. (Hint: Correct inventory and cost of goods sold.)
b. The prepaid insurance amount of $6,000 was the total premium paid on July 1, 1977, and covered a two-year period from payment date. (The $6,000 was debited to Prepaid Insurance.)
c. Depreciation for 1977.
d. Accrued interest on the note payable. The note was dated November 1, 1977, and the principal plus interest is payable at the end of one year.
e. Corporation income taxes. Assume an average tax rate of 30 percent.

Required:

1. Prepare the appropriate adjusting entry, in journal form, for each item of additional data.
2. Recast the income statements and balance sheet to incorporate the additional data. Suggested format:

		Changes		
Items	*Amounts reported*	*Plus*	*Minus*	*Correct amounts*

3. Draft a brief nontechnical explanation for the management to adequately explain why the second set of statements should replace the first set.

P5–8. This is a case to test your ability to analyze a specific situation and to determine whether an adjusting entry is required and, if so, what the entry should be.

General situation: On December 10, 19A, the company collected cash $1,200 which was for some office space rented to an outsider. The rent collected was for the period December 10, 19A, through January 9, 19B. The annual accounting period ends on December 31.

Required:

1. How much of the $1,200 should be reported as revenue on the 19A income statement? How much of it should be reported as revenue on the 19B income statement?
2. What is the amount of "Rent Collected in Advance" as of December 31, 19A? How should this amount be reported on the 19A financial statements?
3. On December 10, 19A, the company could have recorded the $1,200 collection in one of three different ways as follows:

   Case A:

Cash	1,200	
Rent revenue		1,200

   Case B:

Cash	1,200	
Rent collected in advance		1,200

   Case C:

Cash	1,200	
Rent revenue		800
Rent collected in advance		400

   For each case, give the appropriate adjusting entry (in journal form) at December 31, 19A. If no adjusting entry is required, explain why.
4. For each case, after taking into consideration your adjusting entry, give the entry that could be made in January 19B to correctly reflect rent revenue in 19B.

6

Information processing in an accounting system

PURPOSE OF THE CHAPTER

In Chapters 4 and 5, processing information in an accounting system was introduced and outlined in broad perspective. The purpose of this chapter is to expand those discussions to incorporate all of the phases and procedures in the accounting information-processing cycle. This cycle is repeated each accounting period because it focuses on a systematic approach to periodic recording, measuring, and classifying financial data and generating periodic financial statements.

For those students interested in majoring in accounting, knowledge of accounting information processing is essential from the professional and technical points of view. For other students, particularly those interested in a career in management, a good general knowledge of the information-processing cycle is important because, as managers, they should be able to assess such things as (1) the capabilities and limitations of such a system, (2) the basic adaptations that should be expected for different types and sizes of entities, (3) cost-benefit relationships (i.e., the benefit of financial information versus the cost of generating the information), (4) the internal control implications of the system, and (5) the relationship of the accounting information processing system (a subset) to the overall information system of the entity.

Part One of the chapter will discuss and illustrate the information-processing cycle. Part Two will discuss an optional data processing procedure commonly called "reversing" entries.

PART ONE: INFORMATION PROCESSING

MANUAL, MECHANICAL, AND ELECTRONIC DATA PROCESSING

Information processing refers to the order and ways in which the work is accomplished in collecting the source documents, recording their effects in terms of the accounting model, classifying the data, and, finally, in preparing the periodic financial statements. In most entities an extremely large amount of data must be handled. Although information processing can be time-consuming and costly to the enterprise, a well-designed system provides a smooth, uninterrupted, efficient flow of data from the points of occurrence of the transactions to the various financial reports. The processing of accounting data may be performed in one of three ways, or, as is the usual case, by a combination of them. The three approaches may be briefly described as follows:

1. Manual data processing—When this approach is used, all of the work is performed manually (that is, by hand). In the discussion and illustrations up to this point, manual processing has been employed. The manual approach is used extensively in small entities. Also, in large and medium-sized businesses, certain elements of data processing continue to be performed manually. The manual approach is quite useful for illustrating the application of accounting principles and measurement procedures. It also is convenient for explaining and illustrating the accounting process because the learner can readily see what is being done. One cannot see what is going on inside a computer.
2. Mechanical data processing—Mechanical data processing is used for repetitive transactions that occur in large numbers. Mechanical processing employs accounting machines that vary widely in type and application. They encompass mechanical devices, some of which display a combination typewriter–adding machine keyboard. They encompass not only the strictly mechanical devices, such as posting machines, but also punched-card equipment. The latter consists of (1) key-punch machines, on which cards are punched to record the transactions; (2) sorting machines, which sort the cards in a predetermined order; and (3) tabulating machines, which print the output, such as a listing of the expenses for the period. Although mechanical data processing is widely used today, it is rapidly being superseded by electronic data processing.
3. Electronic data processing—Electronic data processing is based upon use of electronic computers. The manual and mechanical activities in data processing are reduced to a minimum. Because of their large capabilities to store data and the speed with which such data can be manipulated and recalled, electronic data processing

has become widely used in accounting. This process involves the use of "hardware" and "software." The computer and equipment related to it (usually called peripheral equipment) constitute the hardware. Software includes the programs that must be designed as instructions to the computer and other items related to the operation of the system. Other items include materials used in operating the system, training materials, and studies of various sorts. Electronic data processing is widely applied to such accounting problems as payrolls, billings for goods and services, accounts receivable, accounts payable, and inventories.[1]

EXPANDING THE INFORMATION-PROCESSING CYCLE

In this part of the chapter we will expand the information-processing cycle that was outlined in Chapter 4, page 121, to illustrate the additional **phases** of the processing of accounting data. The cycle is expanded to encompass the phases listed below in the order that they are usually completed. (Phases added to those discussed and illustrated in Chapters 4 and 5 are indicated with an asterisk.)

1. Collection of raw economic data generated by transactions.
2. Analysis of all current transactions (as they occur) to determine their economic effects on the entity in terms of the accounting model.
3. Journalizing the results of this analysis of the current transactions. This phase encompasses recording the entries in chronological order in the journal.
4. Posting the current entries from the journal to the ledger.
5. Preparation of an unadjusted trial balance from the ledger.

*6. Preparation of an accounting worksheet:
   a. Collection of data for adjusting entries and analysis of the data in the context of the accounting model.
   b. Segregation of the data for the income statement and balance sheet.

7. Preparation of financial statements:
   a. Income statement.
   b. Balance sheet.
   c. Statement of changes in financial position (discussed in Chapter 15).

*8. Adjusting entries (at the end of the period):
   a. Entered in the journal.
   b. Posted to the ledger.

[1] This subject is discussed in more depth in *Fundamentals of Management Accounting*, Chapter 16.

*9. Closing the revenue and expense accounts in the ledger:
  a. Entered in the journal.
  b. Posted to the ledger.
*10. Preparation of a post-closing trial balance.

The four phases added (6, 8, 9, and 10) are strictly information-processing phases and involve no new accounting concepts and principles beyond those that you have already learned in the first five chapters. These four added phases are designed to provide an orderly flow of the data processing work and generally are quite helpful in completion of the financial statements with minimum effort. They also tend to decrease the potential for errors and omissions. The phases discussed in Chapters 4 and 5 will be reviewed. The added phases will be discussed and illustrated in order. In the illustrations, a manual system is employed for instructional purposes.

COLLECTION OF RAW ECONOMIC DATA GENERATED BY TRANSACTIONS (PHASE 1)

This is a necessary continuing activity that collects source documents for transactions as they occur. It involves all functions of the entity and a large number of employees.

ANALYSIS OF TRANSACTIONS (PHASE 2)

This is a mental activity performed by accountants that identifies and measures the economic impact of each transaction on the entity in terms of the basic accounting model: Assets = Liabilities + Owners' Equity.

JOURNALIZING (PHASE 3)

The results determined in transaction analysis are initially entered into the information system in chronological order. The initial record used for this first data input is called the journal; recording data in the journal is called journalizing.

POSTING (PHASE 4)

The data recorded in the journal is transferred or posted to the ledger to accomplish a classification purpose. The ledger is composed of a number of accounts—one for each kind of asset, liability, and owners' equity. Thus, posting to the ledger reorders the data from a chronological order to the classifications explicit in the fundamental accounting model. The ledger is viewed as the basic accounting record since it provides data classified appropriately for subsequent preparation of the periodic financial statements.

PREPARATION OF AN UNADJUSTED TRIAL BALANCE (PHASE 5)

At the end of the period, after all current transactions are journalized and posted to the ledger, a listing of all ledger accounts and their balances is prepared. This listing is called an unadjusted trial balance since (1) it serves to check the equalities of the accounting model (A = L + OE and Debit = Credit) and (2) it does not include the effects of a particular group of end-of-the-period entries called adjusting entries.

THE WORKSHEET (PHASE 6)

After Phase 5 (above), it is generally desirable, although optional with the accountant, to prepare what is known as a **worksheet.** The worksheet is an efficient **tool** that has as its **only purpose** to provide an organized approach to data manipulation and the grouping of appropriate amounts for the income statement and balance sheet. It brings together in one place, in an orderly way, the (1) unadjusted trial balance, (2) adjusting entries, (3) income statement, (4) balance sheet, and (5) closing entries (explained later). The worksheet normally is prepared by the accountant in pencil (for ease in revision) since it is not presented to the management or to other parties. After the worksheet is completed and determined to be correct, it then becomes the **guide** for completing the subsequent phases in the information-processing cycle (Phases 7, 8, and 9 as listed above).

Preparing the worksheet. A typical worksheet, shown in Exhibit 6–1, is presented for High-Rise Apartments for the year ended December 31, 1977. Note that the ledger accounts are listed vertically in the first column and there is a separate pair of debit and credit columns for the Unadjusted Trial Balance, Adjusting Entries, Adjusted Trial Balance, Income Statement, and Balance Sheet.[2]

The steps involved in developing this worksheet are:

Step 1 – After the current transactions for the year are entered in the journal and posted to the ledger, an unadjusted trial balance is developed. This unadjusted trial balance is entered directly in the first pair of amount

[2] Some accountants prefer to caption the last two parts of columns as follows:

Income Statement		Balance Sheet	
Expenses	Revenues	Assets	Liabilities and Owners' Equity

EXHIBIT 6–1. HIGH-RISE APARTMENTS, INC., For the Year Ended December 31, 1977

Account Titles	Unadjusted Trial Balance		Adjusting Entries		Adjusted Trial Balance		Income Statement		Balance Sheet	
	Debit	Credit	Debit	Credit	Debit	Credit	Debit	Credit	Debit	Credit
Cash	2,297				2,297				2,297	
Prepaid insurance	2,400			(*a*) 1,200	1,200				1,200	
Inventory of maintenance supplies	600			(*c*) 400	200				200	
Land	25,000				25,000				25,000	
Apartment building	360,000				360,000				360,000	
Accumulated depreciation, building		10,000		(*b*) 10,000		20,000				20,000
Notes payable		30,000				30,000				30,000
Rent collected in advance		1,200	(*g*) 600			600				600
Mortgage payable		238,037				238,037				238,037
Capital stock, 500 shares		50,000				50,000				50,000
Retained earnings (balance January 1, 1977, $23,760, less 1977 dividends, $12,000)		11,760				11,760				11,760
Rent revenue		128,463		(*g*) 600 (*h*) 400		129,463		129,463		
Advertising expense	500				500		500			
Maintenance expense	3,000		(*c*) 400		3,400		3,400			
Salary expense	17,400		(*d*) 600		18,000		18,000			
Interest expense	19,563		(*f*) 400		19,963		19,963			
Utilities expense	34,500				34,500		34,500			
Miscellaneous expenses	4,200				4,200		4,200			
Insurance expense			(*a*) 1,200		1,200		1,200			
Depreciation expense			(*b*) 10,000		10,000		10,000			
Salaries payable				(*d*) 600		600				600
Property tax expense			(*e*) 4,700		4,700		4,700			
Property taxes payable				(*e*) 4,700		4,700				4,700
Interest payable				(*f*) 400		400				400
Rent revenue receivable			(*h*) 400		400				400	
	469,460	469,460	18,300	18,300	485,560	485,560	96,463	129,463		
Income tax expense*			(*i*) 9,900				9,900			
Income taxes payable				(*i*) 9,900						9,900
Net Income							23,100			23,100
							129,463	129,463	389,097	389,097

* ($129,463 − $96,463) × 30% = $9,900.

columns on the worksheet. The equality of debits and credits is verified at this point (totals $469,460).

Step 2—The second pair of amount columns, headed "Adjusting Entries," is completed by entering the *adjusting entries* directly onto the worksheet. The adjusting entries for High-Rise Apartments placed on the worksheet were determined as explained in Chapter 5.

Observe on the worksheet that the last adjusting entry is for income taxes. This entry is accomplished as a "loopback" since pretax income must be computed before income tax expense can be determined. This is accomplished as a part of Step 4.

To facilitate examination (for potential errors), future reference, and study, the adjusting entries usually are coded on the worksheet as illustrated in Exhibit 6–1. Some of the adjusting entries require the addition of one or more account titles below the original trial balance listing. After the adjusting entries are completed on the worksheet, the equality of debits and credits for those entries is checked (totals $18,300).

Step 3—Next, the pair of columns headed "Adjusted Trial Balance" are completed. Although not essential, they are used for insuring accuracy. They simply represent, line by line, the combined amounts of the unadjusted trial balance, plus or minus the amounts entered as adjusting entries in the second pair of columns. For example, the Rent Revenue account reflects a $128,463 credit balance under Unadjusted Trial Balance. To this amount is *added* the credit amounts—$600 and $400 (debit amounts would be subtracted)—giving a combined amount of $129,463, which is entered as a *credit* under Adjusted Trial Balance. For those accounts that were unaffected by the adjusting entries, the Unadjusted Trial Balance amount is simply carried across to the Adjusted Trial Balance column. After each line has been completed, the equality of the debits and credits under Adjusted Trial Balance is checked (total $485,560).

Step 4—The amount on each line, under Adjusted Trial Balance, is extended horizontally across the worksheet and entered (*a*) as a debit, if it was a debit under Adjusted Trial Balance, or as a credit, if it was a credit under Adjusted Trial Balance; and (*b*) under the financial statement heading (income statement or balance sheet) on which it must appear. You can see that each amount extended across (1) was entered under *only one* of the four remaining columns, and (2) that debits remain debits and credits remain credits in the extending process.

At this point, the pair of Income Statement columns are summed (subtotals). The difference between the two subtotals represents the pretax income (or loss). Income tax expense is then computed by multiplying this difference by the tax rate. In Exhibit 6–1, the computation was ($129,463 − $96,463) × 30% = $9,900. The adjusting entry for income taxes then was entered at the bottom of the worksheet (we call this a "loopback"). Income tax expense and income taxes payable can now be extended horizontally to the Income Statement and Balance Sheet columns.

After all of the amounts on each line are extended to the last four columns of the worksheet, the four columns are summed vertically. At this point you can observe a very interesting and useful feature of the worksheet: the difference between the debit and credit columns under Income Statement is the after-tax *net income* or *net loss*. Likewise, the difference between the debit and credit columns under Balance Sheet is the net income or net loss. If this result does not occur, there is an error in the extending process.

Step 5—This step completes the worksheet. Observe on Exhibit 6–1 that the last item listed in the left column (Account Titles) is "Net Income" and that the amount of net income after tax (the difference explained above) is entered under *both* the Income Statement and the Balance Sheet in debit and credit format. The amount of net income is entered in the *debit* column under Income Statement in order to make the two columns balance, and as a *credit* under Balance Sheet for the same reason. The credit under Balance Sheet for "Net Income" (or, alternatively, debit if a loss) also indicates that this amount must be added to the balance sheet account Retained Earnings which is a part of owners' equity.

Despite the several balancing features of the worksheet, errors sometimes exist; that is, the balance features are not absolute proofs of accuracy. For example, in extending the amounts to the four remaining columns, one could enter an expense (a debit) under Balance Sheet instead of under the Income Statement (where it should be), and the worksheet would still balance; however, net income would be incorrect. Clearly, special care must be exercised in the extending process.[3]

PREPARING FINANCIAL STATEMENTS FROM THE WORKSHEET (PHASE 7)

The completed worksheet provides all of the amounts needed, in convenient form, to prepare the income statement, balance sheet, and statement of retained earnings. The statement of retained earnings, although not listed as a required statement, generally is prepared by corporations (see pages 62 and 70). It ties together the income statement and the stockholders' equity section of the balance sheet. For example, the Statement of Retained Earnings for High-Rise Apartments would be as follows:

---

[3] The number of amount columns on the worksheet can be minimized to five by (1) omitting the Adjusted Trial Balance caption and (2) using one column for the four remaining major captions (credits are indicated by parentheses).

HIGH-RISE APARTMENTS, INC.
Statement of Retained Earnings
For the Year Ended December 31, 1977

Retained earnings balance January 1, 1977	$23,760
Add net income for 1977	23,100
Total	46,860
Less dividends paid in 1977	12,000
Retained earnings balance, December 31, 1977	$34,860

The task of preparing the income statement and balance sheet is simply one of classifying the data provided by the worksheet. Since such statements were illustrated in Chapter 4, they will not be repeated here.

The worksheet described above does not provide data for the statement of changes in financial position. This statement requires special analytical procedures; as a consequence, a special worksheet must be used to develop it. The special worksheet will be discussed and illustrated in Chapter 15.

RECORDING ADJUSTING ENTRIES IN THE ACCOUNTING RECORDS (PHASE 8)

Next, the adjusting entries reflected on the completed worksheet are entered in the journal and then posted to the ledger. They are "dated" at the last day of the period. This is a clerical task since they are merely copied from the worksheet. The adjusting entries for High-Rise Apartments, showing a folio notation for posting completed, is illustrated in Exhibit 6–2. The ledger, with the adjusting entries posted (in gold to facilitate your identification) is shown in Exhibit 6–4. This phase is done to enter the economic effects of the adjusting entries into the accounting system.

CLOSING THE ACCOUNTS (PHASE 9)

In our study of the fundamental accounting model, we have emphasized that the **revenue** and **expense** accounts are subdivisions of retained earnings which is a part of **owners' equity.** The revenue and expense accounts are "income statement accounts," whereas the remainder of the accounts can be viewed as "balance sheet accounts." The revenue and expense accounts are often called **temporary** or **nominal** accounts in the sense that data are collected in them for the current accounting period only. At the end of each period their balances are transferred, or closed, to the Retained Earnings account. This periodic clearing out, dumping, or closing of their balances to retained earnings serves two purposes: (1) it transfers net income (or loss) to retained earnings (i.e., owners' equity) and (2) it establishes a zero balance in the revenue and expense

EXHIBIT 6–2
Adjusting entries

JOURNAL Page 6

Date 1977	Account Titles and Explanation	Folio	Debit	Credit
Dec. 31	Insurance expense	356	1,200	
	Prepaid insurance	103		1,200
31	Depreciation expense	360	10,000	
	Accumulated depreciation, building	113		10,000
31	Maintenance expenses	351	400	
	Inventory of maintenance supplies	104		400
31	Salary expense	352	600	
	Salaries payable	206		600
31	Property tax expense	361	4,700	
	Property taxes payable	207		4,700
31	Interest expense	353	400	
	Interest payable	209		400
31	Rent collected in advance	204	600	
	Rent revenue	340		600
31	Rent revenue receivable	102	400	
	Rent revenue	340		400
31	Income tax expense	370	9,900	
	Income taxes payable	208		9,900

accounts to start the new accounting period. In this way, the income statement accounts are ready to serve their periodic collection function for the next period.

In contrast, the balance sheet accounts (assets, liabilities, and owners' equity) are not closed; therefore, they are often called **permanent** or **real** accounts. The only time a permanent account has a zero balance is when the item represented (such as machinery or notes payable) is no longer owned or is fully depreciated. The balance at the end of the period in each balance sheet account is carried forward in the ledger as the beginning balance for the next period.

The clearing out, or closing, at the end of the accounting period of all revenue and expense accounts is simply a mechanical phase. To close an account means to transfer its balance to another designated account by means of an entry. For example, an account that has a credit balance (such as a revenue account) would be closed by *debiting* that account for an amount equal to its balance and crediting the account to which the balance is to be transferred. The closing entries are entered in the journal in the normal format and are immediately posted to the ledger.

A special clearing account called "Income Summary" often is used to facilitate the procedure. To illustrate the closing procedure, assume the following summarized data from the accounts of XYZ Corporation at December 31, 1977:

Stockholders' Equity Accounts

Capital stock, 5,000 shares, par $10	$ 50,000
Retained earnings beginning balance January 1, 1977	15,000
Total revenue earned during 1977	100,000
Total expenses incurred during 1977	80,000
Total dividends paid during 1977	10,000

The three closing entries required would be dated December 31, 1977, and would appear in the journal as follows:

a. Revenue	100,000	
Income summary		100,000
To close the Revenue account and transfer its balance to Income Summary.		
b. Income summary	80,000	
Expenses		80,000
To close the Expense account and transfer its balance to Income Summary.		
c. Income summary	20,000	
Retained earnings		20,000
To close the Income Summary account and transfer net income to Retained Earnings.		

After the closing entries are posted from the journal, the ledger accounts affected would appear as follows:

Capital Stock, Par $10

		Balance (5,000 shares)	50,000

Expenses

Balance	80,000	(*b*) Closing	80,000

Revenue

(*a*) Closing	100,000	Balance	100,000

Income Summary

(*b*) Expenses	80,000	(*a*) Revenue	100,000
(*c*) Closing	20,000		

Retained Earnings

Dividend paid	10,000	Balance	15,000
		(*c*) Net income	20,000

In this example, we used only one revenue and one expense account for illustrative purposes. Actually all revenue and expense accounts must be closed at the end of the period using the procedure illustrated above.

Now, let's return to High-Rise Apartments and apply the same closing mechanics. The closing entries are shown in Exhibit 6–3 as they would be entered in the journal; the posting notation (folio) to the ledger also is indicated. Observe that all of the revenue and expense accounts are closed and in the process their balances are transferred to retained earnings.

The ledger accounts with (1) the trial balance totals, (2) the adjusting entries posted (in gold), and (3) the closing entries posted (in black boxes) are shown in Exhibit 6–4 in T-account format. The colors and boxes are used to facilitate your study of the mechanics of each step. You should observe that all of the adjusting and closing amounts are verifiable directly on the completed worksheet (Exhibit 6–1).

There is one point that should be emphasized. The closing entry in the journal for expenses (and for revenues when there is more than one)

EXHIBIT 6–3
Closing entries for High-Rise Apartments

JOURNAL Page 7

Date 1977		Folio	Debit	Credit
Dec. 31	Rent revenue	340	129,463	
	Income summary	330		129,463
	To transfer revenues to Income Summary.			
31	Income summary ($96,463 + $9,900)	330	106,363	
	Advertising expense	350		500
	Maintenance expense	351		3,400
	Salary expense	352		18,000
	Interest expense	353		19,963
	Utilities expense	354		34,500
	Miscellaneous expenses	355		4,200
	Insurance expense	356		1,200
	Depreciation expense	360		10,000
	Property tax expense	361		4,700
	Income tax expense	370		9,900
	To transfer expense accounts to Income Summary.			
31	Income summary	330	23,100	
	Retained earnings	305		23,100
	To transfer net income to Retained Earnings.			

EXHIBIT 6–4

LEDGER

Cash 101

	2,297		

Rent Revenue Receivable 102

(6)	400		

Prepaid Insurance 103

	2,400	(6)	1,200

Inventory of Maintenance Supplies 104

	600	(6)	400

Land 110

	25,000		

Apartment Building 111

	360,000		

Accumulated Depreciation, Building 113

			10,000
		(6)	10,000

Notes Payable 201

			30,000

Rent Collected in Advance 204

(6)	600		1,200

Salaries Payable 206

		(6)	600

Property Taxes Payable 207

		(6)	4,700

Income Taxes Payable 208

		(6)	9,900

Interest Payable 209

		(6)	400

Mortgage Payable 251

			238,037

Capital Stock 301

			50,000

Retained Earnings 305

	12,000		23,760
		(7)	23,100

Income Summary 330

(7)	106,363	(7)	129,463
(7)	23,100		

Rent Revenue 340

(7)	129,463		128,463
		(6)	600
		(6)	400

Advertising Expense 350

	500	(7)	500

Maintenance Expense 351

	3,000	(7)	3,400
(6)	400		

Salary Expense 352

	17,400	(7)	18,000
(6)	600		

Interest Expense 353

	19,563	(7)	19,963
(6)	400		

Utilities Expense 354

	34,500	(7)	34,500

Miscellaneous Expenses 355

	4,200	(7)	4,200

Insurance Expense 356

(6)	1,200	(7)	1,200

Depreciation Expense 360

(6)	10,000	(7)	10,000

Property Tax Expense 361

(6)	4,700	(7)	4,700

Income Tax Expense 370

(6)	9,900	(7)	9,900

For illustrative purposes:

- Unadjusted balances are in black.
- Adjusting entries are in gold.
- Closing entries are enclosed in boxes.

is in a compound entry, which saves closing time and space (of course, a separate closing entry could be made for each separate expense account). Notice that the total debit to Income Summary in that entry is taken directly from the worksheet.

After the closing process is completed, observe that all of the nominal (i.e., the income statement) accounts are closed and are ready for reuse during the next accounting period for accumulating the revenues and expenses of that period. The Retained Earnings account now has an ending balance of $34,860 which will be reported on the December 31, 1977, balance sheet as a part of stockholders' equity.[4]

POST-CLOSING TRIAL BALANCE (PHASE 10)

Despite the guidance provided by the worksheet, occasional errors are made in the adjusting and closing mechanics. After the completion of these two phases, it is desirable to retest the equality of the ledger account balances. This is normally accomplished by using the computer or simply running an adding machine tape on the ledger—the debits are entered as plus and the credits as minus, and the resultant total should be zero. Instead, some individuals prefer to prepare another formal trial balance, called a post-closing trial balance, before starting the new period. Since all of the revenue and expense accounts have been closed to retained earnings, the post-closing trial balance will only reflect account balances for the assets, liabilities, and owners' equity. These balances will be identical with those as reflected in the last two columns of the worksheet, with the exception of the Retained Earnings account, which must be calculated as the net of the beginning balance plus net income minus dividends paid. Observe that the ending balances reflected in the ledger accounts, after the closing process, will be the beginning balance for the next period.

OVERVIEW

We cannot emphasize too strongly that the worksheet, the closing entries, and the post-closing trial balance steps are only mechanical data

[4] A common bookkeeping approach to "ruling a permanent T-account" with a carry-forward balance is as follows:

Retained Earnings 305

Dividends (1977)	12,000	Jan. 1, 1977, balance	23,760
Balance carried forward to 1978	34,860	Net income (1977)	23,100
	46,860		46,860
		Jan. 1, 1978, balance	34,860

processing procedures and do not involve any new accounting principles or measurement approaches.

The ten phases discussed above constitute the information-processing cycle repeated each accounting period in all accounting information systems. It is a processing model that captures the economic essence of all transactions at their point of incurrence and carries those effects to the end result—the periodic financial statements. Numerous adaptations of the procedures used to implement the cycle are to be found in the entity having different characteristics such as size, type of industry, complexity, and the sophistication of the management.

Implementation of the cycle and organization of the information-processing activities in a particular entity can be efficient, effective, and timely in terms of the outputs (the financial statements) or the opposite depending on the competence of those performing the data processing tasks and the importance attached by the management and owners to financial measurement of the operating results. In this context, the information-processing system of the entity is significant to all parties interested in the entity because the end results—the financial statements—are important.

PART TWO: REVERSING ENTRIES

After completion of Phase 10 of the information-processing cycle (i.e., the post-closing trial balance), an *optional phase* may be added as Phase 11 (see page 173). This final phase is known as "reversing entries." Reversing entries are dated at the beginning of the *next period* and relate *only* to certain adjusting entries made at the end of the immediate prior period. Certain adjusting entries may be reversed on the first day of the next period solely to simplify or facilitate the recording of a subsequent related entry. Unlike most of the phases in the information-processing cycle already discussed, reversing entries are strictly optional and involve only bookkeeping mechanics rather than accounting principles or concepts.

The reversing entry phase is presented because (1) it introduces a common data processing mechanism used in most companies, whether the system is manual, mechanical, or computerized; and (2) a knowledge of the circumstances under which it may be used gives some additional insight into certain relationships in the efficient processing of accounting information.[5]

Reversing entries are given this name because they reverse, at the start of the next accounting period, the effects of certain adjusting entries made at the end of the previous period. Reversing entries are always the

---

[5] Knowledge of reversing entries is of importance primarily to those students who plan to study accounting at the advanced level. This knowledge is not significant for study of the remaining chapters in this book.

EXHIBIT 6–5
Purpose of reversing entries illustrated

DAY COMPANY

a. *The preceding adjusting entry:*
The payroll was paid on December 28, 1977; the next payroll will be on January 13, 1978. At December 31, 1977, there were wages earned of $3,000 for the last three days of the year that had not been paid or recorded.

With reversing entry	*Without reversing entry*

December 31, 1977, adjusting entry to record the $3,000 accrued (unpaid) wages:

Wage expense.............. 3,000		Wage expense.............. 3,000		
Wages payable		Wages payable		
(a liability)	3,000	(a liability)...............	3,000	

b. *The closing entry:*
The revenue and expense accounts are closed to Income Summary after the adjusting entries are completed and posted to the ledger.

December 31, 1977, closing entry:

Income summary.......... 3,000		Income summary........... 3,000		
Wage expense	3,000	Wage expense........	3,000	

c. *The reversing entry:*
The information-processing cycle in 1977 is complete. All closing entries have been posted and the post-closing trial balance has been verified. At this point in time, January 1, 1978, the accountant should decide whether it is desirable to make any reversing entries to simplify the subsequent entries. Question: Would a reversing entry on January 1, 1978, simplify the entry to be made on January 13, 1978, when the wages are paid?

January 1, 1978, reversing entry:

Wages payable		No reversing entry to be made.
(a liability) 3,000		
Wage expense	3,000	

d. *The subsequent entry that was facilitated:*
The payroll of $25,000 was completed and paid on January 13, 1978. This subsequent payment entry is to be recorded. Question: Did the reversing entry simplify this entry?

January 13, 1978, payroll entry:

Wage expense 25,000		Wages payable 3,000		
Cash..................	25,000	Wage expense.......... 22,000		
		Cash..................	25,000	

Explanation—Observe that with the reversing entry having been made, this last entry required only one debit, contrasted with two debits when no reversing entry was made. This difference was due to the fact that the reversing entry served to (1) clear out the liability account "Wages Payable," and (2) set up a temporary *credit* in the Wage Expense account. After the last entry, to record the payment of the payroll, both accounts affected—Wage Expense and Wages Payable—are identical in balance under both approaches. If the reversing entry is not made, the company must go to the trouble of identifying how much of the $25,000 paid on January 13, 1978, was expense and how much of it was to pay the liability set up in the adjusting entry at the end of the prior period (*a* above).

opposite of the related adjusting entry. It may be desirable to "reverse" only certain adjusting entries; the other adjusting entries should not be reversed.

To illustrate reversing entries and the type of situation where a reversing entry will simplify the subsequent accounting entry, assume that Day Company is in the process of completing the information-processing cycle at the end of its accounting period, December 31, 1977. To place the reversing entry in context, Exhibit 6–5 presents a tabulation of a series of related entries that show (1) an adjusting entry on December 31, 1977; (2) the reversing entry that could be made on January 1, 1978; and (3) the subsequent entry on January 13, 1978, that was simplified. To demonstrate the facilitating effect of a reversing entry, we have presented entries in the tabulation reflecting the same situation without the reversing entry. You should study carefully the two sets of entries and the explanatory comments in Exhibit 6–5.

Another example is given of a situation where a reversing entry simplifies recording of a subsequent related entry. This example will illustrate both the journal entries and the related ledger accounts.

Situation: On September 1, 19A, Company X loaned $1,200 on a one-year, 10 percent, interest-bearing note. On August 31, 19B, the company will collect the $1,200 principal plus $120 interest revenue. The annual accounting period ends December 31.

The related journal entries, explanations, and ledger accounts are given on page 187. Study them carefully.

The facilitating feature is clear if we observe that without the reversing entry on January 1, 19B, the collection entry on August 31, 19B, would have to be:

Cash	1,320	
Note receivable		1,200
Interest receivable		40
Interest revenue		80

In the above discussion it was indicated that certain adjusting entries could be reversed to simplify subsequent entries and that certain adjusting entries would not be reversed. How does one decide the entries that may be reversed to advantage? There is no inflexible rule that can be provided. The accountant must analyze each situation and make a rational choice. In general it can be said that short-term accruals and deferrals are candidates for reversal.

The adjusting entry to record depreciation and entries of this type should never be reversed. In these situations the adjusting entry is not followed by a subsequent "payment" entry; therefore, it would be not only pointless to reverse it but would also introduce an error into the accounts because the accumulated depreciation account would reflect a zero balance throughout the period. Thus, most adjusting entries are

JOURNAL

a. September 1, 19A—To record the loan:

Note receivable	1,200	
Cash...............		1,200

b. December 31, 19A—Adjusting entry for four months' interest revenue accrued but not collected ($1,200 × 10% × 4/12 = $40):

Interest receivable...	40	
Interest revenue..........		40

c. December 31, 19A—To close interest revenue:

Interest revenue......	40	
Income summary.........		40

d. January 1, 19B—To reverse adjusting entry of December 31, 19A:

Interest revenue......	40	
Interest receivable		40

Observe that after this entry, the Interest Receivable account reflects a zero balance and Interest Revenue reflects a *debit* balance of $40 (four months interest).

e. August 31, 19B—Subsequent entry; to record collection of note plus interest for one year:

Cash.....................	1,320	
Note receivable		1,200
Interest revenue..........		120

Observe that after this entry the Note Receivable account has a zero balance and the Interest Revenue an $80 balance which represents eight months' interest revenue earned in 19B.

LEDGER

Cash

		x,xxx	(*a*)	9/1/19A	1,200
(*e*)	8/31/19B	1,320			

Note Receivable

(*a*)	9/1/19A	1,200	(*e*)	8/31/19B	1,200

Interest Receivable

(*b*)	12/31/19A	40	(*d*)	1/1/19B	40

Interest Revenue

(*c*)	12/31/19A	40	(*b*)	12/31/19A	40
(*d*)	1/1/19B	40	(*e*)	8/31/19B	120

Income Summary

			(*c*)	12/31/19A	40

not candidates for reversal, and those that are candidates are easily identified if one considers the nature of the subsequent related entry.

Perhaps the most compelling reason for reversing entries is to reduce the likelihood that the effects of certain adjusting entries will be overlooked when recording the next related transaction in the following period.

In this part of the discussion of reversing entries, we will refer to the illustrations in Chapter 5 for High-Rise Apartments. Reversal of adjusting entries (*b*) (page 147), (*f*) (page 150), and (*g*) (page 151) would simplify the subsequent entries related to them. The remaining entries for High-Rise would not be reversed.

To explain further the type of entry that may be reversed, we will analyze the facilitating feature in terms of a computerized system. Refer to entry (*f*) (page 150) for High-Rise. First, let's look at the adjusting entry that was made on December 31, 1977:

Salary expense	600	
Salaries payable		600
To record the salary expense and the liability for December salary not yet paid.		

On the date of payment, January 11, 1978, it would be correct to record payment of the salary as follows:

Salaries payable	600	
Cash		600

Let us assume, however, the accounts for High-Rise are maintained on a computer (a common situation) and that the computer is programmed to make the following entry **every time** a salary payment is made:

Salary expense	XXX	
Cash		XXX

Such a program is completely logical for all of the salary payments for the year; yet, the payment entry on January 11, 1978, as given above, debits Salaries Payable rather than Salary Expense. It may make little economic sense to write a special program for the once-a-year January payment entry and separate programs for the remaining 11 monthly payments during the year, or to manually interrupt the January computer run to make a "special" payment entry. This undesirable effect can be avoided by utilizing a reversing entry. A reversing-entry computer routine can be included in the end-of-the-period information-processing cycle. The reversing procedure can be included in the same group of computer runs as those to record the closing entries with no additional cost. The computer would be programmed to effect the following reversing entry as of the first day of the next period:

Salaries payable	600	
Salary expense		600

As demonstrated in Exhibit 6–5, the ledger accounts then would reflect appropriate balances for the continuation of the routine entry programmed to debit Salary Expense for all salary payments. Thus, adjusting entries should be reversed only in those situations where *an analysis* of the *subsequent entry* shows that the subsequent recording would be simplified and the clerical or computer costs reduced.

In contrast, let's examine a situation where reversals should not be made. Examine adjusting entry (*g*) (page 151) for Property Tax Expense for High-Rise Apartments on December 31, 1977; it was as follows:

Property tax expense	4,700	
Property taxes payable		4,700

When the payment is made on January 15, 1978, the payment entry would be:

Property taxes payable	4,700	
Cash		4,700

As property tax payments are made only once each year in most communities, the computer input would be written to debit Property Taxes Payable for the payment. Thus, future bookkeeping would not be simplified (nor the cost reduced) by using a reversing entry.

In summary, reversing entries are optional and are made for the sole purpose of simplifying subsequent related entries. When appropriate, they are the reverse of the related adjusting entry and are dated the first day of the following period. They represent a data processing mechanism and do not involve accounting principles or practice.

SUMMARY

Part One of the chapter focused on the accounting information cycle which must be accomplished in situations where periodic financial statements for both external and internal users are developed. The cycle captures raw economic data on transactions as they occur and processes the economic effects on the entity to the final effective communication by means of the periodic financial statements. The information system must be designed to accurately and effectively measure net income, financial position, and funds flow. An information system also must be designed to fit the characteristics of the entity.

Part Two discussed a data processing procedure called "reversing entries." They involve only bookkeeping mechanics rather than accounting principles and concepts. A reversing entry is used only when it will facilitate making a subsequent related entry in the accounts. They are made on the first day of the new period, and only selected adjusting entries are reversed.

IMPORTANT TERMS

Manual data processing
Mechanical data processing
Electronic data processing
Real or permanent accounts
Nominal or temporary accounts
Closing entries
Reversing entries

QUESTIONS FOR DISCUSSION

1. Basically, what is meant by an "accounting information system?"
2. Distinguish between manual, mechanical, and electronic data processing. Basically, how does each relate to accounting information processing?
3. Briefly identify, in sequence, the ten phases of the information-processing cycle.
4. Contrast transaction analysis with journalizing.
5. Compare the objectives of journalizing with posting.
6. Explain in what way posting reflects a change in classification of the data.
7. Contrast an unadjusted trial balance with an adjusted trial balance. What is the basic purpose of each?
8. What is the purpose of the worksheet?
9. Why are adjusting entries entered on the worksheet?
10. Why are adjusted entries entered in the journal and posted to the ledger even though they are entered on the worksheet?
11. What are the purposes of closing entries? Why are they entered in the journal and posted to the ledger?
12. Distinguish between (*a*) real, (*b*) nominal, (*c*) permanent, and (*d*) temporary accounts.
13. Explain why the income statement accounts are closed but the balance sheet accounts are not.
14. What is a post-closing trial balance? Is it a useful part of the information processing cycle?
15. What are reversing entries? When are they useful? Give an example of an adjusting entry that (*a*) should be reversed and (*b*) that should not be reversed.

EXERCISES

PART ONE: EXERCISES 6-1 TO 6-6

E6-1. Prepare a chart that reflects the ten sequential steps in the information-processing cycle and that relates the steps to an annual accounting period starting with January 1, 19A. Assume you plan to use the chart as a visual aid in explaining the overall cycle. Be prepared for a brief explanation of the topic should your professor call on you. Use a form similar to the following:

Steps	*Brief description*	*Time frame*
1. Raw economic data	Collect source documents	January 1, 19A

E6-2. Assume that the worksheet at December 31, 19B, for Toby Realty Corporation has been completed through "Adjusted Trial Balance" and you are ready to extend each amount to the several columns to the right. These columns that will be used are listed below with code letters:

Code	*Columns*
a	Income statement, debit
b	Income statement, credit
c	Balance sheet, debit
d	Balance sheet, credit

Below are listed representative accounts to be extended on the worksheet. You are to give, for each account, the code letter that indicates the proper worksheet column to the right of "Adjusted Trial Balance" to which the amount in each account should be extended.

Account Titles	*Code*
Cash	
Inventory of office supplies	
Interest payable	
Capital stock	
Commissions earned	
Rent revenue collected in advance	
Salary expense	
Return sales	
Retained earnings	
Building	
Mortgage payable	
Income taxes payable	
Sales commissions receivable	
Accumulated depreciation on building	
Contributed capital in excess of par	

Account Titles	*Code*
Unearned (prepaid) sales commissions	
Income tax expense	
Net income:	
Code number for the debit	
Code number for the credit	
Net loss:	
Code number for the debit	
Code number for the credit	

E6–3. Dacy Corporation, a small company, is completing the information-processing cycle for 19B. The worksheet, as reflected below, has been started. Note that the number of columns has been reduced to five by using single columns (a common practice).

Account Titles	Unadjusted Trial Balance (credits)	Adjusting Entries Debit	Adjusting Entries Credit	Income Statement (credits)	Balance Sheet (credits)
Cash	10,000				
Accounts receivable	15,000				
Equipment	20,000				
Accumulated depreciation	(6,000)				
Other assets	54,500				
Accounts payable	(9,000)				
Income taxes payable					
Long-term note payable	(15,000)				
Capital stock, par $10	(30,000)				
Contributed capital in excess of par	(1,500)				
Retained earnings	(18,000)				
Revenues	(70,000)				
Expenses	50,000				
Income tax expense					
Net income					
	-0-				

Data not yet recorded:

a. Depreciation for 19B, $2,000.

b. Income tax rate, 30 percent.

Required:

Complete the worksheet in every respect.

E6–4. Z Corporation has just completed the following worksheet for the year ended December 31, 19D:

Account Titles	Unadjusted Trial Balance (credits)	Adjusting Entries Debit	Adjusting Entries Credit	Income Statement (credits)	Balance Sheet (credits)
Cash	15,000				15,000
Prepaid insurance	300		100		200
Accounts receivable	20,000				20,000
Machinery	80,000				80,000
Accumulated depreciation	(24,000)		8,000		(32,000)
Other assets	13,700				13,700
Accounts payable	(7,000)				(7,000)
Rent collected in advance			200		(200)
Interest payable			450		(450)
Income taxes payable			3,375		(3,375)
Notes payable, long term	(10,000)				(10,000)
Capital stock, par $10	(50,000)				(50,000)
Retained earnings	(18,000)				(18,000)
Revenues	(80,000)	200		(79,800)	
Expenses (not detailed)	60,000	100		60,100	
Depreciation expense		8,000		8,000	
Interest expense		450		450	
Income tax expense		3,375		3,375	
Net income				7,875	(7,875)
Totals	-0-	12,125	12,125	-0-	-0-

Required:

a. Prepare the adjusting entries in journal form for December 31, 19D. Write a brief explanation with each entry.

b. Prepare the closing entries for December 31, 19D.

E6–5. All-Purpose Service Company is in the process of completing the information-processing cycle at the end of the fiscal year, December 31, 19B. The worksheet and financial statements have been prepared, and the next step is journalization of the adjusting entries. The two trial balances given below were taken directly from the completed worksheet.

Account Titles	December 31, 19B Unadjusted Trial Balance Debit	Credit	Adjusted Trial Balance Debit	Credit
a. Cash	$ 8,000		$ 8,000	
b. Accounts receivable			700	
c. Prepaid insurance	300		250	
d. Equipment	120,200		120,200	
e. Accumulated depreciation, equipment		$ 21,500		$ 25,500
f. Income taxes payable				4,000
g. Capital stock, par $10		50,000		50,000
h. Retained earnings, January 1, 19B		14,000		14,000
i. Service revenues		60,000		60,700
j. Salary expense	17,000		17,000	
k. Depreciation expense			4,000	
l. Insurance expense			50	
m. Income tax expense			4,000	
	$145,500	$145,500	$154,200	$154,200

Required:

By examining the amounts in each trial balance, reconstruct the four adjusting entries that were made between the unadjusted trial balance and the adjusted trial balance. Give a brief explanation of the reason the adjusting entry was made.

PART TWO: EXERCISES 6–6 TO 6–9

E6–6. This exercise has three cases that relate to the closing procedure. Case A deals with a sole proprietorship; Case B, with a partnership; and Case C, with a corporation.

Case A – Smith Cleaners (sole proprietorship) accounts reflected the following on December 31, 1977, end of the fiscal year: capital, $15,000; withdrawals, $8,000; revenues, $40,000; and expenses, $29,000.

Case B – Bob and Ray (partnership) accounts reflected the following on December 31, 1977, end of the fiscal year: capital, Bob, $14,000; capital, Ray, $15,000; withdrawals, Bob, $9,000; withdrawals, Ray, $10,000; revenues, $68,000; and expenses, $50,000. Profits are divided equally.

Case C – Stein Corporation accounts reflected the following on December 31, 1977, end of the fiscal year: capital stock, $100,000; contributed capital in excess of par, $10,000; retained earnings, January 1, 1977, $43,000; cash dividends paid (during 1977), $25,000; revenues, $160,000; and expenses, $130,000 (income taxes already deducted).

Required:

1. For each separate case, enter the above amounts in the following accounts:

Sole proprietorship	*Partnership*	*Corporation*
Capital, Smith	Capital, Bob	Capital stock
Withdrawals, Smith	Withdrawals, Bob	Contributed capital in excess of par
Income summary	Capital, Ray	Retained earnings
Revenues	Withdrawals, Ray	Dividends paid*
Expenses	Income summary	Income summary
	Revenues	Revenues
	Expenses	Expenses

* Close to retained earnings.

Next enter the closing entries in the accounts for each case. Key the closing entries with letters as (*a*), (*b*), and so on. (Hint: After the closing entries for a sole proprietorship and a partnership only the assets, liabilities, and individual capital accounts have balances.)

2. Prepare the owners' equity section of the balance sheet for each separate case. Show how you think the various items in owners' equity should be reported to meet the full-disclosure principle.

E6–7. B Company has completed the information-processing cycle for the year ended December 31, 19A. Reversing entries are now under consideration (for January 1, 19B) for two different accounts. For case purposes, the relevant data are given in T-accounts, viz:

Prepaid Insurance

1/1/19A Balance	600	(*a*) 12/31/19A Adj. entry	400

Insurance Expense

(*a*) 12/31/19A Adj. entry	400	(*c*) 12/31/19A Closing entry	400

Accrued Wages Payable

		(*b*) 12/31/19A Adj. entry	1,000

Wage Expense

Paid during 19A	18,000	(*d*) 12/31/19A Closing entry	19,000
(*b*) 12/31/19A Adj. entry	1,000		

Income Summary

12/31/19A		12/31/19A	
(*c*)	400	Closed to Retained	
(*d*)	19,000	Earnings	19,400

Required:

Would a reversing entry on January 1, 19B, facilitate the next related entry for (*a*) Prepaid Insurance and (*b*) Accrued Wages Payable? Explain why.

E6–8. On August 1, 19A, W Corporation borrowed $20,000 on a one-year, 9 percent, interest-bearing note. The principal plus interest is payable on July 31, 19B. The accounting period ends December 31.

Required:

1. Give the following entries in journal form with respect to the note:
   a. August 1, 19A—to record the loan.
   b. December 31, 19A—to record the adjusting entry.
   c. January 1, 19B—to record the reversing entry.
   d. July 31, 19B—to record payment of the principal plus interest.
2. Give the entry for July 31, 19B, assuming no reversing entry was made on January 1, 19B.
3. Do you prefer to use the reversing entry in this situation? Explain why.

E6–9. Dikins Corporation is completing the information-processing cycle at December 31, 1977. The adjusting entries have been made and posted to the ledger. Following that phase, the closing entries also were entered in the journal and posted to the ledger. The post-closing trial balance has been verified as to be correct.

This case focuses on two of the adjusting entries that were made at December 31, 1977. They were:

a. Rent revenue amounting to $10,000 was collected on December 15, 1977. The amount collected was for the period December 15, 1977, to January 14, 1978. At the date of collection they were processed through the computer, which was programmed to make the following entry for rent revenue:

Cash	10,000	
Rent revenue		10,000

b. Depreciation expense of office equipment for the year was $8,000.

Required:

1. Give the adjusting entry for each of the above items on December 31, 1977.
2. Give the closing entry for each item.

3. Give the reversing entry that could be made on January 1, 1978, to simplify the subsequent entry. If no reversing entry is advantageous, explain why not.
4. Give the next entry (*a*) for the monthly collection of rent again from these tenants on January 15, 1978, amounting to $10,000; and (*b*) the next adjusting entry for $8,000 depreciation at the end of 1978.

PROBLEMS

PART ONE: PROBLEMS 6–1 TO 6–6

P6–1. J Corporation has partially completed the following worksheet for the year ended December 31, 19E:

Account Titles	Unadjusted Trial Balance (credits)	Adjusting Entries		Income Statement (credits)	Balance Sheet (credits)
		Debit	Credit		
Cash	18,570				
Accounts receivable	18,000				
Supplies inventory	180		(*a*) 110		
Interest receivable		(*b*) 80			
Long-term note receivable, 8%	6,000				
Equipment	75,000				
Accumulated depreciation	(30,000)		(*c*) 7,500		
Accounts payable	(11,000)				
Short-term notes payable, 9%	(8,000)				
Interest payable			(*d*) 120		
Income taxes payable			(*e*) 363		
Capital stock, par $10	(40,000)				
Contributed capital in excess of par	(2,000)				
Retained earnings	(7,000)				
Service revenue	(60,000)				
Interest revenue	(400)		(*b*) 80		
Expenses (not detailed)	40,050	(*a*) 110			
Depreciation expense		(*c*) 7,500			
Interest expense	600	(*d*) 120			
Income tax expense		(*e*) 363			
Totals	-0-	8,173	8,173		

Required:

1. Complete the above worksheet.
2. Prepare a single-step income statement and unclassified balance sheet.
3. Give the adjusting and closing entries in general form.
4. Explain why the adjusting and closing entries must be journalized and posted.

P6–2. You are to complete the following worksheet by (*a*) entering the adjusting entries (key these (*a*), (*b*), (*c*), etc.) and (*b*) extending appropriate amounts to the income statement column.

Account Titles	Unadjusted Trial Balance (credits)	Adjusting Entries Debit	Adjusting Entries Credit	Income Statement (credits)	Balance Sheet (credits)
Cash	30,380				30,380
Prepaid insurance	80				60
Interest receivable					300
Long-term note receivable, 9%	10,000				10,000
Machinery	70,000				70,000
Accumulated depreciation	(21,000)				(28,000)
Long-term note payable, 8%	(9,000)				(9,000)
Rent revenue collected in advance					(120)
Interest payable					(180)
Income taxes payable					(5,232)
Capital stock	(40,000)				(40,000)
Retained earnings	(16,000)				(16,000)
Revenues	(85,000)				
Expenses	60,000				
Depreciation expense					
Interest expense	540				
Income tax expense					
Net income					(12,208)
Totals	-0-				-0-

P6–3. BK Corporation is completing the information processing cycle for the year ended December 31, 19C. The unadjusted trial balance, taken from the ledger, was as follows:

Account No.	Account Titles	Unadjusted Trial Balance Debit	Unadjusted Trial Balance Credit
101	Cash	$ 43,650	
103	Accounts receivable (net)	17,000	
105	Prepaid insurance	450	
107	Interest receivable		
120	Long-term note receivable, 10%	6,000	
150	Equipment	90,000	
151	Accumulated depreciation		$ 20,000
170	Other assets	30,000	
201	Accounts payable		14,000
203	Wages payable		
205	Interest payable		
207	Income taxes payable		
210	Long-term note payable, 9%		10,000
300	Capital stock, par $10		80,000
301	Contributed capital in excess of par		12,000
310	Retained earnings (Balance January 1, 19C, $24,000; less cash dividends paid during 19C, $8,000)		16,000
320	Service revenue		150,000
322	Interest revenue		400
350	Expenses (not detailed)	115,000	
351	Depreciation expense		
360	Interest expense	300	
370	Income tax expense		
		$302,400	$302,400

Additional data for adjusting entries:

a. Unexpired insurance at December 31, 19C, was $150.

b. Interest on the long-term note receivable (dated September 1) is collected annually each August 30.

c. The equipment was acquired on January 1, 19A (assume no estimated residual value).

d. At December 31, 19C, wages earned but not yet paid or recorded amounted to $1,000.

e. Interest on the long-term note payable (dated May 1) is paid annually each April 30.

f. Assume a 40 percent average income tax rate.

Required:

1. Complete a worksheet for the year ended December 31, 19C. Key the adjusting entries with letters. (Hint: Net income is $14,040.)
2. Prepare a single-step income statement, a statement of retained earnings, and a balance sheet.
3. Write a brief explanation of each adjusting entry reflected on the worksheet.
4. Give the closing entries in journal form. Explain why they must be journalized and posted to the ledger.

P6–4. (Note: This is a longer case selected to review Chapters 3, 4, 5, and 6.)

R&S Service Company was organized as a corporation three years ago by three individuals. During the first two years, practically no records were kept. In June 1977 they employed on a part-time basis a college student who was majoring in accounting "to get an accounting system going." With the advice of an accounting professor, the student has been able to establish a simple, yet efficient, system that will provide monthly financial statements for internal purposes and financial statements for the stockholders at the end of each year. The shortened list of accounts (and simplified amounts) used in this case are representative of operations for 1977. The first set of financial statements will be prepared for the year ended December 31, 1977. The student has worked diligently to gather the raw data for the year and to record it in the newly designed information-processing system.

This case starts with the worksheet, which has been completed through the columns headed "Adjusted Trial Balance, December 31, 1977." However, income taxes have not been recorded; assume a 30 percent average tax rate. You are to start there and complete the requirements listed below. The Adjusted Trial Balance on the worksheet follows:

Debit		*Credit*	
Cash	$ 28,700	Accumulated depreciation	$ 4,500
Accounts receivable	6,000	Accounts payable	1,900
Supplies inventory	1,200	Income taxes payable	
Prepaid insurance	800	Precollected service fees	100
Land (future building site)	20,000	Interest payable	200
Equipment	25,000	Note payable, long term	10,000
Salary expense	30,000	Capital stock, par $10	30,000
Rent expense	4,800	Retained earnings	2,000
Insurance expense	500	Service fees earned	73,000
Advertising expense	1,400		
Utilities expense	900		
Depreciation expense	1,500		
Interest expense	800		
Income tax expense			
Miscellaneous expenses	100		
	$121,700		$121,700

Required:

a. Set up a worksheet starting with "Adjusted Trial Balance" as given above and complete the worksheet in every respect.

b. Prepare an unclassified income statement, statement of retained earnings, and balance sheet based upon the worksheet.

c. Based upon the worksheet, prepare the closing entries in journal form. Date and provide a brief explanation for each entry.

d. Prepare a post-closing trial balance.

P6–5. (Note: This is an extended case selected to review Chapters 3, 4, 5, and 6.)

W&P Moving and Storage Service, Incorporated, has been in operation for several years. Revenues have gradually increased from both the moving and storage services. The *annual* financial statement is inadequate for management needs. Therefore, during 1977, the current year, the president decided to have the accounting system improved so that it will provide *monthly* income, balance sheet, and cash-flow statements for internal purposes. The first step was to employ a full-time bookkeeper, and they called upon a local CPA firm for assistance. It is now December 31, 1977, the end of the current fiscal year. The bookkeeper has developed a trial balance. A member of the staff of the CPA firm will advise and assist the bookkeeper in completing the information processing cycle for the first year. The unadjusted trial balance at December 31, 1977, follows:

Debit		*Credit*	
Cash	$ 25,850	Accumulated depreciation	$ 18,000
Accounts receivable	2,030	Accounts payable	6,000
Office supplies inventory	150	Wages payable	
Prepaid insurance	600	Interest payable	
Land for future building site	6,000	Precollected storage fees	
Equipment	68,000	Income taxes payable	
Other assets (not detailed)	27,000	Note payable	30,000
Salary expense	74,000	Capital stock, par $10	20,000
Advertising expense	1,000	Retained earnings, January 1, 1977	18,600
Utilities expense	1,300	Hauling fees	106,400
Maintenance expense	6,500	Storage fees	14,000
Miscellaneous expenses	570		
Insurance expense			
Wage expense			
Depreciation expense			
Interest expense			
Income tax expense			
	$213,000		$213,000

Examination of the records and related documents provided the following additional information that should be considered for adjusting entries:

a. A physical count of office supplies inventory at December 31, 1977, reflected $40 on hand. Office supplies used are considered to be a miscellaneous expense. No office supplies were purchased during the year.

b. On July 1, 1977, a two-year insurance premium was paid amounting to $600.

c. The equipment cost $68,000 when acquired. It is estimated to have a ten-year useful life to the company and an $8,000 residual value.

d. Unpaid and unrecorded wages at December 31, 1977, amounted to $1,200.

e. The $30,000 note payable was signed on October 1, 1977, for an 8 percent bank loan, principal and interest due at the end of 12 months from that date.

f. Storage fees collected and recorded as earned before December 31, 1977, included $400 collected in advance from one customer for storage time in 1978. (Hint: This $400 should be regarded as Precollected Storage Fees.)

g. Gasoline, oil, and fuel purchased for the vehicles and used during the last two weeks of December 1977 amounting to $300 have not been paid for nor recorded.

h. The average income tax rate is 30 percent.

Required:

1. Enter the unadjusted trial balance on a worksheet; then, based on the above data, enter the adjusting entries. Complete the worksheet. (Hint: EPS is $9.89.)
2. Using the worksheet, prepare a single-step income statement, statement of retained earnings, and balance sheet. (Hint: The balance sheet total is $105,370.)
3. Using the worksheet, enter the adjusting entries in the journal.
4. Using the worksheet, prepare closing entries in journal form.
5. Prepare a post-closing trial balance.

P6–6. (Note: This is an extended case selected to review Chapters 3, 4, 5, and 6.)

Charter Air Service, Incorporated, was organized to operate a charter service in a city of approximately 350,000 population. The ten organizers were issued 7,500 shares of $10 par-value stock for a total of $75,000 cash. The company rents hangar and office space at the airport for a flat monthly rental. The business has prospered because of the excellent service and the high level of maintenance on the planes. It is now December 31, 1977, end of the annual fiscal period, and the information-processing cycle is in the final phases. Following are representative accounts and unadjusted amounts selected from the ledger at December 31, 1977, for problem purposes:

Debit		*Credit*	
Cash	$ 14,600	Accumulated depreciation, aircraft	$ 60,000
Prepaid insurance	6,000	Notes payable, long term	90,000
Maintenance parts inventory	18,000	Capital stock, par $10	75,000
Aircraft	260,000	Retained earnings, January 1, (balance January 1, 1977, $20,600; less dividends paid during 1977, $15,000)	5,600
Salary expense	90,000	Charter revenue	262,400
Maintenance expense	24,000		
Fuel expense	63,000		
Advertising expense	2,000		
Utilities expense	1,400		
Rent expense	14,000		
	$493,000		$493,000

For the adjusting entries, the following additional data were developed from the records and supporting documents:

a. On January 1, 1977, the company paid a three-year insurance premium amounting to $6,000.
b. The aircraft, when purchased on January 1, 1974, cost $260,000; and it is estimated that the useful life to the company is approximately ten years. At that time the equipment will have an estimated residual value of $60,000.
c. On March 1, 1977, the company borrowed $90,000 from the bank on a five-year, 8 percent loan. Interest is payable annually starting on March 1, 1978.
d. Charter revenue, on occasion, is collected in advance. On December 31, 1977, collections in advance amounted to $1,000; when collected this amount was recorded as charter revenue.
e. Rent amounting to $14,000 on hangar and office space was paid during the year and recorded as Rent Expense. This included rent paid in advance amounting to $2,000 for January and February 1978. The total amount was recorded as Rent Expense in 1977.
f. The inventory of maintenance parts on December 31, 1977, showed $7,000. All parts purchased are debited to Maintenance Parts Inventory when purchased.
g. For case purposes, assume an average income tax rate of 30 percent.

Required:

1. Enter the above accounts and unadjusted balances from the ledger on a worksheet. (The following accounts should be added to the worksheet since they will be needed for the adjusting entries: Insurance Expense, Depreciation Expense, Interest Expense, Interest Payable, Precollected Charter Revenue, Prepaid Rent Expense, Income Tax Expense, and Income Taxes Payable.)
2. Based on the additional data given above, enter the adjusting entries on the worksheet.
3. Complete the worksheet. (Hint: Net income is $21,000.)
4. Based on the worksheet, prepare a single-step income statement, a statement of retained earnings, and a classified balance sheet. (Hint: The total on the balance sheet is $207,600.)
5. Journalize the adjusting entries.
6. Journalize the closing entries.

PART TWO: PROBLEMS 6–7 TO 6–9

P6–7. Brookshire Manufacturing Company operates two separate plants that manufacture specialty tools sold through hardware outlet channels. Their line of tools appeals to mechanics, machinists, and general repair specialists. One of their most popular small tools has been their "nut cracker," a tool designed to cut the nuts off of corroded bolts without damaging the bolt and other parts when disassembling machinery. The company has a large number of individuals on hourly pay; and as a consequence, a payroll is prepared each week for payment on Friday. At the end of each accounting period, there is a significant amount of wages earned but not yet paid. This is due to the fact that the accounting period ends on the last day of the period, which is seldom on Friday. Accordingly, an adjusting entry must be made at the end of each period for the wages earned (accrued) but not yet paid. The adjusting entry at the end of the last period was:

December 31, 1977:

Wage expense	29,000	
Wages payable		29,000

To record wages earned in 1977 but not yet paid.

The next Friday, in this particular case, was on January 3, 1978; accordingly, the following "regular payroll" entry was made for January 3, 1978:

Wages payable	29,000	
Wage expense (1978)	47,000	
Cash		76,000

To record weekly payroll, including unpaid wages carried over from 1977 (Monday and Tuesday).

The bookkeeper has presented you with a problem in respect to these two entries. "When I go to make the payroll entry, there is a tremendous amount of time spent and inconvenience in keeping up with the amount of the cash disbursement that must be matched with the debit to Wages Payable ($29,000 in this instance). Is there some way that we can simplify the procedure to make it less inconvenient?" Your immediate response is: "Sure, it's very simple; just back out the adjusting entry. Here is how it is done!"

Required:

Illustrate and explain "how it is done" using the above situation.

P6–8. Starnes Corporation has completed all information processing including the annual financial statements at December 31, 19D. The adjusting entries recorded at that date were as follows:

a. Insurance expense	150	
Prepaid insurance		150
b. Interest receivable	200	
Interest revenue		200
c. Supplies expense	80	
Supplies inventory		80
d. Depreciation expense	2,000	
Accumulated depreciation		2,000
e. Wage expense	500	
Accrued wages payable		500
f. Interest expense	300	
Interest payable		300
g. Income tax expense	4,000	
Income taxes payable		4,000

Required:

For each of the above adjusting entries, indicate whether it would normally be reversed. Give the reversing entry (if none, so state) and explain the basis for your response.

P6–9. BV Corporation was organized in January 19A. The annual accounting period ends December 31. The following transactions occurred during 19C:

1. January 1 – BV Corporation purchased a special machine at a cash cost of $24,000. The estimated useful life is three years and no residual value.
2. September 1 – BV Corporation borrowed $12,000 on a two-year, 10 percent, interest-bearing note dated September 1, 19C. Interest is payable on August 31, 19D, and 19E; the principal is payable on August 31, 19E.
3. September 1 – BV Corporation paid a $480 two-year insurance premium on equipment used in operations.

Required:

Give entries, in journal form, on the following dates:

a. January 1, 19C, and September 1, 19C – to record each of the three transactions and provide an explanation for each entry.

b. December 31, 19C – to record the required adjusting entry for each item at the end of the accounting period; include an explanation for each adjusting entry. If no adjusting entry is required, so state and explain why.

c. January 1, 19D – to record an appropriate reversing entry for each item. If no reversing entry is appropriate, so state. Explain the basis for your treatment of each item.

d. August 31, 19D – to record payment of the annual interest on the loan including an explanation.

e. December 31, 19D – to record the required adjusting entry for each item including an explanation.

7

Accounting for sales revenue and measurement of revenue deductions

PURPOSE OF THE CHAPTER

The dominant features of many business entities are the purchasing and selling functions, whether the business is a retail, wholesale, or manufacturing entity. Decision makers that use financial reports focus considerable attention on the marketing successes and failures of a business. Retail or wholesale merchandising businesses devote much of their energies to buying and selling goods. Practically all manufacturing businesses also devote significant efforts and resources to purchasing and selling activities. Generally, a manufacturing business purchases raw materials for conversion into finished products, which then are sold. It is not uncommon for a service business also to sell some merchandise. For example, a retail appliance store frequently includes a combined sales-and-service-type operation.

Although the discussions and illustrations in the preceding chapters relating to the measurement of resources, liabilities, and net income are as appropriate for merchandising and manufacturing enterprises as for service businesses, for instructional reasons they were limited primarily to service businesses. This chapter will focus on the measurement and reporting problems for the selling and purchasing functions irrespective of the type of business. It will not consider manufacturing activities. That topic is discussed in *Fundamentals of Management Accounting.*

PART ONE: ACCOUNTING FOR SALES REVENUE

This part focuses on the accounting for sales revenue. Marketing activities have two aspects the accountant must consider in measuring net income. One aspect is revenue, and the other is expenses directly related to revenue generation. The revenue aspect requires careful measurement of economic effects of each sale of goods and services in accordance with the **revenue principle.** On the expense side, under the **matching principle,** the cost of the merchandise sold and the selling and administrative expenses incurred in making those sales must be measured and reported in the same period in which the revenue was realized. The cost of the merchandise sold is an expense usually called **cost of goods sold** on the income statement, and on the multiple-step format it is reported immediately after the sales revenue amount.[1] Selling or distribution expenses are reported on the multiple-step income statement as a subclassification of operating expenses.[2] Exhibit 7–1 is presented to

EXHIBIT 7–1

CAMPUS CORNER, INCORPORATED
Income Statement (Multiple-Step Format)
For the Year Ended December 31, 1977

Gross sales		$808,000
Less: Sales returns		8,000
Net sales		800,000
Cost of goods sold:*		
Beginning inventory of merchandise, January 1, 1977	$ 40,000	
Purchases of merchandise during 1977†	515,000	
Goods available for sale	555,000	
Less: Ending inventory of merchandise, December 31, 1977	35,000	
Cost of goods sold		520,000
Gross margin on sales		280,000
Operating expenses:		
Selling expenses	110,000	
Administrative expenses	90,000	
Income tax expense‡	31,900	231,900
Net Income		$ 48,100
Earnings per share ($48,100 ÷ 10,000 shares)		$ 4.81

* This illustration assumes a periodic inventory system (see page 218).
† In a manufacturing company this is called "Cost of goods manufactured."
‡ Often reported after pretax income; see pages 34 and 57.

---

[1] Some accountants prefer the designation "Cost of sales."

[2] In this chapter, to simplify the illustrations, we shall not ordinarily show the detailed operating expenses. In the single-step format for the income statement, revenues would be reported as above under a major caption "Revenues." However, all expenses, including cost of goods sold, would be reported under a major caption "Expenses." Therefore, in the single-step format, gross margin on sales is not reported.

emphasize the purchasing and selling activities of a typical small business. Observe the detail in respect to sales revenue and cost of goods sold. Compare this income statement with one for a service type of business such as Exhibit 2–2, page 32. There are two primary differences: (1) revenue is represented by an amount for sales rather than by service fees, and (2) inclusion of an additional expense captioned **"Cost of goods sold."** This feature makes it feasible to utilize a "step," or difference, called **"Gross margin on sales"** (or simply **gross margin**).[3] This amount is the difference between **net sales** and cost of goods sold. It shows the average markup **above cost** realized on the goods sold during the period. The relationship between gross margin and net sales is called the **gross margin ratio** or percent. To illustrate, for Campus Corner, Inc., the gross margin ratio is $280,000 ÷ $800,000 = 0.35. From this it can be said that for each $1 of net sales the gross margin is $0.35.

On published financial statements the net sales amount, without the revenue details shown on Exhibit 7–1, normally is reported. However, there is a trend to reporting sales revenue by major product lines because this information is considered particularly useful information for external decision makers.

REPORTING AND ACCOUNTING FOR REVENUES FROM SALES

Exhibit 7–1 reports gross sales revenue less sales returns and sales allowances. In accordance with **revenue principle,** a sale generally is considered to be realized and, therefore, recorded as revenue in the accounts when ownership of the goods passes from the seller to the buyer, regardless of when the cash is collected. Thus, under the revenue principle, sales would be recorded as follows:

a. Cash sales for the day per cash register totals:

Jan. 15	Cash	12,760	
	Sales (or sales revenue)		12,760

b. Credit sales for the day per charge tickets:

Jan. 15	Accounts receivable	4,120	
	Sales (or sales revenue)		4,120

Alternatively, if it is desired to maintain a separate sales account in the ledger for the sales by each department, entry (*a*), for example, could be as follows:[4]

Jan. 15	Cash	12,760	
	Sales, Department 1		4,120
	Sales, Department 2		7,890
	Sales, Department 3		750

[3] Occasionally the obsolete designation "Gross profit on sales" is used.

[4] See Appendix A to this chapter for an applicable data processing procedure.

Sales returns and allowances. Many businesses permit a customer to return unsatisfactory or damaged merchandise and receive a cash or credit refund. In some cases, rather than taking back such merchandise, a cash or credit adjustment may be given to the customer. To correctly measure sales revenue, such transactions must be recorded, whether or not the goods are returned. Although the Sales account could be debited (i.e., reduced) in recording these reductions in sales, for management control purposes (that is, so that management will be informed of the volume of returns and allowances), a separate account entitled "Sales Returns and Allowances" often is used. This account is always viewed as a deduction from **gross sales revenue** since it is a contra revenue account. To illustrate, assume a customer returned unsatisfactory merchandise that was sold for $25; the entry to record the return would be:[5]

Jan. 18	Sales returns and allowances	25	
	Cash (or Accounts receivable, if applied to the customers' account)		25

See later section for perpetual inventory system.

Sales discounts. A substantial portion of the sales made by some businesses are on credit. When merchandise is sold on credit, the terms of payment should be definite so there will be no misunderstanding as to the amounts and due dates. In fact, credit terms usually are printed on each credit document. Frequently, credit terms are abbreviated by symbols such as, "n/10, EOM," which means the net amount (i.e., the sales amount less any sales returns) with no discount is due not later than ten days after the end of the month (EOM) in which the sale was made. In other cases the terms may be "n/30," which means that the net amount is due 30 days after the date of the invoice (i.e., after date of sale). In still other cases, **sales discounts** (often called cash discounts) are granted to the purchaser for early payment. For example, the credit terms may be "2/10, n/30," which means that if payment is made within 10 days from the date of sale, the customer (debtor) may deduct 2 percent from the invoice price; however, if not paid within the 10-day discount period, the full sales price (less any returns) is due in 30 days from date of sale.

When a cash discount is granted, a customer is motivated to pay within the discount period because by doing so the savings are substantial. For example, with terms 2/10, n/30, 2 percent is saved by paying 20 days early, which equates to approximately 36 percent annual interest. As a consequence, the usual case is that credit customers take advantage of the sales discount. A favorable economic effect may result even when cash must be borrowed so that the cash discount can be taken.

---

[5] If the goods were returned in the year following the year of sale, the matching principle would be violated; however, no special accounting is undertaken since the amount generally is not material.

In accounting for sales discounts, the normal situation should govern the accounting procedure. The revenue principle holds that sales revenue is measured by the cash or cash equivalent received (or to be received) for the sales of goods. Since the sales discount will almost always be taken, to properly measure revenue the Sales Revenue account should be credited (i.e., increased) for the cash that will probably be received rather than for the gross sales amount. To illustrate, assume a sale is made for $1,000 with terms 2/10, n/30. The sequence of entries would be as follows:[6]

a. January 18, date of sale on credit:

Accounts receivable	980	
Sales revenue		980

Terms: 2/10, n/30 ($1,000 × 0.98 = $980).

b. January 27, date of collection (within the discount period):

Cash	980	
Accounts receivable		980

Alternatively, assuming the collection is after the discount period, entry *b* would be:

January 31, date of collection (after the discount period):

Cash	1,000	
Sales discount revenue*		20
Accounts receivable		980

* Interest revenue sometimes is used since conceptually it is in the nature of interest earned.

Cash discounts should be distinguished from **trade discounts.** A cash discount is a price concession given to encourage early payment of an account. A trade discount is a device sometimes used by vendors for quoting sales prices; the amount *after* the trade discount is the sales price. For example, an item may be quoted at $10 per unit subject to a 20 percent trade discount on orders of 100 units or more; thus, the price for the large order would be $8 per unit.

In recent years there has been a trend toward more credit sales, particularly at the retail level. However, the use of cash discounts appears to be declining. In some jurisdictions, they are not legal in certain situations. The extension of credit usually entails a significant increase in the amount of recordkeeping required. Unless the business has its credit sales handled by a credit card company, which charges a fee for this

[6] In this type of situation, some people prefer to record sales revenue at date of sales as $1,000. If the payment date is *within* the discount period, a debit of $20 to a "Sales Discount" account would be recorded at payment dates. Sales discount is then deducted from sales revenue on the income statement. This approach is conceptually deficient since it often overstates both the sales and accounts receivable amounts.

service, detailed records must be maintained for each credit customer. Appendix A discusses the nature of these detailed records.

Measuring bad debt losses. When goods and services are sold on credit, despite careful credit investigation, there will be a few customers who do not pay their obligations. When an account receivable proves uncollectible, the business incurs a **bad debt loss.** Businesses that extend substantial amounts of credit do so with the expectation that there will be a certain **average rate** of bad debt losses on credit sales. As a matter of fact, an unusually low rate of losses due to uncollectible accounts may give evidence of too tight a credit policy. If the credit policy is too restrictive, many credit customers who would pay their bills may be turned away. In the measurement of net income for the period, the bad debt expense (losses) of that period must be measured.

In bad debt losses, the matching principle requires that the bad debt expense be matched with the period's sales that gave rise to those losses. This requirement is difficult to implement because a bad debt loss may not materialize until one or more years after the particular sale was made. To illustrate, assume credit sales in 1977 amounted to $100,000. All of these accounts were collected except one from John Doe for $100, which was not determined to be uncollectible until the end of 1978. One approach in accounting for this sequence of events would be as follows:

1977:

Accounts receivable	100,000	
Sales revenue		100,000

1977–78:

Cash	99,900	
Accounts receivable		99,900

End of 1978:

Bad debt expense	100	
Accounts receivable (John Doe)		100

The above approach is known as the **direct charge-off method.** Note that the bad debt expense is reported one year after the related revenue was recognized. Therefore, it is clearly deficient because it violates the **matching principle.** The charge-off method should not be used except when the bad debt losses are not material in amount.

To satisfy the matching principle in credit situations, the **allowance method** was developed to measure bad debt expense. It recognizes that bad debt losses really are incurred in the year in which the sales that generated those losses were made. Since there is no way of telling in advance which individual accounts ultimately will prove worthless, the method is based upon the concept of **estimating** in each accounting period what the probable amount of bad debt losses due to uncollectible accounts will be during the collection period. The estimate is made on an aggregate basis (i.e., based on total credit sales for the period), because the individual accounts that will be bad will not be known in the period of sale. The question is: What percent of the aggregate credit sales for the period probably will become bad debts?

Estimating the probable amount of losses due to uncollectible accounts generally is not complex nor fraught with major uncertainties. For a company that has been operating for some years, past experience provides a sound basis for projecting probable future bad debt losses related to credit sales. For example, an analysis of accounting data on aggregate **credit** sales and aggregate uncollectible accounts for the past five years indicated an average bad debt loss of 1.2 percent of aggregate credit sales, viz:

Prior year	*Bad debt losses*	*Credit sales*
1	$ 640	$ 54,000
2	680	57,000
3	620	53,000
4	800	66,000
5	860	70,000
	$3,600	$300,000

Aggregate: $3,600 ÷ $300,000 = 1.2 percent average loss rate.

This bad debt loss rate could simply be used for the coming year, or alternatively, assuming more care will be exercised in credit granting and more efficient collection efforts, the rate may be estimated at 1 percent.

Now, let's see how the allowance method would be applied to the above example. Assuming net **credit** sales in 1977 of $100,000, we would record bad debt expense of $100,000 × 1% = $1,000 **in 1977.** This would require the following *adjusting entry* at the end of the accounting period, December 31, 1977:

Bad debt expense	1,000	
Allowance for doubtful accounts..................................		1,000

To record the estimated bad debt loss for 1977 based on credit sales and an average expected loss rate of 1 percent ($100,000 × 1% = $1,000).

Bad debt expense would be reported on the 1977 income statement as an expense and thus would be matched with the sales revenue of the year in which the credit was granted (1977 in this case). The Bad Debt Expense account would be closed at the end of each accounting period along with the other expense accounts.

In the above entry, rather than crediting the Accounts Receivable account, the credit was made to an **offset,** *or* **contra, account** descriptively titled "Allowance for doubtful accounts" because there is no way of knowing *which* account receivable is involved. Other acceptable titles are "Allowance for bad debts" and "Allowance for uncollectible accounts." The balance in Allowance for Doubtful Accounts is **always** considered as an offset or deduction to the balance of Accounts Receivable. Thus, the two accounts would be reported on the balance sheet, under current assets, as follows:

Current Assets:		
Cash		$ 34,000
Accounts receivable	$148,600	
Less: Allowance for doubtful accounts	2,400	146,200

Allowance for Doubtful Accounts carries a cumulative **credit** balance; and since it is a balance sheet account, it is not closed. It is sometimes described as a contra account, an asset reduction account, an offset account, or a negative asset account, but more frequently as a **valuation account.** These titles, particularly the last one, derive from the fact its cumulative credit balance is always deducted from Accounts Receivable and thus serves to measure the net realizable value of accounts receivable. In the above example, the difference between the two accounts –$146,200–represents the expected **net realizable value** of accounts receivable (sometimes called book value).

In the above illustration the bad debt estimate was based on credit sales. Occasionally, a company bases the loss rate on total sales (i.e., cash plus credit sales). This approach is illogical since (1) it is impossible to have a bad debt loss on a cash sale, and (2) a shift in the relative proportion between cash and credit sales would render such a rate meaningless. Since the total amount of credit sales for each period can be determined (because they are also recorded in Accounts Receivable as debits), there is no reason for not using credit sales as the base. Another method of estimating bad debt losses is known as "aging accounts receivable"; this method is explained and illustrated in Appendix B to this chapter.

Recording an uncollectible account. Whenever a particular receivable from a customer ultimately is determined to be uncollectible, the amount should be removed from Accounts Receivable. At this time no bad debt loss should be recorded in respect to this particular account since the loss was estimated and recorded earlier in the period in which the sale was made. The Allowance for Doubtful Accounts was established to absorb this loss. Accordingly, the entry to record an uncollectible account in the period in which uncollectibility is determined would be:

Dec. 30	Allowance for doubtful accounts	100	
	Accounts receivable		100
	To write off a receivable from John Doe determined to be uncollectible.		

Observe that this entry does not affect the income statement since the expense had already been recorded (when the adjusting entry was made). Also, the entry does not change the net realizable value (i.e., the book value) of the accounts receivable. The difference between accounts receivable and the allowance account remains the same as before the entry, viz:

	Before write-off	*After write-off*
Accounts receivable	$148,600	$148,500
Less: Allowance for doubtful accounts	2,400	2,300
Difference—estimated net realizable value	$146,200	$146,200

Actual write-offs compared with estimate. The uncollectible accounts actually written off seldom will agree exactly in amount with the estimates previously recorded. If the accounts actually written off are less than the allowance provided, the Allowance for Doubtful Account will have a credit balance.[7]

Terminology. The caption "Accounts receivable" often appears on the balance sheet under current assets without additional descriptive terms; however, a more descriptive designation such as "Receivables from trade customers" is preferable. Receivables from other than the regular trade customers, such as loans to officers or employees, should not be included in the accounts receivable category. Rather, as a special kind of receivable, they should be reported as separate items.

PART TWO: MEASUREMENT OF REVENUE DEDUCTIONS

In measuring income for a period, in addition to carefully measuring all aspects of the revenue generated, the **revenue deductions** must be measured and reported. The revenue deductions, directly related to sales activities for the period, are comprised of two categories of expense: cost of goods sold and selling expenses. This section focuses on the measurement of cost of goods sold. It is often the largest single item of expense to be measured and reported for the period.

MEASURING INVENTORY AND COST OF GOODS SOLD

In the income statement, shown in Exhibit 7–1, the component amounts making up **cost of goods sold** (inventories and purchases) were

[7] On the other hand, if the amount written off is more than the allowance balance, there will be a temporary debit balance in the allowance account. This situation will be resolved when the next "allowance entry" is made. It indicates that the estimated loss rate used may be too low.

reported separately. The components represent important concepts in the measurement of net income. Cost of goods sold, as an expense, is a relatively simple concept. It is the **cost** of the merchandise **sold** during the period; therefore, it excludes all goods remaining on hand at the end of the period (i.e., the ending or final inventory). Typically, a business will start each period with a supply of merchandise on hand, which generally is called the **beginning,** or **initial, inventory.** To that stock will be **added** the merchandise purchased (or manufactured) during the period.

Clearly the beginning inventory plus the purchases of merchandise (or goods manufactured) during a period represent the **goods available for sale** during that period. If all the merchandise available for sale were sold during the period, there would be no ending inventory. In a typical situation, however, a quantity of the goods remains unsold (on hand) at the end of each period. Thus, we must subtract the ending inventory from the goods available for sale to determine the cost of goods sold for the period.

To compute cost of goods sold, three amounts must be known: (1) beginning inventory, (2) purchases of merchandise during the period, and (3) ending inventory. **The ending inventory of one accounting period is the beginning inventory of the next period.** Therefore, the beginning inventory amount will be available from the prior period. The amount of purchases for the period will be accumulated in the accounting system. Determining the amount of the **final inventory** presents a special problem.

There are two distinctly different systems that are used in measuring inventories. They are:

1. Perpetual inventory system—This approach involves the maintenance of detailed inventory records in the accounting system. For each type of goods stocked, a detailed record is maintained that shows (*a*) units and cost of each purchase, (*b*) units and cost of the goods for each sale, and (*c*) the units and amount on hand at any point in time. This continuous record is maintained on a transaction-by-transaction basis throughout the period. Thus, the inventory record provides both the amount of ending inventory and the cost of goods sold for the period.
2. Periodic inventory system—Under this approach, no detailed record of inventory is maintained during the year. An actual physical count of the goods remaining on hand is required at the end of each period. The number of units of each type of goods on hand then is multiplied by their purchase cost per unit to compute the dollar amount of the final inventory. Thus, the balance of goods on hand is not known until the last day of the period when the inventory count is completed. Also the amount of cost of goods sold cannot be determined until the inventory count is completed.

PERPETUAL INVENTORY SYSTEM

A perpetual inventory system may involve a considerable amount of clerical effort; however, it is effective in measuring inventory and cost of goods sold. The maintenance of a separate inventory record for each type of goods stocked on a transaction-by-transaction basis can be time-consuming and costly. In businesses stocking very few items, a manual system may be feasible; however, many perpetual inventory systems are computerized. Whether manual, mechanical, or computerized, the data

EXHIBIT 7–2

PERPETUAL INVENTORY RECORD

Item Mower (heavy) Code No. 330 Minimum stock 10
Location Storage No. 4 Valuation basis Cost Maximum stock 40

Date	Explanation	Goods Purchased			Goods Sold			Balance on Hand		
		Units Rec'd	Unit Cost	Total Cost	Units Sold	Unit Cost	Total Cost	Units	Unit Cost	Total Cost
Jan. 1	Beginning inventory							10	300	3,000
14	Purchase	30	300	9,000				40	300	12,000
30	Sale				20	300	6,000	20	300	6,000
31	Return sale				(1)	300	(300)	21	300	6,300
Recap: Total purchases		30		9,000						
Total cost of goods sold					19		5,700			
Final inventory								21		6,300

to be recorded and reported are the same. For instructional purposes let's look at a manual approach. For example, Modern Equipment Company sells heavy construction equipment. It maintains a separate **perpetual inventory record** for each type of machine stocked. The inventory record for a mower, code 330, is shown in Exhibit 7–2.[8]

The perpetual inventory record shown in Exhibit 7–2 reflects an ending inventory balance of 21 units and a total inventory cost of $6,300. Similar records of purchases, sales, and inventory balances for the various types of equipment carried in stock would provide the total inventory for the company. The computer does exactly what was done manually

[8] Measuring inventories and cost of goods sold when there are different *unit* purchase costs is deferred to Chapter 8.

in Exhibit 7–2; however, a computerized system does it with tremendous speed and has considerable capacity to handle voluminous data. The perpetual inventory approach is widely used because it can be programmed for computer-based systems and it measures both inventory and cost of goods sold amounts effectively.

A perpetual inventory system may be described as follows:

1. During the period, the purchase cost of each type of goods bought is entered in the Inventory ledger account as an increase and in a detailed perpetual inventory record (Exhibit 7–2). Thus, a cash or credit purchase of goods for resale would be recorded as follows (refer to Exhibit 7–2):

   January 14, 1977:

Inventory* (mower No. 330)	9,000	
Accounts payable (or Cash)		9,000

   * Also entered in the perpetual inventory record as shown in Exhibit 7–2.

2. During the period, each sale is recorded by means of **two companion entries.** One entry is to record the **sales revenue at sales price,** and the other entry is to record the **cost of goods sold at purchase cost.** The sales revenue is accumulated in the Sales Revenue account, and the cost of goods sold is accumulated in the Cost of Goods Sold account. Thus, a credit or cash sale would be recorded as follows (refer to Exhibit 7–2):

   January 30, 1977:

   a. To record the sales revenue at the sales price of $400 per unit:

Accounts receivable (or Cash)	8,000	
Sales revenue (20 units × $400)		8,000

   b. To record the cost of goods sold (at cost per the perpetual inventory record–Exhibit 7–2):

Cost of goods sold	6,000	
Inventory (mower No. 330)*		6,000

   * Also entered in the perpetual inventory record as shown in Exhibit 7–2.

3. During the period, **purchase returns** and **sales returns** are recorded in the Inventory account and on the perpetual inventory record at cost. For example, the return by a customer of one mower on January 31 would be recorded as follows (refer to Exhibit 7–2):

   January 31, 1977:

   To record the return of one mower:

Sales returns and allowances	400	
Accounts receivable (or Cash)		400

Inventory (mower No. 330)	300*	
Cost of goods sold		300

*This amount was provided by the perpetual inventory record; also restored to the perpetual inventory record as shown in Exhibit 7–2.

4. At the end of the period, the balance in the Cost of Goods Sold account would measure the total amount of that expense to be reported on the income statement. No computations would be needed of cost of goods sold like those shown on page 219 since they are in situations where the periodic inventory system is used. Similarly, the Inventory account would reflect the ending inventory amount that would be reported on the balance sheet. The sum of all the inventory balances on the various perpetual inventory records should equal the balance in the Inventory account in the ledger each point in time.

This illustration demonstrates that when a perpetual inventory system is used, it is not necessary to take a physical inventory count of the merchandise remaining on hand at the end of the accounting period in order to measure the inventory amount and cost of goods sold. However, since clerical errors, theft, and spoilage may occur, a physical inventory should be taken from time to time to check upon the accuracy of the perpetual inventory records. When an error is found, the perpetual inventory records and the inventory account are adjusted to agree with the physical count.

PERIODIC INVENTORY SYSTEM

For various reasons some companies do not use a perpetual inventory system. One of the primary reasons is the nature of the business. For example, a variety store or a grocery store could experience considerable difficulties and cost in implementing such a system because of the large number of low-priced items stocked and the high stock turnover rates. For example, when groceries are sold for cash, usually no record is made at the cash register of the quantity of items sold. Rather, the dollar amount of sales revenue is recorded on the cash register tape. Clearly, the grocery store in this instance is not accumulating the physical quantity of goods sold that would be needed for each type of item to implement a perpetual inventory system. Businesses that do not use a perpetual inventory system necessarily use a **periodic inventory system.** A periodic inventory system, in many respects, is more difficult to understand, and more accounts are required. Also, a periodic inventory system does not provide an important element of **inventory control** that can be attained through a perpetual system.[9]

A periodic inventory system may be described as follows:

[9] Because of these important advantages and others, large chain stores now have a computerized inventory system tied in directly to the cash register.

1. During the period, the purchase cost of all goods bought is accumulated in an account called Purchases (or Merchandise purchases). Thus, a credit or cash purchase would be recorded as follows:

   January 14, 1977:

Purchases	9,000	
Accounts payable (or Cash)		9,000

2. During the period, the sales price received for all goods sold is accumulated in a Sales Revenue account. In contrast to the perpetual inventory approach, no companion entry is made at the date of sale to record the cost of goods sold since the periodic system cannot provide such unit cost data during the period. Thus, a credit or cash sale would be recorded as follows:

   January 30, 1977:

Accounts receivable (or Cash)	8,000	
Sales revenue		8,000

3. At the end of the period, the **Inventory account** balance still reflects the inventory amount carried over from the prior period since no entries were made to the Inventory account during the current period. Thus, to measure the ending inventory for the current period, a physical count must be made of all goods on hand. This count is made at the end of each period for which financial statements are to be prepared. A physical count is necessary since, under the periodic inventory system, a transaction-by-transaction **unit record** is not maintained for purchases, cost of goods sold, and the inventory balance. Taking a physical inventory is discussed later.
4. The **dollar amount** of the ending inventory quantities is computed by multiplying the number of units found as determined by physical count to be on hand times their unit purchase cost. The dollar amounts, thus determined for all of the types of goods stocked, are summed to measure the total ending inventory for the company.
5. After the ending inventory is measured, as in 4, cost of goods sold for the period can be computed as follows:

Beginning inventory (carried over from the last period in the Inventory account)	$ 40,000*
Add purchases for the period (accumulated balance in the Purchases account)	515,000
Goods available for sale	555,000
Less ending inventory (determined by physical count)	35,000
Cost of goods sold	$520,000

* Based on the data shown in Exhibit 7–1.

To summarize, there are **two** basic differences between perpetual and periodic inventory systems:

1. Inventory:
   a. Perpetual – During the period, the Inventory account is increased for each purchase and decreased (at cost) for each sale. Thus, at at the end of the period, it measures ending inventory.
   b. Periodic – During the period, the Inventory account is not changed; thus, it reflects the beginning inventory amount. During the period, each purchase is recorded in the Purchases account. As a consequence, the ending inventory each period must be measured by physical count, then "costed" at unit purchase cost.
2. Cost of goods sold:
   a. Perpetual – During the period, cost of goods sold is recorded at the time of each sale and the Inventory account is reduced (at cost). Thus the system measures the cost of goods sold amount for the period.
   b. Periodic – During the period, no entry is made for cost of goods sold (in this instance a Cost of Goods Sold account is not used). At the end of the period, after the physical inventory count, cost of goods sold is measured as:

$$\text{Beginning Inventory} + \text{Purchases} - \text{Ending Inventory} = \text{Cost of Goods Sold}$$

SOME ISSUES IN MEASURING PURCHASES

In accordance with the cost principle, goods purchased for resale are recorded at the date that ownership passes to the buyer. Normally, ownership is considered to pass when the goods are received and not when the purchase order is placed. The goods should be recorded at their **cash equivalent cost** in accordance with the cost principle. Cost, as defined, includes the cash equivalent price paid to the vendor plus other amounts paid for freight and handling in order to get the goods to their intended location. Cost does not include financing expenditures, such as interest paid on funds borrowed to make the purchase. In accounting for purchases, several measurement problems frequently are encountered; they are discussed below.

Purchase returns and allowances. Goods purchased may be returned to the vendor because they do not meet specifications, arrive in unsatisfactory condition, or are otherwise unsatisfactory. When the goods are returned or when the vendor makes an allowance because of the circumstances, the effect on the cost of purchases must be measured. The purchaser will receive a cash refund or a reduction in the liability to the vendor for the purchase. To illustrate, assume Company A returned to Company B, for credit, unsatisfactory goods that cost $160. The return would be recorded by Company A as follows:

Accounts payable	160	
Purchase returns and allowances*		160

* Inventory is credited when perpetual inventory procedures are being used.

Purchase returns and allowances are viewed as a deduction to the cost of Purchases.

Transportation-in. Under the cost principle, assets acquired should be measured and recorded at their **cash equivalent cost.** Thus, the **purchase cost** of goods acquired for resale should include all freight and other transportation-in costs incurred by the purchaser. When a perpetual inventory system is used, transportation costs paid on goods purchased should be included in the inventory cost amount entered in the perpetual inventory if feasible. When a periodic inventory system is used, such costs should be entered as a debit (i.e., increase) to the Purchases account. However, for control and reporting purposes, and because of problems of apportioning a freight bill to the several items it may cover, it may be more practical to use a separate ledger account entitled "Transportation-In," or "Freight-In." Thus, in this situation the journal entry to record a payment for transportation charges upon delivery of merchandise acquired for resale would be:

Jan. 17	Transportation-in	18	
	Cash		18

At the end of the period, the balance in the Transportation-In account would be reported as an addition to the cost of Purchases.

Assuming freight-in and purchase returns, cost of goods sold may be reflected as follows on the income statement when periodic inventory procedures are used:

Cost of goods sold:			
Beginning inventory		$10,000	
Purchases	$60,000		
Add: Freight-in	3,000		
Deduct: Purchase returns	(1,000)		
Net purchases		62,000	
Goods available for sale		72,000	
Less: Ending inventory		11,000	
Cost of goods sold			$61,000

Purchase discounts. Recall the discussion of cash discounts on sales (page 209). Essentially, a corresponding situation occurs when merchandise is purchased for resale—except that the cash discount is **received** rather than given. When merchandise is purchased on credit, terms such as 2/10, n/30 are sometimes specified. This means that if payment of the purchase invoice cost is made within ten days from date of purchase, a 2 percent discount may be taken. If payment is not made within the discount period; then the full purchase invoice cost is due 30 days after purchase. To illustrate, assume Company A purchases goods from a number of suppliers. The company always pays cash at date of purchase or within the discount period. On January 17, the company purchased goods from Vendor B that had a $1,000 invoice price with terms 2/10, n/30. Under these terms, Company A, following its own payment policy, will pay $980 for the goods. Therefore, the purchase should be recorded on the net basis by Company A as follows:[10]

January 17—date of purchase:

Purchases*	980	
Accounts payable		980

* Inventory is debited when a perpetual inventory system is used.

January 26—date of payment, within the discount period:

Accounts payable	980	
Cash		980

If for any reason Company A did not pay within the ten-day discount period, the following entry would result:

Feb. 1	Accounts payable	980	
	Purchase discounts lost (similar to Interest expense)	20	
	Cash		1,000

Purchase discounts lost should be reported on the income statement as a *financial expense* along with regular interest expense.

Taking a physical inventory. We explained above that whether a periodic or perpetual inventory system is used, a physical inventory count must be taken from time to time. When a periodic inventory system is used, the inventory must be counted (and costed) at the end of each period because the financial statements cannot be prepared without this key amount. When a perpetual inventory system is used, the inventory count may be scheduled at various times to verify the perpetual inventory records. The two steps in taking a *physical inventory* are:

1. Quantity count—The count of merchandise is made after the close of business on the last day of the period. Normally, it would be difficult to accurately count goods during business hours when sales are taking place. A physical count is made of all items of merchandise on hand and entered on an appropriate form. For example, an **inven-**

[10] Some people prefer to record the transaction at the date of purchase at the gross amount, that is, at $1,000. In this instance, payment within the discount period would result in credit to an account called Purchase Discounts, $20. The purchase discount credit would than be reported as a revenue, or as a deduction from purchases. This credit is not revenue and if deducted in full from purchases on the income statement would tend to misstate both inventory and purchases. For these reasons it is conceptually deficient. Also, in contrast, the net basis has the distinct advantage in that recording the *purchase discount lost* calls direct attention to inefficiency—failure to take the discount.

tory sheet, such as the one shown in Exhibit 7–3, may be used. The quantity determined to be on hand by actual count is recorded in a quantity column as shown in the exhibit. Special care must be exercised in the quantity count to be sure that all of the merchandise owned by the business is included, wherever located, and that all items for which the entity does not have legal ownership are excluded. Occasionally, a business will have possession of goods it does not own (see discussion of consignments in Chapter 8).

2. Inventory costing—After the physical count to determine the quantity of goods on hand has been completed, each kind of merchandise must be assigned a **unit cost.** The quantity of each kind of merchandise is multiplied by the unit purchase cost to derive the **inventory amount** as illustrated in Exhibit 7–3. The sum of the inventory amounts for all merchandise on hand measures the total ending inventory amount for the business. Exhibit 7–3 reflects computation of the ending inventory shown on the income statement for Campus Corners (Exhibit 7–1). In costing inventory quantities, the cost principle is applied; therefore, unit purchase cost, as defined above, must be used. However, there are several ways to identify unit purchase cost for inventory purposes such as the *first-in, first-out* (*Fifo*), *last-in, first-out* (*Lifo*), or *average cost* approaches. These alternative approaches to costing inventories are discussed in detail in Chapter 8.

Inventories, since they frequently represent large amounts of tied-up resources (cash), often present management with complex planning and

EXHIBIT 7–3

Campus Corner
PHYSICAL INVENTORY SHEET

Date of Inventory 12/31/77 Department #4 Taken by M. R.

Location	Identification of Merchandise	Quantity on Hand	Date Purchased	Unit Cost	Unit Market Price*	Unit Cost (LCM)	Inventory Amount
1	Headsets #8-16	20	12/2/74	$20	$21	$20	$400
2	Television sets #17-961	7	11/5/74	300	300	300	2,100
2	Radios #23-72	4	10/26/74	52	50	50	200
	Total Department Inventory	XXX	XXX	XXX	XXX	XXX	6,000
	TOTAL INVENTORY VALUE--ALL DEPARTMENTS 12/31/77						$35,000

* Price that would have to be paid if the item were being purchased on the inventory date (see lower-of-cost-or-market discussion in Chapter 8).

control problems. For example, decisions should be made as to the maximum and minimum levels of inventory that should be observed; when to reorder; how much to reorder; and the characteristics of the items to stock, such as size, color, style, and specifications. Some of these issues are discussed in *Fundamentals of Management Accounting.* From the viewpoint of the investor, creditor, and other interested parties, the investment in inventory frequently is important in decision making. Thus, explanatory footnotes related to inventories are frequently included in the financial reports.

DATA PROCESSING—ADJUSTING AND CLOSING ENTRIES

In this chapter some new accounts related to selling and purchasing activities were introduced. Further explanation, in terms of the adjusting and closing phases of the information-processing cycle, is needed.

The Sales Revenue and Sales Return and Allowance accounts normally do not require any adjusting entries (see discussion in Chapter 6). These accounts are closed to the Income Summary account along with the other revenue and expense accounts. Thus, these new accounts do not present new problems for you in the adjusting and closing phases of the information-processing cycle. In contrast to the revenue accounts, however, the Inventory and Cost of Goods Sold accounts do require new procedures in the adjusting and closing phases. The adjusting and closing phases for these two items are affected by the inventory system used.

Adjusting and closing phases for a perpetual inventory system

When a perpetual inventory system is used, no additional adjusting entries are required. The only new closing entry needed is to transfer the balance in Cost of Goods Sold to the Income Summary account. Since the Cost of Goods Sold account is an expense, it is closed in the same manner as each of the other expense accounts. To illustrate, assuming a debit balance of $150,000 in the Cost of Goods Sold account at the end of the period, the closing entry would be:

Income summary	150,000	
Cost of goods sold		150,000

Under the perpetual inventory system there are no directly related adjusting entries and only one directly related closing entry (for Cost of Goods Sold), because the perpetual Inventory account is updated after each purchase and sale so that the ending balance in the Inventory account reflects the ending inventory as reported on the balance sheet as a current asset. Similarly, the Cost of Goods Sold account balance reflects the accumulated cost of all goods sold for the period.

Adjusting and closing phases for a periodic inventory system

When a periodic inventory system is used, **two directly related adjusting entries** are required: (1) the beginning inventory amount, which has remained in the Inventory account throughout the period (since no entries are made to it during the period), must be transferred to Income Summary; and (2) the ending inventory amount, which has been determined by physical count, must be recorded in the Inventory account as an asset. Specifically, appropriate adjusting entires must be made to replace the beginning inventory balance in the Inventory account with the ending inventory amount.

To illustrate, assume that the Inventory account (periodic inventory system) reflects a $40,000 debit on the unadjusted trial balance taken from the ledger at the end of the period on December 31, 1977. Since no entries are made in the Inventory account during the year, under the periodic approach, this balance reflects the **beginning** inventory. That is, it is the amount of inventory that was carried over from the last period. Assume further that the ending inventory on December 31, 1977, determined by physical count, amounted to $35,000. The two adjusting entries needed would be as follows (these amounts agree with those shown on page 207).

a. To transfer the beginning inventory balance:

Income summary	40,000	
Inventory (beginning)		40,000

b. To record the ending inventory:

Inventory (ending)	35,000	
Income summary		35,000

In respect to **closing entries** under a periodic inventory system, the ending balance in the Purchases account is closed to Income Summary along with the other expense accounts. To illustrate, assuming an ending balance in the Purchases account of $515,000, the closing entry would be as follows:

c.	Income summary	515,000	
	Purchases		515,000

After these entries are posted, the Inventory, Purchases, and Income Summary accounts would appear as follows:

Inventory (periodic system)

1/1/77	40,000	(*a*) To close	40,000
(*b*) 12/31/77	35,000		

Purchases

Balance	515,000	(*c*) To close	515,000

Income Summary

Operating expenses (not illustrated)		Revenues (not illustrated)	
(*a*) Beginning inventory	40,000	(*b*) Ending inventory	35,000
(*c*) Purchases	515,000		

Observe that the net of the three amounts shown above in the Income Summary account is a debit of $520,000, which is the amount of Cost of Goods Sold (see page 207).[11] If there are accounts for Transportation-In and Purchase Returns and Allowances, they would be closed to Income Summary along with the Purchases account.

Inventory shrinkage. Inventory shrinkage sometimes occurs as a result of theft, breakage, and spoilage. The measurement of inventory shrinkage is important for internal management uses. The amount of shrinkage is reported on *internal* financial statements, but seldom if ever are such amounts reported separately on *external* financial statements. Accurate measurement of this loss is directly related to the inventory system used.

When the periodic inventory system is used, measurement of shrinkage loss is often difficult, and may be impossible. The inventory, as counted at the end of the period, does not, in itself, provide a basis for measurement of shrinkage. Under this system, since cost of goods sold is a residual amount (i.e., Beginning Inventory + Purchases − Ending Inventory = Cost of Goods Sold), shrinkage loss necessarily is buried in the cost of goods sold amount.

Alternatively, a perpetual inventory system will provide data on shrinkage loss. The inventory record provides both cost of goods sold and the ending inventory. These data make it possible to measure shrinkage loss. To illustrate, assume the perpetual inventory records show cost of goods sold for the period to be 19 units, $5,700 (Exhibit 7–2) and the ending inventory to be 21 units, $6,300. Assume further that an inventory count is taken at the end of the period which shows 20 units on hand. In the absence of clerical error, an inventory shrinkage would be reported as 1 unit, $300. Further investigation may convince the management that the shrinkage is due to theft. The entry to record the shrinkage, assuming a perpetual inventory system, would be:

Inventory shrinkage (or loss due to theft)	300	
Inventory		300

[11] Some accountants prefer to set up a *temporary* Cost of Goods Sold account under the periodic inventory system to facilitate the three adjusting and closing entries illustrated above. Under this procedure the three amounts, beginning inventory, ending inventory, and purchases would be transferred to it. The resultant balance in the Cost of Goods Sold account ($520,000 in the above instance) would then be closed to the Income Summary account.

DEMONSTRATION CASE FOR SELF-STUDY

Rote's Appliance Store, Incorporated

(Try to resolve the case before studying the suggested solution that follows.)

Rote's Appliance Store has been operating for a number of years. It is a relatively small but profitable retail outlet for major appliances, such as refrigerators and air conditioners. Approximately 40 percent of the sales are on short-term credit. This case has been selected and simplified to demonstrate information processing when there are significant selling activities; the service activities have been deleted. The case has been structured to illustrate the application of both perpetual and periodic inventory systems with the same data. The annual accounting period ends December 31, 1977. Two independent cases will be assumed:

Case A – Perpetual inventory system is assumed.
Case B – Periodic inventory system is assumed.

The trial balance derived from the ledger at December 31, 1977, was:

	Unadjusted Trial Balance			
	Case A – Perpetual inventory system used		*Case B – Periodic inventory system used*	
Account Titles	*Debit*	*Credit*	*Debit*	*Credit*
Cash	$ 34,100		$ 34,100	
Accounts receivable	5,000		5,000	
Allowance for doubtful accounts		$ 1,000		$ 1,000
* Merchandise inventory:				
January 1, 1977			20,000	
December 31, 1977	16,000			
Store equipment	30,000		30,000	
Accumulated depreciation, store equipment		9,000		9,000
Accounts payable		8,000		8,000
Income taxes payable				
Capital stock, par $10		40,000		40,000
Retained earnings, January 1, 1977		9,000		9,000
Sales revenue		102,000		102,000
Sales returns and allowances	2,000		2,000	
* Cost of goods sold	60,000			
* Purchases			57,000	
* Purchases returns and allowances				1,000
Expenses (not detailed)	21,900		21,900	
Depreciation expense				
Income tax expense				
	$169,000	$169,000	$170,000	$170,000

* These account balances are different between the cases because of the effects of the inventory system used.

Data developed as a basis for the adjusting entries at December 31, 1977, were:

a. Credit sales in 1977 amounted to $40,000; the average loss rate for bad debts is estimated to be 0.25 percent of credit sales.
b. The store equipment is being depreciated on the basis of an estimated ten-year useful life with no residual value.
c. On December 31, 1977, the periodic inventory count of goods remaining on hand reflected $16,000.
d. The corporate average income tax rate is 20 percent.

The beginning inventory, January 1, 1977, was as shown on the trial balance.

Required:

a. Based upon the above data, complete a worksheet at December 31, 1977, similar to that shown in Exhibit 6–2. If you prefer, you may omit the pair of columns for Adjusted Trial Balance. Prepare a separate worksheet for each separate case.
b. Based upon the completed worksheets, present an income statement for each case. Use a single-step format for Case A and a multiple-step format for Case B.
c. Based upon the two worksheets, present, in parallel columns, the adjusting entries for each case at December 31, 1977.
d. Based upon the two worksheets, present, in parallel columns, the closing entires for each situation at December 31, 1977.

In preparing the worksheet when a **perpetual inventory system** is used no new complications are presented. The inventory amount is extended across the worksheet as an asset since the balance in the Inventory account reflects the ending inventory when a perpetual inventory system is used. The expense—cost of goods sold—is extended to the Income Summary, debit column along with the other expenses. See Exhibit 7–4.

In preparing the worksheet with a **periodic inventory system,** both the beginning and ending inventory amounts must be used. First, the beginning inventory amount must be transferred to Income Summary. This may be done by means of an adjusting entry that credits the Inventory account and debits Income Summary. A special line, "Income summary—inventories," is added to the bottom of the worksheet to accommodate this debit. Next, the ending inventory (determined by physical count) must be entered on the worksheet. This may be done by means of another adjusting entry that debits the Inventory account and credits Income Summary. On the worksheet this credit is entered on the special line that was added—"Income summary—inventories." To extend this special line (at the bottom of the worksheet), the beginning inventory amount is carried across as a debit to the Income Statement column because it is an *addition* to cost of goods sold. In contrast, the ending inventory amount is carried across as a credit to the Income Statement because it is a *deduction* from cost of goods sold. The balance in the merchandise inventory

Requirement (*a*):

EXHIBIT 7–4
Worksheets compared for perpetual and periodic inventory systems

ROTE'S APPLIANCE STORE, INCORPORATED
Worksheet, December 31, 1977
Case A—Assuming Perpetual Inventory System Is Used

Account Titles	Trial Balance		Adjusting Entries		Income Statement		Balance Sheet	
	Debit	Credit	Debit	Credit	Debit	Credit	Debit	Credit
Cash	34,100						34,100	
Accounts receivable	5,000						5,000	
Allowance for doubtful accounts		1,000		(*a*) 100				1,100
Merchandise inventory	16,000						16,000	
Store equipment	30,000						30,000	
Accumulated depreciation, equipment		9,000		(*b*) 3,000				12,000
Accounts payable		8,000						8,000
Income taxes payable				(*d*) 3,000				3,000
Capital stock		40,000						40,000
Retained earnings, January 1, 1977		9,000						9,000
Sales revenue		102,000				102,000		
Sales returns and allowances	2,000				2,000			
Cost of goods sold	60,000				60,000			
Expenses (not detailed)	21,900		(*a*) 100		22,000			
Depreciation expense			(*b*) 3,000		3,000			
Income tax expense			(*d*) 3,000		3,000			
Net Income					12,000			12,000
Totals	169,000	169,000	6,100	6,100	102,000	102,000	85,100	85,100

EXHIBIT 7–4 (*continued*)

ROTE'S APPLIANCE STORE, INCORPORATED
Worksheet, December 31, 1977
Case B—Assuming Periodic Inventory System Is Used

Account Titles	Trial Balance		Adjusting Entries		Income Statement		Balance Sheet	
	Debit	Credit	Debit	Credit	Debit	Credit	Debit	Credit
Cash	34,100						34,100	
Accounts receivable	5,000						5,000	
Allowance for doubtful accounts		1,000		(*a*) 100				1,100
Merchandise inventory	20,000		(*c*-2) 16,000	(*c*-1) 20,000			16,000	
Store equipment	30,000						30,000	
Accumulated depreciation, equipment		9,000		(*b*) 3,000				12,000
Accounts payable		8,000						8,000
Income taxes payable				(*d*) 3,000				3,000
Capital stock		40,000						40,000
Retained earnings, January 1, 1977		9,000						9,000
Sales revenue		102,000				102,000		
Sales returns and allowances	2,000				2,000			
Purchases	57,000				57,000			
Purchases returns and allowances		1,000				1,000		
Expenses (not detailed)	21,900		(*a*) 100		22,000			
Depreciation expense			(*b*) 3,000		3,000			
Income tax expense			(*d*) 3,000		3,000			
Income summary—inventories			(*c*-1) 20,000	(*c*-2) 16,000	20,000	16,000		
Net Income					12,000			12,000
Totals	170,000	170,000	42,100	42,100	119,000	119,000	85,100	85,100

account (fourth line on Exhibit 7–4, Case B) is extended as a balance sheet debit because it is the amount of the asset—Inventory—at the end of the period.[12] See Exhibit 7–4.

Requirement (*b*):

ROTE'S APPLIANCE STORE, INCORPORATED
Income Statement
For the Year Ended December 31, 1977
Case A—Perpetual Inventory System and Single-Step Format

Revenues:		
Sales	$102,000	
Less: Sales returns and allowances	2,000	
Net sales		$100,000
Expenses:		
Cost of goods sold	60,000	
Expenses (not detailed for case purposes)	22,000	
Depreciation expense	3,000	
Income tax expense	3,000	
Total Expenses		88,000
Net Income		$ 12,000
Earnings per share ($12,000 ÷ 4,000 shares)		$3.00

ROTE'S APPLIANCE STORE, INCORPORATED
Income Statement
For the Year Ended December 31, 1977
Case B—Periodic Inventory System and Multiple-Step Format

Gross sales		$102,000
Less: Sales returns and allowances		2,000
Net sales		100,000
Cost of goods sold:		
Inventory, January 1, 1977	$ 20,000	
Purchases	57,000	
Purchase returns and allowances	(1,000)	
Goods available for sale	76,000	
Less: Inventory, December 31, 1977	16,000	
Cost of goods sold		60,000
Gross margin on sales		40,000
Operating expenses:		
Expenses (not detailed for case purposes)	22,000	
Depreciation expense	3,000	25,000
Pretax income		15,000
Income tax expense ($15,000 × 20%)		3,000
Net Income		$ 12,000
Earnings per share ($12,000 ÷ 4,000 shares)		$3.00

[12] There are several mechanical ways of handling the inventories on the worksheet when a periodic inventory system is used. Some accountants view the inventory entries as closing rather than adjusting entries. The various approaches arrive at the same net result, and each has its particular mechanical advantages and disadvantages.

Suggested Solution:

Requirement (*c*):

Adjusting Entries
December 31, 1977

	Case A *Perpetual Inventory*		*Case B* *Periodic Inventory*	
a. Expenses (bad debt loss)	100		100	
Allowance for doubtful accounts...........		100		100
Bad debt loss estimated, $40,000 × 0.25% = $100.				
b. Depreciation expense	3,000		3,000	
Accumulated depreciation, store equipment		3,000		3,000
Depreciation for one year, $30,000 ÷ 10 years = $3,000.				
c-1. Income summary.......................................	(Not applicable)		20,000	
Inventory (beginning)...........................				20,000
Transfer beginning inventory to income summary.				
c-2. Inventory (ending)	(Not applicable)		16,000	
Income summary.................................				16,000
Record ending inventory per physical count.				
d. Income tax expense....................................	3,000		3,000	
Income taxes payable		3,000		3,000
Income taxes for year, $15,000 × 20% = $3,000.				

Requirement (*d*):

Closing Entries
December 31, 1977

	Case A		Case B	
1. Sales revenue	102,000		102,000	
Sales returns and allowances		2,000		2,000
Income summary.................................		100,000		100,000
To transfer the revenue accounts to income summary.				
2. Income summary..	(Not applicable)		56,000	
Purchase return and allowances			1,000	
Purchases..				57,000
To transfer purchase amounts to income summary.				
3. Income summary..	60,000		(Not applicable)	
Cost of goods sold		60,000		
4. Income summary..	28,000		28,000	
Expenses (not detailed)........................		22,000		22,000
Depreciation expense		3,000		3,000
Income tax expense.............................		3,000		3,000
To transfer expense accounts to income summary.				
5. Income summary..	12,000		12,000	
Retained earnings		12,000		12,000
To transfer net income to retained earnings.				

SUMMARY

This chapter focused on the measurement of the effects on net income of the selling and purchasing activities in various types of businesses. A new expense on the income statement was introduced: "Cost of Goods Sold." It measures the *cost* of the merchandise included in the sales revenue amount. In conformity with the matching principle, the total cost of the items sold during the period must be matched with the total sales revenue earned during the period. When cost of goods sold is deducted from sales revenue for the period, the difference is known as gross margin on sales. From this amount, the other expenses must be deducted to derive net income.

The chapter also discussed and illustrated the effect on cost of goods sold of the beginning and ending inventory amounts. We observed that the ending inventory of one period is the beginning inventory of the next period. Two inventory systems were discussed for measuring the merchandise remaining on hand at the end of the period and the cost of goods sold for the period: (1) the perpetual inventory system, which is based on the maintenance of detailed and continuous inventory records for each kind of goods stocked; and (2) the periodic inventory system, which is based upon a physical count of the goods remaining on hand at the end of each period.

IMPORTANT TERMS

Revenue principle
Matching principle
Cost of goods sold
Gross margin on sales
Gross margin ratio (or percent)
Net sales
Gross sales
Sales returns and allowances
Sales discounts
Trade discounts
Bad debt losses
Allowance method
Offset (or contra) account
Allowance for doubtful accounts
Revenue deductions
Beginning (or initial) inventory
Ending (or final) inventory
Perpetual inventory system
Periodic inventory system
Goods available for sale
Purchases returns and allowances
Transportation-in
Cash equivalent cost
Purchase discounts
Physical inventory
Inventory shrinkage

APPENDIX A

Data processing—controlling accounts and subsidiary ledgers

This appendix explains an accounting procedure designed to facilitate recordkeeping and internal control in situations where a large number of similar transactions recur continuously. It does not involve accounting theory, principles, or standards, but deals only with the mechanics of data processing. The use of *control accounts* and *subsidiary ledgers* will be explained and illustrated for accounts receivable; however, the procedure is also applicable in any situation that involves numerous transactions that are similar and require detailed recordkeeping, such as accounts payable and fixed assets.

In the preceding discussions and illustrations, charge sales and services were credited to a revenue account with the corresponding debit to an account designated *"Accounts Receivable."* Subsequently, upon payment, the Accounts Receivable account was decreased (a credit). We did not illustrate the manner in which the account receivable for each *individual customer* was maintained. Some businesses carry thousands of individual customers on a credit status. The business could maintain some kind of "filing system" that would show (1) the amount of sales and services provided each customer on credit, (2) the cash collections from each customer on credit previously extended, and (3) the balance owed by each customer at each point in time. Alternatively, it could maintain a separate receivable account for each customer in the *general ledger.* This would require, in the above example, several thousand such accounts in that ledger.

A more efficient procedure involves the use of a single *control account* in the general ledger for Accounts Receivable and a separate *subsidiary ledger* that carries an individual account for each credit customer. Thus, in the above example, the general ledger would include Accounts Receivable as a *single control account* and the *subsidiary ledger* would include several thousand *individual receivable accounts.* At any given point, the *sum* of the *individual account balances* in the receivable subsidiary ledger, in the absence of error, would equal the *single balance* in the *Accounts Receivable control account* in the general ledger. The Accounts Receivable account in the general ledger is called a control account because it controls the subsidiary ledger. The individual customer accounts, as subdivisions of it, are subsidiary to the control account; thus the designation, subsidiary ledger.

To illustrate data processing with a control account and a subsidiary ledger for Accounts Receivable, we will assume several transactions for the Mayo Department Store. Although most businesses that have a large volume of transactions such as these will use a computerized system, we will illustrate a manual system for instructional purposes. First, assume that on January 5, 1977, credit sales were made to six different customers. These sales could be recorded in the general journal as follows:

GENERAL JOURNAL Page 1

Date	Account Titles and Explanation		Folio	Debit	Credit
Jan. 5	Accounts receivable		102	2,400	
	Sales		610		2,400
	To record the following credit sales:				
	Adams, J. K.	$ 740	102.1		
	Baker, B. B.	120	102.2		
	Ford, C. E.	340	102.3		
	Moore, W. E.	320	102.4		
	Price, V. T.	430	102.5		
	Ward, B. L.	450	102.6		
	Total	$2,400			

Posting of the above journal entry to the control account in the general ledger is indicated by entering the account numbers in the folio column in the usual manner, and posting to the individual customer accounts in the subsidiary ledger is indicated by entering an individual customer's account number in the folio column of the journal. Thus, we posted the total amount to the control account, Accounts Receivable (a debit total of $2,400), and we posted the several single amounts to the subsidiary ledger as illustrated below. Note that the debit-credit-balance form is used rather than the T-account form that is often used for instructional purposes.

GENERAL LEDGER

Date			Folio	Debit	Credit	Balance
1977		Cash # 101				
Jan	12		3	1 000		
		Accounts Receivable Control # 102				
Jan	5		1	2 400		2 400
	7		2		140	2 260
	12		3		1 000	1 260
		Sales # 610				
Jan	5		1		2 400	2 400
		Sales Returns # 620				
Jan	7		2	140		140

SUBSIDIARY LEDGER

		Adams, J.K. 102.1				
Jan	5		1	740		740
	7	Return	2		140	600
	12		3		400	200
		Baker, B. R. 102.2				
Jan	5		1	120		120
		Ford, C. E. 102.3				
Jan	5		1	340		340
	12		3		340	-0-
		Moore, W. E. 102.4				
Jan	5		1	320		320
	12		3		220	100
		Price, V. T. 102.5				
Jan	5		1	430		430
	12		3		40	390
		Ward, B. L. 102.6				
Jan	5		1	450		450

Now, assume that on January 7 one customer, J. K. Adams, returned as unsatisfactory some of the goods purchased on January 5. Mayo accepted the goods and gave him a credit memorandum. The resultant journal entry was:

GENERAL JOURNAL Page 2

Jan. 7	Sales returns	620	140	
	Accounts receivable	102		140
	To record the return of goods:			
	Adams, J. K. $140	102.1		

The folio column reveals that the above entry has been posted in total to the control account in the general ledger and that the single amount has been posted to the individual customer account in the subsidiary ledger.

Now, let's complete the example by assuming subsequent collections on accounts from some of the customers. The collections are recorded in the journal entry given below. The folio column indicates that the entry has been posted in total to the control account and each single amount to the individual customer accounts in the subsidiary ledger.

GENERAL JOURNAL Page 3

Jan. 12	Cash	101	1,000	
	Accounts receivable	102		1,000
	To record collections on accounts as follows:			
	Adams, J. K. .... $ 400	102.1		
	Ford, C. E. 340	102.3		
	Moore, W. E. 220	102.4		
	Price, V. T. 40	102.5		
	Total $1,000			

The subsidiary ledger should be frequently reconciled with the control account. This is accomplished by summing the balances in the subsidiary ledger to determine whether that total agrees with the total shown by the control account in the general ledger. This check can be done by simply running an adding machine tape from the subsidiary ledger or by preparing a schedule or listing of the individual customer account balances. When there are a large number of credit sales and collections, a frequent reconciliation is advisable. A reconciliation schedule for Mayo follows:

MAYO DEPARTMENT STORE
Schedule of Accounts Receivable
January 28, 1977

Account No.	*Customer*	*Amount (per subsidiary)*
102.1	Adams, J. K.	$ 200
102.2	Baker, B. B.	120
102.4	Moore, W. E.	100
102.5	Price, V. T.	390
102.6	Ward, B. L.	450
102	Total Accounts Receivable (per control account)	$1,260

In this instance the subsidiary ledger total agrees with the balance in the control account. If there is disagreement, of course, an error is indicated; however, the mere fact of agreement does not necessarily mean there are no errors. One could post a debit or credit to the wrong individual account and the two ledgers would still reconcile in total.

In the above situation, the *Sales* account also could have been established as a control account supported by a subsidiary ledger that would contain separate accounts for the sales of *each department* or for *each product*. A very common application also relates to *accounts payable* when there are numerous purchases on credit.

Another common application relates to *fixed assets*. For example, the Office Equipment account is included in the general ledger, usually as a control account. In such instances, the control account is supported by a subsidiary ledger of office equipment that incorporates an account for each different kind of office equipment, such as copiers, typewriters, calculators, and furniture. You can appreciate from these examples that the control account/subsidiary ledger procedure is an important element of the information-processing system of most enterprises.

A particular advantage of the use of subsidiary ledgers in a manual system is that it facilitates the subdivision of work. A person can be trained in a short time to maintain a subsidiary ledger since a knowledge of the broad field of accounting is not required for such routine record-keeping tasks.

In the journal entries given above, the individual amounts relating to each individual customer account were listed in the "Explanation" column of the journal and were then posted to the subsidiary ledger. There are two approaches to simplifying this particular phase of the record-keeping. Obviously, one could transfer directly from the charge tickets and credit memoranda to the subsidiary ledger accounts and thus avoid the detailed listing in the journal entry. This approach is used sometimes by small companies that use a manual system. Another approach involves the use of a related procedure known as *special journals*. This procedure is explained and illustrated in Appendix B to Chapter 9.

Although our illustration used a manual approach to subsidiary ledgers, such is not the usual case. Most companies of any size apply the procedure by means of accounting machines or electronic computers. The computer can be programmed to process credit sales, returns, collections on account, reconciliation of account balances, and a printout of monthly bills to be mailed to the customers.

APPENDIX B

Aging accounts receivable

Generally the older an account receivable, the greater the probability of its uncollectibility. Therefore, an analysis of accounts receivable, in terms of "age," provides management with valuable information in respect to probable cash inflows, losses due to uncollectible accounts, and the general effectiveness of the credit and collection activities of the company. Aging analysis also is used by some companies to provide information needed to make the *adjusting entry* at the end of each period for estimated bad debt expense.

Instead of relating bad debt losses to credit sales for the period, as illustrated on pages 211–14, an aging approach is used that relates bad debt losses to the uncollected accounts (i.e., the balance in Accounts

Receivable) at the end of each period. The approach addresses the problem of analyzing the individual uncollected balances in order to *estimate* the portion that will ultimately be worthless. The amount estimated to be ultimately uncollectible represents the balance that should be in the account "Allowance for Doubtful Accounts" at the end of the period. The *difference* between the actual balance in that account and the amount estimated that should be reflected in it is the amount needed for the adjusting entry at the end of the period.

To illustrate, assume the general ledger for Macon Appliance Store, whose fiscal year ended December 31, 1977, reflected the following account balances:

Accounts receivable	$ 40,000 (debit balance)
Allowance for doubtful accounts	900 (credit balance)
Sales on credit for 1977	200,000

The adjusting entry for bad debt *expense* is being prepared at December 31, 1977. The company utilizes the accounts receivable aging method for determining the amount for the adjusting entry to record estimated bad debt expense. As a consequence, the following aging analysis of accounts receivable was completed:

Analysis of Accounts Receivable by Age, December 31, 1977

Customer	Total	Not Yet Due	1–30 Days Past Due	31–60 Days Past Due	61–90 Days Past Due	Over 90 Days Past Due
Adams, A. K.	$ 600	$ 600				
Baker, B. B.	1,300	300	900	100		
Cox, R. E.	1,400			400	900	100
Day, W. T.	3,000	2,000	600	400		
Zoe, A. B	900					900
Total	$40,000	$17,200	$12,000	$8,000	$1,200	$1,600
Percent	100%	43%	30%	20%	3%	4%

The management, on the basis of past experience and knowledge of specific situations, can use the above analysis as a basis for realistically estimating the probable *rates of uncollectibility for each age group.* Assume the Management estimated the following loss rates: not yet due, 1 percent; 1–30 days past due, 3 percent; 31–60 days, 6 percent; 61–90 days, 10 percent; over 90 days, 25 percent. Now the following estimating schedule can be prepared:

Estimate of Probable Uncollectible Accounts, December 31, 1977			
Age	Amount of Receivable	Percent Estimated to Be Uncollectible	Balance Needed in Allowance for Doubtful Accounts
Not yet due	$17,200	1	$172
1–30 days past due	12,000	3	360
31–60 days past due	8,000	6	480
61–90 days past due	1,200	10	120
Over 90 days past due	1,600	25	400
Total	$40,000		$1,532

The resultant adjusting entry on December 31, 1977, would be:

Dec. 31	Bad debt expense	632	
	Allowance for doubtful accounts		632
	To adjust allowance for doubtful accounts to estimated balance needed:		
	Balance needed (per schedule above)	$1,532	
	Balance before adjustment	900	
	Difference—adjustment needed (increase)	$ 632	

Some would argue that this approach to estimating the amount of bad debt expense does not comply with the *matching principle* as effectively as the method discussed in the chapter. There the estimate was based on the amount of credit sales for the period from which uncollectible accounts will ultimately occur. This matches bad debt expense with the period's sales revenues.

In contrast, the aging method, since it is based on the balance in Accounts Receivable, tends to match bad debt expense with credit sales for a number of periods; hence the matching principle may not be well served each period. However, it produces a good measurement of the net realizable value of accounts receivable since it takes into account probable losses by actual age distribution of the amounts in each account.

QUESTIONS FOR DISCUSSION

1. In an enterprise characterized by extensive selling and purchasing activities, cost of goods sold must be matched with sales revenue. Explain.
2. Explain the difference between gross sales and net sales.
3. What is gross margin on sales? How is the gross margin ratio computed?
4. Explain what is meant by sales discount. Use 1/10, n/30 in your explanation.
5. What is the distinction between sales allowances and sales discount?

6. A sale is made for $500; terms are 2/10, n/30. At what amount should the sale be recorded?

7. Since the actual time of cash collection is not relevant in determining the date on which a sale should be given accounting recognition, what factor is relevant?

8. Why is it essential that bad debt losses be estimated?

9. Briefly contrast the direct charge-off method with the allowance method in accounting for bad debt losses.

10. Why does the direct charge-off method of accounting for bad debt losses violate the matching principle?

11. What is a contra account? Give two examples.

12. Define the book value of accounts receivable.

13. Why should estimated bad debt losses be based on credit sales rather than on total sales for the period?

14. Briefly distinguish between a perpetual and a periodic inventory system. Basically, how does each measure (a) inventory and (b) cost of goods sold?

15. What is the purpose of a perpetual inventory record for each item stocked?

16. What account is debited for a purchase of goods for resale (a) when a perpetual inventory system is used and (b) when a periodic inventory system is used?

17. What accounts are debited and credited for a sale of goods on credit (a) when perpetual inventory system is used and (b) when a periodic inventory system is used?

18. Why is transportation-in considered to be a cost of purchasing merchandise?

19. Why is it necessary to take an actual physical inventory count at the end of the period when the periodic inventory system is used?

20. Under the cost principle, at what amount should a purchase be recorded?

21. Why is there no Purchases account when the perpetual inventory system is used?

$$S - CGS = GM) - OEx = Pre\ tax\ income)$$

$$BI + P = GAS - EI$$

EXERCISES

E7–1. Supply the missing dollar amounts for the income statement of Joplin Retailers for each of the following independent cases:

Case	Sales	Beginning Inventory	Pur-chases	Total Avail-able	Ending Inventory	Cost of Goods Sold	Gross Margin	Ex-penses	Pretax In-come or (Loss)
A	900	100	700	800	200	?	?	200	?
B	900	180	750	930	?	?	?	100	0
C	900	140	?		300	650	?	100	?
D	900	?	600		210	?	?	150	50
E	900	?	650		100	?	100	?	(50)

E7–2. Supply the missing dollar amounts for the income statement of Swazey Company for each of the following independent cases:

	Case A	Case B	Case C
Sales	6,000	6,000	6,000
Sales returns and allowances	150	?	?
Net sales	?	?	?
Beginning inventory	9,000	9,500	8,000
Purchases	5,000	?	5,300
Freight-in	?	120	120
Purchase returns	40	30	?
Goods available for sale	?	14,790	13,370
Ending inventory	10,000	9,000	?
Cost of goods sold	?	?	5,400
Gross margin	?	110	?
Expenses	690	?	520
Pretax income	1,000	(500)	-0-

E7–3. The following data were taken from the records of Reo Corporation on December 31, 1977:

Sales of merchandise for cash	$240,000
Sales of merchandise for credit	150,000
Sales returns and allowances	2,000
Operating expenses	140,500
From perpetual inventory records:	
Merchandise inventory, January 1, 1977	50,000
Cost of goods sold	230,000
Merchandise inventory, December 31, 1977	60,000

Estimated bad debt loss, 1% of net credit sales.
Average income tax rate, 20%.
Number of shares of common stock outstanding, 20,000.

Required:

a. Based on the above data, prepare an income statement. There were no extraordinary items.

b. Compute the gross margin ratio and the profit margin ratio.

E7–4. The following summarized data were provided by the records of Melody's Music Store, Incorporated, for the year ended December 31, 1977:

Sales of merchandise for cash	$120,000
Sales of merchandise on credit	40,000
Purchases	96,000
Operating expenses	60,000
Merchandise inventory, January 1, 1977	40,000
Sales returns and allowances	3,000
Purchase returns and allowances	1,000
Freight-in	4,000

Average income tax rate, 20%.
Number of shares of common stock outstanding, 10,000.
Physical inventory of goods on hand, December 31, 1977, $63,000. (The company uses a periodic inventory system.)

Required:

a. Based upon the above data, prepare an income statement. Show income tax expense separately. There were no extraordinary items.
b. Compute the gross margin ratio and the profit margin ratio.

E7–5. During the month of January, the WZ Corporation sold goods to two customers. The sequence of events was as follows:

Jan. 6 Sold goods for $800 to J. Doe and billed that amount subject to terms, 2/10, n/30.
6 Sold goods to R. Roe for $600 and billed that amount subject to terms, 2/10, n/30.
14 Collected cash due from J. Doe.
Feb. 2 Collected cash due from R. Roe.

Required:

Give the appropriate entry for each date. Assume a periodic inventory system is used.

E7–6. The following list of transactions involving College Store were selected from the records for January 1977:

1. Sales: cash, $130,000; and on credit, $40,000 (terms, n/30).
2. Merchandise sold on credit in 1 and subsequently returned for credit, $800.
3. Purchases: cash, $80,000; and on credit $15,000 (terms, n/60).
4. Merchandise purchased and subsequently returned for credit: $500.
5. Shipping costs paid in cash on the merchandise purchased, $400.
6. Bad debt losses, on the basis of past experience, are estimated to be one half of 1 percent of credit sales net of sales returns and allowances.
7. An account receivable amounting to $150 was written off as uncollectible. The sale was made two years earlier.

Required:

a. Give the journal entry that would be made for each transaction, assuming the company uses a periodic inventory system.
b. Prepare an income statement for January 1977, through the caption "Gross margin on sales." The December 31, 1976, inventory of merchandise was $75,000; and the physical inventory count of merchandise taken on January 31, 1977, amounted to $90,000.

E7–7. During 1977, Mae's Ready-to-Wear Shop sold merchandise amounting to $110,000, of which $40,000 was on credit. At the start of 1977, Accounts Receivable reflected a debit balance of $12,000 and the Allowance for Doubtful Accounts a $600 credit balance. Collections on accounts receivable during 1977 amounted to $33,000.

Data during 1977:

1. December 31, 1977, an account receivable of $700 from a prior year was determined to be uncollectible; therefore, it was written off immediately.
2. December 31, 1977, on the basis of past experience, it was decided to continue the accounting policy of basing estimated bad debt losses on 1 percent of net credit sales for the year.

Required:

a. Give the required entries for the two items on December 31, 1977 (end of the accounting period).
b. Show how the amounts related to accounts receivable and bad debt expense would be reported on the income statement and balance sheet for 1977. Disregard income tax considerations.
c. On the basis of the data available does it appear that the 1 percent rate used is too high or too low? Explain. What other ways can you think of to estimate bad debt losses.

E7–8. Swift Sport Shop sells on credit terms of 2/10, n/30. A sale of $800 was made to K. Williams on February 1, 1977. In due time the account was paid in full.

Required:

a. Give the entry to record the credit sale.
b. Give the entry assuming the account was collected in full on February 9, 1977.
c. Give the entry assuming, instead, the account was collected in full on March 2, 1977.

On March 4, 1977, Swift purchased from a supplier, on credit, sporting goods costing $6,000; the terms were 1/10, n/30.

Required:

d. Give the entry to record the purchase on credit. Assume periodic inventory system.
e. Give the entry assuming the account was paid in full on March 12, 1977.
f. Give the entry assuming, instead, the account was paid in full on March 28, 1977.

E7–9. Palmer Company uses a perpetual inventory system. Since it is a small business and sells only five different high-cost items, a perpetual inventory record is maintained for each item. The following selected data relate to Item A for the month of January:

a. Beginning inventory—quantity 5, cost $77 each.
b. Purchased—quantity 4, cost $72 each; paid $20 total freight.

c. Sold—quantity 6, sales price $150 each.
d. Returns—one sold in (*c*) was returned for full credit.

Required:

1. Give the journal entries for the above transactions assuming a perpetual inventory system and cash transactions.
2. Prepare the perpetual inventory record to Item A.
3. For January, give the following amounts for Item A:

a.	Sales revenue	$________
b.	Cost of goods sold	$________
c.	Gross margin	$________
d.	Ending inventory	$________

4. Was there any inventory shrinkage? Explain.

E7–10. Rose Company uses a perpetual inventory system that provides amounts for the period for (*a*) cost of goods sold and (*b*) ending inventory. Physical inventory counts are made from time to time to verify the perpetual inventory records. On December 31, 1977, the end of the fiscal year, the perpetual inventory record for Item No. 18 showed the following (summarized):

	Units	*Unit cost*	*Total cost*
Beginning inventory	500	$2	$1,000
Purchases during the period	900	2	1,800
Sales during the period (sales price $3.50)	800		

Required:

a. Give the entry to record the purchases for cash during the period.
b. Give the entry to record the sales for cash during the period.
c. Assume a physical inventory count was made after the above transactions and it reflected 590 units of Item No. 18 on hand. Give any entry required.
d. Give the following amounts for 1977 related to Item No. 18:

1.	Ending inventory	units ______	$______
2.	Cost of goods sold	units ______	$______
3.	Shrinkage loss	units ______	$______

e. As a manager, would you investigate in this situation? How?

E7–11. The trial balance for Home Appliances, Incorporated, at December 31, 1977 (end of the fiscal year), is given below. Only selected items have been used in order to shorten the case. The company uses a perpetual inventory system. All of the accounts you will need are listed in the trial balance.

Trial Balance
December 31, 1977

Cash	$ 6,800	
Accounts receivable	12,000	
Allowance for doubtful accounts		$ 700
Merchandise inventory	64,000	
Fixed assets	40,000	
Accumulated depreciation		12,000
Accounts payable		8,000
Income taxes payable		
Capital stock, par $10		60,000
Retained earnings, January 1, 1977		14,300
Sales revenue		105,000
Sales returns and allowances	1,200	
Cost of goods sold	56,000	
Expenses (not detailed)	20,000	
Bad debt expense		
Depreciation expense		
Income tax expense		
	$200,000	$200,000

Additional data developed for the adjusting entries:

a. Estimated bad debt expense is 2 percent of net credit sales. Net credit sales for 1977 amounted to $35,000.
b. The fixed assets are being depreciated $4,000 each year.
c. The average income tax rate is 20 percent.

Required:

Set up a worksheet similar to the one in the demonstration problem (omit columns for Adjusted Trial Balance). Enter the trial balance and the adjusting entries and complete the worksheet.

E7–12. During 1977, XY Corporation records reflected the following for one product stocked:

a.	Beginning inventory	1,000 units, unit cost $2
b.	Purchases	8,000 units, unit cost $2
c.	Sales	7,000 units, unit sales price $3
d.	Purchase returns	10 units, for $2 per unit refund from the supplier
e.	Sales returns	5 units, for $3 per unit refund to the customer

Required:

1. Assuming all transactions are cash, give the entries for the above transactions for:

   Case A – a perpetual inventory system.
   Case B – a periodic inventory system.

2. How would the amount of cost of goods sold be determined in each case?

E7–13. The trial balance for Variety Store, Incorporated, at December 31, 1977 (the end of the fiscal year), is given below. Only selected and summary accounts are given in order to shorten the case. Also, the amounts have been simplified for this same purpose. The company uses a periodic inventory system. With the exception of the ending inventory, all of the accounts you will need are listed in the trial balance.

Debit		*Credit*	
Cash	$ 7,600	Allowance for doubtful accounts	$ 150
Accounts receivable	3,000	Accumulated depreciation	900
Merchandise inventory, January 1, 1977	4,000	Accounts payable	5,000
Store supplies inventory	250	Wages payable	
Store equipment	3,000	Income taxes payable	
Sales returns	150	Capital stock, par $10	6,000
Purchases	6,000	Retained earnings	1,870
Bad debt expense		Sales	13,000
Depreciation expense		Purchases returns	80
Freight-in (on purchases)	100		
Income tax expense			
Other operating expenses	2,900		
	$27,000		$27,000

Data developed as a basis for the adjusting entries at December 31, 1977, were:

a. Estimated bad debt expense for 1977 was 1 percent of net credit sales of $12,000.
b. An inventory of store supplies on hand taken at December 31, 1977, reflected $50.
c. Depreciation on the store equipment is based on an estimated useful life of ten years and no residual value.
d. Wages earned up to December 31, 1977, but not yet paid or recorded amounted to $500.
e. Inventories: The beginning inventory is shown in the above trial balance. A physical inventory of merchandise on hand and unsold, taken at December 31, 1977, reflected $2,000.
f. Assume an average income tax rate of 20 percent.

Required:

1. Set up a worksheet similar to the one in the demonstration case (omit columns for Adjusted Trial Balance). Enter the trial balance, adjusting entries, and ending inventory, and complete the worksheet.
2. Prepare a partial income statement through gross margin on sales.

PROBLEMS

P7–1. Red Equipment Company, Incorporated, sells heavy construction equipment. There are 10,000 shares of capital stock outstanding. The company uses a perpetual inventory system for inventory control and accounting purposes. The annual fiscal period ends on December 31. The following condensed trial balance was taken from the general ledger on December 31, 1977:

	Debit	*Credit*
Cash	$ 11,000	
Accounts receivable	20,000	
Allowance for doubtful accounts		$ 1,000
Inventory	90,000	
Fixed assets	40,000	
Accumulated depreciation		8,000
Liabilities		17,000
Capital stock		100,000
Retained earnings, January 1, 1977		20,000
Sales		204,000
Sales returns and allowances	4,000	
Cost of goods sold	120,000	
Selling expenses	37,000	
Administrative expenses	10,000	
Interest expense	3,000	
Extraordinary loss, storm damage	5,000	
Income tax expense*	10,000	
	$350,000	$350,000

* Assume a 40 percent average tax rate on both operations and the extraordinary loss.

Required:

a. Prepare a multiple-step income statement. (Hint: Reflect the income tax effect of the extraordinary loss.)

b. Prepare the following ratio analysis:
1. Gross margin on sales ratio.
2. Profit margin ratio.
3. Return on investment (on owners' equity).

c. In the ratio analysis, what amount did you use for income? Explain why.

P7–2. White's Corporation is a local grocery store organized seven years ago as a corporation by three individuals. At that time, a total of 10,000 shares of common stock was issued to the organizers. The store is in an excellent location, and sales have increased each year. At the end of 1977 the bookkeeper prepared the following statement (assume all amounts are correct):

WHITE'S INCORPORATED
Profit and Loss
December 31, 1977

	Debit	Credit
Sales		$301,000
Purchase returns and allowances		700
Merchandise inventory, per count, December 31, 1977		112,300
Sales returns and allowances	$ 1,000	
Purchases	181,700	
Freight-in	800	
Selling expenses	60,000	
Administrative and general expenses	30,000	
Interest expense	500	
Merchandise inventory, per count, December 31, 1976	100,000	
Extraordinary loss	4,000	
Income tax expense (on operations $12,000 less $1,200 saved on the extraordinary loss)	10,800	
Net profit	25,200	
	$414,000	$414,000

Required:

a. Prepare a multiple-step income statement. The company utilizes periodic inventory procedures. Assume an average 30 percent income tax rate.

b. Prepare the following ratio analysis:

1. Profit margin on sales ratio.
2. Gross margin on sales ratio.
3. Return on investment (on owners' equity of $150,000).

c. In computing the above ratios, what amount did you use for income? Explain why.

d. Which ratio do you think has the highest information content for a typical investor? Why?

P7-3. The transactions listed below have been selected from those occurring during the month of January 1977 for the OK Department Store, Incorporated. A wide line of goods is offered for sale. A periodic inventory system is used. Credit sales are extended to a few select customers; however, the usual credit terms are n/EOM. Selected transactions (summarized for January) are:

1. Sales to customers:	
Cash	$350,000
On credit	20,000
2. Unsatisfactory merchandise returned by customers:	
Cash	4,000
Credit	1,000
3. Merchandise purchased from vendors on credit; terms, 1/20, n/30:	

AB Supply Company, amount billed, before deduction of cash discount	1,000
From other vendors, amount billed, before deduction of cash discount	120,000
4. Freight paid on merchandise purchased; paid cash (set up a separate account for this item)	2,000
5. Collections on accounts receivable	17,000
6. The accounts payable were paid in full during the period as follows:	
AB Supply Company, paid after the discount period	1,000
Other vendors, paid within the discount period	118,800
7. Purchased two new typewriters for the office; paid cash	900
8. An account receivable from a customer from a prior year amounting to $300 was determined to be uncollectible and was written off.	
9. At the end of January the adjusting entry for estimated bad debts is to be made. The loss rate, based on past experience, is one half of 1% of net credit sales for the period (i.e., on credit sales less credit returns).	

Relevant account balances on January 1, 1977, were: Accounts Receivable, $3,200 (debit); and Allowance for Doubtful Accounts, $900 (credit). Total assets at the end of the period, $250,000.

Required:

a. Prepare journal entries for the above items assuming a periodic inventory system.

b. Determine the following amounts at January 31, 1977 (show computations):
   1. Bad debt expense.
   2. Balance in accounts receivable.
   3. Balance in allowance for doubtful accounts.
   4. Book or carrying value of accounts receivable.
   5. Estimated net realizable value of accounts receivable.

c. Explain why bad debt expense for January is not debited for the $300 bad debt.

P7–4. This problem is designed to demonstrate the accounting for cash discounts by both the seller and purchaser. Observe the consistency between both parties to the same transactions—one party's sales discount is another party's purchase discount.

Assume the following summarized transactions between Company A, the vendor, and Company B, the purchaser. Use the letters to the left as the date notations. Assume both companies use a periodic inventory system.

1. Company A sold Company B merchandise for $10,000; terms, 2/10, n/30.
2. Prior to payment, Company B returned $1,000 (one tenth) of the merchandise for credit because it did not meet their specifications.

Required:

Give the following entries for each party:

a. The sale/purchase transaction.
b. The return transaction.
c. Payment in full assuming made within the discount period.
d. Payment in full assuming, instead, after the discount period.

Use a form similar to the following:

		Co. A—vendor		*Co. B—purchaser*	
Date	*Accounts*	*Debit*	*Credit*	*Debit*	*Credit*

P7–5. College Shop, Incorporated, is a "student co-op." It has been operating successfully for a number of years. The board of directors is composed of faculty and students. On January 1, 1977, when this case starts, the beginning inventory was $200,000; the Accounts Receivable debit balance was $3,000; and the Allowance for Doubtful Accounts credit balance was $400. A periodic inventory system is used.

The following transactions (summarized) have been selected from 1977 for case purposes:

a. Merchandise sales for cash	$220,000
b. Merchandise returned by customers as unsatisfactory, for cash refund	1,400
c. Merchandise purchased from vendors on credit; terms, 2/10, n/30:	
May Supply Company, invoice price, before deduction of cash discount	4,000
Other vendors, invoice price, before deduction of cash discount	115,000
d. Purchased equipment for use in the store; paid cash	1,800
e. Purchased office supplies for future use in the store; paid cash	600
f. Freight on merchandise purchased; paid cash (set up a separate account for this item)	500
g. Accounts payable paid in full during the period as follows:	
May Supply Company, paid after the discount period	4,000
Other vendors, paid within the discount period	98,000

Required:

1. Prepare journal entries for each of the above items.
2. Give the adjusting entries required at December 31, 1977 for:
   a. Beginning inventory.
   b. Ending inventory (assume $210,000).
   c. Ending inventory of supplies (assume $200 and no beginning inventory).
3. Prepare a partial income statement through gross margin on sales.
4. Did you record merchandise purchases at net or at gross? Explain why.

P7–6. Strong Distributing Company uses a perpetual inventory system for the ten different kinds of items it sells. The following selected data relate to a small but high-cost item stocked during the month of January 1977. To simplify we will refer to this item as Item No. 10.

a. Beginning inventory—quantity 70; cost, $50 each.
b. Purchases—quantity 90; cost, $48 each plus $180 total freight-in.
c. Sales—quantity 120; sales price, $95 each.
d. Returns—Strong accepted a return of two of the items sold in (*c*) because it was not needed by the customer and it had not been used.
e. At the end of January 1977, a physical inventory count showed 37 items remaining on hand.

Required (assume all transactions were cash):

1. Prepare the perpetual inventory record for Item No. 10.
2. Give entries for each of the above transactions.
3. Prepare the income statement for January 1977 through gross margin on sales as it relates to Item No. 10. What was the gross margin ratio on sales?
4. As the responsible manager, would you investigate the inventory shrinkage? How? What alternatives would you consider for corrective action?
5. Assume also that you observe quite often that the required items are out of stock. How can a perpetual inventory system be helpful in avoiding this problem?

P7–7. MRW Company uses a perpetual inventory system. During the month of January 1977, the perpetual inventory record for Item A, which is one of the 23 items stocked, showed the following (summarized):

PERPETUAL INVENTORY RECORD

		Goods Purchased		Goods Sold		Balance	
Date	Explanation	Units	Total Cost	Units	Total Cost	Units	Total Cost
a.	Beginning inventory					40	3,200
b.	Purchase (at $80 each)	20					
c.	Sale (sales price $150 each)			31			
d.	Purchase return (one unit)						
e.	Purchase (at $80 each)	30					
f.	Sale return (one unit)						
g.	Sale (sales price $150 each)			29			
h.	Inventory shortage (two units)						

Required:

1. Complete the above perpetual inventory record.
2. Give the journal entry for each transaction (assume transactions are cash).

3. Complete the following:

Income Statement:	
Sales	$______
Cost of goods sold	$______
Gross margin on sales	$______
Gross margin ratio	$______
Balance Sheet:	
Inventory	$______

4. How should the inventory shortage be reported?
5. As the responsible manager, would you investigate this situation? How? What alternatives would you consider for corrective action?
6. Assume "stockout" has been a problem. What would you recommend?

P7–8. The following transactions, relating to one product sold by Robbins Company, were completed in the order given during January:

a. Purchased—quantity 100; cost, $20 each.
b. Sold—quantity 80; $30 each.
c. Purchase return—returned one of the units purchased in (*a*) because it was the wrong size.
d. Sales return—accepted two units from a customer that were sold in (*b*). The customer did not need them, and they were not damaged.
e. Inventories:
  Beginning inventory, January 1—30 units at total cost of $600.
  Ending inventory, January 31—per periodic inventory count, 51 units @ $20 = $1,020.
f. Cost of goods sold for January—78 units @ $20 = $1,560.

Required:

You are to compare the journal entries that would be made for the above transactions assuming: Case A—a perpetual inventory system is used; and Case B—a periodic inventory system is used. To do this, set up the following form (assume cash transactions):

		Amounts			
		Perpetual		*Periodic*	
Date	*Explanation*	*Debit*	*Credit*	*Debit*	*Credit*
a.	To record the purchase				
b.	To record the sale				
c.	To record the purchase return				
d.	To record the sales return				
e.	To record the adjusting entries for inventories				
f.	To record the closing entry for cost of goods sold				

P7–9. Long Retailers' Incorporated is completing the information-processing cycle for the year ended December 31, 1977. The worksheet given below has been completed through the adjusting entries:

Account Titles	Trial Balance Debit	Trial Balance Credit	Adjusting Entries Debit	Adjusting Entries Credit	Income Statement Debit	Income Statement Credit	Balance Sheet Debit	Balance Sheet Credit
Cash	26,000							
Accounts receivable	11,700							
Allowance for doubtful accounts				(*a*) 400				
Merchandise inventory	30,000		(*b*) 32,000	(*b*) 30,000				
Equipment	22,500							
Accumulated depreciation, equipment		7,500		(*c*) 1,500				
Other assets	20,000							
Accounts payable		8,000						
Interest payable				(*d*) 300				
Income taxes payable				(*e*) 4,000				
Note payable, long term, 9%		10,000						
Capital stock, par $10		50,000						
Contributed capital in excess of par		7,500						
Retained earnings, January 1, 1977 (less $6,000 cash dividends paid during January 1977)		7,000						
Sales revenue		95,000						
Sales returns and allowances	1,000							
Purchases	52,000							
Freight-in	2,000							
Purchase returns and allowances		1,100						
Operating expenses (not detailed)	20,300							
Bad debt expense			(*a*) 400					
Depreciation expense			(*c*) 1,500					
Interest expense	600		(*d*) 300					
Income summary—inventories			(*b*) 30,000	(*b*) 32,000				
Income tax expense			(*e*) 4,000					
Net Income								
Totals	186,100	186,100	68,200	68,200				

Required:

1. Complete the worksheet.
2. Write a brief explanation for each adjusting entry.
3. Based on the worksheet, respond to the following questions:
   a. What kind of inventory system was used? What is the basis for your response?

b. How long has the equipment been used by Long assuming no residual value?
c. What is the interest date for the long-term note payable?
d. What was the average income tax rate?
e. What was the balance in retained earnings on January 1, 1977?
4. Prepare a multiple-step income statement.
5. Prepare a classified balance sheet.
6. Give the closing entries.

P7–10. (Note: This is an extended problem designed to review Chapters 4, 5, 6, and 7.) Quality Furniture Store, Incorporated, has been in operation for a number of years and has been quite profitable. The losses on uncollectible accounts and merchandise returns are about the same as for other furniture stores. The company uses a perpetual inventory system. The annual fiscal period ended December 31, 1977, and the end-of-the-period information-processing cycle has been started. The following trial balance was derived from the general ledger at December 31, 1977:

Cash	$ 16,880	
Accounts receivable	36,000	
Allowance for doubtful accounts		$ 4,600
Merchandise inventory	120,000	
Store equipment	20,000	
Accumulated depreciation		8,000
Accounts payable		10,000
Income taxes payable		
Interest payable		
Notes payable, long term		48,000
Capital stock, par $100		70,000
Retained earnings, January 1, 1977*		1,400
Sales revenue		441,000
Sales returns and allowances	25,000	
Cost of goods sold	213,350	
Selling expenses	102,700	
Administrative expenses	49,070	
Bad debt expense		
Depreciation expense		
Interest expense		
Income tax expense		
	$583,000	$583,000

* After deducting $10,000 cash dividends declared and paid during January 1977.

Data for adjusting entries:

a. The bad debt losses due to uncollectible accounts are estimated to be $6,000.
b. The store equipment is being depreciated over an estimated useful life of ten years with no residual value.
c. The long-term note of $48,000 was for a two-year loan from a local bank. The interest rate is 8 percent, payable at the end of each

12-month period. The note was dated April 1, 1977. (Hint: Accrue interest for nine months.)

d. Assume an average 40 percent corporate income tax rate.

Required:

1. Based upon the above data, complete a worksheet similar to the one illustrated in the chapter for the demonstration case (you may omit columns for Adjusted Trial Balance). The company uses a perpetual inventory system. (Hint: Net income is $24,000.)
2. Based upon the completed worksheet, prepare a multiple-step income statement, statement of retained earnings, and balance sheet.
3. Based upon the completed worksheet, prepare the adjusting and closing entries for December 31, 1977.

P7–11. (Note: This is an extended problem designed to review the materials discussed in Chapters 4, 5, 6, and 7.) Central Appliances, Incorporated, is owned by six local investors. It has been operating for four years and is at the end of the 1977 fiscal year. For case purposes, certain accounts have been selected to demonstrate the information-processing activities at the end of the year for a corporation that sells merchandise rather than services. The following trial balance, assumed to be correct, was taken from the ledger on December 31, 1977. The company uses a periodic inventory system.

Debit		*Credit*	
Cash	$ 18,000	Allowance for doubtful accounts	$ 600
Accounts receivable	28,000	Accumulated depreciation	12,000
Merchandise inventory, January 1, 1977	80,000	Accounts payable	15,000
Prepaid insurance	300	Notes payable, long term	30,000
Store equipment	40,000	Capital stock, par $10	40,000
Sales returns	3,000	Retained earnings, January 1, 1977*	2,000
Purchases	250,000	Sales	400,000
Freight-in	11,000	Purchase returns	7,000
Operating expenses	76,300		
	$506,600		$506,600

* After deducting cash dividends of $12,000 declared and paid during January 1977.

Additional data for adjusting entries:

a. Credit sales during the year were $100,000; based on past experience, a 1 percent loss rate on credit sales has been established.

b. Insurance amounting to $100 expired during the year.

c. The store equipment is being depreciated over a ten-year estimated useful life with no residual value.

d. The long-term note payable for $30,000 was dated May 1, 1977, and carries an 8 percent interest rate per annum. The note is for three years and interest is payable at April 30 each year.

e. Assume an average tax rate of 30 percent.

f. Inventories:

Beginning inventory, January 1, 1977 (per above trial balance), $80,000.

Ending inventory, December 31, 1977 (per physical inventory count), $75,000.

Required:

1. Prepare a worksheet at December 31, 1977, similar to the one shown in the demonstration problem in the chapter. You may omit columns for Adjusted Trial Balance. In order to save time and space, all operating expenses have been summarized. However, you should set up additional expense accounts for depreciation, bad debts, interest, and income taxes. Also, you will need additional liability accounts for interest payable and income taxes payable. (Hint: Net income is $38,500.)
2. Based upon the completed worksheet, prepare a multiple-step income statement, statement of retained earnings, and classified balance sheet.
3. Based upon the completed worksheet, prepare the adjusting and closing journal entries at December 31, 1977.

P7–12. (Related to Appendix A.) Town's Department Store, Incorporated, is a large department store located in a midwestern town of approximately 200,000 population. The store carries top brands and attempts to appeal to "quality customers." Approximately 80 percent of the sales are on credit. As a consequence, there is a significant amount of detailed recordkeeping related to charge sales, returns, collections, and billings. Some years ago the accounts receivable records were maintained manually. A change was made to a mechanized system, and now the store is considering computerizing this phase of the information system. Included in the general ledger is a control account for accounts receivable. Supporting the control account is an accounts receivable subsidiary ledger that carries individual accounts for over 20,000 customers. For case purposes only, a few accounts and transactions with simplified amounts have been selected. The case requirement is intended to indicate the nature of the data processing work that is to be computerized; however, here it will be completed manually.

On January 1, 1977, the Accounts Receivable control account (No. 52), in the general ledger, reflected a debit balance of $4,000 and the subsidiary ledger reflected the following balances:

52.1	Akins, A. K.	$400	52.5	May, O. W.	$800
52.2	Blue, V. R.	700	52.6	Nash, G. A.	100
52.3	Daley, U. T.	900	52.7	Roth, I. W.	600
52.4	Evans, T. V.	300	52.8	Winn, W. W.	200

During the month of January, the following transactions and events relating to sales activities occurred (use notation at left for date):

a. Sales of merchandise on credit:

Akins, A. K.	$300	Daley, U. T.	$ 70
Blue, V. R.	250	Roth, I. W.	370
Winn, W. W.	730	Evans, T. V.	410
May, O. W.	140		

b. Unsatisfactory merchandise returned:

Roth, I. W.	$ 30	Akins, A. K.	$ 20
Winn, W. W.	70		

c. Collections on accounts receivable:

Winn, W. W.	$800	Roth, I. W.	$700
May, O. W.	940	Blue, V. R.	750
Akins, A. K.	200	Daley, U. T.	600

d. The account with G. A. Nash has been inactive for several years. After an investigation, the management decided that it was uncollectible; therefore, it is to be written off immediately.

e. The bad debt losses are based on credit sales; the estimated loss rate is 2 percent of net credit sales (i.e., on credit sales less returns for credit).

Required:

1. Set up the general ledger control account for Accounts Receivable. Also set up the general ledger account for Allowance for Doubtful Accounts (No. 53) with a credit balance of $600. Indicate the beginning balance as "Bal." and for convenience use T-accounts.
2. Set up an accounts receivable subsidiary ledger in good form; use three columns—Debit, Credit, and Balance. Enter the beginning balances with the notation "Bal."
3. Prepare journal entries for each of the above transactions. Include a folio number for posting to both the control account and the subsidiary ledger. Assume periodic inventory.
4. Post the entries prepared in 3 to the Accounts Receivable control account, Allowance for Doubtful Accounts, and the subsidiary ledger. Use folio numbers.
5. Prepare a schedule of accounts receivable to show how much each customer owed at the end of January.
6. Show how accounts receivable and the related allowance would be reported in the January balance sheet.

8

Costing methods for measuring inventory and cost of goods sold

PURPOSE OF THE CHAPTER

In measuring the amount of inventory at a given date, whether a perpetual or periodic inventory system is used, the following basic questions must be considered:

1. What items should be included in the inventory and in cost of goods sold?
2. What cost should be assigned to those items included in the inventory and in cost of goods sold?

In this chapter we will focus on answers to these two questions and their implementation in the information-processing system.[1]

INVENTORY EFFECTS ON THE MEASUREMENT OF INCOME

Inventory often is the largest single asset owned by a business. Its measurement directly affects the amount of income reported for the period. The amount of inventory, measured at the end of the accounting period, affects not only the income for that period but also the amount of income for the **following period.** This two-period effect is due to the fact that the ending inventory for one period is the beginning inventory for the

[1] *Fundamentals of Management Accounting* discusses inventory measurement in a manufacturing business.

next period. To illustrate these effects, assume that the 1976 and 1977 income statements for Company A reflected incomes of $5,000 and $6,500, respectively, measured as follows:

		1976		*1977*
Sales		$100,000		$110,000
Cost of goods sold:				
Beginning inventory	$ -0-		$10,000	
Purchases	70,000		58,000	
Goods available for sale	70,000		68,000	
Ending inventory	10,000		-0-	
Cost of goods sold		60,000		68,000
Gross margin		40,000		42,000
Expenses		35,000		35,500
Pretax income		$ 5,000		$ 6,500

Observe that the ending inventory, as measured and reported at December 31, 1976, amounted to $10,000. This amount also is reported as the inventory at the **beginning** of 1977.

Now, let's assume that there was an error in measuring the ending inventory at December 31, 1976, and that the correct amount was determined to be $11,000 (i.e., $1,000 more than shown above). The changed amount in the inventory could have been due to either one or a combination of the following factors:

1. In physically counting the inventory items, some were incorrectly left out. They had a cost of $1,000.
2. Although the physical count was correct, in applying the unit costs, a higher purchase cost should have been used. This higher cost increased the amount of the inventory by $1,000.

We now will see how this error of $1,000 in the 1976 ending inventory will affect the income amounts for each of the two years. The income statements may be restated to reflect the increased inventory amount as follows:

		1976		*1977*
Sales		$100,000		$110,000
Cost of goods sold:				
Beginning inventory	$ -0-		$11,000	
Purchases	70,000		58,000	
Goods available for sale	70,000		69,000	
Ending inventory	11,000		-0-	
Cost of goods sold		59,000		69,000
Gross margin		41,000		41,000
Expenses		35,000		35,500
Pretax income		$ 6,000		$ 5,500

Observe that in comparison with the preceding income statements, the income for 1976 is greater by $1,000 and less by the same amount for 1977. Thus, a comparison of the two sets of income statements demonstrates the following generalizations:

1. In the period of the change: An increase in the amount of the ending inventory for a period increases income for that period by the same amount. To the contrary, a decrease in the amount of inventory decreases pretax income for that period by the same amount.
2. In the next period: An increase in the amount of the ending inventory for a period decreases the income of the *next period* by the same amount. To the contrary, a decrease in the amount of the ending inventory for a period increases pretax income of the *next period* by the same amount.

Observe that in any period there is a direct relationship between ending inventory and pretax income. Conversely, there is an inverse relationship between beginning inventory and pretax income.

The above illustrations indicate the importance of careful measurement of inventory. Care must be exercised in (1) measuring the quantity of items that should be included in the inventory, and (2) applying the dollar unit cost to the units counted as remaining on hand.

WHAT ITEMS SHOULD BE INCLUDED IN INVENTORY

Inventory usually is represented by tangible personal property that is held for sale in the ordinary course of business or is to be consumed in the near future in producing goods or services for sale. Inventory is reported on the balance sheet as a current asset because it normally will be converted into cash within one year or within the next operating cycle of the business, whichever is the longer. It usually is listed below accounts receivable because it is less liquid (i.e., less readily convertible to cash).

The kinds of inventory normally held depend upon the characteristics of the business:[2]

Retail or wholesale business:

Merchandise inventory—goods (or merchandise) held for resale in the ordinary course of business. The goods usually are acquired through purchase as completely manufactured and ready for sale without further processing.

Manufacturing business:

Finished goods inventory—goods manufactured by the business, completed and ready for sale.

[2] Supplies on hand are reported as prepaid expenses. This topic is discussed on page 284.

Goods in process inventory—goods (or work) in the process of being fabricated or manufactured but not yet completed as finished goods. Goods in process inventory, when completed, becomes finished goods inventory.

Raw materials inventory—items acquired by purchase, extraction of natural resources, or growth (such as food products) for the purpose of processing into finished goods. Raw materials inventory, when used, flows into goods in process inventory; then, when processing is completed, to finished goods inventory.

The discussions to follow focus on merchandise and finished goods inventories.

In measuring the **physical quantity** of goods in the inventory, a company should include all items to which it has **legal ownership;** irrespective of their location. In business transactions involving inventories and cost of goods sold, accounting focuses on when legal ownership passes. When ownership passes, one party has made a sale and the other party has made a purchase. In a purchase/sale transaction, the basic guideline is that ownership to the goods passes at the *time intended by the parties* to the transaction. Generally, ownership passes when the goods are delivered by the seller to the buyer; however, there are situations where this is not the case.

There are situations where the intentions of the parties as to the time of passage of ownership are not clear. In such situations, all of the circumstances must be assessed and judgment applied as to when the buyer and seller intended ownership to pass. For example, goods may be sold on credit and the buyer requests the vendor to hold the goods pending shipping instructions. In this instance, ownership appears to have passed, irrespective of the delivery date. A similar question arises when a third party, usually a transportation company, has physical possession of the goods for a period of time. The question is: Who owns goods during the period in transit? If the terms of the sale provide that the buyer must pay the transportation charges (known as FOB shipping point), then ownership generally is assumed to pass when the vendor delivers the goods to the transportation agent. In contrast, if the terms of the sale are FOB destination (i.e., the seller must pay the freight), ownership generally is assumed to pass when the goods are delivered to the buyer at destination.[3]

The passage-of-ownership test is a part of the revenue principle previously discussed (Exhibit 2–1). The passage-of-ownership guideline has a legal basis and prevails in the accounting process in respect to both the sale and purchase of goods. In the absence of the passage-of-ownership test, the financial statements could be manipulated to overstate

[3] FOB stand for "free on board"; it is used in business to indicate who is responsible for paying the transportation charges: FOB destination, seller pays the freight; FOB shipping point, buyer pays the freight.

income by entering all **sales orders** received up through the last day of the period, irrespective of the fact that ownership to the goods ordered may not have passed. Conversely, purchases may not be recorded intentionally even though ownership to the goods has passed.

A company may have possession of goods that it does not own; these should be excluded from the inventory. The usual situation here is when goods are held **on consignment** for sale on a commission basis. When goods are on consignment, the supplier (known as the consignor) legally retains ownership to the goods although they are in the physical possession of the party that will sell them (known as the consignee). The consignor, although the goods are not in his or her physical possession, should include them in the inventory. The consignee, although having possession of them, should exclude them from the inventory since ownership still resides with the consignor.

In summary, in identifying the goods to be included in the inventory at a specific date, ownership, rather than physical possession, is controlling. The inventory should include only, but all of, the goods to which the entity has legal ownership.

INVENTORY COST

In Chapter 7 we discussed the application of the cost principle to the purchase of goods for resale. Goods in inventory are costed in accordance with the *cost principle.* Its application to inventories has been stated as follows:

> The primary basis of accounting for inventory is cost, which has been defined generally as the price paid or consideration given to acquire an asset. As applied to inventories, cost means, in principle, the sum of the applicable expenditures and charges directly or indirectly incurred in bringing an article to its existing condition and location.[4]

We also explained that in accordance with the cost principle, indirect expenditures related to the purchase of goods, such as freight, insurance, and storage, conceptually should be included in measuring the purchase cost of the goods acquired. When any of those goods remain in inventory, these elements should be included in measuring the inventory cost. However, since these incidental amounts frequently are not *material in amount* (recall the materiality concept; Exhibit 2–1) when related to the total purchase cost, and since there is often no convenient method of apportioning such costs to each item of goods, they often are not assigned to the inventory cost. Thus, for practical reasons, some companies use the *net invoice price* when assigning a unit cost to goods purchased or to inventory.

---

[4] AICPA, *Accounting Research Bulletin No. 43* (New York, 1961), chap. 4, statement 3.

Assigning cost to the inventory

The previous chapter discussed the perpetual and periodic inventory systems. In addition to other purposes, these two systems are used for **measuring** the amounts for cost of goods sold and for the ending inventory. Even though the mechanics of applying the two systems differ, the fundamental accounting submodel on which they focus is the same. That submodel is:

$$\text{Cost of Beginning Inventory} + \text{Cost of Additional Inventory Acquired (purchases)} - \text{Cost of Ending Inventory} = \text{Cost of Goods Sold}$$

Algebraically, this model can be rearranged as follows to represent each of the two systems:

Perpetual inventory system:

$$BI + P - CGS = EI$$

(since this particular system focuses on measuring and recording the amount of cost of goods sold *currently during the period* for each separate sale).

Periodic inventory system:

$$BI + P - EI = CGS$$

(since this particular system focuses on measuring, that is, physically counting, the ending inventory at the *end of the period* and then determining cost of goods sold by subtracting the ending inventory from goods available for sale.)

Thus, both systems focus on the central objective of the measurement of both cost of goods sold and ending inventory. The perpetual inventory system accomplishes the objective on a *current* basis by means of detailed inventory records. In contrast, the periodic inventory system accomplishes the objective on a *end-of-the-period* basis by means of a physical count of the goods remaining on hand.

In the discussions to follow we must constantly remember that the central objective is not solely to measure the amount of goods on hand in order to obtain the balance sheet amount, but it also is to measure cost of goods sold, which is an important element on the income statement in the measurement of income.

The unit cost problem

In Chapters 6 and 7, to simplify the illustrations, we assumed that the beginning inventory and the additional purchases of goods during the period were at the same **unit cost.** The usual situation, however, is that goods will be purchased during the period at different unit costs. To illustrate, assume the data given in Exhibit 8–1 for one product stocked and sold regularly by Summer's Retail Store.

EXHIBIT 8–1

SUMMER'S RETAIL STORE
Unit Cost Data

Transactions	*Symbol*	*Number of units*	*Unit cost*	*Total cost*	
Beginning inventory (carried over from last period)	BI	100	$6		$ 600
Purchases during the current period:					
January 3, first purchase	P	50	7	$ 350	
June 12, second purchase	P	200	8	1,600	
December 20, third purchase	P	120	9	1,080	3,030
Goods available for sale	GA	470			3,630
Sales during the period:					
January 6, unit sales price, $10	S	40	$?		$?
June 18, unit sales price, 12	S	220	?		$?
December 25, unit sales price, 14	S	60	?		$?
Goods sold	CGS	320			$?
Ending inventory	EI	150	$?		$?

In the above example there are four different unit cost prices that make up the $3,630 amount for **goods available for sale** (i.e., $6, $7, $8, and $9). The accounting objective is to recognize these different unit costs in apportioning the total amount of goods available for sale ($3,630) between **cost of goods sold** and **ending inventory** on a rational basis. As explained above, the perpetual and periodic inventory systems represent two different approaches for accomplishing this measurement objective. However, when *unit costs* change over time, as they did for Summer's, *either* system obviously must cope with this vexing problem. This problem of measuring the cost of goods sold and the ending inventory can be portrayed graphically as in Exhibit 8–2.

The apportionment of cost of goods available for sale between cost of goods sold and ending inventory requires the use of an **inventory costing method.** The four inventory costing methods commonly used are known as: (1) specific identification; (2) average; (3) first-in, first-out (Fifo); and (4) last-in, first-out (Lifo). First, we will discuss the characteristics of each of these inventory costing methods. Following that discussion, we will illustrate the application of each method separately for the perpetual and periodic inventory systems. Throughout these discussions we will use the data given in Exhibit 8–1 for Summer's Retail Store.

EXHIBIT 8–2

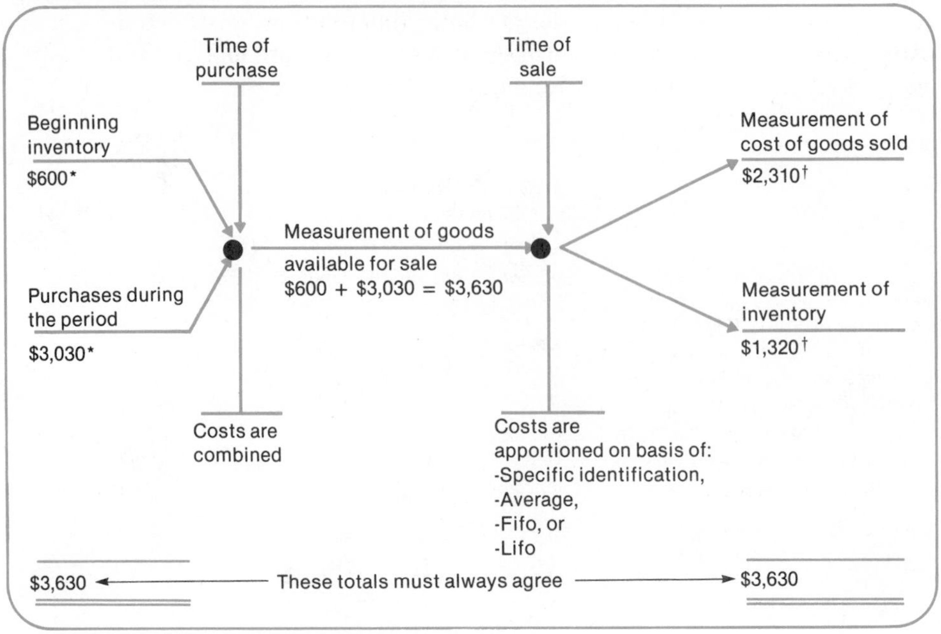

* Data from Exhibit 8–1.
† Fifo basis, Exhibit 8–5.

Inventory costing methods

A choice among the inventory costing methods is necessary only when there are different unit costs in the beginning inventory and/or purchases during the current period. These are *cost-assignment* methods and do not necessarily relate to the physical flow of goods on and off the shelves. Although the actual *physical flow* of goods is usually first-in, first-out, a company can use any one of the four inventory costing methods. Generally accepted accounting principles require that the inventory costing method used must be rational and systematic.

Specific identification method. One way of assigning unit costs to cost of goods sold and the ending inventory is to keep track of the units of the beginning inventory and each separate purchase—that is, specific identification of the purchase cost of each item. This is done either by simply coding the purchase cost on each unit before placing it in stock or by keeping a separate record of the unit and identifying it with a serial number. When a sale is made, the cost of that unit is identified and recorded. For example, using the data given in Exhibit 8–1, if the 40 units sold on January 6 were identified specifically as, say, units that were purchased for $6 (i.e., from the beginning inventory), the cost of goods sold amount for that sale would be measured as 40 units × \$6 = \$240. Alternatively, if 20 of the units were identified as costing \$6 (from the beginning inventory) and the other 20 as costing \$7 (from the January 3 purchase), cost of goods sold would be measured as (20 units × \$6) + (20 units × \$7) = \$260.

The specific identification method would be rather tedious and impractical where (1) unit costs are low; (2) unit costs change frequently; and (3) a large number of different items are stocked. On the other hand, where there are "big-ticket" items such as automobiles and expensive jewelry, it is especially appropriate since each item tends to be different from the other items. In such situations, it is rational because the *selling price* generally is based on a markup over specific cost. However, the method may not be systematic when the units are identical because one can manipulate the cost of goods sold and the ending inventory amounts simply by "picking and choosing" from among the several available unit costs, even though the goods are identical in every other respect. To illustrate, in the above example, cost of goods sold was either \$240 or \$260, depending on the choices made. In that example, assuming identical items, income would be different by \$20, depending on an arbitrary "identification."

Average-cost method. This method involves computation of the **weighted average unit cost** of the goods available for sale. The average unit cost computed is then applied to (1) the number of units sold to measure cost of goods sold, and (2) the number of units in the ending inventory to measure the dollar inventory amount. To illustrate, at the end of the period, the method would be applied to the data given in Exhibit 8–1 as follows:[5]

To compute average cost:

$$\frac{\text{Total Goods Available for Sale—at Cost}}{\text{Total Goods Available for Sale—Units}} = \frac{\$3{,}630}{470} = \$7.72 \left\{\begin{array}{l}\text{Average Cost}\\ \text{per Unit for}\\ \text{the Period}\end{array}\right.$$

The cost assignment then would be:

	Units		*Amount*
Cost of goods sold	320	@ \$7.72 =	\$2,470
Ending inventory	150	@ \$7.72 =	1,158
Goods available for sale	470	@ \$7.72 =	\$3,628

Observe that the same \$7.72 unit cost applies to (1) goods available for sale, (2) cost of goods sold, and (3) ending inventory.

[5] This illustration shows the application when the periodic inventory system is used. For the perpetual inventory system a moving weighted average is used. Both applications are illustrated in detail in subsequent paragraphs.

The average-cost method is used often since it is rational, systematic, easy to apply, and not subject to manipulation. It weights the number of units purchased and unit costs during the period (including the beginning inventory). Thus, it is representative of costs during the entire period (including the beginning inventory) rather than of the cost only at the beginning, end, or at one point during the period.[6]

First-in, first-out method. This method, frequently referred to as **Fifo,** assumes that the oldest units (i.e., the first costs in) are the first units sold (i.e., the first costs out). In other words, the units in the beginning inventory are treated as if they were sold first, the units from the first purchase sold next, and so on until the units left in the ending inventory all come from the latest purchases. It follows that the oldest unit costs are apportioned to cost of goods sold and the latest unit costs apply to the ending inventory.

Frequently, Fifo is justified on the basis that it is consistent with the actual physical flow of the goods. It is said that the first goods placed in stock tend to be the first goods sold. However, the method is applied irrespective of the actual physical inflow and outflow of goods because it is not a flow of goods concept but is a *cost assignment* procedure used to measure cost of goods sold and ending inventory.

To illustrate, using the data given in Exhibit 8–1, the Fifo method would be applied as follows for the sale of January 6:

Goods available for sale on January 6:			
January 1, beginning inventory	100 units @ $6 =		$600
January 3, first purchase	50 units @ $7 =		350
Total			$950*
Cost of goods sold for 40 units sold on January 6:			
At the oldest unit cost	40 units × $6 =		$240
Inventory remaining after sale of January 6:			
At latest unit costs	60 units × $6 =	$360	
	50 units × $7 =	350	710
			$950*

* These totals must always agree.

The Fifo method is widely used since it is rational, systematic, easy to apply, and not subject to manipulation. On the balance sheet, under Fifo, the ending inventory amount is at the most **recent unit costs** and, therefore, it is likely to be a realistic value prevailing at the balance sheet date. In direct contrast, on the income statement, cost of goods sold is at the oldest unit costs. The significance of the impact of Fifo on the income

[6] A weighted average unit cost rather than a simple average of the units costs must be used. For example, ($6 + $7 + $8 + $9) ÷ 4 = $7.50 would be incorrect because it does not consider the number of units at each unit cost.

statement (i.e., cost of goods sold and net income) and the balance sheet (i.e., the inventory amount under current assets) depends on the extent to which unit costs increase or decrease during the period. These effects are illustrated later.

Last-in, first-out method. This method, frequently referred to as **Lifo,** assumes that the most recently acquired goods are sold first. Irrespective of the physical flow of goods, Lifo treats the **costs** of the most recent units acquired as the cost of goods sold. This leaves the unit costs of the beginning inventory and the earliest purchases in the ending inventory. Thus, the Lifo method attains results that are inverse to Fifo. That is, under Lifo, the total ending inventory cost is measured at the oldest unit costs and cost of goods sold is measured at the newest unit costs.

To illustrate, using the data in Exhibit 8–1, the Lifo method would be applied as follows for the sale of January 6:

Goods available for sale on January 6:			
January 1, beginning inventory	100 units @ $6 =		$600
January 3, first purchase	50 units @ $7 =		350
Total			$950
Cost of goods for 40 units sold on January 6:			
At the newest unit cost	40 units × $7 =		$280
Inventory remaining after sale of January 6:			
At oldest unit costs	100 units × $6 =	$600	
	10 units × $7 =	70	670
Total			$950

The Lifo method is acceptable since it is deemed rational and systematic. However, it is amenable to manipulation by buying, or not buying, goods at the end of a period when unit costs have changed in order to affect cost of goods sold and, hence, reported income. On the income statement under Lifo, cost of goods sold is based on the latest unit costs. In contrast, on the balance sheet the ending inventory amount is based on the earliest unit costs. The significance of the impact of Lifo will be discussed later.

Costing inventory and cost of goods sold with a perpetual inventory system

To measure cost of goods sold and inventory continuously throughout the period, a perpetual inventory system may be used. This system requires the maintenance of a detailed **perpetual inventory record** for each kind of goods or merchandise stocked and sold. This record is designed to show units and dollars, at all times, for (1) the goods received (purchased), (2) the goods sold (issued), and (3) the balance of goods on hand on a continuing basis. Each purchase and each sale transaction is entered on the perpetual inventory record when it occurs. The perpetual inventory record may be maintained manually, mechanically, or by means of the electronic computer. The perpetual inventory record is designed so that cost of goods sold and the inventory are measured on a perpetual or continuous basis.

In the discussions to follow, a perpetual inventory record will be illustrated for each of the four inventory costing methods. To illustrate each application, we will use the data for Summer's Retail Store given in Exhibit 8–1. We also will use a manual system for instructional purposes. The beginning inventory of 100 units at a unit cost of $6 would have been carried over in the records from the prior period. Recall from Chapter 7 that each purchase would be recorded as follows and, at the same time, entered on the perpetual inventory record (see Exhibit 8–5):

Jan. 3	Inventory (50 units @ $7)	350	
	Cash (or Accounts payable)		350

Also recall that a sale generates *two* companion entries when a perpetual inventory system is used:

Jan. 6	Cash	400	
	Sales revenue (40 units @ $10)		400
	Cost of goods sold (Fifo basis)	240	
	Inventory (40 units @ $6)		240

Specific identification method applied. When this method is applied, as each unit is sold it is identified, usually by a code on the item, with a specific prior purchase unit cost. Exhibit 8–3 illustrates application of the specific identification method. The inventory reflects the beginning

EXHIBIT 8–3

Specific identification method—perpetual inventory system

PERPETUAL INVENTORY RECORD

Item: Item A — Cost Basis—Specific Identification
Location: 320 — Minimum Level
Code: 13 — Maximum Level

Date	Received (purchases)			Issued (sales)			Inventory Balance		
	Units	Unit Cost	Total Cost	Units	Unit Cost	Total Cost	Units	Unit Cost	Total Cost
1/1 Balance							100	6	600
1/3	50	7	350				50	7	350
1/6				20	6	120	80	6	480
				20	7	140	30	7	210

inventory in units and dollars in the column headed Inventory Balance. The January 3 purchase of 50 units at $7 each is recorded under the Received column and the Balance column is changed to reflect the new balance. The Balance column is maintained so that the number of units on hand at each unit cost is reflected at all times. Now, assume that the sale of 40 units on January 6 was "identified" as consisting of 20 units that cost $6 each (from the beginning inventory) and 20 units that cost $7 each (from the January 3 purchase). The perpetual inventory would reflect this transaction as shown in Exhibit 8–3. The cost of goods sold for this transaction of $260 is reflected in the Issued column, and the inventory level, in units and amounts, is shown in the Balance column. The companion entries for the sale on January 6 would reflect sales revenue of $400 and cost of goods sold of $260 (from the inventory record). The inventory immediately after the sale of 110 units is valued at $690 ($480 + $210). Specific identification, applied in a perpetual inventory system requires (1) considerable clerical effort and (2) arbitrary selection of unit costs.

Average-cost method applied. When the average-cost method is applied with a perpetual inventory system, a **weighted moving average** unit cost usually is used. This is used because the cost of goods sold amount must be measured and recorded at the time of each sale. Instead, if one were to apply the concept of an *annual* weighted average, the recording of costs of goods sold would be delayed until year-end since it is not until that time that such an annual average can be computed.

In applying a weighted moving average, a *new* average unit cost is computed during the period at the time of *each purchase.* Cost of goods sold and the remaining inventory are measured at the then prevailing moving average unit cost. An illustration of the perpetual inventory record on a weighted moving average basis for the data given in Exhibit 8–1 is shown in Exhibit 8–4. The weighted moving average was recomputed three times during the period since there were three purchases. Units sold are removed from the inventory record at the then average unit cost. For example, the moving average was computed on the date of the first purchase as follows:

	Units	Cost
Beginning inventory	100	$600
Purchase, January 3	50	350
Totals	150	$950

Moving average unit cost: $950 ÷ 150 units = $6.33 per unit.

The companion entries for the sale on January 6 would reflect sales revenue of $400 and cost of goods sold of $253 (from the inventory record) as follows:

Jan. 6	Cash	400	
	Sales revenue (40 units @ $10)		400
	Cost of goods sold (moving average basis)	253	
	Inventory		253
	From Exhibit 8–4.		

The moving average method is used widely with the perpetual inventory system.

EXHIBIT 8–4

Moving average method—perpetual inventory system

PERPETUAL INVENTORY RECORD

(heading—same as in Exhibit 8–3, except cost basis—moving average)

Date	Received (purchases)			Issued (sales)			Inventory Balance		
	Units	Unit Cost	Total Cost	Units	Unit Cost	Total Cost	Units	Unit Cost	Total Cost
1/1 Bal.							100	6.00	600
1/3	50	7.00	350				150	6.33*	950
1/6				40	6.33	253	110	6.33	697
6/12	200	8.00	1,600				310	7.41*	2,297
6/18				220	7.41	1,630	90	7.41	667
12/20	120	9.00	1,080				210	8.32*	1,747
12/25				60	8.32	499	150	8.32	1,248
Total cost of goods sold						2,382			
Total ending inventory									1,248

* New average computed.

Fifo method applied. When the Fifo method is applied with a perpetual inventory system, the remaining quantities on hand must be identified separately after each issue on the perpetual inventory record for *each unit cost*. These groups frequently are referred to as "inventory cost layers." The identification of inventory cost layers is necessary because goods sold are removed from the inventory record in Fifo order; that is, the oldest unit cost is taken off first. An illustration of the perpetual inventory record on a Fifo basis is shown in Exhibit 8–5. Each purchase and each sale of goods is entered on the record at the time of occurrence. At each time, the balance column on the perpetual inventory record is restated to show the units and amount on hand for each different unit cost. At the same time, each transaction would be recorded in the accounts.

EXHIBIT 8–5
Fifo method—perpetual inventory system

PERPETUAL INVENTORY RECORD
(heading—same as in Exhibit 8–3, except cost basis—Fifo)

Date	Received (purchases)			Issued (sales)			Inventory Balance		
	Units	Unit Cost	Total Cost	Units	Unit Cost	Total Cost	Units	Unit Cost	Total Cost
1/1 Bal.							100	6	600
1/3	50	7	350				100	6	600
							50	7	350
1/6				40	6	240	60	6	360
							50	7	350
6/12	200	8	1,600				60	6	360
							50	7	350
							200	8	1,600
6/18				60	6	360			
				50	7	350			
				110	8	880	90	8	720
12/20	120	9	1,080				90	8	720
							120	9	1,080
12/25				60	8	480	30	8	240
							120	9	1,080

The companion entries to record the sale of June 18 are:

June 18	Cash	2,640	
	Sales revenue (220 units @ $12)		2,640
	Cost of goods sold (fifo basis)	1,590	
	Inventory		1,590

From Exhibit 8–5, $360 + $350 + $880 = $1,590.

The perpetual inventory record in Exhibit 8–5 reflects the following measurements at the end of the period:

a. Cost of goods sold for the year (sum of the column Issued, Total Cost—$240 + $360 + $350 + $880 + $480) $2,310
b. Final inventory (last balance amounts—$240 + $1,080) 1,320
c. Goods available for sale (beginning inventory plus the sum of the purchases column) $3,630

Lifo method applied. When the Lifo method is applied with a perpetual inventory system, the inventory cost layers must be identified separately on the perpetual inventory record, as was the case with Fifo. This identification is necessary so that the **unit costs** for the number of units for each sale can be removed at that time from the inventory record in the **reverse order** that they came in; that is, the newest unit cost is removed from the record.[7] To illustrate, the perpetual inventory record on a Lifo basis is shown in Exhibit 8–6.

EXHIBIT 8–6

Lifo method costed currently—perpetual inventory system

PERPETUAL INVENTORY RECORD

(heading—same as in Exhibit 8–3, except cost basis—Lifo)

	Received (purchases)			Issued (sales)			Inventory Balance		
Date	Units	Unit Cost	Total Cost	Units	Unit Cost	Total Cost	Units	Unit Cost	Total Cost
1/1 Bal.							100	6	600
1/3	50	7	350				100	6	600
							50	7	350
1/6				40	7	280	100	6	600
							10	7	70
6/12	200	8	1,600				100	6	600
							10	7	70
							200	8	1,600
6/18				200	8	1,600			
				10	7	70			
				10	6	60	90	6	540
12/20	120	9	1,080				90	6	540
							120	9	1,080
12/25				60	9	540	90	6	540
							60	9	540

[7] This discussion and the illustration of Lifo assumes an item-by-item application and costing of cost of goods sold currently throughout the period. Although the concepts are the same, many companies use an application known as dollar-value Lifo, and the costing is at the end of the year. These complexities are beyond the scope of this book. See Welsch, Zlatkovich, and White, *Intermediate Accounting* (Homewood, Ill.: Richard D. Irwin, Inc., 1976). Also see footnote 8.

The Lifo method required that the sale of 40 units on January 6 be measured, recorded in the accounts, and removed from the perpetual inventory card at the latest unit purchase price, which was $7 per unit. The record measures cost of goods sold for the year as $2,550 (sum of the Issued column) and the ending inventory as $1,080 (Balance column).

To summarize, in respect to the four inventory pricing methods, let's recall that the central objective was to measure cost of goods sold for the income statement and ending inventory for the balance sheet. Each method applied with the perpetual inventory system met this objective on a continuing basis as each transaction happened. With the same data for beginning inventory, purchases, and sales, however, each method provided *different* amounts for costs of goods sold (and hence for income) and for ending inventory (and hence current assets on the balance sheet).

Costing inventory and cost of goods sold with a periodic inventory system

Recall that in a periodic inventory system the measurement and recording of the ending inventory and cost of goods sold is deferred until the end of the period. At that time, the ending inventory in units is determined by physical count and then **costed** by using one of the inventory costing methods. Goods available for sale (i.e., beginning inventory plus purchases during the period) less the amount of the ending inventory, thus determined, is the cost of goods sold amount. Thus, the inventory costing methods with a periodic inventory system are applied to measure the dollar cost of the units remaining on hand as determined by the physical inventory count, and cost of goods sold is measured as the difference between goods available for sale and the ending inventory amount.

To illustrate, using the data for Summer's Retail Store given in Exhibit 8–1, application of the four inventory costing methods with the periodic inventory system may be brought into sharp focus as follows:

Goods available for sale:		
Beginning inventory (carried over from last year)	100 units @ $6 =	$ 600
Purchases during the current year (from the Purchases account):		
January 3	50 units @ $7 =	350
June 12	200 units @ $8 =	1,600
December 20	120 units @ $9 =	1,080
Total—goods available for sale	470	$3,630
Ending inventory:		
Units by physical inventory count	150	
Dollar amount		$?
Difference—cost of goods sold	320	$?

Having completed the physical inventory count and found 150 units remaining on hand, the **dollar amount** of the ending inventory must be determined by applying one of the inventory pricing methods.

Application of specific identification method. When this method is used with a periodic inventory system, the unit cost of each item in the ending inventory must be identified with a specific unit purchase price. For example, assume that when the physical count was made at December 31 by Summer's, the unit costs for the 150 units on hand were identified from the "code" on each item as follows:

Units	*Unit cost*	*Total cost*
20	$6	$ 120
50	8	400
80	9	720
150		$1,240

With these data, cost of goods sold can be derived as follows:

Goods available for sale (per above)	$3,630
Less ending inventory (specific identification)	1,240
Cost of goods sold	$2,390

Application of weighted average-cost method. When this method is used with the periodic inventory system, the weighted average is computed at year-end; thus, it is an *annual* weighted average rather than a series of moving weighted averages as is used with a perpetual inventory system. In computing the annual weighted average, the beginning inventory and all of the purchases during the year are included in the average. To illustrate, using the data given in Exhibit 8–1, the annual weighted average would be computed as follows:

	Units	*Total cost*
Beginning inventory	100	$ 600
Purchases:		
January 3	50	350
June 12	200	1,600
December 20	120	1,080
Totals	470	$3,630

Annual weighted average: $3,630 ÷ 470 units = $7.72 per unit.

With these data, cost of goods sold can be derived as follows:

Goods available for sale (per above)	$3,630
Less ending inventory (average):	
150 units @ $7.72 =	1,158
Cost of goods sold	$2,472

Application of Fifo method. When this method is applied with a periodic inventory system, the number of units in the ending inventory are costed from the latest inventory layers, starting with the unit cost for the last purchase, then moving to the next to last one, and so on, until all units in the ending inventory are costed. To illustrate, for Summer's the 150 units physically counted as remaining on hand would be costed as follows:

	Units	*Unit cost*	*Total cost*
From December 20 purchase	120	$9	1,080
From June 12 purchase	30	8	240
Ending inventory amount	150		$1,320

With these data, cost of goods sold can be derived as follows:

Goods available for sale (per above)	$3,630
Less ending inventory (Fifo)	1,320
Cost of goods sold	$2,310

Application of Lifo. When this method is used with periodic inventory procedures, the units in the ending inventory are costed at the oldest unit costs for the period starting with the beginning inventory, then to the first purchase, and so on. To illustrate, using the data from Exhibit 8–1, the 150 units remaining in the ending inventory would be costed as follows:

	Units	*Unit cost*	*Total cost*
From beginning inventory	100	$6	$600
From January 3 purchase	50	7	350
Ending inventory amount	150		$950

With these data, cost of goods sold can be derived as follows:

Goods available for sale (per above)	$3,630
Less ending inventory (Lifo)	950
Cost of goods sold	$2,680

Comparison of inventory cost methods

Four alternative inventory costing methods were explained and illustrated in the preceding paragraphs. Each method is in accordance with generally accepted accounting principles, although they may produce significantly different income and asset (i.e., ending inventory) amounts.

With the same data assumed, the moving weighted average used with a perpetual inventory system will derive a different result than the annual weighted average used with a periodic system. Similarly, Lifo applied with a perpetual system (costed currently) usually will derive a somewhat different result than when applied with a periodic system (on an end-of-period basis).[8] In contrast, Fifo will always derive the same result under both systems, as will specific identification.

To illustrate, the comparative results for Summer's Retail Store are as follows:

	Sales revenue	*Cost of goods sold*	*Gross margin*	*Balance sheet (inventory)*
Perpetual inventory system:				
Specific identification	$3,880	$2,390	$1,490	$1,240
Moving average	3,880	2,382	1,498	1,248
Fifo	3,880	2,310	1,570	1,320
Lifo (currently)	3,880	2,550	1,330	1,080
Periodic inventory system:				
Specific identification	3,880	2,390	1,490	1,240
Weighted average	3,880	2,472	1,408	1,158
Fifo	3,880	2,310	1,570	1,320
Lifo (end of period)	3,880	2,680	1,200	950

A comparison of the results shown above for the four **methods** will increase our understanding of their characteristics. First, we can readily perceive that in the case of a constant inventory cost, all methods would provide the same income and the same inventory amounts. Second, in the case of changing unit cost, each method tends to give different income and different inventory amounts. On this point, observe that the difference in *pretax income* among each of the methods is the same as the difference as in the inventory amounts. The method that provides the higher ending inventory amount also provides the higher income amount. Third, the income and inventory amounts may be affected by both the inventory *system* used (perpetual versus periodic) and the costing method

[8] When a perpetual inventory system is used, Lifo is costed on a current basis throughout the period. Therefore, the cost of goods sold for each sale will be in terms of the then most recent unit cost. In contrast, when a periodic inventory system is used, Lifo is costed only at the end of the period. Therefore, the cost of goods sold for the entire period is in terms of the highest unit costs (by layers) at the end of the period. Because of this difference in "ordering" unit costs, the two systems usually will give different inventory and cost of goods sold amounts. Also see footnote 7.

used (i.e., compare the Lifo results with Fifo results). Fourth, the average-cost method tends to give income and inventory amounts that fall between the Fifo and Lifo extremes.

We will now focus on a comparison of the Fifo and Lifo methods since they usually represent the extreme, and opposite, effects. Note in the comparison above that unit costs were *increasing* and that Lifo provided the lower income and inventory amounts, whereas Fifo provided the higher income and inventory amounts. In comparing the effects of Fifo and Lifo, it is important to note that the comparative effects will depend upon the direction of change in unit cost. *When unit costs are rising, Lifo will result in lower income and a lower inventory valuation than will Fifo. Conversely, when unit costs are declining, Lifo will result in higher income and higher inventory valuation than will Fifo.*

INCOME TAX EFFECTS

Let's turn our attention to the income tax effects for the moment. The effect of different inventory costing methods on income taxes to be paid in particular years often is significant. Of course, over the long term only the actual cost incurred for goods for resale is deductible as an expense for tax purposes. We have seen that income is allocated between periods in a different way by the several inventory costing methods. Thus, when prices are rising Lifo often is used for income tax purposes since an early tax deduction is to be preferred to a later tax deduction. Due to the time value of money, the shifting of tax liability to later years becomes important.

Since all four methods are acceptable for income tax purposes, why have some businesses opted for Lifo in recent years? Clearly, the reason is that it tends to minimize early income tax payments. Prices have been rising; and with rising prices, Lifo charges higher costs to cost of goods sold. This in turn reduces income so the income tax bill is lower. Of course, the inventory effect suggests that should prices decline at some future date, those businesses may want to change from Lifo to Fifo to minimize income taxes on the downward trend of prices. It is difficult, however, to obtain permission from the Internal Revenue Service to change the inventory costing method (except when the change is to Fifo).

To illustrate the income tax effects, assume the following for X Corporation for the year 19XX (when prices rose rapidly):

a. Sales revenue	$900,000
b. Cost of goods sold:	
Fifo basis	400,000
Lifo basis	600,000
c. Remaining expenses (excluding income taxes)	250,000
d. Average income tax rate	45%

	Inventory Costing Method	
	Fifo	Lifo
Revenue	$900,000	$900,000
Cost of goods sold	400,000	600,000
Gross margin	500,000	300,000
Less: Expenses (except income taxes)	250,000	250,000
Pretax income	250,000	50,000
Income tax expense (45% rate)	112,500	22,500
Net Income	$137,500	$ 27,500
EPS (100,000 shares common stock outstanding)	$1.375	$.275

Reduction in income tax expense ($112,500 − $22,500) = $90,000
Cash saved ($112,500 − $22,500) = $90,000

WHICH METHOD OF COSTING IS THE BEST

No one method of inventory costing can be considered as the "best." It would be impractical to assume that the tax consequences are not important in the choice of method. Many observers believe that businesses, in setting selling prices, often do so within a "Lifo assumption" since the goods sold must be replaced on the shelf at the latest cost rather than at earlier cost.

Many accountants believe that the best inventory costing method is the one that best matches the sales pricing policy of the company. Companies do price units for sale in each of the ways implied by these four costing methods. These accountants believe that the only conceptually sound basis for selecting the best costing method for a particular company depends upon the sales pricing policy followed. Other accountants believe that the choice should be based upon whether the measurement emphasis should be on the income statement or on the balance sheet. Those who believe that the income statement should be accorded primary emphasis tend to defend Lifo since it matches the most recent purchase cost with current sales revenue. To the contrary, those who prefer to emphasize the balance sheet tend to prefer Fifo since it reports the inventory (an asset) at the most current cost price. Also there is a problem where one is comparing companies in the same industry when they use different methods. Because of these considerations, it is not difficult to understand why the accounting profession, and the income tax laws, have accepted several alternative inventory costing methods.

Inventories at net realizable value

Merchandise on hand that is damaged, obsolete, or shopworn should not be measured and reported at original cost but at present **net realizable value** when it is below cost. Net realizable value is the *estimated* *amount* that is expected to be realized when the goods are sold in their deteriorated condition, less disposal costs. For example, assume a company selling television sets has on hand two sets that have been used as demonstrators; when purchased, the sets cost $200 each. In the light of their present condition, realistic estimates are:

	Per set
Sales value in present condition	$140
Estimated selling costs	30
Estimated net realizable value	$110

On the basis of these estimates, the two television sets would be included in the inventory at $110 each, or a total of $220, rather than at the total original cost of $400. Net realizable value is used because it records the loss in the period in which it occurred rather than in the period of sale and does not overstate the asset.

If a periodic inventory system is used, the item is simply included in the ending inventory at estimated net realizable value and the loss is automatically reflected in cost of goods sold. However, if a perpetual system is used, the following entry would be made:

Inventory of damaged goods (2 × $110)	220	
Loss on damaged goods (an expense) ($400 − $220)	180	
Inventory (2 × $200)		400

The perpetual inventory record also would be changed to reflect this entry.[9]

Inventories at lower of cost or market

We have emphasized that inventories should be measured at their unit purchase cost in accordance with the cost principle. However, when the new goods remaining in the ending inventory can be replaced new at a lower cost at inventory date, that lower unit cost should be used. This is known as measuring inventories on a **lower-of-cost-or-market basis.** It is a departure from the cost principle in favor of the exception principle—conservatism (see Exhibit 2–1). It serves to recognize a "holding" loss in the period when the replacement cost dropped, rather than in the period when the goods are actually sold. To illustrate, assume that an office equipment dealer has ten new electronic calculators remaining in the ending inventory. The calculators were purchased for $150 each about a year earlier and were marked to sell at $199.95. At the date of the ending inventory, however, the same new calculators can be purchased for $100

[9] Net realizable value is used in applying the lower-of-cost-or-market basis discussed in the next section; however, here the focus is on damaged or deteriorated goods rather than a drop in the market replacement cost of new goods.

EXHIBIT 8–7
Effect of inventory measurement at lower of cost or market

	Inventory measured at—			
	Cost (Fifo)		Lower of cost or market	
Sales		$12,500		$12,500
Cost of goods sold:				
Beginning inventory	$6,750		$6,750	
Add purchases	2,250		2,250	
Goods available for sale	9,000		9,000	
Less ending inventory (ten computers):				
At purchase cost of $150	1,500			
At lower of cost or market of $100			1,000	
Cost of goods sold		7,500		8,000
Gross margin on sales		5,000		4,500
Expenses		4,000		4,000
Pretax Income		$ 1,000		$ 500

and will be marked to sell for $129.95. Under the lower-of-cost-or-market basis the ten calculators should be costed in the ending inventory at $100 each. In this context, market is defined as the current market replacement cost of the new item in the quantities usually purchased.

Let's look carefully at the effect of using a replacement cost of $100 against using the original purchase cost of $150 for the ten computers to be included in the ending inventory. By costing them at $50 per unit below their purchase cost, pretax income will be $500 (10 × $50), less than it would have been had they been costed in the inventory at $150 per unit. This $500 loss in **economic utility** of the inventory was due to a decline in the replacement cost. Because it is included in the cost of goods sold, pretax income will be reduced by $500 in the period in which the cost fell, rather than in the later period when the goods are sold. Thus, the loss is matched with the revenues generated in the accounting period in which the drop in economic utility occurred. These effects are demonstrated in Exhibit 8–7. Lower of cost or market must be applied to all inventories.

ESTIMATING INVENTORY

When a periodic inventory system is used, a physical inventory count is essential for each date on which financial statements are to be prepared. Taking a physical inventory at the end of each period for which financial statements are derived is a time-consuming task in many businesses. As a consequence, physical inventories may be taken only once a year. Nevertheless, the management of many businesses desire financial statements for internal use on a monthly or, at least, a quarterly basis. When a periodic, rather than a perpetual, inventory system is used, some businesses *estimate* the ending inventory for the monthly or quarterly financial statements. The **gross margin method** has been developed for this purpose. The method uses an **estimated gross margin ratio** as the basis for the computation.

Recall that the gross margin ratio is derived by dividing gross margin on sales by net sales (page 208). The gross margin method assumes that the *gross margin ratio* for the current period should be essentially the same as it was in the immediate past. Therefore, based on the *ratio* in the immediate past, a gross margin ratio is estimated for the current period. This estimated ratio can then be used to compute *estimated amounts* for (1) gross margin on sales, (2) cost of goods sold, and (3) ending inventory.

To illustrate the gross margin method, assume Patz Company is preparing *monthly* financial statements at January 31, 1977. The accounting records would provide the sales, beginning inventory, purchases, and expense amounts as listed below.

PATZ COMPANY
Income Statement
For the Month Ended January 31, 1977

Net sales		$100,000*
Cost of goods sold:		
Beginning inventory	$15,000*	
Add purchases	65,000*	
Goods available for sale	80,000	
Less ending inventory	To be estimated	
Cost of goods sold		?
Gross margin on sales		?
Expenses		30,000*
Pretax Income		$?

* Provided by the accounts.

The amount of the ending inventory each month is to be *estimated* rather than determined by physical count. Assume that the net sales for 1976 amounted to $1,000,000 and gross margin was $400,000; therefore, the actual gross margin ratio for 1976 was $400,000 ÷ $1,000,000 = 0.40. Now assume that the management decides that this value is a realistic estimate for 1977. Using the 0.40 as our estimate for 1977, we can compute an *estimated* inventory valuation. The computational steps, in lettered sequence, are shown below.

PATZ COMPANY
Income Statement
For the Month of January 1977 (estimated)

			Computations (sequence a, b, c)
Net sales		$100,000	Per accounts
Cost of goods sold:			
Beginning inventory	$15,000		Per accounts
Add purchases	65,000		Per accounts
Goods available for sale	80,000		
Less ending inventory	20,000		c. $80,000 − $60,000 = $20,000
Cost of goods sold		60,000	b. $100,000 − $40,000 = $60,000*
Gross margin on sales		40,000	a. $100,000 × 0.40 = $40,000
Expenses		30,000	Per accounts
Pretax Income		$ 10,000	

* Or alternatively, $100,000 × (1.00 − 0.40) = $60,000.

The balance sheet is completed by reporting the $20,000 estimated ending inventory amount as a current asset.

The gross margin method has several other uses apart from preparation of the monthly or quarterly financial statements. Auditors and accountants may use it to test the reasonableness of the amount of the inventory determined by other means. If the current gross margin ratio has changed materially from past experience, it may suggest an error in the inventory determination. As another example, the method also is used in the case of a fire where an inventory of goods is burned and its valuation must be estimated for settlement purposes with the insurance company.[10]

SUPPLIES INVENTORIES

The term **inventory,** as commonly used, means only merchandise inventory (either purchased or manufactured), raw materials to be used directly in the manufacture of goods for resale, and goods in process in varying stages of completion. Other types of inventories do exist; they include unused office supplies, janitorial supplies, store supplies, and maintenance supplies.

When supplies are purchased for *immediate use,* an appropriately designated expense account is debited at the date of purchase of the supplies. On the other hand, supplies may be purchased for *future use*

[10] Another method, known as the retail inventory method, is widely used to estimate the ending inventory by department stores. It is essentially the same as the gross margin method, but differs in detail. Discussion of it is deferred to more advanced books.

in the business. Supplies purchased for future use have been briefly discussed in the previous chapters as **prepaid expenses.** Recall that a prepaid expense is reported on the balance sheet as a current asset. When supplies are purchased for future use, an appropriately designated prepaid expense account is charged (i.e., debited). As the supplies are used, the prepaid expense account is credited and an expense account is debited. To illustrate, assume on January 1, 1977, Company X had $100 office supplies on hand (beginning inventory) and purchased additional office supplies during 1977 that cost $200. Supplies purchased are placed in inventory for future use as needed. The purchase would be recorded as follows:

Office supplies inventory	200	
Cash		200

Now, assume it is December 31, 1977, end of the fiscal period. A count of the office supplies still unused and costed at their purchase price showed $130. Thus, the supplies actually used during 1977 amounted to $100 + $200 − $130 = $170. Therefore, an adjusting entry must be made on December 31, 1977, as follows:

Office supplies expense	170	
Office supplies inventory		170

The effect of these entries on the financial statements for 1977 will be:

Income Statement:	
Office supplies expense	$170
Balance Sheet:	
Current Asset:	
Prepaid expenses (office supplies inventory)	130

Office and other supplies on hand are not included with the "inventories" because they are not held for resale.

CONSISTENCY IN ACCOUNTING

In this and the two preceding chapters, several alternative approaches in measuring cost of goods sold and inventory were discussed and illustrated. Some of these alternatives produce different income statement and balance sheet results under identical situations (see page 278). In addition to these situations, there are accounting alternatives in other areas of accounting. Recall that in Chapter 3 we illustrated different accounting policies that were reported by Carborundum Company. Some of the policies reflected the company's choice of one of several alternatives available. In view of the **consistency principle** (Exhibit 2–1), a company cannot capriciously shift from one accounting alternative to another. The consistency principle holds that in the accounting process all concepts, principles, and measurement approaches should be applied in a similar or consistent way from one period to the next in order to assure that the data reported in the financial statements are reasonably comparable over time. This principle prevents "willy-nilly" changes from one accounting or measurement approach to another. The consistency principle is not inflexible. It permits changes in accounting when the change tends to improve the measurement of financial results and financial position. Consistency is a difficult concept to precisely define and poses troublesome problems in application.

DEMONSTRATION CASE FOR SELF-STUDY

Metal Products, Incorporated

(Try to resolve the requirements before proceeding to the suggested solution.)

This case focuses on the effects of a misstatement of the ending inventory. It does not introduce any new accounting concepts or procedures.

Metal Products, Incorporated, has been operating for eight years as a distributor of a line of metal products. It is now the end of 1977 and for the first time the company will undergo an audit by an independent CPA. The company uses a periodic inventory system. The annual income statements, prepared by the company, were:

	For the Year Ended December 31	
	1977	*1976*
Sales	$800,000	$750,000
Cost of goods sold:		
Beginning inventory	40,000	45,000
Add purchases	484,000	460,000
Goods available for sale	524,000	505,000
Less ending inventory	60,000	40,000
Cost of goods sold	464,000	465,000
Gross margin on sales	336,000	285,000
Operating expenses	306,000	275,000
Pretax income	30,000	10,000
Income tax expense (30%)	9,000	3,000
Net Income	$ 21,000	$ 7,000

During the early stages of the audit, the independent CPA discovered that the ending inventory for 1976 had been understated by $15,000.

Required:

a. Based on the above income statement amounts, compute the gross margin ratio on sales for each year. Do the results suggest the inventory error? Explain.

b. Reconstruct the two income statements on a corrected basis.
c. Answer the following questions.

1. What are the corrected gross margin ratios?
2. What effect did the $15,000 understatement of the ending inventory have on 1976 pretax income? Explain.
3. What effect did it have on 1977 pretax income? Explain.
4. How did the error affect income tax expense?

Suggested Solution:

Requirement (*a*), gross margin ratios as reported:
1976: $285,000 ÷ $750,000 = 0.38
1977: $336,000 ÷ $800,000 = 0.42

The change in the gross margin ratio from 0.38 to 0.42 suggests the possibility of an inventory error in the absence of any other explanation for this significant change.

Requirement (*b*), income statements corrected:

	For the Year Ended December 31	
	1977	*1976*
Sales	$800,000	$750,000
Cost of goods sold:		
Beginning inventory	55,000	45,000
Add purchases	484,000	460,000
Goods available for sale	539,000	505,000
Less ending inventory	60,000	55,000
Cost of goods sold	479,000	450,000
Gross margin on sales	321,000	300,000
Operating expenses	306,000	275,000
Pretax income	15,000	25,000
Income tax expense (30%)	4,500	7,500
Net Income	$ 10,500	$ 17,500

Requirement (*c*):

1. Corrected gross margin ratios:
   1976: $300,000 ÷ $750,000 = 0.40
   1977: $321,000 ÷ $800,000 = 0.401

   The inventory error of $15,000 was responsible for the variation in the gross margin ratios reflected in Requirement (*a*). The inventory error in 1976 affected gross margin for both 1976 and 1977, in the opposite direction but by the same amount ($15,000).
2. Effect on pretax income in 1976: *Ending inventory understatement*

($15,000) caused an *understatement of pretax income* by the *same amount.*

3. Effect on pretax income in 1977: Beginning inventory *understatement* (by the same $15,000 since the inventory amount is carried over from the prior period) caused an *overstatement* of pretax income by the same amount.
4. Total income tax was the same ($12,000) regardless of the error. However, there was a shift of $4,500 ($15,000 × 30 percent) income tax expense from 1976 to 1977.

An inventory misstatement in one year affects pretax ending income by the amount of the error and in the next year affects pretax income again by the same amount but in the opposite direction.

SUMMARY

This chapter focused on the problem of measuring cost of goods sold and ending inventory. The inventory should include all the items remaining on hand for resale to which the entity has ownership. Costs flow into inventory when goods are purchased (or manufactured) and flow out (as expense) when the goods are sold or otherwise disposed of. When there are several unit cost amounts representing the inflow of goods for the period, one is confronted with the necessity of using a rational and systematic method to assign unit cost amounts to the units remaining in inventory and to the units sold (cost of goods sold). The chapter discussed and illustrated four different cost-flow methods under both a perpetual inventory system and a periodic inventory system. The methods discussed were specific identification, average cost, Fifo, and Lifo. Each of the cost-flow methods is in accordance with the cost principle. The method of inventory costing used is particularly important since it will affect reported income, income tax expense (and hence cash flow), and the inventory valuation reported on the balance sheet. In a period of rising prices, Fifo gives a higher income than does Lifo; in a period of falling prices the opposite results occur.

Damaged, obsolete, and deteriorated items in inventory should be assigned a unit cost that represents their current estimated net realizable value. Also, when new market value (i.e., replacement cost) has declined below the actual cost of the goods remaining on hand, the inventory should be measured on a lower of cost or market basis.

This chapter presented another fundamental accounting principle (Exhibit 2–1) known as the consistency principle. This principle holds that in the accounting process all concepts, principles, and measurement approaches should be applied in a similar or consistent way from period to period so that the financial statements will be reasonably comparable over time.

IMPORTANT TERMS

Merchandise inventory
Finished goods inventory
Goods in process inventory
Raw materials inventory
Passage of ownership
Specific identification
Average cost
Weighted average cost
Moving average cost
First-in, first-out (Fifo)
Last-in, first-out (Lifo)
Inventory costing methods
Perpetual inventory record
Net realizable value
Lower of cost or market
Gross margin method
Consistency principle

QUESTIONS FOR DISCUSSION

1. Match the type of inventory with the type of business in the following matrix.

Type of Inventory	Type of Business	
	Trading	Manufacturing
Merchandise		
Finished goods		
Goods in process		
Raw materials		

2. Why is inventory an important item to both internal management and external users of financial statements?
3. Fundamentally, what items should be included in inventory?
4. In measuring cost of goods sold and inventory, why is passage of ownership an important issue? When does ownership to goods usually pass? Explain.
5. Explain the application of the cost principle to an item in the ending inventory.
6. When a perpetual inventory system is used, unit costs must be known at the date of each sale. In contrast, when a periodic inventory system is used, unit costs must be known at the end of the accounting period. Explain.
7. The chapter discussed four inventory costing methods: (*a*) specific identification, (*b*) average cost, (*c*) Fifo, and (*d*) Lifo. Briefly explain each.
8. Some accountants believe the specific identification method is subject to manipulation. Explain.
9. When a perpetual inventory system is used, a *moving weighted average* is used. In contrast, when a periodic inventory system is used, an *annual weighted average* is used. Explain why the different averages are used.

10. Contrast the balance sheet effects of Lifo versus Fifo on reported assets (i.e., the ending inventory) when (*a*) prices are rising and (*b*) prices are falling.
11. Contrast the income statement effects of Lifo versus Fifo (i.e., on pretax income) when (*a*) prices are rising and (*b*) prices are falling.
12. Contrast the effects on cash outflow and inflow between *Fifo* and *Lifo.*
13. When should net realizable value be used in costing an item in the ending inventory?
14. The chapter discussed the gross margin method to estimate inventories. Briefly explain it and indicate why it is used.
15. Briefly explain the consistency principle. How might it relate to the inventory costing methods?

EXERCISES

E8–1. The records at the end of January 1977 for Z Company showed the following for a particular kind of merchandise:

	Units	*Total cost*
Inventory, December 31, 1976	30	$390
Purchase, January 9, 1977	60	900
Sale, January 11, 1977 (at $35 per unit)	40	
Purchase, January 20, 1977	35	490
Sale, January 27, 1977 (at $36 per unit)	41	

Required:

Assuming a periodic inventory system, compute the amount of (1) goods available for sale, (2) ending inventory, and (3) cost of goods sold at January 31, 1977, under each of the following inventory costing methods (show computations):

a. Specific identification (assume the sale on January 11 was "identified" with the purchase of January 9, the sale of January 27 was "identified" with the purchase of January 20, and any excess identified with the beginning inventory).
b. Weighted average cost.
c. First-in, first-out.
d. Last-in, first-out.

E8–2. Western Company uses a perpetual inventory system and Fifo. The records reflected the following for January 1977.

	Units	*Unit cost*
Beginning inventory, January 1	100	$1.00
Purchase, January 6	200	1.20
Sale, January 10 (at $2.40 per unit)	110	
Purchase, January 14	100	1.30
Sale, January 29 (at $2.60 per unit)	160	

Required:

a. Prepare the perpetual inventory record for January.

b. Give journal entries indicated by the above data for January (assume cash transactions).

c. Prepare a summary income statement for January through gross margin.

E8–3. Use the data given in Exercise 8–1 for this exercise (assume cash transactions, a perpetual inventory system, and moving average cost).

Required:

a. Prepare the perpetual inventory record for January on a moving average basis. Round to the nearest cent on unit costs and the nearest dollar on total cost.

b. Give journal entry to record the purchase of January 9.

c. Give the journal entries to record the sale on January 11.

d. Prepare a summarized income statement for January through gross margin.

e. Explain why a moving average rather than a weighted average for the period was used.

E8–4. Use the data given in Exercise 8–1 for this exercise (assume cash transactions and perpetual inventory system).

Required:

a. Prepare a perpetual inventory record on a Lifo basis (costed currently). What is the amount for (1) cost of goods sold and (2) ending inventory?

b. Assume a perpetual inventory system and Fifo, compute (1) cost of goods sold and (2) ending inventory.

c. Give in parallel columns, journal entries for the transactions on January 9 and 11 assuming a perpetual inventory system for (1) Lifo and (2) Fifo. Set up captions as follows:

	Lifo		*Fifo*	
Accounts	*Debit*	*Credit*	*Debit*	*Credit*

d. Explain why the results are different between (*c*) (1) and (*c*) (2) immediately above.

e. Which inventory system would be preferred for tax purposes? Explain.

E8–5. Following is a partial computation of cost of goods sold for the income statement under three different inventory costing methods assuming a periodic inventory system:

	Fifo	*Lifo*	*Weighted average*
Cost of goods sold:			
Beginning inventory (480 units)........	$ 9,600	$ 9,600	$ 9,600
Purchases (520 units)......................	13,000	13,000	13,000
Goods available for sale...........			
Ending inventory (530 units)......			
Cost of goods sold			

Required:

a. Compute cost of goods sold for each costing method.
b. Rank the three methods (results) in decreasing order of pretax income.
c. Rank the three methods in order of favorable cash flow.

E8–6. During January 1977, BR Company reported sales revenue of $400,000 for the one item stocked. The inventory for December 31, 1976, showed 7,500 units on hand, valued at $165,000. During January 1977, two purchases of the item were made: the first was for 1,500 units at $24 per unit; and the second was for 7,600 units at $25 each. The periodic inventory count reflected 8,600 units remaining on hand on January 31, 1977. Operating expenses for the month summed to $62,100.

Required:

a. On the basis of the above information, complete single-step income statements under Fifo and Lifo. Use a single list of side captions including computation of cost of goods sold. Set up three separate column headings as follows: Units; Fifo; Lifo. Show your computations of the ending inventory.
b. Which method gives the higher pretax income? Why?
c. Which method gives the most favorable cash-flow effects? By how much, assuming a 40 percent tax rate?

E8–7. DB Company uses a periodic inventory system. Data for 1977 were: merchandise inventory, December 31, 1976, 1,600 units @ $15; purchases during 1977, 6,000 units @ $18; expenses (excluding income taxes), $51,800; ending inventory per physical count at December 31, 1977, 1,800 units; Sales price per unit, $33; and average income tax rate of 30 percent.

Required:

1. Complete income statements under the Fifo, Lifo, and average costing methods. Use a format similar to the following:

		Inventory Costing Method		
Income Statement	*Units*	*Fifo*	*Lifo*	*Average*
Sales revenue	____	$____	$____	$____
Cost of goods sold:				
Beginning inventory	____	____	____	____
Purchases	____	____	____	____
Goods available for sale	____	____	____	____
Ending inventory	____	____	____	____
Cost of goods sold	____	____	____	____
Gross margin	____	____	____	____
Expenses		____	____	____
Pretax income		____	____	____
Income tax expense		____	____	____
Net income		====	====	====

2. Which method is preferable in terms of (*a*) net income and (*b*) cash flow? Explain.
3. What would be your answer to Requirement 2 assuming prices were falling? Explain.

E8–8. In November 1977 a fire destroyed the inventory of Mason Retail Store. The accounting records were not destroyed; hence, they provided the following information:

	1975	*1976*	*1977 to date of fire*
Sales	$120,000	$142,000	$115,000
Cost of goods sold	73,200	85,200	?
Gross margin on sales	46,800	56,800	?
Expenses	34,800	42,800	37,000
Pretax income	$ 12,000	$ 14,000	?
Ending inventory	$ 20,000	$ 22,000	?
Purchases during year	70,000	87,200	68,000

Required:

a. Prepare an income statement for 1977 up to the date of the fire. Show detail for the cost of goods sold. Disregard income taxes.

b. What was the amount of the fire loss? Explain.

E8–9. The income statements for four consecutive years for Swan Company reflected the following summarized amounts:

	1974	*1975*	*1976*	*1977*
Sales	$60,000	$70,000	$80,000	$65,000
Cost of goods sold	36,000	38,300	50,100	39,000
Gross margin	24,000	31,700	29,900	26,000
Expenses	15,000	16,700	19,100	15,800
Pretax income	$ 9,000	$15,000	$10,800	$10,200

Subsequent to development of the above amounts, it has been determined that the physical inventory taken on December 31, 1975, was overstated by $4,000.

Required:

a. Recast the above income statements to reflect the correct amounts, taking into consideration the inventory error.

b. Compute the gross margin ratio for each year (1) before the correction and (2) after the correction. Do the results lend confidence to your corrected amounts? Explain.

c. What effect would the error have had on the income tax expense assuming a 20 percent average rate?

E8–10. White Company is completing the annual information-processing cycle on December 31, 1977. The company uses large quantities of store supplies in regular operations. To obtain lower prices, store supplies are bought in large quantities far in advance of actual use. When purchased, the cost is debited to a store supplies inventory account. At December 31, 1977, the account reflected the following debits:

Balance, January 1, 1977	$ 750
Purchases during 1977	1,600

A physical count at December 31, 1977, costed at purchase price, reflected supplies on hand amounting to $900.

Required:

a. What entry should be made on December 31, 1977, to reflect the effect of the inventory count?

b. What would have been the effect on the income statement and balance sheet had the entry in Requirement (*a*) not been made?

c. What entry should be made on December 31, 1977, assuming the 1977 purchases were debited to Store Supplies expense?

PROBLEMS

P8–1. Samson Company has just completed a physical inventory count at year-end, December 31, 1977. Only the items on the shelves, in storage, and in the receiving area were counted and extended at cost on a Fifo basis. The inventory summed to $82,000. During the audit the independent CPA developed the following additional information:

a. Goods costing $350 were out on trial by a customer; hence, they were excluded from the inventory count at December 31, 1977.

b. Goods in transit on December 31, 1977, from a supplier, with terms FOB destination, amounted to $400. Since these goods had not arrived, they were excluded from the physical inventory count.

c. On December 31, 1977, goods in transit to customers, with terms FOB shipping point, amounted to $900 (expected delivery date January 10, 1978). Since the goods had been shipped, they were excluded from the physical inventory count.

d. On December 28, 1977, a customer purchased goods for cash amounting to $1,200 and left them "for pickup on January 3, 1978." Samson had paid $700 for the goods and, since they were on hand, included the latter amount in the physical inventory count.

e. Samson Company, on the date of the inventory, received notice from a supplier that goods ordered earlier, at a cost of $2,100, had been delivered to the transportation company on December 27, 1977; the terms were FOB shipping point. Since the shipment had not arrived by December 31, 1977, it was excluded from the physical inventory.

f. On December 31, 1977, Samson shipped $750 worth of goods to a customer, FOB destination. The goods are expected to arrive at destination no earlier than January 8, 1978. Since the goods were not on hand, they were not included in the physical inventory count.

g. One of the items sold by Samson has such a low volume that the management planned to drop it last year. In order to induce Samson to continue carrying the item, the manufacturer-supplier provided the item on a consignment basis. At the end of each month, Samson (the consignee) renders a report to the manufacturer on the number sold and remits cash for the cost. At the end of December 1977, Samson had five of these items on hand; hence, they were included in the physical inventory count at $1,600 each.

Required:

Begin with the $82,000 inventory amount and compute the correct amount for the ending inventory. Explain the basis for any changes that you make. (Hint: The correct amount is $76,500. Set up three columns: Items, Amount, and Explanation.)

P8–2. Eatman Company has just completed taking the periodic inventory count of merchandise remaining on hand at the end of the fiscal year, December 31, 1977. Questions have arisen concerning inventory costing for five different items. The inventory reflected the following:

	Units	*Original unit cost*
Item A–The two units on hand are damaged because they were used as demonstrators. It is estimated that they may be sold at 20 percent below cost and that disposal costs will amount to $60 each.	2	$260
Item B–Because of a drop in the market, this item can be replaced from the original supplier at 10 percent below the original cost price. The sales price also was reduced.	20	70
Item C–Because of style change, it is highly doubtful that the four units can be sold; they have no scrap value.	4	20
Item D–This item will no longer be stocked; as a consequence it will be marked down from the regular selling price of $110 to $50. Cost of selling is estimated to be 20 percent of the original cost price.	3	80
Item E–Because of high demand and quality, the cost of this item has been raised from $120 to $144; hence, all replacements for inventory in the foreseeable future will be at the latter price.	15	120

The remaining items in inventory pose no valuation problems; their costs sum to $45,000.

Required:

Compute the total amount of the ending inventory. List each of the above items separately and explain the basis for your decision with respect to each item.

P8–3. At the end of January 1977, the records of Stanford Company showed the following for a particular item that sold at $15 per unit:

	Units	Amount
Inventory, January 1, 1977	500	$3,000
Sale, January 10	(400)	
Purchase, January 12	600	4,200
Sale, January 17	(550)	
Purchase, January 26	310	2,790
Purchase return, January 28	(10)	Out of Jan. 26 purchase

Required:

a. Assuming a periodic inventory system, prepare a summarized income statement through gross margin on sales under each method of inventory: (1) specific inventory, (2) average cost, (3) Fifo, and (4) Lifo. For specific identification, assume the first sale was out of the beginning inventory and the second sale was out of the January 12 purchase. Show the inventory computations in detail.

b. Between Fifo and Lifo, which method will derive the higher pretax income? Which would derive the higher EPS?

c. Between Fifo and Lifo, which method will derive the lower income tax expense? Explain, assuming a 40 percent average tax rate.

d. Between Fifo and Lifo, which method will produce the more favorable cash flow? Explain.

P8–4. Clark Company executives are considering their inventory policies. They have been using the moving average method with a perpetual inventory system. They have requested an "analysis of the effects of using Fifo versus Lifo." Selected financial statement amounts (rounded) for the month of January 1977 based upon the moving average method are as follows:

	Units	Amounts
Income Statement:		
Sales	180	$9,400
Cost of goods sold	180	5,710
Gross margin on sales		3,690
Less: Expenses		1,700
Pretax income		$1,990
Balance Sheet:		
Merchandise inventory		$2,620

Transactions during the month were:

Beginning inventory 50 units @ $30

Jan. 6 Sold 40 units @ $50

9 Purchased 100 units @ $32

16 Sold 80 units @ $52

Jan. 20 Purchased 110 units @ $33
28 Sold 60 units @ $54

Required:

a. Copy the above statement data and extend it to the right by adding columns for Fifo and Lifo (costed currently) using perpetual inventory system. This will provide one basis for analyzing the different results among the three inventory costing methods.
b. Which method produces the higher pretax income? Explain.
c. Between Fifo and Lifo, which one provides a more favorable cash position for 1977? Explain.

P8–5. Stover Appliance Store uses a perpetual inventory system. In this problem, we will focus on one item stocked, which is designated as Item A. The beginning inventory was 2,000 units @$4. During January, the following transactions occurred that affected Item A:

Jan. 5 Sold 500 units at $10 per unit.
10 Purchased 1,000 units at $5 per unit.
16 Sold 1,800 units at $10 per unit.
18 Purchased 2,300 units for $13,800.
24 Sold 600 units at $12 per unit.

Required (assume cash transactions):

a. Prepare a perpetual inventory record for January on (1) a Fifo basis and (2) a Lifo basis.
b. Give the entry for each basis for the purchase on January 10.
c. Give the entries for each basis for the sale on January 16.
d. Complete the following financial statement amounts for each basis:

	January	
	Fifo	Lifo
Income Statement:		
Sales	$?	$?
Cost of goods sold	$?	$?
Gross margin	$?	$?
Expenses	$12,000	$12,000
Pretax income	$?	$?
Balance Sheet:		
Current Assets:		
Merchandise inventory	$?	$?

e. Which method derives the higher pretax income? Under what conditions would this comparative effect be the opposite?
f. Assume a 40 percent average tax rate, which method would provide the more favorable cash position? By how much? Explain.
g. Which basis would you recommend for Stover? Why?

P8–6. This case is designed to demonstrate the effect on pretax income of (*a*) rising prices and (*b*) falling prices in comparing Fifo with Lifo. Income is to be evaluated under four different situations as follows:

Prices are rising:
  Situation A – Fifo is used.
  Situation B – Lifo is used.
Prices are falling:
  Situation C – Fifo is used.
  Situation D – Lifo is used.

The basic data common to all four situations are: sales, 600 units for \$5,300; beginning inventory, 500 units; purchases, 500 units; ending inventory, 400 units; and expenses, \$3,000. The following tabulated income statements for each situation have been set up for analytical purposes:

	Prices rising		*Prices falling*	
	Situation A Fifo	*Situation B Lifo*	*Situation C Fifo*	*Situation D Lifo*
Sales	\$5,300	\$5,300	\$5,300	\$5,300
Cost of goods sold:				
Beginning inventory	1,000	?	?	?
Purchases	1,500	?	?	?
Goods available for sale	2,500	?	?	?
Ending inventory	1,200	?	?	?
Cost of goods sold	1,300	?	?	?
Gross margin	4,000	?	?	?
Expenses	3,000	3,000	3,000	3,000
Pretax income	1,000	?	?	?
Income tax expense (20%)	200	?	?	?
Net Income	\$ 800	?	?	?

Required:

1. Complete the above tabulation for each situation. In Situations A and B (prices rising), assume the following: beginning inventory, 500 units @ \$2 = \$1,000; and purchases, 500 units @ \$3 = \$1,500. In Situations C and D (prices falling), assume the opposite; that is, beginning inventory, 500 units @ \$3 = \$1,500; and purchases, 500 units @ \$2 = \$1,000. Use periodic inventory procedures.
2. Analyze the relative effects on pretax income and on net income as demonstrated by Requirement 1 when prices are rising and when prices are falling.
3. Analyze the relative effects on the cash position for each situation.
4. Would you recommend Fifo or Lifo? Explain.

P8–7. The president of DT Company has just been presented with the March 1977 financial statements. They reflect data for three months as summarized below:

Income statements

	January	*February*	*March*	*Quarter*
Sales	$100,000	$106,000	$90,000	$296,000
Cost of goods sold	61,000	59,360	?	?
Gross margin on sales	39,000	46,640	?	?
Expenses	32,000	33,500	32,000	97,500
Pretax Income	$ 7,000	$ 13,140	$?	$?
Gross margin ratio	0.39	0.44	0.43 (estimated)	
Ending inventory	$ 14,000	$ 16,000		

The company uses a periodic inventory system. Although monthly statements are prepared, a monthly inventory count is not made. Instead, the company uses the gross margin method for monthly inventory purposes.

Required:

a. Complete computations in the following form to estimate the results for March.

	Amounts		*Computations*
Cost of goods sold:			
Beginning inventory	$16,000		From records
Purchases	51,000		From records
Goods available for sale	?		?
Ending inventory	?		?
Cost of goods sold		?	

b. Complete the income statements given above: assume a 45 percent average income tax rate.

c. What level of confidence do you think can be attributed to the results for March? Explain.

d. Would you recommend continued use of the method for the company? Explain.

P8–8. The income statement for Mason Company summarized for a four-year period showed the following:

	1974	*1975*	*1976*	*1977*
Sales	$1,000,000	$1,200,000	$1,300,000	$1,100,000
Cost of goods sold	600,000	610,000	870,000	650,000
Gross margin	400,000	590,000	430,000	450,000
Expenses	300,000	328,000	362,000	317,000
Pretax income	100,000	262,000	68,000	133,000
Income tax expense (45%)	45,000	117,900	30,600	59,850
Net Income	$ 55,000	$ 144,100	$ 37,400	$ 73,150

An audit revealed that, in determining the above amounts, the ending inventory for 1975 was overstated by $50,000. The company uses a periodic inventory system.

Required:

a. Recast the above income statements on a corrected basis.
b. Did the error affect cumulative net income for the four-year period? Explain.
c. Did the error affect cash inflows or outflows? Explain.

P8–9. XY Company uses a perpetual inventory system. Below is a perpetual inventory record for the period for one product sold at $6 per unit.

PERPETUAL INVENTORY RECORD

Date									
a.							400		1,200
b.	800	3.30					1,200		
c.				500		1,600	700		2,240
d.	300		1,050						3,290
e.				200			800		2,632
f.				300		987	500		
g.	100	3.65					600		

Required:

1. Complete the column captions for the perpetual inventory record.
2. What inventory costing method is being used?
3. Enter all of the missing amounts on the perpetual inventory record.
4. Complete the following:

	Units	Per unit	Amount
a. Beginning inventory............	______	______	______
b. Ending inventory	______	______	______
c. Total purchases..................	______	______	______
d. Total cost of goods sold.......	______	______	______

5. Give the entry(s) for date (*b*).
6. Give the entry(s) for date (*c*).
7. Complete the following tabulation:

Assumption	Cost of goods sold	Ending inventory
a. Fifo	______	______
b. Lifo (end of period)........	______	______
c. Annual weighted average (for the period).............	______	______

8. Assume a periodic inventory taken at the end of the period reflected 590 units on hand. Give any entry(s) required. (Disregard Requirement 7.)
9. Disregard Requirements 7 and 8 and assume that on date (*h*) 10 units of the beginning inventory were returned to the supplier and a cash refund of $2.90 per unit was recovered. Give the required entry.

9

Cash, short-term investments in securities, and receivables

PURPOSE OF THE CHAPTER

In this chapter our attention is focused on the measurement and reporting of a group of assets known as liquid assets: cash, short-term investments in securities, and receivables. They are designated as liquid assets because of their primary characteristic: they are either money or relatively close to conversion to money. Thus, they possess the characteristics of a current asset. The chapter will discuss these topics in three parts.

PART ONE: SAFEGUARDING AND REPORTING CASH

Cash is the most liquid asset that a business owns. Cash includes money and any instrument, such as a check, money order, or a bank draft, that banks normally will accept for deposit and immediately credit to the depositor's account. Cash *excludes* such items as notes receivable, IOUs, and postage stamps (a prepaid expense) and is generally divided into three categories: cash on hand, cash deposited in banks, and other instruments that meet the above definition. It is not unusual for a business to have several bank accounts. Even though a separate cash account may be maintained for each bank account, they are combined as one amount for financial reporting purposes.

Because cash is the most liquid asset and is continuously generated and used, it imposes heavy responsibilities on the management of an entity. They may be summarized as follows:

1. Safeguarding to prevent theft, fraud, loss through miscounting, and so on.
2. Accurate accounting so that relevant reports of cash inflows, outflows, and balances may be prepared periodically.
3. Control to assure a sufficient amount of cash on hand to meet (*a*) current operating needs, (*b*) maturing liabilities, and (*c*) unexpected emergencies.
4. Planning to prevent excess amounts of idle cash from accumulating—idle cash produces no revenue. In many cases, idle cash is invested in securities to derive a return, pending future need for the cash.

INTERNAL CONTROL OF CASH

Internal control refers to those policies and procedures of the business designed primarily to safeguard the assets of the enterprise. Internal control should extend to all assets: cash, receivables, investments, fixed assets, and so on. An important phase of internal control focuses on cash. Effective internal control of cash normally should include:

1. Complete separation of the *function* of receiving cash from the function of disbursing cash.
2. Definite and clear-cut assignment to designated *individuals* of the responsibilities for all activities related to cash handling and accounting for cash.
3. Establishment of definite and separate *routines* for (*a*) handling the inflow of cash, (*b*) handling the outflow of cash, and (*c*) the accounting process for both cash receipts and disbursements.
4. Separation of the physical handling of cash (in all forms) from the *accounting function.* Individuals that handle cash receipts or make cash disbursements (whether cash or by check) should not have access to the cash records. Similarly, those involved in maintaining the records should not have access to cash.
5. Require that all cash receipts be deposited in a bank daily. Keep cash on hand under strict controls.
6. Require that all significant cash payments be made by numbered checks with a separate approval requirement. For example, the person authorized to approve payments should be different from the person authorized to sign checks.

The separation of responsibilities and the use of prescribed routines are particularly important phases in the control of cash. A clear-cut separation of duties and responsibilities between people would require collusion between two or more persons if cash is to be embezzled and the theft concealed in the accounting records. Prescribed routines are designed so that the work done by one individual automatically is checked by the results reported by other individuals. For example, the routine for handling cash received through the mail may be designed so that one designated person opens the mail and makes a list of the cash. Then the cash received must follow a prescribed channel to the bank deposit, and another channel is prescribed for the flow of the related cash forms and documents. Finally, the accounting process for cash is another prescribed routine. Thus, the individuals that handle the cash should be separated at all times from those that maintain the related records in the cash-processing cycle.

To indicate how easy it is to conceal cash theft when internal control is lacking, we use two examples. Example 1—Employee X handles both cash receipts and the recordkeeping. Cash amounting to $100 was collected from J. Doe in payment of an account receivable. Employee X pocketed the cash and made an entry for $100 crediting Accounts Receivable (J. Doe) and debiting Allowance for Doubtful Accounts. Example 2—Occasionally Employee X would send a fictitious purchase invoice through the system. The resulting check, to a fictitious person, would be cashed by Employee X (using a fictitious endorsement and perhaps a partner in crime).

All cash disbursements should be made with prenumbered checks. For cash payments there should be separate routines and responsibilities for (1) payment approvals, (2) check preparation, and (3) check signing. If procedures similar to these are followed, it is difficult to conceal a fraudulent cash disbursement without the collusion of two or more persons. The level of internal control, which is subject to close scrutiny by the independent auditor, increases the reliability that users can accord to the financial statements of the business.

BANK ACCOUNTS

When a depositor opens a bank account, a signature card must be completed that lists the names and signatures of persons authorized to sign checks against the account. When a deposit is to be made, the depositor must fill out a deposit slip that includes the name of the account, the account number, and a listing of the coins, currency, and checks deposited. In recent years most banks have converted almost exclusively to personalized checks; that is, the name, address, and account number of the depositor is preprinted on each check. Obviously, this is an important safety feature for all parties concerned.

The bank statement

Each month the bank provides the depositor with a bank statement that lists (1) each deposit made during the period, (2) each check cleared during the period, and (3) a running balance of the depositor's account. The bank statement also will reflect any bank charges or deductions (such

EXHIBIT 9–1
Bank statement

BANK CAPITAL
THE CAPITAL NATIONAL BANK

John Doe Company
1000 Blank Road
Austin, Texas 78703

ACCOUNT NUMBER	STATEMENT DATE	PAGE NO.
877-95861	6-30-77	1

STATEMENT OF ACCOUNT
Please examine statement and checks promptly. If no error is reported within ten days, the account will be considered correct. Please report change of address.

ON THIS DATE	YOUR BALANCE WAS	DEPOSITS ADDED NO.	DEPOSITS ADDED AMOUNT	CHECKS AND DEBITS SUBTRACTED NO.	CHECKS AND DEBITS SUBTRACTED AMOUNT	SERVICE COST	RESULTING BALANCE
6-1-77	7,562.40	5	4,050.00	23	3,490.20	6.00	8,122.20

CHECKS AND DEBITS			DEPOSITS	DATE	DAILY BALANCE
				6-1-77	7 562 40
			3 000 00	6-2-77	10 562 40
500 00				6-4-77	10 062 40
55 00	5 00	40 00		6-5-77	9 962 40
100 00			500 00	6-8-77	10 362 40
8 20	16 50	160 00		6-10-77	10 177 70
2150 00	10 00		*100 00CM	6-12-77	8 177 70
7 50	15 30			6-16-77	8 094 90
35 00	1 50		150 00	6-17-77	8 208 40
40 20	15 00	6 00		6-18-77	8 147 20
*18 00NC				6-20-77	8 129 20
125 50	80 00	2 00		6-21-77	7 921 70
18 90			300 00	6-24-77	8 202 80
7 52	19 60			6-27-77	8 175 68
15 00	32 48			6-28-77	8 128 20
*6 00SC				6-30-77	8 122 20

Code:
CM - Credit Memo--Customer note collected
NC - Insufficient funds
SC - Service charge

* Note to student: John Doe Company did not record these items until the bank statement was received. See page 310.

as service charges) made directly to the depositor's account by the bank. Also included with the bank statement are copies of the deposit slips and all checks that cleared through the bank during the period covered by the statement. A typical bank statement (excluding the deposit slips and canceled checks) is shown in Exhibit 9–1.

On Exhibit 9–1 there are three items that require comment. First, observe that on June 20 there is listed under "Checks and Debits" a deduction for $18 coded with "NC."[1] This code indicates an "NSF check charge" (in slang, a "hot" or "rubber" check); NSF stands for Not

[1] These codes vary between banks.

Sufficient Funds. A check for $18 was received and deposited by John Doe Company from a customer, say R. Roe. Capital National Bank processed it through banking channels to Roe's bank. Roe's account did not have sufficient funds to cover it; therefore, the bank used by Roe returned it to the Capital National Bank, which then charged it back to John Doe Company. The NSF check is now a receivable, and John Doe Company must make an entry debiting Receivables (R. Roe) and crediting Cash for the $18.

The second item on Exhibit 9–1 that requires comment is the $6 listed under Checks and Debits and coded "SC." This is the code for bank service charges. Included with the bank statement was a memo prepared by the bank explaining this charge. John Doe Company must make an entry to reflect this $6 decrease in the bank balance by debiting an appropriate expense account, such as Bank Service Expenses, and crediting Cash.

The third item to be noted is the $100 listed on June 12 under Deposits and coded "CM" for "credit memo." In this instance, John Doe Company had asked the bank to collect a note receivable held by Doe that had been received from a customer. The bank collected the note and increased the depositor account in favor of John Doe Company. The bank service charge mentioned above was in part for this service. John Doe Company must record the collection by making an entry debiting Cash and crediting Notes Receivable (customer's name) for the $100.

Reconciling the bank balance

Normally, when the bank statement arrives, the ending cash balance shown on the bank statement will not agree with the ending balance shown by the Cash ledger account on the books of the depositor. For example, assume the Cash ledger account at the end of June of John Doe Company reflected the following:

Cash

June 1	Balance	7,010.00*	June	Checks written	3,800.00
June	Deposits	5,750.00			

(Ending balance, $8,960.00)

* Including $200 undeposited cash held for change.

The $8,122.20 **ending cash balance** shown on the **bank statement** is different from the $8,960.00 **ending book balance** shown on the **books of the John Doe Company** because (1) some transactions affecting cash may have been recorded in the books of the depositor but have not been recognized on the bank statement, and (2) some transactions may have been recognized on the bank statement but have not been recorded in the books of the depositor. The most common causes of a difference between the ending bank balance and the ending book balance of cash are:

1. Outstanding checks—checks written by the depositor and recorded in the Cash account as credits (in the depositor's books) but have not yet cleared the bank (hence they have not been deducted from the bank statement). The outstanding checks are determined by comparing the canceled checks returned with the bank statement with record of checks drawn (such as the check stubs) maintained by the depositor.
2. Deposits in transit—deposits taken to the bank by the depositor, and recorded in the Cash account as debits (in the depositor's books) but not yet recorded by the bank (hence they have not been reflected on the bank statement). This usually happens when deposits are made one or two days before the close of the period covered by the bank statement. These are known as **deposits in transit** and are determined by comparing the deposits listed on the bank statement with the copies of the deposit slips retained by the depositor.
3. Bank service charges—explained above.
4. NSF checks—explained above.
5. Errors—both the bank and the depositor are susceptible to errors, especially when the volume of cash transactions is large.

In view of these several factors, a **bank reconciliation** should be made by the depositor (whether for a business or a personal account) immediately after each bank statement is received. A bank reconciliation is an important element of internal control and is needed for accounting purposes. To encourage bank reconciliation by depositors, many banks provide a format on the back of the bank statement for such purposes. Instructions for completing the reconciliation also may be given. A typical form is shown in Exhibit 9–2.

Bank reconciliation illustrated. A bank reconciliation prepared by John Doe Company to reconcile the ending bank balance (Exhibit 9–1, \$8,122.20) with the ending book balance (page 306, \$8,960) is shown in Exhibit 9–3. A bank reconciliation has two accounting purposes: (1) to reconcile the ending bank and book cash balances, and (2) to develop the *correct balance* for the Cash account for reporting on the balance sheet. Observe on the completed reconciliation, Exhibit 9–3, that the *correct* cash balance is \$9,045, which is different from both the reported bank and book balances before the reconciliation.

Although the layout of a bank reconciliation can vary, the most simple and flexible one follows a balancing format with the "Depositor's Books" and the "Bank Statement" identified separately. This format starts with two different amounts: (1) the reported ending balance per books and (2) the reported ending balance per bank statement. Provision then is made for additions to, and subtractions from, each balance so that the

EXHIBIT 9–2

Sample form and instructions for bank reconciliation

THIS IS PROVIDED TO HELP YOU BALANCE YOUR BANK STATEMENT.

BANK BALANCE SHOWN ON THIS STATEMENT $______

ADD + (IF ANY) DEPOSITS NOT SHOWN ON THIS STATEMENT ______

TOTAL ______

SUBTRACT - (IF ANY) CHECKS OUTSTANDING ______

BALANCE $______

SHOULD AGREE WITH YOUR CHECKBOOK BALANCE

CHECKS OUTSTANDING	
NO	AMOUNT
TOTAL	

THIS IS PROVIDED TO HELP YOU BALANCE YOUR CHECKBOOK

CHECKBOOK BALANCE AT STATEMENT DATE $______

SUBTRACT - (IF ANY) ACTIVITY CHARGE ______

SUB-TOTAL ______

SUBTRACT - (IF ANY) OTHER BANK CHARGES ______

BALANCE $______

SHOULD AGREE WITH YOUR STATEMENT BALANCE

IF YOUR ACCOUNT DOES NOT BALANCE
PLEASE CHECK THE FOLLOWING CAREFULLY

- ☐ HAVE YOU CORRECTLY ENTERED THE AMOUNT OF EACH CHECK ON YOUR CHECKBOOK STUB?
- ☐ ARE THE AMOUNTS OF YOUR DEPOSITS ENTERED ON CHECKBOOK STUBS THE SAME AS IN YOUR STATEMENT?
- ☐ HAVE ALL CHECKS BEEN DEDUCTED FROM YOUR STUBS?
- ☐ HAVE YOU DEDUCTED ALL BANK CHARGES FROM YOUR STUBS?
- ☐ HAVE YOU CARRIED THE CORRECT BALANCE FORWARD FROM ONE CHECKBOOK STUB TO THE NEXT?
- ☐ HAVE YOU CHECKED ALL ADDITIONS AND SUBTRACTIONS ON YOUR CHECKBOOK STUBS?

last line reflects the same correct cash balance (for the bank and the books). This correct balance represents the amount that finally *should be* reflected in the Cash account after the reconciliation. It is also the amount of cash that should be reported on the balance sheet. Exhibit 9–3 for the John Doe Company reflects these features.

John Doe Company followed these steps in completing the bank reconciliation:

1. Identification of the outstanding checks—A comparison of the canceled checks returned by the bank with the records of the company of all checks drawn revealed the following checks still outstanding (not cashed) at the end of June:

Check No.	*Amount*
101	$ 145.00
123	815.00
131	117.20
Total	$1,077.20

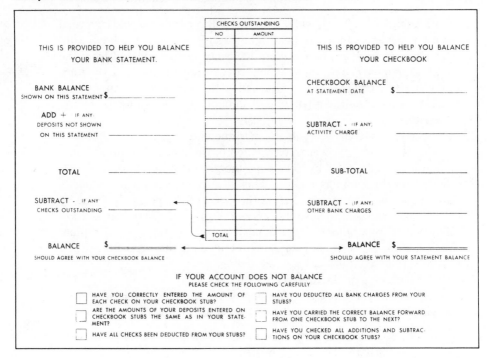

EXHIBIT 9–3

JOHN DOE COMPANY
Bank Reconciliation
For the Month Ending June 30, 1977

Depositor's Books			Bank Statement	
Ending cash balance per books		$8,960.00	Ending cash balance per bank statement	$ 8,122.20
Additions:			Additions:	
Proceeds of customer note collected by bank		100.00	Deposit in transit	1,800.00
Error in recording check No. 137		9.00	Cash on hand	200.00
		9,069.00		10,122.20
Deductions:			Deductions:	
NSF check of R. Roe	$18.00		Outstanding checks	1,077.20
Bank service charges	6.00	24.00		
Correct cash balance		$9,045.00	Correct cash balance	$ 9,045.00

This total was entered on the reconciliation as a deduction from the bank account (the checks will be deducted by the bank when they clear).

2. Identification of the deposits in transit—A comparison of the deposit slips on hand with those listed on the bank statement revealed that a deposit made on June 30 for $1,800 was not listed on the bank statement. This amount was entered on the reconciliation as an addition to the bank account (it will be added by the bank when it is recorded by them).
3. Cash on hand—On the date of the bank statement, cash on hand (i.e., undeposited cash held for making change) amounted to $200. Since this amount is included in the company's Cash account but was not included in the bank statement balance, it was entered on the reconciliation as an addition to the bank balance (as it would be, if deposited).
4. Items on bank statement not yet recorded in the books of John Doe Company:

   a. Proceeds of note collected, $100 (explained on page 306)—entered on the bank reconciliation as an addition to the book balance; it was already included in the bank balance. A journal entry is required to increase the Cash account balance for this item.

   b. NSF check of R. Roe, $18 (explained on page 305)—entered on the bank reconciliation as a deduction from the book balance; it was already deducted from the bank statement balance. A journal entry is required to reduce the Cash account balance for this item.

c. Bank service charges, \$6 (explained above)—entered on the bank reconciliation as a deduction from the book balance; it has already been deducted from the bank balance. A journal entry is required to reduce the Cash account balance for this item.

5. Error—At this point John Doe Company found that the reconciliation did not balance by \$9. Since this amount is divisible by 9, they suspected a transposition. (A transposition, such as writing 65 for 56, will always cause an error that is divisible by 9.) Upon checking the journal entries made during the month, they found that a check was written by John Doe Company for \$56 to pay an account payable for that amount. The check was recorded in the company's accounts as \$65. The incorrect entry made was a debit to Accounts Payable and a credit to Cash for \$65 (instead of \$56). Therefore, \$9 (i.e., \$65 − \$56) must be added to the book cash balance on the reconciliation; the bank cleared the check for the correct amount, \$56. The following correcting entry also must be made in the accounts: Cash debit \$9 and Accounts Payable credit \$9.

Note that the "Depositor's Books" and the "Bank Statement" now reconcile at \$9,045. This amount will be reported on the balance sheet. After the following journal entries have been made and posted to the ledger, the Cash account will reflect this balance:

	Journal entries from bank reconciliation	
	Debit	*Credit*
Entries from the reconciliation:		
Cash	100.00	
Notes receivable		100.00
To record note collected by bank.		
Accounts receivable (R. Roe)	18.00	
Cash		18.00
To record NSF check.		
Bank service expense	6.00	
Cash		6.00
To record bank service charges.		
Cash	9.00	
Accounts payable (name)		9.00
To correct transposition made in prior journal entry.		

Cash (after recording results of bank reconciliation)

June 1	Balance	7,010.00	June	Checks written	3,800.00
June	Deposits	5,750.00	June 30	NSF check	18.00
June 30	Note collected	100.00	June 30	Bank service charge	6.00
June 30	Correcting entry	9.00			

(Correct cash balance, $9,045.00)

Observe that all of (and only) the additions and deductions on the "Depositor's Books" side of the reconciliation require journal entries to correct the Cash account balance. Otherwise, the correct cash balance will not agree with what should be reported on the balance sheet and reflected in the Cash account. All other reconciling differences are adjustments to the "Bank Statement" side and will automatically work out when they clear the bank.

The importance of the bank reconciliation procedure in generating entries to *update* the Cash account should not be overlooked. This feature is important in measuring the correct cash balance for reporting on the balance sheet.

CASH OVER AND SHORT

Irrespective of the care exercised, when a large number of cash transactions is involved, errors in handling cash inevitably occur. These errors cause cash shortages or cash overages at the end of the day when the cash is counted and compared with the cash records for the day. Cash overages and shortages must be recognized in the accounts. To illustrate, assume that at the end of a particular day the cash from sales, as counted, amounted to $1,347.19 and the cash register tapes for sales totaled $1,357.19 – a cash *shortage* of $10 is indicated. The sales for the day should be recorded as follows:

Cash	1,347.19	
Cash over and short	10.00	
Sales		1,357.19

To record cash sales and cash shortage.

Alternatively, in the case of a cash *overage,* the Cash Over and Short account would be credited. It is important to note that sales revenue should be recorded for the correct amount reflected on the register tapes. At the end of the period, the Cash Over and Short account, in the case of a cumulative debit balance, usually is reported as a miscellaneous expense. If a credit balance exists, it would be reported as a miscellaneous revenue.

PETTY CASH

In the discussion of internal control we stated that all major disbursements of cash should be made by prenumbered checks. Many businesses find it quite inconvenient and costly in terms of paperwork and employee time to write checks for small payments for items such as taxi fares, newspapers, and small amounts of supplies. To avoid this inconvenience and cost, businesses frequently establish a **petty cash fund** to handle these small, miscellaneous cash payments. To establish a petty cash fund a check should be drawn "Pay to the order of: Petty Cash" for the amount desired and cashed; whenever cash runs low and at the end of each period, the expenditures from the fund are summarized and an accounting entry is made to reflect the activities of the fund and to record the check written to reimburse the fund for the total amount spent. The details of accounting for a petty cash fund are included in Appendix A to this chapter.

COMPENSATING BALANCES

A recent accounting issue that has created some concern has to do with the disclosure of **compensating balances.** Until recently, information concerning compensating balances has not been included in the financial statements. A compensating balance is the minimum amount of cash a bank requires the business to maintain in its bank account. A minimum, or compensating balance, may be required by the bank explicitly (by a loan agreement), or implicitly (by informal understanding), as part of a credit-granting arrangement. Often, it is difficult for the independent auditor to know whether or not an informal understanding exists. Information on compensating balances is important to statement users since there are two major effects on the business: (1) a compensating balance requirement imposes a restriction on the amount of cash readily available in the checking account; and (2) if it arises in connection with a loan, it increases the real rate of interest on the loan since not all of the cash borrowed can be used because some must remain on deposit.

Information concerning compensating balances must be reported in the financial statements because of its importance to statement users.

DATA PROCESSING FOR CASH

In small businesses the processing of accounting information on cash inflows and cash outflows often is done manually. In medium-sized companies much of the cash information processing may be mechanized through the use of various accounting machines. In the still larger businesses much of the cash information processing is accomplished by means of electronic computers. The nature of these data processing activities broadly is the same whether manual, mechanical, or electronic approaches are used. For instructional purposes their characteristics are best viewed in terms of a manual system. Appendix B to this chapter presents a data processing procedure known as "special journals." Two of these special journals relate to data processing for cash inflows and outflows. As you read the appendix, although a manual system is illustrated, mechanical or electronic computer applications should be apparent.

PART TWO: MEASURING AND REPORTING SHORT-TERM INVESTMENTS

To employ idle cash and for other business reasons, a company may invest in commercial paper (such as certificates of deposit), or in the capital stock or bonds of another company. Such investments are facilitated because commercial paper is sold by local banks, and the stocks and bonds of most of the large corporations are "listed" on the New York or American stock exchanges. Capital stock of smaller unlisted companies frequently can be bought and sold "over the counter" or between individuals and companies directly.

When bonds of another company are acquired, the purchaser has become a creditor of the issuing company, since bonds represent debt owed by the other company similar to a long-term note payable. As the holder of a bond, the investor is entitled to receive interest on the principal of the bond and the principal if held to maturity. In contrast, when shares of capital stock are purchased as an investment, the purchaser becomes one of the owners (frequently called stockholders, shareholders, or equity holders) of the company that issued the stock. As an owner, the stockholder receives dividends when they are declared and paid by the board of directors of the other company. Since most capital stock confers voting rights, the stockholder is provided an opportunity to exercise some control over the issuing company. The amount of control, obviously, is dependent upon the number of voting shares owned by the shareholder in relationship to the total number of such shares of stock outstanding.

Investments made by one company in the stocks or bonds of another company may be either (1) short-term investments (also called temporary investments) or (2) long-term investments (sometimes called permanent investments). This chapter discusses the measurement and reporting of short-term investments; long-term investments are discussed in Chapter 14.

SHORT-TERM INVESTMENTS DEFINED

To be classified as a short-term (or temporary) investment a security must meet a twofold test of (1) marketability and (2) a short-term holding period. **Marketability** means that the security must be regularly traded on the market so that there is a continuous market available and a determinable market price. Therefore, short-term investments generally are listed stocks and bonds, or short-term government securities. A **short-term holding period** means that it must be the **intention** of the management to convert the securities into cash in the near future for normal operating purposes.[2] Short term refers to the longer of the normal operating cycle of the business or one year as specified in the definition of current assets (Chapter 3, page 60). The distinction between short-term and long-term investments is important because (1) there are accounting differences that must be observed and (2) short-term investments must be classified as a current asset, whereas the long-term investments are reported under a noncurrent caption, "Investments and Funds."

Measurement of short-term investments. In accordance with the cost principle, short-term investments, when acquired, are measured and recorded at their cost. Cost includes the market price paid plus all additional costs incurred to purchase the security. To illustrate, assume the Brown Corporation had approximately $50,000 in cash that would not be needed for operations for the next eight to ten months. Brown purchased 1,000 shares of American Telephone and Telegraph (AT&T) stock for $55,000, including all broker's fees, transfer costs, and taxes related to the purchase.

The transaction would be recorded in the accounts as follows:

Short-term investments (1,000 shares @ $55)	55,000	
Cash		55,000
Purchase of 1,000 shares of AT&T stock at $55 as a short-term investment.		

Assume that two months after the purchase a quarterly cash dividend of $0.70 per share is received. The revenue on the temporary investment would be recorded as follows:

Cash	700	
Investment revenue		700
Cash dividend of $0.70 per share on short-term investment (AT&T stock); $0.70 × 1,000 shares = $700.		

Short-term investments held at the end of the accounting period are reported, at lower of cost or market, on the balance sheet as a current asset (lower of cost or market is discussed later). The current market value at that date should be shown parenthetically. For example, Brown Corporation would report the short-term investment of AT&T stock as follows:

[2] We shall see later that long-term investments also include marketable securities. Thus, the primary distinction between short-term and long-term investments turns primarily on the intention of management in respect to their expected disposal date. The same kind of security may be a short-term investment in one company and a long-term investment in another company, depending upon the intentions of the respective managements.

Current Assets:

Cash	$62,000
Short-term investments, at cost (current market value $55,800)	55,000

Investment revenue earned is reported on the income statement under "Financial revenue."

When a short-term investment is sold, if there is a loss or gain on the sale, it must be recognized. To illustrate, assume Brown sold one fourth of the short-term investment in AT&T stock for $14,000 cash, after deducting broker's fees, transfer costs, and taxes it would be recorded as follows:

Cash	14,000	
Short-term investments (250 shares @ $55)		13,750
Gain on sale of investments		250
Sale of 250 shares of AT&T stock at $56 per share.		

When a company owns short-term securities in several other companies, the securities held generally are referred to collectively as the **short-term portfolio.** A portfolio of short-term investments is managed (i.e., acquired, held, and sold) with the objective of maximizing the return while minimizing the risk. Thus, a portfolio of securities tends to be managed and accounted for as a whole rather than as a number of separate investments.

Short-term investments valued at lower of cost or market. Although short-term investments are measured and recorded at cost when acquired and are measured thereafter in conformity with the cost principle, there is an important exception. The exception occurs when the *current* market value of the portfolio drops below the recorded acquisition cost.[3]

In Chapter 8, relating to inventories of merchandise, we explained that items of merchandise in the inventory for which the *replacement cost* had dropped below acquisition cost should be measured on a lower-of-cost-or-market basis. The same principle applies to other current assets, including the short-term investment portfolio. It is reasoned that because of the drop in market value, the short-term investment portfolio has lost a part of its value as a short-term source of cash. The drop in value is viewed as a **holding or unrealized loss** that should be recognized in the period in which the drop occurred. However, a corresponding line of reasoning is not applied when the current market value is *above* the acquisition cost. Although this practice is an exception to both the *cost principle* and the *consistency principle,* the lower-of-cost-or-market basis in this situation is applied because the **principle of conservatism** (see page

[3] FASB *Statement of Accounting Standards No. 12,* "Accounting for Certain Marketable Securities," December 1975.

323) is permitted to override the other principles. Thus, the short-term investment portfolio is restated on a lower-of-cost-or-market basis.

To illustrate, let's return to the above example. Recall that Brown Corporation still owns 750 shares of AT&T stock at a cost of $41,250 (i.e., $55 per share). Assume that it is at the end of the accounting period and the financial statements are to be prepared. Assume further that the current market value of the stock is $53.50 per share; the total market value, therefore, is 750 shares × $53.50 = $40,125. Although the stock is not sold at this date, under the lower-of-cost-or-market (LCM) basis, a **holding loss** would be recognized at the end of the accounting period in an adjusting entry as follows:

Loss on short-term investments—reduction to LCM	1,125	
Short-term investments*		1,125
To reduce short-term investments to lower-of-cost-or-market basis ($41,250 − $40,125 = $1,125).		

* Note: A contra account, Allowance to Reduce Investments to LCM, often is used. The net effect is the same.

After the write-down illustrated above, the balance sheet would report the short-term investment as follows:

Current Assets:	
Short-term investment, at lower of cost or market (cost $41,250)	$40,125

When the lower-of-cost-or-market basis is applied to short-term investments, the measurement is based upon the *total portfolio cost* versus *total portfolio market* amount rather than on an item-by-item basis. To illustrate, assume Brown Company (see above) has three separate stocks, A, B, and C (rather than AT&T) in its short-term investment portfolio. The measurement at the end of the accounting period would be derived as follows:

	Portfolio	
Security	*Acquisition cost*	*Current market*
A Company common stock	$10,000	$10,000
B Company preferred stock	25,000	23,875
C Company common stock	6,250	7,250
Totals	$41,250	$41,125

Under the lower-of-cost-or-market basis, the Short-Term Investments account would be written down to $41,125 as illustrated above.[4] Should

[4] In contrast, when the lower-of-cost-or-market rule is applied to merchandise inventories, the item-by-item basis generally is used since merchandise is not viewed "as a single item" but as separate items.

a short-term investment in equity securities held at the end of the next period following a write-down to lower of cost or market experience an *increase* in market value, it would be written up for the increase (and i.e., a loss recovery) but not in excess of the original acquisition cost. It would appear this would seldom happen because of the limited holding period permitted for a security classified as a short-term investment.

At the end of the accounting period, no adjustment is made for dividend revenue on capital stock held as an investment because dividends (1) do not accrue on the basis of time and (2) are not paid unless formally declared by the board of directors of the issuing corporation. In contrast, when bonds (or other forms of debt) are held, an adjusting entry is required for accrued interest revenue as illustrated previously and in Part Three for notes receivable.

Certificates of deposit. In recent years a common short-term investment strategy to employ idle cash has been to purchase **certificates of deposit (CDs).** A "CD" is an investment contract (a certificate is received) that an investor may purchase from a bank for cash. The contract specifies (1) a limited period of time for the investment, such as 90 days, 6 months, 1 year, and so on; and (2) a guaranteed interest rate. Generally, the larger the amount of the certificate (the amount invested), the higher the interest rate. The interest rate also tends to be higher for longer time periods to maturity. Certificates of deposit and similar commercial paper are widely used for the short-term employment of idle cash because of the relatively high interest return and the liquidity factor.

Certificates of deposit are measured and accounted for in a manner similar to that discussed above for other short-term investments. They are accounted for separately from the regular cash. The interest earned is reported on the income statement as investment revenue. For external reporting purposes, certificates of deposit are reported as a current asset as follows:

Current Assets:	
Cash	$200,000
Certificates of deposit	300,000

or

Current Assets:	
Cash and certificates of deposit	$500,000

PART THREE: MEASURING AND REPORTING RECEIVABLES

Broadly speaking, receivables encompass all claims of the entity for money, goods, or services from other entities or persons. In most businesses there are two types of receivables: trade receivables and special (nontrade) receivables. Either type may include both short-term receivables (i.e., classified as current assets) and long-term receivables (i.e., classified as long-term investments or other assets). For example, a balance sheet may report the following receivables:

Current Assets:		
Trade accounts receivable	$40,000	
Less: Allowance for doubtful accounts	3,000	$37,000
Trade notes receivable		5,000
Special receivables:		
Due from employees		400
Equipment note receivable		600
Long-term Investments:		
Note receivable		10,000
Other Assets:		
Utility deposits		2,000
Due from company officers		1,000

TRADE RECEIVABLES

Trade receivables include trade accounts receivable (usually called accounts receivable) and trade notes receivable. Either may be short term or long term, although the latter is relatively rare in most situations. Trade receivables arise from the regular operating activities of the business; that is, from the sale of merchandise and/or services.

Trade accounts receivable and the contra account, Allowance for Doubtful Accounts, were discussed in detail in Chapter 7.

Many businesses *factor* their accounts receivable instead of holding them until due date for collection. **"Factoring"** is a term used for the sale of accounts receivable, usually at the date of the sale transaction, to a financial institution. It is widely used because the business receives the cash immediately for sales; however, the rate of interest for factoring arrangements tends to be high. A discussion of the detailed accounting involved is beyond the objectives of this book.

SPECIAL RECEIVABLES

Special (or nontrade) receivables arise from transactions other than the sale of merchandise and/or service. Special receivables may be short term or long term and should be given descriptive titles similar to those illustrated above. They should not be included in the caption "Accounts receivable."

Other than for appropriate classification on the balance sheet, special receivables generally do not involve unusual measurement or reporting problems.

NOTES RECEIVABLE

Notes receivable may be either trade notes receivable or special notes receivable, depending upon the source of the note. A promissory note is an unconditional promise in writing (i.e., a formal document) to pay a definite sum of money (known as the face amount or principal) on demand or at a definite future date known as the maturity or due date. The person who signs a promissory note is known as the **maker,** and the person to whom payment is to be made is known as the **payee.** The maker views the note as a "note payable," whereas the payee views the note as a "note receivable." Notes are said to be either interest bearing or noninterest bearing. In the case of long-term notes, interest frequently is paid annually or semiannually.

Interest calculations. Interest represents the **time cost of money.** To the maker of a promissory note, interest is an expense; whereas to the payee, it is a revenue. The formula for computing interest is:

Principal × Annual Rate of Interest × Fraction of Year = Interest Amount

It is important to remember that **interest rates** are quoted on an **annual basis** and, therefore, must be restated for time periods of less than one year. Thus, the interest on a $1,500, 8 percent, 90-day promissory note would be calculated as follows:

$$\$1{,}500 \times 0.08 \times 90/360 = \$30$$

When a note specifies a number of days, the exact days must be counted on the calendar to determine the due date and then related to the number of days in the year. For computing interest, it is often assumed that the year encompasses 360 days, so that each day's interest is $1/360$ of a year rather than $1/365$. This has the effect of making the actual interest cost for a short-term loan slightly higher than the stated amount of interest.[5]

All commercial notes involve interest, either explicitly or implicitly, because money borrowed, or loaned, has a time value that cannot be avoided.

An *interest-bearing note* is one that explicitly specifies (1) a stated rate of interest (such as 8 percent) on the note itself and (2) that the interest is to be paid at maturity, or in future installments, *in addition* to the face or principal amount of the note. For example, a $1,000, 8 percent, one-year, interest-bearing note would (1) provide the borrower with $1,000 cash, (2) have a face or principal amount of $1,000, and (3) require the payment of the principal ($1,000) plus interest for one year ($80)—a total of $1,080.

In contrast, in a *noninterest-bearing note,* the interest is implicit; that is, it is a note that (1) does not specify a rate of interest on the note itself

[5] For simplicity throughout this book, interest dates are given so as to avoid the needless counting of exact days on a calendar. Currently a trend appears to be developing toward using 365 days in the calculations.

and (2) includes the interest in the face amount of the note. For example, a \$1,000, one-year, noninterest-bearing note (assuming a going rate of interest of 8 percent) (1) would provide the borrower with \$925.93 (i.e., \$1,000 ÷ 1.08) and (2) would require the payment of only the face amount of the note at maturity date \$1,000. Observe that the interest (\$1,000 − \$925.93 = \$74.07) is included in the face amount of the note.[6]

An overdue *noninterest*-bearing note immediately draws interest at a legal rate (usually specified by law) from due date.

Accounting for notes receivable. Notes receivable usually arise in a business as a result of selling merchandise or services. Although most businesses use open accounts (i.e., accounts receivable), those selling high-priced items on credit frequently require notes from their customers. Assuming a \$1,500, 8 percent, interest-bearing promissory note was received from a customer as a result of the sale of goods, the payee would record it on the date of the sale as follows:

Notes receivable (trade)	1,500	
Sales revenue		1,500

To record 90-day, 8 percent, interest-bearing note received from customer.

(Note: Assuming the note was in settlement of an open account receivable, which frequently happens, the credit would have been to Accounts Receivable instead of to Sales.)

When collection is made at maturity date 90 days later, the entry would be:

Cash	1,530	
Notes receivable (trade)		1,500
Interest revenue		30

To record collection of a 90-day, 8 percent, interest-bearing note receivable plus interest (\$1,500 × 0.08 × 90/360 = \$30).

Default of a note receivable. A note receivable that is not collected at maturity is said to be **dishonored** or **defaulted** by the maker. Immediately after default, an entry should be made by the payee transferring the amount due from the Notes Receivable account to a special account such as, Special Receivable – Defaulted Trade Notes. Since the maker is responsible for both the unpaid principal and the unpaid interest, the receivable account should reflect the full amount owed to the payee. To

[6] This may be verified as follows:

Amount of cash received (true principal)	\$ 925.93
Interest expense (\$925.93 × 8%)	74.07
Amount of cash disbursed at due date	\$1,000.00

(Note: In some cases the interest is computed on the \$1,000 face amount; this would result in cash of \$920 and would serve to increase the interest cost to \$80 and a true interest rate of \$80 ÷ \$920 = 8.6957 percent. For further discussion, see Chapter 11.)

illustrate, assuming the above note was defaulted by the maker, the entry in the accounts of the holder or payee would be:[7]

Special receivable – defaulted trade notes	1,530	
Notes receivable (trade)		1,500
Interest revenue		30
To record the principal and interest earned on defaulted note		

Special Receivable – Defaulted Trade Notes is reported as a current or noncurrent asset depending upon the probable collection date.

Discounting a note receivable. Many businesses prefer a negotiable note receivable rather than an open account receivable from customers involved in large amounts of credit. The primary reasons are (1) the note provides formal evidence of the receivable, and (2) notes often can be sold to a financial institution, such as a bank, or to individuals in order to obtain needed cash *before* the maturity date. Selling a note receivable to a financial institution frequently is referred to as **discounting** a note receivable.

Promissory notes are almost always negotiable. A *negotiable* instrument is one that can be transferred by endorsement (there are other technical legal requisites for negotiability). The most common negotiable instrument is a check. Notes and a number of other instruments generally can be transferred by endorsement. An endorsement may be simply by signature of the holder, in which case it is said to be "with recourse." This means that in case of default, as in the case of a "hot" check (i.e., one that the depositor's bank has turned down because of insufficient funds in the depositor's account), the endorser is liable contractually for repayment. In contrast, an endorsement may be made "without recourse" by writing this phrase on the instrument before the endorsement signature. This means that the endorser cannot be held liable contractually in the case of default by the maker.[8] Entities and individuals seldom will accept endorsements without recourse; that is, a discounted note receivable usually is endorsed with recourse and, as a result, the financial institution can rely on both the maker and the endorser. An endorsement with recourse makes the endorser **contingently liable;** that is, if the maker does not pay the note at maturity, the endorser must do so. The full-disclosure principle (Exhibit 2–1) requires that such **contingent liabili-**

[7] From date of default, the amount due at that date (principal plus interest) continues to draw interest either at the stipulated rate or the legal rate as specified by the law of the state. There may be a question about the propriety of recognizing the interest revenue until collection is made when there is a reasonable probability that collection will not be made.

[8] The endorser or transferor may not be held liable contractually. However, the transferor may be held liable under *warranty* liability since the endorsement "without recourse" does not disclaim warranties such as title to the instrument. These legal distinctions are beyond the scope of this course.

ties be reported on the financial statements. This is usually done by means of a note to the financial statements, as illustrated below.

To illustrate the discounting of a note receivable, assume that the $1,500, 8 percent, 90-day interest-bearing note receivable (page 320) was sold to the Capital National Bank after 30 days at a **discount rate** of 9 percent per annum. The discount rate is the annual rate of interest required by the bank and may be more or less than the interest rate specified on the note. The discount rate is applied to the **maturity value**—that is, the principal amount of the note *plus* the amount of interest due at maturity. The discount rate of interest applies to the number of days the bank will hold the note (in this case, 60 days). Computation of the amount the bank will pay for the note is:[9]

Discounting a note receivable

Note: principal, $1,500; annual interest rate, 8%; term, 90 days.
Discounted: thirty days after date; discount rate, 9% per year.

Principal amount	$1,500.00
Plus: Interest due at maturity ($1,500 × 0.08 × 90/360)	30.00
Maturity value—amount subject to discount rate	1,530.00
Less: Discount—interest charged by bank ($1,530 × 0.09 × 60/360)	22.95
Proceeds—amount the bank pays for the note	$1,507.05

The discounting or sale of the note receivable would be recorded by the payee as follows:[10]

Cash	1,507.05	
Notes receivable (trade)		1,500.00
Interest revenue		7.05
To record discounting of a note receivable.		

Although the note was sold by the endorser, he or she must disclose the *contingent liability* on the note by means of a footnote to the financial statements similar to the following:

Note: At December 31, 1977, the company was contingently liable for notes receivable discounted in the amount of $1,530.

---

[9] This is the "commercial" approach which is almost always used. Conceptually, the proceeds should be computed on a present value basis as follows: $1,530 ÷ 1.015 = $1,507.39. This computes the interest on the present value of $1,507.39 rather than on the maturity value of $1,530 (i.e., $1,507.39 × 1.015 = $1,530).

[10] The credit of $7.05 to Interest Revenue may be explained as follows: Had the note been held to maturity, the payee would have earned $30 interest revenue; however, the bank charged interest amounting to $22.95. The difference is $7.05, which is the net interest earned by the payee for holding it 30 of the 90 days. Also the discount rate is applied to the maturity value of the note since that is the amount the bank will advance, less the interest required by the bank.

EXCEPTION PRINCIPLE

In the preceding chapters, the terms **materiality** (or material amount) and **conservatism** were used often. The principle of conservatism was discussed on pages 281 and 315 as the reason for using the lower-of-cost-or-market basis in measuring inventory and short-term investments. These terms, materiality and conservatism, refer to one of the fundamental accounting principles listed in Chapter 2 (Exhibit 2–1). It was designated there as the "exception principle."

The exception principle is comprised of the following three subprinciples: (1) materiality, (2) conservatism, and (3) industry peculiarities.

Although accounting must recognize that measurement and compliance with the specified accounting principles are essential, from a practical point of view the benefits of extremely high accuracy in measurement and absolute compliance with concepts sometimes are offset by practical considerations. Under certain limited conditions, the exception principle may override one or more of the other principles. These conditions are specified in the three subprinciples as follows:

1. Materiality—The fundamental accounting principles must be followed without exception for each transaction when the amount involved in the transaction is material (i.e., significant) in relationship to the overall financial effect. Although immaterial amounts must be accounted for, they need not be accorded theoretically correct treatment. For example, a pencil sharpener that cost $5.95 and having a five-year estimated life need not be depreciated under the matching principle; rather the $5.95 can be expensed in the period of acquisition because the amount is not material. The clerical cost alone of recording depreciation over the five-year period would exceed, by far, the cost of the asset. Additionally, the $1.19 annual depreciation amount would not impact on any important decisions by statement users.
2. Conservatism—This concept holds that where more than one accounting or measurement alternative is permissible for a transaction, the one having the least favorable immediate effect on net income or owners' equity usually should be selected. For example, in measuring the amount of a short-term investment or a merchandise inventory, the lower-of-cost-or-market basis is used. In this case, conservatism overrides the cost principle so that any market or holding loss that occurs before the asset is sold is recorded and reported.
3. Industry peculiarities—This concept holds that the unique characteristics of an industry may require use of special accounting approaches and measurement procedures in order to produce realistic financial reporting. For example, in the insurance mutual fund industry, the investment portfolio is accounted for and reported at fair market value (rather than cost or lower of cost or market).

DEMONSTRATION CASE FOR SELF-STUDY

Dotter's Equipment Company, Incorporated

(Try to resolve the case before studying the suggested solution that follows.)

Dotter's Equipment Company, Incorporated, has been selling farm machinery for over 30 years. The company has been quite successful in both sales and repair services. A wide range of farm equipment, including trucks, is sold. The company policy is to seek "high volume and quality service, at the right price." Credit terms with varying conditions are typical. Although most of the credit granted is carried by several financial institutions. Dotter's will carry the credit in special circumstances. As a result, the company occasionally accepts a promissory note and keeps it to maturity. However, if a cash need arises, some of these notes may be sold (i.e., discounted) to the local bank with which Dotter's carries its checking account. This case focuses on two farm equipment notes that were received during 1977. By following these notes from date of sale of farm equipment to final collection, we can see the various measurement problems posed and the accounting for them. The fiscal year for accounting purposes ends December 31, 1977.

The series of transactions in respect to the two notes follows:

Equipment Note No. 1:

1977

Jan. 15 Sold a farm tractor to S. Scott for $8,000 and received a 25 percent cash down payment plus a $6,000 equipment note receivable for the balance. The note was due in nine months and was interest bearing at 8 percent per annum. A mortgage on the tractor was executed as a part of the agreement.

Apr. 15 The Scott equipment note was sold to the local bank at an $8\frac{1}{2}$ percent per annum discount rate. Dotter endorsed the note, with recourse, and the proceeds were deposited in Dotter's checking account.

Oct. 15 Scott paid the bank the face amount of the note plus the interest ($6,000 + $360 = $6,360).

Required:

a. Give appropriate journal entries on each of the three dates. Show the interest computations and give an explanation for each entry.

b. Assume, that instead of payment on October 15, 1977, S. Scott defaulted on the note. The bank contacted Dotter's, which paid the note and interest in full. Give the appropriate entry for this assumption and one for the further assumption—that Scott later paid Dotter's in full on December 1, 1977.

Equipment Note No. 2:

1977

Oct. 1 Sold a farm truck to B. Day for $4,000; received a down payment of $400 and set up an account receivable for the balance; terms, n/30.

Nov. 1 Day came in and wanted an extension on the account receivable "until he sold some products." After some discussion it it was agreed to settle the account with a six-month, 8 percent, interest-bearing note. Day signed the note and a mortgage on this date.

Dec. 31 End of the fiscal period. An adjusting entry is required.

1978

Jan. 1 Start of the new fiscal period.

May 1 Since this was the due date, Day came in and paid the note plus interest in full. The note was marked paid and the mortgage was canceled.

Required:

c. Give appropriate journal entries on each date, including any adjusting entries at year-end. Omit closing entries at year-end. Provide an explanation for each journal entry.

Suggested Solution:

Requirement (*a*)—Equipment Note No. 1:

January 15, 1977:

Cash	2,000.00	
Equipment notes receivable	6,000.00	
Sales revenue		8,000.00

Sale of tractor to S. Scott for cash and equipment note; terms of note, nine months, 8 percent interest, including a mortgage.

April 15, 1977:

Cash	6,089.70	
Equipment notes receivable		6,000.00
Interest revenue		89.70

Discounted Scott equipment note receivable at bank discount rate of $8\frac{1}{2}$ percent.

Proceeds computed:

Principal amount	$6,000.00
Interest to maturity ($6,000 × 0.08 × $^9/_{12}$)	360.00
Maturity value	6,360.00
Discount ($6,360 × 0.085 × $^6/_{12}$)	270.30
Proceeds	$6,089.70

October 15, 1977: No entry required; Scott paid the bank that owned the note. During the period from April 15, 1977, until the note was paid, Dotter's was contingently liable for the note should Scott default.

Requirement (*b*)—Equipment Note No. 1:

Under the assumption that Scott defaulted on the note on due date, Dotter's would have to pay the principal plus interest in full and make the following entry:

October 15, 1977:

Special receivable (defaulted note)	6,360	
Cash		6,360

Scott note defaulted; payment to bank of the $6,000 principal plus interest ($\$6,000 \times 0.08 \times 9/12 = \$360$).

December 1, 1977:

Cash	6,360	
Special receivable (defaulted note)		6,360

Payment received in full on Scott note in default.

(Note: In most states, Dotter's could have also assessed Scott interest at the *legal* rate on the $6,360 amount overdue; in this case, there would be a credit to Interest Revenue.)

Requirement (*c*)—Equipment Note No. 2:

October 1, 1977:

Cash	400	
Accounts receivable	3,600	
Sales revenue		4,000

Sold truck to B. Day; terms of the receivable, n/30.

November 1, 1977:

Equipment notes receivable	3,600	
Accounts receivable		3,600

Settled account receivable with a six-month, 8 percent, interest-bearing note.

December 31, 1977:

Interest receivable	48	
Interest revenue		48

Adjusting entry for two months' interest accrued at 8 percent on Day equipment note ($\$3,600 \times 0.08 \times 2/12$).

January 1, 1978: No entry is required on this date; however, a reversal of the adjusting entry could be made to facilitate the subsequent entry when the interest is collected. The *optional reversing entry* would be (see Chapter 6, Part Two).

Interest revenue	48	
Interest receivable		48

May 1, 1978: This entry to record collection of the principal plus interest will vary depending on whether the above reversing entry was made:

a. Assuming reversing entry was not made:

Cash	3,744	
Equipment notes receivable		3,600
Interest receivable ($3,600 × 0.08 × 2/12)		48
Interest revenue ($3,600 × 0.08 × 4/12)		96

Collection of Day equipment note plus interest.

b. Assuming reversing entry was made:

Cash	3,744	
Equipment notes receivable		3,600
Interest revenue ($3,600 × 0.08 × 6/12)		144

SUMMARY

This chapter focused on the measurement and reporting of cash, short-term investments, and receivables. Since cash is the most liquid of all assets and is continually flowing in and out of a business, it can be one of the most critical control problems facing the management. It is also of critical importance to the decision maker relying on the financial statements for relevant information. The measurement and reporting of cash includes such problems as control of cash, safeguarding cash, reconciliation of bank balances, petty cash, and recording of all cash inflows and outflows.

The use of short-term investments to employ idle cash was discussed. Marketability and the intention of management in respect to the holding period are fundamental in the classification of an investment as short term as opposed to long term. Short-term investments are accounted for in accordance with the cost principle; however, in accordance with the principle of conservatism, the lower-of-cost-or-market basis is applied to the portfolio at the end of each accounting period. Long-term investments are deferred for discussion in a later chapter.

Receivables include trade receivables (usually called accounts receivable), special receivables, and notes receivable. Each of these should be accounted for separately. Interest calculations and discounting of notes receivable were discussed and illustrated.

The chapter emphasized the importance of careful measurement of these liquid assets and the importance of examining their characteristics before classifying them as current assets for reporting purposes. Financial statement users often are faced with decisions in which these liquid assets are critical; therefore, they should be properly measured and adequately reported.

IMPORTANT TERMS

Internal control	**Investment portfolio**
Bank reconciliation	**Lower of cost or market**
Cash over and short	**Principle of conservatism**
Petty cash	**Certificates of deposit (CDs)**
Compensating balances	**Contingent liability**
Short-term investments	**Materiality**
Holding or unrealized loss	

APPENDIX A

Petty cash

A petty cash fund is established to avoid the inconvenience and cost of writing checks for the many small payments that occur daily in some businesses. This appendix discusses and illustrates the detailed accounting and recordkeeping for a petty cash fund.

Establishing the petty cash fund. To establish a petty cash fund (sometimes called an imprest fund), a check should be written for the estimated amount needed to meet the expected payments, say for an average month. The check, made payable to "Petty Cash," is cashed and the money kept in a safe place under the direct control of a *designated individual* as the *custodian.* The entry for the initial check would be:

Petty cash	100	
Cash		100
To record establishment of a petty cash fund.		

Disbursements from the petty cash fund. The petty cash system should require that the custodian responsible for disbursements from the fund maintain a running record of all disbursements and the amount of cash on hand. No entry is made in the regular accounts at the time each payment is made from the petty cash fund by the custodian. Rather, the custodian maintains a *petty cash record* in which each disbursement is recorded when made. This record is supported by signed bills, vouchers, and receipts for each payment made. As an internal control feature, the custodian should expect occasional surprise counts of the fund and examinations of the records of disbursements. "Borrowing" from the fund by the custodian or others should not be allowed. Careless handling of petty cash has often led to defalcations and theft.

Replenishment of the petty cash fund. When the amount of petty cash on hand gets low, and at the end of each accounting period, the fund should be reimbursed, or replenished, with an amount of cash sufficient to restore it to the original amount (to $100 in the example). This is accomplished by having the custodian turn in the petty cash record and the supporting documents. On the basis of these records, a check to "Petty Cash" is written for the amount of cash needed for replenishment. The check is cashed, and the money is given to the custodian. An entry in the regular accounts for the amount of the check is made to record the expenditures. The petty cash documents turned in by the custodian provide the underlying support for this entry.

To illustrate, assume that by the end of the month, there remained \$8.50 petty cash on hand of the \$100. This means that cash expenditures by the custodian amounted to \$91.50 for the month. Assuming no shortage or overage, the bills, vouchers, and receipts accumulated by the custodian should sum to this amount. They provide the supporting documents for the additional check to petty cash for \$91.50. These supporting documents provided the detailed data for recording the replenishment check in the following journal entry:

Telephone and telegraph expense	12.40	
Office expense (coffee)	6.32	
Postage expense	21.45	
Freight-in	6.33	
Taxi fare expense	14.87	
Repair expense, office equipment	5.00	
Supply expense for coffee bar	10.04	
Miscellaneous expenses	15.09	
Cash		91.50

It should be emphasized that the Petty Cash account is debited *only* when the petty cash fund is first established. The Petty Cash account carries a stable balance at all times (\$100 in the above example). Expense accounts, not Petty Cash, are debited and the *regular* Cash account is credited when the fund is replenished. Hence, there will be no further entries in the petty cash fund once it is established unless it is decided to discontinue the fund or to increase or decrease the original amount on a permanent basis. The fund must be replenished when the balance of cash in the fund is low, and always at the end of the accounting period, whether low or not. The latter is necessary in order to record the expenses incurred by the fund up to the date of the financial statements. The petty cash fund should be subject to rigid internal control procedures to remove all temptations to misuse it.

In a bank reconciliation, petty cash should be included in the "Ending cash balance per books" and as an addition under "Bank Statement" along with cash on hand because this reflects the amount of cash to be reported on the balance sheet (see Exhibit 9–3).

APPENDIX B

Special journals

Up to this point in your study of accounting, we have utilized the *general journal* to record all transactions in chronological order (i.e., by order of date). The general journal is flexible in that any transaction can be recorded in it. However, it is inefficient if used for recording transactions that have a very high rate of occurrence, such as credit sales, credit purchases, cash receipts, and cash payments. It is inefficient in three ways: (1) in recording the same journal entry repeatedly (except for changed amounts), (2) in posting to the ledger, and (3) in facilitating division of labor. Special journals are designed to reduce these inefficiencies as will be demonstrated below.

In discussing and illustrating special journals, we emphasize that no accounting principles or concepts are involved—we are simply dealing with the mechanics of data processing. Although special journals can, and should, be designed to meet a special need when a particular type of data processing problem arises, we will limit this discussion to the four special journals that are often used: credit sales, credit purchases, cash receipts, and cash payments.

Sales journal. This journal is designed to accommodate *only credit sales.* Cash sales are entered in the cash receipts journal as explained below. You will recall that the journal entry to record a credit sale is:[11]

Jan. 3	Accounts receivable (customer's name)	100	
	Sales		100
	To record credit sale; Invoice No. 324; terms, n/30.		

The sales journal is designed specifically to simplify (1) recording only this kind of entry and (2) subsequent posting to the ledger. The design of a sales journal is shown in Exhibit 9–4. Observe the saving in space, time, and accounting expertise required to journalize a credit sale (all of these are minimized).

Posting the sales journal. Posting the special sales journal involves two distinct phases. First, the *individual charges* (i.e., debits) must be posted daily to the customers individual accounts in the *accounts receivable subsidiary ledger.* Observe here the potential for division of labor. Second, periodically (usually weekly or monthly), the *totals* are posted to the *general ledger* accounts: Accounts Receivable (debit) and Sales (credit). In this activity, there is a significant saving in time.

Posting on a daily basis to the subsidiary ledger is indicated in the folio column by entering the account number for each individual customer. Daily posting to the subsidiary ledger is necessary because the customer may, on any day, want to pay the current balance then owed.

Thus, the control account and the subsidiary ledger would agree only when both the totals and the daily postings are complete.

---

[11] For instructional purposes, we will utilize simplified amounts, a limited number of transactions and customers, and T-accounts. We remind you again that a manual system and T-accounts are illustrated for instructional purposes. In many companies these procedures are completely computerized.

EXHIBIT 9–4

SALES JOURNAL Page 9

Date		Customer Name	Terms	Invoice Number	Folio	Amount
Jan.	3	Adams, K. L.	n/30	324	34.1	100
	4	Small, C. C.	n/30	325	34.6	60
	6	Baker, C. B.	n/30	326	34.2	110
	10	Roe, R. R.	n/30	327	34.5	20
	11	Mays, O. L.	n/30	328	34.3	200
	16	Roe, R. R.	n/30	329	34.5	90
	18	Null, O. E.	n/30	330	34.4	30
	20	Baker, C. B.	n/30	331	34.2	180
	21	Small, C. C.	n/30	332	34.6	150
	31	Null, O. E.	n/30	333	34.4	260
		Total				1,200
		Posting				(34) (81)
Feb.	1	Etc.				

The daily posting during January to the accounts receivable subsidiary ledger is shown below.

ACCOUNTS RECEIVABLE SUBSIDIARY LEDGER

Adams, K. L. 34.1

Jan. 3		9	100		

Baker, C. B. 34.2

Jan. 6		9	110		
20		9	180	290	

Mays, O. L. 34.3

Jan. 11		9	200		

Null, O. E. 34.4

Jan. 18		9	30		
31		9	260	290	

Roe, R. R. 34.5

Jan. 10		9	20		
16		9	90	110	

Small, C. C. 34.6

Jan. 4		9	60		
27		9	150	210	

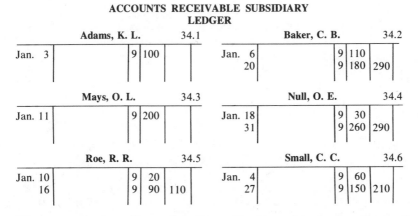

The second phase in posting the sales journal is to transfer to the general ledger the total credit sales for the month. Thus, the $1,200 total will be posted to the general ledger as (1) a debit to the Accounts Receivable *control account* and (2) as a credit to the Sales account. This posting is shown below; note in the sales journal that two ledger account numbers were entered for the $1,200 total to indicate the posting procedure.

Accounts Receivable (control) 34	
Jan. 31 9 1,200	

Sales 81	
	Jan. 31 9 1,200

The sales journal can be readily adapted to record sales taxes by adding a column headed "Sales Taxes Payable," and separate sales columns can be added to accumulate sales by department or product. You should observe the following efficiencies attained: (1) recording in the sales journal is much less time-consuming than separately entering each credit sale in the general journal; (2) posting is significantly reduced by transferring the *total* to the ledger as opposed to posting separate debits and credits for each sales transaction; and (3) the potential for division of labor.

Purchases journal. Following exactly the same pattern as described above, the purchases journal may be designed as shown below to accommodate the entry common to all purchases on credit, viz:

Jan. 8	Purchases*	392	
	Accounts payable		392
	To record purchase on credit from C. B. Smith, Purchase Order No. 139; invoice dated January 5, 1977; terms, 2/10, n/30. Recorded at net of discount, $400 × 0.98 = $392.		

* This assumes a periodic inventory system; if a perpetual inventory system is used, this account would be Merchandise Inventory.

Only credit purchases would be recorded in the purchases journal. Cash purchases would be entered in the cash payments journal as illustrated later. The design of a purchases journal generally is as shown in Exhibit 9–5.

EXHIBIT 9–5

PURCHASES JOURNAL Page 4

Date		Creditors Account	Purchase Order No.	Date of Invoice	Terms	Folio	Amount
Jan	8	Smith C. B.	139	Jan. 5	2/10, n/30	91.8	392
		Etc.					
		Total					784
		Posting					(6) (5)

Observe that purchases are recorded net of the purchase discount as explained in Chapter 7, page 221. The cash payments journal will provide for recording the subsequent payment of cash for the purchase including situations where the purchase discount is lost.

Exhibit 9–5 was not completed in detail for illustrative purposes since it follows essentially the same pattern already illustrated for the sales journal, both in respect to entries therein and the two phases in posting. Daily posting would involve transfer to the creditors' individual accounts in the *accounts payable subsidiary ledger.* Periodically, the total would be posted to the *general ledger* as (1) a debit to the Purchases account and (2) a credit to the Accounts Payable control account. The efficiencies cited for the sales journal are also realized by a purchases journal.

Cash receipts journal. The design of a special journal to accommodate *all* cash receipts is more complex since there are a number of different accounts that are individually *credited* when the Cash account is debited. In order to resolve this problem, more than one credit column is necessary to accommodate the various credits. The number and designation of the debit and credit columns will depend upon the character of the repetitive cash receipts transactions in the particular business.

A typical cash receipts journal with some usual transactions recorded is shown in Exhibit 9–6. Notice in particular that there are separate debit and credit sections. Each column illustrated is used as follows:

EXHIBIT 9–6

CASH RECEIPTS JOURNAL — Page 14

Date		Explanation	DEBITS	CREDITS				
			Cash	Account Title	Folio	Accounts Receivable	Sundry Accounts	Cash Sales
Jan.	2	Cash sales	1,237					1,237
	3	Cash sales	1,482					1,482
	4	Sale of land	2,500	Land	43		2,000	
				Gain on sale of land	91		500	
	4	Cash sales	992					992
	6	Invoice #324	100	Adams, K. L.	34.1	100		
	6	Cash sales	1,570					1,570
	10	Bank loan	1,000	Notes payable	54		1,000	
	15	Invoice #328	200	Mays, O. L.	34.3	200		
	26	Cash sales	1,360					1,360
	31	Invoice #326	110	Baker, C.B.	34.2	110		
	31	Cash sales	1,810					1,810
		Totals	12,361			410	3,500	8,451
		Posting	(12)			(34)	(NP)	(81)

1. Cash debit—This column is used for *every* debit to cash. The column is totaled at the end of the period and posted as one debit amount to the Cash account in the general ledger. The posting number at the bottom indicates the total was posted to account number "12," the Cash account.[12]
2. Accounts Receivable credit—This column is used to enter the individual amounts collected and to be posted to the individual customer accounts in the accounts receivable *subsidiary* ledger (as indicated by the posting numbers in the folio columns). The total of this column is posted at the end of the period as a credit to the Accounts Receivable control account in the general ledger as indicated by the posting number "34."
3. Sundry Accounts credit—This column is used for recording credits to all accounts other than those for which special credit columns are provided (in this example Accounts Receivable and Sales). The titles of the accounts to be credited as listed in this column are entered under the column "Account Title." Since the Sundry Accounts column represents a number of *accounts,* the *total* is not posted; rather, each individual amount must be posted as a credit directly to the indicated general ledger accounts. Account numbers entered in the related folio column indicate the posting.
4. Cash Sales credit—This column is used to record *all* cash sales. The total at the end of the month is posted as a credit to the Sales account in the general ledger.

Posting the cash receipts journal involves the same two phases explained previously for the sales and purchases journals. The daily posting phase encompasses posting the individual credits to the accounts receivable subsidiary ledger. The second phase involves posting the totals periodically to the accounts in the general ledger, with the exception of the column total for "Sundry Accounts," as explained above.

The individual accounts shown in the "Sundry Accounts" column can be posted daily or at the end of the period. Posting through January is indicated by account code numbers in the illustrated cash receipts journal.

The representative entries shown in the illustrated cash receipts journal are summarized below, in *general journal form,* for convenience in assessing the increased efficiencies of the cash receipts journal approach in journalizing and posting a large number of individual cash transactions.

Jan. 2	Cash	1,237	
	Sales		1,237
	To record total cash sales for the day.		

[12] This design assumes that the company correctly records credit sales at net of discounts. If credit sales are recorded at "gross," then a Sales Discount debit column would also be needed in this special journal.

Jan. 3	Cash	1,482	
	Sales		1,482
	To record total cash sales for the day.		
4	Cash	2,500	
	Land		2,000
	Gain on sale of land		500
	To record sale of land for $2,500 that originally cost $2,000.		
4	Cash	992	
	Sales		992
	To record total cash sales for the day.		
6	Cash	100	
	Accounts receivable		100
	To record collection of K. L. Adams account for Invoice No. 324 within the discount period.		
6	Cash	1,570	
	Sales		1,570
	To record total cash sales for the day.		
10	Cash	1,000	
	Notes payable		1,000
	To record bank loan, 90-day, 6 percent.		
15	Cash	200	
	Accounts receivable		200
	To record collection of O. L. Mays account for Invoice No. 328 within the discount period.		
26	Cash	1,360	
	Sales		1,360
	To record total cash sales for the day.		
31	Cash	110	
	Accounts receivable		110
	To record collection of C. B. Baker account, Invoice No. 326.		
31	Cash	1,810	
	Sales		1,810
	To record total cash sales for the day.		

Other debit and credit columns can be added to the cash receipts journal to accommodate repetitive transactions that also involve cash receipts.

Cash payments journal. The special cash payments journal (often called the check register) is designed to accommodate efficiently the recording of *all* cash payments. The basic credit column, of course, is

Credits, Cash; other columns are incorporated into the format to accommodate repetitive transactions that involve cash payments. The cash payments journal, of necessity, must also include a column for "Sundry Accounts, debits" to accommodate the nonrecurring transactions involving cash payments (for which a special column is not provided).

A typical cash payments journal with some usual transactions recorded is shown in Exhibit 9–7. Observe that, in common with the cash receipts journal, there are separate debit and credit sections. Each column illustrated is used as follows:

1. Cash credit—This column is for every *credit* to the Cash account. The column is totaled at the end of the month and posted as a credit to the Cash account in the general ledger.
2. Accounts Payable debit—This column is used to enter the individual amounts paid on accounts payable. The individual amounts are posted as debits to the accounts payable subsidiary ledger (as indicated by the account numbers under folio), and the total at the end of the period is posted as a debit to the Accounts Payable control account in the general ledger.
3. Sundry Accounts debit—This column is used to record all accounts debited for which special columns are not provided (in this example Accounts Payable and Purchases). The titles of the accounts to be

EXHIBIT 9–7

CASH PAYMENTS JOURNAL — Page 16

Date		Check No.	Explanation	CREDITS	DEBITS				
				Cash	Account Title	Folio	Accounts Payable	Sundry Accounts	Cash Purchases
Jan.	2	101	Purchased mdse.	1,880					1,880
	4	102	Invoice #37	2,970	Ray Mfg. Co.	51.3	2,970		
	5	103	Jan. Rent	1,200	Rent Expense	71		1,200	
	8	104	Purchased mdse.	250					250
	10	105	Freight on mdse.	15	Freight in	63		15	
	14	106	Invoice #42	980	Bows Supply Co.	51.1	980		
	15	107	Bank loan plus	2,464	Notes Payable	54		2,400	
			interest paid		Interest Expense	79		64	
	20	108	Insurance premium	600	Prepaid Insurance	19		600	
	26	109	Purchased mdse.	2,160					2,160
	29	110	Invoice #91 - after	500	Myer Corp.	51.2	490		
			discount period		Discount lost	80		10	
	31	111	Wages	1,000	Wage Expense	76		1,000	
			Totals	14,019			4,440	5,289	4,290
			Posting	(12)			(51)	(NP)	(61)
Feb.	1		Etc.						

debited are entered under the column "Account Titles." Since this column represents a number of accounts, the total cannot be posted; rather, each individual amount is posted as a debit directly to the indicated general ledger account.

4. Cash Purchase debit—All cash purchases are entered in this column. The total at the end of the month is posted as a debit to the Purchases account in the ledger.

Posting the cash payments journal involves two phases: (1) daily posting of the individual credit amounts to the accounts payable subsidiary ledger; and (2) periodic posting of the totals to the general ledger, with the exception of the total of "Sundry Accounts." The posting of the individual amounts in the "Sundry Accounts" column can be done during the period, say daily.

The illustrative transactions entered in the cash payments journal were:

Jan. 2 Issued Check No. 101 for cash purchase of merchandise costing $1,880.
4 Issued Check No. 102 to pay account payable owed to Ray Manufacturing Company within the discount period. Discount allowed, 1 percent; Invoice No. 37, $3,000.
5 Issued Check No. 103 to pay January rent, $1,200.
8 Issued Check No. 104 for cash purchase of merchandise costing $250.
10 Issued Check No. 105 for freight-in on merchandise purchased, $15.
14 Issued Check No. 106 to pay account payable owed to Bows Supply Company within the discount period. Discount allowed, 2 percent; Invoice No. 42, $1,000.
15 Issued Check No. 107 to pay $2,400 note payable plus 8 percent annual interest for 120 days.
20 Issued Check No. 108 to pay three-year insurance premium, $600.
26 Issued Check No. 109 for cash purchase of merchandise costing $2,160.
29 Issued Check No. 110 to pay account payable to Myar Corporation; terms, 2/10, n/30; Invoice No. 91, $500. Therefore, accounts payable to Myar was credited for $490 at the purchase date (see Chapter 7, page 221). The payment was made after the discount period; therefore, the full invoice price of $500 was paid and purchase discount lost of $10 was recorded.
31 Issued Check No. 111 to pay wages amounting to $1,000.

Additional debit and credit columns can be added to the cash payments journal to accommodate other repetitive transactions involving cash disbursements.

Many companies use a *voucher system* for controlling expenditures rather than the purchases and the cash payments journals. A voucher system is particularly adaptable to computerized accounting and provides tight control mechanisms on the sequence of events for each transaction from incurrence until final cash payment. The voucher system is explained and illustrated in Chapter 11, Appendix B.

In summary, special journals do not involve new accounting principles or concepts. Rather, they represent a mechanical technique designed to increase the efficiency in the data processing cycle. Special journals are not standardized; they should be especially designed to fit each particular situation. Although a manual approach has been illustrated for instructional purposes, many companies have fully computerized the procedures represented by special journals. In computerized systems, essentially the same mechanics illustrated for the manual system are accomplished by the computer.

QUESTIONS FOR DISCUSSION

1. Define cash in the accounting context and indicate the types of items that should be included.
2. Explain the purpose and nature of internal control.
3. What are the primary characteristics of an effective internal control system for cash?
4. Why should cash-handling and cash-recording activities be separated? Generally, how is it accomplished?
5. What is the purpose and nature of a bank reconciliation? Specifically, what balances are reconciled?
6. Define a short-term investment. What is the twofold test for classification as a short-term investment?
7. Is a marketable security always a short-term investment? Explain.
8. How does the cost principle apply in accounting for short-term investments?
9. What is the rationale for application of the lower-of-cost-or-market basis to the short-term investment portfolio?
10. Distinguish between accounts receivable and special receivables.
11. Define a promissory note indicating the names of the parties and explain what is meant by principal, maturity date, and interest rate.
12. Distinguish between an interest-bearing and noninterest-bearing note.
13. What is a negotiable promissory note?
14. What is a defaulted note? Who is responsible for its payment? Explain.
15. What is meant by discounting a note receivable?
16. What is a contingent liability? How does one arise in respect to a note receivable?

17. What is the purpose of petty cash? What safeguards should be prescribed?
18. Why are special cash journals frequently needed?

EXERCISES

PART ONE: EXERCISES 9–1 TO 9–5

E9–1. Davis Service Company prepared a balance sheet that reported cash, $5,849. The following items were found to have been included in the reported cash balance:

1.	Bank account balance at City Bank	$3,734
2.	A deposit made to the local electric utility	600
3.	Postage stamps on hand	40
4.	Check signed by a customer, returned for NSF	30
5.	Petty cash on hand	150
6.	IOUs signed by employees	80
7.	Check signed by the company president for an advance to him; to be held until he "gives the word to cash it."	1,000
8.	Money orders on hand (received from customers)	45
9.	A signed receipt from a freight company that involved a $10 overpayment to them. They have indicated "a check will be mailed shortly."	10
10.	A money order obtained from the post office to be used to pay for a special purchase upon delivery; expected within the next five days	160
	Total	$5,849

Required:

The reported cash balance has been questioned. Compute the correct balance in the Cash account (prior to the bank reconciliation) and give appropriate reporting for any items that you exclude.

E9–2. Williamson Company operates several branches and, as a consequence, has cash in several locations. The general ledger at the end of 1977 showed the following accounts: Petty Cash – Home Office, $200; City Bank – Home Office, $27,300; Petty Cash – Branch A, $50; National Bank – Branch A, $1,458; Petty Cash – Branch B, $75; Southwest Bank – Branch B, $864; Petty Cash – Branch C, $100; State Bank – Branch C, $965; and Metropolitan Bank – General, $2,500.

Instead of the multiple cash accounts in the general journal; a single cash account is to be used with an appropriate subsidiary ledger.

Required:

1. Explain how the multiple accounts would be consolidated into one. Give an appropriate entry.
2. Explain how the subsidiary ledger should be organized.

3. What amount of cash should be reported on the balance sheet after consolidation?

E9–3. Thompson Company has just received the June 30, 1977, bank statement, which is summarized below:

	Checks	*Deposits*	*Balance*
Balance, June 1			$ 4,800
Deposits during June		$17,000	21,800
Checks cleared through June	$17,700		4,100
Bank service charges	12		4,088
Balance, June 30			4,088

The Cash account in the ledger showed the following for June:

Cash

June 1	Balance	4,400	June	Checks written	18,000
June	Deposits	19,000			

Required:

a. Reconcile the bank account, assuming that a comparison of the checks written with the checks that have cleared the bank show outstanding checks to be $800 and that cash on hand on June 30 is $100. (Note: Some of the checks that cleared in June were written prior to June; there were no deposits in transit carried over from May.)

b. Give any entries that would be made as a result of the bank reconciliation.

c. What is the balance in the Cash account after the reconciliation entries?

d. What amount of cash would be reported on the balance sheet at June 30?

E9–4. Baker Company has just received the September 30, 1977, bank statement, which is summarized below:

	Checks	*Deposits*	*Balance*
Balance, September 1			$ 5,100
Deposits recorded during September		$27,000	32,100
Checks cleared during September	$27,300		4,800
NSF check—J. J. Jones	80		4,720
Bank service charges	13		4,607
Balance, September 30			4,607

Cash on hand on September 1 and September 30 amounted to $200. There were no outstanding checks and no deposits in transit carried over from August.

The Cash account in the ledger reflected the following for September:

Cash

Sept. 1	Balance	5,300	September	Checks written	28,000
September	Deposits	29,500			

Required:

a. Reconcile the bank account. (Hint: You may find an error made by either the bank or the company.)

b. Give any entries that would be made based upon the bank reconciliation.

c. What should be the balance in the Cash account after the reconciliation entries?

d. What amount of cash should be reported on the September 30 balance sheet?

E9–5. Frazier Company has just received the March 31, 1977, bank statement, which is summarized below:

	Checks	*Deposits*	*Balance*
Balance, March 1			$ 8,590
Deposits during March		$28,000	36,590
Note collected for depositor (including $24 interest)		924	37,514
Checks cleared during March	$32,200		5,314
Bank service charges	14		5,300
Balance, March 31			5,300

The Cash account in the ledger showed the following for March:

Cash

Mar. 1	Balance	8,200	March	Checks written	32,500
March	Deposits	31,000			

A comparison of deposits recorded with deposits on the bank statement showed deposits in transit to be $3,000. Similarly, outstanding checks at the end of March were determined to be $900. Cash on hand was $190 at March 31.

Required:

a. Prepare a bank reconciliation for March. (Hint: There is a cash overage or shortage involved; however, the bank figures have been verified to be correct.)

b. Give any entries that should be made based on the reconciliation.

c. What amount should be reflected as the ending balance of cash after the reconciliation entries? What amount of cash should be reflected on the balance sheet at the end of March?

PART TWO: EXERCISES 9–6 TO 9–8

E9–6. Ritter Company, in July 1977, had accumulated approximately $10,000 in cash that would not be needed for 10 to 15 months. In order to employ the idle cash profitably, the management decided to purchase some shares of stock as a short-term investment. This series of transactions occurred:

1977

July 30 Purchased 3,000 shares of the common stock of XY Corporation on the exchange. The cash price, including fees and transfer costs related to the acquisition, amounted to $13,500.

Dec. 15 Received a cash dividend of $0.30 per share on the XY shares.

30 Sold 1,000 of the XY shares at $5 per share for cash.

Required:

a. Give appropriate journal entries on each date for this short-term investment.

b. How would the short-term investment be reported on the balance sheet at December 31, 1977? Assume the same market value as on December 30.

E9–7. Dowd Company, to put some idle cash to work, decided to purchase some common stock in RS Corporation as a short-term investment. The following transactions reflect what happened following this decision:

1977

Feb. 1 Purchased for cash 6,000 shares of RS Corporation common stock at a cost of $30,000.

Aug. 15 Received a cash dividend on the RS stock of $0.20 per share.

Dec. 30 Sold 2,000 shares of the RS stock at $4.80 per share.

31 End of the fiscal year for accounting purposes. RS stock was selling at $4.75.

Required:

a. Give appropriate journal entries for each date for the investment in RS stock. Dowd Company had no other short-term investments.

b. How would the short-term investment be reported on the balance sheet at December 31, 1977?

c. Give the entry on January 15, 1978, assuming the remaining shares were sold for $20,000 cash.

E9–8. Wilson Company, in order to use some idle cash, in March 1977 acquired 200 shares of common stock in each of three corporations: Corporation A, cost $8,000; Corporation B, cost $6,000; and Corporation C, cost $12,000. At the end of the fiscal period, December 31, 1977, the quoted market prices per share were: Corporation A, $40; Corporation B, $25; and Corporation C, $61.

Required:

a. Give entry to record the acquisition of these short-term investments.

b. Give entry to reflect the investments at lower of cost or market. Show computations.

c. Show how the investments would be reported on the balance sheet at December 31, 1977.

d. Give the entry on January 5, 1978, assuming all of the shares were sold for $25,000 cash.

PART THREE: EXERCISES 9–9 TO 9–11

E9–9. Approximately 40 percent of the merchandise sold by Topp Company is on credit. Accounts that are overdue, if material in amount, are "converted" to notes receivable when possible. This case traces one sale through accounts receivable, to notes receivable, and to final collection. The related transactions during 1977 were:

Jan. 10	Sold merchandise on account to J. K. Mier for $9,000; terms, n/30.
Mar. 1	The account was unpaid; therefore, Topp Company asked Mier to sign a 120-day, 8 percent, interest-bearing note for the account. Mier executed the note on this date.
July 1	Mier paid the note plus interest.

Required:

a. Give the entry required on each of the three dates.

b. Give the entry that would have been made on July 1, 1977, assuming Mier defaulted.

E9–10. Robbins Company sells a line of products that have a high unit sales price. Credit terms are traditional in the industry; accordingly, Robbins frequently takes a promissory note for the sales price. This exercise follows one promissory note, taken at date of sale, through final collection. The fiscal year for accounting purposes ends December 31. The series of transactions and events were:

1977	
Dec. 1	Sold merchandise to J. Doe on a 90-day, 10 percent, interest-bearing note for $2,400.
31	End of fiscal period; adjusting entry.
1978	
Jan. 1	Start of new fiscal period.
Mar. 1	Collected the note, plus interest, in full.

Required:

a. Give appropriate entries at each of the four dates; if none, so state.

b. With respect to the note, what item(s) and amount(s) would be reported on the 1977 income statement?

c. With respect to the note, what item(s) and amount(s) would be reported on the balance sheet at December 31, 1977?

E9–11. Logan Company frequently sells merchandise on a promissory note, which is later sold (i.e., discounted) to the local bank to obtain cash needed before maturity date. The following series of transactions relates to one note that followed this pattern:

1977

Apr.	1	Sold merchandise for $6,000 to D. E. Day; took a six-month, 10 percent, interest-bearing note.
June	1	Discounted the note at the local bank at a 9 percent discount rate; received the proceeds upon endorsement of the note to the bank.
Oct.	1	Due date of the note plus interest.

Required:

a. Give appropriate journal entries at each date assuming D. E. Day paid the bank for the note on due date.

b. Give appropriate entry on October 1, 1977, assuming Day defaulted on the note and Logan Company had to make payment plus a $10 protest fee.

c. Give the appropriate entry assuming Day came in and paid Logan in full on October 5, 1977.

E9–12. (Based on Appendix A.) On January 1, 1977, Exalto Company established a petty cash fund amounting to $150 by writing a check to "Petty Cash." The fund was assigned to J. Wright, an employee, to administer as custodian. At the end of January there was $20 cash remaining in the fund. Signed receipts for expenditures during January were summarized as follows: postage, $43; office supplies, $18; transportation, $31; newspapers, $24; and miscellaneous (coffee for the office), $14.

Required:

a. Give the entry to establish the fund on January 1, 1977.

b. Give the entry to replenish the fund on January 31, 1977.

c. What balance would be reflected in the Petty Cash account in the ledger at January 31? Explain.

d. How would petty cash be reported on the balance sheet at January 31, 1977?

e. What effect did the petty cash fund have on the January 1977 income statement?

PROBLEMS

PART ONE: PROBLEMS 9–1 TO 9–3

P9–1. The bookkeeper at Sawhill Company has not reconciled the bank statement with the Cash account, saying, "I don't have time." You have been asked to prepare a reconciliation and review the procedures with the bookkeeper.

The April 30, 1977, bank statement just received showed the following (summarized):

	Checks	Deposits	Balance
Balance, April 1			$21,500
Deposits during April		$38,000	59,500
Note collected for depositor (including $80 interest)		1,080	60,580
Checks cleared during April	$44,700		15,880
NSF check—A. B. Cage	100		15,780
Bank service charges	23		15,757
Balance, April 30			15,757

The Cash account in the ledger for the month of April showed the following:

Cash

Apr. 1	Balance	20,750	April	Checks written	44,500
April	Deposits	42,000			

The balance in the Petty Cash account, and the amount of cash held by the custodian, at the beginning and end of April was $300. A comparison of checks written before and during April with the checks cleared reflected outstanding checks at the end of April to be $600. No deposits in transit were carried over from March. Cash on hand, held for change, at the end of April was $50.

Required:

a. Prepare a detailed bank reconciliation.

b. Give any entries that are indicated to be needed as a result of the reconciliation. Why are they necessary?

c. What are the balances in the cash accounts in the ledger at the end of April?

d. What amount of cash should be reported on the balance sheet at the end of April?

P9–2. Murray Company has just received the following bank statement for the month of August 1977:

	Checks	Deposits	Balance
Aug. 1			$15,000
2	$ 300		14,700
3		$7,000	21,700
4	400		21,300
5	200		21,100
9	900		20,200
10	300		19,900
15		9,000	28,900
21	700		28,200
24	21,000		7,200
25		8,000	15,200
30	800		14,400
31		1,080*	15,480
31	25†		15,455

* $1,000 note collected plus interest.
† $25 bank service charge.

The Cash account in the ledger (detailed) reflected the following for August:

Cash

Aug. 1 Balance	14,300	Checks written:	
Deposits:		Aug. 2	300
Aug. 2	7,000	4	900
12	9,000	15	600
24	8,000	17	500
31	6,000	18	800
		18	700
		23	21,000

Cash on hand at the end of August amounted to $200. There were three outstanding checks at the end of July: $200, $400, and $300. There were no deposits in transit at that time. Petty cash on hand was $100, and the Petty Cash account showed that amount at the end of August.

Required:

a. Determine the deposits in transit at the end of August.
b. Determine the outstanding checks at the end of August.
c. Prepare a bank reconciliation for August.
d. Give any entries that are indicated on the reconciliation that should be made. Why are they necessary?
e. After the reconciliation entries, what balances would be reflected in the Cash accounts in the ledger?
f. What amount of cash should be reported on the August 31, 1977, balance sheet?

P9–3. Foster Company has just received the following bank statement for the month of December 1977:

Date	*Checks*	*Deposits*	*Balance*
Dec. 1			$41,000
2	400, 150	16,000	56,450
4	7,000, 80		49,370
6	120, 180, 1,500		47,570
11	900, 1,200, 90	21,000	66,380
13	450, 700, 1,900		63,330
17	17,000, 2,000		44,330
23	40, 23,500	36,000	56,790
26	1,800, 2,650		52,340
28	2,200, 4,800		45,340
30	13,000, 1,890, 180[a]	19,000	49,270
31	1,650, 1,200, 20[c]	6,600[b]	53,000

[a] NSF check, J. Doe, a customer.
[b] Note collected, principal, $6,000 plus interest.
[c] Bank service charge.

The Cash accounts in the ledger reflected the following:

Cash

Dec. 1 Balance	55,850	Checks written during December:		
Deposits:		40	5,000	2,650
Dec. 11	21,000	13,000	4,800	1,650
23	36,000	700	1,890	2,200
30	19,000	4,400	1,500	7,000
31	15,000	1,200	120	150
		180	80	450
		17,000	23,500	2,000
		90	700	1,900
		1,800	1,200	

Petty Cash

Dec. 1 Balance	200	

The November 1977 bank reconciliation showed the following:

True cash balance (including petty cash) at November 30....	$55,900
Deposits in transit (November 30)......................................	16,000
Outstanding checks ($400 + $900).....................................	1,300

At the end of December 1977, cash held on hand for change at all times (in addition to $200 in Petty Cash) amounted to $150.

Required:

a. Determine the deposits in transit December 31, 1977.
b. Determine the outstanding checks at December 31, 1977.
c. Prepare a bank reconciliation at December 31, 1977.
d. Give any entries that are indicated on the reconciliation that should be made. Why are they necessary?
e. After the reconciliation entries, what balances would be reflected in the Cash accounts in the ledger?
f. What amount of cash should be reported on the December 31, 1977, balance sheet?

PART TWO: PROBLEMS 9–4 TO 9–6

P9–4. Swan Company, in order to use idle cash, usually acquires common stocks as a short-term investment. This case focuses on the purchase of three different common stocks during 1977. The annual fiscal period for accounting purposes ends December 31. The sequence of transactions was:

1977
Apr. 2 Purchased for cash, as a short-term investment, the following common stocks:

Corporation	Number of shares	Total price per share
X	300	$50
Y	400	70
Z	100	90

Sept. 8 Received a cash dividend of $3 per share on Corporation Z stock.

Dec. 30 Sold the stock in Corporation Y for $75 per share.

Dec. 31 Quoted market prices on this date were: Corporation X stock, $46; Corporation Y stock, $75; and Corporation Z stock, $95.

Required:

a. Give the appropriate entry on each date.

b. Illustrate how the effects of these investments would be reflected on the income statement (single step) and the balance sheet (classified) at December 31, 1977.

c. What was the amount of the holding loss? Explain.

P9–5. On July 1, 1977, Katy Corporation purchased, as a short-term investment, ten, $1,000, 6 percent bonds of Lowe Corporation at par (i.e., at $1,000 each). The bonds mature on June 30, 1980. Annual interest is payable on June 30 each year. The accounting period ends on December 31.

Required:

a. Give entries required on the following dates (if no entry is required, explain why): July 1, 1977; December 31, 1977; and June 30, 1978.

b. Show how the effects of this investment would be reported on the income statement and the balance sheet for 1977.

c. How much investment revenue (if any) would be reported on the income statement for 1978 assuming the bonds were sold for $9,850 on July 1, 1978? Explain.

P9–6. Jones Manufacturing Company produces and sells one main product. Demand is seasonal and the unit price is relatively high. The fiscal year for accounting purposes ends December 31. Typically, in the high months of the cycle the company generates cash, which is idle during the low months. As a consequence, they consistently acquire short-term investments in order to earn a return on what would otherwise be idle cash. Recently, the company purchased 1,000 shares of common stock in each of two other corporations, designated for case purposes as Corporations A and B. The prices per share, including fees and related costs, were: A, $30; and B, $70. In addition, Jones purchased a $10,000 bond of Kamas Corporation. The bond pays 6 percent annual interest on each March 31. The bond was purchased on April 1, 1977, for $10,000 cash (i.e., at par).

The sequence of transactions was:

1977

Apr. 1 Purchased the common stocks and the bond.

Oct. 3 Received a cash dividend of $0.50 per share on the stock of Corporation B.

Nov. 30 Sold 600 shares of the stock of Corporation A at $26 per share and 600 shares of the stock of Corporation B at $75 per share.

Dec. 31 End of fiscal period. The market prices on this date were: A stock, $29; B stock, $69; and Kamas bonds, 100 (i.e., at par). (Hint: Do not overlook accrued interest.)

Required:

a. Give appropriate entries at each of the dates. Omit any closing entries.

b. Illustrate how the effects of the investment would be reported on the balance sheet at December 31, 1977.

c. What items and amounts would be reported on the 1977 income statement?

PART THREE: PROBLEMS 9–7 TO 9–8

P9–7. Lawson Company sells approximately 60 percent of the merchandise marketed on credit; terms, n/30. Occasionally, as a part of the collection process of a delinquent account, a promissory note will be received. This case focuses on two different sales that ultimately generated promissory notes. The annual fiscal period for accounting purposes ends December 31. The sequence of transactions was:

Note No. 1:

1977

Feb. 15 Sold merchandise for $1,800 to A. B. Cline; received $600 cash, and the balance was charged to Accounts Receivable.

Apr. 1 Received an interest-bearing note in settlement of the overdue account of A. B. Cline. Terms of the note were four months, 10 percent interest.

July 31 Due date for note; Cline defaulted.

Oct. 1 Cline paid the defaulted note plus interest, plus 6 percent interest on the defaulted amount for the period July 31–October 1. The 6 percent is the legal rate of interest on overdue obligations.

Required:

a. Give appropriate entries on each date. Show interest calculations.

Note No. 2:

1977

Oct. 1 Sold merchandise for $1,000 to W. D. Mason; received $400 cash, and the balance was charged to Accounts Receivable (terms, n/EOM).

Nov. 1 Received an interest-bearing note in settlement of the overdue account from Mason. The terms of the note were 90 days, 10 percent interest.

Dec. 31 End of fiscal period.

1978

Jan. 1 Start of new fiscal period.

30 Maturity date of the note. Mason paid the principal plus interest.

Required:

b. Give appropriate entries on each date (omit any closing entries). Show interest calculations. Specify any accounting assumptions you make.

c. How much interest revenue will be reported on the 1977 income statement?

d. Show how the notes will affect the balance sheet at December 31, 1977.

P9–8. Eastern Machinery Company sells heavy machinery. Credit terms are customary and generally involve promissory notes and a mortgage on the machinery sold. Down payments of 20 percent to 33⅓ percent are required. The annual fiscal period for accounting purposes ends December 31. This problem focuses on two different promissory notes that were received in 1977. The transactions were:

Note No. 1:

1977

Feb. 1 Sold equipment to B. R. Rite for $12,000; received a 25 percent cash down payment and a 120-day, 10 percent, interest-bearing note for the balance.

Mar. 1 Sold the note to the local bank at a 9 percent discount rate; endorsed the note to the bank and received the cash proceeds.

June 1 Due date of the note plus interest; Rite paid the note.

Required:

a. Give appropriate entry on each date. Show interest computations. Assume that Rite paid the bank for the principal plus interest on due date.

b. Give entry on due date, June 1, 1977, assuming Rite defaulted on the note and Eastern paid the note plus interest, plus a $15 protest fee.

c. How much interest revenue will be reported on the income statement for 1977?

Note No. 2:

1977

Dec. 1 Sold equipment to W. T. Owens for $20,000; received $5,000 cash down payment and a 90-day, 10 percent, interest-bearing note for the balance.

31 End of fiscal period for accounting purposes.

1978
Jan. 1 Start of new fiscal period.
Mar. 1 Due date of the principal plus interest; Owens paid the note plus interest in full.

Required:

d. Give appropriate entries on each of the four dates (omit any closing entries). State any assumptions you make. Use 30-day months for interest purposes to avoid counting on the calendar.
e. How much interest revenue will be reported on the 1977 income statement?
f. Show how the note will affect the balance sheet at December 31, 1977.

P9–9. (Special case.) Evans Manufacturing Company is a relatively small local business that specializes in the repair and renovation of antique jewelry, brass objects, and silverware. The owner is an expert craftsman. Although a number of skilled workers are employed, there is always a large backlog of work to be done. A long-time employee, who serves as clerk-bookkeeper, handles cash receipts, keeps the records, and writes checks for disbursements. The checks are signed by the owner. Small claims are paid in cash by the clerk-bookkeeper, subject to approval of the owner. Approvals generally are made in advance; however, routine payments are approved later. Approximately 100 regular customers are regularly extended credit. Although credit losses are small, in recent years the bookkeeper has established an allowance for doubtful accounts.

Recently, Hall, the owner, decided to construct a building for the business that would provide many advantages over the presently rented space and would make possible needed expansion of facilities. As a part of the considerations in financing, the financing institution asked for "audited financial statements." There had never been an audit of the company. Early in the audit, the independent CPA found numerous errors and one combination of amounts, in particular, that worried him. There appeared to be evidence that a job billed at $500 had been charged to a new customer. The account was credited with a $500 collection a few days later. The new account was never active again. The auditor also observed that at about the same time there had been three write-offs of Accounts Receivable balances to the Allowance account as follows: Jones, $125.32; Adams, $269.88; and Coster, $104.80. These write-offs triggered the attention because the auditor knew the customers involved and believed they would not default on their accounts.

Required:

a. Can you determine what caused the CPA to be "worried"? Explain.
b. What recommendations would you make in respect to internal control procedures for this small company?

P9–10. (Based on Appendix B.) Alexander Company has a wide variety of transactions each year. A number of them are repetitive in nature; therefore, the company utilizes five journals: general, sales, purchases, cash receipts, and cash payments. Selected transactions are listed below that are to be entered in the appropriate journal. To shorten the case, amounts have been simplified and the number of transactions limited.

Selected transactions (use letter at left in lieu of a date and use the letter *v* for the last day of the period) are:

a. Sold merchandise to K. K. May at invoice cost of $250; terms, 2/10, n/20; Invoice No. 38.
b. Received merchandise from Sable Company at invoice cost of $300; credit terms, 1/10, n/20; Purchase Order No. 17.
c. Sold merchandise to B. B. Wise for $200 on credit; terms, 2/10, n/20; Invoice No. 39.
d. Received merchandise from Rex Supply Company at an invoice cost of $200 on credit; terms, 1/10, n/20; Purchase Order No. 18.
e. Sold merchandise to A. B. Cox for $150 cash.
f. Received merchandise from Baker Manufacturing Company at a cost of $360; paid cash (number the checks consecutively starting with No. 81).
g. Purchased a fixed asset (machinery) at a cost of $800; gave a 90-day, 8 percent, interest-bearing promissory note for the purchase price.
h. Sold a tract of land for $9,000 that originally cost $3,000; collected cash.
i. Collected account receivable from B. B. Wise within the discount period; Invoice No. 39.
j. Paid $600 for a three-year insurance premium.
k. Obtained a $5,000 bank loan; signed a one-year, 8 percent, interest-bearing note.
l. Paid account payable to Rex Supply Company within the discount period.
m. Paid monthly rent, $650.
n. Sold merchandise for cash, $1,400.
o. Purchased merchandise for cash, $980.
p. Sold merchandise on credit to C. C. Coe for $700; terms, 2/10, n/20; Invoice No. 40.
q. Received merchandise on credit from Stubbs Company at an invoice cost of $400; terms, 2/10, n/30; Purchase Order No. 19.
r. Collected account receivable from K. K. May after the discount period.
s. Paid account payable to Sable Company after the discount period.
t. Paid monthly salaries, $2,400.
u. By year-end, six months of the prepaid insurance had expired.

Use the following general ledger account code numbers for posting: Cash, 11; Accounts Receivable, 14; Prepaid Insurance, 16; Machinery, 17; Land, 19; Accounts Payable, 21; Notes Payable, 22; Purchases, 31; Purchases Discount Lost, 33; Sales, 41; Sales Discount Revenue, 43; Expenses, 51; and Gain on Sale of Fixed Assets, 53. For journals, use the following page numbers: General, 15; Sales, 18; Purchases, 14; Cash Receipts, 21; and Cash Payments, 34.

Required:

1. Draft a format for each of the journals, including a general journal, following the illustrations in Appendix B. Include folio columns.
2. Set up T-accounts for the general ledger accounts listed above.
3. Set up T-accounts for the subsidiary ledgers as follows:

Accounts Receivable (14)	*Accounts Payable (21)*
Coe—14.1	Sable—21.1
May—14.2	Stubbs—21.2
Wise—14.3	Rex—21.3

4. Enter each transaction in the appropriate journal. Sales and purchases are recorded net of discount.
5. Indicate all postings to the *subsidiary ledgers* by entering appropriate account numbers in the folio columns.
6. Sum the special journals and indicate all postings to the *general ledger* accounts by entering the account code numbers in the folio columns and below totals posted. Utilize the account code numbers given above.

10

Operational assets—plant and equipment, natural resources, and intangibles

PURPOSE OF THE CHAPTER

Operational assets are the **noncurrent assets** that a business retains more or less permanently (not for sale) for use (physically or in terms of rights) in the course of normal operations. Thus, operational assets include land in use, plant and equipment, furniture and fixtures, natural resources, and certain intangibles (such as a patent) used in operating the business. The degree of efficiency in the utilization of the operational assets will influence the earnings of the business. The nature and cost of the operational assets, their age and state of repair, and the future demands for funds needed to replace them loom large in many important decisions. The expense of maintaining and operating these assets often has a major effect on income.

An operational asset is acquired by a business because of the **future services** potentially available from it to generate future revenue through use by the entity. Thus, such assets can be viewed as a bundle of services that is purchased *in advance of usage* for generating revenue. As those services are used, as in the use of a machine, the **prepaid cost** of the asset is allocated to the periods of utilization as an expense. To illustrate, assume a truck is purchased at a cost of $5,000 for use in the business. The cost is debited to an asset account and, assuming a five-year useful life, each year a part of the prepaid cost is apportioned to expense. This apportionment of the prepaid cost of operational assets to expense is known as **depreciation, depletion,** or **amortization,** depending on the characteristics of the asset.

The financial statements provide information in respect to operational assets. The economic impact of operational assets on the balance sheet, income statement, and statement of changes in financial position is useful information to decision makers. This chapter focuses on the measurement and reporting problems related to operational assets and discusses the measurement of cost at acquisition date and the apportionment of that cost to expense as the assets are used in the revenue generation process.

CATEGORIES OF OPERATIONAL ASSETS

Effective management of a business requires a combination of assets with different characteristics and purposes. Each type of asset—be it current, long-term investments, or operational—serves a particular purpose not served by the other types of assets. The optimum combination of assets varies with each business, and its determination is a central responsibility of the management. An objective of the financial statements is to report the different assets classified by types and the amount of resources committed to each type. For measurement and reporting purposes, operational assets may be classified as follows:

1. Fixed assets—those assets that are **long-lived** and **tangible** acquired for use in the normal operations of the business and not intended for resale. Examples are land, buildings, equipment, furniture, tools, vehicles, and mineral deposits. There are three kinds of fixed assets: land—not subject to depreciation; plant, equipment, and fixtures—subject to depreciation; and natural resources—the wasting assets used in the operation of the business, such as mines, gravel pits, oil wells, and timber tracts. Natural resources are subject to depletion.
2. Intangible assets—the assets held by the business because of the special rights they confer. They have no physical substance. Examples are patents, copyrights, franchises, licenses, and trademarks. Intangible assets are subject to amortization.

PRINCIPLES UNDERLYING ACCOUNTING FOR OPERATIONAL ASSETS

The primary aspects of accounting for operational assets are:

1. Measuring and recording the cost of the asset at acquisition date.
2. After acquisition, measurement of the expense of using it during its useful life.
3. Recording disposals of operational assets.

At the date of acquisition, an operational asset is measured and recorded in conformity with the **cost principle.** After acquisition, a portion of the cost of an operational asset (except land) is matched periodically with the revenues generated during its useful life in accordance with the **matching principle.**

MEASURING AND RECORDING ACQUISITION COST

Under the cost principle, all reasonable and necessary costs incurred (excluding interest on borrowed funds) in acquiring an operational asset and in placing it in its operational setting, less any cash discounts, should be recorded in an appropriate asset account. Cost represents the net cash equivalent paid or to be paid (excluding interest charges). Cost is easily determined when an operational asset is purchased for cash. For example, the acquisition cost of a machine may be measured as follows:

Invoice price of the machine	$10,000
Less: Cash discount ($10,000 × 0.02)	200
Net cash invoice price	9,800
Add: Transportation charges paid by purchaser	150
Installation costs paid by purchaser	200
Sales tax paid ($10,000 × 0.02)	200
Cost—amount debited to the Machinery account	$10,350

The acquisition of this fixed asset would be recorded as follows:

January 1, 1977:

Machinery	10,350	
Cash		10,350

When an operational asset is purchased and a *noncash* consideration is included in part, or in full, payment for it, cost is the cash equivalent measured as any cash paid plus the **fair-market value** of the noncash consideration. To illustrate, assume a tract of timber (a natural resource) was acquired by Fuqua Corporation. Payment in full was made as follows: $28,000 cash plus 2,000 shares of Fuqua nopar stock.[1] At the date of the purchase, Fuqua stock was selling at $12 per share. The cost of the tract would be measured as follows:

Cash paid	$28,000
Fair-market value, noncash consideration given (2,000 shares nopar stock @ $12)	24,000
	52,000
Title fees, legal fees, and other costs paid in cash (incidental to the acquisition)	1,000
Cost—amount debited to the asset account	$53,000

[1] See Chapter 13 for discussion of capital stock.

The journal entry to record the acquisition of this natural resource would be:

January 1, 1977:

Timber tract (#20)	53,000	
Cash		29,000
Capital stock, nopar (2,000 shares @ $12)		24,000

When land is purchased, all of the incidental costs paid by the purchaser, such as title fees, sales commissions, legal fees, title insurance, delinquent taxes, and surveying fees, should be included in the cost of the land.

Not infrequently, an old building or used machinery is purchased for operational use in the business. Renovation and repair costs incurred by the purchaser *prior to use* should be debited to the asset account as a part of the cost of the asset. Repair costs incurred *after* the asset is placed in use usually are normal operating expenses.

Basket purchases. When two or more kinds of operational assets are acquired in a single transaction and for a single lump sum, the cost of each kind of asset acquired must be separately measured and recorded. For example, when a building and the land on which it is located are purchased for a lump sum, at least two separate accounts must be established: one for the building (which is subject to depreciation) and one for the land (which is not subject to depreciation). This means that the single sum must be apportioned between the land and the building on a rational basis.

Relative fair-market value of the several assets at the date of acquisition is the most logical basis on which to allocate the single lump sum. Appraisals or tax assessments often have to be used as indications of the fair-market values. To illustrate, assume Fox Company purchased a building suitable for an additional plant and the land on which the building is located for a total of $150,000 cash. Since the separate, true fair-market values of the building and land were not known, a professional appraisal was obtained that showed the following *estimated* fair-market values: building, $99,000; and land, $81,000 (apparently the buyer got a good deal). The apportionment of the $150,000 purchase price should be made as follows:

	Appraised value		*Apportionment of lump-sum acquisition cost*	
Asset	*Amount*	*Ratio*	*Computation*	*Apportioned cost*
Building	$ 99,000	0.55*	$150,000 × 0.55 =	$ 82,500
Land	81,000	0.45†	150,000 × 0.45 =	67,500
	$180,000	1.00		$150,000

* $99,000 ÷ $180,000 = 0.55
† $81,000 ÷ $180,000 = 0.45

The journal entry to record the acquisition would appear as follows:

Plant building	82,500	
Land-plant site	67,500	
Cash		150,000

MATCHING THE COST OF AN OPERATIONAL ASSET WITH FUTURE REVENUES

The acquisition cost of an operational asset having a limited useful life represents the prepaid cost of a bundle of **future services** or benefits (i.e., future economic usefulness to the entity). The **matching principle** requires that the acquisition cost of such assets be apportioned as expense to the periods in which revenue is generated as a result of using those assets. Thus, the acquisition cost of this kind of operational asset is matched in the future with the future revenues to which it contributes by way of services and benefits.

We should make clear the distinction among three different terms that generally are used to describe the cost apportionment required by the matching principle for the different types of operational assets:

1. Depreciation—the systematic and rational apportionment of the acquisition cost of tangible **fixed assets** (other than natural resources) to future periods in which the services or benefits contribute to revenue. Example—depreciation of the cost of a machine over its useful life of ten years and no residual value (see page 356):

   December 31, 1977:

Depreciation expense	1,035	
Accumulated depreciation, Machinery		1,035

2. Depletion—the systematic and rational apportionment of the acquisition cost of **natural resources** to future periods in which the use of those natural resources contribute to revenue. Example—depletion of the cost of a timber tract over the period of cutting based on "cutting" rate (see page 357):

   December 31, 1977:

Depletion expense	10,600	
Timber tract (No. 20)		10,600

   (Note: A contra account could be used such as Allowance for Depletion.)

3. Amortization—The systematic and rational apportionment of the acquisition cost of **intangible assets** to future periods in which the benefits contribute to revenue. Example—amortization of the cost of a patent over its economic life (based on economic useful life):

December 31, 1977:

Patent expense	500	
Patents		500

(Note: A contra account could be used such as Allowance for Patent Amortization.)

Each of these terms relates to the same basic objective; namely, the apportionment of the acquisition cost of an operational asset to the future periods in which the benefits of its use contributes to the earning of revenue.

The amounts of depreciation, depletion, and amortization measured and recorded during each period are reported as expenses or costs for the period. On the balance sheet, the amounts of depreciation, depletion, and amortization *accumulated since acquisition date* are reported as a deduction from the assets to which they pertain. To illustrate, a fixed asset, such as the machine illustrated above, would be reported on the balance sheet (at the end of the second year in the example) as follows:

Balance Sheet
At December 31, 1978

Fixed Assets:		
Machinery	$10,350	
Less: Accumulated depreciation	2,070	$8,280

or

Machinery (less accumulated depreciation, $2,070)	$8,280

We emphasize that the amounts for operational assets reported on the balance sheet do not represent their fair-market values at balance sheet date but, rather, are book, or carrying, values. *Book value* is their acquisition cost (which was their fair-market value at acquisition date), less the accumulated apportionments to expense of that cost from acquisition date to the date of the balance sheet. This is in accordance with the cost principle. Under it, the cost of an operational asset is measured and recorded at acquisition date at the then fair-market value. It is not remeasured on a fair-market value basis at subsequent balance sheet dates, rather the acquisition cost is reduced by an expense allocation for depreciation, depletion, or amortization each period.

FIXED ASSETS SUBJECT TO DEPRECIATION

Three kinds of fixed assets were identified on page 355. In this section the discussion will be limited to land and those fixed assets subject to depreciation. The term "fixed asset" refers to all kinds of buildings, machinery, furniture, and other equipment used in the operation of the business. Although the term fixed asset is used widely, a more descriptive term, **"property, plant, and equipment,"** is often used when applicable in published financial statements.

Buildings, machinery, furniture, and other fixed assets (except land) decrease in economic "use utility" to the user because of a number of causative factors, such as wear and tear, the passage of time, effects of the elements (such as the weather), obsolescence (i.e., becoming out-of-date), technological changes, and inadequacy. These causative factors are always bearing down on a fixed asset during the period it is being used to generate revenues. Thus, under the matching principle, at the end of each accounting period an **adjusting entry** is needed to record these expense-causing effects. In developing the adjusting entry, generally accepted accounting principles require that a *rational and systematic* measurement approach be used to match the acquisition cost of a fixed asset with periodic revenues.

Because of the wide diversity of fixed assets subject to depreciation and the varying effects of the causative factors listed above, a number of **depreciation methods** have been developed that are acceptable for both accounting and income tax purposes. In the paragraphs to follow, we will discuss and illustrate the methods of measuring and recording depreciation that are commonly used.

To measure depreciation expense each period, the methods require three amounts for each fixed asset: (1) **actual acquisition cost,** (2) **estimated net residual amount,** and (3) **estimated useful life.** It is important to observe that of these three amounts, two are *estimates* (residual value and useful or service life); thus, the depreciation expense that is recorded and reported is an estimate. To illustrate, depreciation expense may be measured as follows:

Actual acquisition cost	$625
Less: Estimated residual value	25
Amount to be depreciated over useful life	$600
Estimated useful life	3 years
Annual depreciation expense: $600 ÷ 3 =	$200

Estimated residual value[2] must be deducted from acquisition cost because it represents that part of the acquisition cost that is expected to be recovered by the user upon disposal of the asset at the end of its estimated useful life to the entity. *Residual value* is the total estimated amount to be recovered less any estimated costs of dismantling, disposal, and selling. Because these costs may approximately equal the gross residual amount recovered, many fixed assets are assumed to have no residual value. It is important to realize that the estimated net residual value

[2] Residual value is also called "scrap value" or "salvage value," however, "residual value" is a more descriptive term because the asset may not be scrapped upon disposition; a subsequent buyer may renovate it and reuse it for many years.

is not the value of the fixed asset as scrap, but, rather, it is the expected net recovery to be realized at the date that the *current user* intends to dispose of it. For example, a company whose policy is to replace all trucks at the end of three years normally would use a higher estimated residual value than would a user of the same kind of truck whose policy is to replace the trucks at the end of five years.

Estimated useful or service life should be viewed as the *economic* useful life to the *present owner* rather than as the total useful life to all potential users. In the truck example above, for accounting purposes, one user would utilize a three-year useful life, whereas the other user would utilize a five-year useful life.

Several **methods of depreciation** will be discussed and illustrated. For this purpose we will use a common set of facts and notations:

	Symbols	Illustrative amounts
Acquisition cost of a particular machine	*C*	\$625
Estimated net residual value at end of useful life	*R*	\$ 25
Estimated service life:		
Life in years	*N**	3
Life in units of productive output	*P**	10,000
Depreciation rate	*r*	
Dollar amount of depreciation expense per period	*D*	

* Lowercase letters will be used for the current period.

Straight-line depreciation. This method has been widely used because of its simplicity and apparent relationship to what actually happens to many kinds of fixed assets. Under this method, an *equal portion* of the acquisition cost less the residual value is allocated to each period during the useful life. Thus, the annual depreciation expense is measured as follows:

$$D = \frac{C - R}{N} \quad \text{or} \quad D = \frac{\$625 - \$25}{3} = \underline{\underline{\$200}} \text{ Depreciation per Year}$$

A **depreciation schedule** covering the entire useful life of the machine can be developed as follows:

Depreciation schedule—straight-line method

		End of year	
Year	Depreciation expense	Balance in accumulated depreciation	Book value
At acquisition			\$625
1	\$200	\$200	425
2	200	400	225
3	200	600	25
	\$600		

The adjusting entry for depreciation expense on this machine would be for the same for each of the three years of the useful life, viz:

	Year 1		Year 2		Year 3	
Depreciation expense	200		200		200	
Accumulated depreciation, machinery		200		200		200

The straight-line method is simple, rational, and systematic (i.e., logical, stable, consistent, and realistically predictible from period to period). It is especially appropriate where the asset is used essentially at the same rate each period. It implies an approximately equal decline in the economic usefulness of the asset each period.

Productive-output method. This method, sometimes called the units-of-production method, is based upon the assumption that the revenue-generating benefits derived each period from the fixed asset are directly related to the periodic **output** of the asset. For example, many persons believe that certain equipment, such as a delivery truck, should be depreciated on the basis of miles driven each period (i.e., based on a measure of output) rather than on the mere passage of time as is assumed by the straight-line method. They feel that many productive assets do not contribute to the generation of revenues merely because time is passing but, rather, only when they are used productively.

Since the productive-output method relates acquisition cost less residual value to the estimated productive life of the asset in terms of units of output, a **depreciation rate per unit of output** is computed as follows:

$$r = \frac{C - R}{P} \quad \text{or} \quad r = \frac{\$625 - \$25}{10{,}000 \text{ Units}} = \$0.06 \text{ per Unit of Output}$$

Assuming 3,000 units of output in Year 1, depreciation expense for Year 1 would be:

$$D = r \times p \quad \text{or} \quad D = \$0.06 \times 3{,}000 = \underline{\underline{\$180}}$$

Assuming output to be 5,000 units in Year 2 and 2,000 units in Year 3, the depreciation schedule would be as follows:

Depreciation schedule—productive-output method

			End of year	
Year		*Depreciation expense*	*Balance in accumulated depreciation*	*Book value*
At acquisition				$625
1	(3,000 × $0.06)	$180	$180	445
2	(5,000 × 0.06)	300	480	145
3	(2,000 × 0.06)	120	600	25
		$600		

The *adjusting entry* for depreciation at the end of each year would be:

	Year 1		*Year 2*		*Year 3*	
Depreciation expense	180		300		120	
Accumulated depreciation, machinery		180		300		120

The productive-output method is simple, rational, and systematic. It is appropriate where output of the asset can be measured realistically and where the economic use utility of the asset tends to decrease with productive use rather than with the passage of time. Also, where use is significantly variable from period to period, a more realistic measurement of expense to be matched with revenue is attained.

Accelerated depreciation. Accelerated depreciation is based upon the notion that there should be relatively large amounts of depreciation expense reported in the early years of the useful life of the asset and correspondingly reduced amounts of depreciation expense in the later years. The basis for this conclusion is that a fixed asset is more efficient in generating revenue in the early years than in the later years of its life. Also, repair expense tends to be low in the early years and higher in the later years. Therefore, it is contended that the *combined effect,* of decreasing depreciation expense and increasing repair expense, is relatively constant, from period to period over the life of the asset.

Accelerated depreciation has considerable appeal from the income tax viewpoint. Higher depreciation expense means lower reported profits in the early years and lower income taxes. Of course, the effect reverses in the later years; however, an early tax deduction is to be preferred over a later tax deduction because of the time value of money.[3]

There are several variations of accelerated depreciation; however, the two methods generally used are the sum-of-the-years'-digits method and the double-declining balance method.

Sum-of-the-years'-digits method. This method, frequently referred to as the SYD method, is used primarily because it is simple and produces a significantly accelerated effect compared to straight-line depreciation. Depreciation expense each year is computed by multiplying the acquisition cost, less residual value, by a fraction that is successively *smaller* each year. The decreasing fractions are determined by using the sum of the digits comprising the useful life as the denominator and the specific year of life in *inverse order* as the numerator. The computations may be demonstrated by using the illustrative data previously given, as follows:[4]

---

[3] The time value of money refers to interest that can be earned on money when invested or used in the business.

[4] The sum of the digits can be computed by using the formula: $SYD = n\left(\frac{n+1}{2}\right)$. For example, a five-year life would be: $SYD = 5\left(\frac{5+1}{2}\right) = 15$.

Denominator: Sum of digits (comprising the useful life): $1+2+3=6$.
Numerators: Digits (specific year of life) in inverse order: 3, 2, 1.

Year of life	*Fraction*
1	$^3/_6$
2	$^2/_6$
3	$^1/_6$
Total	$^6/_6$

Therefore, the depreciation expense each year for the useful life of the illustrative machine would be: Year 1, $600 × $^3/_6$ = $300; Year 2, $600 × $^2/_6$ = $200; and Year 3, $600 × $^1/_6$ = $100.

The accelerated effects of SYD depreciation can be readily observed in the following depreciation schedule:

Depreciation schedule—sum-of-the-years'-digits method

			End of year	
Year	*Computations*	*Depreciation expense*	*Balance in accumulated depreciation*	*Book value*
At acquisition				$625
1	$600 × $^3/_6$ =	$300	$300	325
2	600 × $^2/_6$ =	200	500	125
3	600 × $^1/_6$ =	100	600	25
Total		$600		

The adjusting entry for depreciation expense by year would be:

	Year 1		*Year 2*		*Year 3*	
Depreciation expense	300		200		100	
Accumulated depreciation, machinery		300		200		100

Double-declining balance method. This accelerated method, often called DDB depreciation, came directly from a provision in the Internal Revenue Code. For income tax purposes, accelerated depreciation is permitted; however, depreciation expense for each period may not be more than double the rate that would result under the straight-line method, ignoring residual value. Since this approach is permitted for income tax purposes, and because it gives a significant accelerating effect, it has been widely used on tax returns. Although considered by many accountants as not theoretically sound, it nevertheless has become widely used for accounting purposes. This is the only method that ignores residual value in computing the rate.

Depreciation expense is measured each year by multiplying a constant rate by the decreasing undepreciated cost of the asset (i.e., the book value), ignoring residual value. The rate used is *double* the straight-line rate, ignoring residual value. Depreciation stops when the book value equals (or approximates) the estimated residual value. Thus, depreciation expense would be computed as follows, utilizing the illustrative data:[5]

Straight-line rate: 3 years = 1 ÷ 3 years = 0.333.
Double straight-line rate: 0.333 × 2 = 0.667.
Annual depreciation: 0.667 × the decreasing book value of the asset.

Depreciation schedule—double-declining balance method

			End of year	
Year	*Computations*	*Depreciation expense*	*Balance in accumulated depreciation*	*Book value*
At acquisition				$625
1	0.667 × $625	$417	$417	208
2	0.667 × 208	139	556	69
3	0.667 × 69	44*	600	25*

* Although .667× $69=$46, depreciation expense in the last year is the amount necessary to leave the book value equal to the residual value of $25 (or zero if there is no residual value).

CHANGE IN DEPRECIATION ESTIMATE

Recall that depreciation is based on two estimates—useful life and residual value—made when an operational asset is acquired. It is sometimes necessary to revise one, or both, of the initial estimates as experience with the asset accumulates. When it is clear that either estimate should be revised (to a material degree), the undepreciated, or unamortized, balance at that date should be apportioned over the remaining estimated life. This is considered to be a "change in estimate."

To illustrate, assume the following for a particular machine:

Cost when acquired	$33,000
Estimated life	10 years
Estimated residual value	$ 3,000
Accumulated depreciation at end of Year 6 (assuming the straight-line method is used)	$18,000

Shortly after the start of Year 7, the estimates were changed to the following:

Revised estimated life	14 years
Revised estimated residual value	$1,000

[5] Accelerated depreciation is limited for tax purposes to assets having a useful life of three years or more; the short period was used to simplify the illustrations. There are other special tax provisions that are too detailed to be considered in this book.

The adjusting entry at the end of Year 7 would be:

Depreciation expense	1,750	
Accumulated depreciation		1,750

Computations:

Acquisition cost	$33,000
Accumulated depreciation, Years 1–6	18,000
Undepreciated balance	15,000
Less: Revised residual value	1,000
Balance to be depreciated	$14,000
Annual depreciation:	
$14,000 ÷ (14 years − 6 years) =	$ 1,750

Although the four methods of computing depreciation are different ways of measuring depreciation expense for each period, the total expense for all periods combined is the same irrespective of the method used (cost less residual value). They have different impacts on the measurement of periodic income, even though the asset cost, estimated life, and residual value are the same. This demonstrates how the selection of a particular accounting approach will cause a difference in the measurement of income for each period (but the same in total for all methods). The comparative effects of each method on the income statement (depreciation expense) and the balance sheet (book value) for the illustrative data are shown quantatively in the table below and graphically in Exhibit 10–1.

Depreciation methods—comparative expense and book value results

	Straight line		*Productive output*		*Sum-of-the-years'-digits*		*Double declining*	
Year	*Depreciation expense*	*Book value*	*Depreciation expense*	*Book value*	*Depreciation expense*	*Book value*	*Depreciation expense*	*Book value*
At acquisition		$625		$625		$625		$625
1	$200	425	$180	445	$300	325	$417	208
2	200	225	300	145	200	125	139	69
3	200	25	120	25	100	25	44	25
At end	$600	$ 25	$600	$ 25	$600	$ 25	$600	$ 25

Depreciation for interim periods. The preceding illustrations assumed that a full year's depreciation is recorded at the end of each year by means of an adjusting entry. Some businesses record depreciation monthly. Also, a fixed asset may be acquired or disposed of during the year. These situations may require that depreciation expense be recorded for periods of less than one year. Therefore, it is customary to compute depreciation on a proportional basis to either the nearest month or six-month period. For example, depreciation for a full month may be assumed to start or end at the nearest first of the month. For all of the methods illustrated,

EXHIBIT 10–1

Depreciation methods—comparative results graphed (including a typical repair curve)

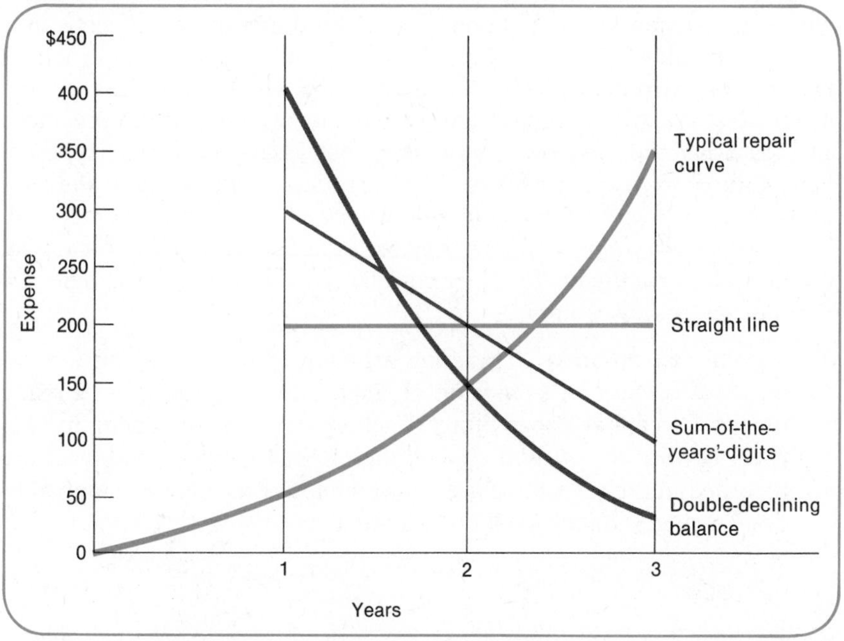

except productive output, monthly depreciation normally is determined by computing the annual amount of depreciation as illustrated, then dividing by 12 to obtain the monthly amount.[6] For example, in the above illustration for double-declining balance depreciation, the depreciation for the first year was determined to be $417. Assume the asset was acquired on August 12, 1977, with a December 31 fiscal year ending. The depreciation expense for 1977 would be (even-month basis):

$$\frac{\$417}{12} \times 5 = \$174$$

Since depreciation expense is an estimate, one should never record depreciation to amounts below one dollar, since to do so would suggest a higher degree of accuracy than is warranted. For this reason, depreciation amounts should always be rounded to even amounts—one, ten, or hundred dollars—depending upon the cost of the fixed asset compared with total assets and/or income. The **materiality concept** also applies in this situation.

[6] Under the productive output method, monthly depreciation is derived by multiplying the unit depreciation rate by the output for the particular month.

REPAIRS AND MAINTENANCE

After the acquisition of a fixed asset, related cost outlays often must be made for such items as ordinary repairs and maintenance, major repairs, replacements, and additions. The central measurement problem is the determination of which of these items should be recorded as an expense of the current period when incurred, and which should be recorded as an asset (i.e., as a prepayment) to be matched with future revenues. In measuring the cost of using operational assets, two basic types of expenditures must be considered. The term **expenditure** means the payment of cash or the incurring of a debt for an asset or service received. The purchase of a machine or a service, such as repairs on a truck, may be for cash or on credit. In either case there is an expenditure. The *two* types of expenditures are:

1. Capital expenditures—These are expenditures for the acquisition of an asset or for the expansion or improvement of an asset already owned. A capital expenditure benefits one or more accounting periods *beyond the current period;* therefore, capital expenditures are recorded in the respective asset accounts. For example, a plant addition costing $20,000 would be recorded as follows:

Plant	20,000	
Cash		20,000

2. Revenue expenditures—These are expenditures for normal operating items such as ordinary repairs, maintenance, and salaries that benefit *only* the current period; therefore, revenue expenditures are debited when incurred directly to appropriate expense accounts.[7] For example, the payment of $150 for ordinary repairs to the plant would be recorded in the current period as follows:

Repair expense	150	
Cash		150

Each expenditure made subsequent to the acquisition of an operational asset must be carefully evaluated in order to classify it properly as either capital or revenue. The distinction between capital and revenue expenditures is essential in order to conform with the matching principle. The expenditures must be matched with the periodic revenues to which they relate. The purpose and nature of the expenditure is the controlling factor in its classification. In the next few paragraphs we will discuss the common types of outlays subsequent to acquisition of a fixed asset.

Extraordinary repairs. Extraordinary repairs are classified as capital expenditures and are debited to the related *asset* account and depreciated

---

[7] The term "revenue expenditure" is widely used. It suggests that the expenditure is to be deducted in the current period from revenue in deriving income. However, a term such as "expense expenditure" would be more descriptive.

over the *remaining* life of that asset. *Extraordinary repairs* occur infrequently, involve relatively large amounts of money, and tend to increase the economic usefulness of the asset in the future because of either greater efficiency or longer life, or both. They are represented by major overhauls, complete reconditioning, and major replacements and betterments. For example, the complete replacement of a roof on the factory building would constitute an extraordinary repair, whereas patching the old roof would constitute an ordinary repair.

To illustrate the accounting for extraordinary repairs, assume a machine is being used that originally cost $20,000 and is being depreciated on a straight-line basis over ten years with no residual value. At the beginning of the seventh year, a major reconditioning was completed at a cost of $3,400. The estimated useful life was changed from 10 years to 12 years. A typical sequence of entries would be:

At acquisition of the asset:

Machinery	20,000	
Cash		20,000
Purchase of machinery.		

Depreciation—annually at end of Years 1 through 6:

Depreciation expense	2,000	
Accumulated depreciation, machinery		2,000
Adjusting entry to record annual depreciation ($20,000 ÷ 10).		

Extraordinary repair—at start of seventh year:[8]

Machinery	3,400	
Cash		3,400
Expenditure for major repair.		

Revised depreciation—annually at end of Years 7 through 12:

Depreciation expense	1,900	
Accumulated depreciation		1,900
Adjusting entry to record annual depreciation.		

Computations

Original cost	$20,000	
Depreciation, Years 1–6	12,000	
Book value remaining		$ 8,000
Extraordinary repair		3,400
Balance to be depreciated over remaining life		$11,400

Annual depreciation: $11,400 ÷ (12 − 6) years = $1,900.

[8] Some accountants prefer to debit the related asset account, as illustrated above, only when the major repair increases the efficiency above normal. In contrast, when it is estimated that the useful life is extended, the related accumulated depreciation account is debited. This distinction often is not made because the distinction is difficult to apply practically. Also subsequent book value and depreciation expense would be the same, irrespective of which account is debited because the remaining book value to be depreciated would be the same.

Additions. Additions are extensions to, or enlargements of, existing assets, such as the addition of a wing to a present building. Since these are capital expenditures, the cost of such additions should be debited to the existing account for the asset and depreciated over the remaining life of the asset.

Ordinary repairs and maintenance. Ordinary repairs and maintenance are always classified as revenue expenditures and debited to an appropriate *expense* account in the period in which incurred. *Ordinary* repairs and maintenance are those relatively small recurring outlays essential to keep a fixed asset in *normal* operating condition. Ordinary repairs do not materially add to the economic value of the asset or to its originally contemplated useful life. Rather, they tend to restore and repair the effects of normal wear and tear that occurred in the past. As a consequence, normal repair and maintenance tend to assure the expected useful life and operating efficiencies. These reasons justify the matching of current repair and maintenance expenditures with revenues of the current period.

DISPOSALS OF FIXED ASSETS

Fixed assets may be disposed of in one of two ways: voluntarily by sale, trade-in, or retirement; or involuntarily as a result of a casualty, such as a storm, fire, or accident. Whatever the nature of the disposal, the cost of the asset and any accumulated depreciation must be removed from the accounts at the date of disposal. The difference between any resources received upon disposal of a fixed asset and the **book value** of the asset at the date of disposal represents a "gain or loss on disposal of fixed assets." To illustrate, assume a machine is sold for $3,500 cash when the account balances showed: Machine, $10,000; and Accumulated Depreciation, Machine, $7,000 (i.e., a book value of $3,000). The entry to record the disposal would be:

Cash	3,500	
Accumulated depreciation, machine	7,000	
Machine		10,000
Gain on disposal of fixed asset		500

Gain Computed

Sale price	$3,500
Book value at date of sale ($10,000 − $7,000)	3,000
Difference—gain	$ 500

When a fixed asset is disposed of at any date other than the end of the accounting period, it may be necessary to record depreciation for the fraction of the year to the date of disposal. After this entry is made, the entry to record the disposal can be made. To illustrate, assume a machine that cost $6,000 when acquired on January 1, 1970, was disposed of through sale for $1,000 cash on June 30, 1977. The machine had been depreciated on a straight-line basis assuming an estimated useful life of ten years and no residual value. The sequence of entries from date of purchase through date of disposal would be as follows:

January 1, 1970:

Machinery	6,000	
Cash		6,000
Purchase of machinery.		

Annually December 31, 1970 through 1976:

Depreciation expense	600	
Accumulated depreciation		600
Adjusting entry to record annual depreciation (repeated each year for seven years).		

June 30, 1977:

Depreciation expense	300	
Accumulated depreciation		300
Depreciation from end of last accounting period to date of disposal, $\$600 \times 6/12 = \$300$. This assumes depreciation is computed on even months.		

June 30, 1977:

Cash	1,000	
Accumulated depreciation: ($\$600 \times 7$ years) + $300	4,500	
Loss on disposal of fixed asset	500	
Machinery		6,000
Sale of fixed asset, including removal from the accounts of original cost and accumulated depreciation.		

In the above illustration, the fixed asset when sold had a book value of $\$6,000 - \$4,500 = \$1,500$. The difference between this book value and the sales price of $1,000 was the amount of the loss on disposal ($500).

The gain or loss on disposal of fixed assets would be reported on the income statement, and the machinery would no longer be reported on the balance sheet.

TRADING IN USED ASSETS

It is not unusual when acquiring a new (or used) asset to trade in an old asset. Although there may be a direct trade of two assets, the typical case involves the trading in of an old asset plus the payment of a cash difference (often called "boot"). In such transactions, the asset acquired must be recorded in the accounts and the old asset removed from the accounts.

Accounting for the exchange of one asset for another asset depends on two factors:[9]

1. Whether the two assets are similar or dissimilar.
2. Whether a cash difference (boot) is paid or received.

The trading in of an old truck on a new truck would involve similar assets. In contrast, the trading in of a plot of land on a new truck would involve dissimilar assets.

The basic principle for recording the exchange of assets can be stated as follows: If the assets exchanged are *similar,* the exchange should be recorded on a "book value" basis because there is no completed earning process.[10] If the assets exchanged are *dissimilar,* the exchange should be recorded on a "fair-market value" basis because there is a completed earning process.

Four cases will be presented to illustrate application of the basic principle. The four cases will be based on the following fact situation:

Transaction: Company T acquired new Asset X and traded in old Asset A. At the date of the transaction, the accounts of Company T reflected the following:

Asset A:	
Cost when acquired	$5,000
Accumulated depreciation	3,000
Estimated fair-market value	2,200

Case A—*Similar assets* are exchanged; *no* cash boot paid.

Principle applied:

The asset acquired is recorded at the *book value* of the asset traded in.

Entry:

Asset X	2,000	
Accumulated depreciation, Asset A	3,000	
Asset A		5,000

[9] APB *Opinion No. 29,* "Accounting for Nonmonetary Transactions," May 1973, specifies the appropriate accounting for transactions that involve the exchange of assets when either or both of these factors are present.

[10] In the case of an exchange of similar productive assets, since the asset acquired performs essentially the same productive function as the asset given up, the exchange is only one step in the earning process. The earning process in these situations is completed when the goods or services are sold that the similar productive assets helped to produce. In contrast, in the case of an exchange of dissimilar productive assets, the earning process is completed because the productive function of the productive asset given up is terminated. The asset acquired serves a different economic purpose for the entity and begins a new earning process of its own.

Case B—*Dissimilar assets* are exchanged; *no* cash boot paid.

Principle applied:
The asset acquired is recorded at the *fair-market value* of the asset traded in.

Entry:

Asset X	2,200	
Accumulated depreciation, Asset A	3,000	
Asset A		5,000
Gain on disposal of fixed asset		200

Case C—*Similar assets* are exchanged; $50 cash boot is *paid.*

Principle applied:
The asset acquired is recorded at the *book value* of the asset traded in *plus* the cash boot paid.

Entry:

Asset X ($2,000 + $50)	2,050*	
Accumulated depreciation, Asset A	3,000	
Asset A		5,000
Cash		50

* This amount cannot exceed the fair-market value of the asset acquired.

Case D—*Dissimilar assets* are exchanged; $50 cash boot is *paid.*

Principle applied:
The asset acquired is recorded at the *fair-market value* of the asset traded in *plus* the cash boot paid.

Entry:

Asset X ($2,200 + $50)	2,250*	
Accumulated depreciation, Asset A	3,000	
Asset A		5,000
Cash		50
Gain on sale of fixed asset		200

* This amount cannot exceed the fair-market value of the asset acquired.

These four cases are sufficient for our objective to explain the exchange of assets. Sometimes the terms of the transaction includes the *receipt* of boot in which case the recording becomes more complex. Note particularly that under generally accepted accounting principles (APB *Opinion No. 29*) an asset, when acquired, should never be recorded at an amount greater than its fair-market value (i.e., its cash equivalent price). In some instances, this constraint will serve to reduce a gain (or increase a loss) on disposal.

In the above illustration, fair-market value of old Asset A was $200 in excess of book value. Therefore, in Cases B and D (relating to dissimilar assets), this amount was recorded as a gain. In contrast, if the fair-market value of old Asset A was $1,900 (i.e., $100 below book value), a loss of $100 would be reported in Cases B and D. This is true also for Cases A and C (similar assets) when the fair market value of either asset is below book value and it indicates an impairment of value.

NATURAL RESOURCES

A natural resource, such as a mineral deposit, oil well, or timber tract, often is referred to as a "wasting asset" since it is physically consumed, or **depleted,** as it is used. When acquired or developed, a natural resource is measured and recorded in the accounts in accordance with the cost principle. As the resource is consumed or used up, the acquisition cost, in accordance with the matching principle, must be apportioned to the periods in which the resulting revenues are recognized. The term **"depletion"** is used to describe this process of cost assignment over the period of use of a natural resource. A **depletion rate** per unit is computed by dividing the total acquisition and development cost by the *estimated* units that can be economically withdrawn from the resource. The depletion rate, thus computed, is then multiplied each period by the number of units actually withdrawn. This procedure is the same as the productive output method of calculating depreciation (see page 362).

To illustrate, assume that a gravel deposit was developed at a cost of $80,000 and that a reliable estimate was made that 100,000 tons of gravel could be economically withdrawn from it. The depletion rate per unit would be computed as follows:

$80,000 ÷ 100,000 Tons = $0.80 per Ton (Depletion Rate per Unit)

Depletion expense for the first year, assuming 5,000 tons of gravel were withdrawn during the year, would be recorded by means of the following adjusting entry:[11]

Depletion expense	4,000	
Gravel pit		4,000
Depletion for the year, 5,000 tons × $0.80.		

At the end of the first year, this natural resource should be reported as follows:

Fixed Assets:

Gravel pit (cost $80,000 – $4,000 accumulated depletion) $76,000

[11] Consistent with the procedure for recording depreciation, an Accumulated Depletion account may be used. However, as a matter of precedent, the asset account itself generally is credited directly for the periodic amortization. Either procedure is acceptable. The same is true for Intangible Assets.

Because changes in the estimate of recoverable units from a natural resource are made frequently, the depletion rate must be revised often. This is a "change in estimate" rather than an error; hence, the undepleted acquisition cost is spread over the estimated remaining recoverable units by computing a new depletion rate. For example, assume in year 2 that the estimate of recoverable units remaining was changed from 95,000 to 150,000 tons. The depletion rate to be applied to the tons of gravel withdrawn in year 2 would be:

($80,000 − $4,000) ÷ 150,000 Units = $0.51 per Ton

When buildings and similar improvements are constructed in connection with the development and exploitation of a natural resource, they should be recorded in separate asset accounts and *depreciated*—not depleted. Their estimated useful lives cannot be longer than time required to exploit the natural resource.

INTANGIBLE ASSETS

An intangible asset, like any other asset, has value because of certain rights and privileges conferred by law upon the owner of the asset. However, an intangible asset has no corporeal existence (i.e., no material or physical substance) as do tangible assets such as land and buildings. Thus, intangible assets are characterized by their lack of physical substance and the special rights that ownership confers. Examples of intangible assets are patents, copyrights, franchises, licenses, trademarks, and goodwill. An intangible asset usually requires the expenditure of resources. For example, an entity may purchase a patent from the inventor. The cost of an intangible asset should be measured and recorded in the accounts and reported on the financial statements of the entity in the same way as a tangible asset.

At acquisition, an intangible fixed asset is recorded at its cost in accordance with the cost principle. Cost is defined as the sum of all expenditures made to acquire the rights or privileges.

Each type of intangible asset should be recorded in a separate asset account when acquired. To illustrate, assume that on January 1, 1977, Mason Company purchased a patent from its developer, John Doe, at a cash price of $1,700. The acquisition of this intangible asset would be recorded as follows:

January 1, 1977:

Patents	1,700	
Cash		1,700
Purchase of patent rights from John Doe.		

Under the cost principle, an intangible right or privilege, although it may have value, is not recorded unless there has been an identifiable expenditure of resources to acquire or develop it. For example, the demise of a competitor's patent may cause the company's patent to be more valuable. This increase in value would not be recorded since there was no expenditure of resources incident to it.

Research and development (R&D) costs are recorded as expenses in the period incurred, even though they sometimes result in the development of a patent.

AMORTIZATION OF INTANGIBLES

Intangible assets normally have a limited life similar to tangible fixed assets; however, intangible assets seldom, if ever, have a residual value at the end of their useful life. Intangible assets have a limited life because the **rights or privileges** that give them value terminate or simply disappear. For example, a patent has a *legal* life of 17 years from the date it is granted; however, the right may cease to have economic utility, although still legally alive, before the end of the legal life. Therefore, the cost of a patent must be apportioned over its *economic life,* which cannot be longer (but may be less) than 17 years. The systematic write-off of the cost of an intangible asset over its economically useful life is referred to as **amortization.** To illustrate, assume the patent acquired by Mason Company, recorded above, had an estimated ten-year remaining economic life. At the end of 1977 the adjusting entry to record amortization for one year would be (see footnote 11):

December 31, 1977:

Patent expense	170	
Patents		170

Adjusting entry to record amortization of patent over the estimated economic life of ten years.

The amount of patent amortization expense recorded for 1977 would be reported on the income statement as an operating expense. The patent would be reported on the balance sheet as follows on December 31, 1977:

Intangible Assets:	
Patents (cost $1,700, less amortization)	$1,530

Formerly, certain kinds of intangibles, such as trademarks, were not amortized. In 1970, however, the APB recognized that all intangible assets, for all practical purposes, have a limited economic life. To stop certain abuses, the APB issued *Opinion No. 17,* which requires that each intangible be amortized over the period of its benefit. The *Opinion* specifies that the estimated useful life of an intangible asset cannot exceed 40 years. The *Opinion* does not permit an arbitrary and immediate write-off of an intangible asset down to, say, a nominal amount of $1. Prior to *Opinion No. 17,* this sometimes was done under the guise of conservatism.

Although an intangible asset may be amortized by using any "systematic and rational" method that reflects the actual expiration of its economic usefulness, the straight-line method is used almost exclusively.

Copyrights. A copyright is similar to a patient. A copyright gives the owner the exclusive right to publish, use, and sell a literary, musical, or artistic piece of work for a period not exceeding 50 years beyond the author's death. The same principles and procedures used in accounting for and reporting the cost of patents also are appropriate for copyrights.

Franchises and licenses. Franchises and licenses frequently are granted by governmental and other units for a specified period and purpose. For example, a city may grant one company a franchise to distribute gas to homes for heating purposes, or a company may sell franchises, such as the right to operate a Kentucky Fried Chicken restaurant to local outlets. Franchises and licenses generally require the expenditure of resources by the franchisee to acquire them; therefore, they represent an intangible asset that should be accounted for as illustrated earlier for patents.

Leaseholds. Leasing is a common type of business contract whereby one party, the owner or lessor, for a consideration known as rent, extends to another party, the lessee, certain rights to use specified property. Leases may vary from simple arrangements, such as the month-to-month lease of an office or apartment or the daily rental of an automobile, to long-term leases having complex contractural arrangements. The rights granted to a lessee frequently are referred to as a **leasehold.**

In the case of long-term leases, a lump-sum advance rental payment sometimes is required. The lessee should debit the advance payment to an intangible asset account (frequently called Leaseholds) and then amortize it over the life of the lease. The true amount of annual rent expense includes the amortization of the leasehold; therefore, the annual amortization is debited to Rent Expense. To illustrate, assume that Favor Company leased a building for its own use on January 1, 1977, under a five-year contract that required a payment in advance of $20,000. The advance payment would be recorded as follows:

January 1, 1977:

Leasehold (or Rent paid in advance)	20,000	
Cash		20,000
Rent paid in advance.		

At the end of 1977, and at the end of each of the remaining four years, the following adjusting entry would be made to reflect amortization of this intangible asset:[12]

[12] This discussion presumes the normal or operating type of lease. In some instances, a lease is in effect a sale/purchase agreement. Such leases, known as financing leases, involve complex accounting problems that are deferred to more advanced accounting books.

December 31, 1977:

Rent expense	4,000	
Leasehold (or Rent paid in advance)		4,000
Adjusting entry to record amortization of leasehold over five years.		

Leasehold improvements. In most instances, when buildings, improvements, or alterations are constructed by the lessee on leased property, they legally revert to the owner of the property at the end of the lease. The lessee has full use of such improvements during the term of the lease, and they should be recorded in an intangible asset account entitled "Leasehold Improvements." These expenditures should be amortized over the estimated useful life of the improvement or the remaining life of the lease, whichever is shorter.

Goodwill. Generally, a successful business, if sold as a unit, will command a price somewhat in excess of the sum of the fair-market values of the recorded assets less the liabilities. The reason a business may command the excess price is that an intangible called goodwill attaches to a successful business.

Goodwill represents the potential of a business to earn above a normal rate of return on the recorded assets. It arises from such factors as customer confidence, reputation for dependability, efficiency and internal competencies, quality of goods and services, and financial standing. From the date of organization, a successful business is continually building goodwill. In this context, the goodwill is said to be "internally generated at no identifiable cost." On the other hand, when a business is purchased as an entity, the purchase price presumably will include a payment for any goodwill that exists at that time. *In conformance with the cost principle, goodwill is recorded as an intangible asset only when it is actually purchased.*

To illustrate, assume Richard Roe purchased the College Men's Store on January 1, 1977, for $200,000 cash. At date of purchase, it was determined that the recorded assets had a total fair-market value of $160,000, comprised of inventory, $110,000; fixtures, $35,000; prepaid rent expense, $1,000; and other assets, $14,000. The purchase would be recorded by Roe as follows:

January 1, 1977:

Inventory	110,000	
Furniture and fixtures	35,000	
Prepaid rent expense	1,000	
Other assets	14,000	
Goodwill	40,000	
Cash		200,000
Purchase of College Men's Store.		

The intangible asset—goodwill—must be amortized over its estimated economic life but not to exceed 40 years (APB *Opinion No. 17*). Assuming a 40-year economic life, the amortization for 1977 would be recorded in an adjusting entry as follows:

December 31, 1977:

Goodwill amortized (expense)	1,000	
Goodwill		1,000

Adjusting entry to record goodwill amortization for one year based on 40-year economic life.

Many other types of intangible assets may be observed in financial statements. Examples are formulas, processes, and film rights. These are not discussed in detail since they are accounted for, and reported, as illustrated above.

DEFERRED CHARGES

An asset category called **deferred charges** is reported occasionally on balance sheets. A deferred charge, like a prepaid expense, is an *expense paid in advance;* that is, goods or services are acquired that will be used to generate future revenues. A deferred charge is a long-term prepaid expense and, therefore, cannot be classified as a current asset. A prepaid expense is a short-term prepayment and, for this reason, is classified as a current asset. Thus, the only difference between the two is time. For example, a $1,000 insurance premium for five years' coverage paid out at the start of Year 1 would be reported as follows at the end of Year 1:

Income Statement:	
Insurance expense	$200
Balance Sheet:	
Current asset—prepaid insurance	$200
Deferred charge	$600

Common examples of deferred charges are bond issuance costs (Chapter 12), start-up costs, organization costs, and plant rearrangement costs. In conformance with the matching principle, deferred charges are amortized to expense each period over the number of future periods benefited.

DEMONSTRATION CASE FOR SELF-STUDY

Diversified Industries, Incorporated

(Try to resolve the requirements before turning to the suggested solution that follows.)

Diversified Industries, Incorporated, has been in operation for a number of years. It started as a construction firm, and in recent years has expanded into a number of related activities. For example, in addition to heavy construction, its operations now include ready-mix concrete, sand and gravel, construction supplies, and earth-moving services.

The transactions given below were selected from those completed during 1977. They focus on the primary issues discussed in this chapter. Amounts have been simplified for case purposes.

1977

Jan. 1 The management decided to purchase a building that was approximately ten years old. The location was excellent, and there was adequate parking space. The company bought the building and the land on which it was situated for $305,000 cash. A reliable appraiser appraised the property at the following fair-market values: land, $136,500; and building, $188,500.

Jan. 12 Paid renovation costs on the building amounting to $38,100.

June 19 Purchased a third location (designated No. 3) for a gravel pit at a cost of $50,000 cash. The location had been carefully surveyed, and it was estimated that 100,000 square yards of gravel could be removed from the deposit.

July 10 Paid $1,200 ordinary repairs on the building.

Aug. 1 Paid $10,000 for costs of preparing the gravel pit, acquired in June 1977, for exploitation.

Dec. 31, 1977 (end of the annual accounting period)—the following data were developed as a basis for the adjusting entries:

a. The building will be depreciated on a straight-line basis over an estimated useful life of 30 years. The estimated residual value is $35,000.

b. During 1977, 12,000 square yards of gravel were removed from gravel pit No. 3. Use an Accumulated Depletion account.

c. The company owns a patent right that is used in operations. The Patent account on January 1, 1977, reflected a balance of $3,300. The patent has an estimated remaining life of six years (including 1977).

Required:

1. Give the journal entries for the transactions completed during 1977.
2. Give the adjusting entries on December 31, 1977.
3. Show the classification and amount for each of the following items as they should be reflected on the balance sheet, December 31, 1977: land, building, gravel pit, and patent.

Suggested Solution:

Requirement (1)—entries during 1977:

January 1, 1977:

Land (building site)	128,100	
Building	176,900	
Cash		305,000

Allocation of purchase price based on appraisal:

Item	*Appraisal value*	*Percent*	*Computation*	*Allocation*
Land	$136,500	42	× $305,000 =	$128,100
Building	188,500	58	× 305,000 =	176,900
Totals	$325,000	100		$305,000

January 12, 1977:

Building	38,100	
Cash		38,100
Renovation costs on building.		

June 19, 1977:

Gravel pit (No. 3)	50,000	
Cash		50,000
Purchased gravel pit; estimated production, 100,000 square yards.		

July 10, 1977:

Repair expense	1,200	
Cash		1,200

August 1, 1977:

Gravel pit (No. 3)	10,000	
Cash		10,000
Development costs.		

Requirement (2)—adjusting entries, December 31, 1977:

a. Depreciation expense, building	6,000	
Accumulated depreciation		6,000

Computation:

Cost ($176,900 + $38,100)	$215,000
Less: Residual value	35,000
Cost to be depreciated	$180,000

Annual depreciation: $180,000 ÷ 30 years = $6,000

b. Depletion expense	7,200	
Accumulated depletion gravel pit (No. 3)		7,200

Computation:

Cost ($50,000 + $10,000)	$60,000
Depletion rate:	
$60,000 ÷ 100,000 yards =	$ 0.60
Depletion expense:	
$0.60 × 12,000 yards =	$ 7,200

c. Patent expense	550	
Patent		550

Computation:

$3,300 ÷ 6 years = $550

Requirement (3)—balance sheet, December 31, 1977:

Assets

Fixed Assets:			
Land		$128,100	
Building	$215,000		
Less: Accumulated depreciation	6,000	209,000	
Gravel pit	60,000		
Less: Accumulated depletion	7,200	52,800	
Total Fixed Assets			$389,900
Intangibles:			
Patent ($3,300 − $550)			2,750

SUMMARY

This chapter focused on accounting for operational assets. These are the noncurrent assets that a business retains more-or-less permanently (rather than for sale) for use in the course of normal operations. They include fixed assets and intangible assets. At acquisition, operational assets are measured and recorded in the accounts at cost, in conformity with the cost principle. Cost includes the purchase price plus all reasonable and necessary incidental expenditures made in acquiring the asset.

An operational asset is, in nature, a bundle of future services and benefits that has been paid for in advance. As an operational asset is used, this bundle of benefits gradually is used up in the generation of revenue. Therefore, in accordance with the matching principle, the asset cost (less any residual value) is apportioned to periodic expense over the periods benefited. In this way the expense associated with the use of operational assets is matched with the revenues generated. This apportionment process is known as depreciation in the case of plant, equipment, and furniture; as depletion in the case of natural resources; and as amortization in the case of intangibles.

Four methods of depreciation are widely used: straight line, productive output, sum-of-the-year's-digits, and double-declining balance depreciation.

Expenditures after acquisition of a fixed asset are classified either as:

1. Capital expenditures—those expenditures that provide benefits for one or more periods beyond the current period; consequently, they are debited to appropriate asset accounts and depreciated, depleted, or amortized over their useful life; or
2. Revenue expenditures—those expenditures that provide benefits during the current period only; consequently, they are debited to appropriate current expense accounts when incurred.

Ordinary repairs and maintenance costs are revenue expenditures, whereas extraordinary repairs and additions are capital expenditures.

Operational assets may be disposed of voluntarily by sale or retirement, or involuntarily through casualty, such as storm, fire, or accident. Upon disposal, such assets must be depreciated, depleted, or amortized up to the date of disposal. The disposal transaction is recorded by removing the cost of the old asset and the related accumulated depreciation, depletion, or amortization amount from the accounts. Normally, a gain or loss on disposal of an operational asset will result since the disposal price generally is different from the book value of the old asset; however, special rules apply to direct exchanges (swaps) of similar assets.

IMPORTANT TERMS

Operational assets	**Straight-line depreciation**
Fixed assets	**Productive-output depreciation**
Natural resources	**Sum-of-years'-digits depreciation**
Intangible assets	**Double-declining balance depreciation**
Basket purchase	
Depreciation	**Extraordinary repairs**
Depletion	**Ordinary repairs**
Amortization	**Leaseholds**
Residual value	**Deferred charges**

QUESTIONS FOR DISCUSSION

1. Define operational assets. Explain how they may be considered to be a "bundle of future services."

2. What are the classifications of operational assets? Briefly explain each.
3. Relate the cost principle to accounting for operational assets.
4. Relate the matching principle to accounting for operational assets.
5. Define and illustrate the book value of a fixed asset that has an estimated residual value. Relate it to fair-market value.
6. Under the cost principle, what amounts should be included in the acquisition cost of a fixed asset?
7. What is a "basket purchase"? What measurement problem does it pose?
8. Briefly distinguish between: depreciation, depletion, and amortization.
9. In computing depreciation, three values must be known; identify and explain the nature of each.
10. Estimated useful life and residual value of a fixed asset relate to the current owner or user rather than to all users. Explain.
11. What kind of a depreciation-expense pattern is provided under the straight-line method? When would its use be particularly appropriate?
12. What kind of depreciation-expense pattern emerges under the productive-output method? When would its use be particularly appropriate?
13. What are the arguments in favor of accelerated depreciation?
14. What kind of depreciation-expense pattern emerges under the accelerated methods? When would their use be particularly appropriate?
15. Explain how monthly depreciation should be computed using the sum-of-the-years'-digits method for an asset having a ten-year life.
16. Over what period should an addition or enlargement to an existing fixed asset be depreciated? Explain.
17. Distinguish between a capital expenditure and a revenue expenditure.
18. Distinguish between ordinary and extraordinary repairs. How is each accounted for?
19. Define an intangible asset.
20. What period should be used to amortize an intangible asset?
21. Define goodwill. When is it appropriate to record goodwill as an intangible asset?
22. Distinguish between a leasehold and a leasehold improvement.
23. Over what period should a leasehold improvement be amortized? Explain.

EXERCISES

E10–1. For each asset listed below, enter a code letter to the left to indicate the allocation procedure for each asset. Use the following letter codes:

A—Amortization
D—Depreciation
P—Depletion
N—None of these

____ 1. Land	____ 9. Franchise	____ 16. Deferred charge
____ 2. Patent	____ 10. Plant site in use	____ 17. Leasehold improvements
____ 3. Building	____ 11. Copyright	____ 18. Timber tract
____ 4. Cash	____ 12. Investment in common stock	____ 19. Tools
____ 5. Oil well	____ 13. Mineral deposit	____ 20. Gravel pit
____ 6. Trademark	____ 14. Machinery	____ 21. Organization costs
____ 7. Goodwill	____ 15. License right	
____ 8. Leasehold		

E10–2. A machine was purchased by X Company on March 1, 1977, at an invoice price of $16,000. On date of delivery, March 2, 1977, X Company paid $10,000 on the machine and the balance was an open account at 10 percent interest. On March 3, 1977, $100 was paid for freight on the machine, and on March 15 installation costs relating to the machine were paid amounting to $600. On September 1, 1977, X Company paid the balance due on the machine plus the interest.

Required:

a. Give the journal entries on each of the above dates through September 1977.

b. Give the adjusting entry for straight-line depreciation at the end of 1977, assuming an estimated useful life of ten years and a net residual value of $3,200. Depreciate to the nearest month. The fiscal period ends December 31, 1977.

c. What would be the book value at the end of 1978?

E10–3. Rayborn Company purchased a building and the land on which it is located for a total cash price of $180,000. In addition, they paid transfer and acquisition costs of $600. Renovation costs on the building amounted to $5,000. An independent appraiser provided fair-market values of building, $160,000; and land, $40,000.

Required:

a. Apportion the cost of the property on the basis of the appraised values. Show computations.

b. Give the entry to record the purchase of the property, including all expenditures. Assume all expenditures were cash when purchased at the start of year 1.

c. Give entry to record straight-line depreciation at the end of one year assuming a 20-year useful life and no residual value.

d. What would be the book value at the end of Year 2?

E10–4. Duke Corporation purchased a machine at a cost of $1,350. The estimated useful life was four years, and the residual value, $150. Assume that the estimated productive life of the machine is 50,000 units and each year's production was Year 1, 20,000 units; Year 2, 15,000 units; Year 3, 9,000 units; and Year 4, 6,000 units. 12000

Required:

a. Determine the amount for each cell in the following table. Show your computations and round to even dollars.

	Depreciation Expense			
Year	Straight Line	Productive Output	Sum-of-the-Years'-Digits	Double-Declining Balance
1				
2				
3				
4				
Total				

b. Assuming the machine was used in the production of a product manufactured and sold by the company, which method would you recommend? Why?

E10–5. Smith Company purchased a machine that cost $18,000. The estimated useful life was five years, and the residual value, $3,000. Assume the estimated useful life in productive units to be 50,000. Units actually produced were Year 1, 9,000; and Year 2, 11,000.

Required:

a. Determine the appropriate amounts for the table below. Show your computations.

	Depreciation expense		*Book value at end of:*	
Method of depreciation	*Year 1*	*Year 2*	*Year 1*	*Year 2*
Straight line..........................	____	____	____	____
Productive output.................	____	____	____	____
Sum-of-the-years'-digits........	____	____	____	____
Double-declining balance......	____	____	____	____

b. Which method would result in the lowest EPS for Year 1? for Year 2?

E10–6. Raven Company acquired a machine that cost $1,000 on July 1, 1977. The estimated useful life is four years with a residual value of $160.

Required:

Compute monthly depreciation expense for July 1977 and September 1978, assuming (*a*) the straight-line method and (*b*) the SYD method.

E10–7. White Company owns an existing building that was constructed at an original cost of $85,000. It is being depreciated on a straight-line basis over a 20-year estimated useful life and has a $5,000 estimated residual value. At the end of 1976, the building was one-half depreciated. In January 1977, an addition to the existing building was completed at a cash cost of $15,000. It is estimated that this addition will last for the remaining life of the existing structure and will add $1,000 to the residual value.

Required:

a. Give the entry to record completion of the addition in January 1977.

b. Compute the amount of depreciation that should be recorded in 1977, assuming the annual accounting period ends December 31. Show computations.

c. Give the adjusting entry for depreciation at December 31, 1977.

d. Under what conditions would the addition be depreciated over a different life from the one you used in (*a*)?

E10–8. Fuller Company operates a small manufacturing facility as a supplement to its regular service activities. At the beginning of 1977, a fixed asset account for the company showed the following balances:

Manufacturing equipment	$78,000
Accumulated depreciation through 1976 (11 years)	(55,000)

During 1977 the following expenditures were incurred for repairs and maintenance:

1. Routine maintenance and repairs on the equipment	$1,000
2. Major overhaul of the equipment	6,000

The equipment is being depreciated on a straight-line basis over 15 years with a $3,000 estimated residual value. The annual accounting period ends on December 31.

Required:

a. Give the adjusting entry for depreciation for the manufacturing equipment that was made at the end of 1976.

b. Give the entries to appropriately record the two expenditures for repairs and maintenance during 1977.

c. Give the adjusting entry to be made at the end of 1977 for depreciation of the manufacturing equipment, assuming no change in the estimated life or residual value. Show computations.

E10–9. AB Company owns the office building occupied by the administrative office. The office building was reflected in the accounts on the December 31, 1976, balance sheet as follows:

Cost when acquired	$250,000
Accumulated depreciation (based on estimated life of 30 years and $40,000 residual value)	105,000

During January 1977, on the basis of a careful study, the management decided that the estimated useful life should be changed to 25 years and the residual value reduced to $35,000.

Required:

a. Give the adjusting entry for straight-line depreciation at the end of 1977. Show computations.
b. Explain the rationale for your response to (*a*).

E10–10. For each item listed below, enter the appropriate letter to the left to indicate the type of expenditure. Use the following:

A—Capital expenditure
B—Revenue expenditure
C—Neither

____ 1. Paid $500 for regular repairs.
____ 2. Paid $6,000 for major repairs.
____ 3. Addition to old building; paid cash, $10,000
____ 4. Routine maintenance; cost, $300; on credit.
____ 5. Purchased a machine, $6,000; gave long-term note.
____ 6. Paid $2,000 for organization costs.
____ 7. Paid three-year insurance premium, $600.
____ 8. Purchased a patent, $3,400 cash.
____ 9. Paid $10,000 for monthly salaries.
____ 10. Paid cash dividends, $15,000.

E10–11. At the end of the annual accounting period, December 31, 1976, the records of Scott Company reflected the following:

Machine A:	
Cost when acquired (estimated useful life, 6 years, residual value, $1,000)	$13,000
Accumulated depreciation (four years)	8,000

During January 1977, the machine was extensively renovated including several major improvements at a cost of $6,000. As a result, the estimated life was increased from six years to eight years and the residual value was increased from $1,000 to $1,800.

Required:

a. Give the entry to record the renovation.
b. Give the adjusting entry at the end of 1977 to record straight-line depreciation for the year.
c. Explain the rationale for your response to (*a*) and (*b*).

E10–12. Franklin Company sold a large truck that had been used in the business for three years. The records of the company reflected the following:

Delivery truck	$4,500
Accumulated depreciation	3,000

Required:

a. Give the entry for disposal of the truck, assuming the sales price was $1,500.
b. Give the same entry but assume that the sales price was $1,750.

c. Give the same entry but assume that the sales price was $1,100.
d. Summarize the conclusions that can be drawn from the three different situations above.

E10–13. On June 30, 1977, a delivery truck owned by King Corporation was a total loss as a result of an accident. On January 1, 1977, the records reflected the following:

Truck	$7,000
Accumulated depreciation (straight line, two years)	2,400

Since the truck was insured, King Corporation collected $4,200 cash from the insurance company on July 20.

Required:

Give all entries with respect to the truck from January 1, through July 20, 1977. Show computations.

E10–14. The records of the Bye Company on December 31, 1976, reflected the following data in respect to a particular machine:

Machine, original cost	$20,000
Accumulated depreciation	10,800*

* Based on a five-year estimated useful life, a $2,000 residual value and straight-line depreciation.

On May 1, 1977, the machine was sold for $8,500 cash. The accounting period ends on December 31.

Required:

a. How old was the machine on January 1, 1977? Show computations.
b. Give entry, or entries, incident to the sale of the machine.
c. Give entry, or entries, incident to the sale of the machine assuming the price was $7,500.

E10–15. Dodson Company has a particular machine (designated Machine R for case purposes) which no longer meets the needs of the company. On December 31, 1976, the records reflected the following:

Machine R:	
Original cost	$20,000
Accumulated depreciation	15,000

On January 3, 1977, the company acquired a new machine (Machine S) and traded in the old machine. On this date, a reliable estimate of the fair-market value of Machine R was $6,500.

Required:

a. Give the entry for Dodson to record the transaction on January 3, 1977, for each of the following independent cases:

Case A—The machines were similar and no cash difference was paid or received by Dodson.

Case B—The machines were dissimilar and no cash difference was paid or received by Dodson.

b. For each case, explain the underlying reason for the amount that you recorded as the cost of Machine S.

E10–16. Use the facts and requirements given in Exercise 10–15 except that for each case assume Dodson paid a $1,000 cash difference (boot). The fair-market value of Machine S was $7,500.

E10–17. The records of Davidson Company reflected the following data in respect to a fixed asset:

Equipment (at cost)	$3,600
Accumulated depreciation	(2,800)

Davidson Company decided to purchase a new vehicle; the dealer demonstrated a vehicle that was suitable to needs. The new vehicle had a special list price of $4,500. However, the cash price without a trade-in was $4,200. The dealer required a cash payment of $3,200 in addition to the old asset.

Required:

a. Give the entry for Davidson Company to record the exchange and the cash payment assuming similar assets.
b. Give the entry to record the exchanges and the cash payment assuming the two assets were dissimilar.
c. Explain the basis for the amounts recorded as the cost of the new vehicle in (*a*) and (*b*).

E10–18. In February 1977, Kleen Extractive Industries paid $300,000 for a mineral deposit. During March, $50,000 was spent in preparing the deposit for exploitation. It was estimated that 700,000 tons could be extracted economically. During 1977, 20,000 tons were extracted. During January 1978, another $16,000 was spent for additional developmental work. After conclusion of the latest work, the estimated recovery was increased to 800,000 tons over the remaining life. During 1978, a total of 30,000 tons was extracted.

Required:

Give the appropriate journal entry at the following dates:

a. February 1977 for acquisition of the deposit.
b. March 1977 for developmental costs.
c. Year 1977 for annual depletion (show computations).
d. January 1978 for developmental costs.
e. Year 1978 for annual depletion (show computations).

E10–19. Utah Manufacturing Company has three intangible fixed assets at the end of 1977 (end of the accounting fiscal year):

1. Patent—Purchased from J. Smith on January 1, 1977, for a cash cost of $4,080. Smith had registered the patent with the U.S. Patent Office on January 1, 1972. Amortize over remaining legal life.
2. A franchise acquired from the local community to provide certain services for ten years starting on January 1, 1977. The franchise cost $15,000 cash.

3. On January 1, 1977, the company leased some property for a five-year term. They immediately spent $3,500 cash for permanent improvements. At the termination of the lease, there will be no recovery for these improvements.

Required:

a. Give entry to record the acquisition of each intangible. Provide a brief explanation with the entries.

b. Give adjusting entry at December 31, 1977, for amortization of each intangible. Show computations.

c. Show how the effects of these assets should be reported on the financial statements for 1977.

E10–20. Center Company is in the process of preparing the balance sheet at December 31, 1977. The following are to be included:

Prepaid insurance	$ 450
Investment in common stock of X Corporation, at cost (market $6,200)	6,000
Patent (at cost)	3,400
Accumulated amortization of patents	800
Accounts receivable	20,000
Allowance for doubtful accounts	600
Franchise (at cost)	1,000
Accumulated amortization of franchises	300
Land–site of building	10,000
Building	280,000
Accumulated depreciation, building	150,000
Organization costs deferred	2,000

Required:

Show how each of the above assets would be reflected on the balance sheet at December 31, 1977. Use the following subcaptions: Current Assets, Investments and Funds, Fixed Tangible Assets, Intangible Assets, Deferred Charges, and Other Assets. The company prefers to use the "accumulated" accounts as listed above. (Hint: Intangible assets sum to $3,300 on the balance sheet.)

E10–21. Ray Company has three intangibles that are to be accounted for during 1977. The relevant facts are:

1. On January 1, 1977, the company purchased a patent from R. Baker for $2,550 cash. Baker had developed the patent and registered it with the Patent Office on January 1, 1975. Amortize over the remaining legal life.
2. On January 1, 1977, the company purchased a special copyright for a total cash cost of $7,560 and the remaining legal life was 25 years. The company executives estimated that the copyright would be of no value by the end of 20 years.
3. The company purchased another small company in January 1977 at a cash cost of $50,000. Included in the purchase price was $8,000 for goodwill; the balance was for plant, equipment, and fixtures. Amortize the goodwill over the maximum period permitted.

Required:

a. Give the entry to record the acquisition of each intangible.

b. Give the adjusting entry that would be required at the end of the annual accounting period, December 31, 1977, in respect to each intangible. Include a brief explanation and show computations.

E10–22. Swat Company conducts operations in several different localities. In order to expand into still another city, the company obtained a ten-year lease, starting January 1, 1977, on a very good downtown location. Although there was a serviceable building on the property, the company had to construct an additional structure to be used for storage purposes. The ten-year lease required a $10,000 cash advance rental payment, plus cash payments of $2,000 per month during occupancy. During January 1977, the company spent $30,000 cash constructing the additional structure. The new structure has an estimated life of 12 years with no residual value (straight-line depreciation).

Required:

a. Give the entry for Swat Company to record the payment of the $10,000 advance on January 1, 1977.

b. Give the entry to record the construction of the new structure.

c. Give any adjusting entries required at the end of the annual accounting period for Swat Company on December 31, 1977, in respect to (1) the advance payment and (2) the new structure. Show computations.

PROBLEMS

P10–1. Dawson Company purchased three used machines from J. Evers for a cash price of $26,400. Transportation costs on the machines amounted to $600. The machines were immediately overhauled, installed, and started operating. Since the machines were essentially different, each had to be recorded separately in the accounts. An appraiser was employed to estimate their fair-market value at date of purchase. The book value reflected on Evers books also are available. The book values, appraisal results, installation costs, and renovation expenditures were:

	Machine A	*Machine B*	*Machine C*
Book value—Evers	$5,000	$ 9,000	$6,000
Appraised value	6,000	15,000	9,000
Installation costs	200	300	100
Renovation costs	800	500	600

Required:

a. Compute the cost of each machine by making a realistic allocation. Explain the rationale for the allocated basis used.

b. Give the journal entry to record the purchase of the three machines assuming all payments were cash. Set up a separate asset account for each machine.

P10–2. Mays Company purchased a machine that cost $34,375. The estimated useful life is ten years, and the estimated residual value is 4 percent of cost. The machine has an estimated useful life in productive output of 110,000 units. Actual output was Year 1, 15,000; and Year 2, 12,000.

Required:

a. Determine the appropriate amounts for the table below. Show your computations.

	Depreciation expense		*Book value at end of:*	
Depreciation method	*Year 1*	*Year 2*	*Year 1*	*Year 2*
Straight line	$_____	$_____	$_____	$_____
Productive output	_____	_____	_____	_____
Sum-of-the-years'-digits	_____	_____	_____	_____
Double-declining balance	_____	_____	_____	_____

b. Give the adjusting entries for Years 1 and 2 under each method.

c. Which method would you recommend in terms of the effect on (1) income taxes and (2) EPS? Explain.

P10–3. Nance Company purchased a machine that cost $9,200. The estimated useful life was three years, and the residual value, $200. The management is considering several depreciation methods and is concerned about the choice of a method.

Required:

a. You have been asked to prepare a table that will reflect the relevant income statement and balance sheet amounts over the life of the machine. Accordingly, you have designed the following table to be completed (show computations):

Comparison of depreciation methods

	Relevant amounts		
Depreciation methods and effects	*Year 1*	*Year 2*	*Year 3*
Straight line:			
Depreciation expense on income statement......	_____	_____	_____
Income tax expense on income statement........	_____	_____	_____
EPS on income statement	_____	_____	_____
Net asset amount reported on balance sheet....	_____	_____	_____
Double-declining balance depreciation:			
Depreciation expense on income statement......	_____	_____	_____
Income tax expense on income statement........	_____	_____	_____
EPS on income statement..............................	_____	_____	_____
Net asset amount reported on balance sheet	_____	_____	_____

Additional data:
Income before depreciation and before income taxes (average rate, 30 percent):
Year 1, $30,000; Year 2, $33,000; and Year 3, $35,000.
Common stock outstanding for all three years, 10,000 shares.

b. Analyze the effect of each method on (1) cash outflow for income taxes and (2) EPS.

P10–4. Thames Manufacturing Company was organized a number of years ago. It is a local manufacturer of seat covers, floor mats, and similar items for automobiles and boats. There are two manufacturing operations: one does custom work and the other manufactures standard items that are distributed through retail channels in a number of states. In January 1975, the company purchased land, including a building that was approximately 15 years old, at a cost of $300,000. Transfer costs, surveys, appraisals, titles, and legal fees amounted to another $6,000.

The property was appraised, at acquisition date, for loan purposes, with the following results: land, $72,000; building, $288,000; estimated remaining life, 20 years; and estimated residual value, $20,000.

In January 1977, major renovations on the building were completed at a cost of $80,050. The estimated remaining life of the building after renovation was 22 years, and the estimated residual value was the same as before, $20,000.

Straight-line depreciation is used, and a full years' depreciation for 1975, 1976, and 1977 seemed reasonable since the property was placed in use immediately.

Required:

a. Give the entry to record the fixed asset in January 1975. Show computations.
b. Give the adjusting entry for depreciation on December 31, 1975. Show computations.
c. Give entry to record the renovation in January 1977.
d. Give the adjusting entry for depreciation on December 31, 1977. Show computations. (Hint: Depreciation expense is $12,835.)

P10–5. Mills Company found it necessary to do some extensive repairs on its existing building and to add a new wing suitable for use during the next ten years. The existing building originally cost $150,000; and by the end of 1976, it was one-half depreciated on the basis of a 20-year useful life and no residual value. During 1977 the following expenditures were made that were related to the building:

1. Ordinary repairs and maintenance expenditures for the year, $9,000 cash.
2. Extensive and major repairs to the roof of the building, $18,000 cash. These repairs were completed on June 30, 1977.
3. The new wing was completed on June 30, 1977, at a cash cost of $40,140.

Required:

a. Record each of the 1977 transactions.
b. Give the adjusting entry that would be required at the end of the annual accounting period, December 31, 1977, for the building

after taking into account your entries in (*a*) above. Assume straight-line depreciation. The company computes depreciation to the nearest one-half year.

c. Show how the assets would be reported on the December 31, 1977, balance sheet. (Hint: The book value of the building is $122,580.)

P10–6. Neil Company has a machine which is no longer needed (designated for case purposes as Machine N). The company decided to dispose of it when the accounts showed the following:

Machine N:	
Original cost	$18,000
Accumulated depreciation (straight line)	14,000

A reasonable estimate was obtained that indicated a $4,500 fair-market value for Machine N at date of disposal.

Required:

Following are several independent cases involving alternative ways of disposing of Machine N. For each independent case for Neil Company, you are to (1) give the entry to record the disposal and (2) provide an explanation of the underlying reason (i.e., accounting justification) for the way in which you recorded the disposal.

Case A – Sold the machine for $4,500.

Case B – Traded in the old machine on a new machine (Machine O) that was similar, and no cash difference was paid or received.

Case C – Traded in the old machine on a new machine that was similar and paid $400 cash difference.

Case D – Traded in the old machine on Machine O that was dissimilar, and no cash difference was paid or received.

Case E – Traded in the old machine on Machine O that was dissimilar and paid a $400 cash difference.

P10–7. Assume the same requirements and facts as given in Problem 10–6, except that the fair-market value of Machine O at date of acquisition was $3,700 and there was no established fair-market value on the old machine. Omit Case A.

P10–8. Slick Manufacturing Company operates a number of machines. One particular bank of machines consists of five identical machines acquired at the same date. At the beginning of 1977 the fixed asset account for the five machines showed the following:

Machinery (Type A, five machines)	$160,000
Accumulated depreciation (Type A machines)	105,000*

* Based on ten-year estimated useful life and $2,000 residual value per machine and straight-line depreciation.

One of the Type A machines was disposed of on September 1, 1977.

Required:

a. How old were the Type A machines at the end of 1976? Show computations.

b. What was the book value of the machines at the date of disposal? Show computations. The company computes depreciation to even months.

c. Give all entries incidental to disposal of the machine under two independent assumptions:

1. It was sold outright for $7,000 cash.
2. It was exchanged for a new machine having a "quoted" price of $44,000; however, it was determined that it could be purchased for $40,000 cash. A trade-in allowance of $11,000 and the balance of $33,000 was paid in cash. Assume the machines were similar.

P10–9. During 1977, Bowen Company disposed of three different assets. On January 1, 1977, prior to their disposal, the accounts reflected the following:

Assets	*Original cost*	*Residual value*	*Estimated life*	*Accumulated depreciation (straight line)*
Machine A..........	$20,000	$2,000	10 years	$12,600(7 years)
Machine B..........	35,400	3,000	9 years	21,600(6 years)
Machine C..........	65,200	6,000	14 years	59,200(14 years)

The machines were disposed of in the following ways:

Machine A: Sold on January 1, 1977, for $6,500 cash.

Machine B: Exchanged for a new machine of similar type on May 1, 1977. The new machine had a quoted price of $48,000; however, was determined that it could be purchased for $45,000 cash. A trade-in of $18,000 was allowed on the old machine, and the balance was paid in cash, $30,000.

Machine C: On January 2, 1977, this machine suffered irreparable damage from an accident. On January 10, 1977, it was given to a salvage company at no cost. The salvage company agreed to remove the machine immediately at no cost. Since the machine was insured, $3,000 cash was collected from the insurance company.

Required:

1. List each machine and its book value on the date of disposal. Show computations. The company computes depreciation to even months.
2. Give all entries incident to the disposal of each machine. Explain the accounting rationale for the way that you recorded each disposal.

P10–10. Glidden Company has six different intangible assets to be accounted for and reported on the financial statements. At issue is a decision by the management in respect to the amortization of the cost of each of the six intangibles. Certain facts concerning each intangible are:

1. Patent—The company purchased a patent for a cash cost of \$23,800 on January 1, 1977. The patent had a legal life of 17 years from date of registration with the U.S. Patent Office, which was January 1, 1974. Amortize over the remaining legal life.
2. Copyright—On January 1, 1977, the company purchased a copyright at a cost of \$8,100. The legal life remaining from that date is 27 years. It is estimated that the copyrighted item will have little or no value by the end of 20 years.
3. Franchise—The company obtained a franchise from X Company to make and distribute a special item. The franchise was obtained on January 1, 1977, at a cash cost of \$4,500 and was for a ten-year period.
4. License—The company secured a license on January 1, 1977, from the city to operate a special service for a period of five years. Total cash expended in obtaining the license was \$8,000.
5. Goodwill—The company started business in January 1975 by purchasing another business for a cash lump sum of \$300,000. Included in the purchase price was the item "Goodwill, \$80,000." Glidden executives believe that "the goodwill is an important long-term asset to us." Amortize over maximum period permitted.
6. Organization costs—The company is a corporation and was organized in January 1975 to purchase the company mentioned in 5 above. During organization, \$4,000 was expended for legal, accounting, charter, and other organizational activities. Debit a deferred charge and amortize over five years.

Required:

a. Give the entry for each of the acquisitions.

b. Give the adjusting entry for each intangible asset that would be necessary at the end of the annual accounting period, December 31, 1977. Provide a brief explanation and show computations. If no entry is required for a particular item, explain the basis for your conclusion.

c. Determine the book value of each intangible on January 1, 1978. (Hint: The total book value for the six intangibles is \$115,845.)

P10–11. On January 1, 1977, Jackson Corporation was organized by five individuals for the purpose of purchasing and operating a successful business known as The Quality Store. The name was retained and all of the assets, except cash, were purchased for \$200,000 cash. The liabilities were not assumed by Jackson Corporation. The transaction was closed on January 5, 1977, at which time the balance sheet of The Quality Store reflected the book values shown below:

THE QUALITY STORE
January 5, 1977

	Book value	Fair-market value*
Accounts receivable (net)	$ 30,000	$ 30,000
Inventory	100,000	100,000
Fixed assets (net)	9,000	25,000
Other assets	1,000	5,000
Total Assets	$140,000	
Liabilities	$ 35,000	
Owners' equity	105,000	
	$140,000	

* These values for the assets purchased were provided to Jackson Corporation by an independent appraiser.

As a part of the negotiations, the former owners of The Quality Store agreed not to engage in the same or similar line of business in the same general region.

Required:

a. Give the entry by Jackson Corporation to record the purchase of the assets of The Quality Store. Include goodwill.

b. Give the adjusting entries that would be made by Jackson Corporation at the end of the annual accounting period, December 31, 1977, for:

(*a*) Depreciation of the fixed assets (straight line), assuming an estimated remaining useful life of 20 years and no residual value.

(*b*) Amortization of goodwill assuming a 40-year amortization period.

P10–12. (Note: This is a complex problem to test your analytical ability.)

It is the end of the annual fiscal period (December 31, 1977) for XY Company. The following items must be resolved before the financial statements can be prepared:

1. On January 1, 1977, a used machine was purchased for $3,900 cash. This amount was debited to a fixed asset account, Machinery. Cash was expended for (*a*) repairing the machine, $300, and (*b*) for installation, $150, which was debited to Expense. The machine has an estimated remaining useful life of five years and a 10 percent residual value. Straight-line depreciation will be used.
2. A small warehouse (and the land site on which it is located) was purchased on January 1, 1977, at a cash cost of $40,000 which was debited to an asset account, Warehouse. The property was appraised for tax purposes near the end of 1976 as follows: warehouse, $21,250; and land, $8,250. The warehouse has an estimated remaining useful life of 10 years and a 10 percent residual value. Double-declining balance depreciation will be used.

3. During 1977 repair costs were paid as follows: Usual recurring repairs, $1,200; during January 1977, major repairs on the warehouse purchased in 2 above, $1,000. Repair expense was debited $2,200, and cash was credited.
4. On June 30, 1977, the company purchased a patent for use in the business at a cash cost of $2,040. The patent was dated July 1, 1972. The Patent account was debited.
5. On December 30, 1977, the company acquired a new truck that had a firm cash price of $4,300 (estimated life, five years; residual value, $300). The company paid for the truck with cash, $3,000, and traded in an old truck (similar) that had a book value on December 31, 1977, as follows:

Original cost, January 1, 1973	$3,500
Accumulated depreciation, December 31, 1977	2,000*

* Includes 1977 depreciation, five-year life and no residual value.

The transaction was recorded as follows:

Truck (new)	4,500	
Accumulated depreciation (old)	2,000	
Truck (old)		3,500
Cash		3,000

Required:

For each of the above items, give the following:

a. Entry or entries that should be made to correct the accounts. If none is required, so state.

b. Adjusting entry at December 31, 1977.

P10–13. (Note: This is a comprehensive problem covering several issues discussed in the chapter.)

On January 1, 19A, AB Company purchased four identical machines. The costs were:

Invoice price per machine (subject to 2% cash discount)	$400
Installation costs (total wages paid to AB employees for installation time)	168
Freight on machines, per machine	50

Due to a careless oversight, the 2 percent cash discount was lost. Sales tax paid on invoice price, 4 percent.

Required:

a. Give the entry to record the acquisition of the four machines on January 1, 19A (round amounts to even dollars).

b. Give the adjusting entries to record depreciation for Years A, B, and C. Assume a five-year estimated life, no residual value, and the straight-line method.

c. On July 1, 19D, three of the machines (each in essentially the same condition) were disposed of as follows:

Machine No. 1 – Sold for $215 cash. (Hint, there was a gain on disposal of $65.)

Machine No. 2 – Traded in on a new similar machine (improved) and paid $250 cash difference (including sales taxes and other acquisition costs).

Machine No. 3 – Since this machine was no longer needed, it was traded for an electric typewriter (assume dissimilar) that had a firm cash price of $520 and paid a $200 cash difference.

Give the entry to record the disposal of each machine.

d. During the first week of January 19E, a major overhaul of Machine No. 4 was completed at a cost of $140 which extended its estimated useful life by an additional two years (over the original estimate).

Give the entry to record the major overhaul of Machine No. 4 and depreciation for 19E. Show computations.

11

Measurement and reporting of liabilities

PURPOSE OF THE CHAPTER

A business generates or receives resources from three distinct sources: contributions by owners, extension of credit by creditors, and sale of goods and services. Creditors provide resources to the business through cash loans and by providing property, goods, and services to the entity on credit. These borrowing activities create for the entity liabilities to various creditors. *Liabilities can be defined as obligations that result from transactions requiring the future payment of assets or the future performance of services, which are definite as to amount or are subject to reasonable estimation. Liabilities generally have a definite and known payment date known as the maturity or due date.*

From the point of view of the user of the financial statements, the liabilities reported on the balance sheet, and the expense incurred from borrowing funds (i.e., interest expense), reported on the income statement, often are important factors in evaluating the financial performance of the entity. Usually there are a number of different kinds of liabilities and a wide range of creditors; therefore, those interested in the business necessarily must rely on the financial statements for relevant information on this important facet of the financial activities of an entity. The accounting model, coupled with the audit made by an independent accountant, provides the user with a good level of confidence that all liabilities are identified, properly measured, and fully reported.

This chapter focuses on the measurement and reporting problems associated with the various classifications of liabilities. Throughout this chapter the discussions will emphasize (1) identification of liabilities, (2) measurement of the amount of each liability, (3) accounting for the various types of liabilities, and (4) appropriate reporting. The chapter is divided into two parts: Part One discusses the accounting for liabilities; and Part Two focuses on an important concept in the measurement of liabilities, present and future value.

PART ONE: ACCOUNTING FOR LIABILITIES

Although there are various ways to classify liabilities, for accounting and reporting purposes the following classifications are widely recognized:

1. Current liabilities:
   a. Accounts payable.
   b. Short-term notes payable.
   c. Other short-term obligations.
2. Long-term liabilities:
   a. Long-term notes payable and mortgages.
   b. Bonds payable.
   c. Other long-term obligations.

Bonds payable will be discussed in Chapter 12. Each of the other classifications will be separately discussed and illustrated in this chapter.

MEASUREMENT OF LIABILITIES

Identification of the liabilities of an entity at the balance sheet date generally is not difficult for the accountant; however, aside from identification, the problem of **measurement** of the amount of each liability may be more complex. Conceptually, the amount of a liability, at any point in time, is the **present value** of the future outlays of assets required to pay the liability in full; that is, the present value of the principal plus all future interest payments. This present value amount may be called the **current cash equivalent amount.**[1]

A liability that requires the "going rate of interest" will always have a present value equal to its maturity amount. However, when the required rate of interest is different from the going rate, or interest is unspecified, the present value will be different from the maturity amount. As such liabilities approach maturity or due date the present value, or

[1] Some persons find it useful to think of the current cash-equivalent amount of a liability as the figure that the two parties involved (the debtor and the creditor) would settle the obligation for at a given date (between the beginning and due date) on a fair and equitable basis. This figure may be constant over the life of the debt, as in the case of an interest-bearing note. In the case of a bond payable, issued at a discount or premium, the carrying amount would be different each date (see Chapter 12).

current cash equivalent amount, approaches the maturity amount. These concepts are discussed and illustrated in Part Two.

Fundamentally, liabilities are measured in accordance with the *cost principle.* That is, the amount of a liability, when initially incurred, is equivalent to the current value of the resources received when the transaction occurred. Although the amount of most liabilities is definitely specified in the initial transaction (such as in a note payable), there are situations where a liability is known to exist but the exact amount is not determinable until a later date. For example, television sets may be sold with a one-year guarantee against defects. For the vendor, the guarantee creates a liability, the actual amount of which depends on the performance of the sets during the year. Thus, liabilities can be said to be comprised of known obligations of a definite amount and known obligations of an estimated amount.

CURRENT LIABILITIES

Current liabilities are short-term obligations that will be paid within the **current operating cycle** of the business or within one year of the balance sheet date, whichever is the longer. Thus, the definition presumes that current liabilities will be paid with existing current assets.[2]

An important financial relationship on the balance sheet is known as working capital. **Working capital is the dollar difference between total current assets and total current liabilities.** The relationship between current assets and current liabilities also is measured as the **working capital ratio** (sometimes called the **current ratio**). The current ratio is computed by dividing total current assets by total current liabilities. To illustrate, assume the balance sheet for XY Company on December 31, 1977, reported total current assets of $900,000 and total current liabilities of $300,000. The amount of working capital would be $900,000 − $300,000 = $600,000. The current ratio would be: $900,000 ÷ $300,000 = 3.00, or 3 to 1. That is, at balance sheet date, for each $1 of current liabilities there were $3 of current assets. These relationships often assist creditors in assessing the ability of a company to meet its short-term maturing obligations.[3]

Current liabilities commonly encountered are trade accounts payable,

[2] Current assets and current liabilities were defined and discussed in Chapter 4. Current assets are defined as cash and other resources reasonably expected to be realized in cash or sold or consumed within one year from the date of the balance sheet or during the *normal operating cycle,* whichever is the longer. Current liabilities are defined as those liabilities normally to be paid out of the current assets as reported on the balance sheet. The AICPA Committee on Accounting Procedure defined current liabilities as follows: The term "current liabilities" is used principally to designate obligations whose liquidation is reasonably expected to require the use of existing resources properly classifiable as current assets, or the creation of other current liabilities.

[3] Interpretation of financial ratios is discussed in Chapter 16.

short-term notes payable, accrued liabilities (such as wages payable, taxes payable, and interest payable), cash dividends payable, and revenues collected in advance (i.e., deferred or unearned revenues).

Accounts payable

Trade accounts payable were discussed in Chapter 7 since they are created by the purchases of goods and services. The term "accounts payable" is used in accounting to mean *trade* accounts payable. Typical entries are:

March 6, 1977:

Purchases (or Inventory)	980	
Accounts payable		980
Purchase of merchandise on credit; terms, 2/10, n/30. (Invoice price, $1,000 × 0.98 = $980.)		

March 11, 1977:[4]

Accounts payable	980	
Cash		980
Payment of account payable within the discount period.		

Accrued liabilities

Accrued liabilities arise from expenses that have been incurred but are not yet paid or recorded at the end of the accounting period. They appeared in Chapter 5 in the discussion of **adjusting entries.** To illustrate a typical accrued liability, assume that the amount of property taxes for 1977 was determined to be $1,600. At the end of the accounting period, December 31, 1977, the current liability must be recorded and reported, although the amount will not be paid until January 15, 1978. Therefore, the following adjusting entry must be made:

December 31, 1977:

Property tax expense	1,600	
Property taxes payable		1,600
Adjusting entry to record property taxes incurred in 1977 but not yet recorded or paid.		

The entry in the next year for payment of the accrued liability would be:

[4] In case of payment after the discount period, the entry would be:

Accounts payable	980	
Purchase discounts lost (or Interest expense)	20	
Cash		1,000

January 15, 1978:

Property taxes payable	1,600	
Cash		1,600
Payment of liability for property taxes accrued in 1977.		

Accrued liabilities also arise when salaries and wages are incurred. When employees perform services, the employer incurs an obligation to them that normally is paid on a weekly or monthly payroll basis. In the preceding discussions and illustrations, accounting for wage and salary expense has been simplified by disregarding payroll taxes and payroll deductions.

In addition to the obligation to the employee, payrolls create other liabilities that are directly related to the payment of salaries and wages. These additional liabilities generally arise as a result of federal and state laws (social security taxes), and contractual obligations (such as pension plans and union dues). Some of these liabilities are paid by the employee through the employer (as payroll deductions); others must be paid by the employer and are additional expenses to the business.

The take-home pay of most employees is considerably less than the gross salary or wages because of **payroll deductions** for such items as employee income taxes withheld, social security taxes that must be paid by the employee, and other employee deductions such as insurance and union dues. The employer is required to pay the amounts deducted from the wages to the designated governmental agencies and other organizations such as the union. From the date of the payroll deduction until the date of payment to the agencies or organizations, the employer must record and report the current liabilities that are owed to the designated units. Thus, a typical journal entry for a $80,000 payroll would be as follows:

January 31, 1977:

Salaries expense	50,000	
Wages expense	30,000	
Liability for income taxes withheld—employees		16,000
Liability for union dues withheld—employees		300
F.I.C.A. taxes payable—employees		4,800
Cash		58,900
To record the payroll including employee deductions.		

In addition to the payroll taxes that the *employees* must pay through the employer, the *employer* is required by law to pay *additional* specified payroll taxes. These constitute an operating expense for the business. Therefore, a second entry related to the payroll is needed to record the taxes to be paid by the employer. A typical entry, related to the above payroll, would be as follows:

January 31, 1977:

Payroll tax expense	7,600	
F.I.C.A. taxes payable—employer		4,800
F.U.T.A. taxes payable—employer		400
State unemployment taxes payable—employer		2,400
Employer payroll taxes for January payroll.		

The six current liabilities created in the two entries immediately above are paid in the near future when the company remits the requisite amount of cash to the appropriate agencies. Details involved in payroll accounting are discussed and illustrated in Appendix A to this chapter. Payroll accounting does not entail any new concepts or accounting principles; however, there is a significant amount of procedural detail involved.

Deferred revenues

Deferred revenues (frequently called unearned revenues) arise from revenues that have been collected in advance during the current period but will not be earned until a later accounting period. A more descriptive title preferred by many accountants is Revenue Collected in Advance.

Deferred revenues constitute a liability since the cash has been collected but the revenue has not been earned; therefore, there is a *present obligation* to render, in the future, the services or to provide the goods. To illustrate, assume that during December 1977 rent revenue collected amounted to $6,000, which was debited to Cash and credited to Rent Revenue. Assume further that at the end of 1977 it was determined that $1,000 of this amount was for January 1978 rent. Thus, there is a current liability for deferred rent revenue that must be recognized. The sequence of entries for this situation would be as follows:

December 1977:

Cash	6,000	
Rent revenue		6,000
Collection of rent revenue.[5]		

[5] The credit could be made to Rent Revenue Collected in Advance, in which case the adjusting entry to give the same results on December 31, 1977, would be:

Rent revenue collected in advance	5,000	
Rent revenue		5,000

Alternatively, the entry could have been made on payment date in such a way as to avoid the need for an adjusting entry, viz:

Cash	6,000	
Rent revenue		5,000
Rent revenue collected in advance		1,000

December 31, 1977 (adjusting entry):

Rent revenue	1,000	
Rent revenue collected in advance (deferred revenue)		1,000
Adjusting entry to record unearned rent revenue at the end of the accounting period.		

LONG-TERM LIABILITIES

Long-term liabilities encompass all obligations of the entity not properly classified as current liabilities. Long-term liabilities sometimes are referred to as fixed liabilities. They generally arise from the purchase of fixed assets or the borrowing of large amounts of cash to be used for the acquisition of operational assets and major expansions of the business. Long-term liabilities usually are long-term notes payable or bonds payable. Frequently, a long-term liability is supported by a mortgage on specified assets of the borrower *pledged* as security for the liability. The mortgage involves a separate document that is appended to the note payable. A liability supported by a mortgage is said to be a "secured debt." An unsecured debt is one for which the creditor relies primarily on the integrity and general earning power of the borrower.

Long-term liabilities are reported on the balance sheet under a separate caption below "Current Liabilities." As a long-term debt approaches the maturity date, the portion of it that is to be paid in the next current period is reclassified as a current liability. To illustrate, assume a five-year note payable of $50,000 was signed on January 1, 1975. Repayment is to be in two installments as follows: December 31, 1978, $25,000; and December 31, 1979, $25,000. The December 31, 1976, 1977, and 1978 balance sheets would report the following:

December 31, 1976:	
Long-Term Liabilities:	
Note payable	$50,000
December 31, 1977:	
Current Liabilities:	
Maturing portion of long-term note	$25,000
Long-Term Liabilities:	
Long-term note	$25,000
December 31, 1978:	
Current Liabilities:	
Maturing portion of long-term note	$25,000

Notes payable may be either short term or long term. A short-term note payable usually has a maturity date within one year from the balance sheet date and generally arises as a result of borrowing cash or from purchasing merchandise or services on credit. Bonds payable (see

Chapter 12) are always long-term liabilities, except for any currently maturing portion as illustrated above for the long-term note payable.

NOTES PAYABLE

A note payable (short term or long term) is a written promise to pay a stated sum at one or more specified dates in the future. A note payable may require a single-sum repayment at the due or maturity date or it may call for installment payments. To illustrate, assume the purchase of a sailboat for $3,000, with a $1,000 cash down payment and a note payable for the balance. The note may be drawn to call for a single payment at the end of 12 months or, alternatively, for 12 monthly payments.

Notes payable require the payment of interest and, hence, the recording of interest expense. Interest expense is incurred on liabilities because of the **time value of money.** The word "time" is significant because the longer money is borrowed (used), the larger the total dollar amount of interest expense. Thus, one must pay more interest for a two-year loan of a given amount, at a given **interest rate,** than for a one-year loan. To the borrower, interest is an expense; whereas to the lender (creditor), interest is a revenue. In calculating interest we must consider three variables: (1) the principal, (2) the interest rate, and (3) the duration of time. Therefore the formula is:

$$\text{Interest} = \text{Principal} \times \text{Rate} \times \text{Time}$$

To illustrate, assume $6,000 cash is borrowed by Baker Company on November 1, 1977, and a six-month, 8 percent, interest-bearing, note payable is given. The interest is payable at the due date of the note. The computation of interest expense would be: $\$6{,}000 \times 0.08 \times 6/12 = \$240$. This note would be recorded in the accounts as follows:

November 1, 1977:

Cash	6,000	
Note payable, short term (8 percent, interest bearing)		6,000
Borrowed on short-term note; terms, six months at 8 percent per annum; interest is payable at maturity.		

Since interest is an expense of the period when the money is used (unpaid), it is measured, recorded, and reported on a *time basis* rather than when the cash is actually paid or borrowed. This is based on legal as well as on economic considerations. For example, were the $6,000 loan cited above to be paid off in two months instead of in six months, interest amounting to $\$6{,}000 \times 0.08 \times 2/12 = \$80$ would have to be paid. It is on the time basis that the *adjusting entry* for accrued interest payable would be made at the end of the accounting period. To illustrate, assume the accounting period ends December 31, 1977. Although the $240 interest for the six months will not be paid until April 30, 1978, two months' unpaid interest must be accrued by means of the following adjusting entry:

December 31, 1977:

Interest expense	80	
Interest payable		80
Adjusting entry to accrue two months' interest, $\$6,000 \times 0.08 \times 2/12 = \$80$.		

At maturity date the payment of principal plus interest would be recorded as follows:[6]

April 30, 1978:

Notes payable, short term	6,000	
Interest payable (per above)	80	
Interest expense ($\$6,000 \times 0.08 \times 4/12$)	160	
Cash ($6,000 + $240)		6,240
To record payment of note payable including interest.		

The accounting for a note payable is the same whether it is classified as a current or as a long-term liability. Accounting for a note payable also is the same irrespective of the purpose for which the note was executed.

Interest on notes. A note may be either interest bearing or noninterest bearing. All commercial notes involve interest, either explicitly or implicitly, because money loaned, or borrowed, has a time value that cannot be avoided.

An *interest-bearing note* is one that explicitly specifies (1) a stated rate of interest (such as 8 percent) on the note itself, and (2) that the interest is to be paid at maturity, or in future installments, *in addition to the face or principal amount* of the note. For example, a $30,000, 8 percent, one-year, interest-bearing note would (1) provide the borrower with $30,000 cash, (2) have a face or principal amount of $30,000, and (3) require the payment of the principal ($30,000) plus interest for one-year ($2,400)—a total of $32,400.

In contrast, in a *noninterest-bearing note,* the interest is implicit; that is, it is a note that (1) does not specify a rate of interest on the note itself and (2) includes the interest in the face amount of the note. For example, a $30,000, one-year, noninterest-bearing note (assuming a stated rate of interest of 8 percent) (1) will provide the borrower with

---

[6] This assumes no reversing entry was made on January 1, 1978. (See Chapter 6, Part Two.) If a reversing entry of the accrual was made on January 1, 1978, the payment entry would have been:

Notes payable, short term	6,000	
Interest expense	240	
Cash		6,240

$27,600 cash (i.e., $30,000 – $2,400 interest) and (2) would require the payment of only the face amount of the note at maturity date ($30,000). Observe that the interest is included in the face amount of the note.[7] The entries for the two different types of notes payable cited above are:

Transactions	*Interest bearing*		*Noninterest bearing*	
November 1, 1977, date of note:				
Cash	30,000		27,600	
Discount on note payable (or deferred interest expense)			2,400	
Note payable, short term		30,000		30,000
(Eight percent interest; term, one year.)				
December 31, 1977, end of accounting period:				
Interest expense (two months)	400		400	
Accrued interest payable		400		
Discount on note payable				400
Adjusting entry for 2 months' accrued interest; $30,000 × 8% × 2/12 = $400.				
October 31, 1978, maturity date of note:*				
Notes payable	30,000		30,000	
Interest expense (ten months)	2,000		2,000	
Accrued interest payable	400			
Discount on note payable				2,000
Cash		32,400		30,000
Payment of note at maturity.				

* It would have simplified this entry if a *reversing entry* of the accrual of December 31, 1977, had been made on January 1, 1978.

The above illustration suggests two important concepts in the measurement of liabilities and interest expense. The concept of *present value* is important in the measurement of liabilities. The present value of a note is the value today of its future cash flows. In the case of the interest-bearing note, the present value and the face amount of principal are the same at all dates, that is, $30,000 (at 8 percent). However, in the case of the noninterest-bearing note, the present value on the date of the note (November 1, 1977) is $27,600, the amount of cash received, although the face amount is $30,000. As time passes, the present value gradually increases

[7] In some instances, interest is computed on the cash received. Cash received would be computed as: $30,000 ÷ 1.08 = $27,778. When this basis is used, the effective interest rate is ($30,000 – $27,778) ÷ $27,778 = 8 percent. Also see Chapter 9, Part Three.

to the face amount of $30,000 on maturity date. The concepts of present value are discussed and illustrated in Part Two of this chapter.

In the measurement of interest cost, the concepts of the *stated* (or nominal) *interest rate* and the *effective* (or real) *interest rate* are important. The stated interest rate is the rate specified on the note (in the above illustration it was 8 percent per year). The effective interest rate is the real or true rate of interest. In the above example the stated and effective rates were the same for the interest-bearing note, viz:

Stated interest rate 8%

Effective interest rate:

$$\frac{\text{Annual Interest Payable}}{\text{Cash Proceeds Received}} = \frac{\$2{,}400}{\$30{,}000} = 8\%$$

In contrast, the stated and effective interest rates on the noninterest-bearing note are different, viz:

Stated interest rate (given as the going rate) 8%

Effective interest rate:

$$\frac{\text{Annual Interest Payable}}{\text{Cash Proceeds Received}} = \frac{\$2{,}400}{\$27{,}600} = 8.6957\%$$

DEFERRED INCOME TAXES

Throughout the preceding chapters, income taxes paid by corporations have been discussed and illustrated. In those illustrations, income tax expense was reflected on the income statement and income taxes payable was reflected on the balance sheet. In addition to income taxes payable, most corporate balance sheets report another tax liability called deferred income taxes.

The concept of deferred income taxes is that income tax expense should be based on the *taxable* income reported on the income statement, whereas income taxes payable necessarily must be based on the taxable income per the tax return (i.e., as specified in the tax laws). Often there is a difference between the time when certain revenues or expenses appear on the income statement and when they appear on the tax return. Thus, when a taxable revenue or expense appears on the income statement before or after it appears on the tax return, a deferred income tax amount will result. When it later appears in the other place, the deferred income tax amount will automatically be offset (i.e., it will "reverse" or "turn around").

To illustrate, XY Company reported income taxes as follows at the end of 19A, 19B, and 19C:[8]

[8] For illustrative purposes and to focus on income taxes only, the illustration has two simplifying assumptions: (1) pretax income is held constant for the three years and (2) income taxes payable at the end of each period are paid in the next period.

	19A	19B	19C
Income Statement:			
Pretax income	$30,000	$30,000	$30,000
Income tax expense (30%)	9,000	9,000	9,000
Net Income	$21,000	$21,000	$21,000
Balance Sheet:			
Liabilities:			
Income taxes payable	$ 8,400	$ 9,000	$ 9,600
Deferred income taxes	600	600*	

* Cumulative balance.

Observe that income tax expense (on the income statement) does not agree with income taxes payable on the balance sheet in years 19A and 19C. However, the totals for the three years agree ($27,000). Also observe that in 19A a second tax liability, "Deferred income taxes," of $600 was reported; this additional liability disappears in 19C.

The difference between "Income tax expense" on the income statement and "Income taxes payable" on the balance sheet in the example above was due to a single expense—depreciation. XY Corporation purchased an asset at the beginning of 19A that cost $12,000 and had a useful life of three years with no residual value. The company used straight-line depreciation in the accounts (and hence on the income statement) and sum-of-the-years'-digits on its tax return. This caused a difference between income tax expense and income taxes payable as follows:

Year	*Straight-line depreciation*	*SYD depreciation*
A	$12,000 × 1/3 = $4,000	$12,000 × 3/6 = $6,000
B	12,000 × 1/3 = 4,000	12,000 × 2/6 = 4,000
C	12,000 × 1/3 = 4,000	12,000 × 1/6 = 2,000

	19A	*19B*	*19C*
Computation of tax expense as reported on the income statement:			
Income before depreciation expense and before income tax expense	$34,000	$34,000	$34,000
Less: Depreciation expense (straight line)	4,000	4,000	4,000
Amount subject to tax	30,000	30,000	30,000
Income tax *expense* (30%)	$ 9,000	$ 9,000	$ 9,000
Computation of taxes payable as reported on the tax return:			
Income before depreciation expense and before income taxes	$34,000	$34,000	$34,000
Less: Depreciation expense (SYD)	6,000	4,000	2,000
Amount subject to tax	28,000	30,000	32,000
Income taxes *payable* (30%)	$ 8,400	$ 9,000	$ 9,600

Since income tax *expense* (on the income statement) in years 19A and 19C is different from income taxes *payable* (on the tax return) for years 19A and 19C, *deferred income taxes* must be recorded as follows:

	19A		*19B*		*19C*	
Income tax expense (from income statement)	9,000		9,000		9,000	
Income taxes payable (from tax return)		8,400		9,000		9,600
Deferred income taxes (the difference)		600			600	

Observe that the liability account, Deferred Income Taxes, would appear as follows for the three-year period:

Deferred Income Taxes

		Dec. 31, 19A and B	600
Dec. 31, 19C	600		

Observe that the $600 liability, Deferred Income Taxes, recorded in 19A, reversed or turned around in 19C. This occurred because the advantage of increased depreciation deduction in early years using SYD for tax purposes was offset in 19C. Recall that, irrespective of the method of depreciation used, only the cost of the asset (less any residual value) can be depreciated for both accounting and tax return purposes ($12,000 in the example above). Also this illustration demonstrates what has been noted before—the tax advantage of SYD (or DDB) is only the time value of money. That is, the tax savings resulting from SYD in early years can be invested to earn a certain return.

From the above illustration, it can be seen that deferred taxes are recorded only when there are one or more items of expense or revenue that appear on the income statement in one period and on the income tax return of another period. Also observe that Deferred Income Taxes may have a debit balance (an infrequent occurrence) in which case it would be reported under Assets as a prepaid expense or deferred charge. This situation would have occurred in the above example had XY Corporation used SYD on the income statement and straight-line depreciation on the tax return (permissible by the tax regulations but not a likely choice by the taxpayer).

APB *Opinion No. 11,* "Accounting for Income Taxes," (December 1967) specifies that deferred income taxes shall be recorded *only* when there is a *timing difference* between the income statement and the tax return. A timing difference occurs only when an item of revenue or expense will be included on *both* the income statement and the tax return in different years so that the deferred tax effect will automatically reverse (as illustrated above). Another type of difference between the income statement and tax return is called a *permanent difference.* A permanent difference does not create deferred income taxes because it appears on either the income statement or the tax return but not both. For example, interest revenue on tax-free municipal bonds is included on the income statement of the recipient, but is not reported on the recipient's federal income tax return.

On the balance sheet, the total amount of deferred income taxes must be reported in part as a current liability (or asset) and in part as a long-term liability (or asset) depending upon the length of time before it will automatically reverse or turn around.[9]

This discussion of deferred income taxes was presented so that you will understand the nature of deferred income taxes reported on the balance sheets of most medium and large corporations. Income taxes payable (as a liability) is easy to comprehend; however, many statement users have difficulty understanding the other tax item—deferred income taxes.

LEASE LIABILITIES

In recent years the practice of leasing equipment, rather than purchasing it, has increased by leaps and bounds. There are a number of economic reasons why businesses have increasingly obtained operational assets by leasing. A primary reason has been that leasing does not require an immediate outflow of cash or, in the opinion of many people, the incurrence of a large debt as would be the case if the asset is purchased outright.

The trend in leasing has posed some difficult problems in measuring and reporting liabilities. As a result, leasing has been called "off balance sheet financing." To illustrate the issues, assume Daly Construction Company urgently needs a heavy machine that costs $40,000 new. It has an estimated useful life of five years and no residual value. The management of the company is considering three alternative ways of acquiring the machine:

a. Purchase the machine outright—Since the company is short of cash, this would entail borrowing approximately all of the purchase price at 10 percent on a two-year repayment schedule. If this alternative

---

[9] It is unfortunate that the accounting profession has adopted the term "deferred income taxes" because it is not descriptive since the item may be reported as either a liability or an asset. More descriptive (but less succinct) titles are:

Liabilities:
Estimated future income taxes payable on revenues deferred and expenses accrued for tax purposes.

Assets:
Estimated future income tax savings on revenues accrued and expenses deferred for tax purposes.

is selected, the machine would be recorded in the accounts as follows assuming the full amount is borrowed:

Machinery	40,000	
Note payable, long term		40,000

Each period, payments for maintenance, operating insurance, taxes, interest expense, and so on, would be made and reported as operating expenses on the income statement and tax return.

b. Lease the machine on a month-to-month or year-to-year basis—It has been determined that the rental payments would be as follows:

Monthly basis	$ 2,500 (per month)
Yearly basis	18,000 (per year)

Each period, payments for maintenance and operating expenses (but not for insurance, taxes and interest; these would be paid by the lessor) would be paid in addition to the rental payment. These payments would be included on the tax return.

c. Lease the machine on a long-term (five-year), noncancelable lease contract—This contract would provide that Daly be fully responsible for paying all expenses for maintenance, operating, insurance, taxes, and so on, for the full five years and, in addition, would pay an annual rental of $10,018 based on an 8 percent interest assumption (see footnote 10). At the end of the five years, the machine would be returned to the lessor.

In this situation, after preparing comparative cost and cash-flow analyses, the management of Daly Construction Company tentatively selected the third alternative. Let's look at some of the considerations given by the management that influenced the decision. Note that this does not mean that their reasoning was sound in every respect nor that they considered all of the important issues.

Alternative (*a*) was considered undesirable by the management because (1) of the immediate cash demand if borrowing is not feasible; (2) the 10 percent interest rate was unfavorable when compared with the average rate currently being paid by the company; (3) the anticipated difficulty in obtaining a $40,000 loan even at 10 percent; and (4) the undesirability of increasing the long-term liabilities on the balance sheet by $40,000, which may affect their current credit standing with the banks and probably would increase the interest rate on other loans.

Alternative (*b*) was given very little consideration because of the extremely high rental payments required. Although the machine could be returned at any time with no further obligation under this alternative, the high rental payments would cause a significant decrease in income. In the view of the management, the income statement effect would be "more than the company could stand," even though there would be no liability reflected on the balance sheet.

Alternative (*c*) was tentatively selected by the management; the reasons given were (1) no cash or loan would be required to obtain the machine; (2) the rental payment would be deductible in full on the income tax return each period; (3) the amount of the annual rental payment "appears to be reasonable;" and (4) no liability needs to be recorded on the balance sheet.

The third alternative is typical of many current leasing contracts that involve high-cost machinery and equipment. It is a situation that has caused some difficult accounting and reporting problems. In the past, some companies viewed the situation outlined in alternative (*c*) as an ordinary or **operating type of lease** just as is alternative (*b*). This is the way the Daly management viewed it in its analysis which was the usual case prior to APB *Opinions No. 5* and *No. 7*. If this view prevailed, no entry would be made in the accounts at the inception of the lease. Each period, when the rental payment is made, the entry would be:

Rental expense	10,018	
Cash		10,018

The APB *Opinions* specify that this constitutes inappropriate measurement and reporting of the liability that is implicit in the situation outlined in alternative (*c*). They specify that the essence of the long-term, noncancelable lease, for the life of the equipment, is in fact a **purchase/sale transaction.** The rationale is the leasing company is providing financing for Daly; therefore, it is a **financing type of lease** rather than an *operating type of lease.* When classified as a financing type of lease, the following entries would be necessary:

At date of inception of the lease:

Asset – machinery	40,000	
Discount on financing lease obligations	10,090*	
Liability – obligations on financing lease ($10,018 × 5 years)		50,090*

*Note: The liability is reported on the balance sheet as the net of these two balances.

At date of first rental payment:

Liability – obligations on financing lease	10,018	
Cash		10,018
Interest expense ($50,090 − $10,090) × 8%	3,200	
Discount on financing lease obligations		3,200
Depreciation expense ($40,000 ÷ 5 years)	8,000	
Accumulated depreciation		8,000

Thus, one of the reasons (the liability) given by the Daly management is no longer valid. We emphasize that correct accounting as specified by the APB *Opinions* reports the asset and the long-term liability on the balance sheet.[10] This result essentially follows the accounting effect of alternative (*a*) in that it reports the financing on the balance sheet.

There was widespread opposition by companies, such as Daly, to accounting for this kind of transaction as a *financing lease* because of the effect on their financial statements. It is interesting to note that the leasing company would record the long-term lease, outlined in alternative (*c*), as a sale at the date of the lease transaction. There are many related complexities; however, the above illustration should be sufficient to comprehend the basic measurement and reporting issues of long-term noncancelable leases.

CONTINGENT LIABILITIES

A contingent liability is not a legal or effective liability; rather it is a **potential future liability.** The amount of a contingent liability may be known or estimated. A contingent liability is defined as a potential future liability that has arisen as a result of an event or transaction that has *already occurred* but its conversion to an effective liability is dependent upon the occurrence of one or more *future* events or transactions (i.e., a future contingency). To illustrate, assume that in 1977 Baker Company was sued for $100,000 damages arising from an accident involving one of the trucks owned by the company. The suit is scheduled for trial during March 1978. Whether there is a legal liability will depend upon the decision of the court at the termination of the trial. When financial statements are prepared at December 31, 1977, a contingent liability must be disclosed. Because of the accident, the company is contingently liable for the payment of damages.

A contingent liability is *not* recorded in the accounts unless there is a high probability of loss. Rather, it is reported in a note to the financial statements. For example, the contingent future liability arising from the lawsuit may be disclosed by a note to the balance sheet similar to the following:

> The company is contingently liable for $100,000 because of a lawsuit based on an accident involving a company vehicle. Legal counsel believes that the suit is lacking in merit. Trial is scheduled for March 1978.

---

[10] Lease accounting requires the use of present value concepts. For example, the annual rental was computed as: $40,000 ÷ 3.99271 = $10,018. The present value of an annuity of 1 for 5 periods at 8 percent = 3.99271 (see Part Two).

CONTROLLING EXPENDITURES

The purchase of merchandise, services, and fixed assets often requires the recording of either a short-term or long-term liability. As a consequence, in addition to the cash transactions a large number of **cash payments** such as on liabilities are made in a business. In a company of any size, control over cash expenditures is essential to prevent the misapplication of cash in the cash-disbursement process. In a very small business it is often possible for the owner to personally give attention to each transaction when it is incurred and to make each cash payment. This personal attention may assure that the business is getting what it pays for, that cash is not being disbursed carelessly, and that there is no theft or fraud involving cash.

As a business grows and becomes more complex, the owner or chief executive cannot give personal attention to each transaction involving the acquisition of goods and services and the processing of cash disbursements. In such situations these activities must be assigned to various employees. The assignment of these responsibilities to others creates a need for systematic and effective procedures for the control of cash expenditures. This is an important function of a well-designed accounting system.

In Chapter 9, the essential features of effective **internal control** were discussed. That chapter emphasized the control of cash receipts. Similar procedures were discussed in respect to cash disbursements: the separation of duties, disbursement of cash by check, petty cash, and the two special journals—the purchases journal and the cash disbursements journal. In larger companies and in computerized accounting systems, the method usually used for maintaining control over cash expenditures is known as the **voucher system.** This system replaces the cash disbursements journal procedures that was explained in Chapter 9, Appendix B.

The voucher system

The voucher system is designed to establish strict control over the incurrence of every legal obligation to make an expenditure and all disbursements of cash. The system requires that a **written authorization,** called a **voucher,** be approved by one or more designated managers at the time each such transaction occurs. An approved voucher is required regardless of whether the transaction involves the purchase of merchandise or services, the acquisition of fixed assets, investments, or the payment of a liability. The system permits checks to be issued only in payment of properly prepared and approved vouchers. Check writing is kept completely separate from the voucher-approval, check-approval, and check-distribution procedures.

The voucher system requires that every obligation be supported by a voucher and that each transaction be recorded when incurred. The incurrence of each obligation is treated as an independent transaction, and each payment of cash is treated as another independent transaction. This sequence of voucher approval, followed by payment by check, is required even in strictly cash-disbursement transactions. To illustrate, the *cash* purchase of merchandise for resale would be recorded under the voucher system as follows:

1. To record the incurrence of an obligation:

Purchases (or Inventory)	1,000	
Vouchers payable		1,000

2. To record payment of the obligation by check (immediately thereafter):

Vouchers payable	1,000	
Cash		1,000

In the voucher system, the account designated **Vouchers Payable** replaces the account entitled Accounts Payable; but "Accounts payable," as the designation on the balance sheet, continues to be used. Entries of the first type are entered in a **voucher register,** and entries of the second type are entered in a **check register.**

The primary objective of the voucher system is to attain continuous control over each step in an expenditure from the incurrence of an obligation to the final disbursement of cash to satisfy the obligation. Thus, every single transaction leading to a cash payment, and the cash payment itself, is systematically reviewed, then subjected to an approval system based on separately designated responsibilities. Appendix B to this chapter discusses and illustrates the *mechanics* of the voucher system.

PART TWO: CONCEPTS OF FUTURE VALUE AND PRESENT VALUE

The measurement and reporting of liabilities, when they are first recorded in the accounts and during the period the debt is outstanding, often involve application of the concepts of future value and present value. These concepts also are used in measuring the effects of long-term investments in bonds, leases, pension plans, and sinking funds. However, most of the applications in accounting involve either the establishment of a fund or the measurement of a liability or a receivable.

1. Establishment of a fund—A company may decide to set aside a certain amount of cash to be used in the future for a specific purpose, such as to pay off a large debt that will mature ten years hence. Funds of this type were reported on the balance sheet shown in Exhibit

3–2 and were discussed on page 63. They are also discussed further in Chapter 12 (page 470).

2. Measurement of a liability or a receivable—Long-term liabilities and receivables usually involve significant amounts of principal and interest. The measurement of these two related amounts often requires the use of future and present value concepts.

The concepts of future and present value focus on the **time value of money,** which is another name for **interest.** The time value of money refers to the fact that a dollar received today is worth more than a dollar to be received one year from today (or at some other later date). A dollar received today can be invested, say at 8 percent, so that it grows to $1.08 in one year. In contrast, a dollar to be received one year from today denies one the opportunity to earn the $0.08 interest for the year. The difference is due to interest, which is the cost of the use of money for a specific period of time, just as rent represents the cost for use of a tangible asset for a period of time. Interest may be specified (i.e., it is explicitly stated), as in the case of an interest-bearing note, or it may be unspecified, as in a noninterest-bearing note (but it is paid nonetheless; i.e., it is present implicitly).

For many years the time value of money was largely overlooked in accounting for some of the transactions cited above. In recent years, several *Opinions* issued by the APB have required the application of present value determinations. Of particular significance was *Opinion No. 21,* issued in August 1971, entitled "Interest on Receivables and Payables." This *Opinion* requires the application of present value determinations to a number of transactions. For example, the *Opinion* states: "In the absence of established exchange prices for the related property, goods, or service or evidence of the market value of the note, the present value of a note that stipulates either no interest or a rate of interest that is clearly unreasonable should be determined by *discounting* all future payments on the notes using an imputed rate of interest. . . ." To illustrate, assume a machine is purchased for $12,000 and the purchaser is given two years in which to make payment. What amount should be debited to the Machine account in order to conform to the cost principle assuming an imputed interest rate of 8 percent is used? Answer: The present value of the debt, which is the **current cash equivalent cost,** $10,288 (see page 427).

BASIC CONCEPTS

Time value of money relates to four different concepts that involve interest calculations:

1. Future amount of $1.
2. Present value of $1.

3. Future amount of an annuity of $1.
4. Present value of an annuity of $1.

Tables, using $1 as the base, provide values for each of these situations for different periods of time (n) and at different rates of interest (i). Extracts from the four tables are shown on pages 424–25. Let's examine each of these concepts.

Future amount of $1

This concept is generally referred to as **compound interest.** The future amount is the amount to which $1 will increase at i interest rate for n periods. The future amount will be the **principal plus interest.**

To illustrate, assume that on January 1, 1977, you deposited $1,000 in a savings account at 6 percent annual interest, compounded each year. How much would you have at the end of the third year; that is, on December 31, 1979? We can calculate the compound amount to be $1,191 as follows:

	Amount at Start of Year	+	*Interest during the Year*	=	*Amount at End of Year*
Year 1	$1,000	+	$1,000 × 0.06 = $60	=	$1,060
Year 2	1,060	+	1,060 × 0.06 = 64	=	1,124
Year 3	1,124	+	1,124 × 0.06 = 67	=	1,191

However, we can avoid the detailed arithmetic by referring to Table 11–1, *"Future amount of $1,"* as shown on page 424. For $i = 6$ percent, $n = 3$, we find the value 1.191; therefore, we can compute the balance at the end of Year 3 as $1,000 × 1.191 = $1,191. The increase of $191 was due to the time value of money; it would be interest revenue to you and interest expense to the savings institution. Assuming a positive interest rate, the future amount of 1 will always be greater than 1. The symbol used for an amount of 1 usually is a. Exhibit 11–1 presents a summary of the concept.

Present value of $1

Present value of $1 is the value now (i.e., the present) of a dollar to be received at some date in the future. It can be said to be the inverse of the future amount of $1 concept. To compute the present value of a sum to be received in the future, the future sum is subjected to **compound discounting** at i interest rate for n periods. In compound discounting, the interest is subtracted rather than added, as in compounding. To illustrate, assume that today is January 1, 1977, and that you will receive $1,000 cash on December 31, 1979—that is, three years from now. Assuming

EXHIBIT 11–1. Time value of money determinations

Table No	*Designation*	*Definition and graphic representation*	*Usual symbol*	*Table formula*
11–1	Future amount of \$1	The future amount (worth or value) of \$1 at the end of n periods at i compound interest rate. This is simply the principal plus compound interest. Graphic representation:	a	$(1+i)^n$

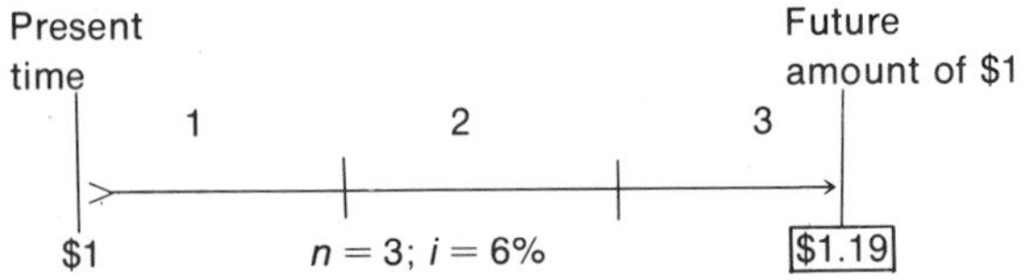

11–2	Present value of \$1	The present value (worth now) of \$1 due n periods hence, discounted at i compound interest rate. This is simply a future amount with compound discount subtracted from it.	p	$\frac{1}{(1+i)^n}$

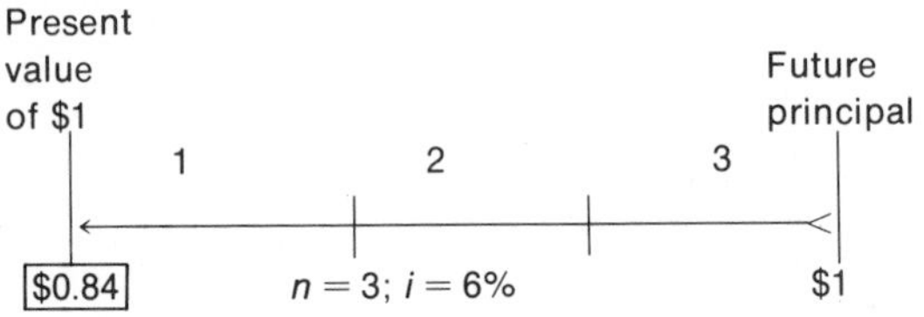

11–3	Future amount of annuity of \$1	The future amount (worth or value) of n periodic contributions (i.e., rents) of \$1 each plus accumulated compound interest at i rate. The first rent is at the end of the current period and the future value is on the date of the last rent.	A	$\frac{(1+i)^n-1}{i}$

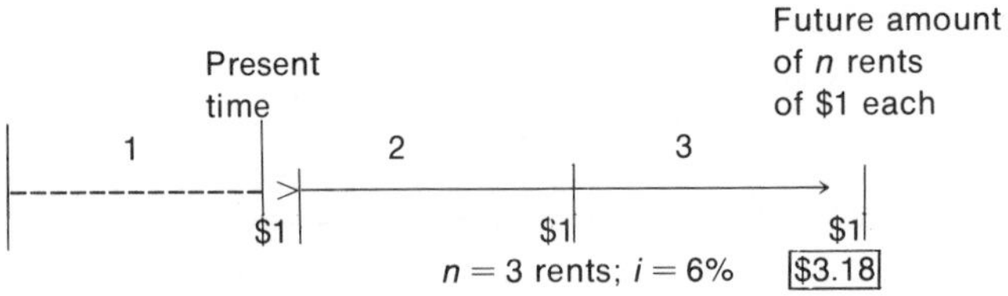

11–4	Present value of annuity of \$1*	The present value (worth now) of n periodic rents of \$1 each to be received (or paid) each period, discounted at i compound discount rate per period. The first rent is at the end of the first period.	P	$\frac{1-\frac{1}{(1+i)^n}}{i}$

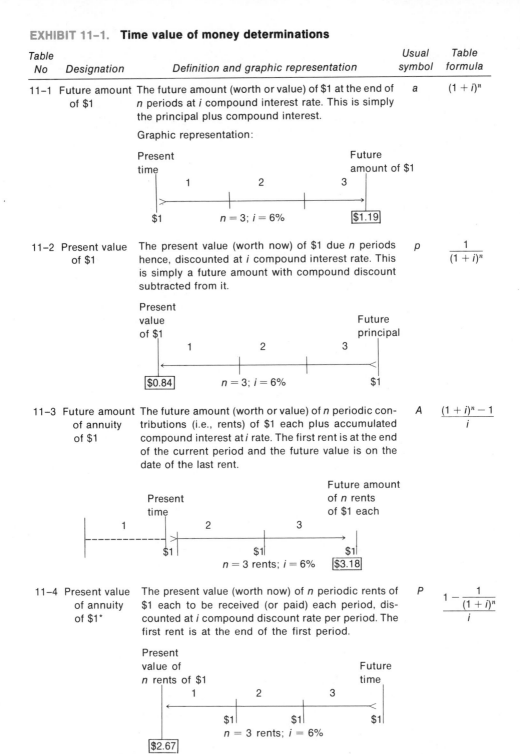

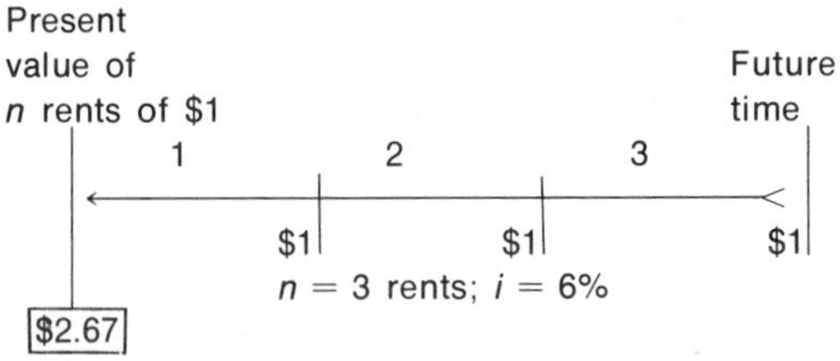

* Observe that these are *ordinary* annuities; that is, they are often called "end-of-the-period" annuities. Thus, for A, the future amount is on the date of the last rent; and for P, the present value is at the beginning of the period of the first rent. Annuities *due* assume the opposite; that is, they are "beginning-of-the-period" annuities. Ordinary annuity values can be converted to annuities due simply by multiplication by $(1+i)$. Annuities due are deferred to the next level of accounting sophistication in intermediate accounting.

an interest rate of 6 percent per year, how much would the $1,000 be worth today; that is, what is its present value (today, on January 1, 1977)? We could set up a discounting computation, year by year, that would be the inverse to that shown on page 421. However, to facilitate the computation, we can refer to a present value of $1 table, like the one shown on page 424, Table 11–2. For $i = 6$ percent, $n = 3$, we find the present value of $1 to be 0.8396. The $1,000, to be received three years hence, has a present value of $\$1,000 \times 0.8396 = \$839.60$. The difference (i.e., the discount) of $160.40 is due to the time value of money; it is the interest. The symbol commonly used for present value of $1 is p. The concept of the present value of $1 is summarized in Exhibit 11–1.

Future amount of an annuity of $1

Basically, the future amount of an annuity of $1 is the same as the future amount of $1, except for the addition of the concept of an **annuity.** The word "annuity" refers to a series of payments characterized by (1) an *equal amount each period* (for two or more future periods), (2) equal length of the periods and (3) an equal interest rate each period. In contrast to an amount of $1, which involves a single contribution at the start, an annuity involves an equal contribution each period. A future amount of an annuity of $1 involves *compound interest* on *each* contribution. To illustrate, assume that you decide to put $1,000 cash in a savings account each year for three years at 6 percent interest per year (i.e., a total of $3,000). The first $1,000 contribution is to be made on December 31, 1977; the second one on December 31, 1978; and the third and last one on December 31, 1979. How much would you have in the savings account immediately after the third (and last) deposit on December 31, 1979? In this situation, the first $1,000 contribution would draw compound interest for two years (1977 and 1978); the second deposit would draw interest for one year (1978); and the third deposit would draw no interest (since we desire to know the amount in the savings account *immediately* after the third deposit). We could laboriously compute the interest for each contribution to derive the future value of this annuity. However, we can refer to Table 11–3 (page 425), "*Future amount of annuity of $1.*" For $i = 6$ percent, $n = 3$, where we find the value 3.1836.[11] This is the future amount of $1 at $i = 6$ percent, $n = 3$. Therefore, the total of your three contributions (of $1,000 each) would have increased to $\$1,000 \times 3.1836 = \$3,183.60$ on December 31, 1979. The increase of $183.60 was due to the time value of money; it is interest

[11] The equal amounts for each period implicit in all annuities often are referred to in the literature as "rents."

TABLE 11–1
Future amount of $1, $a = (1 + i)^n$

Periods	*2%*	*3%*	*4%*	*5%*	*6%*	*7%*	*8%*	*9%*
0	1.	1.	1.	1.	1.	1.	1.	1.
1	1.02	1.03	1.04	1.05	1.06	1.07	1.08	1.09
2	1.0404	1.0609	1.0816	1.1025	1.1236	1.1449	1.1664	1.1881
3	1.0612	1.0927	1.1249	1.1576	1.1910	1.2250	1.2597	1.2950
4	1.0824	1.1255	1.1699	1.2155	1.2625	1.3108	1.3605	1.4116
5	1.1041	1.1593	1.2167	1.2763	1.3382	1.4026	1.4693	1.5386
6	1.1262	1.1941	1.2653	1.3401	1.4185	1.5007	1.5869	1.6771
7	1.1487	1.2299	1.3159	1.4071	1.5036	1.6058	1.7138	1.8280
8	1.1717	1.2668	1.3686	1.4775	1.5938	1.7182	1.8509	1.9926
9	1.1951	1.3048	1.4233	1.5513	1.6895	1.8385	1.9990	2.1719
10	1.2190	1.3439	1.4802	1.6289	1.7908	1.9672	2.1589	2.3673

TABLE 11–2
Present value of $1, $p = \frac{1}{(1 + i)^n}$

Periods	*2%*	*3%*	*4%*	*5%*	*6%*	*7%*	*8%*	*9%*
1	0.9804	0.9709	0.9615	0.9524	0.9434	0.9346	0.9259	0.9174
2	0.9612	0.9426	0.9246	0.9070	0.8900	0.8734	0.8573	0.8417
3	0.9423	0.9151	0.8890	0.8638	0.8396	0.8163	0.7938	0.7722
4	0.9238	0.8885	0.8548	0.8227	0.7921	0.7629	0.7350	0.7084
5	0.9057	0.8626	0.8219	0.7835	0.7473	0.7130	0.6806	0.6499
6	0.8880	0.8375	0.7903	0.7462	0.7050	0.6663	0.6302	0.5963
7	0.8706	0.8131	0.7599	0.7107	0.6651	0.6227	0.5835	0.5470
8	0.8535	0.7894	0.7307	0.6768	0.6274	0.5820	0.5403	0.5019
9	0.8368	0.7664	0.7026	0.6446	0.5919	0.5439	0.5002	0.4604
10	0.8203	0.7441	0.6756	0.6139	0.5584	0.5083	0.4632	0.4224

revenue to you on the $3,000. The symbol commonly used for the future amount of an annuity of $1 is *A*. This concept is summarized in Exhibit 11–1 (page 422).

Present value of annuity of $1

The present value of an annuity of $1 is the value now of a series of *equal amounts* (i.e., rents) to be received each period for some specified number of periods in the future. It can be said to be the inverse of the future amount of an annuity of $1 explained immediately above. It involves **compound discounting** of each of the equal periodic amounts.

To illustrate, assume now is January 1, 1977, and that you are to re-

TABLE 11–3

Future amount of annuity of $1 (ordinary), $A = \dfrac{(1+i)^n - 1}{i}$

*Period rents**	*2%*	*3%*	*4%*	*5%*	*6%*	*7%*	*8%*	*9%*
1	1.	1.	1.	1.	1.	1.	1.	1.
2	2.02	2.03	2.04	2.05	2.06	2.07	2.08	2.09
3	3.06	3.0909	3.1216	3.1525	3.1836	3.2149	3.2464	3.2781
4	4.1217	4.1836	4.2465	4.3101	4.3746	4.4399	4.5061	4.5731
5	5.2040	5.3091	5.4163	5.5256	5.6371	5.7507	5.8666	5.9847
6	6.3081	6.4684	6.6330	6.8019	6.9753	7.1533	7.3359	7.5233
7	7.4343	7.6625	7.8983	8.1420	8.3938	8.6540	8.9228	9.2004
8	8.5830	8.8923	9.2142	9.5491	9.8975	10.2598	10.6366	11.0285
9	9.7546	10.1591	10.5828	11.0266	11.4913	11.9780	12.4876	13.0210
10	10.9497	11.4639	12.0061	12.5779	13.1808	13.8164	14.4866	15.1929

* There is one rent each period.

TABLE 11–4

Present value of annuity of $1 (ordinary), $P = \dfrac{1 - \dfrac{1}{(1+i)^n}}{i}$

*Period rents**	*2%*	*3%*	*4%*	*5%*	*6%*	*7%*	*8%*	*9%*
1	0.9804	0.9709	0.9615	0.9524	0.9434	0.9346	0.9259	0.9174
2	1.9416	1.9135	1.8861	1.8594	1.8334	1.8080	1.7833	1.7591
3	2.8839	2.8286	2.7751	2.7232	2.6730	2.6243	2.5771	2.5313
4	3.8077	3.7171	3.6299	3.5460	3.4651	3.3872	3.3121	3.2397
5	4.7135	4.5797	4.4518	4.3295	4.2124	4.1002	3.9927	3.8897
6	5.6014	5.4172	5.2421	5.0757	4.9173	4.7665	4.6229	4.4859
7	6.4720	6.2303	6.0021	5.7864	5.5824	5.3893	5.2064	5.0330
8	7.3255	7.0197	6.7327	6.4632	6.2098	5.9713	5.7466	5.5348
9	8.1622	7.7861	7.4353	7.1078	6.8017	6.5152	6.2469	5.9952
10	8.9826	8.5302	8.1109	7.7217	7.3601	7.0236	6.7101	6.4177

* There is one rent each period.

ceive $1,000 in cash on each December 31, 1977, 1978, and 1979. How much would these three $1,000 future amounts be worth now, on January 1, 1977 (i.e., the present value), assuming an interest rate of 6 percent per year? We could laboriously calculate the discounting on each rent; however, we can compute the present value readily by referring to Table 11–4, *"Present value of annuity of $1."* For $i = 6$ percent, $n = 3$ rents, we find the value 2.673. This is the present value of an **annuity** of $1 at $i = 6$ percent, and three equal periodic rents. Therefore, your three

$1,000 amounts to be received in the future have a present value of $1,000 × 2.673 = $2,673. The difference (i.e., the discount) of $327 was due to the interest factor. The symbol commonly used for the present value of an annuity of $1 is *P*. This concept is summarized in Exhibit 11–1 (page 422).

SOME MEASUREMENT AND ACCOUNTING APPLICATIONS

We have said that there are numerous transactions where the concepts of future and present value are used for accounting measurements. Below are cited four different situations where they must be used.

Case A—Company A, on January 1, 1977, set aside $150,000 cash in a special building fund (an asset) to be used at the end of five years to construct a new building. The fund is expected to earn 6 percent interest per year, which will be added to the fund balance. On the date of deposit the company made the following entry.

January 1, 1977:

Special building fund	150,000	
Cash		150,000

Required:

1. What will be the balance of the fund at the end of the fifth year?
   Answer: This situation involves the future amount of $1 concept.

   Principal × Table 11–1 value ($i = 6\%$; $n = 5$) = Future Amount
   $150,000 × 1.3382 = $200,730

2. How much interest revenue was earned on the fund during the five years?
   Answer:

   $200,730 − $150,000 = $50,730

3. What entry would be made on December 31, 1977, to record the interest revenue for the first year?
   Answer: Interest for one year on the fund balance is added to the fund and recorded as follows:

   December 31, 1977:

Special building fund	9,000	
Interest revenue ($150,000 × 0.06)		9,000

4. What entry would be made on December 31, 1978, to record interest revenue for the second year?
Answer:

December 31, 1978:

Special building fund	9,540	
Interest revenue [($150,000 + $9,000) × 0.06]		9,540

Case B—On January 1, 1977, Company B purchased a new machine to be used in the plant at a list price of $12,000, which was payable at the end of two years. The going rate of interest was 8 percent.

Required:

1. The company accountant is preparing the following entry:

Machinery	$?	
Accounts payable (special)		$?

What amount should be used in this entry?
Answer: This situation requires application of the present value of $1 concept. Under the cost principle, the cost of the machine is the current cash equivalent price, which is the present value of the future payment. The present value of the $12,000 is computed as follows:

Future Amount × Table 11–2 ($i = 8\%$; $n = 2$) = Present Value
$12,000 × 0.8573 = $10,288

Therefore, the entry would be as follows:

January 1, 1977:

Machinery	10,288	
Accounts payable (special)		10,288

2. What entry would be made at the end of the first and second years for interest expense on the accounts payable?
Answer: Interest expense for each year on the amount in the Accounts Payable account would be recorded by means of an adjusting entry, as follows:

December 31, 1977:

Interest expense	823	
Accounts payable (special)		823

$10,288 × 0.08 = $823.

December 31, 1978:

Interest expense	889	
Accounts payable (special)		889

(\$10,288 + \$823) × 0.08 = \$889.

The effect of these two entries is to increase the balance in Accounts Payable to the new **current cash equivalent amount.** By maturity date the balance will have been increased to the maturity amounts, \$12,000, which is the current cash equivalent amount at due date.[12]

3. What entry would be made to record the payment on due date?

Answer: At this date the amount to be paid as the balance of Accounts Payable is the current cash equivalent amount, which is the same as the maturity amount on the due date; that is, \$10,288 + \$823 + \$889 = \$12,000.

The entry would be:

December 31, 1978:

Accounts payable (special)	12,000	
Cash		12,000

Case C—Company C decided to make five annual deposits of \$20,000 each with a financial institution to create a debt retirement fund. The deposits will be made on each December 31, starting on December 31, 1977. The fifth and last deposit will be made on December 31, 1981. The financial institution will pay 5 percent annual compound interest, which will be added to the fund at the end of each year.

[12] These entries could also be made as follows with the same ultimate result:

January 1, 1977:

Machinery	10,288	
Discount on accounts payable	1,712	
Accounts payable (special)		12,000

December 31, 1977:

Interest expense	823	
Discount on accounts payable		823

At the end of 1977, the liability would be reported at net as \$12,000 − \$823 = \$11,177.

December 31, 1978:

Interest expense	889	
Discount on accounts payable		889

Required:

1. What entry should be made to record the first deposit?
   Answer:

   December 31, 1977:

Debt retirement fund	20,000	
Cash		20,000

2. What will be the balance in the fund immediately after the fifth and last deposit (i.e., on December 31, 1981)?
   Answer: This situation requires application of future amount of an annuity of $1.

   Rent × Table 11–3 ($i = 5\%$; $n = 5$) = Future Amount
   $20,000 × 5.5256 = $110,512

3. What entries would be made at the end of 1978?
   Answer:
   a. Interest for one year on the fund balance would be added to the fund and recorded as follows:

   December 31, 1978:

Debt retirement fund	1,000	
Interest revenue ($20,000 × 0.05)		1,000

   b. The second deposit would be recorded as follows:

   December 31, 1978:

Debt retirement fund	20,000	
Cash		20,000

4. What would be the amount of interest revenue to be recorded at the end of the 1979?
   Answer: Interest would be computed on the increased fund balance as follows:

   ($20,000 + $1,000 + $20,000) × 0.05 = $2,050

Case D—On January 1, 1977, Company D purchased a new machine at a cash price of $30,000. Since the company was short of cash, arrangements were made to execute a $30,000 note payable to be paid off in three equal yearly installments. Each installment would include principal plus interest on the unpaid balance at 7 percent per year. The equal annual installments are due on December 31, 1977, 1978, and 1979. The acquisition was recorded as follows:

January 1, 1977:

Machinery	30,000	
Note payable, 7 percent		30,000

Required:

1. What would be the amount of each annual installment?
   Answer: The $30,000 is the amount of the debt today; hence, it is the present value of the three future installment payments required (i.e., the rents). Therefore, $n = 3$, $i = 7$ percent, and the present value is $30,000. To compute the equal rents required, the present value of an annuity of $1 must be used as follows:

   Rent × Table 11–4 Value ($i = 7\%$; $n = 3$) = Present Value
   Substituting:
   Rent × 2.6243 = $30,000
   Rent = $30,000 ÷ 2.6243
   = $11,432 (amount of each annual payment)

2. What was the amount of interest expense in dollars?
   Answer:

   ($11,432 × 3) − $30,000 = $4,296

3. What entry would be made at the end of each year to record the payment of this $30,000 note payable?
   Answer:
   a. To record the first installment payment on the note:

   December 31, 1977:

Note payable	9,332	
Interest expense ($30,000 × 0.07)	2,100	
Cash (computed above)		11,432

   b. To record the second installment on the note:

   December 31, 1978:

Note payable	9,985	
Interest expense ($30,000 − $9,332) × 0.07	1,447	
Cash (computed above)		11,432

   c. To record final installment on the note:

   December 31, 1979:

Note payable	10,683	
Interest expense	749	
Cash (computed above)		11,432

   Interest: ($30,000 − $9,332 − $9,985) × 0.07 = $749 (rounded).

4. Prepare a debt payment schedule that shows the effect on interest expense and the unpaid amount of principal each period.

Debt payment schedule

Date	Payment cash (cr.)	Interest expense (dr.)	Reduction of principal (dr.)	Unpaid principal
1/1/77				30,000
12/31/77	11,432[a]	2,100[b]	9,332[c]	20,668[d]
12/31/78	11,432	1,447	9,985	10,683
12/31/79	11,432	749	10,683	-0-
Totals	34,296	4,296	30,000	

Sequential computations:
[a] Annual payment: Computed above.
[b] Interest expense: Unpaid principal $30,000 × 0.07 = $2,100.
[c] Reduction of principal: Annual payment $11,432 − Interest $2,100 = $9,332.
[d] New unpaid balance: Prior Balance $30,000 − Reduction $9,332 = $20,668.

Although there are many other applications of the concept of the time value of money in the recording and reporting processes, the above examples are typical. The application of these concepts to **capital budgeting** is deferred to *Fundamentals of Management Accounting.*

SUMMARY

This chapter focused on accounting for three types of obligations: current, long-term, and contingent liabilities. The treatment of bonds payable has been deferred to Chapter 12. Liabilities are obligations of either a known or estimated amount. Detailed information concerning the liabilities of an entity is especially important to decision makers, whether internal or external to the enterprise. Identification by the decision maker of the kinds and amounts of liabilities would be practically impossible without reliable financial statements. The existence and amount of liabilities sometimes are easy to conceal from outsiders. The accounting model and the verification by the independent CPA constitute the best assurance that liabilities are fully disclosed.

Current liabilities are those obligations that will be paid from the resources reported on the balance sheet as current assets. Thus, they are short-term obligations that will be paid within the coming year or within the normal operating cycle of the business, whichever is the longer. All other liabilities (except contingent liabilities) are reported as long-term liabilities. A contingent liability is not a liability, it is a potential claim due to some event or transaction that has already happened, but whether it will materialize as a legal liability is not certain and depends upon some future event or transaction. Contingent liabilities must be fully disclosed on the financial statements. Disclosure usually is by note to the financial statements.

IMPORTANT TERMS

Current cash equivalent amount
Current liabilities
Working capital
Long-term liabilities
Deferred taxes
Lease liabilities
Operating lease
Financing lease
Contingent liabilities
Voucher system
Future amount of $1
Present value of $1
Annuity
Future amount of an annuity of $1
Present value of an annuity of $1

APPENDIX A

Payroll accounting

Accurate and detailed payroll accounting, although it does not involve any new accounting concepts or principles, is particularly important in most enterprises because of the necessity to pay the employees for their services promptly and correctly. In addition, detailed payroll accounting is necessary in order to fulfill legal requirements under federal and state laws with respect to withholding taxes, social security taxes, and unemployment taxes. Further, the management of an enterprise, for planning and control purposes, must have detailed and accurate cost figures for wages and salaries. Frequently, this is the largest category of expense in an enterprise. As a consequence of these requirements, payroll accounting is characterized by a large amount of detailed recordkeeping. Payroll accounting is computerized, including the production of individual checks for the employees, in many businesses.

Payroll accounting requires that a detailed payroll record be maintained for each employee. The payroll record varies with the circumstances in each company; however, it must include for each individual such data as social security number, number of dependents (for income tax withholding), rate of pay, a time record (for hourly paid employees), deductions from gross pay, and so on.

To understand payroll accounting, a distinction must be made between (1) payroll deductions and taxes that must be paid by the *employee* (i.e., deducted from the employee's gross earnings); and (2) payroll taxes that must be paid by the *employer*. Both types of payroll items must be transmitted to the governmental unit or other party to whom the amount is owed. Payroll taxes and deductions apply only in situations where there is an employer-employee relationship. Independent contractors that are not under the direct supervision of the client, such as outside lawyers, independent accountants, and building contractors, are not employees; hence, amounts paid to them are not subject to payroll taxes and related deductions.

An employee generally receives take-home pay that is much less than the gross earnings for the period. This is due to two types of payroll deductions:

1. Deductions for taxes that must be paid by the employee as required by state and federal laws.
2. Deductions authorized by the employee for special purposes.

Deductions for taxes paid by employees

There are two categories of taxes that the employee must pay and thus are deducted from the employee's gross earnings; they are income taxes and social security taxes. The employer must remit the amount deducted to the appropriate government agency.

Employee income taxes. Practically every employee must submit a federal income tax return annually. Wages and salaries earned during the year must be included on the tax return as income. For many years, federal laws have required the employer to deduct an appropriate amount of income taxes each period from the gross earnings of each employee. The amount of the deduction for income taxes is determined from a tax table (provided by the Internal Revenue Service) based upon the earnings and number of exemptions (for self and dependents) of the employee. The amount of income taxes withheld from the employee's wages is recorded by the employer as a current liability between the date of deduction and the date the amount withheld is remitted to the government. The total amount withheld must be paid to the Internal Revenue Service within a specified short period of time. An especially designed form to accompany each remittance is provided by the Internal Revenue Service to identify the employees and the amounts withheld. Some states also require withholding for state income taxes.

Employee F.I.C.A. taxes. The social security taxes paid by the employee generally are called F.I.C.A. taxes since they are a result of the Federal Insurance Contributions Act. That act provides that persons who are *qualified* under the provisions of the act, upon reaching age 62, may retire and receive the minimum monthly benefits for life, plus certain medical benefits after age 65.[13] Retirement at age 65 provides maximum pension

[13] In order to qualify under the act for retirement and medical benefits, the employee must be in "covered" employment for a specified period of time. Covered employment requires payroll deductions for these taxes. The amount of benefits and the F.I.C.A. tax deductions are frequently changed by the U.S. Congress.

benefits. It also provides benefits for the family of a deceased person who was qualified.

The funds required by the government to provide the benefits under the Social Security Act are obtained by payroll taxes, which are imposed in equal amounts on **both the employee and the employer.** Effective January 1, 1977, the F.I.C.A. rate was 5.85 percent on the first $16,500 paid to each employee during the year. Since F.I.C.A. rates and the wage maximum change frequently, for convenience in calculations we will use a flat rate of 6 percent for illustrative and problem purposes.

At the end of each year, the employer is required to provide each employee with a **Withholding Statement, Form W-2,** which reports to the employee (1) gross earnings for the year, (2) earnings subject to F.I.C.A. taxes, (3) income taxes withheld, and (4) F.I.C.A. taxes withheld. A copy of this form also is sent to the Internal Revenue Service.

Employee deductions for special purposes

Many companies encourage programs of voluntary deductions from earnings by employees. Typical of these voluntary deductions are savings funds, insurance premiums, charitable contributions, supplementary retirement programs, repayment of loans, stock purchase plans, and the purchase of U.S. savings bonds. The employer agrees to make these deductions, subject to authorization as a matter of convenience to the employees. The amounts deducted are remitted in a short time to the organization or agency in whose honor the deduction was authorized. Another type of deduction, not always voluntary, is for union dues as specified in the union contract. The employer is required to remit the deductions, along with the employee list, to the union each month.

Accounting for employee deductions

The employer must maintain detailed and accurate records of all deductions from the earnings of each employee. From the employer's viewpoint, the employee deductions are *current liabilities* from the date of the payroll deduction to the date of remittance to the government or other entity.

To illustrate the basic accounting entry to be made for the payment of a payroll and the accrual of liabilities for the *employee* deductions, assume that X Company accumulated the following data in the detailed payroll records for the month of January 1977:

Gross earnings:	
Salaries	$50,000
Wages (hourly paid employees)	30,000
Income taxes withheld	16,000

Union dues withheld	300
F.I.C.A. taxes (rate 6%; assume no maximums were exceeded in January)	4,800

The entry to record the payroll and employee deductions would be:

January 31, 1977:

Salaries expense	50,000	
Wages expense	30,000	
Liability for income taxes withheld—employees		16,000
Liability for union dues withheld—employees		300
F.I.C.A. taxes payable—employees ($80,000 × 6%)		4,800
Cash		58,900
Payroll for January, including employee payroll deductions.		

Payroll taxes paid by employer

Remember that the payroll taxes illustrated above are those levied on the *employees*. The employer simply serves as a tax collector with respect to them. In addition, specific payroll taxes are also levied on the employer. These taxes represent operating expenses for the business. The liability is extinguished when the taxes are remitted to the designated agencies of the state and federal governments. Generally, three different payroll taxes must be paid by the employer—F.I.C.A. taxes, F.U.T.A. taxes, and state unemployment compensation taxes.

Employer F.I.C.A. taxes. The employer must pay an additional F.I.C.A. tax equal to the amount withheld from the employee's wages. Thus, the F.I.C.A. tax paid by the employer is at the same rate as the F.I.C.A. employee tax and on the same amount of wages (i.e., 5.85 percent on the first $16,500 of gross earnings of each employee).

Employer F.U.T.A. taxes. The Social Security Act provides for another program known as unemployment compensation. This program derives its monetary support under the provisions of the Federal Unemployment Tax Act. The F.U.T.A., or unemployment tax, is paid *only by the employer.* Currently, the federal tax amounts to 0.5 percent of the first $4,200 in wages paid to each employee during the year.

State unemployment compensation taxes. The unemployment program specified in the Federal Unemployment Tax Act is a joint federal-state program; consequently, each state participates in the program by sharing both in providing benefits and in funding the program through payroll taxes. Although state laws vary as to both benefits and tax rates, most states have either a 2.5 percent or 3.0 percent rate on the first $4,200 wages paid during the year. Most states have a merit-rating plan that provides for a reduction in the tax rate for employers that establish a record of stable employment over a period of time.

Accounting for employer payroll taxes

Payroll taxes paid by the employer are debited to an expense account and credited to a current liability when the payroll is paid each period. To illustrate, the January entry for the employer's payroll taxes for X Company (data shown on page 434), assuming a 3 percent state unemployment tax rate, would be as follows:[14]

Payroll tax expense	7,600	
F.I.C.A. taxes payable—employer ($80,000 × 6%)		4,800
F.U.T.A. taxes payable—employer ($80,000 × 0.5%)		400
State unemployment taxes payable—employer ($80,000 × 3%)		2,400
To record employer payroll taxes.		

When the taxes are remitted to the government, the liability accounts are debited and Cash is credited.

APPENDIX B

The voucher system

The voucher system is designed to attain strict control over cash expenditures from the point of incurrence of an obligation (by means of purchase of merchandise for resale, services, fixed assets, investments, etc.) through the payment of cash to satisfy it. The incurrence of an obligation and the payment of cash to satisfy it are viewed as separate and independent transactions. When a voucher system is used, an account called *Vouchers Payable* replaces the account *Accounts Payable* in the ledger. Similarly, a *voucher register* and a *check register* replace the purchases journal and the cash disbursements journal, respectively (see Chapter 9, Appendix B).

The basic document in the voucher system is the *voucher*. A voucher is a form, prepared and used within the business, on which a transaction is (1) summarized and adequately supported, (2) approved, (3) analyzed for recording, and (4) approved for payment. Thus, it is a comprehensive document that follows a transaction from the transaction date to the final cash payment. A voucher is prepared for *each* transaction involving the payment of cash, such as the purchase of assets, the use of services, the incurrence of expenses, and the payment of debt. The form of a voucher varies between companies since it should be designed to meet the internal requirements of the individual company. For control purposes, all

[14] In this and the preceding entries, it was assumed that none of the employees received remuneration above the $16,500 and $4,200 maximums for the year.

voucher forms and checks should be numbered consecutively when printed.

Each voucher, after approval, is entered in the voucher register in order of number. The voucher register is designed to record the basic information from the voucher, including the accounts to be debited and credited.

To illustrate the mechanics of a voucher system, we will follow a purchase of merchandise for resale through the system from the order date to the final cash payment date. Each step in the sequence may be illustrated and explained as follows:

1977

Jan. 10 Merchandise ordered from Box Supply Company, cost $1,000; terms, n/15. A purchase order is prepared and approved.

12 Merchandise ordered from Box Supply Company on January 10 is received; invoice is received. Voucher No. 47 is drawn and the purchase order is attached (see Exhibit 11–2). Goods are checked for quantity and condition; a receiving report is prepared.

12 Receiving report and invoice sent to accounting department; they are attached to the voucher. Voucher is approved, and then recorded in the voucher register (see Exhibit 11–3).

26 Voucher is approved by designated manager for payment on January 27 and sent to disbursements department; Check No. 90 is prepared.

27 Check No. 90 is signed by treasurer and mailed.

28 The accounting department enters Check No. 90 in the check register (see Exhibit 11–4). Enters payment notation in the voucher register (see Exhibit 11–3). Files the voucher in the *Vouchers Paid File*.

For illustrative purposes, two more transactions are recorded in the voucher register, one of which remains unpaid.

At the end of the month the voucher register and the check register are totaled and the equality of the debits and credits are verified. Posting to the ledger from these two special journals follows the same pattern explained in Chapter 9, Appendix B, for the special journals illustrated there. Posting involves two separate phases:

1. Current posting—During the period, and perhaps daily, the details in the Voucher Register columns are posted to (*a*) the selling expense subsidiary ledger (under the selling expense control); (*b*) the administrative expense subsidiary ledger (under the administrative expense control); and (*c*) other accounts to be debited. No current posting is required from the check register as illustrated.

EXHIBIT 11–2
Voucher

MAY DEPARTMENT STORE
Boston, Mass.

Voucher No. 47

Date of Voucher Jan. 12, 1977 Date Paid Jan 27, 1977
Pay to: Box Supply Company Check No. 90
1119 Brown Street
Philadelphia, Pa.

For the following goods or services: (attach all supporting documents)

Date Incurred	Terms	Explanation of Details	Amount
Jan. 12	n/15	Merchandise, Dept. 8	1,000.00
		Invoice No. 17-8132	
		Receiving Report No. 123	
		Net payable	1,000.00

Approvals:

Voucher Approval: Date 1/12/77 Signature R. C. Roe

Payment Approval: Date 1/26/77 Signature A.B. Doe

Accounting Analysis:

Account Debited:	Acct. No.	Amount
Purchases	91	1,000.00
Office Supplies		
Sales Salaries		
Fixed Assets		
Etc.		
Total, Voucher Payable Credit	41	1,000.00

EXHIBIT 11–3
Voucher register

Date	Vou. No.	Payee	Payment		Vouchers Payable (Credit)	Purchases (Debit)	Selling Expense Control			Adm. Expense Control			Other Accounts to Be Debited			
			Date	Check No.			Account Code	Folio	Amount (Debit)	Account Code	Folio	Amount (Debit)	Account Name	Folio No.	P	Amount (Debited)
Jan 12	47	Box Supply Co.	1/27	90	1,000	1,000										
Jan 14	48	John Day-Salary	1/15	89	600		64	✓	600							
Jan 31	98	Capital Nat'l			2,160								Notes payable	44	✓	2,000.00
		Bank-Note											Interests expense	82	✓	160.00
		Totals			27,605.00	14,875.00			7,410.00			3,160.00				2,160.00
		Posting notations			(41)	(91)			(60)			(70)				(✓)

EXHIBIT 11–4
Check register

Date		Payee	Voucher No. Paid	Check No.	Vouchers Payable (Debit)*	Cash (Credit)*
Jan	15	John Day	48	89	600	600
	27	Box Supply Co.	47	90	1,000	1,000
	31	Totals			18,751.00	18,751.00
		Posting notation			(41)	(11)

* These two columns could be combined.

2. Monthly posting—The totals from the voucher register, except for the "Other Accounts to Be Debited" are posted at the end of each month. The account number to which each total is posted is entered below the amount. The column for "Other Accounts" was posted individually; hence, the total should not be posted. The totals from the check register are posted to the accounts at the end of each month as indicated by the account numbers entered below the total.

The balance in the ledger account Vouchers Payable is reported on the balance sheet as a liability and on the financial statement is designated as Accounts Payable. The amount should be appropriately classified between current and long-term liabilities.

The Vouchers Payable accounts is a control account, the balance of which represents all of the *unpaid* vouchers at any given time. The total of all vouchers in the *Unpaid Vouchers File* must agree with the balance of the Vouchers Payable account; therefore, the Vouchers Payable account replaces the Accounts Payable control account in the ledger (see Chapter 7, Appendix A).

In studying the mechanics of the voucher system, as illustrated above, you should not overlook its most important aspect—the high degree of control attained through formalization of the sequence of acquiring fixed assets, services, and merchandise, and in making the cash payments. The control feature rests upon (1) clear-cut separation and designation of specific approval responsibilities; (2) a prescribed routine for carrying out these responsibilities; and (3) accounting for the results.

Although a manual approach was illustrated, we emphasize again that these routines are easily adapted to the computer. The computer program is designed to accomplish the same steps and procedures illustrated above. Most companies of any size have computerized the voucher system in order to attain a high degree of control over expenditures and to accelerate the processing of a large volume of transactions, including cash disbursements.

QUESTIONS FOR DISCUSSION

1. Define a liability and distinguish between a current liability and a long-term liability.
2. How can external parties be informed in respect to liabilities of an enterprise? Explain.
3. Liabilities are measured and reported at their current cash equivalent amount. Explain.
4. A liability is a known obligation of either a definite or estimated amount. Explain.
5. What is working capital?
6. What is the current ratio? What is another name for the current ratio? How is it related to the classification of liabilities?
7. What is an accrued liability? What kind of an entry generally reflects an accrued liability?
8. What is a deferred revenue? Why is it a liability?
9. Define a note payable and distinguish between a secured and unsecured note payable.
10. Distinguish between an interest-bearing note and a noninterest-bearing note.
11. Define deferred income taxes. Explain why deferred income taxes are said to reverse, or turn around, in subsequent periods.
12. What is a lease liability?
13. What is meant by a financing lease?
14. What is meant by "off balance sheet financing" in respect to long-term leases?
15. What is a contingent liability? How is a contingent liability reported?
16. Briefly explain the primary purpose of a voucher system.
17. When a voucher system is used, the account Vouchers Payable replaces Accounts Payable. Explain.
18. Briefly explain what is meant by the time value of money.
19. Explain the basic difference between present value and future value.
20. What is an annuity?

EXERCISES

PART ONE: EXERCISES 11–1 TO 11–9

E11–1. Anderson Company sells a wide range of goods through two retail stores that are operated in two adjoining cities. Most purchases of goods for resale are on invoices with credit terms of 2/10, n/30. Occasionally, a short-term note payable is executed to obtain cash for current use. The following transactions were selected from those occurring during 1977:

1. On January 10, 1977, purchased merchandise on credit, $14,000; terms, 2/10, n/30. Record at net; the company uses the periodic inventory system.
2. On March 1, 1977, borrowed $40,000 cash from City Bank and gave an interest-bearing note payable; face value, $40,000; due at the end of six months, with an annual interest rate of 9 percent payable at maturity.

Required:

a. Give the entry for each of the above transactions. Record purchases and accounts payable at net.
b. Give the entry assuming the account payable of January 10, 1977, was paid within the discount period.
c. Give the entry assuming the account payable of January 10, 1977, was paid after the discount period.
d. Give the entry for the payment of the note payable plus interest on the maturity date.

E11–2. During 1977, the two transactions given below were completed by Best Company. The annual accounting period ends December 31.

1. Wages paid and recorded during 1977 amounted to $50,000; however, at the end of December 1977, there were two days' wages unpaid and unrecorded because the weekly payroll will not be paid until January 6, 1978. Wages for the two days amounted to $2,000.
2. On December 10, 1977, Best Company collected rent revenue amounting to $600 on some office space that it rented to another party. The rent collected was for the month from December 10, 1977, to January 10, 1978, and was credited to Rent Revenue.

Required:

a. Give (1) the adjusting entry required on December 31, 1977, and (2) the January 6, 1978, entry for payment of any unpaid wages from December 1977.
b. Give (1) the entry for the collection of rent on December 10, 1977, and (2) the adjusting entry on December 31, 1977 (compute rent to even ten days).
c. Show how any liabilities related to the above transactions should be reported on the balance sheet at December 31, 1977.

E11–3. On November 1, 1977, Super Auto Parts Company borrowed $18,000 cash from the City Bank for working capital purposes and gave an interest-bearing note with a face amount of $18,000. The note was due in six months, and the interest rate was 9 percent per annum payable at maturity.

Required:

a. Give the entry to record the note on November 1.
b. Give the adjusting entry that would be required at the end of the annual accounting period, December 31, 1977.
c. Give a reversing entry, if you deem one desirable, on January 1, 1978.
d. Give the entry to record payment of the note and interest on the maturity date, April 30, 1978, assuming: Case A, a reversing entry was made, and Case B, no reversing entry was made.

E11–4. On November 1, 1977, Ace Auto Parts Company borrowed cash from the City Bank for working capital purposes and gave a noninterest-bearing note payable. The note was due in six months, and the face amount was $10,000. The going rate of interest was 9 percent per year. Cash received was $9,550.

Required:

a. Give the entry to record the note on November 1.
b. Give the adjusting entry that would be required at the end of the annual accounting period, December 31, 1977.
c. Show how the note should be reported on the December 31, 1977, balance sheet.
d. Give a reversing entry, if you deem one desirable, on January 1, 1978.
e. Give the entry to record payment of the note at maturity on April 30, 1978.
f. Compute the true or effective rate of interest. If it is not 9 percent per annum, explain why.

E11–5. Assume you needed to borrow exactly $1,800 cash on a one-year note payable. The City Bank charges 10 percent interest per annum on such loans. You are to respond to the following questions (show computations):

Required:

a. What would be the face amount of the note, assuming the bank agreed to accept an interest-bearing note?
b. What would be the face amount of the note, assuming the bank insisted on a noninterest-bearing note? Assume interest is Case A, based on the face amount of the note; and Case B, based on the cash received.
c. What would be the journal entry to record the note in (*a*)? In (*b*), Case A.
d. What would be the journal entry at date of maturity in (*a*)? In (*b*), Case A.
e. What would be the real or effective rate of interest paid in (*a*)? In (*b*) for Case A and Case B.

E11–6. James Corporation reported the following income statement data (summarized):

	Income statement for year ended December 31		
	19A	*19B*	*19C*
Revenues	$150,000	$150,000	$150,000
Expenses (including depreciation)	(110,000)	(110,000)	(110,000)
Pretax Income	$ 40,000	$ 40,000	$ 40,000

Depreciation expense included on the income statement was computed as follows:

Machinery cost (acquired on January 1, 19A)	$60,000
Estimated useful life, three years; no residual value	
Annual depreciation (straight line) $60,000 ÷ 3 years	20,000

The company uses sum-of-the-years'-digits depreciation on the income tax return and has an average income tax rate of 40 percent.

Required:

a. For each year, compute (1) income tax expense for the income statement and (2) income taxes payable for the tax return (show computations).

b. Give the entry for each year to record income taxes including any deferred taxes.

c. What kind of "tax difference" was involved? Explain.

d. What advantage was gained by using SYD depreciation on the tax return? Explain.

E11–7. The comparative income statement for Oakland Company at December 31, 19B reflected the following data (summarized and excluding income taxes):

	Annual income statement for	
	19A	*19B*
Sales	$50,000	$60,000
Expenses	40,000	48,000
Pretax Income	$10,000	$12,000

Included on the 19B income statement given above was an expense amounting to $4,000 that had to be included as a deduction on the income tax return in 19A rather than in 19B. Assume an average tax rate of 30 percent.

Required:

a. For each year compute (1) income tax expense, (2) income taxes payable, and (3) any deferred taxes.

b. Give the entry for each year to record income taxes, including any deferred taxes.

c. Show how the income tax liabilities would be shown on the balance sheet for each year assuming the tax is paid the following April.

E11–8. The comparative income statement for Northern Company at December 31, 19B, reflected the following data (summarized and excluding income taxes):

	Annual income statement for	
	19A	*19B*
Revenues	$90,000	$94,000
Expenses	75,000	78,000
Pretax Income	$15,000	$16,000

Included on the 19B income statement given above was a revenue item amounting to $6,000 that had to be included on the income tax return for 19A rather than in 19B. Assume an average income tax rate of 30 percent.

Required:

a. For each year, compute (1) income tax expense, (2) income taxes payable, and (3) deferred taxes. (Hint: Deferred taxes will have a debit balance for 19A.)

b. Give the entry for each year to record income taxes, including any deferred taxes.

c. Show how income taxes would be reported on the balance sheet each year assuming the tax is paid the following April.

E11–9. Midwest Manufacturing Company has completed the payroll for January 1977, reflecting the following data:

Salaries and wages earned	$60,000
Employee income taxes withheld	10,000
Union dues withheld	1,500
F.I.C.A. payroll taxes*	4,200
F.U.T.A. payroll taxes	350
State unemployment taxes	1,750

* Assessed on both employer and employee at a 6 percent rate for each.

Required:

a. Give the entry to record payment of the payroll and employee deductions.

b. Give the entry to record employer payroll taxes.
c. What was the amount of additional labor expense to the company due to tax laws? Explain.

PART TWO: EXERCISES 11–10 TO 11–13

E11–10. On January 1, 1977, you deposited $5,500 in a savings account. The account will earn 5 percent annual compound interest, which will be added to the fund balance at the end of each year. You recorded the deposit as follows:

Savings account	5,500	
Cash		5,500

Required:

a. What will be the balance in the savings account at the end of ten years?
b. What is the time value of money in dollars for the ten years?
c. How much interest revenue did the fund earn in 1977? 1978?
d. Give the entry to record interest revenue at the end of 1977 and 1978.

E11–11. On each December 31, you plan to deposit $500 in a savings account. The account will earn 5 percent annual interest, which will be added to the fund balance at the end of each year. You recorded the first deposit as follows:

December 31, 1977:

Savings account	500	
Cash		500

Required:

a. What will be the balance in the savings account on the date of the tenth deposit?
b. What is the time value of money in dollars for the ten deposits?
c. How much interest revenue did the fund earn in 1978? 1979?
d. Give the entry for interest revenue at the end of 1978 and 1979.

E11–12. You have decided to take a trip around the world upon graduation, four years from now. Your grandfather desires to deposit sufficient funds for the purpose in a savings account for you now. A carefully drawn budget on your part indicates that you will need $5,000 at that time. The savings account will draw 5 percent annual interest, which will be added to the savings account at the end of each year.

Required (round to even dollars for convenience):

a. How much should your grandfather deposit in the savings account now so that there will be a $5,000 balance at the end of four years? (Indicated entry: debit, Savings Account, $?; and credit, Cash, $?).

b. What is the time value of money in dollars for the four years?

c. How much interest revenue would the fund earn in Year 1? Year 2?

d. Give the accounting entry for the interest revenue at the end of Year 1 and Year 2.

E11–13. You have decided to attend college for four years and have budgeted the cost at $1,500 per year. This amount will be needed each September 1, starting in 1977. Your father has decided to deposit a single sum of money now, which will pay you the $1,500 each September 1. The savings account will earn 5 percent annual interest, which will be added to the savings account at the end of each year. Your father will make the single deposit on September 1, 1976. (Indicated entry: debit, Savings account, $?; and credit, Cash, $?).

Required:

a. How much should your father deposit in the savings account?

b. What is the time value of money in dollars?

c. How much interest revenue would the fund have earned at the end of Year 1 and Year 2?

d. Give the accounting entry for interest revenue at the end of Year 1 and Year 2.

PROBLEMS

PART ONE: PROBLEMS 11–1 TO 11–7

P11–1. Dakota Company completed the transactions listed below during 1977. The annual accounting period ends on December 31, 1977.

1977

Jan. 8 Purchased merchandise for resale at an invoice cost of $30,000; terms, 2/10, n/60. Record at net (see Chapter 7); assume a periodic inventory system.

17 Paid invoice of January 8.

Apr. 1 Borrowed $20,000 from the National Bank for general use; executed a 12-month, 9 percent, interest-bearing note payable.

June 3 Purchased merchandise for resale at an invoice cost of $20,000; terms, 1/20, n/30; record at net.

July 5 Paid invoice of June 3.

Aug. 1 Rented two rooms in the building owned by Baker and collected six months' rent in advance amounting to $2,400.

Dec. 20 Received a $500 deposit from a customer as a guarantee to return a large trailer "borrowed" for 30 days.

31 Wages earned but not paid on December 31 amounted to $3,000 (disregard payroll taxes).

Required:

a. Prepare journal entries for the above transactions.
b. Prepare all adjusting entries required on December 31, 1977.
c. Show how all of the liabilities arising from the above transactions would be reported on the balance sheet at December 31, 1977.

P11–2. Stereo Retailers' sold a Super-set to a customer for $1,500 cash on December 30, 19A. Stereo gave the customer a one-year guarantee on the Super-set. Past experience with this set by Stereo indicates that to maintain the warranty would cost approximately 5 percent of the sales price.

Assume a perpetual inventory system and that the Super-set cost Stereo $900.

Actual cash for warranty expenditures (parts and labor) to make good the warranty on the set during 19B amounted to $70.

Required:

a. Give entry or entries required on December 30, 19A. Explain the basis for your entries.
b. Give entry (or entries) required on December 31, 19A, end of the annual accounting period. Explain the bases for your responses.
c. Show how the income statement and balance sheet for 19A would reflect the above data.
d. Give the entry to record the repair made to the set in 19B.

P11–3. Stanley Company completed the transactions listed below during 1977. The annual accounting period ends on December 31.

Jan.	20	Purchased merchandise for resale at an invoice cost of $40,000; terms, 2/10, n/30; record at net and assume a perpetual inventory system (see Chapter 7).
	28	Paid invoice of January 20.
May	1	Purchased an operational asset (fixtures) for $60,000; paid $20,000 cash and gave a 12-month, 9 percent, interest-bearing note payable for the balance.
June	5	Purchased an operational asset (machine) at an invoice cost of $10,000; terms, 3/10, n/60.
	20	Paid invoice of June 5.
Sept.	1	Collected rent revenue on some office space rented to another company; the rent of $2,400 was for the next six months.
Dec.	31	Received a tax bill for property taxes for 1977 in the amount of $800; the taxes are payable no later than March 1, 1978.

Required:

a. Give the journal entries for the above transactions.
b. Prepare any adjustment entries required on December 31, 1977 (exclude depreciation).
c. Show how all liabilities arising from the above transactions would be reported on the balance sheet at December 31, 1977.

P11–4. On April 1, 1977, Miller Company purchased equipment at a cost of $110,000. A cash down payment in the amount of $30,000 was made. An interest-bearing note (including a mortgage on the equipment) for $80,000 was given for the balance. The note specified 9 percent annual interest. Two payments of $40,000 each on the principal plus interest on the unpaid balance on March 31, 1978, and March 31, 1979 are required. (Note: These will be unequal cash payments.)

Required:

a. Give the indicated entries at the following dates: April 1, 1977; December 31, 1977 (end of the annual accounting period); and March 31, 1978.

b. Show how the liabilities related to the purchase should be shown on the balance sheet at December 31, 1977.

P11–5. This situation was designed to illustrate accounting for (*a*) an interest-bearing note payable, and (*b*) a noninterest-bearing note payable. The annual accounting period ends December 31 in both cases.

Assume Company X executed a note payable in favor of the City Bank for a loan of cash on April 1, 1977. The loan was for 12 months with a maturity date of March 31, 1978. The bank charges a 9 percent annual rate on loans of this type. The amount of cash borrowed was $20,000. We will assume:

Case A—The note was interest bearing—that is, the principal plus the interest is payable at maturity. The face amount of note was $20,000.

Case B—The note was noninterest bearing—that is, the interest was included in the face amount of the note. The face amount of note was $21,800.

Required:

a. Record the issuance of the note on April 1, 1977, under each of the two cases. Your solution can be simplified by setting up five columns: Account Titles; Case A (debit and credit); and Case B (debit and credit). Thus, the two cases can be presented in your solution in parallel columns.

b. Give the journal entry to record the adjusting entry that would be required for each case on December 31, 1977.

c. Give the appropriate reversing entry for each case on January 1, 1978, if you deem this useful.

d. Give the entry to record payment of the note under each case at maturity, March 31, 1978; consider your response to (*c*).

e. In respect to each case show the following:

1. Liabilities that would be reported on the balance sheet at December 31, 1977.
2. Interest expense that would be reported on the income statements for 1977 and 1978 (separately).

f. Compute the true or effective interest rate in each case. If they differ, explain why.

P11–6. Foster Company is in the process of preparing comparative statements at December 31, 19B. The records reflect the following summarized income statement date, exclusive of income tax expense:

	19A	*19B*
Revenues	$150,000	$160,000
Expenses	(110,000)	(129,000)
Extraordinary item	(10,000)	4,000
Income before income taxes	$ 30,000	$ 35,000

Included in the 19B revenues of $160,000 is an item of revenue amounting to $10,000 that was required to be included on the income tax return for 19A rather than 19B. Also included in the 19B expenses of $129,000 was an item of expense amounting to $6,000 that had to be deducted on the income tax return for 19A rather than 19B. Assume an average 30 percent income tax rate. Assume there were no deferred taxes in the extraordinary items.

Required:

a. For each year, compute (1) income tax expense, (2) income tax liability, and (3) deferred taxes.

b. Give the entry for each year to record income tax expense, including any deferred taxes.

c. Restate the above comparative income statement, including the appropriate presentation of income taxes for each year. (Hint: Allocate income tax expense between operations and extraordinary items.)

d. What kind of "tax difference" was represented by the two items. Explain.

P11–7. At December 31, 1977, the records of XY Corporation provided the following pretax information:

1.	Revenues	$150,000
2.	Expenses (including $13,000 depreciation expense)	113,000
3.	Depreciation expense was computed as follows for income statement purposes:	
	Fixed asset cost (acquired January 1, 1977)	52,000
	Four-year useful life (no residual value)	
	Depreciation expense per year $52,000 ÷ 4 years	13,000
4.	Extraordinary loss	10,000
5.	The revenues given in 1 include $3,000 interest on tax free municipal bonds.	
6.	Assume an average income tax rate of 40% on both ordinary income and extraordinary income.	
7.	Sum-of-the-years'-digits depreciation on the fixed asset will be used on the income tax return and straight line on the income statement.	

Required:

a. Compute income tax expense.

b. Compute income taxes on the tax return.

c. Give the entry to record income taxes including any deferred taxes.
d. Prepare a single-step income statement.
e. What kind of "tax differences" were involved? Explain the basis for your treatment of them.

PART TWO: PROBLEMS 11–8 TO 11–14

P11–8. On January 1, 1977, Nash Company signed a contract with Z Company. Nash Company was required to deposit with an independent trustee $20,000 cash as a performance guarantee. The trustee agreed to pay 4 percent annual interest on the fund and to add it to the fund balance at the end of each year. At the end of the third year, the contract was satisfactorily completed and the trustee returned the balance of the fund to Nash Company. The entry to record the deposit was as follows:

Performance fund	20,000	
Cash		20,000

Required:

a. What was the balance of the fund at the end of the three years?
b. What was the time value of money in dollars for the three years?
c. How much interest revenue did the fund earn in each year?
d. Give the following accounting entries for Nash Company:
1. To record interest revenue for each of the three years.
2. To record receipt of the fund balance at the end of 1979.

P11–9. On January 1, 1977, the management of Noah Company agreed to set aside a special fund in order to provide sufficient cash to pay off a $50,000 long-term debt due at the end of five years. The single deposit will be made with an independent party (a bank), which will pay 5 percent annual interest on the fund balance. The interest will be added to the fund balance at the end of each year. The indicated entry for the single deposit on January 1, 1977, is as follows:

Debt retirement fund	$?	
Cash		$?

Required:

a. How much must be deposited as a single sum on January 1, 1977, to satisfy the agreement?
b. What was the time value of money in dollars for the five years?
c. How much interest revenue would the fund earn in 1977? 1978?
d. Give accounting entries for the following for Noah Company:
1. To record the deposit.
2. To record the interest revenue for 1977 and 1978.
3. To record payment of the maturing liability at the end of 1981.

P11–10. On December 31, 1977, the management of Strawn Company agreed to set aside, in a special fund, sufficient cash to pay a $50,000 debt due on December 31, 1981. Strawn Company will make five equal deposits on each December 31, 1977, 1978, 1979, 1980, and 1981. The fund will earn 5 percent annual interest, which will be added to the balance of the fund at the end of each year. The fund needed must be available immediately after the last deposit. Deposits will be recorded as follows:

Date:

Debt retirement fund	$?	
Cash		$?

Required:

a. How much must be deposited each December 31? (Hint: Use Table 11–3 and divide instead of multiplying; round table value to three places.)

b. What will be the time value of money in dollars for the fund?

c. How much interest revenue will the fund earn in 1978 and 1979?

d. Give accounting entries for the following for Strawn Company:
1. To record the first deposit on December 31, 1977.
2. To record interest revenue at the end of 1978 and 1979.
3. To record payment of the debt on December 30, 1981.

P11–11. On January 1, 1977, Kevin Company sold to K Company a new machine for $40,000. A cash down payment of $10,000 was made by K Company. A $30,000, 8 percent note was signed by K Company for the balance due. The note is to be paid off in three equal installments due on December 31, 1977, 1978, and 1979. Each payment is to include principal plus interest on the unpaid balance. The sale was recorded as follows:

January 1, 1977:

Cash	10,000	
Notes receivable	30,000	
Sales revenue		40,000

Required:

a. What is the amount of the equal annual payment that must be made by K Company? (Hint: Use Table 11–4 and divide instead of multiplying.)

b. What was the time value of money, in dollars, on the note?

c. Give the entry for Kevin Company to record the collection of (1) the first installment (on December 31, 1977) and (2) the second installment (on December 31, 1978).

P11–12. On January 1, 1976, you purchased a new Super-Whiz automobile for $4,000. You paid a $1,000 cash down payment and signed a $3,000 note to pay the balance in four equal installments on each December 31, the first payment to be made on December 31, 1976. The interest rate is 7 percent per year on the unpaid balance. Each payment will include payment on principal plus the interest.

Required:

a. Compute the amount of the equal payments that you must make.
b. What is the time value of money in dollars for the installment debt?
c. Complete a debt amortization and interest expense schedule using the following format.

Date	Cash Payment	Interest Expense	Reduction of Principal	Unpaid Principal
1/1/76				$3,000
12/31/76	$886	$3,000 × 0.07 = $210	$886 − $210 = $676	2,324
12/31/77				
12/31/78				
12/31/79				-0-

Note: After completing the table, explain the fact that interest expense decreases each year, whereas, reduction of principle increases each year.

P11–13. (Based on Appendix A.) Tappen Company has just completed the salary and wage payroll for March 1977. Details provided by the payroll were as follows:

Salaries and wages earned	$100,000*
Employee income taxes withheld	24,000
Union dues withheld	1,000
Insurance premiums withheld	500

F.I.C.A. tax rate, 6%
F.U.T.A. tax rate, 0.5%
State unemployment tax rate, 2.5% (based on same amount of wages as F.U.T.A. taxes)

* Subject in full to payroll taxes.

Required:

a. Give the entry to record the payroll for March, including employee deductions. Show computations.
b. Give the entry to record the employer's payroll taxes.
c. Give a combined entry to reflect remittance of amounts owed to governmental agencies and other organizations.
d. What was the total labor cost for Tappen Company? Explain.

P11–14. (Based on Appendix B.) Holt Company uses a voucher system to attain control of expenditures. The following transactions have been selected from December 1977 for problem purposes. The accounting year ends December 31.

You are to design a voucher register and a check register similar to those shown in Appendix B. The transactions to follow will be entered in these two special journals.

Dec. 2 Purchased merchandise from AB Wholesalers for resale $2,000; terms, 2/10, n/30; record purchases at net and assume a periodic inventory system (see Chapter 9); Invoice No. 14; start with Voucher No. 11.

7 Approved contract with Ace Plumbing Company for repair of plumbing, $450; account, Building Repairs, No. 77.

11 Paid Voucher No. 11; start with Check No. 51.

22 Purchased store supplies for future use from Crown Company; Invoice No. 21 for $90; account, Store Supplies Inventory, No. 16.

23 Advertising for pre-Christmas sale $630; bill received from Daily Press and payment processed immediately; account, Advertising Expense, No. 54.

31 Monthly payroll voucher, total $2,500; $1,500 was selling expense (Sales Salaries, No. 52) and $1,000 was administrative expense (Administrative Salaries, No. 62). Voucher was supported by the payroll record; therefore, one voucher is prepared for the entire payroll. Voucher was approved for immediate payment. Six checks with consecutive numbers were issued.

Required:

a. Enter the above transactions in the voucher register and the check register.

b. Total the special journals and check the equality of the debits and credits. Set up T-accounts and post both registers. Complete all posting notations. The following accounts may be needed:

Account Titles	*Account No.*
Cash	01
Store supplies inventory	16
Vouchers payable	30
Purchases	40
Selling expense control	50
Subsidiary ledger:	
Sales salaries	52
Advertising expense	54
Administrative expense control	60
Subsidiary ledger:	
Administrative salaries	62
Building repairs	77

c. Reconcile the Vouchers Payable account balance with the Unpaid Vouchers File at the end of December.

12

Measurement and reporting of bonds payable

PURPOSE OF THE CHAPTER

The sale of bonds is a primary way of obtaining resources for growth and expansion by businesses, nonprofit organizations (such as colleges), and public subdivisions (such as municipalities and water districts). Bonds are evidences of long-term debt. When bonds are sold, they become an investment to the buyer and an obligation to the issuer. Accounting for bonds as debt is complex because of the wide range of characteristics they may possess. To be efficient in their decision making, both the issuing entity and the investor need to understand the characteristics of bonds and their varying economic effects. Accounting seeks to measure and report these economic effects.

Because of the special characteristics of bonds and the complexities in accounting for them, they were deferred for separate consideration. The purposes of this chapter are (1) to impart a knowledge of the characteristics of bonds payable and (2) to explain the accounting approaches used to measure, record, and report their economic impact. To provide flexibility the chapter is divided into two parts: Part One presents the fundamentals of measuring and reporting bonds payable; Part Two presents some accounting complexities often encountered in measuring and reporting bonds payable.

PART ONE: FUNDAMENTALS OF BONDS PAYABLE

NATURE OF BONDS PAYABLE

Funds required for long-term purposes, such as the acquisition of high-cost machinery or the construction of a new plant, may be obtained

EXHIBIT 12–1
Typical bond certificate

by issuing long-term notes payable (discussed in Chapter 11) or **bonds payable.** Bonds payable represent a long-term liability and may be secured by a mortgage on specified assets. Bonds are usually in denominations of $1,000 or $10,000 and, occasionally, in denominations of $100,000. They usually are negotiable (i.e., transferable by endorsement) and are bought and sold daily by investors. The bonds of most leading companies are quoted on the security exchanges.[1] A typical bond is shown in Exhibit 12–1.

The **principal** of a bond is the amount payable at the maturity or due date as specified on the bond certificate. This amount also is called its **par value,** maturity value, or its **face amount.** Throughout the life of a bond, the issuing company makes periodic interest payments, usually semiannually, to the bondholders.

A company desiring to sell a **bond issue** must draw up a **bond indenture,** which specifies the legal provisions of the bonds, such as due date, rate of interest to be paid, dates of interest payments, and conversion privileges (explained later). When a bond is sold, the investor receives a

[1] In addition to bonds that are issued by corporations, bonds are also issued by governmental units, such as federal and state governments, cities, counties, school districts, water districts, and nonprofit institutions. The discussions in this chapter apply to both types, although we will focus mainly on those issued by corporations.

bond certificate (i.e., a bond). All of the bond certificates for a single bond issue are identical in that there is specified on the face of each certificate the same maturity date, interest rate, interest dates, and the other provisions. When a company issues bonds, it normally sells them to an **underwriter,** who, in turn, markets them to the public. A third party, called the **trustee,** usually is appointed to represent the bondholders. The duties of an independent trustee are to ascertain that the issuing company fulfills all of the provisions of the bond indenture.

CLASSIFICATION OF BONDS

Bonds may be classified in a number of different ways, depending upon their characteristics. The following classifications should be understood:

1. On the basis of the underlying security:
   a. Unsecured bonds—bonds that do not include a mortgage or pledge of specific assets as a guarantee of repayment at maturity date. These often are called **debentures.**
   b. Secured bonds—bonds that include a mortgage or a pledge of specific assets as a guarantee of repayment. Secured bonds tend to be designated on the basis of the type of assets pledged, such as real estate mortgage bonds and equipment trust bonds.
2. On the basis of repayment of principal:
   a. Ordinary or single-payment bonds—the principal is payable in full at a single specified due date in the future.
   b. Serial bonds—the principal is payable in installments on a series of specific dates in the future.
3. On the basis of early retirement:
   a. Callable bonds—bonds that may be called for early retirement at the option of the *issuer.*
   b. Redeemable bonds—bonds that may be turned in for early retirement at the option of the *bondholder.*
   c. Convertible bonds—bonds that may be converted to other securities of the issuer (such as common stock) after a specified date in the future at the option of the *bondholder.*
4. On the basis of payment of interest:
   a. Registered bonds—the name and address of the owner must be currently on file (registered) with the issuing company. Payment of interest is made by check, which is mailed only to the person shown in the bond register.
   b. Coupon bonds—bonds to which a printed coupon is attached for each interest payment throughout the life of the bond. When an interest date approaches, the bondholder "clips" the coupon, signs it, and mails it to the issuing company. In turn, an interest check is sent to the person and address shown on the completed coupon.

ADVANTAGES OF ISSUING BONDS

Bonds payable often represent an attractive avenue for obtaining large amounts of funds needed by a corporation. The advantages of issuing bonds stem from the fact that the bondholders are creditors and not owners, as are stockholders. A bondholder does not share in the management, the accumulated earnings, or the growth in assets, as does the shareholder. Payments of resources to bondholders are limited to (1) the amount of interest specified on the bond and (2) the principal or face amount of the bond at maturity. The rate of interest paid to bondholders may be more or less than the dividend rate being paid to shareholders.

Using borrowed assets (i.e., assets acquired with funds obtained from creditors) to enhance the return to the owners' equity is called **leverage.** When leverage is positive, an important financial advantage to the shareholders occurs. Leverage is positive when the net after-tax interest rate on borrowed funds is less than the after-tax rate of return earned by the company on total assets.

To illustrate, assume X Corporation earns a 15 percent return on total assets, while at the same time it is paying an average interest rate of 9 percent on borrowed funds and has an average income tax rate of 40 percent. The interest differential on the portion of total assets provided by the creditors clearly is a significant benefit to the shareholders. The precise nature and economic effects of leverage are shown for X Corporation in Exhibit 12–2.

Observe in the illustration that the use of debt (Case B) increased earnings per share and return on stockholders' equity by approximately 43 percent. This favorable leverage effect was due to the fact that 40 percent (i.e., $200,000) of the assets employed were obtained at a net after-tax interest rate of 5.4 percent (i.e., 9% × 0.6) and the company earned 15 percent on total assets employed. The difference benefited the shareholders' so that there was a 6 percent leverage factor in their favor. The significance of the economic effects of leverage depends upon the (1) difference between net after-tax interest rate and the earnings on total assets employed and (2) the relative amount of total assets provided by creditors.

Dividends normally are paid to stockholders only if profits have been earned. In contrast, interest payments to bondholders legally must be paid each period, irrespective of whether the corporation earns a profit or incurs a loss. This "fixed charge" to expense each period is a distinct disadvantage of bonds; however, there is an important compensating factor for the issuing company. Interest expense is *deductible* on the income tax return whereas dividends paid to stockholders are not deductible for tax purposes. This fact serves to reduce significantly the net cost of funds acquired by issuing bonds. For example, a corporation in the 48 percent tax bracket, paying 7 percent interest per annum on bonds

EXHIBIT 12-2
Effects of leverage

X Corporation

		Case A: No debt		*Case B: Debt $200,000 @ 9%*
Total debt (9% interest rate)		None		$200,000
Total stockholders' equity	(10,000 shares)	$500,000	(6,000 shares)	300,000
Total assets*		$500,000		$500,000
Interest expense (net of average income tax @ 40%)			$200,000 × 9% × (1.00 − .40)	$10,800
Net income (after interest expense and income taxes)		$ 75,000	($75,000 − $10,800)	64,200
Return earned on total assets	($75,000 ÷ $500,000)	15%	($64,200 + $10,800) ÷ $500,000†	15%
Earnings available to shareholders:				
Amount		$ 75,000		$ 64,200
Per share	($75,000 ÷ 10,000)	7.50	($64,200 ÷ 6,000)	10.70
Return on stockholders' equity	($75,000 ÷ $500,000)	15%	($64,200 ÷ $300,000)	21%

* Same as debt plus owners' equity.
† Interest on debt is added back to derive total return to all fund providers (see Chapter 16).
Leverage factor: Case A, 15% − 15% = 0%; Case B, 21% − 15% = 6% favorable (see Chapter 16).

payable, would incur a net interest cost on the bonds of 7 percent × 52 percent = 3.64 percent. Despite the advantages of leverage, sound financing of a large business requires a realistic *balance* between the amounts of debt (including bonds payable) and owners' equity (i.e., common and preferred stock and retained earnings).

MEASURING BONDS PAYABLE AND BOND INTEREST EXPENSE

The accounting approach used in measuring, recording, and reporting bonds payable is determined primarily by the cost and matching principles. When a bond is issued (i.e., sold), the issue price (or proceeds) is the net cash received, plus the fair-market value of any noncash resources received. Under the cost principle, bonds payable are recorded at their issue price; that is, at their **current cash equivalent amount.** Subsequent to issuance, the bonds usually are measured and reported at their current net liability amount. This amount will change from period to period if the bonds were issued at a discount or at a premium.

Bonds may be sold at **par;** that is, at the face or maturity amount. If sold above par, they are said to have been issued at a **premium.** If sold below par, they are said to have been issued at a **discount.** To illustrate, if the issuing corporation received $1,000 cash for a bond having a $1,000 face or par value, there would be no premium or discount. Alternatively, if the corporation received $960 for the bond, there would be a discount of $40; or if $1,050 cash were received, there would be a premium of $50. Typically, bond prices are quoted on the security exchanges as a percent of par or face amount. A bond quoted at 100 sells at par; if quoted at 96 it sells at a discount of 4 percent below its face amount; if quoted at 105 it sells at a premium of 5 percent above its face amount.

Each period the bond interest is measured, recorded, and reported in conformance with the matching principle. Since interest is incurred on the basis of time, at the end of each period the amount of interest unpaid must be accrued and reported as expense so that it will be matched with the period in which it was incurred. The measurement and reporting of interest has already been discussed in respect to both notes receivable and notes payable. When bonds are issued at a premium or discount, however, an additional measurement problem arises, because these affect both the price of the bond and the amount of interest expense. This measurement problem is discussed subsequently.

In the paragraphs to follow, we will utilize a common set of illustrative data for Mason Corporation. Assume the board of directors and the shareholders of the corporation approved a bond issue with the following provisions:

Bonds payable authorized ($1,000 per bond)	$500,000
Date on each bond	January 1, 1977

Maturity in ten years, on December 31, 1986.
Interest, 6% per annum, payable 3% each six months on June 30 and December 31.
Mason Corporation, end of the annual accounting period: December 31.

Using the above data, we will discuss and illustrate three different assumed situations: (1) the bonds are sold at par, (2) the bonds are sold at a discount, and (3) the bonds are sold at a premium.

Bonds sold at par

Bonds sell at their par value when the buyers (investors) are willing to invest in them at the **stated interest rate** on the bond. To illustrate, assume that on January 1, 1977, Mason Corporation issued $400,000 of the bonds payable and received $400,000 in cash for them. The bonds were dated to start interest on January 1, 1977. The entry by Mason Corporation to record the issuance of the bonds would be:

January 1, 1977:

Cash	400,000	
Bonds payable		400,000
Sold $400,000, 6 percent, ten-year bonds payable at par.		

Subsequent to the sale of the bonds, interest at 3 percent on the face amount of the bonds must be paid on each June 30 and December 31 until maturity. The entries to record the interest payments during 1977 would be as follows:

June 30, 1977:

Bond interest expense	12,000	
Cash		12,000
Paid semiannual interest on bonds payable ($400,000 × 0.03 = $12,000).		

December 31, 1977:

Bond interest expense	12,000	
Cash		12,000
Paid semiannual interest on bonds payable ($400,000 × 0.03 = $12,000).		

At the end of the accounting period, December 31, 1977, the financial statements would report the following:

Income Statement:	
Bond interest expense	$ 24,000
Balance Sheet:	
Long-Term Liabilities:	
Bonds payable, 6% (due December 31, 1986)	$400,000

In this situation, Mason Corporation received $1,000 cash for each $1,000 bond sold and will pay back $1,000 + ($30 × 20) = $1,600. The $600 difference is the amount of interest expense for the ten years; therefore, the interest cost was $60 per year and the *effective rate of interest* was $60 ÷ $1,000 = 6 percent per year. The *stated* or *nominal rate* called for on the bond also was 6 percent.

Bonds sold at a discount

Bonds sell at a discount when the buyers (investors) are willing to invest in them only at a rate of interest that is *higher* than the stated interest rate on the bond. This situation may occur when the stated interest rate is lower than the interest rate that investors could obtain by investing in other securities of similar risk. In this situation the **effective rate of interest** is more than the *stated interest rate* on the bonds. To comprehend this situation you must understand that the *dollar amount* of interest paid on a bond remains the same each period. The dollar amount of interest paid each period is the face or par amount multiplied by the interest rate *stated* on the bond. To illustrate, for each $1,000 bond payable, Mason Corporation will pay semiannual interest amounting to $1,000 × 0.03 = $30. This is true whether the bond was sold at par, at a discount, or at a premium. With this fact in mind, let's see what the approximate *effective rate of interest* would be, assuming Mason Corporation issued a $1,000 bond for $980 (i.e., issued at 98). An analysis of the issuance of this $1,000 bond could be made as follows:

Cash received when bond was sold		$ 980
Cash paid back: Principal at maturity	$1,000	
Interest ($1,000 × 3% × 20)	600	1,600
Difference: Amount of interest paid		$ 620

Approximate effective rate of interest: $620 ÷ 10 years = $62 per year
$62 ÷ $980 = 6.33% per year

This computation suggests that Mason Corporation, because it had to pay $60 a year for the use of $980 (the bond sold at a discount), incurred an approximate *effective rate of interest* of 6.33 percent, although the stated rate on the bond was 6 percent per year.[2] The additional $20 paid at maturity is just more interest. The discount served to increase the effective rate above the nominal rate of interest. From this illustration you can see that the investor who desires a *higher* effective rate of interest than the *stated interest rate* on the bond will invest in these bonds only if they can be bought at a discount.

To illustrate the effect on the accounting and reporting of bonds payable sold at a discount, assume $400,000 of the Mason bonds were issued for $392,000 (i.e., at 98) on January 1, 1977. The entry to record the issuance would be:

January 1, 1977:

Cash	392,000	
Discount on bonds payable	8,000*	
Bonds payable		400,000*

Sold $400,000, 6 percent, ten-year bonds payable at 98;
$400,000 × 0.98 = $392,000, cash received.

* Note: In effect the bonds are recorded at their issue price because the liability is reported on the balance sheet of the net of these two balances.

[2] This is a straight-line approximation of the effective interest rate. A precise and conceptually preferable computation can be made based on present value concepts explained in Chapter 11. The effective rate of interest is sometimes called the real rate.

In the above entry the amount of the discount was recorded in a separate contra account (Discount on Bonds Payable) as a *debit* because it must be accorded special treatment and because the accounts should reflect the maturity amount of $400,000 and the current cash equivalent of $400,000 − $8,000 = $392,000.

The analysis presented on page 462 demonstrated that the discount had the effect of increasing the effective rate of interest; therefore, bond discount, in the economic sense, represents an *increase in bond interest expense*. To give accounting effect to this, the $8,000 debit to Bond Discount on Bonds Payable must be apportioned to each interest period as an increase in bond interest expense from the date of issuance to maturity date. There are two different methods for doing this: (1) *straight-line* amortization and (2) *effective-interest* amortization. Straight-line amortization is easy to understand and compute; however, it is conceptually deficient. Effective-interest amortization requires use of the future and present value concepts (discussed in Part Two of Chapter 11) and is therefore difficult to understand. It is, however, the required method when the amounts are material. Nevertheless, to introduce the subject we will use straight-line amortization because it is easy to follow. The more complex effective-interest method will be presented in Part Two of this chapter.

Straight-line amortization. To amortize the $8,000 bond discount over the period from date of issuance to maturity date on a straight-line basis, an equal dollar amount is allocated to each interest period. Since there are 20 six-month interest periods, the computation would be: $8,000 ÷ 20 periods = $400, amortization on each semiannual interest date. Therefore, the payments of interest on the bonds during 1977 would be recorded as follows:[3]

June 30, 1977:

Bond interest expense	12,400	
Discount on bonds payable ($8,000 ÷ 20 periods)		400
Cash ($400,000 × 0.03)		12,000

Payment of semiannual interest on bonds payable and amortization of bond discount for six months.

[3] The amount of interest expense each semiannual period may be confirmed as follows:

Cash to be paid out by the borrower:	
Face amount of the bonds—payable at maturity	$400,000
Interest payments ($12,000 × 20 semiannual payments)	240,000
Total cash payments	640,000
Cash received by the borrower	392,000
Total interest expense over ten years	$248,000
Interest expense per semiannual period ($248,000 ÷ 20 periods)	$ 12,400

December 31, 1977:

Bond interest expense	12,400	
Discount on bonds payable		400
Cash		12,000
Payment of semiannual interest on bonds payable and amortization of bond discount for six months.		

In accordance with the thrust of APB *Opinion No. 21,* "Interest on Receivables and Payables," bonds payable should be measured and reported on the balance sheet at their *net liability amount;* that is, the maturity amount less any unamortized bond discount. Therefore, at the end of the accounting period, December 31, 1977, the financial statements would report the following:

Income Statement:		
Bond interest expense		$ 24,800
Balance Sheet:		
Long-Term Liabilities:		
Bonds payable, 6%, due December 31, 1986	$400,000	
Less unamortized discount	7,200	$392,800
Or, alternatively:		
Bonds payable, 6%, due December 31, 1986 (maturity amount $400,000, less unamortized discount)		$392,800*

* This is called the net liability.

Each succeeding year the unamortized discount will *decrease* by $800; and as a consequence, the net liability will *increase* each year by $800. At the maturity date of the bonds, the unamortized discount (i.e., the balance in the Discount on Bonds Payable account) will be zero. At that time the maturity or face amount of the bonds and the current net liability amount will be the same—$400,000.

Bonds sold at a premium

When lenders are willing to accept an effective rate of interest that is *lower* than the stated interest rate on the bonds, the bonds will sell at a premium. This situation occurs when the stated rate of interest is higher than the rate being paid on investments with comparable risk. When the issue price is greater than par, the cash received is greater than the base amount (par) on which the dollars of interest to be paid is calculated. Therefore, when the cash received is related to the dollars of interest paid, based on the lesser par amount, the effective rate of interest is lower than the stated rate of interest.

To illustrate the issuance of bonds at a premium, assume Mason Corporation issued $400,000 of the bonds on January 1, 1977, and received $408,000 in cash (i.e., issued at 102). An analysis of this issuance could be made as follows:

Cash received when bonds were sold		$408,000
Cash paid back:		
Principal at maturity	$400,000	
Interest ($400,000 × 3% × 20 periods)	240,000	640,000
Difference: Amount of interest paid		$232,000

Approximate effective rate of interest:
$232,000 ÷ 10 years = $23,200
$23,200 ÷ $408,000 = 5.69% per year (see footnote 2)

Although the bonds carried a stated rate of interest of 6 percent per year, the approximate effective rate of interest was 5.69 percent. The lesser amount reflects the effect of the issuance premium (computations based on straight-line amortization).

The measurement and recording of the issuance of these bonds at a premium for 1977 and the first two interest payments (assuming straight-line amortization) would be:

January 1, 1977:

Cash	408,000	
Premium on bonds payable		8,000
Bonds payable		400,000
Sold $400,000, 6 percent, bonds payable at 102; $400,000 × 1.02 = $408,000.		

June 30, 1977:

Bond interest expense	11,600	
Premium on bonds payable	400	
Cash		12,000
To record payment of interest for six months ($400,000 × 0.03 = $12,000) and to amortize bond premium for six months ($8,000 ÷ 20 periods = $400).		

December 31, 1977:

Bond interest expense	11,600	
Premium on bonds payable	400	
Cash		12,000
To record payment of interest for six months and to amortize bond premium for six months as computed above.		

In the entry to record the sale of the bonds, the premium was recorded in a separate account, Premium on Bonds Payable, as a *credit*. The premium has the effect of *decreasing* interest expense; therefore, in each period a portion of it is amortized to interest expense. Observe that in the above illustration bond interest expense is reduced by $400 each semiannual period since straight-line amortization was assumed.[4] At the end of 1977, the financial statements will reflect the following:

Income Statement:		
Bond interest expense		$ 23,200
Balance Sheet:		
Long-Term Liabilities:		
Bonds payable, 6% (due December 31, 1986)	$400,000	
Add unamortized premium	7,200	$407,200
Or, alternatively:		
Bonds payable, 6%, due December 31, 1986 (maturity amount $400,000 plus unamortized premium)		$407,200*

* This is called the net liability.

At maturity date, after the last interest payment, the bond premium of $8,000 will be fully amortized and the maturity or face amount and the current net liability for the bonds will be the same—$400,000. At maturity, December 31, 1986, the bonds will be paid off, resulting in the same entry whether originally sold at par, a discount or a premium, viz:

December 31, 1986:

Bonds payable	400,000	
Cash		400,000
To retire 6 percent bonds payable at maturity date.		

The discussions and illustrations in this part of the chapter have focused on the fundamental issues in measuring and reporting bonds payable. The background essential to understanding the economic impact on the issuing company and to comprehending financial statements that report bonds payable is provided. The next part focuses on some complexities often encountered in accounting for bonds payable.

PART TWO: SOME COMPLEXITIES IN ACCOUNTING FOR BONDS PAYABLE

This part of the chapter focuses primarily on three complexities usually encountered in accounting for bonds payable because important

---

[4] The amount of interest expense each semiannual period may be confirmed as follows:

Cash paid out by the borrower:	
Face amount of bonds at maturity	$400,000
Interest payments ($12,000 × 20 periods)	240,000
Total cash payments	640,000
Cash received by the borrower	408,000
Total interest expense over ten years	$232,000
Interest expense per semiannual period ($232,000 ÷ 20 periods)	$ 11,600

EXHIBIT 12-3

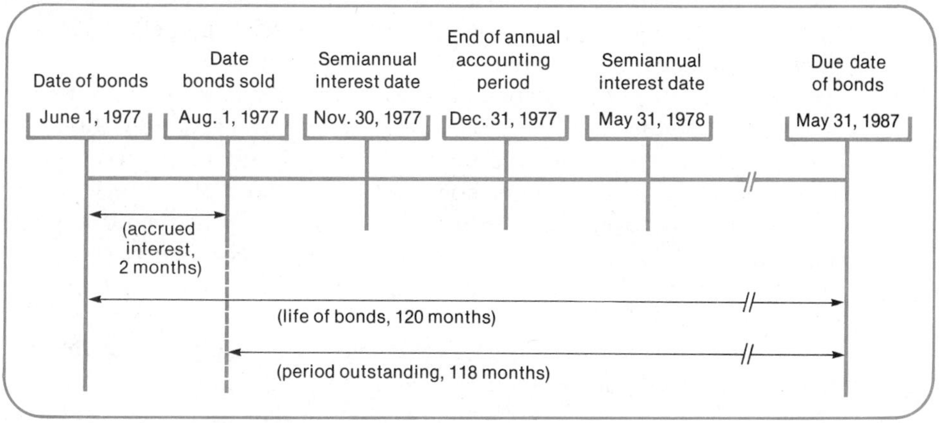

dates related to the bond issue are not the same as the date of issuance or the ending of the accounting period. Bonds payable sold between interest dates, adjusting entries for accrued bond interest, and effective-interest amortization will be discussed and illustrated. Also treated will be a related issue—bond sinking funds.

As a basis for the discussions to follow, we will utilize a common set of data for Mendez Corporation. Assume that the following bond issue was approved:

Bonds payable authorized ($1,000 per bond)	$100,000
Date on each bond	June 1, 1977

Maturity in ten years on May 31, 1987.
Interest, 6% per annum, payable 3% each May 31 and November 30.
Additional data:
Mendez Corporation: End of the annual accounting period, December 31,
Bonds issued: Entire issue sold August 1, 1977, for $96,460.

In order to focus on the effect of different dates on the accounting for a bond issue, the time scale shown in Exhibit 12-3 may be helpful.

ACCOUNTING FOR BONDS SOLD BETWEEN INTEREST DATES

The bond certificates specify the date and amount of each interest payment. Although bonds may be sold on an interest date, generally market factors cause them to be sold *between* interest dates. Nevertheless, the exact amount of interest specified on the bond certificate for each interest date will be paid, irrespective of whether a bond is sold on or between an interest date. Therefore, when bonds are sold between two interest dates, the lender (i.e., the buyer) must *pay the accrued interest* since the last interest date in addition to the market price of the bond. Because the amount of the next interest payment will be for a full interest period, the accrued interest is then effectively returned to the buyer. The net effect is that the investor will realize interest revenue only for the number of months the bonds were held by the investor from the date of sale. Similarly, the issuing corporation will incur interest expense for the same period. This situation presents two complexities in accounting for bonds: (1) the amount of accrued interest charged to the buyer must be included in the entry to record the sale of bonds; and (2) any premium or discount is amortized over the remaining **period outstanding**–that is, the period from date of sale to date of maturity of the bonds.

To illustrate, the above data for Mendez Corporation state that the bonds were sold for $96,460 (i.e., issued at a discount of $3,540) on August 1, 1977, which was *two* months after the date of the bonds.

On August 1, 1977, date of the sale of the bonds, Mendez Corporation would receive cash for the sales price of the bonds, *plus* two months accrued interest (June 1, 1977 to July 31, 1977), computed as follows (refer to the time scale above):

Market price	$96,460
Add accrued interest for 2 months:	
$100,000 × 6% × 2/12	1,000
Total cash received	$97,460

The entry to record the issuance of the bonds payable would be as follows:

August 1, 1977:

Cash (per above)	97,460	
Discount on bonds payable ($100,000 – $96,460)	3,540	
Bonds payable		100,000
Bond interest expense (per above)		1,000
Sale of bonds two months after interest date.		

In this entry, Bond Interest Expense is credited because the $1,000 accrued interest collected will be refunded to the investor when the following interest payment is made. That payment will be recorded as a credit to Cash and a debit to Bond Interest Expense. This is illustrated below.

The $3,540 recorded in the Discount on Bonds Payable account is amortized over the *period outstanding* of 118 months; therefore, straight-line amortization would be $3,540 ÷ 118 months = $30 per month. The entry to record the following interest payment would include amortization of discount only for the four months that the bonds have been outstanding. Therefore, the following interest payment would be recorded as follows:

November 30, 1977:

Bond interest expense	3,120	
Discount on bonds payable ($30 × 4 months)		120
Cash ($100,000 × 0.03)		3,000

Payment of bond interest for six months and amortization of discount for four months.

After the two entries are posted, the Bond Interest Expense account would reflect a balance of $2,120, which is equivalent to four months' interest ($100,000 × 6% × 4/12 = $2,000) plus four months' discount amortization ($30 × 4 = $120), viz:

Bond Interest Expense

11/30/77	3,120	8/1/77	1,000

(Balance, 11/30/77, $2,120)

ADJUSTING ENTRY FOR ACCRUED BOND INTEREST

In accounting for notes payable, recall that at the end of each accounting period, an adjusting entry must be made for any interest expense accrued since the last interest payment date. The same adjustment procedure must be applied to bonds payable. However, in the case of bonds, the adjusting entry must include both the accrued interest and amortization of the bond discount or premium. To illustrate for 1977 for Mendez Corporation, recall that the last interest payment date was November 30, 1977; therefore, on December 31, 1977, there is accrued interest for one month. Bond discount also must be amortized for one more month. The adjusting entry would be:

December 31, 1977:

Bond interest expense	530	
Discount on bonds payable		30
Bond interest payable		500

Adjusting entry to record bond interest payable for one month, $100,000 × 6% × 1/12 = $500; and to amortize bond discount for one month, $30.

After this entry is posted on December 31, 1977, the Bond Interest Expense account will reflect a debit balance of $2,650, which represents interest expense for the five months that the bonds have been outstanding during 1977 (August 1 to December 31). This amount may be verified as follows:

4/12 3 4

Interest: $100,000 × 6% × 5/12	$2,500
Add discount amortized: $30 × 5	150
Total Interest Expense for 1977	$2,650

This amount is closed to Income Summary and will be reported on the income statement for 1977 as "Bond interest expense."

BOND SINKING FUND

On the maturity date of bonds payable, the issuing company must have available a large amount of cash to pay off the bondholders. Such a large cash demand might place the issuing company in a severe financial strain. In order to avoid this situation, some companies build up a separate **cash fund** in advance by making equal contributions each year over a period of time in advance of maturity date. Such a separate cash fund generally is known as a **bond sinking fund.** A sinking fund is an asset that is invested pending the due date; it is reported on the balance sheet under the caption "Investments and Funds."

A bond sinking fund also adds a measure of security for the bondholders since it assures them that funds will be available for retirement of the bonds at maturity. Each cash contribution usually is deposited with an independent trustee, a designated third party such as a bank or another financial institution. The trustee invests the funds received and pays interest to the fund each year on the balance of the fund. Interest earned on a sinking fund is recorded as an increase in the fund balance (the debit) and as interest revenue (the credit). Thus, a bond sinking fund typically has the characteristics of a regular savings account. At maturity of the bonds, the balance of the fund is used to pay off the bondholders. Any excess is returned to the issuing corporation, or, in the case of a deficit, it must be made up by the issuer.

To illustrate a bond sinking fund, assume Mendez Corporation, in order to pay off the $100,000 bonds payable due May 31, 1987, decided to set up a bond sinking fund. The fund is to be built up over the last five years that the bonds are outstanding by making five equal annual deposits each December 31, starting in 1982. The sinking fund is to be deposited with City Bank, as trustee, which will pay 5 percent annual interest on the fund balance. The amount of each deposit required was calculated to be $18,098. This was based on the time value of money concepts discussed and illustrated in Chapter 11, Part Two. If the fund earned no interest, obviously each deposit would have to be $100,000 ÷ 5 contributions = $20,000. Instead of $20,000, the annual deposit required is $18,098 because the interest earned each year will be added to the fund balance. (Note: This was computed to provide a $100,000 fund balance five months before maturity date.) The required annual deposit was computed as follows:

Situation:

Future amount needed	$100,000
Period of accumulation; equal annual contributions	5 rents
Assumed interest earnings rate on the fund balance	5% per year

Computation (application of amount of annuity):

Future Amount = Periodic Rent × $A_{\substack{n=5\\i=5\%}}$ Amount of Annuity of $1

Substituting:

$100,000 = ? × 5.5256 (from Table 11–3)

Periodic Rent = $100,000 ÷ 5.5256

= $18,098

The entries for 1982 and 1983 to be made by Mendez Corporation for this sinking fund would be:

December 31, 1982 (first deposit):

Bond sinking fund	18,098	
Cash		18,098
To establish a bond sinking fund; first deposit.		

December 31, 1983 (interest added to the fund):

Bond sinking fund	905	
Interest revenue		905
To record sinking fund earnings during first year ($18,098 × 0.05 = $905).		

December 31, 1983 (second deposit):

Bond sinking fund	18,098	
Cash		18,098
To record second deposit in bond sinking fund.		

Identical entries with different interest amounts, because of the increasing balance in the fund, would be made for each of the five years of the accumulation period. At maturity date of the bonds, the following entry would be made upon payment to the bondholders:

At maturity date:

Bonds payable	100,000	
Cash	2,500	
Bond sinking fund		102,500
To record payment of bonds payable at maturity from the bond sinking fund and the return of the $2,083 excess in the bond sinking fund (i.e., 5 percent interest on $100,000 in the fund for the last five months).		

At December 31, 1983, the financial statement would reflect:

Income Statement:	
Interest revenue	$ 905
Balance Sheet:	
Investments and Funds:	
Bond sinking fund	$37,101*

* Computation: $18,098 + $905 + $18,098 = $37,101.

The bond sinking fund is only one of several funds that a company may establish from time to time to meet future needs. For example, it is not uncommon for a company to accumulate, in a similar manner, a "building fund" in anticipation of the future cash needs for the construction of a large building. All such funds, appropriately labeled, are accounted for and reported as discussed and illustrated above.[5]

EFFECTIVE-INTEREST AMORTIZATION ON BONDS PAYABLE

Effective-interest amortization of bond discount or bond premium is a conceptually sound approach for measuring both (1) the true or effective interest expense on bonds and (2) the carrying amount of the bonds (at the current net liability amount). It uses the concept of present value discussed in Chapter 11, Part Two. Conceptually, it is somewhat complex; however, APB *Opinion No. 21,* "Interest on Receivables and Payables," requires this approach when the discount or premium amount is material. At this stage in your study of accounting, we are not concerned with all of the computational complexities but, rather, stress understanding of the concept. It is similar to this situation when one purchases an automobile on an installment payment basis where equal monthly payments are made on the debt. Each equal payment made on the debt consists of two parts: (1) a payment on the principal and (2) payment of interest.

Let's see how this same concept applies to bonds payable (also a debt). We will use a simplified situation to illustrate the concept. Assume that Company X issued a $1,000 bond payable on January 1, 1977, and received $948 cash. Assume also that the bond carried a **stated interest rate** of 6 percent, payable at the end of each year, and that the life of the bond is three years. A $1,000, 6 percent bond issued at an effective rate of 8 percent will have an issue price of $948 (the $948 was taken from a bond table). The issuance of the bond was recorded as follows:

[5] In connection with such funds, a company may also restrict, or appropriate, an equivalent amount of retained earnings as a dividend restriction. The restriction of retained earnings by a corporation is discussed in Chapter 13.

January 1, 1977:

Cash	948	
Bonds payable (maturity amount, $1,000)........................		948

Issued $1,000, 6 percent bond at $52 discount.

(Note: The discount could have been set up separately as a debit to a bond discount account as illustrated in a prior paragraph. In either case, the effect will be the same.)

The three annual interest payments, assuming effective-interest amortization, would be recorded as follows:

	Year 1		*Year 2*		*Year 3*	
Bond interest expense	76		77		79	
Cash ($1,000 × 0.06)		60		60		60
Bonds payable*		16		17		19

* Computed below.

The financial statements at the end of each year would reflect the following:

	Year 1	*Year 2*	*Year 3*
Income Statement:			
Bond interest expense	$ 76	$ 77	$ 79
Balance Sheet:			
Bonds payable (maturity amount, $1,000), less unamortized discount......................	$964	$981	$1,000*

* Just prior to retirement of the bonds.

The underlying concept of the measurement of interest expense is indicated on the income statement above; the dollar amount of interest expense changes each year. Had straight-line amortization been used, interest expense would have been a constant dollar amount each year. The underlying concept of the measurement of the **current net liability amount** of the debt is reflected in an increasing amount on the balance sheet from the issue price to the maturity or face amount of the bond (at maturity date).

Computations of the effective interest amortization amounts reflected above for each of the three years is shown in the tabulation below. Observe that the stated interest rate is 6 percent; however, the effective rate of 8 percent is used to compute the amounts of interest expense and amortization.[6]

[6] The $948 was taken from a published bond table that gives the selling price of bonds with the following bond specifications: (1) face amount, (2) nominal interest rate, (3) effective interest rate, and (4) time to maturity. Alternatively, the effective interest rate of a bond selling at a given price also can be determined from the bond table.

The *approximate* yield to maturity can be computed by using the following formula:

Date	Cash paid for interest each period	Effective interest each period; based on unpaid balance and effective rate	Amount applied to restate the principal	Amount of unpaid principal
1/1/77 (issuance)				$ 948
End Year 1	$ 60*	$948 × 8% = $ 76	$16†	964‡
End Year 2	60	964 × 8% = 77	17	981
End Year 3	60	981 × 8% = 79	19	1,000
Totals...............	$180	$232	$52	

* $1,000 × 6% = $60.
† Col. 2, $76 minus Col. 1, $60 = $16.
‡ $948 plus Col. 3, $16 = $964.

The first amount column reflects the cash outflow at each interest payment date; the second column shows the effective interest amount to be reported on the income statement each period; and the last column shows the amount of the net liability (face amount less the unamortized bond discount or plus bond premium) to be reported on the balance sheet at the end of the period.

Effective-interest amortization is conceptually superior to straight-line amortization because, for each period, consistent with the issue price of the bonds, it measures (1) the true amount of interest expense on the income statement and (2) the true current net carrying amount of the bonds outstanding (net liability) on the balance sheet. Straight-line amortization provides only approximations of these amounts and can be used only when the difference between the two methods is deemed not material (refer to exception principle, materiality). In such situations, straight-line amortization is used because it is less complex.

DEMONSTRATION CASE FOR SELF-STUDY

Reed Company, Inc.

(Try to resolve the requirements before studying the suggested solution that follows.)

$$\frac{\text{Nominal Interest in \$1 } (i) -^{*} \dfrac{\text{Discount } (D) \text{ or Premium } (P)}{\text{Time to Maturity } (M)}}{\dfrac{\text{Bond Cost } (C) + \text{Maturity Value } (M)}{2}} = \text{Approximate Yield to Maturity}$$

* Plus if discount; minus if premium.

To illustrate:

$$\frac{\$60 + \dfrac{\$52}{3}}{\dfrac{\$948 + \$1{,}000}{2}} = \frac{\$77.33}{\$974.00} = 8 \text{ Percent}$$

In order to raise funds to construct a new plant, the management of Reed Company, Inc., decided to issue bonds. Accordingly, a proposed bond indenture was submitted to the board of directors and approved. The provisions in the bond indenture and specified on the bond certificates were:

Face value of bonds to be issued ($1,000 bonds)..............	$600,000
Date of bond issue—February 1, 1977, due in ten years on January 31, 1987.	
Interest—6% per annum, payable 3% on each January 31 and July 31.	

The bonds were sold on June 1, 1977, at 102½ plus accrued interest. The annual accounting period for Reed Company, Inc., ends on December 31.

Required:

a. How much cash was received by Reed Company, Inc., from the sale of the bonds payable on June 1, 1977? Show computations.
b. What was the amount of premium on the bonds payable? Over how many months will it be amortized?
c. Compute the amount of amortization of premium per month and for each six-month interest period; use straight-line amortization. Round to even dollars.
d. Give entry on June 1, 1977, to record the sale of the bonds payable.
e. Give entry for payment of interest and amortization of premium for the first interest payment on July 31, 1977.
f. Give adjusting entry required on December 31, 1977, at the end of the accounting period.
g. Give the optional reversing entry that could be made on January 1, 1978.
h. Give entry to record second interest payment and amortization of premium on January 31, 1978.
i. Show how bond interest expense and bonds payable would be reported on the financial statements at December 31, 1977.

Suggested Solution:

Requirement (*a*):

Sales price of the bonds: ($600,000 × 102.5%)..................	$615,000
Add accrued interest for four months (February 1 to May 31) ($600,000 × 6% × 4/12)..................................	12,000
Total cash received from the bonds payable...........	$627,000

Requirement (*b*):

Premium on the bonds payable ($600,000 × 2.5%)	$ 15,000
Months amortized: From date of sale, June 1, 1977, to maturity date, January 31, 1987: 120 months − 4 months =	116 months

Requirement (*c*):

Premium amortization: $15,000 ÷ 116 months = $129 per month, or $774 each six-month interest period (straight-line).

Requirement (*d*):

June 1, 1977:

Cash (per Req. [*a*] above)	627,000	
Premium on bonds payable (per Req. [*b*] above)		15,000
Interest expense (per Req. [*a*] above)		12,000
Bonds payable		600,000
To record sale of bonds payable at $102\frac{1}{2}$ plus accrued interest for four months, February 1 to May 31, 1977.		

Requirement (*e*):

July 31, 1977:

Bond interest expense	17,742	
Premium on bonds payable ($129 × 2 months)	258	
Cash ($600,000 × 3%)		18,000
To record payment of semiannual interest and to amortize premium for two months, June 1 to July 31, 1977.		

Requirement (*f*):

December 31, 1977:

Bond interest expense	14,355	
Premium on bonds payable ($129 × 5 months)	645	
Accrued bond interest payable ($600,000 × 6% × 5/12)		15,000
Adjusting entry for five months' interest accrued plus amortization of premium, August 1 to December 31, 1977.		

Requirement (*g*):

January 1, 1978:

Accrued bond interest payable	15,000	
Premium on bonds payable		645
Bond interest expense		14,355
Reversing entry; optional.		

Requirement (*h*):

January 31, 1978 (assuming reversing entry [*g*] was made):[7]

Bond interest expense	17,226	
Premium on bonds payable (per Req.[*c*])	774	
Cash ($600,000 × 6% × 6/12)		18,000
To record payment of semiannual interest and to amortize premium for 6 months.		

Requirement (*i*):

Interest expense to be reported on the 1977 income statement should be for the period outstanding during the year (i.e., for seven months, June 1 through December 31). Interest expense, per the above entries, is $17,742 + $14,355 − $12,000 = $20,097; or, alternatively, ($600,000 × 6% × 7/12 = $21,000) minus ($129 × 7 months = $903) = $20,097.

Income Statement for 1977:		
Interest expense		$ 20,097
Balance Sheet, December 31, 1977:		
Long-Term Liabilities:		
Bonds payable, 6% (due January 31, 1987)	$600,000	
Add unamortized premium*	14,097	$614,097

* $15,000 − ($258 + $645) = $14,097.

SUMMARY

In this chapter we discussed bonds payable, the issuance of which is one of the primary ways to obtain funds needed for acquiring long-term assets and to expand the business. An important advantage of bonds payable is that the cost of the funds—interest expense—is deductible for income tax purposes. This serves to reduce the net interest cost to the business. Bonds are measured and reported at their current cash-equivalent amount.

Bonds may be sold at their face, or par, amount; at a premium; or at a discount, depending upon the stated interest rate on the bonds when compared with the effective or market rate of interest that the bond buyers demand. The price of a bond varies inversely with the effective or market rate of interest. If the market rate is higher than the stated rate on the bond, the bonds will sell at a discount. Conversely, if the market rate is lower than the stated rate on the bond, the bonds will sell at a premium.

[7] If no reversing entry was made on January 1, 1978, this entry would be:

Accrued bond interest payable	15,000	
Premium on bonds payable	129	
Bond interest expense	2,871	
Cash		18,000

Discount and premium on bonds payable, in effect, are adjustments to the interest expense incurred by the issuing company. As a consequence, discount or premium on bonds payable is amortized to interest expense over the *outstanding* life of the bonds (i.e., from issue date to maturity date).

To pay off bonds payable at maturity, a company may set aside cash in advance by means of equal periodic contributions to a bond sinking fund. Such a fund is similar to a savings account. The bond sinking fund normally is administered by an independent third party, such as a bank (called the trustee). Interest earned on the fund balance is added to the fund each period. At the maturity date of the bonds, the fund is used to pay off the bondholders. Such a fund is reported on the balance sheet under the caption "Investments and Funds." Interest earned on the fund is reported on the income statement as "Interest revenue."

IMPORTANT TERMS

Bond indenture
Leverage
Bond premium
Bond discount
Stated rate of interest
Effective rate of interest
Straight-line amortization
Bond sinking fund
Effective-interest amortization

QUESTIONS FOR DISCUSSION

1. What is a bond payable? For what purpose are bonds payable usually issued?
2. What is the difference between the bond indenture and the bond certificates?
3. Distinguish between secured and unsecured bonds.
4. Distinguish between callable, redeemable, and convertible bonds.
5. Distinguish between registered and coupon bonds.
6. What are some advantages to the issuer in raising funds by the issuance of bonds, as compared with issuing capital stock?
7. The higher the tax bracket, the lower the net cost of borrowing money. Explain.
8. At date of issuance, bonds are recorded at their current cash-equivalent amount. Explain.
9. What is the nature of discount and premium on bonds payable?
10. What is the difference between the stated interest rate and the effective interest rate on a bond?
11. Distinguish between the stated and effective rates of interest on a bond payable (*a*) sold at par, (*b*) sold at a discount, and (*c*) sold at a premium.
12. Why is bond discount or bond premium amortized over the outstanding life of the bonds payable?

13. In respect to bonds payable, what is meant by "net liability"?
14. Why is the lender (i.e., the purchaser of a bond payable) charged for the accrued interest from the last interest date to date of purchase of the bonds?
15. Explain the basic difference between straight-line amortization and effective-interest amortization of bond discount or premium.

EXERCISES

PART ONE: EXERCISES 12–1 TO 12–6

E12–1. Dawson, Incorporated, is considering borrowing $60,000 on a three-year note payable. The interest rate will be 8½ percent per annum, payable each year. The company computed its return on total investment (i.e., net income ÷ liabilities + owners' equity) to be 12 percent. The average tax rate for the company is 40 percent.

Required:

a. What amount of interest would be paid the first year?
b. Considering the effect of income taxes, what would be the net interest cost and the net interest rate?
c. Would leverage be present in this situation? Explain.
d. List two advantages to Dawson in favor of the note payable versus selling more of its capital stock.

E12–2. AB Company, Inc., has approved a $100,000, 6 percent bond issue. The bonds are dated January 1, 1977, and are for ten years. Interest is paid each January 1. They have not yet been placed on the market. Assume they are issued on January 1, 1977, under three different assumptions:

Assumption A—They sell at 100.
Assumption B—They sell at 99.
Assumption C—They sell at 102.

Required:

1. Give the entries to record the issuance under each assumption.
2. What were the stated and approximate effective rates of interest for each assumption?
3. Why were the two rates different in each case?

E12–3. Adams, Incorporated, sold a $150,000, 6 percent bond issue on July 1, 1977, at 98. The bonds were dated July 1, 1977, and pay interest each December 31 and June 30. The bonds mature ten years from July 1, 1977.

Required:

a. Give the entry to record the issuance of the bonds.
b. Give the entry to record the interest payment on December 31, 1977. Assume straight-line amortization.
c. Show how the bond interest expense and the bonds payable would be reported on the December 31, 1977, annual financial statements.

d. What were the stated and approximate effective rates of interest? Why were they different?

E12–4. XY Company, Inc., sold a $60,000, 7 percent bond issue on July 1, 1977 at 103. The bonds were dated July 1, 1977, and pay interest each December 31 and June 30. The bonds mature in 15 years from July 1, 1977.

Required:

a. Give the entry to record the issuance of the bonds.
b. Give the entry for the interest payment on December 31, 1977. Assume straight-line amortization.
c. Show how the bond interest expense and the bonds payable would be reported on the December 31, 1977, annual financial statements.
d. What were the stated and approximate effective rates of interest? Why were they different?

E12–5. Vieux-Carre, Incorporated, issued $100,000 bonds payable on January 1, 1977, that were due in ten years. The bonds sold for $106,000 on that date. Interest at 6 percent per annum payable each June 30 and December 31.

Required:

a. Give the entry to record the issuance of the bonds on January 1, 1977.
b. Give the entry to record the first interest payment on June 30, 1977. Assume straight-line amortization.
c. Show how the bonds would be reported on the balance sheet December 31, 1977.
d. What were the stated and approximate effective rates of interest? Why were they different?

E12–6. In order to obtain cash for a purchase of fixed assets, Blye Corporation, whose annual accounting period ends on December 31, issued the following bonds:

Date of bonds: January 1, 1977.
Maturity amount and date: $100,000, due in ten years (December 31, 1986).
Interest: 6 percent per annum payable each June 30 and December 31.
Date sold: January 1, 1977.

Required:

a. Give the entry to record the issuance and the first two interest payments under each of three different assumptions. Assume straight-line amortization.

1. The bonds sold at par.
2. The bonds sold at 96.
3. The bonds sold at 104.

b. Provide the following amounts to be reported on the financial statements at the end of 1977:

	Assumption 1	*Assumption 2*	*Assumption 3*
Interest expense	$______	$______	$______
Bonds payable	______	______	______
Unamortized premium or discount	______	______	______
Net liability	______	______	______
Stated rate of interest	______	______	______
Approximate effective rate of interest	______	______	______

c. Why are the two rates different in each situation?

PART TWO: EXERCISES 12–7 TO 12–10

E12–7. Dawson Corporation issued the following bonds payable:

Bonds payable authorized	$50,000
Date on each bond	Jan. 1, 1977
Maturity date (ten years)	Dec. 31, 1986
Interest, 6% per year, payable each December 31.	

Dawson sold all of the bonds on March 1, 1977, and received $51,180 cash plus any accrued interest.

Required:

a. What was the amount of discount or premium?
b. Over what period of time should the discount or premium be amortized?
c. What would be the amortization amount per month assuming straight-line amortization?
d. Give entry to record the issuance.
e. Give entry on first interest payment date.
f. What amount should be reported as interest expense for 1977?
g. What amount of net liability should be shown on the balance sheet at December 31, 1977?
h. What was the approximate effective rate of interest? Why was it different from the stated rate?

E12–8. WT Corporation issued $10,000, 6 percent bonds payable dated April 1, 19A. Interest is paid each March 31. The bonds mature in 3 years on March 31, 19C. The bonds were sold on June 1, 19A, for $9,660 plus accrued interest. The accounting period ends each December 31.

Required:

a. Give the entry to record the issuance on June 1, 19A.
b. Give the adjusting entry required on December 31, 19A, assuming straight-line amortization.

c. What amount of interest expense should be reported on the income statement for 19A?

d. What amount of net liability should be reported on the balance sheet at December 31, 19A?

e. Give the entry to record the first interest payment on March 31, 19B.

E12-9. Smith Corporation has a $50,000 bond issue outstanding that is due four years hence. They desire to set up a bond sinking fund for this amount by making five equal annual contributions. The first contribution will be made immediately and the last one on the due date. They will deposit the contributions with a bank as trustee, which will increase the fund at the end of each year for 6 percent on the fund balance that existed at the beginning of the year.

Required:

a. Compute the annual contribution or rent.

b. Give entry for the first and second contributions, including interest.

c. Show how the effects of the fund would be reported on the financial statements at the end of the second year.

E12-10. Fluger Corporation issued a $1,000 bond payable on January 1, 1977. The bond specified an interest rate of 7 percent payable at the end of each year. The bond matures in three years. It was sold at an effective rate of 5 percent per year. In respect to the issuance of the bond, the following computation has been completed:

Date	*Cash*	*Interest*	*Principal*	*Balance*
January 1, 1977 (issuance) ...				$1,054
End of Year 1	$70	$53	$17	1,037
End of Year 2	70	52	18	1,019
End of Year 3	70	51	19	1,000

Required:

Respond to the following questions:

a. What was the issue price of the bond?

b. Did the bond sell at a discount or a premium? How much?

c. What amount of cash was paid each year for bond interest?

d. What amount of interest expense should be shown each year on the income statement?

e. What amount(s) should be shown on the balance sheet for bonds payable at each year-end (for Year 3, show the balance just before retirement of the bond)?

f. What method of amortization was used? Explain.

g. Show how the following amounts were computed for Year 2: (1) $70, (2) $52, (3) $18, and (4) $1,019.

h. Is the method of amortization used preferable? Explain why.

PROBLEMS

PART ONE: PROBLEMS 12–1 TO 12–5

P12–1. The financial statements of WT Corporation for 19A reflected the following:

Income Statement		Balance Sheet	
Revenue	$200,000	Assets	$150,000
Expenses	(139,000)		
Interest expense	(1,000)	Liabilities (average interest rate 10%)	$ 10,000
Pretax income	60,000	Common stock, par $10	100,000
Income taxes (40%)	(24,000)	Retained earnings	40,000
	$ 36,000		$150,000

To demonstrate leverage, assume that WT Corporation during 19A had $60,000 liabilities (instead of $10,000) and common stock of $50,000 (5,000 shares). That is, they financed the business more with debt.

Required:

a. Complete a table similar to the following to demonstrate the economic effects of financial leverage.

Item	*Actual results for 19A*	*Results assuming an increase in debt of $50,000*
a. Total debt		
b. Total assets		
c. Total stockholders' equity		
d. Interest expense (total)		
e. Net income (after interest and income tax)		
f. Return on total assets		
g. Earnings available to stockholders':		
1. Amount.		
2. Per share.		
3. Return on stockholders' equity.		

b. Write an explanation of the advantages and disadvantages of higher debt financing (i.e., higher leverage) in this situation.

P12–2. On January 1, 19A, XY Corporation sold and issued $100,000, 6 percent, five-year bonds payable. The bond interest is payable annually on each December 31. Assume the bonds were sold under three separate and independent cases: Case A, at par; Case B, at 95; and Case C, at 105.

Required:

a. Complete a tabulation similar to the following for each separate case assuming straight-line amortization of discount and premium. Disregard income taxes.

						At End of 19D	
	At Start of 19A	At End of 19A	At End of 19B	At End of 19C	At End of 19D	Prior to Payment of Principal	Payment of Principal
Case A—Sold at par (100): Cash inflow	$	$	$	$	$	$	$
Cash outflow							
Interest expense on income statement							
Net liability on balance sheet							
Case B—Sold at a discount (95): Cash inflow							
Cash outflow							
Interest expense on income statement							
Net liability on balance sheet							
Case C—Sold at a premium (105): Cash inflow							
Cash outflow							
Interest expense on income statement							
Net liability on balance sheet							

b. For each separate case, respond to each of the following:

	Case A	*Case B*	*Case C*
1. Total cash outflow	$_____	$_____	$_____
2. Total cash inflow	_____	_____	_____
3. Difference—net cash outflow	_____	_____	_____
4. Total interest expense	_____	_____	_____

c. 1. As between the three cases, explain why the net cash outflows are different.
2. For each case, explain why the net cash outflow is the same amount as total interest expense.

d. For each case, complete the tabulation similar to the following assuming an average income tax rate of 40 percent:

	Case A	*Case B*	*Case C*
Total interest expense	$____	$____	$____
Total income taxes saved	____	____	____
Net interest cost:			
In dollars	____	____	____
As an average net rate	____%	____%	____%

P12–3. Ward, Incorporated, issued bonds with the following provisions:

Maturity value:	$200,000.
Interest:	6% per annum payable semiannually each June 30 and December 31.
Terms:	Bonds dated January 1, 1977, due in ten years from that date.

The annual accounting period for Ward ends December 31. The bonds were sold on January 1, 1977, for $208,000.

Required:

a. Give journal entry to record the issuance of the bonds.

b. Give journal entries at the following dates (assume straight-line amortization): June 30, 1977; December 31, 1977; and June 30, 1978.

c. How much interest expense would be reported on the income statement for 1977? Show how liabilities relating to the bonds would be reported on the December 31, 1977, balance sheet.

d. What were the stated and approximate effective interest rates? Why were they different?

P12–4. May, Incorporated, issued $100,000 bonds payable, due in ten years, at 3 percent interest per semiannual period. The bonds were dated March 1, 1977, and interest is payable each February 28 and August 31.

The bonds were sold on April 1, 1977, at 98 plus accrued interest. The annual accounting period ends December 31.

Required:

a. Give the entry to record the issuance of the bonds on April 1, 1977.

b. Give the entry to record the first interest payment and amortization of discount on August 31, 1977. Assume straight-line amortization.

c. Give the required adjusting entry on December 31, 1977.

d. Give the amounts that should be reported on the 1977 financial statements for:

Interest expense.
Bonds payable.
Unamortized discount.
Net liability.

e. What were the stated and approximate effective interest rates? Why were they different?

P12–5. Assume a $200,000, 6 percent bond issue was sold on March 1, 1977. The bonds pay interest each February 28 and August 31 and will mature ten years from March 1, 1977. Using these data, complete the table below under three separate cases as follows (show computations and assume straight-line amortization):

Case A – The bonds sold at par.
Case B – The bonds sold at 97.
Case C – The bonds sold at 103.

	Case A	*Case B*	*Case C*
Cash inflow at issue date	______	______	______
Total cash outflow through maturity	______	______	______
Difference – total interest expense	______	______	______
Income Statement for 1977:			
Bond interest expense	______	______	______
Balance Sheet at December 31, 1977:			
Long-Term Liabilities:			
Bonds payable, 6%	______	______	______
Unamortized discount	______	______	______
Unamortized premium	______	______	______
Net liability	______	______	______
Stated interest rate	______	______	______
Approximate effective interest rate	______	______	______

PART TWO: PROBLEMS 12–6 TO 12–10

P12–6. Suber Corporation plans to sell a $300,000, ten-year bond issue dated July 1, 19A. The bonds will pay 6 percent interest each June 30. The accounting period ends December 31. Assume the bonds will be sold on August 1, 19A, under three different assumptions as follows:

Case A – sold at par.
Case B – sold at 98.
Case C – sold at 102.

Required:

On a separate sheet of paper, complete a table similar to the following assuming straight-line amortization.

	Case A	Case B	Case C
1. Cash received at issuance date	$______	$______	$______
2. Amount of accrued interest at issuance date	______	______	______
3. Amount of premium or discount at issuance date	______	______	______
4. Stated rate of interest	______%	______%	______%
5. Approximate effective rate of interest	______%	______%	______%
6. Interest expense reported for 19A	$______	$______	$______
7. Bonds payable reported at end of 19A	______	______	______
8. Unamortized premium or discount reported at end of 19A	______	______	______
9. Net liability reported at end of 19A	______	______	______
10. Accrued interest payable reported at end of 19A	______	______	______

P12–7. In order to expand to a new region, Goode Manufacturing Company decided to construct a new plant and warehouse. It was decided that approximately 60 percent of the resources required would be obtained through a $600,000 bond issue. Accordingly, the company developed and approved a bond indenture with the following provisions:

Date of bonds	March 1, 1977, due in ten years
Amount authorized	$600,000 (maturity amount)
Interest	6% per annum, payable 3% each February 28 and August 31

The annual accounting period ends on December 31. The bonds were sold on March 1, 1977, at 102.

Required:

a. How much cash was received by Goode on March 1, 1977?

b. What was the amount of the premium? Over how many months will it be amortized?

c. Complete the following tabulation (use straight-line amortization):

	Per month
Interest payment	$______
Premium amortization	$______
Net interest expense	$______

d. What were the stated and approximate effective interest rates? Why were they different?

e. Give entries, if any, at each of the following dates: March 1, 1977; August 31, 1977; December 31, 1977; January 1, 1978; and February 28, 1978.

f. In respect to the financial statements for December 31, 1977;

1. How much interest expense would be reported?
2. Show how the liabilities related to the bonds would be reported on the balance sheet.

P12–8. On January 1, 1966, Boston Corporation issued $500,000, 6 percent bonds payable due at the end of 15 years. The bonds specified semiannual interest payments on each June 30 and December 31. The bonds originally sold at 103. Additionally, the bond indenture called for the establishment of a bond sinking fund to be accumulated over the last five years by deposits of $90,000 on each January 1, starting in 1977. Interest on the fund is to be added to the fund at the end of each year.

Required:

a. Give entry for issuance of the bonds on January 1, 1966.
b. Give entry for the semiannual interest payment on the bonds on June 30, 1977. Assume straight-line amortization.
c. Give entry on January 1, 1977, for the first contribution of cash to the sinking fund.
d. Give the sinking fund entry at the end of 1977, assuming the interest earned on the first contribution amounted to $4,000.
e. Give the entry to retire the bonds at maturity assuming the total bond sinking fund accumulation to be $493,000.

P12–9. Johnson, Incorporated, in order to obtain funds to acquire additional long-term assets, approved the following bond indenture:

Maturity value authorized:	$600,000 (in $1,000 denominations)
Interest:	6% per annum, payable 3% each May 31 and November 30
Maturity:	Ten years from June 1, 1977
Bond sinking fund:	Starting at the beginning of the eighth bond year, deposit $150,000 annually in a bond sinking fund under the control of Trustee X. Interest earned by the fund shall be deposited in the fund. The bond sinking fund shall be used only to retire the bonds at maturity.

The annual accounting period for Johnson ends on December 31. The bonds were sold on August 1, 1977, for $623,700, which included two months' accrued interest (May 31 to August 1).

Required:

a. Give the entry to record issuance of the bonds.
b. Give the entries at the following dates (assume straight-line amortization):
   1. First interest date.
   2. End of first annual accounting period (1977).
   3. Beginning of second accounting period (1978).
   4. Second interest date.
c. In respect to the 1977 financial statements:
   1. How much interest expense would be reported on the 1977 income statement?

2. Show how the liabilities related to the bonds would be reported on the December 31, 1977, balance sheet.

d. Give the entry to record:
1. The first contribution to the sinking fund.
2. Interest earned on the sinking fund on the first contribution; amount, $6,000.

e. Give the entry to retire the bond issue at the end of the tenth year assuming the bond sinking fund has a balance of $510,000. (Note: The fund earnings rate varied from year to year).

P12–10. Foster Corporation issued bonds payable and received cash in full for the issue price. The bonds were dated and issued on January 1, 1977. The stated interest rate was payable at the end of each year. The bonds mature at the end of four years. In respect to the issuance of the bonds, the following computations have been completed:

Date	*Cash*	*Interest*	*Principal*	*Balance*
January 1, 1977				$5,173
End of Year 1	$350	$310	$40	5,133
End of Year 2	350	308	42	5,091
End of Year 3	350	305	45	5,046
End of Year 4	350	304	46	5,000

Required:

Respond to the following questions:

a. What was the maturity amount?

b. How much cash was received upon issuance?

c. Was there a premium or a discount? If so, which and how much?

d. How much cash will be disbursed for interest each period? In total for the life of the bond issue?

e. What method of amortization is being used? Explain.

f. What is the stated rate of interest?

g. What is the effective rate of interest?

h. Show how the following amounts for Year 3 were computed: (1) $350, (2) $305, (3) $45, and (4) $5,046.

i. What amount of interest expense should be reported on the income statement each year?

j. Show how the bonds should be reported on the balance sheet at the end of each year (show the last year immediately before retirement of the bonds).

k. Why is the method of amortization being used preferable to other methods? When must it be used?

13

Measurement and reporting of owners' equity

PURPOSE OF THE CHAPTER

Owners' equity is defined as the excess of total assets over total liabilities. It is a residual amount that represents the **book value** of the owners' interest in the business enterprise. Owners' equity appears somewhat differently on the balance sheet (and in the accounts) for a sole proprietorship, partnership, and corporation. With the same set of transactions, however, the *total amount* of owners' equity on a given date would be the same (except for income tax effects), irrespective of the type of business organization. The accounting entries and financial reporting for the three types of business organizations essentially are the same in all situations, *except for those entries that directly affect owners' equity.* This commonality exists because the underlying fundamentals of accounting (Exhibit 2–1) apply equally to each of the three types of business organizations.

Because of certain legal requirements and the full-disclosure principle, owners' equity for each of the three types of business organizations must be accounted for and reported in slightly different ways. Accounting for the owners' equity of a corporation is more complex than for a sole proprietorship or a partnership. The purpose of this chapter is to expand the prior discussions of owners' equity. Part One will focus on corporations, and Part Two on sole proprietorships and partnerships.

PART ONE: STOCKHOLDERS' EQUITY

CHARACTERISTICS OF A CORPORATION

In terms of volume of business the corporation is the dominant type of business organization in the United States. This is because the corporate form has three important advantages over the sole proprietorship and the partnership. First, the corporate form facilitates the bringing together of large amounts of funds through the sale of ownership interests (capital stock) to the public. Second, it facilitates the transfer of separate ownership interests because the shares can be easily transferred to others. Third, it affords the investor or stockholder limited liability.[1]

In contrast to a sole proprietorship or partnership, a corporation is recognized in law as a separate legal entity. Legally, it is separate and distinct from the owners and enjoys a continuous existence separate and apart from them. It may own property, sue others, be sued, and execute contracts independently of the stockholder owners.

Ownership in a corporation is evidenced by shares of **capital stock,** which are freely transferable without affecting the corporation. The owners of a corporation are known as stockholders or shareholders.

Each state has laws that govern the organization and operation of corporations. The laws of each state establish the requirements that must be met to organize a corporation. To form a corporation, an **application for a charter** must be submitted to the appropriate state official. The application must specify the name of the corporation, the purpose (type of business), kinds and amounts of capital stock authorized, and certain minimum financial contributions that must be made (through the sale of capital stock) at date of organization. Most states require a minimum of three stockholders initially. Upon approval of the application, the state issues a **charter** (sometimes called the **articles of incorporation**). The governing body of a corporation is the board of directors, which is elected by the shareholders.

When a person acquires shares of capital stock, a **stock certificate** is received as evidence of ownership interest in the corporation. The certificate will indicate the name of the stockholder, date purchased, type of stock, number of shares represented, and a description of the characteristics of the stock. Exhibit 13–1 shows a stock certificate for 100 shares of common stock. On the back of the certificate are instructions and blanks to be completed when the shares are sold or transferred to another party.

The charter granted by the state specifies the maximum number of shares of stock the corporation can issue. To illustrate, assume the charter for Rogers Corporation specified "authorized capital stock, 10,000 shares; par value, $10 per share." Assume further that the corporation immediately sold and issued 6,000 shares. The following terms are used to describe the status of the 10,000 shares permitted:

---

[1] In case of insolvency of a corporation, the creditors have recourse for their claims only to the assets of the corporation. Thus, the stockholders stand to lose, as a maximum, only their equity in the corporation. In contrast, in the case of a partnership or sole proprietorship, creditors have recourse to the personal assets of the owners in case the assets of the business are insufficient to meet the outstanding debts of the business.

EXHIBIT 13–1
Stock certificate

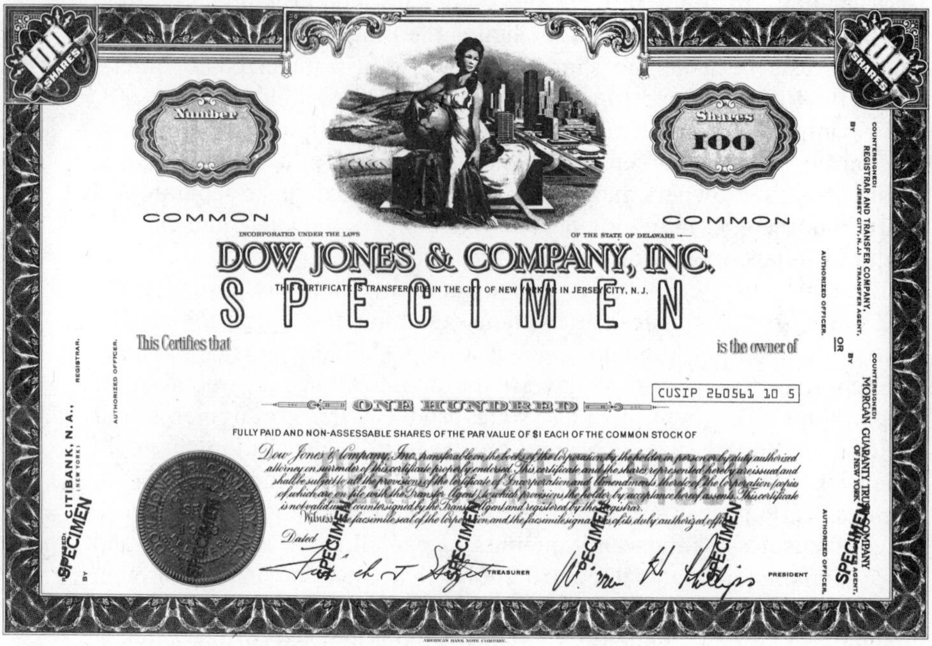

1. Authorized shares – the maximum number of shares of stock that can be sold and issued as specified in the charter of the corporation. For Rogers Corporation, the authorized shares would be 10,000.

2. Issued shares – the number of shares of capital stock that have been issued by the corporation to date. For Rogers Corporation, the issued shares at this time would be 6,000.

3. Unissued shares – the number of authorized shares of capital stock that have not been issued by the corporation to date. For Rogers Corporation, the unissued shares would be 4,000.

4. Subscribed shares – A corporation may sell some stock on credit and not issue it until payment is received. These are called subscribed shares. To illustrate, assume Rogers Corporation sold 500 shares to an individual and has not issued them because the sales price has not been collected. In this instance there would be 500 subscribed shares.

5. Treasury stock – A corporation may buy back some of its own shares previously sold. Shares of the corporation that have been sold and issued and subsequently repurchased and held by the issuing corporation are referred to as treasury stock. They are considered issued but not outstanding. To illustrate, assume Rogers Corporation purchased 200 of its own shares from a stockholder. The corporation then would have 200 shares of treasury stock.

6. Outstanding shares—the number of shares currently owned by stockholders. It is the number of shares *issued* less the number of shares of treasury stock held by the corporation. For example, for the Rogers Corporation, outstanding shares would be:

Issued shares	6,000
Less treasury stock	200
Outstanding shares	5,800

TYPES OF CAPITAL STOCK

The capital stock of a corporation may consist of only one kind of stock, which would be known as **common stock;** or it may consist of two kinds of stock—common stock and **preferred stock.** Common stock may be conveniently viewed as the "usual" or "normal" stock of the corporation. In contrast, preferred stock is distinguished because it grants certain **preferences.** These preferences generally specify that the preferred shareholders must receive their dividends *before* any dividends can be paid to the common shareholders. Because of the important differences between common and preferred stock, they are separately identified in the accounting and reporting processes.

Common stock

When only one class of stock is issued, it must be common. It has the voting rights and often is called the **residual equity** since it ranks after the preferred stock for dividends and assets distributed upon dissolution. However, since common stock has no dividend limits comparable with those associated with preferred, it has the possibility of higher dividends and increases in market value. The two primary classifications of common stock are par value and nopar value.

Par value and nopar value stock. Many years ago, all capital stock was par value. Par value is a **nominal** value per share established for the stock in the charter of the corporation and is printed on the face of each stock certificate. Stock that is sold by the corporation to investors above par value is said to sell at a premium, whereas, stock sold below par is said to sell at a discount. In recent years the laws of all states have been changed to forbid the initial sale of stock by the corporation to investors below par value.[2] Originally, the concept of par value was established as a protection to creditors and investors by means of a "cushion" of assets that could not

[2] The discussions throughout this chapter in respect to the sale of stock refer to the initial sale of the stock by the corporation rather than to later sales between investors as is the common situation in the day-to-day transactions of the stock markets. Since the sale of stock by a corporation at a discount is no longer legal, no further discussion of it is included. The sale of stock between individuals is not recorded in the accounts of the corporation.

be impaired. Par value does not establish market value or worth, and the idea that it represented a financial cushion was ill-conceived. Today, par value, when specified, only serves to identify the stated or legal capital of the corporation.

The par value concept proved to be ineffective in protecting either creditors or stockholders. For that reason, many states enacted legislation permitting **nopar value** stock. Nopar value common stock does not have an amount per share specified in the charter; therefore, it may be issued at any price without involving a **discount.** It also avoids giving the impression of a value that is not present. When nopar stock is used by a corporation, the legal, or stated, capital is as defined by the state law. State laws generally define it as (1) a stated amount per share set by the corporation itself or (2) as the amount for which the stock was sold originally.

In recent years, when par value stock is used, the par value is set at a very low amount (such as $1 per share) and the issuing (asking) price is set much higher (such as $10 per share). This avoids the possibility of a discount.

The term **legal capital,** or **stated capital,** is a matter of specification by the state incorporation laws. It varies between states; however, it is generally viewed as the par value of the stock outstanding (in the case of par value stock) or in the case of nopar value stock, the stated value set by the company or the amount for which the stock was originally sold. We shall see later that legal capital generally cannot be used as the basis for dividends. The stock certificate shown in Exhibit 13–1 is for common stock, par $1.

Preferred stock

When one or more classes of stock in addition to common are issued, the additional classes are called preferred stock. Preferred stock involves some modification that makes it different from the common stock. The usual modifications, (i.e., characteristics or features) of preferred stock are:

1. Dividend preferences.
2. Conversion privileges.
3. Asset preferences.
4. Nonvoting specifications.

Preferred stock generally has both favorable and unfavorable characteristics, in comparison with common stock.[3] Preferred stock almost

---

[3] A majority of corporations issue only common stock. Large corporations tend to have both common and preferred in their financial structure. Some large companies also issue more than one class of preferred stock in addition to the common stock.

always has a par value. For example, a corporation charter may specify "Authorized capital stock: nonvoting, 5 percent preferred stock, 5,000 shares, par value $20 per share; common stock, 100,000 shares, nopar value."

A corporation may choose to issue more than one class of stock (1) to obtain favorable control arrangements from its own point of view; (2) to issue stock without voting privileges; and (3) to appeal to a wide range of investors with the special provisions on the preferred stock.

The dividend preferences of preferred stock will be discussed and illustrated later in the chapter. The other features may be briefly explained as follows:

Convertible preferred stock extends to the preferred stockholders the option to turn in their preferred shares and receive in return shares of common stock of the corporation. The terms for the conversion will specify dates and a conversion ratio. To illustrate, in the example above, the charter could have read: "Each share of preferred stock, at the option of the shareholder, can be converted to two shares of the nopar common stock anytime after January 1, 1980."

Asset preferences almost always are specified for preferred stock. It is a preference as to the distribution of assets (1) in the event that the corporation *dissolves* or (2) in the event the corporation "calls" the preferred stock. The asset preference often is somewhat higher than the par value; that is, upon redemption of the preferred stock or dissolution of the corporation, the preferred stockholders would receive cash equal to the asset preference of their stock before any distribution could be made to the common stockholders. To illustrate, in the above example, the asset preference could have been specified as $25 per share. If it were, then a holder of the preferred stock would be entitled to receive on call or dissolution, $25 per share before a shareholder of common stock would receive anything.

Nonvoting preferred stock is customary, despite the fact that the nonvoting feature is undesirable to the investor. This feature denies the preferred stockholder the right to vote at stockholder meetings. It is one avenue for obtaining capital without lessening the control of the common stockholders.

ACCOUNTING AND REPORTING CAPITAL STOCK

In accounting and reporting for shareholders' equity, accountants follow the concept of **sources.** Under this concept, the capital or owners' equity from different sources is recorded in separate accounts and reported separately in the stockholders' equity section of the balance sheet. The two basic sources of stockholders' equity are:

1. Contributed capital—the amount invested by stockholders through the purchase of shares of stock from the corporation. It is comprised of two basic separate elements: (*a*) stated capital—amounts derived from the sale of capital stock and (*b*) additional contributed capital—amounts derived from the sale of stock above par. This is also sometimes referred to as **paid-in capital.**
2. Retained earnings—the cumulative amount of net income earned since organization of the corporation less the cumulative amount of dividends paid by the corporation since organization.

First, we will discuss and illustrate contributed capital. For illustrative purposes in this section, we will use Siesta Corporation. Assume the charter specified two types of capital stock as follows:

Authorized capital stock:
Preferred stock, 5%, 1,000 shares, $10 par value per share.
Common stock, 200,000 shares, $1 par value per share.

Sale of capital stock

When par value stock is sold and issued, Cash is debited and an appropriately designated contributed capital account for each type of stock is credited. The difference between the selling price and the par value of the stock is credited to a separate contributed capital account entitled "Contributed Capital in Excess of Par." To illustrate, assume Siesta Corporation sold 400 shares of preferred stock at $15 per share and 100,000 shares of common stock at $5 per share. The entry would be:

Cash ($6,000 + $500,000)	506,000	
Preferred stock (400 shares × $10 par value)		4,000
Contributed capital in excess of par, preferred (400 shares × [$15 − $10])		2,000
Common stock (100,000 shares × $1 par value)		100,000
Contributed capital in excess of par, common (100,000 shares × [$5 − $1])		400,000

Observe in the above entry that the two capital stock accounts were credited for the *par value* of the shares sold and the differences between selling price and the par value were credited to two other contributed capital accounts. There were *two* basic "sources" to be recognized—preferred and common stock—and each source was subdivided between the par value and the excess received over par.[4]

Now, assume a balance sheet is prepared after the above entry. The **stockholders' equity** would be reported as follows:

[4] Contributed capital in excess of par sometimes is called "premium on stock" or "paid-in capital above par."

Stockholders' Equity

Contributed Capital:		
5% preferred stock, par $10; authorized 1,000 shares, issued and outstanding, 400 shares	$ 4,000	
Common stock, par $1; authorized 200,000 shares, issued and outstanding, 100,000 shares	100,000	
Contributed capital in excess of par:		
Preferred stock	2,000	
Common stock	400,000	
Total Contributed Capital		$506,000
Retained earnings (illustrated later).		

Capital stock sold for noncash assets or services. When noncash considerations, such as buildings, land, machinery, and services (e.g., attorney fees), are received in payment for capital stock issued, the assets received (or expenses, in the case of services) should be recorded by the issuing corporation at the **fair-market value** of the stock issued at the date of the transaction in accordance with the cost principle. Alternatively, if the fair-market value of the stock issued cannot be determined, then the fair-market value of the consideration received should be used. To illustrate, assume Siesta Corporation issued 50 shares of common stock for legal services when the stock was regularly selling at $5 per share. The entry would be:

Legal expense (50 shares × $5)	250	
Common stock (50 shares × $1 par)		50
Contributed capital in excess of par, common stock (50 shares × [$5 − $1])		200

Accounting for nopar stock. Nopar stock does not have a particular "value" specified in the charter of the corporation. As a consequence, when nopar stock is sold and issued, it may be recorded in one of two ways, depending on the laws of the particular state that granted the charter. In some states the law requires the corporation, after the charter is granted for nopar stock, to set a *stated* value per share. This stated value becomes the *legal* capital and is credited to the nopar capital stock and any excess is credited to "Contributed Capital in Excess of Stated Value." To illustrate, assume that Elgin Corporation sold and issued 1,000 shares of its nopar common stock at $25 per share. Assume further that the corporation established a *stated value* of $20 per share. The sale and issuance of the nopar stock would be recorded as follows:

Cash	25,000	
Nopar common stock (1,000 shares × $20)		20,000
Contributed capital in excess of stated value, nopar common stock		5,000

Sale and issuance of 1,000 shares of nopar common stock at $25 per share; stated value, $20 per share.

In contrast, the corporation may be chartered in a state where the law requires that the corporation must credit *all* of the proceeds from the sale of its nopar capital stock to the Nopar Capital Stock account. In this situation there would be no "stated" value. To illustrate, under these circumstances, Elgin Corporation would record the sale and issuance of the nopar common stock at $25 per share as follows:

Cash	25,000	
Nopar common stock		25,000
Sale and issuance of 1,000 shares of nopar common stock at $25 per share		

At this point it may be emphasized that there is no difference in accounting between preferred and common stock, except that each is recorded in separate accounts. On the financial statements, common and preferred stock are reported in the same manner, although separately.

TREASURY STOCK

Treasury stock is a corporation's own capital stock that was sold, collected for, issued, and subsequently reacquired by the corporation. Corporations frequently purchase shares of their own capital stock for sound business reasons—to obtain shares needed for employee bonus plans; to influence the market price of the stock; to increase their earnings per share amount; or to have shares on hand for use in the acquisition of other companies. Treasury stock, while held by the issuing corporation, has no voting, dividend, or other stockholder rights.[5]

When a corporation purchases its own capital stock, the assets (usually cash) of the corporation and the stockholders' equity are reduced by equal amounts. When treasury stock is sold, the opposite effects occur. Purchases of treasury stock generally are recorded by debiting the cost to a *negative* stockholders' equity account called Treasury Stock (by type of stock) and crediting Cash. Since the Treasury Stock account has a debit balance, it is often referred to as a negative stockholders' equity account. When treasury stock is sold, the Treasury Stock account is credited at cost and Cash is debited. Generally, the purchase and selling prices will be different, necessitating recognition of the difference in an appropriately designated contributed capital account in the entry to record the sale. To illustrate accounting for treasury stock, assume the balance sheet for May Corporation reflected the following on January 1, 1977:[6]

[5] The laws of most states impose certain restrictions on the amount of treasury stock a corporation can hold at any one time since this is an avenue for taking resources out of the corporation by the owners (stockholders), which may jeopardize the rights of creditors. The law in some states limits the cost of treasury stock that can be purchased to the balance reflected in the Retained Earnings account.

[6] There are two alternative approaches to accounting for treasury stock—the cost method and the par value method. We will limit our discussions to the cost method since it

MAY CORPORATION
Summarized Balance Sheet
January 1, 1977

Assets		*Stockholders' Equity*	
Cash	$ 30,000	Contributed Capital:	
Other assets	70,000	Common stock, par $10, authorized 10,000 shares, issued 8,000 shares	$ 80,000
		Retained earnings	20,000
Total Assets	$100,000	Total Stockholders' Equity	$100,000

Assume that on January 2, 1977, May Corporation purchased 300 of the outstanding shares of its own common stock at $12 per share. The transaction would be recorded as follows:

January 2, 1977:

Treasury stock, common (300 shares at cost)	3,600	
Cash		3,600
Purchased 300 shares of treasury stock at $12 per share.		

The effect of this entry is to reduce both the assets and stockholders' equity by $3,600. Now, assume that on February 14, 1977, one third of the treasury shares were resold at $13 per share. This transaction will have the effect of expanding both assets and stockholders' equity by $1,300. These effects are reflected in the following entry to record the resale of 100 of the treasury shares:

February 14, 1977:

Cash	1,300	
Treasury stock, common (100 shares at cost)		1,200
Contributed capital, treasury stock transactions		100
Sold 100 shares of treasury stock at $13; cost, $12 per share.		

The Treasury Stock account has a debit balance, although owners' equity accounts normally carry a credit balance. Since the balance in the Treasury Stock account reflects a **contraction** of stockholders' equity, it is a negative equity account and is **subtracted** from total stockholders' equity. To illustrate, a balance sheet at February 15, 1977 assuming no other transactions by May Corporation, would be:[7]

is less complex and more widely used. The par value method is discussed in most accounting texts at the intermediate level.

[7] Some people argue that the debit balance in the Treasury Stock account should be reported on the balance sheet as an asset rather than as a reduction in stockholders' equity. This position is supported by the argument that the treasury stock could be sold for cash just as readily as the shares of other corporations. The argument is fallacious; all *unissued* stock of the corporation presumably also could be sold for cash, yet it is not considered to be an asset.

MAY CORPORATION
Summarized Balance Sheet
February 15, 1977

Assets		*Stockholders' Equity*	
Cash	$27,700	Contributed Capital:	
Other assets	70,000	Common stock, par $10, authorized 10,000 shares, issued 8,000, of which 200 shares are held as treasury stock	$ 80,000
		Contributed capital, treasury stock transactions	100
		Total Contributed Capital	80,100
		Retained earnings	20,000
		Total	100,100
		Less cost of treasury stock held	2,400
Total Assets	$97,700	Total Stockholders' Equity	$ 97,700

Upon resale of the 100 shares of treasury stock, **contributed capital** was increased by $100, which was the difference between cost and sales price of the treasury shares sold. Observe that this difference was *not* recorded as a gain as would be done for the sale of an asset. The basic accounting concept is that "gains or losses" on transactions involving a corporation's own stock are balance sheet (*stockholder equity*) items and not income statement items.

Also observe in the preceding balance sheet that May Company, on February 15, 1977, has both **treasury stock** and **unissued stock;** there are 200 shares of treasury stock held and 2,000 shares of unissued stock. The purchase and/or resale of treasury stock does not affect the number of shares of unissued (or issued) stock; however, the number of shares of *outstanding* stock is affected. The only difference between treasury stock and unissued stock is that treasury stock has been sold at least once and recorded in the accounts.

To illustrate the resale of treasury stock at a price *less than cost,* assume that an additional 50 shares of the treasury stock were resold by May Corporation on March 1, 1977, at $11 per share; that is, $1 per share below cost. The resulting entry would be:

March 1, 1977

Cash	550	
Contributed capital, treasury stock transactions	50	
Treasury stock, common (50 shares)		600
Sold 50 shares of treasury stock at $11 per share; cost, $12 per share.		

Note that the difference was debited to the same contributed capital account to which the difference in the preceding entry was credited. Retained Earnings would be debited for the amount of the deficiency only if there is no credit balance or there is an insufficient credit balance in the account Contributed Capital, Treasury Stock Transactions.

ACCOUNTING FOR DIVIDENDS

A dividend is a distribution to stockholders by a corporation. Dividends must be voted by the board of directors of the corporation before they can be paid. Dividends may involve the distribution of cash, other assets of the corporation, or the corporation's own stock (i.e., a stock dividend). The term *"dividend,"* without a qualifier, generally is understood to mean a cash dividend, which is the most common type. Dividends normally are stated in terms of so many dollars per share, or as a percent of par value.

For illustrative purposes in this section, we will use Monarch Corporation and will assume capital stock outstanding and retained earnings as follows:

5% preferred stock, par $20, shares outstanding 2,000	$40,000
Common stock, par $10, shares outstanding 5,000	50,000
Retained earnings	40,000

To illustrate the payment of a cash dividend, assume the board of directors voted the following:

"On December 1, 1977, the Board of Directors of the Monarch Corporation hereby declares an annual cash dividend of $2 per share on the common stock and 5 percent per share on the preferred stock to the stockholders on date of record, December 10, 1977, payable on December 15, 1977." The entry to record the declaration and payment of the cash dividend would be:

December 15, 1977:

Dividends paid, common stock	10,000	
Dividends paid, preferred stock	2,000	
Cash		12,000

To record payment of a cash dividend:
Common stock, 5,000 shares × $2 = $10,000
Preferred stock, $40,000 × 0.05 = $2,000

In the above entry the debits were to a temporary account, Dividends Paid. This account is closed to Retained Earnings at the end of the period. Many accountants prefer to make the debits directly to Retained Earnings rather than using the temporary Dividends Paid accounts. The effect is precisely the same in either case. The important point to observe is that the payment of a cash dividend has two effects: (1) assets are decreased and (2) retained earnings (i.e., owners' equity) is decreased by the same amount.

NATURE OF A CASH DIVIDEND

An investor expends cash to acquire shares of stock as an investment. The incentive for buying the shares is to earn an economic return on the investment. Specifically, the investor expects cash inflows in the future that will return both the initial investment and a gain. The investor's cash inflows in the future from the stock investment are expected to come from two sources: (1) current cash inflows in the form of dividends on the shares; and (2) a cash inflow at the time the stock is sold. Thus the investor anticipates that the sum of these two cash inflows will be greater than the original investment in the shares. The cash inflow from dividends is considered by the investor to be revenue. The other cash inflow (from sale of the shares) usually will result in a **market** gain or loss, depending on whether the investor sells the shares above or below the acquisition price. The amounts and frequency of dividends paid by a corporation generally have an effect on the market price of the stock.

Now, let's look at a cash dividend from the viewpoint of the corporation. A corporation has the earning of income on the resources provided by the stockholders as a primary objective. The ability to attract and retain resources from present and potential stockholders in the long run depends in good measure on the earnings record. The profits of a corporation may be retained in the business for corporate expansion or paid to the shareholders as dividends. One of the significant decisions faced by the board of directors of a corporation is how much of the earnings should be retained and how much should be distributed to the shareholders as dividends each year.

In the entry above to record the cash dividend, it is significant to note that both assets (i.e., cash) and owners' equity (i.e., retained earnings) are decreased by the amount of the dividend. This fact suggests that there are two fundamental requirements for the payment of a cash dividend:

1. Sufficient retained earnings—The corporation must have accumulated a sufficient amount of retained earnings to cover the amount of the dividends. State laws place a restriction on cash dividends. The laws tend to limit dividends to the balance in Retained Earnings. As a matter of financial policy, and to meet growth objectives, corporations seldom disburse more than 40–60 percent of the average net income amount as dividends.
2. Sufficient cash—The corporation must have access to cash sufficient to pay the dividend, and in addition, adequate cash to meet the continuing operating needs of the business. The mere fact that there is a large *credit* in the Retained Earnings account does not indicate sufficient cash. The cash generated by earnings represented in the Retained Earnings account may have been expended in acquiring inventory, purchasing fixed assets, or paying liabilities. There is no necessary relationship between the balance of retained earnings and the balance of cash.

DIVIDENDS ON PREFERRED STOCK

Recall that preferred stock grants to its holders certain rights that have precedence over the rights granted by common stock. The primary distinguishing characteristic of preferred stock are dividend preferences. The **dividend preferences** may be classified as follows:[8]

1. Current dividend preference.
2. Cumulative dividend preference.
3. Participating dividend preference.

Preferred stock may have one or a combination of these three dividend features. The charter of the corporation must state specifically the distinctive features of the preferred stock.

Current dividend preference

Preferred stock usually carries a current dividend preference. This preference assures the preferred shareholders that, if any *current dividends* are paid, their current dividend must be paid before any dividends can be paid on the common stock. When the current dividend preference is met and no other preference is operative, dividends can then be paid to the common stock shareholders. The current dividend preference almost always is a specified percent of the par value of the preferred stock. To illustrate, the preferred stock of the Monarch Corporation was: "5 percent perferred stock, par $20 per share, 2,000 shares outstanding, total par value outstanding $40,000." The current dividend preference is $20 × 0.05 = $1 per share of preferred. Therefore, current dividends paid by Monarch Corporation, under four different assumptions in respect to the total dividends paid, would be divided between the preferred and common shareholders as follows:

MONARCH CORPORATION
Current Dividend Preference

Assumption		*Amount of dividend paid to shareholders*	
Designation	*Total dividends paid*	*5% preferred stock (2,000 shares @ $20 par = $40,000)**	*Common stock (5,000 shares @ $10 par = $50,000)*
A	$1,000	$1,000	$ -0-
B	2,000	2,000	-0-
C	3,000	2,000	1,000
D	8,000	2,000	6,000

* Preferred dividend preference, $40,000 × 0.05 = $2,000.

[8] A dividend preference does not mean that dividends will be paid automatically. Dividends are paid only when *formally* declared by the corporation's board of directors. Thus, the declaration of a dividend is discretionary. A typical dividend problem involves the allocation of a total amount of dividends declared between the preferred and common stock as illustrated above.

Cumulative dividend preference

If preferred stock has this feature, it is said to be "cumulative preferred stock." This means that if all or a part of the specified dividend (5 percent in the above example) is not paid in a given year, the unpaid amount becomes dividends **in arrears.** If the preferred stock is cumulative, the dividends in arrears must be paid at subsequent dates before any dividends can be paid to the common shareholders. To illustrate, assume in the above example for Monarch Corporation that no dividends were paid in the two preceding years. Therefore, a dividend payment, assuming two years in arrears, under four different assumptions, would be divided between the preferred and common stock as follows:

MONARCH CORPORATION
Cumulative Preferred Stock

Assumption		*Amount of dividend paid to shareholders*	
Designation	*Total dividends paid*	*5% preferred stock (2,000 shares @ $20 par = $40,000)**	*Common stock (5,000 shares @ $10 par = $50,000)*
A	$ 4,000	$4,000	$ -0-
B	6,000	6,000	-0-
C	8,000	6,000	2,000
D	15,000	6,000	9,000

* Current dividend preference, $40,000 × 0.05 = $2,000; dividends in arrears preference, $2,000 × 2 years = $4,000.

Of course, if the preferred stock is noncumulative, dividends can never be in arrears and, in effect, are lost to the preferred stockholders. Because of this highly unfavorable feature for the preferred stockholders, preferred stock usually is cumulative.

Participating dividend preference

Preferred stock may be (1) nonparticipating, (2) fully participating, or (3) partially participating. These features relate to dividends that might be paid to preferred shareholders *above* the current dividend preference (i.e., above the 5 percent of par value in the above example) and above any cumulative dividends in arrears.

Most preferred stock is **nonparticipating;** that is, the amount of dividends payable to preferred shareholders in any one year is limited, in the absence of dividends in arrears, to the specified rate or amount. If the stock is cumulative, the preferred dividends are limited to the amount in arrears plus the specified dividend preference for the current year. To illustrate, assume Monarch 5 percent preferred stock is nonparticipating and *non*cumulative. Under this assumption, dividends on the preferred stock would be limited to the maximum of 5 percent of par (i.e., $1 per share) in any one year. However, if Monarch preferred stock were nonparticipating and cumulative, the preferred shareholders would be limited to the $1 per share for the current dividend *plus* the dividends in arrears.

Alternatively, preferred stock may be **fully participating.** This means that the preferred stock participates pro rata with common stock above the specified preference rate (5 percent in the above example) and with no specified upper limit to the annual dividend rate. When the preferred stock is fully participating, after the specified preference on the preferred stock is satisfied each year, the common stockholders then would receive an equivalent percentage amount, after which each group of stockholders would participate on an equivalent pro rata basis. To illustrate, dividends for Monarch Corporation under two different assumptions as to the preferred stock would be divided between the preferred and common shareholders as follows:

MONARCH CORPORATION
Participating Preferred Stock

		Amount of dividend paid to	
Assumptions	*Total dividends paid*	*Preferred shareholders (total par $40,000)*	*Common shareholders (total par $50,000)*
Case A—Preferred stock is cumulative and nonparticipating (two years in arrears). Total dividends paid $13,000.			
Arrears	$ 4,000	$4,000	
Current dividend	9,000	2,000	$7,000
Totals	$13,000	$6,000	$7,000
Case B—Preferred stock is cumulative and fully participating (two years in arrears). Total dividends paid $13,000.			
Arrears	$ 4,000	$4,000	
Current preference	2,000	2,000	
Equivalent amount to common ($50,000 × 5%)	2,500		$2,500
Subtotal	8,500		
Balance divided in ratio of par value:			
($40,000/$90,000) × ($13,000 − $8,500)	2,000	2,000	
($50,000/$90,000) × ($13,000 − $8,500)	2,500		2,500
Totals	$13,000	$8,000	$5,000

Partially participating preferred stock is the same as fully participating, except that the participating preference above the current dividend rate is limited to a stated percent of par. For example, the charter may read, ". . . and partially participating up to an additional two percent." Fully participating and partially participating preferred stock preferences are rather rare.[9]

STOCK DIVIDENDS

Instead of paying a cash dividend, the board of directors of a corporation may decide to distribute to the stockholders, on a *pro rata basis,* additional shares of the corporation's own unissued stock. This is known as a **stock dividend.** Stock dividends almost always consist of common stock being distributed to holders of common stock. To illustrate, assume Monarch Corporation distributed a 10 percent common-stock dividend to the shareholders. For each ten shares of common stock held, one additional common share would be issued.

In contrast to a cash dividend, a stock dividend does *not affect the assets* of a corporation or the *total* amount of stockholders' equity. A stock dividend causes only an internal change in stockholders' equity. In accounting for a stock dividend, *Retained Earnings* is decreased (i.e., debited) and *Contributed Capital* is increased (i.e., credited) by the amount of the stock dividend. The 10 percent stock dividend for Monarch Corporation would require the company to issue 500 additional shares (i.e., 5,000 shares outstanding × 10 percent) of the unissued common stock. The entry to record the distribution of the stock dividend, assuming a current market value of $15 per share, would be:[10]

Retained earnings, or dividends paid (500 shares × $15)	7,500	
Common stock (500 shares × $10 par)		5,000
Contributed capital in excess of par, common stock (500 shares × $5)		2,500
Common stock dividend of 10 percent distributed when market value per share was $15.		

The transfer of retained earnings to permanent or contributed capital by means of a stock dividend often is referred to as **capitalizing earnings.** To restate: The only effects on the corporation issuing a stock dividend is to reshuffle the internal content of stockholders' equity and to increase the number of shares outstanding. From the viewpoint of the stockholder, additional shares of stock are received; however the stockholder owns the same *proportion* of the total common shares outstanding after the stock dividend as before.

[9] Refer to more advanced books for additional discussion and illustrations of the participating features and the payment of a dividend in assets other than cash, such as property and stock of other corporations being held as an investment.

[10] Some accountants prefer to debit an account called "Stock Dividends Distributed," which is closed to Retained Earnings at the end of the period. The effect is precisely the same.

Observe in the above illustration that the amount for the stock dividend transferred from Retained Earnings to Contributed Capital was the *current fair-market value* of the shares issued (i.e., $15 × 500 shares = $7,500). This amount is considered appropriate when the stock dividend is "small"; that is, when it is less than 25 percent of the previously outstanding shares. In those cases where a stock dividend is "large" (i.e., over 25 percent), some accountants believe that the amount transferred should be the par value of the shares issued. Par value is considered to be the absolute minimum since stock cannot be issued at a discount. Fair-market value is preferred by many accountants primarily because (1) it is the amount that would be credited to Contributed Capital if the stock were sold at the current price, and (2) it is the amount that would be debited to Retained Earnings for a cash dividend equal to the current cash equivalent of the stock issued.

Reasons for stock dividends. Stock dividends are fairly common because they serve useful purposes both from the viewpoint of the corporation and the individual stockholder. The two primary purposes of a stock dividend are:

1. To maintain dividend consistency—Many corporations prefer to declare dividends each year. In the case of a cash shortage, the dividend record may be maintained by issuing a stock dividend. Stock dividends tend to satisfy the demands of stockholders for continuing dividends and yet avoid the demand on cash. Also, a stock dividend is not considered to be revenue to the shareholder for income tax purposes. Shareholders view stock dividends as quite different than a cash dividend.
2. To "capitalize" retained earnings—A stock dividend is used to transfer retained earnings to permanent capital and thus remove such earnings from cash dividend availability. When a corporation consistently retains a substantial percent of its earnings for growth, the related funds are, more or less, permanently invested in long-term assets such as plant and other property. Therefore, it is considered realistic to transfer those accumulated earnings to permanent capital. A stock dividend is a convenient approach for doing this. In profitable corporations that are expanding rapidly, this may be the fundamental reason for stock dividends.

Stock split. A stock dividend should not be confused with a **stock split.** In a stock split, the number of shares is increased by a specified amount, such as a two-for-one split. In this instance, each share held is called in and two shares are issued in its place. A stock split is accomplished by reducing the par or stated value per share, so that the total par value outstanding is unchanged. For example, assuming $20 par value stock before a split, the two-for-one split would involve reducing the par value of the two shares received to $10 per share. In contrast to a stock dividend, a stock split does not result in a transfer of Retained Earnings to Contributed Capital. No transfer is needed in view of the change in the par value per share to accomplish the increased number of shares. The primary reason for a stock split is to reduce the market price *per share,* which tends to increase the market activity of the stock.

DIVIDEND DATES

The preceding discussions assumed that a dividend was paid immediately after its declaration by the board of directors. There often is a time lag involved. For example, a typical dividend declaration would be as follows: "On November 20, 1977, the Board of Directors of XY Corporation declared a $0.25 per share cash dividend on the 200,000 shares of nopar common stock outstanding. The dividend will be paid to stockholders of record at December 15, 1977 on January 15, 1978." In this declaration there are three identified dates. Strict accounting in respect to each date would be:

1. Declaration date – November 20, 1977: This is the date on which the board of directors officially voted the dividend. As soon as public announcement of the declaration is made, legally it is nonrevocable; hence, a dividend *liability* immediately comes into existence. Accordingly, on this date the **declaration** by XY Corporation would be recorded as follows:

   November 20, 1977:

Retained earnings (or dividends paid)	50,000	
Dividends payable		50,000

   Cash dividend declared: 200,000 shares × $0.25 = $50,000.

   The December 31, 1977, balance sheet would report Dividends Payable as a current liability.
2. Date of record – December 15, 1977: This date follows the declaration date, usually by about one month, as specified in the declaration. It is the date on which the corporation takes from its stockholders' records the list of individuals owning shares. The dividend is payable only to those names listed on the record date. Thus, share transfers between buyers and sellers reported to the corporation before this date result in the dividend being paid to the new owner. Changes reported after this date are not recognized for this particular dividend; they will be effective for subsequent dividends. No accounting entry would be made on this date.
3. Date of payment – January 15, 1978: This is the date on which the cash will be disbursed to pay the dividend. It follows the date of

record as specified in the dividend announcement. The entry to record the cash disbursement by XY Corporation would be as follows:

January 15, 1978:

Dividends payable	50,000	
Cash		50,000

Paid dividend declared and recorded on November 20, 1977.

For instructional purposes this time lag usually is disregarded since it does not pose any substantive issues. Also when all of the dates fall in the same accounting period, a single entry on the date of payment usually is made in practice.

STOCKHOLDER RECORDS

A corporation must maintain a record of each stockholder. The record includes at least the name, address, number of shares purchased of each type of stock, certificate numbers, dates acquired, and shares sold. Such a record is known as the **stockholders' subsidiary ledger.** The Capital Stock account serves as the controlling account in the general ledger for this subsidiary ledger. Sales of shares by a stockholder to others must be reported to the corporation so that new stock certificates can be issued and the stockholders' subsidiary ledger can be changed accordingly. Dividends are sent only to the names and addresses shown in the stockholders' subsidiary ledger. Large corporations with thousands of stockholders generally pay an independent **stock transfer agent** to handle the transfer of shares, to issue new stock certificates, and to maintain the equivalent of a stockholders' subsidiary ledger.

A particularly important record that must be maintained by all corporations is called the **minute book.** This is an official record of the actions taken at all meetings of the board of directors and of the stockholders. The independent auditor is required to inspect the minute book as a part of the audit program.

REPORTING RETAINED EARNINGS

The preceding chapters have emphasized that the income statement reports two *income* amounts: (1) income before extraordinary items and (2) net income (i.e., after extraordinary items). Net income is closed to the Income Summary account and is also reported on the statement of retained earnings. APB *Opinion No. 30* (dated June 1973) defines extraordinary items as those transactions and events that meet two criteria: (1) unusual in nature for the business and (2) infrequency of occurrence. They are set out separately on the income statement to help the statement

EXHIBIT 13–2

FERRARI CORPORATION
Statement of Retained Earnings
For the Year Ended December 31, 1977

Retained earnings balance, January 1, 1977		$240,000
Prior period adjustment:		
Deduct adjustment for additional 1972 federal income taxes		24,000
Balance as restated		216,000
Net income for 1977		34,000
Total		250,000
Deduct dividends declared in 1977:		
On preferred stock	$ 6,000	
On common stock	12,000	18,000
Retained earnings balance, December 31, 1977 (see Note 5)		$232,000

Note 5. Restrictions on retained earnings; total, $137,400:

a. Treasury stock—The corporation has treasury stock that cost $37,400. The state law requires that retained earnings be restricted from dividend availability by the cost of all treasury stock held.

b. Bonds payable—The bond indenture requires that retained earnings be restricted in accordance with an agreed schedule. The schedule amount for 1977 and 1978 is $100,000.

user to focus on recurring normal operations since this is the best measure of earnings potential. We have also explained and illustrated the requirement by APB *Opinion No. 15* that earnings per share amounts be reported on the income statement for a corporation.

Similarly, we have discussed and illustrated the **statement of retained earnings.** Although not a required statement, it is almost always presented in conformity with the full-disclosure principle. Since retained earnings is one of two basic components of stockholders' equity, we should extend our knowledge of it at this point. A typical statement of retained earnings is shown in Exhibit 13–2.

The statement of retained earnings shown in Exhibit 13–2 reports two kinds of items that have not been discussed: (1) prior period adjustments and (2) restrictions on retained earnings.

Prior period adjustments. This category of events is defined in APB *Opinion No. 9* essentially as follows:

> Prior period adjustments are those rare adjustments, material in amount, which (a) are directly related to prior periods, (b) are not the result of events in the current or future periods, (c) resulted from determinations of persons other than the management of the business, and (d) were not susceptible to reasonable estimation as to their economic effect when the prior event occurred. Since a prior period adjustment must meet *all* of these criteria, they very rarely occur.

Examples of prior period adjustments given in APB *Opinion No. 9* are: (1) tax adjustments from prior years, (2) settlement of lawsuits initiated in prior periods, and (3) correction of accounting errors. Prior period adjustments are recorded in a special account which is closed directly to Retained Earnings at the end of the period rather than to Income Summary. Consistent with this, they *must* be reported on the statement of retained earnings as illustrated in Exhibit 13–2 rather than on the income statement. Observe in the definitions above that they are quite different in concept from extraordinary items.

Restrictions on retained earnings. Corporations frequently have restrictions on retained earnings. Basically, such a restriction removes that amount of retained earnings from availability for dividends. When the restriction is removed, the amount that was restricted then resumes dividend-availability status. Restrictions on retained earnings may be voluntary or involuntary. For example, the two restrictions reported on Exhibit 13–2 would be considered involuntary; one was imposed by law (i.e., the treasury stock restriction) and the other was imposed by contract. On occasion, the management or the board of directors may voluntarily establish a restriction on retained earnings for expansion of the business attained by using internally generated funds such as "Retained earnings appropriated for profits invested in plant and equipment." Of course, this restriction can be removed at will by the management.

The full-disclosure principle requires that restrictions on retained earnings be reported directly on the financial statements or as a separate note to the financial statements. The approach most widely used follows the illustration in Exhibit 13–2.

A practice widely used in past years, but used now infrequently, was to set up a special retained earnings account for each appropriation. Such accounts, somewhat illogically, were often called "reserves." To illustrate, if Ferrari Corporation had followed this approach, it would have made the following entry:

Retained earnings	137,400	
Reserve for cost of treasury stock		37,400
Reserve for bonds payable		100,000

In preparing the statement of retained earnings, these two accounts would be listed on the statement of retained earnings and the footnote would be unnecessary. When the restrictions are removed, the above entry is reversed.

PART TWO: OWNERS' EQUITY FOR SOLE PROPRIETORSHIP AND PARTNERSHIP

OWNER'S EQUITY FOR A SOLE PROPRIETORSHIP

A sole proprietorship is a business owned by one person. As a consequence, accounting for owner's equity is simple. The only owner's equity accounts needed are: (1) a capital account for the proprietor (for example, J. Doe, Capital; or J. Doe, Owner's Equity), and (2) a drawing account for the proprietor (for example, J. Doe, Drawings; or J. Doe, Withdrawals). The capital account is used to record investments by the owner and it absorbs the net income (or loss) for each period. Thus, the **Income Summary** account is closed to the capital account at the end of each accounting period. The drawing account is used to record withdrawals of cash or other assets by the owner from the business or the payment of the owner's personal obligations with assets of the business. The drawing account is closed to the capital account at the end of each accounting period; thus, the capital account cumulatively reflects all investments by the owner, plus all earnings of the entity, less all withdrawals of resources from the entity by the owner. In all other respects the accounting for a sole proprietorship is the same as for a corporation.

The following sequence of selected entries for Doe's Retail Store is presented to illustrate the accounting and reporting of owner's equity for a single proprietorship:

January 1, 1977:

J. Doe started a retail store by investing $150,000 of personal savings. The accounting entry would be as follows:

Cash	150,000	
J. Doe, capital		150,000
Investment by owner.		

During 1977:

Each month during the year, Doe withdrew $1,000 cash from the business for personal living costs. Accordingly, each month the following entry was made:

J. Doe, drawings	1,000	
Cash		1,000
Withdrawal of cash by owner for personal use.		

(Note: At December 31, 1977, after the last withdrawal, the drawing account will reflect a debit balance of $12,000.)

December 31, 1977:

Normal accounting entries for the year, including adjusting and closing entries for the revenue and expense accounts, resulted in an $18,000 *credit balance* in the Income Summary account (i.e., $18,000 net income). The next closing entry will be:

Income summary	18,000	
J. Doe, capital		18,000
Closing entry to transfer net income for the year to the owner's equity account.		

December 31, 1977:

The entry required on this date to close the drawing account would be:

J. Doe, capital	12,000	
J. Doe, drawings		12,000
Closing entry to transfer drawings for the year to the capital account.		

The financial statements of a sole proprietorship basically follow the same format as for a corporation, **except in respect to owner's equity** on the balance sheet. In conformity with the full-disclosure principle, the balance sheet at December 31, 1977, for Doe's Retail Store would report the owner's equity as follows:[11]

Owner's Equity

J. Doe, capital, January 1, 1977	$150,000	
Add: Net income for 1977	18,000	
Total	168,000	
Less: Withdrawals for 1977	12,000	
J. Doe, capital, December 31, 1977		$156,000

Since a sole proprietorship, as a business entity, does not pay income taxes, the financial statements will not reflect income tax expense or income taxes payable. The net income of a sole proprietorship must be included on the personal income tax return of the owner. Also, since an employer/employee contractual relationship cannot exist with only one party involved, a "salary" to the owner is not recognized as an expense of a sole proprietorship.

OWNERS' EQUITY FOR A PARTNERSHIP

The Uniform Partnership Act, which has been adopted by most states, defines a partnership as "an association of two or more persons to carry on as co-owners of a business for profit." The partnership form of business is used by small businesses and professional people, such as doctors, lawyers, and accountants. A partnership is formed by two or more persons reaching mutual agreement as to the terms of the partnership. The law does not require an application for a charter as in the case for a corporation. The agreement between the partners constitutes a **partnership contract,** and it should be in writing. The partnership contract or agreement should specify such matters as division of profits, management responsibilities, transfer or sale of partnership interests, disposition of assets upon liquidation, and procedures to be followed in case of the death of a partner. The primary advantages of a partnership are (1) ease of formation, (2) complete control by the partners, and (3) no income taxes on

[11] Alternatively, the balance sheet may reflect only "J. Doe, capital, December 31, 1977, $156,000," with a supplemental or supporting *statement of owner's equity* that would be the same as this illustration.

the business itself. The primary disadvantage is the unlimited liability feature discussed in Chapter 1.

As with a sole proprietorship, accounting for a partnership follows the same underlying fundamentals of accounting as any other form of business organization, **except for those entries that directly affect owners' equity.** Accounting for partners' equity follows the same pattern as illustrated earlier for a sole proprietorship, except that separate partner capital and drawing accounts must be established for *each* partner. Investments by each partner are credited to separate capital accounts. Withdrawals of cash and other resources from the partnership by each partner are debited to the respective drawing accounts. The net income for a partnership is divided between the partners in the **profit ratio** specified in the partnership contract. The Income Summary account is then closed to the respective partner capital accounts in accordance with the division of profits. The respective drawing accounts also are closed to the partner capital accounts. Therefore, after the closing process, the capital account of each partner cumulatively reflects all investments of the individual partner, plus the partner's share of all partnership earnings, less all withdrawals by the partner.

The following sequence of selected entries is presented to illustrate the accounting and reporting of partners' equity.

January 1, 1977:

The AB Partnership was organized by A. Able and B. Baker on this date. Able contributed $60,000 and Baker $40,000 cash in the partnership and agreed to divide profits and losses 60 percent and 40 percent, respectively. The accounting entry to record the investment would be:

Cash	100,000	
A. Able, capital		60,000
B. Baker, capital		40,000
Investment to initiate a partnership.		

During 1977:

It was agreed that in lieu of salaries, Able would withdraw $1,000 and Baker $650 per month in cash. Accordingly, *each month* the following entry for the withdrawals was made:

A. Able, drawings	1,000	
B. Baker, drawings	650	
Cash		1,650
Withdrawal of cash by partners for personal use.		

December 31, 1977:

Assume the normal accounting entries for the revenue and expense accounts resulted in a $30,000 *credit balance* in the Income Summary account (i.e., $30,000 net income). The next closing entry would be:

Income summary	30,000	
A. Able, capital		18,000
B. Baker, capital		12,000

Closing entry to transfer net income to the respective capital accounts. Net income divided as follows:

A. Able:	$30,000 × 0.60 =	$18,000
B. Baker:	$30,000 × 0.40 =	12,000
Total		$30,000

December 31, 1977:

The entry required to close the drawings accounts would be:

A. Able, capital	12,000	
B. Baker, capital	7,800	
A. Able, drawings		12,000
B. Baker, drawings		7,800

Closing entry to transfer drawings for the year to the respective capital accounts.

After the closing entries the partners' accounts would reflect the following balances:

Income summary	$ -0-
A. Able, drawings	-0-
B. Baker, drawings	-0-
A. Able, capital	66,000
B. Baker, capital	44,200

The financial statements of a partnership follow the same format as for a sole proprietorship and a corporation, except (1) the income statement includes an additional section entitled "Distribution of net income," and (2) the partners' equity section of the balance sheet is detailed for each partner in conformity with the principle of full disclosure. To illustrate, the income statement and balance sheet for the AB Partnership for 1977 would reflect the following additional information:

Income Statement:

Net income		$30,000
Distribution of net income:		
A. Able (60%)	$18,000	
B. Baker (40%)	12,000	
	$30,000	

Balance Sheet:

Partners' Equity

A. Able, capital	$66,000	
B. Baker, capital	44,200	
Total Partners' Equity		$110,200

A separate statement of partners' capital similar to the following usually is prepared to supplement the balance sheet:

AB PARTNERSHIP
Statement of Partners' Capital
For the Year Ended December 31, 1977

	A. Able	*B. Baker*	*Total*
Investment, January 1, 1977	$60,000	$40,000	$100,000
Add: Additional investments during the year	-0-	-0-	-0-
Net income for the year	18,000	12,000	30,000
Totals	78,000	52,000	130,000
Less: Drawings during the year	12,000	7,800	19,800
Partners' Equity, December 31, 1977	$66,000	$44,200	$110,200

DEMONSTRATION CASE FOR SELF-STUDY

Shelly Corporation

(Try to resolve the case before studying the suggested solution that follows.)

This case focuses on the organization and operations for the first year of Shelly Corporation, which was organized officially on January 1, 1977, the date on which the charter was granted by the state. The laws of the state specify that the legal or stated capital for nopar stock is the full sales amount. The corporation was promoted and organized by ten local entrepreneurs for the purpose of operating a hotel supply business. The charter authorized the following capital stock:

Common stock, nopar value, 20,000 shares authorized.
Preferred stock, 5 percent, $100 par value, 5,000 shares authorized (cumulative, nonparticipating, and nonvoting; liquidation value, $110).

The following summarized transactions, selected from 1977, were completed on the dates indicated:

1. Jan. Sold a total of 7,500 shares of nopar common stock to the ten promoters for cash at $52 per share. Credit the Nopar Common Stock account for the total sales amount.
2. Feb. Sold 1,890 shares of preferred stock at $102 per share; cash collected in full.
3. Mar. Purchased land for a store site and made full payment by issuing 100 shares of preferred stock. Early construction is planned. Assume the preferred stock is selling at $102 per share.
4. Apr. Paid cash for organization costs amounting to $1,980. Set up an account entitled "Organization Costs."

5.	May	Issued ten shares of preferred stock to A. B. Cain in full payment of legal services rendered in connection with organization of the corporation. Assume the preferred stock is regularly selling at $102 per share. Debit Organization Costs.
6.	June 19	Sold 500 shares of nopar common stock for cash to C. B. Abel at $54 per share.
7.	July 19	Purchased 100 shares of preferred stock that had been sold and issued earlier. The stockholder was moving to another state and "needed the money." Shelly Corporation paid the stockholder $104 per share.
8.	Aug.	Sold 20 shares of preferred treasury stock at $105 per share.
9.	Dec.	Purchased fixed assets at a cost of $600,000; paid cash. Assume no depreciation expense in 1977.
10.	Dec. 31	Borrowed $20,000 cash from the City Bank on a one-year, interest-bearing note. Interest is payable at 7 percent at maturity.
11.	31	Gross revenues for the year amounted to $129,300; expenses, including corporation income taxes but excluding organization costs, amounted to $98,000. Assume, for simplicity, that these summarized revenue and expense transactions were cash.
12.	31	Shelly Corporation decided that a "reasonable" amortization period for organization costs, starting as of January 1, 1977, would be ten years. This is an intangible asset that must be amortized over a reasonable period.

Required:

a. Give appropriate entries, with brief explanation for each of the above transactions.
b. Give appropriate closing entries at December 31, 1977.
c. Prepare a balance sheet for Shelly Corporation at December 31, 1977.

Suggested Solution:

Requirement (*a*)—journal entries:

1. January 1977:

Cash	390,000	
Nopar common stock (7,500 shares)		390,000
Sale of nopar common stock ($52 × 7,500 shares = $390,000).		

2. February 1977:

Cash	192,780	
Preferred stock, 5 percent, par $100 (1,890 shares)		189,000
Contributed capital in excess of par, preferred stock		3,780
Sale of preferred stock ($102 × 1,890 shares = $192,780).		

3. March 1977:

Land (store site)	10,200	
Preferred stock, 5 percent, par $100 (100 shares)		10,000
Contributed capital in excess of par, preferred stock		200
Purchased land for future store site; paid in full by issuance of 100 shares of preferred stock; implied fair-market value, $102 × 100 shares = $10,200.		

4. April 1977:

Organization costs	1,980	
Cash		1,980
Paid organization costs.		

5. May 1977:

Organization costs	1,020	
Preferred stock, 5 percent, par $100 (10 shares)		1,000
Contributed capital in excess of par, preferred stock		20
Organization costs (legal services) paid by issuance of ten shares of preferred stock; implied fair-market value, $102 × 10 shares = $1,020.		

6. June 1977:

Cash	27,000	
Nopar common stock (500 shares)		27,000
Sold 500 shares of the nopar common stock ($54 × 500 shares = $27,000).		

7. July 1977:

Treasury stock, preferred (100 shares at $104)	10,400	
Cash		10,400
Purchased 100 shares of preferred treasury stock ($104 × 100 shares = $10,400).		

8. August 1977:

Cash (20 shares at $105)	2,100	
Treasury stock, preferred (20 shares at $104)		2,080
Contributed capital from treasury stock transactions		20

Sold 20 shares of the preferred treasury stock at $105.

9. December 1977:

Fixed assets	600,000	
Cash		600,000

Purchased fixed assets.

10. December 31, 1977:

Cash	20,000	
Notes payable		20,000

Borrowed on one-year, 7 percent, interest-bearing note.

11. December 31, 1977:

Cash	129,300	
Revenues		129,300
Expenses	98,000	
Cash		98,000

To record summarized revenues and expenses.

12. December 31, 1977:

Expenses	300	
Organization costs		300

Adjusting entry to amortize organization expense for one year, $3,000 ÷ 10 years = $300.

Requirement (*b*)—closing entries:

13. December 31, 1977:

Revenues	129,300	
Income summary		129,300
Income summary	98,300	
Expenses ($98,000 + $300)		98,300
Income summary	31,000	
Retained earnings		31,000

Requirement (*c*):

SHELLY CORPORATION
Balance Sheet
At December 31, 1977

Assets		
Current Assets:		
Cash		$ 50,800
Fixed Assets:		
Land	$ 10,200	
Fixed assets (no depreciation assumed in the problem)	600,000	610,200
Intangible Assets:		
Organization costs (cost, $3,000 less amortization, $300)		2,700
Total Assets		$663,700
Liabilities		
Current Liabilities:		
Note payable		$ 20,000
Stockholders' Equity		
Contributed Capital:		
Preferred stock, 5% par value $100, authorized 5,000 shares, issued 2,000 shares of which 80 shares are held as treasury stock	$200,000	
Common stock, nopar value, authorized 20,000 shares, issued and outstanding 8,000 shares	417,000	
Contributed capital in excess of par, preferred stock	4,000	
Contributed capital from treasury stock transactions	20	
Total Contributed Capital	621,020	
Retained earnings	31,000	
Total	652,020	
Less cost of preferred treasury stock held (80 shares)	8,320	
Total Stockholders' Equity		643,700
Total Liabilities and Stockholders' Equity		$663,700

SUMMARY

This chapter focused on accounting for and reporting of owners' equity for corporations, sole proprietorships, and partnerships. Other than owners' equity, the accounting and reporting basically is unaffected by the type of business organization. Accounting for owners' equity is based upon the concept of **source:** each specific source of owners' equity should be accounted for and reported separately. The two basic sources of owners' equity for a corporation are contributed capital and retained earnings. Separate accounts are maintained for each type of capital stock.

The earnings of a corporation that are not retained in the business for growth and expansion are distributed to the stockholders by means of dividends. Dividends are paid only when formally declared by the board of directors of the corporation. A cash dividend results in a decrease in assets (cash) and stockholders' equity (retained earnings). In contrast, a stock dividend does not change either total assets or total stockholders' equity. Significantly, a stock dividend results in a transfer of retained earnings to the permanent or contributed capital of the corporation by the amount of the stock dividend.

Not infrequently a corporation purchases its own stock in the marketplace. Such stock, having been sold and issued by the corporation and subsequently reacquired, is known as treasury stock. The purchase of treasury stock is viewed as a contraction of corporate capital, and the subsequent resale of the treasury stock is viewed as an expansion of corporate capital.

IMPORTANT TERMS

Corporation charter	**Treasury stock**
Common stock	**Cumulative dividends**
Par value	**Participating preferred stock**
Nopar value stock	**Stock dividends**
Preferred stock	**Stock split**
Convertible stock	**Prior period adjustments**

QUESTIONS FOR DISCUSSION

1. Define a corporation and give its primary characteristics.
2. What is the charter of a corporation?
3. Briefly explain each of the following terms: (*a*) authorized capital stock, (*b*) issued capital stock, (*c*) unissued capital stock, and (*d*) outstanding capital stock.
4. Briefly distinguish between common and preferred stock.
5. Briefly explain the distinction between par value and nopar value capital stock.
6. What are the usual features or characteristics of preferred stock?
7. What are the two basic sources of stockholders' equity? Explain them briefly.
8. Owners' equity is accounted for by source. Explain what is meant by source.
9. Define treasury stock. Why do corporations acquire treasury stock?
10. How is treasury stock reported on the balance sheet? How is the "gain or loss" on treasury stock that has been sold reported on the financial statements?
11. What are the fundamental requirements to support a cash dividend? What is the effect of a cash dividend on assets and stockholders' equity?
12. Distinguish between cumulative and noncumulative preferred stock.
13. Distinguish between participating and nonparticipating preferred stock.
14. Define a stock dividend. In what major respects does it differ from a cash dividend?
15. What are the primary purposes in issuing a stock dividend?

16. Identify and briefly explain the three important dates in respect to dividends.
17. Define extraordinary items. Why is it desirable that they be reflected separately on the income statement?
18. Define retained earnings. What are the primary components of retained earnings?
19. Define prior period adjustments. How are they reported?
20. Explain what is meant by restrictions on retained earnings.
21. List and explain the basic purposes of each owner's equity account for a partnership.

EXERCISES

PART ONE: EXERCISES 13–1 TO 13–14

E13–1. Dollins Corporation was organized in 1977 for the purpose of operating an engineering service business. The charter authorized the following capital stock: common stock, par value $20 per share, 10,000 shares. During the first year the following selected transactions were completed:

1. Sold 6,000 shares of common stock for cash at $25 per share; the stock was immediately issued.
2. Issued 200 shares of common stock for a piece of land that will be utilized as a facilities site; construction was started immediately. Assume the stock was still selling at $25 per share. Debit Land.
3. Sold 1,000 shares of common stock for cash at $25 per share; issued the stock.
4. At year-end, the Income Summary account reflected a $8,000 loss. Since a loss was incurred, no income tax expense was recorded.

Required:

a. Give the indicated journal entry for each of the transactions listed above.

b. Assume it is the year-end and the financial statements are being prepared. Show how stockholders' equity would be reported in the balance sheet.

E13–2. Foster Corporation was organized in January 1977 by 12 stockholders to operate an air-conditioning sales and service business. The charter issued by the state authorized the following capital stock:

Common stock, $10 par value, 30,000 shares.
Preferred stock, $20 par value, 5 percent, nonparticipating, noncumulative, 5,000 shares.

During January and February 1977 the following stock transactions were completed:

1. Collected $24,000 cash from each of the 12 organizers and issued each of them 1,000 shares of common stock.
2. Sold 1,000 shares of preferred stock at $30 per share; collected the cash and immediately issued the stock.

Required:

a. Give the journal entries to record the above stock transactions.
b. Assume it is the end of the annual accounting period, December 31, 1977, and net income for the year was $31,000; also assume that cash dividends paid at year-end amounted to $15,000. Prepare the stockholders' equity section of the balance sheet at December 31, 1977.

E13–3. Video Systems, Incorporated, was issued a charter on January 15, 1977, that authorized the following capital stock:

Common stock, nopar, 40,000 shares.
Preferred stock, 5 percent, par value $10 per share, 10,000 shares.
The board of directors established a stated value on the nopar common stock of $5 per share.

During 1977 the following selected transactions were completed in the order given:

1. Sold 15,000 shares of the nopar common stock at $40 per share. Collected the cash and immediately issued the shares.
2. Sold 3,000 shares of preferred stock at $15 per share. Collected the cash and immediately issued the shares.
3. At the end of 1977 the Income Summary account reflected a credit balance of $24,000.

Required:

a. Give the entry indicated for each of the above items.
b. Prepare the stockholders' equity section of the balance sheet at December 31, 1977.

E13–4. Townsend Corporation obtained a charter at the start of 1977 that authorized 20,000 shares of common stock, par value $20 per share, and 5,000 shares of preferred stock, par value $10. The corporation was promoted and organized by six individuals who "reserved" 60 percent of the common stock shares for themselves. The remaining shares are to be sold to the public at $50 per share on a cash basis. During 1977 the following selected transactions occurred:

1. Collected $20,000 cash from each of the six organizers and issued 1,000 shares of common stock to each.
2. Sold 5,000 shares of common stock to an "outsider" at $50 per share. Collected the cash and issued the stock.
3. Sold 2,000 shares of preferred stock at $15 per share. Collected the cash and immediately issued the stock.
4. At the end of 1977, the Income Summary account, after income taxes, reflected a credit balance of $25,000.

Required:

a. Give journal entries indicated for each of the transactions listed above.
b. Prepare the stockholders' equity section of the balance sheet at December 31, 1977.

E13–5. The stockholders' equity section on the December 31, 1977, balance sheet for Stover Corporation was as follows:

Stockholders' Equity

Contributed Capital:	
Preferred stock, par value $30, authorized 5,000 shares; ? issued, of which 100 shares are held as treasury stock	$120,000
Common stock, nopar, authorized 10,000 shares; issued 7,000 shares	630,000
Contributed capital in excess of par, preferred	6,000
Contributed capital, treasury stock transactions	500
Retained earnings	40,000
Less: Treasury stock, preferred	(3,200)
	$793,300

Required:

Complete the following (show computations) on a separate sheet of paper:

a. The number of shares of preferred stock issued was ______.

b. The number of shares of preferred stock outstanding is ______.

c. The average sales price of the preferred stock when issued apparently was $______ per share.

d. Have treasury stock transactions (1) increased corporate resources ______; or (2) decreased resources 2700? By how much? $______.

e. How much did the treasury stock held cost per share? $______.

f. Total stockholders' equity is $______.

E13–6. The balance sheet (summarized) for Tabor Corporation reflected the following:

TABOR CORPORATION
Balance Sheet
At December 31, 1976

Assets		*Liabilities*	
Cash	$100,000	Current liabilities	$ 60,000
All other assets	412,000	Long-term liabilities	80,000
			140,000
		Stockholders' Equity	
		Contributed Capital:	
		Common stock, par $20, authorized 20,000 shares; outstanding 12,000 shares	240,000
		Contributed capital in excess of par	72,000
		Retained earnings	60,000
	$512,000		$512,000

During the next year, 1977, the following selected transactions affecting stockholders' equity occurred:

Feb. 1	Purchased for cash, in the open market, 500 shares of Tabor's own common stock at $40 per share.
July 15	Sold 100 of the shares purchased on February 1, 1977 at $41 per share.
Sept. 1	Sold 20 more of the shares purchased on February 1, 1977, at $38 per share.
Dec. 31	The credit balance in the Income Summary account was $31,000.

Required:

a. Give the indicated entries for each of the four dates listed above.

b. Prepare the stockholders' equity section of the balance sheet at December 31, 1977.

E13–7. Fox, Incorporated, obtained a charter from the state in January 1977 that authorized 100,000 shares of common stock, $1 par value. The stockholders comprised 20 local citizens. During the first year the following selected transactions occurred in the order given:

1. Sold a total of 60,000 shares of the common stock to the 20 shareholders at $5 per share. Collected cash and immediately issued the stock.
2. During the year, one of the 20 stockholders moved to another state and wanted to "get the investment back." Accordingly, the corporation purchased the investor's 5,000 shares at $5.20 per share.
3. Two months later, 3,000 of the shares purchased from the departing stockholder were resold to another individual at $5.50 per share.
4. On December 31, 1977, the end of the first year of business, the Income Summary account reflected a credit balance of $28,000.

Required:

a. Give the indicated journal entries for the above items.

b. Prepare the stockholders' equity section of the balance sheet at December 31, 1977.

E13–8. Scott Manufacturing Company has outstanding (*a*) 50,000 shares of $5 par value common stock and (*b*) 10,000 shares of $10 par value preferred stock (6 percent). On December 1, 1977, the board of directors voted a 6 percent cash dividend on the preferred stock and a 10 percent common stock dividend on the common stock (i.e., for each ten shares of common stock held one additional share of common stock is to be issued as a stock dividend). At the date of declaration, the common stock was selling at $30 and the preferred at $20 per share.

Required:

a. Give the entry to record the payment of the cash dividend. Assume immediate payment.
b. Give the entry to record the distribution of the stock dividend. (Hint: Transfer retained earnings on the basis of market values.)

E13–9. Dement Supply Company records reflected the following balances in the stockholders' equity accounts:

Common stock, par $5 per share, 30,000 shares outstanding.
Preferred stock, 5 percent, par $10 per share, 3,000 shares outstanding.
Retained earnings, $150,000.

On September 1, the board of directors was considering the distribution of a cash dividend amounting to $40,000. No dividends have been paid during the past two years. You have been asked to determine the total and per-share amounts that would be paid to the common stockholders and to the preferred stockholders assuming (show computations):

a. The preferred stock is noncumulative and nonparticipating.
b. The preferred stock is cumulative and nonparticipating.
c. The preferred stock is cumulative and fully participating.

E13–10. The stockholders' equity section of the balance sheet of Farr Corporation, on December 31, 1977, reflected the following:

Common stock, par $10, shares authorized 50,000; shares outstanding 20,000	$200,000
Contributed capital in excess of par	12,000
Retained earnings	100,000

Now, assume a one-for-five (i.e., a 20 percent) stock dividend is declared and issued (that is, one additional share will be issued for each five shares now held). The market value of the stock is $15 per share. Assume the market value is capitalized.

Required:

a. Give the entry to record the distribution of the stock dividend.
b. Reconstruct the stockholders' equity section of the balance sheet (1) immediately before the stock dividend and (2) immediately after the stock dividend. (Hint: Use two columns.)

E13–11. The following account balances were selected from the records of Barker Corporation at December 31, 1977, after all adjusting entries were completed:

Common stock, par $5, authorized 200,000 shares; issued 120,000 shares, of which 500 shares are held as treasury stock	$600,000
Contributed capital in excess of par	360,000
Bond sinking fund	70,000

Dividends paid in 1977	24,000
Retained earnings, January 1, 1977	90,000
Adjustment of prior years' income taxes (additional assessment)	10,000
Treasury stock at cost (500 shares)	3,000
Income summary for 1977 (credit balance)	45,000
Restriction on retained earnings for cost of treasury stock is required by law in this state.	

Required:

Based upon the above data, prepare (*a*) the stockholders' equity section of the balance sheet at December 31, 1977, and (*b*) the statement of retained earnings for 1977. (Hint: Total stockholders' equity is $1,058,000.)

E13–12. The following data were taken from the records of Meany Corporation at December 31, 1977:

Common stock, par $2, authorized 300,000 shares, issued 210,000 shares of which 1,000 are held as treasury stock (purchased at $7 per share)	$420,000
Preferred stock, par $10, authorized 20,000 shares, issued 15,000 shares	150,000
Contributed capital in excess of par:	
Common stock	630,000
Preferred stock	120,000
Dividends paid during 1977	24,000
Net income for 1977	62,000
Retained earnings balance, January 1, 1977	130,000
Prior period adjustment (gain, net of tax)	10,000

Required:

Based upon the above date, prepare (*a*) the stockholders' equity section of the balance sheet and (*b*) the statement of retained earnings for 1977.

E13–13. At December 31, 1977, the records of Raymond Corporation provided the following data:

Common stock, par $5
  Shares authorized, 300,000
  Shares issued 150,000—issue price $12 per share
  Shares held as treasury stock 2,000 shares—cost $15 per share
Net income for 1977, $75,000
Dividends paid during 1977, $30,000
Bond sinking fund balance, $20,000
Prior period adjustment—income tax refund for 1974, $14,000
Retained earnings balance, January 1, 1977, $180,000
State law places a restriction on retained earnings equal to the cost of treasury stock held.

Required:

a. Prepare a statement of retained earnings for 1977.
b. Prepare the stockholders' equity section of the balance sheet at December 31, 1977.

E13–14. Assume that at the beginning of 1977 the stockholders' equity accounts of Lowe Corporation reflected the following:

Common stock, $5 par, 50,000 shares outstanding	$250,000
Retained earnings (including a $50,000 restriction on retained earnings for bonds payable)	185,000

Assume the following transactions were completed in the order given:

1. Paid cash dividends during 1977 amounting to $3 per share.
2. Received a $30,000 cash refund on prior income taxes that had been in litigation for three years.
3. The Income Summary account on December 31, 1977, after closing all revenue and expense accounts, reflected a credit balance of $50,000.

Required:

a. Give the appropriate entries for each of the above items.
b. Prepare a statement of retained earnings, after taking into account the entries made in (*a*).

PART TWO: EXERCISE 13–15

E13–15. This exercise presents three separate cases. Assume in each case that the annual accounting period ended December 31, 1977, and that the Income Summary account at that date reflected a credit balance of $35,000.

Case A—Assume that the company is a sole proprietorship and that, prior to the closing entries, the owner's (D. Doe) equity accounts reflected the following: Capital, $70,000; Drawings, $21,600.

Case B—Assume that the company is a partnership owned by Partner X and Partner Y, who divide profits equally. Prior to the closing entries, the owners' equity accounts reflected the following: X, Capital, $40,000; Y, Capital, $30,000; X, Drawings, $12,000; Y, Drawings, $9,600.

Case C—Assume that the company is a corporation owned by ten stockholders. Prior to the closing entries, the stockholders' equity accounts reflected the following: Capital Stock, 12,000 shares, par value $1 per share originally sold at $5 per share; Retained Earnings, $10,000. Dividends paid during the year, $23,400.

Required:

a. Give all of the closing entries indicated at December 31, 1977, for each of the three separate cases.
b. Show how the owners' equity section of the balance sheet would be reflected on December 31, 1977, for each case.

PROBLEMS

PART ONE: PROBLEMS 13–1 TO 13–10

P13–1. Ace Corporation received its charter during January 1977. The charter authorized the following capital stock:

Preferred stock, 5 percent, par $10, authorized 10,000 shares.
Common stock, par $2, authorized 150,000 shares.

During 1977 the following transactions occurred in the order given:

1. Issued a total of 60,000 shares of the common stock to the six organizers at $5 per share. Cash was collected in full, and the stock was issued immediately.
2. Sold 2,000 shares of the preferred stock at $20 per share. Collected the cash and issued the stock immediately.
3. Sold 2,000 shares of the common stock at $7 per share and 1,000 shares of the preferred stock at $30. Collected the cash and issued the stock immediately.
4. Revenues for 1977 totaled $200,000, and expenses (including income taxes) totaled $160,000.

Required:

a. Give all entries, including closing entries, for the above items.
b. Prepare the stockholders' equity section of the balance sheet at December 31, 1977.

P13–2. Wilson Corporation began operations in January 1977. The charter authorized the following capital stock:

Preferred stock, 5 percent, $10 par, authorized 20,000 shares.
Common stock, nopar, authorized 50,000 shares.
The corporation, in conformance with state laws, established a stated value per share of $5 for the nopar common stock.

During 1977, the following transactions occurred in the order given:

1. Issued 15,000 shares of the nopar common stock to each of the three organizers. Collected $8 per share in full and issued the stock immediately.
2. Sold 3,000 shares of the preferred stock at $15 per share. Collected the cash and issued the stock immediately.

3. Sold 200 shares of the preferred stock at $16 and 1,000 shares of the nopar common stock at $10 per share. Collected the cash and issued the stock immediately.
4. Operating results at the end of 1977 were reflected as follows:

Revenue accounts	$150,000
Expense accounts, including income taxes	115,000

Required:

a. Give the entries indicated, including closing entries, for the above items.

b. Prepare the stockholders' equity section of the balance sheet at December 31, 1977.

P13–3. Lacy Corporation was issued a charter in January 1977 that authorized 50,000 shares of common stock. During 1977, the following selected transactions occurred in the order given:

1. Sold 20,000 shares of the stock for cash at $60 per share. Collected the cash and issued the stock immediately.
2. Acquired land to be used as a future plant site; made payment in full by issuing 500 shares of stock. Assume a market value per share of $60.
3. At the end of 1977, the Income Summary account reflected a credit balance of $25,000.

Three independent cases are assumed as follows:

Case I: Assume the stock was $25 par value per share.
Case II: Assume the stock was nopar and that the total selling price is credited to the Nopar Capital Stock account.
Case III: Assume the stock is nopar with a stated value, specified by the board of directors, of $10 per share.

Required:

For each case:

a. Give the entries for the three transactions.

b. Prepare the stockholders' equity section of the balance sheet at December 31, 1977. (Hint: Total stockholders' equity is the same in amount in each case – $1,225,000.)

P13–4. Richmond Manufacturing Company was granted a charter that authorized the following capital stock:

Common stock, nopar, 50,000 shares. Assume the nopar stock is not assigned a stated value per share.
Preferred stock, 5 percent, par value, $10, 10,000 shares.

During the first year, 1977, the following selected transactions occurred in the order given:

1. Sold 15,000 shares of nopar common stock at $30 per share and 3,000 preferred stock at $22 per share. Collected cash and

issued the stock immediately. For the nopar stock, credit the full selling price to the Nopar Common Stock account.

2. Issued 500 shares of preferred stock as full payment for a plot of land to be used as a future plant site. Assume the stock is selling at $22.
3. Purchased 300 shares of the nopar common stock sold earlier; paid cash, $25 per share.
4. Sold all of the treasury stock (common) purchased in 3 above. The sales price was $27 per share.
5. Purchased 200 shares of preferred stock at $22 per share at the request of a stockholder who was moving to another state.
6. At December 31, 1977, the Income Summary account reflected a credit balance of $21,000.

Required:

a. Give the entries indicated for each of the above items.

b. Prepare the stockholders' equity section of the balance sheet at December 31, 1977, end of the annual accounting period. (Hint: Total stockholders' equity is $544,200.)

P13–5. Korn Equipment Company had the following stock outstanding and retained earnings:

Common stock, $10 par, outstanding 20,000 shares	$200,000
Preferred stock, 5%, $20 par, outstanding 5,000 shares	100,000
Retained earnings	240,000

The board of directors is considering the distribution of a cash dividend to the two groups of stockholders. No dividends have been paid in the past two years. Four different case situations are assumed:

Case A – The preferred is noncumulative and nonparticipating; the total amount of dividends to be $35,000.

Case B – The preferred is cumulative and nonparticipating; the total amount of dividends to be $15,000.

Case C – Same as Case B, except the amount is $50,000.

Case D – The preferred is cumulative and fully participating; total amount, $49,000.

Required:

a. Compute the amount of dividends, in total and per share, that would be payable to each class of stockholders for each case. Show computations.

b. Give the entry to record the cash dividend paid in Case C. Reflect a separate dividend paid account for each class of stock.

c. Give the required entry assuming, instead of a cash dividend, the declaration and issuance of a 10 percent common stock dividend on the outstanding common stock. Assume the market value per share of common stock was $16.

P13–6. The accounts of Foster Corporation reflected the following balances on January 1, 1977:

Preferred stock, 5%, $50 par value, cumulative, authorized 10,000 shares, issued and outstanding 2,000 shares	$100,000
Common stock, $10 par value, authorized 100,000 shares, outstanding 20,000 shares	200,000
Contributed capital in excess of par, preferred stock	5,000
Contributed capital in excess of par, common stock	10,000
Retained earnings	200,000
Total Stockholders' Equity	$515,000

The transactions during 1977 relating to the stockholders' equity are listed below in order:

1. Purchased 100 shares of preferred treasury stock at $115 per share.
2. The board of directors declared and paid a cash dividend to the preferred shareholders. No dividends had been paid during the past two years. The dividend was sufficient to pay the arrears plus the dividend for the current year.
3. The board of directors declared a one-for-ten (i.e., 10 percent) common stock dividend on the outstanding common stock. Fair-market value of $12 per share is to be capitalized.
4. Net income for the year, after taxes, was $30,000.

Required:

a. Give the entry for each of the above transactions, including the closing entries. Show computations.

b. Prepare the stockholders' equity section of the balance sheet at December 31, 1977, and a statement of retained earnings for 1977. (Hint: Total stockholders' equity is $519,250.)

P13–7. Miles, Incorporated, is in the process of completing the year-end accounting, including the preparation of the annual financial statements, at December 31, 1977. The stockholders' equity accounts reflected the following balances at the end of the year:

Common stock, par $10, shares outstanding 50,000	$500,000
Contributed capital in excess of par	50,000
Retained earnings, January 1, 1977 (credit)	300,000
Cash dividends declared and paid during 1977 (debit)	30,000
Income summary account for 1977 (credit balance; after tax)	60,000

The following selected transactions occurred near the end of 1977; they are not included in the above amounts:

1. As a result of litigation in the tax court over the last three years the corporation was assessed additional taxes for 1974 amounting to $35,000. The amount was paid immediately on December 31, 1977.
2. The board of directors voted a voluntary restriction on retained

earnings amounting to $100,000. It is to be designated as "Earnings Appropriated for Plant Expansion" effective for 1977 financial statements.

3. A 10 percent (i.e., one share for ten) stock dividend was issued on December 31, 1977. Capitalize the fair-market value at $15 per share.

Required:

a. Give the appropriate entries for the events listed immediately above. If no entry is given, explain why not.

b. Give the appropriate closing entries, based upon the above data and Requirement (*a*), at December 31, 1977.

c. Prepare the stockholders' equity section of the balance sheet at December 31, 1977, and a statement of retained earnings for 1977.

P13–8. Garland, Incorporated, has completed all of the annual information processing at December 31, 1977, except for preparation of the financial statements. The following account balances were reflected at that date:

Adjusted Trial Balance
December 31, 1977

Cash	$ 62,000	
Accounts receivable (net)	58,000	
Merchandise inventory, December 31, 1977	120,000	
Long-term investment in Company Y	20,000	
Bond sinking fund	40,000	
Land	15,000	
Buildings and equipment (net)	738,000	
Other assets	29,200	
Accounts payable		$ 86,000
Income taxes payable		18,000
Bonds payable, 5%		100,000
Preferred stock, par $10, authorized 50,000 shares		100,000
Common stock, par $5, authorized 200,000 shares		660,000
Contributed capital in excess of par, preferred		6,100
Contributed capital in excess of par, common		19,900
Treasury stock, preferred, 10 shares at cost	1,100	
Retained earnings, January 1, 1977		163,300
1977 net income (after tax)		40,000
1977 cash dividends on preferred	26,000	
1977 common stock dividends distributed (10,000 shares)	70,000	
Adjustment of 1974 income taxes (additional assessment)	14,000	
	$1,193,300	$1,193,300

Note: Retained earnings is restricted to an amount equal to the bond sinking fund per the provisions of the bond indenture.

15
1900
13500
15
265.00
50 14250

Required:

Prepare a classified balance sheet at December 31, 1977, and a statement of retained earnings for 1977. (Hint: Total stockholders' equity is $878,200.)

P13–9. The bookkeeper for Riley Corporation prepared the following balance sheet:

RILEY CORPORATION
Balance Sheet
For the Year 1977

Assets	
Current assets	$ 45,000
Fixed assets (net of depreciation reserves, $70,000)	125,000
Other assets	50,000
Total Debits	$220,000
Liabilities	
Current liabilities	$ 32,000
Other debts	25,000
Capital	
Stock, par $10, authorized 10,000 shares	60,000
Stock premium	30,000
Earned surplus	18,000
Treasury stock (500 shares)	(10,000)
Reserve for expansion of fixed assets	40,000
Reserve for treasury stock	10,000
Refund of 1975 income taxes	7,000
Cash dividends paid during 1977	(12,000)
Net profit	20,000
Total Credits	$220,000

Required:

a. What basic objections do you have of the above statement?
b. Prepare a statement of retained earnings for 1977.
c. Recast the above balance sheet in good form; focus especially on stockholders' equity.

P13–10. You are to refer to the financial statements of Carborundum Company, shown in Chapter 3, and respond to the following:

a. What name was used for the statement of retained earnings?
b. What items caused retained earnings to change during each year?
c. In which year were dividends higher?
d. Approximately what percent of net income was declared as dividends each year? Show computations.
e. At the end of 1975, what kinds and amounts of capital stock were authorized? Indicate the characteristics of each and the status of the shares.

f. Was any stock issued during 1975? How many shares?

g. What amounts were carried to the 1975 balance sheet from the statement referred to in (*b*) above?

PART TWO: PROBLEMS 13–11 TO 13–12

P13–11. KL Partnership is owned and operated by J. Kay and H. Low. The annual accounting period ends December 31, 1977. At the end of December 1977, the accounts reflected the following:

Credit balance in capital accounts (January 1, 1977):	
J. Kay	$50,000
H. Low	30,000
Credit balance in Income Summary account	23,000
Debit balance in drawing accounts:	
J. Kay	7,000
H. Low	6,000

The partners divide net income equally.

Required:

a. Give the closing entries indicated.

b. Prepare the December 31, 1977, statement of partners' capital.

P13–12. Assume for each of the three separate cases below that the annual accounting period ends on December 31, 1977, and that the Income Summary account at that date reflected a debit balance of $30,000 (i.e., a loss).

Case A—Assume that the company is a sole proprietorship owned by Proprietor A. Prior to the closing entries, the capital account reflected a credit balance of $70,000 and the drawings account a balance of $6,000.

Case B—Assume that the company is a partnership owned by Partner A and Partner B. Prior to the closing entries, the owners' equity accounts reflected the following balances: A, Capital, $50,000; B, Capital, $45,000; A, Drawings, $7,000; and B, Drawings, $6,000. Profits and losses are divided equally.

Case C—Assume that the company is a corporation. Prior to the closing entries, the stockholders' equity accounts showed the following: Capital Stock, par $20, authorized 20,000 shares, outstanding 4,000 shares; Contributed Capital in Excess of Par, $2,000; and Retained Earning, $40,000.

Required:

a. Give all of the closing entries indicated at December 31, 1977, for each of the separate cases.

b. Show how the owners' equity section of the balance sheet would appear at December 31, 1977, for each case.

14

Measurement and reporting of long-term investments[1]

PURPOSE OF THE CHAPTER

One corporation may invest in another corporation by acquiring either **debt securities** (e.g., bonds) or **equity securities** (e.g., capital stock) of the other corporation. These investments are classified by the investing entity for measurement and reporting purposes as either short-term investments or long-term investments, depending on the investment intentions of the management. In Chapter 9, short-term (or temporary) investments were defined as those that meet the two tests of ready *marketability* and *management intention* to convert them to cash in the short run. Those not meeting these two tests are classified as long-term investments. Short-term investments are classified on the balance sheet as a current asset. Long-term investments are classified on the balance sheet under the caption "Investments and Funds."

The purpose of this chapter is to discuss the measurement and reporting of long-term investments. In Part One we will focus on long-term investments in equity securities, except for those situations where **consolidated financial statements** must be prepared. This latter topic is deferred to Chapter 17. Part Two discusses long-term investments in bonds.

[1] We suggest that you review the discussion of short-term investments in Chapter 9 prior to studying this chapter.

PART ONE: LONG-TERM INVESTMENTS IN EQUITY SECURITIES

NATURE OF LONG-TERM INVESTMENTS IN THE CAPITAL STOCK OF OTHER CORPORATIONS

A corporation may invest in the equity securities (either the common or preferred stock) of one or more other corporations for reasons such as to use idle cash; to exercise influence or control over the other company; to attain growth through sales of new products and new services; to gain access to new markets and new sources of supply; or to attain other economic purposes. Basically, one corporation may acquire capital stock of another corporation by purchasing outstanding shares from other shareholders for cash (or other assets), or by exchanging some of its own capital stock for outstanding capital stock of the other corporation.

It is important to remember that when one company purchases *outstanding* shares of stock of another company, the transaction is between the acquiring company and the *shareholders* of the other company (not the other company itself). Thus, the accounting problems in focus here are only those of the acquiring company. The accounting of the other company is unaffected.

The investing company (i.e., the investor) may acquire *some or all* of either the preferred or the common stock *outstanding* of the other corporation. If the purpose is to gain influence or control, the typical situation involves investment in the *common stock* because it is the voting stock. The number of shares of outstanding stock acquired by one corporation of another corporation generally depends upon the investment objectives of the investing company (i.e., the acquiring company). For measurement and reporting purposes, **three different levels of ownership** are recognized. Each of these calls for different measurement and reporting approaches. The three levels generally are related to the percentage of shares of voting capital stock owned by the investing company in relationship to the total number of such shares that are outstanding.

MEASURING LONG-TERM INVESTMENTS IN VOTING COMMON STOCK

For long-term investments in voting common stock, measurement of the investment amount to be reported on the balance sheet and the periodic investment revenue to be reported on the income statement depend upon the **relationship** between the investing company and the other company. To effectively interpret and use the periodic financial statements of companies reporting long-term investments, the measurement approaches and their economic impacts must be understood.

In accordance with the cost principle, long-term investments in the capital stock of another company are measured and recorded, at the date of acquisition of the shares, as the total consideration given to acquire them. This total includes the market price, plus all commissions and other buying costs. Subsequent to acquisition, measurement of the investment amount and the investment revenue depends upon the extent to which the investing company can exercise **significant influence or control over the operating and financial policies** of the other company. Significant influence and control are related to the number of voting shares owned of the other company in proportion to the total number of such shares outstanding.

For the measurement and reporting of long-term investments in the voting capital stock of another company, the APB, in *Opinion No. 18* (March 1971), defined the two terms "significant influence" and "control" essentially as follows:

1. Significant influence—the ability of the investing company to affect, in an important degree, the operating and financing policies of another company in which they own shares of the voting stock. Significant influence may be indicated by (*a*) membership on the board of directors of the other company, (*b*) participation in the policy-making processes, (*c*) material transactions between the two companies, (*d*) interchange of management personnel, or (*e*) technological dependency. In the absence of a clear-cut distinction based upon these factors, **significant influence is presumed** if the investing company owns at least 20 percent but not more than 50 percent of the outstanding shares of the other company.
2. Control—the ability of the investing company to determine the operating and financing policies of another company in which they own shares of the voting stock. For all practical purposes, control is assumed when the investing company owns over 50 percent of the outstanding voting stock of the other company.

The way these terms relate to the measurement and reporting of long-term investments in voting capital stock is as follows:

Level of ownership	*Measurement and reporting approach*
1. Neither significant influence nor control	Cost method
2. Significant influence but not control	Equity method
3. Control	Consolidated statement method

Each of these approaches is outlined in Exhibit 14–1. The first two are discussed in the paragraphs to follow, and the third is discussed in Chapter 17.

EXHIBIT 14–1

Measurement and reporting of long-term investments in capital stock

Status of ownership	*Designation of method*	*Measurement at date of acquisition*	*Measurement after date of acquisition* — *Investment*	*Measurement after date of acquisition* — *Revenue*
1. Investor can exercise no significant influence or control. Presumed if investor owns less than 20% of the outstanding voting stock of the other company.	Cost method	Investor records the investment at cost. Cost is the total outlay made to acquire the shares.	Investor measures and reports the investment at cost on the balance sheet each period. Subsequently report at lower of cost or market by recognizing unrealized losses.	Investor recognizes revenue each period when dividends are recorded by the other company. Realized gain or loss recognized when investment is sold.
2. Investor can exercise significant influence, but not control, over the operating and financing policies of the other company. Presumed if investor owns 20% or more, but not more than 50%, of the outstanding voting stock of the other company.	Equity method	Same as above.	Investor measures and reports the investment at cost *plus* the investor's share of the earnings (or less the losses) and *minus* the dividends received from the other company. (Dividends received are not considered revenue. To recognize them as revenue, rather than as a reduction in the investment, would involve double counting.)	Investor recognizes as revenue each period his or her proportionate share of the earnings (or losses) reported each period by the other company.
3. Investor can exercise control over the operating and financing policies of the other company. Control is presumed if the investor owns over 50% of the outstanding voting stock of the other company.	Consolidated financial statement method	Same as above.	Consolidated financial statements required each period. Discussed in Chapter 17.	

COST METHOD—NO SIGNIFICANT INFLUENCE OR CONTROL

When the investment by one corporation in the voting capital stock of another corporation does not give the former the ability to exercise significant influence or control, the **cost method** of accounting and reporting must be used. Under this method of accounting, the investment is measured in the accounts at cost. Subsequent to acquisition, the investment amount is considered to be the current lower of cost or market, and this amount is reported under "Investments and Funds" on the balance sheet for each period. Cash dividends declared by the other corporation are reported by the investing entity as "Revenue from investments" in the period received. The cost method is essentially the same as the accounting and reporting previously discussed and illustrated for short-term investments in Chapter 9.

FASB *Statement No. 12,* "Accounting for Certain Marketable Securities" (December 1975) requires that long-term equity investments accounted for under the cost method be valued at lower of cost or market after acquisition. Thus, at the end of each accounting period, the *entire portfolio* of long-term equity investments, accounted for under the cost method, must be calculated at both total cost and total market. If total market is less than total cost, the difference must be recorded as a credit to a contra account called "Allowance to Reduce Long-Term Investments to Market"; the offsetting deibt is to a contra owners' equity account called "Unrealized Loss on Long-Term Investments." If, at the end of a subsequent period, market exceeds the valuation reported the prior period, the portfolio is written up to the new market but not to exceed the acquisition cost of the securities portfolio. (To repeat, only the recovery to acquisition cost is recognized as a recovery of the unrealized loss previously recorded.) *Market* is measured as the number of shares owned multiplied by the actual market price per share at the balance sheet date.

When long-term securities are sold, the difference between the sales price and acquisition cost is recorded and reported as a *realized* gain or loss.

To illustrate application of the cost method, assume the following transactions by Able Corporation over a two-year period:

February 1, 19A: Purchased long-term investments as follows:

Baker Corporation common stock (nopar), 1,000 shares at $12 per share (this is 10 percent of the shares outstanding).

Cox Corporation preferred stock (par $20), 500 shares at $40 per share (this is 1 percent of the shares outstanding).

Entry:

Long-term investments	32,000	
Cash		32,000

Baker common stock, 1,000 shares × $12 =	$12,000
Cox preferred stock, 500 shares × $40 =	20,000
Total Acquisition Cost	$32,000

November 30, 19A: Received the following dividends on long-term investments:

Baker common stock, $1 per share.
Cox preferred stock 5 percent of par.

Entry:

Cash	1,500	
Revenue from investments		1,500

Baker common stock, 1,000 shares × $1 =	$1,000
Cox preferred stock, 500 shares × $20 × 5% =	500
Total Dividends Received	$1,500

December 31, 19A: Quoted market prices at year-end:

Baker common stock, $13.
Cox preferred stock, $36.

Entry:

Unrealized loss on long-term investments	1,000	
Allowance to reduce long-term investments to market		1,000

	Shares	*Market Dec. 31, 19A*	*Acquisition cost*	*Market at Dec. 31, 19A*
Baker common stock	1,000	$13	$12,000	$13,000
Cox preferred stock	500	36	20,000	18,000
			$32,000	$31,000

Lower of cost or market: $32,000 − $31,000 = $1,000 (balance required in the allowance account).

June 15, 19B: Unexpectedly sold 300 of the Cox preferred stock at $41:

Entry:

Cash (300 shares × $41)	12,300	
Long-term investment (300 × $40)		12,000
Gain on sale of investment		300

November 30, 19B: Dividends received:

Baker common stock, $0.90 per share.
Cox preferred stock, 5 percent of par.

Entry:

Cash	1,100	
Revenue from investments		1,100

Baker common stock, 1,000 shares × $0.90 =	$ 900
Cox preferred stock, 200 shares × $20 × 5% =	200
Total Dividends Received	$1,100

December 31, 19B: Quoted market price at year-end:

Baker common stock, $11.
Cox preferred stock, $43.

Entry:

Allowance to reduce long-term investments to market	600	
Unrealized loss on long-term investments		600

	Shares	*Market Dec. 31, 19B*	*Acquisition cost*	*Market at Dec. 31, 19B*
Baker common stock	1,000	$11	$12,000	$11,000
Cox preferred stock	200	43	8,000	8,600
			$20,000	$19,600

Lower of cost or market: $20,000 − $19,600 = $400 (balance required in the allowance account). Reduction in allowance account: $1,000 − $400 = $600.

The income statement and balance sheet for each year would report the following:

	19A		*19B*	
Income Statement:				
Revenue from investments		$ 1,500		$ 1,100
Gain on sale of investments				300
Balance Sheet:				
Investments and Funds:				
Investments in equity securities	$32,000		$20,000	
Less: Allowance to reduce to market	1,000	31,000	400	19,600
Stockholders' Equity:				
Unrealized loss on long-term investments		(1,000)		(400)

The above entries reflect application of the cost principle at acquisition and application of lower of cost or market subsequent to that time. The investment is carried continuously at lower of cost or market, and revenue is recognized from the investment *only* in periods when dividends are received. In the example above, it was assumed that Baker and Cox Corporations' dividends were paid in the same year as declared.[2]

Recall that the discussions above pertain only to the investing entity—Able Corporation. The fact that Able Corporation purchased 10 percent of the outstanding voting shares of Baker Corporation and 1 percent of the outstanding preferred shares of Cox Corporation had absolutely no affect on the accounting and reporting by either Baker or Cox Corporations.

All *nonvoting* stock owned as a long-term investment, regardless of the level of ownership, is accounted for under the cost method as described above.

EQUITY METHOD—SIGNIFICANT INFLUENCE EXISTS

When the investment by one corporation in another corporation represents at least 20 percent, but not more than 50 percent, of the outstanding voting stock of the latter corporation, we can presume that significant influence is present; therefore, the **equity method** of measuring and reporting must be followed. When 20 percent or more, but not more than 50 percent, of the outstanding voting common stock of another corporation is owned, the degree of ownership is deemed to be sufficient to exercise significant influence but not control over the financing and operating policies (including the dividend policies) of the other company.

When significant influence can be exercised over the dividend policies of another corporation, the net income of the other corporation can be obtained, almost at will (by means of dividends), by the investor company. In order to avoid manipulating income by manipulating dividends, under the equity method, each year the investor company recognizes its proportionate part of the *net income* (or net loss) of the other corporation as a part of its own net income rather than awaiting the receipt of dividends. At the time of recognition, since no cash is received, the offsetting debit is to the investment account (an asset increase). Thus, under the equity method, both the **investment account** and **investment revenue** reflect the investor's proportionate share of the profits (and losses) of the other corporation. When dividends are received, they are debited to Cash and credited to the investment account. Thus, dividends received serve to reduce the investment account balance and they are *not* credited to Revenue from Investments. The revenue was already recognized by the investor in the same period that the other company earned the income.

---

[2] If cash dividends are declared in one year and paid in the following year, the dividend is recognized when declared by debiting Dividends Receivable (a current asset) instead of Cash.

To illustrate the accounting and reporting under the equity method, assume that Crown Corporation (the investor company), on January 15, 1977, purchased in the market 3,000 shares of the outstanding common stock of Davis Corporation (often called the investee company) at a cash price of $120 per share. At the date of purchase, Davis Corporation had outstanding 10,000 shares of common stock (par $100 per share). Since Crown Corporation purchased 30 percent of the outstanding voting stock of the other corporation, the equity method must be used. At the date of acquisition, the investment would be recorded by Crown Corporation **at cost** as follows:[3]

January 15, 1977:

Investment in common stock, Davis Corporation (3,000 shares)	360,000	
Cash		360,000
Purchased 3,000 shares (30 percent) of the common stock of Davis Corporation at $120 per share.		

After the acquisition date, each year when the other corporation reports net income (or net loss), the investor company records its percentage share (i.e., equity in) of the investment revenue. To illustrate, assume that at the end of 1977, Davis Corporation reported a net income of $50,000. The entry by Crown Corporation (the investor company) to recognize its proportionate share of the net income would be:

December 31, 1977:

Investment in common stock, Davis Corporation	15,000	
Revenue from investments		15,000
To record the proportionate share of 1977 net income reported by Davis Corporation ($50,000 × 30% = $15,000).		

The proportionate share of the net income of Davis Corporation was taken up by Crown Corporation as revenue and as an *increase* in the investment account. Therefore, when a dividend is received, to avoid counting the income twice, it is recorded as a debit to Cash and as a **credit to the investment account.** This entry reflects the fact that a dividend represents the conversion of a part of the investment account balance to cash. To illustrate, assume that on December 31, 1977, Davis Corporation paid a cash dividend amounting to $10,000, of which 30 percent, or $3,000, was received by Crown Corporation. Crown Corporation would record the dividend as follows:

[3] This example assumes that the investment was purchased at "book value." The accounting and reporting procedures for other situations are more complex since they involve asset write-ups and write-downs and, perhaps, the recognition of "goodwill." This chapter presents the fundamentals devoid of this complexity. More advanced books devote considerable attention to these complexities.

December 31, 1977:

Cash	3,000	
Investment in common stock, Davis Corporation		3,000
To record the receipt of a cash dividend from Davis Corporation ($10,000 × 30% = $3,000).		

To recapitulate, under the equity method, the balance in the investment account initially starts at cost. Subsequently, it is increased on a proportionate basis by the earnings (or decreased by losses) of the investee company and decreased by the proportionate share of the dividends declared by that company. The investment and revenue accounts on the books of the investor company, the Crown Corporation, would be as follows:

Investment in Common Stock, Davis Corporation

1/15/77	Purchased 3,000 shares	360,000	12/31/77	Proportionate share of dividends of Davis Corp.	3,000
12/31/77	Proportionate share of 1977 net income of Davis Corp.	15,000			

(Debit balance, $372,000)

Revenue from Investments

			12/31/77	Revenue from Davis Corp.	15,000

The financial statements for Crown Corporation, the investor company, at the end of 1977 would reflect the following:

CROWN CORPORATION
Balance Sheet
At December 31, 1977

Investments and Funds:

Investment in common stock, Davis Corporation, equity basis (cost, $360,000; market, $369,000)*	$372,000

Income Statement

Revenue from investments	$ 15,000

* Market is measured as the number of shares owned multiplied by the actual market price per share on the balance sheet date. Lower of cost or market does not apply to the equity method.

In interpreting and using financial statements that report long-term investments, information in respect to the method of measuring the investment and the related investment revenue is important. The financial statement must disclose the method used. In addition, regardless of whether the cost or the equity method is used, the original cost, current market value, and carrying value of the investment should be disclosed; this disclosure is illustrated in the preceding paragraphs.

The different methods used represent a compromise on the part of the accounting profession in respect to measuring the effects of long-term investments. Although not currently acceptable, many accountants believe that marketable securities should be measured and reported at their **fair-market value** at each balance sheet date. Under this approach, both dividends received and changes in the market value of the stock since the last period would be reported as revenue (or loss) on the income statement. They take this position because they believe that it meets most closely the objective of reporting the economic consequences of holding an investment in marketable securities. The *cost method* measures the resources (dividends) received by the investor as revenue, but these may have absolutely no relationship to the earnings of the other company for the period. The cost method does not indicate to the investor or statement user the earnings pattern of the other company. The equity method tends to overcome this objection; however, it does not reflect the impact on the entity of market changes that are significant to the investor. After consideration of these and other factors, the accounting profession, for the present time, has accepted the three different measurement approaches for long-term investments in shares that are outlined in Exhibit 14–1.

PART TWO: LONG-TERM INVESTMENTS IN BONDS

NATURE OF A BOND INVESTMENT

In Chapter 12, the measurement and reporting of bonds as a long-term liability of the issuing corporation were discussed. In this part, we will focus on bonds of another company held as a long-term investment. Bonds purchased as a long-term investment offer significantly different investment risks than does capital stock. Although bonds held as an investment do not confer voting privileges, as does capital stock, they do provide a stated rate of interest and a specified maturity value. As debt, they rank above shares as a claim for both interest and principal. For example, assume that Smith Company issued $100,000, 6 percent, 20-year bonds. At the specified maturity date, the investors in the bonds (i.e., the bondholders) receive exactly $100,000 cash in retirement of the bonds. The 6 percent stated interest on the face amount of the bond is received in cash each year (usually 3 percent semiannually), irrespectively of the market price of the bonds or the earnings of the other company. The owner (i.e., the investor) of one or more of these bonds has no right to vote in the annual stockholders' meeting as would be the case if some of the common stock of Smith Company was owned.

Similar to capital stock, bonds are bought and sold in regular security markets. The market price of bonds fluctuates inversely with changes in the **market rate** of interest since the **stated rate** of interest, paid on the face amount of the bond, remains constant over the life of the bonds (see Chapter 12).

MEASURING AND REPORTING BOND INVESTMENTS

Investors may buy bonds as an investment at their date of issuance or at subsequent dates during the life of the bonds. Irrespective of the timing of their acquisition, the investor must measure the (1) cost plus any amortized discount or minus any amortized premium at each balance sheet date, and (2) interest revenue earned each period, which is reported on the income statement. An understanding of the measurement approaches used is helpful in interpreting and using financial statements.

At date of acquisition, a bond investment is measured, recorded, and reported in accordance with the **cost principle.** The purchase cost, including all incidental acquisition costs (such as transfer fees and broker commissions), is debited to an investment account such as "Long-Term Investment, Bonds of X Corporation." The cost recorded under the cost principle is the **current cash-equivalent amount;** and it may be the same as the maturity amount (if acquired at par), less than the maturity amount (if acquired at a discount), or more than the maturity amount (if acquired at a premium).[4] The premium or discount on a bond investment usually is not recorded in a separate account as is done for bonds payable; rather, the investment account reflects the current book or carrying amount. However, a separate discount or premium account can be used with precisely the same results.

Subsequent to acquisition, a bond investment is measured as the acquisition cost plus or minus any amortized discount or premium at each subsequent date. If the bond investment was acquired at maturity value (at par), the carrying value amount remains constant over the life of the investment because there is no premium or discount to be amortized. In this situation, revenue earned from the investment each period is measured as the amount of cash interest collected (or accrued).

When a bond investment is acquired at a current cash-equivalent amount that is either more or less than the maturity amount (i.e., at a premium or discount), measurement of the carrying value of the investment after date of acquisition necessitates adjustment of the investment account balance from acquisition cost to maturity amount each period over the life of the investment. This adjustment is the periodic amortization of the premium or discount. The periodic amortization is made as

[4] Fees, commissions, and other incidental costs increase the discount, or decrease the premium; hence, they are amortized over the remaining period to maturity. Alternatively, they sometimes are separately recorded and amortized on the same basis as the discount or premium.

a debit or credit to the investment account, depending on whether there was a premium or discount at acquisition, so that the investment account at the end of each period reflects the *then current carrying amount.*

When a bond investment is acquired at a premium or discount, the revenue from interest each period is measured as the cash interest collected (or accrued) plus or minus the periodic amortization of premium or discount. As was illustrated in Chapter 12 for bonds payable, bond premium or discount may be amortized by using either the straight-line or effective-interest approach. The former is simpler, whereas the latter is conceptually preferable. In the paragraphs to follow, we will assume straight-line amortization; effective-interest amortization is explained at the end of this part. In contrast to long-term investments, premium or discount is not amortized on bonds held as a short-term investment since the bonds will be converted to cash (i.e., sold) within the coming year instead of being held to maturity.

The concepts of the carrying value of a bond investment and amortization of a premium and discount may be graphically portrayed as follows:

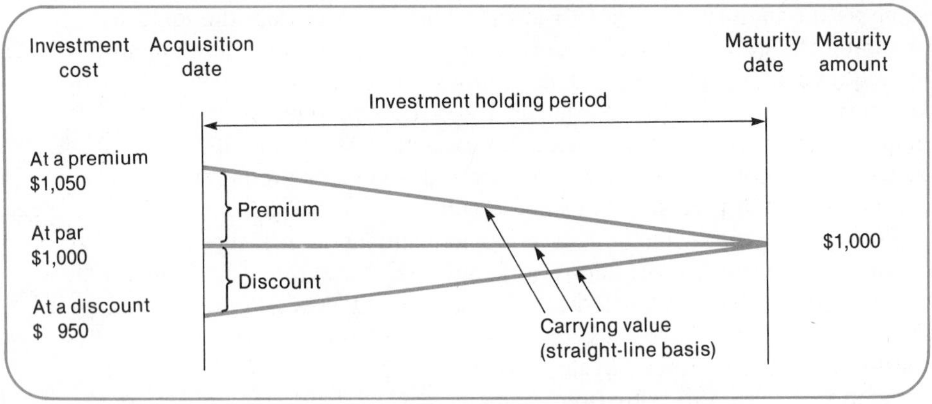

Observe that when the effective interest amortization is used, the carrying value lines, when there is a premium or discount, will be curved instead of straight.

Accrual of interest revenue. After date of acquisition, interest revenue must be accrued (by means of an adjusting entry) for periods between the last date on which interest revenue was collected and the end of the accounting period. The procedure for accruing interest expense and interest revenue was discussed and illustrated in several prior chapters.

BONDS PURCHASED AT PAR

To illustrate a long-term investment in the bonds payable of another company, purchased at par, assume that on July 1, 1977, Roth Company purchased $10,000, 6 percent, 20-year bonds of Smith Company in the open market at a cost of $10,000 cash (i.e., purchased at par). The bonds were originally issued by Smith Company on July 1, 1962, and mature on June 30, 1982; thus, Roth Company purchased the bonds at 100, five years before the maturity date. The bonds call for 6 percent annual interest payable each June 30. Roth Company adjusts and closes its book each December 31. The sequence of entries on the books of Roth Company to account for this long-term investment in bonds payable follows:[5]

July 1, 1977:

Long-term investment, bonds of Smith Company	10,000	
Cash		10,000
Purchased at par, $10,000 maturity value, 6 percent bonds of Smith Company. (Note: Since the bonds were purchased on an interest date, there was no accrued interest.)		

December 31, 1977 (and each year until maturity):

Bond interest receivable	300	
Revenue from investments*		300
Adjusting entry to accrue six months interest revenue on Smith Company bonds ($10,000 × 0.06 × 6/12 = $300).		

* Alternate titles are interest revenue and, sometimes, interest income.

June 30, 1978 (and each year until maturity):[6]

Cash ($10,000 × 0.06)	600	
Bond interest receivable (from December 31 entry)		300
Revenue from investments		300
Receipt of annual interest payment on the Smith Company bonds.		

June 30, 1982:

Cash	10,000	
Long-term investment, bonds of Smith Company		10,000
Retirement of bonds at maturity date (assumes last interest receipt already recorded).		

Since the bond investment was purchased at par or maturity value, there was no premium or discount to be amortized.

At the end of 1977, the financial statements of Roth Company would report the following:

---

[5] Bonds generally pay interest semiannually. Annual interest is used in this illustration to reduce the number of repetitive entries. The concepts are applied the same way in either case.

[6] This entry presumes that there was no reversal on January 1, 1978, of the prior adjusting entry. A reversing entry is optional since it serves only to facilitate the subsequent entry (see Chapter 6).

Balance Sheet

Current Assets:	
Bond interest receivable	$ 300
Investments and Funds:	
Investment in bonds, at cost (market, $10,125)	10,000

Income Statement

Revenue from investments	$ 300

BONDS PURCHASED AT A DISCOUNT

When investors demand a *higher* rate of interest on bonds than the **stated rate,** bonds will sell in the market at a **discount.** When a bond investment is purchased at a discount, say at 98 (this means 98 percent of the bond's par value), the investor receives back in cash the periodic interest payments stated on the bond plus the maturity value (i.e., at 100). The discount serves to increase the interest revenue earned on the bond investment. To illustrate, assume that on July 1, 1977, Roth Company purchased a $10,000, 6 percent bond issued by Smith Company for $9,800 cash. The bond will mature in five years. Interest revenue of $10,000 × 0.06 = $600 will be collected annually. This investment can be analyzed to show that although $600 cash is collected each year, the annual revenue *earned* from the investment is $640, due to amortization of the discount. The analysis, assuming straight-line amortization, is as follows:

Cash inflows from the investment:		
Annual interest collected, July 1, 1977, through June 30, 1982 ($10,000 × 0.06 × 5 years)	$ 3,000	
Collection of bond at maturity date, June 30, 1982	10,000	$13,000
Cash outflow for the investment:		
July 1, 1977—purchase of bond		9,800
Difference—net increase in cash (this is the total interest earned)		$ 3,200

Revenue from investment per year: $3,200 ÷ 5 years = $640 (assuming straight-line amortization).

When a bond is purchased as an investment, the long-term investment account is debited for the current cash-equivalent amount in accordance with the cost principle. Therefore, when a bond investment is purchased at a discount, the investment account balance at purchase date will be less than par or maturity value. Through **amortization** of the discount, the balance of the investment account must be *increased* each period in order to be at the par amount at maturity date. Amortization of the discount each period over the **remaining life** of the bond also *increases* the amount of interest revenue earned. To accomplish this, the amount of discount amortized each period is debited to the investment account and credited to Interest Revenue. The effects of this periodic amortization, over the life of the investment, are (1) to carry the investment account balance at the end of each period at the then current carrying amount, and (2) to increase interest revenue earned each year by the amount of the amortization.

To illustrate, in the preceding example, Roth Company each year must amortize a part of the discount ($10,000 − $9,800 = $200), so that the total will be amortized over the remaining life of the bond investment. Assuming straight-line amortization, the amount of discount amortized each full year would be $200 ÷ 5 years = $40 per year.

The sequence of entries by Roth Company, from the date of acquisition of the bond investment through maturity date, would be:

July 1, 1977:

Long-term investment, bonds of Smith Company (at cost)	9,800	
Cash		9,800

Purchased $10,000 maturity value, 6 percent bonds of the Smith Company at 98.

December 31, 1977 (and each year until maturity):

Bond interest receivable ($10,000 × 0.06 × 6/12)	300	
Long-term investment, bonds of Smith Company (amortization: $40 × 6/12)	20	
Revenue from investments		320

Adjusting entry to (1) accrue interest revenue for six months and (2) to amortize discount on the bond investment for six months (July 1 to December 31).

June 30, 1978 (and each year until maturity):

Cash ($10,000 × 0.06)	600	
Long-term investment, bonds of Smith Company (amortization: $40 × 6/12)	20	
Bond interest receivable (from December 31 entry)		300
Revenue from investments		320

Receipt of annual interest on Smith Company bonds and amortization of discount for six months (January 1 to June 30).

June 30, 1982:

Cash	10,000	
Long-term investment, bonds of Smith Company		10,000

Retirement of bonds at maturity (assumes last interest receipt already recorded).

The increase in the balance in the long-term investment account from cost at date of purchase to par value at maturity date that results from the amortization of the bond discount is reflected in the investment ledger account in Roth's accounts as follows:[7]

Long-Term Investment, Bonds of Smith Company

July 1, 1977 At acquisition	9,800	June 30, 1982 Retirement	10,000
Amortizations:			
Dec. 31, 1977	20		
31 1978	40		
31 1979	40		
31 1980	40		
31 1981	40		
June 30, 1982	20		
	10,000		10,000

At the end of 1977, the financial statements of Roth Company would report the following:

Balance Sheet

Current Assets:	
Bond interest receivable	$ 300
Investments and Funds:	
Investment in bonds, at amortized cost (market, $10,125)	9,820

Income Statement

Revenue from investments	$ 320

BONDS PURCHASED AT A PREMIUM

When investors are willing to invest at a rate of interest *less* than the **stated rate** of interest on the bonds, the bonds will sell at a **premium.** When bonds are purchased at a premium, the investment account is debited for an amount greater than the par or maturity value. Therefore, the premium must be **amortized** over the **remaining life** of the bonds as a *decrease* in the balance in the investment account so that the balance of the investment account is at par value on maturity date. The procedure parallels that illustrated above for a discount, except that each period the investment account is credited and the premium amortization serves to *decrease* interest revenue.

To illustrate the accounting and reporting where there is a premium, assume that in the preceding example, Roth Company purchased Smith

[7] Observe that the amortization of discount or premium on bond investments conceptually is the same as the amortization discussed and illustrated in Chapter 12 in the issuer's accounts. Here, we are simply looking at the other side of the transaction. A minor procedural difference may be noted. In Chapter 12, premium or discount was recorded in a separate account; in this chapter, the *net amount* (i.e., the cost) was recorded in the investment account. Either procedure can be used in either situation with the same results. Common practice follows the procedures illustrated in the respective chapters.

Company bonds for $10,200 cash. The cash outflow and inflows for this investment may be analyzed to reflect the effect of the premium on interest revenue earned as follows:

Cash inflows from the investment:		
Annual interest collected, July 1, 1977, through June 30, 1982 ($10,000 × 0.06 × 5 years)	$ 3,000	
July 30, 1982, collection of bond at maturity	10,000	$13,000
Cash outflow for the investment:		
July 1, 1977—purchase of bond		10,200
Difference—net increase in cash (this is the total interest revenue earned)		$ 2,800

Revenue from investment, per year: $2,800 ÷ 5 years = $560.

The amount of premium amortization each full year, on a straight-line basis would be $200 ÷ 5 years = $40. The sequence of entries by Roth Company for the bond investment, purchased at a premium, would be:

July 1, 1977:

Long-term investment, bonds of Smith Company (at cost)	10,200	
Cash		10,200

Purchased $10,000 maturity value, 6 percent bonds of Smith Company at 102.

December 31, 1977 (and each year until maturity):

Bond interest receivable ($10,000 × 0.06 × 6/12)	300	
Long-term investment, bonds of Smith Company (amortization: $40 × 6/12)		20
Revenue from investments		280

Adjusting entry to (1) accrue interest revenue for six months and (2) amortize premium on the investment for six months (July 1 to December 31).

June 30, 1978 (and each year until maturity):

Cash ($10,000 × 0.06)	600	
Bond interest receivable (per December 31 entry)		300
Long-term investment, bonds of Smith Company (amortization: $40 × 6/12)		20
Revenue from investments		280

Receipt of annual interest revenue on Smith Company bonds and amortization of premium for six months, January 1 to June 30, 1978.

June 30, 1982:

Cash	10,000	
Long-term investment, bonds of Smith Company		10,000

Retirement of bonds at maturity (assuming the last interest receipt has been recorded).

At the end of 1977, the financial statements of Roth Company would report the following:

Balance Sheet	
Current Assets:	
Bond interest receivable	$ 300
Investments and Funds:	
Investment in bonds, at amortized cost (market, $10,225)	10,180
Income Statement	
Revenue from investments	$ 280

BOND INVESTMENT PURCHASED BETWEEN INTEREST DATES

Investors generally purchase bond investments between the interest dates specified on the bonds. In these situations the investor must pay for the amount of **interest accrued** since the last interest date in addition to the purchase price of the bond. The bond market operates in this fashion because the holder of the bond at the interest date receives interest for the full period between interest dates, irrespective of the purchase date. The former owner of the bond is entitled to interest for the period of time that the bond was held (see Chapter 12). To illustrate, assume a $1,000 bond, 6 percent interest, payable 3 percent each March 31 and September 30, is purchased on June 1, 1977, at 100 plus accrued interest. The purchase of the bond investment would be recorded as follows:

June 1, 1977:

	Debit	Credit
Long-term investment, 6 percent bond	1,000	
Revenue from investments ($1,000 × 0.06 × 2/12)	10[8]	
Cash [$1,000 + ($1,000 × 0.06 × 2/12)]		1,010
Purchase of a $1,000, 6 percent bond as a long-term investment at 100 plus accrued interest for two months, March 31 to June 1, 1977.		

It is important to observe in this entry that the long-term investment account is debited for the *cost* of the investment, which excludes the accrued interest. The $10 accrued interest was paid for in cash by the purchaser; however, it will be refunded to the investor at the next interest date on September 30, 1977. At that time, the investor will receive the full amount of interest for six months, although the bond has been owned for only four months (i.e., June 1 to September 30, 1977).

[8] Alternatively, an account, "Bond Interest Receivable," could have been debited on June 1 for $10 and then credited for that amount on September 30. The net effect would have been the same. When the end of the accounting period falls between the purchase date and the next interest date, such a procedure may be less complex.

The entry to record the first interest collection after the purchase would be:

September 30, 1977:

Cash	30	
Revenue from investments		30
Collected interest for six months on bond investment ($1,000 × 0.03 = $30).		

After these two entries are posted, the Revenue from Investments account on Roth's books will reflect $20 interest earned for the four months since purchase as follows:

Revenue from Investments

6/1/77	10	9/30/77	30

(Balance, $1,000 × 0.03 × 4/6 = $20 credit)

SALE OF A BOND INVESTMENT

When bonds are acquired as a long-term investment, they are accounted for with the expectation that they will be held to the maturity date. This is the basis for amortizing any premium or discount over the period from the date of purchase to the maturity date. Nevertheless, such long-term investments may be sold prior to the maturity date. When a bond investment is sold prior to maturity of the bonds, the difference between the sales price and the balance in the investment account is recorded as a "gain (or loss) on the sale of investments."

To illustrate, assume Carson Corporation has two $1,000, 6 percent bonds of Drake Company that are being held as a long-term investment. Each bond was purchased at 104; therefore, the long-term investment account was debited for $2,080. Because of amortization to January 1, 1977, the investment account balance is $2,040. On that date one of the bonds was sold for 100. The entry to record the sale would be as follows:

Cash	1,000	
Loss on sale of investments	20	
Long-term investment, Drake Co. bonds		1,020
Sale of long-term investment.		

EFFECTIVE-INTEREST AMORTIZATION ON BOND INVESTMENTS

Effective-interest amortization of the discount or premium on a bond investment is conceptually identical with that discussed for bonds payable in Chapter 12 (page 472). This method of amortization is conceptually superior because the effective interest rate is used; therefore (1) interest revenue is measured correctly each period for income statement purposes, and (2) the carrying amount of the investment is correctly measured for balance sheet purposes at the end of each period. Each interest revenue collection (in cash) is assumed to be part principal and part interest. To illustrate the effective-interest approach, assume that on January 1, 1977, Company A purchased a three-year, $10,000, 6 percent bond of Company B as a long-term investment. The purchase price, based on a 7 percent effective interest rate, was 97.38. Therefore, the cash paid was $9,738, that is, at a $262 discount. The bond carried a stated rate of interest of 6 percent per year, payable each December 31. The acquisition was recorded as follows:[9]

January 1, 1977:

Long-term investment, bond of Company B (maturity amount $10,000)	9,738	
Cash		9,738
Purchase of long-term investment.		

Computation of effective-interest amortization is shown in the following tabulation. Observe that the effective rate of interest, 7 percent in this example, is used to compute the revenue rather than the stated interest rate.

Period	*Cash received for interest each period*	*Interest revenue each period: Based on investment balance and effective rate*	*Amount added to investment balance*	*Investment balance*
1/1/77 (acquisition)				$ 9,738
12/31/77	$ 600*	$9,738 × 0.07 = $ 682	$ 82†	9,820‡
12/31/78	600	9,820 × 0.07 = 687	87	9,907
12/31/79	600	9,907 × 0.07 = 693	93	10,000
Totals	$1,800	$2,062	$262	

* $10,000 × .06 = $600.
† Col. 2, $682, minus Col. 1, $600 = $82.
‡ $9,738 plus Col. 3, $82 = $9,820.

The first amount column reflects the cash inflow each period for interest (at the stated rate); the second column shows the interest revenue amount to be reported on the income statement each period (i.e., the effective rate on the unpaid balance); and the last column shows the

[9] Given the effective rate of 7 percent, the price of the bond can be determined from a bond table or computed as follows:

$$\$10{,}000 \times p_{n=3,\ i=7\%} = \$10{,}000 \times 0.8163 \text{ (Table 11–2)} = \$8{,}163$$
$$\$\quad 600 \times P_{n=3,\ i=7\%} = \$\quad 600 \times 2.6243 \text{ (Table 11–4)} = \underline{1{,}575}$$
$$\text{Bond price (PV of future cash flows)} \ldots\ \underline{\underline{\$9{,}738}}$$

Alternatively, if the price is known (97.38), the effective rate can be determined from a bond table or computed with certain pocket calculators.

amount of the investment (i.e., the unamortized principal) to be reported on the balance sheet at the end of each period under "Investments and Funds." The entry for interest revenue each period can be taken directly from the table, viz:

	Year 1		*Year 2*		*Year 3*	
Cash	600		600		600	
Long-term investment	82		87		93	
Revenue from investments		682		687		693

Conceptually, this method derives the true or effective-interest revenue earned during each period and the correct current carrying value for the investment at the end of each period. The straight-line approach provides only approximations of these amounts. When the amounts are material, APB *Opinion No. 21,* "Interest on Receivables and Payables," requires use of the effective interest method. Straight-line amortization is often used because the different amounts of premium or discount amortized each period are not material. In such a case, the departure from the conceptually superior method is justified by the exception principle (i.e., materiality) of accounting.

DEMONSTRATION CASE FOR SELF-STUDY

Howell Equipment, Incorporated

(Try to resolve the case before turning to the suggested solution that follows.)

Howell Equipment, Incorporated, has been in operation for 18 years. The company sells a major line of farm equipment. In recent years its service department has expanded significantly. Both sales and services have been quite profitable. At the beginning of 1977, the company had considerable excess cash. At that time the management decided to invest in some securities of two of the manufacturers that supply most of the equipment purchased for resale. The annual accounting period ends on December 31.

This case focuses on the two long-term investments made in 1977. One investment was in equity securities, and the other in debt securities. The transactions follow:

1977

a. Jan. 1 Purchased 2,000 shares of common stock of Dear Company at $40 per share. This was 1 percent of the shares outstanding.

b. Aug. 1 Purchased $100,000, 6 percent bonds payable of the Massey Company at 102, plus accrued interest. The bonds pay semiannual interest on each May 31 and November 30. The bonds mature on May 31, 1982. Brokerage fees amounted to $900.

c.	Nov. 30	Received semiannual interest on Massey Company bonds. Use straight-line amortization.
d.	Dec. 28	Received $4,000 cash dividend on the Dear Company stock.
e.	31	Adjusting entry for accrued interest on the Massey Company bonds.
f.	31	The current market price of the Dear stock is $39 and 103 for the Massey bonds.
g.	31	Closed the revenue from investments account to Income Summary.

Required:

a. Give the journal entry for each of the above transactions.

b. Show how the two investments, the accrued interest receivable and the related revenue, would be reported on the balance sheet and income statement at December 31, 1977.

Suggested Solution:

Requirement (*a*):

a. January 1, 1977:

Long-term investment, stock of Dear Company (2,000 shares)	80,000	
Cash		80,000

Purchased 2,000 shares Dear Company common stock at $40 per share.

b. August 1, 1977:

Long-term investment, bonds of Massey Company	102,900	
Revenue from investments ($100,000 × 0.03 × 2/6)	1,000	
Cash		103,900

Purchased $100,000 bonds of the Massey Company:

Cost ($100,000 × 1.02) + $900	=	$102,900
Accrued interest for 2 months ($100,000 × 0.03 × 2/6)	=	1,000
Total Cash Paid		$103,900

c. November 30, 1977:

Cash	3,000	
Long-term investment, bonds of Massey Company		200
Revenue from investments		2,800

Semiannual interest: $100,000 × 0.03	=	$3,000
Amortization of premium: $2,900 ÷ 58 months = $50 per month; $50 × 4 months*	=	200
Revenue from investments		$2,800

* August 1, 1977, to June 1, 1982 = 58 months remaining life.

d. December 28, 1977:

Cash	4,000	
Revenue from investments		4,000

Received dividend on Dear Company stock.

e. December 31, 1977:

Accrued interest receivable	500	
Long-term investment, bonds of Massey Company		50
Revenue from investments		450

Adjusting entry for accrued interest and premium amortization for one month on Massey Company bonds:

Accrued interest receivable:
$100,000 × 0.03 × 1/6 = $500
Amortization of premium:
$50 × 1 month = 50
Revenue from investments $450

f.

Unrealized loss on long-term investment	2,000	
Allowance to reduce long-term investment to LCM		2,000

To record lower of cost or market on Dear stock:
2,000 shares × ($40 − $39) = $2,000.

g. December 31, 1977:

Revenue from investments	6,250	
Income summary		6,250

Closing entry: (2,800 − $1,000 + $4,000 + $450 = $6,250).

Requirement (*b*):

HOWELL EQUIPMENT, INCORPORATED
Balance Sheet
At December 31, 1977

Current Assets:		
Accrued interest receivable		$ 500
Investments and Funds:		
Stock of Dear Company, at lower of cost or market, 2,000 shares (cost, $80,000)	$ 78,000	
Bonds of Massey Company, at amortized cost ($100,000 maturity value; market, $103,000)	102,650	180,650
Stockholders' Equity:		
Unrealized loss on long-term investments		(2,000)

Income Statement
For Year Ending December 31, 1977

Revenue from investments	$ 6,250

SUMMARY

This chapter discussed the measuring and reporting of two types of long-term investments: the capital stock and the bonds of another company. A company may acquire a part or all of the outstanding capital stock of another corporation through purchase of the shares or by exchanging their own stock for shares in the other company. The measurement and reporting for a long-term investment in shares of capital stock of another company is determined by the percent of shares owned in relation to the total number outstanding.

If the ownership level is less than 20 percent, the **cost method** must be used. Under this method the investment amount reported by the investor company is lower of cost or market, and dividends received from the other company are recognized as investment revenue.

If the ownership is at least 20 percent but not more than 50 percent, the **equity method** is used. Under this method the investment is recorded at cost by the investor company at date of acquisition. Each period thereafter, the investment amount is increased (or decreased) by the proportionate interest in the net income (or loss) reported by the other company and decreased by the proportionate share of the dividends received from the other company. Each period, the investor company recognizes as revenue its proportionate share of the net income reported by the other company.

When there is a controlling interest—that is, over 50 percent ownership of the outstanding stock is held by the investor—the financial statements of the affiliated companies are **consolidated.** The subject is discussed in Chapter 17.

A corporation may purchase the bonds of another entity as a long-term investment. In contrast to capital stock, bonds are a liability of the issuing company, therefore they (1) have a specified maturity date and face amount, (2) require the payment of a stated rate of interest at regular specified interest dates, and (3) do not convey voting privileges. At the date of purchase, a long-term investment in bonds is recorded at cost, which may be at par, at a discount, or at a premium. When purchased at a premium or a discount, amortization of such premium or discount over the remaining life of the bonds is required. The periodic amortization serves to adjust the investment amount to a carrying value which is reported on the balance sheet and interest revenue earned which is reported on the income statement.

IMPORTANT TERMS

Significant influence
Control
Cost method
Equity method
Current cash-equivalent amount
Amortization of bond discount and premium

QUESTIONS FOR DISCUSSION

1. Explain the difference between a short-term investment and a long-term investment.

2. Match the following:

Measurement method	*Level of ownership of capital stock*
______Cost method.	*a.* Over 50% ownership.
______Equity method.	*b.* Under 20% ownership.
______Consolidation.	*c.* At least 20% but not more than 50%.

3. Explain the application of the cost principle to the purchase of shares of capital stock in another company.
4. Under the cost method, why is revenue measured by the investor company only in periods when the other company declares and pays a dividend?
5. Under the equity method, why is revenue measured on a proportionate basis by the investor company when earnings are reported by the other company, rather than when dividends are declared and paid?
6. Under the equity method, dividends received from the investee company are not recorded as revenue. To record dividends as revenue would involve double counting. Explain.
7. Match the following relating to the balance of the long-term investment amount reported on the balance sheet of the investor company:

Measurement method	*Explanation of balance in the investment account*
______Cost method.	*a.* Lower of cost or market.
______Equity method.	*b.* Original cost plus proportionate share of the net income of the subsidiary, less dividends received.

8. Explain why interest revenue must be accrued on a long-term investment in bonds but not on a long-term investment in capital stock.
9. Under what conditions will a bond sell at (*a*) par, (*b*) a discount, and (*c*) a premium?
10. Distinguish between a long-term investment in bonds versus a long-term investment in capital stock of another company.
11. Why is it necessary to amortize premium or discount that arises from the purchase of a long-term bond investment above or below par? Over what period should the premium or discount be amortized?
12. When a bond investment is purchased between interest dates, the purchaser must pay accrued interest plus the purchase price of the bond. Explain why the accrued interest must be paid.

EXERCISES

PART ONE: EXERCISES 14–1 TO 14–5

E14–1. Company P purchased a certain number of the outstanding voting shares of Company S at $15 per share as a long-term investment. Company S had outstanding 10,000 shares of $10 par value stock. On a separate sheet complete the following matrix relating to the measurement and reporting by Company P after acquisition of the shares of Company S stock.

Questions	Method of Measurement		
	Cost Method	Equity Method	Consolidated Statements
a. What is the applicable level of ownership by Company P of Company S to apply the method?	19 %	49 %	100 %
b. At acquisition, the investment account on the books of Company P should be debited at what amount?	$	$	$
c. On what basis should Company P recognize revenue earned on the stock of Company S? Explanation required.	on div	every year	
d. After acquisition date, on what basis should Company P change the balance of investment account in respect to the stock of Company S owned (other than for disposal of the investment)? Explanation required.	Buy Sell	Buy Sell net income Dividends	
For (*e*), (*f*), and (*g*) that follow, assume the following:			
Number of shares acquired of Company S stock	1,000	3,000	
Net income reported by Company S in first year	$40,000	$40,000	
Dividends declared by Company S in first year	$10,000	$10,000	
Market price Company S stock, $13.50			
e. What would be the balance in the investment account on the books of Company P at the end of the first year?	13500 $	45000 / 3000 12000 $ 54000	
f. What amount of revenue from the investment in Company S will Company P report at the end of the first year?	1000 $	12000 $	
g. What amount of unrealized loss will Company P report at the end of the first year?	1500 $	$	

E14–2. National Company acquired some of the 50,000 shares of the common stock, par $10, of Olsen Corporation as a long-term investment. The following transactions occurred during 1977. The accounting period for both companies ends on December 31.

1977

July 2 Purchased 5,000 shares of Olsen common stock at $20 per share.

Dec. 31 Received a copy of the 1977 annual financial statement for Olsen Corporation. It reflected a net income of $40,000.

31 Olsen Corporation declared and paid a cash dividend of $0.50 per share.

31 Market price of Olsen stock, $19.

Required:

a. What accounting method should be used? Why?

b. Give the required entries by National Company for each transaction. If no entry is required, explain why.

c. Show how the long-term investment and the related revenue would be reported on the 1977 financial statements for National Company.

E14–3. Reo Company acquired some of the 40,000 shares of outstanding common stock (nopar) of Sty, Inc., during 1977 as a long-term investment. The annual accounting period for both companies ends on December 31. The following transactions occurred during 1977:

1977

Jan. 10 Purchased 12,000 shares of Sty stock at $30 per share.

Dec. 31 Received the December 31, 1977, financial statement of Sty, Inc. The reported net income was $60,000.

31 Sty, Inc., declared and paid a cash dividend of $1.20 per share.

31 Market price of Sty stock, $29.

Required:

a. What method of accounting should be used? Why?

b. Give the entries by Reo Company for each of the above transactions. State if no entry is required and explain why.

c. Show how the long-term investment and the related revenue would be reported on the 1977 financial statements of Reo Company.

E14–4. During 1977, Ross Company purchased some of the 100,000 shares of common stock, par $10, of Salt Marine, Inc., as a long-term investment. The annual accounting period for each company ends on December 31. The following transactions occurred during 1977:

1977

Jan. 7 Purchased 12,000 shares of Salt stock at $15 per share.

Dec. 31 Received the 1977 financial statement of Salt Marine, Inc. The reported net income was $70,000.

31 Salt paid a cash dividend of $1.10 per share.
31 Market price of Salt stock, $14.50.

Required:

a. What method of accounting is required? Why?
b. Give the entries for Ross Company for each of the above transactions. State if no entry is required and explain why.
c. Show how the long-term investment and the related revenue would be reported on the 1977 financial statements of Ross Company.

E14–5. You are to use the same situation and data given in Exercise 14–4, *except* for the January 7, 1977, transaction. Assume it to be as follows:

1977
Jan. 7 Purchased 30,000 shares of Salt stock at $15 per share.
(The data for December 31 are unchanged.)

Requirements (*a*), (*b*), and (*c*) as given in Exercise 14–4.

PART TWO: EXERCISES 14–6 TO 14–14

E14–6. On July 1, 1977, Kline Company purchased at par a $10,000, 5 percent, 20-year bond of Case Corporation as a long-term investment. The annual bond interest is payable each year on June 30. The accounting period for Kline Company ends on December 31. At the date of purchase, the bond had five years remaining before maturity.

Required:

Give the following entries on the books of Kline Company in respect to the long-term investment:

a. July 1, 1977, for acquisition.
b. December 31, 1977, adjusting entry at the end of the accounting period.
c. June 30, 1978, collection of first interest.
d. Maturity date of the bond, June 30, 1982.

E14–7. On April 1, 19A, Goode Company purchased at par five $1,000, 6 percent, ten-year bonds of Hillside Corporation as a long-term investment. The bond interest is payable semiannually on each March 31 and September 30. The accounting period ends for Goode Company on December 31. At the date of purchase, the bonds had six years remaining before maturity.

Required:

Give the entry for each of the following dates in the accounts of Goode Company in respect to the long-term investment: April 1, 19A; September 30, 19A; December 31, 19A; March 31, 19B; and maturity date.

E14–8. On February 1, 19A, Larson Company purchased at par a $10,000, 6 percent, 20-year bond of Matson Corporation as a long-term investment. The bond interest is payable semiannually on each January

31 and July 31. The accounting period for Larson Company ends on December 31. At the date of purchase, the bonds had four years remaining life.

Required:

Give all entries required in the accounts of Larson Company for the period February 1, 19A, through January 31, 19B, and on the maturity date.

E14–9. On July 1, 1977, Parsons Company purchased three different bonds as long-term investments. Data with respect to the three bonds and the purchase price were:

Bond designation	*Face of bond*	*Annual interest*	*Payable semiannually*	*Remaining years to maturity*	*Purchase price*
A...........	$1,000	6%	Dec. 31 and	5	$1,000
B...........	1,000	5	June 30	5	970
C...........	1,000	7	each year	5	1,020

Required:

a. Give the entries to record separately the purchase of each bond.
b. Give the entries to record separately collection of interest on the first interest date after purchase. Use straight-line amortization.
c. Give the entries to record separately the maturity of each bond.

E14–10. On May 1, 1977, Nance Company purchased $8,000 maturity value bonds of Brown Corporation at 97 as a long-term investment. The bond interest rate is 6 percent per annum payable 3 percent each April 30 and October 31. The bonds mature in four years from May 1, 1977.

Required:

a. Give the entries for Nance Company on May 1, 1977; October 30, 1977; and December 31, 1977 (adjusting entry for accrued interest). Use straight-line amortization.
b. Show how this long-term investment and the related revenue would be shown on the December 31, 1977, annual financial statements of Nance Company.

(Hint: Include the investment, interest receivable, and any revenue.)

E14–11. On May 1, 1977, KC Company purchased $6,000, 6 percent bonds of Cook, Inc., at 104 as a long-term investment. The bonds pay interest each April 30 and October 31. The bonds mature in four years on April 30, 1981.

Required:

a. Give the entries for KC Company on May 1, 1977; October 31, 1977; and December 31, 1977 (adjusting entry for accrued interest). Use straight-line amortization.
b. Show how this long-term investment would be shown on the December 31, 1977, annual financial statements of KC Company.

E14–12. On March 1, 1977, Stutz Corporation purchased $5,000, 6 percent bonds of Taylor Corporation as a long-term investment. The bonds pay 3 percent interest each June 30 and December 31. The bonds mature in ten years on December 31, 1986. The purchase price was $5,236, plus the accrued interest.

Required:

a. Give the entry by Stutz Corporation to record the purchase on March 1, 1977.

b. Give the entry to record the interest received on June 30 and December 31, 1977. Use straight-line amortization.

c. What was the amount of interest revenue in 1977? At what amount would the bonds be reported on the balance sheet at December 31, 1977?

E14–13. On September 1, 1977, Indian Company purchased, as a long-term investment, a $10,000 face value, 6 percent bond issued by Jackson Corporation for par plus any accrued interest. The annual bond pays interest each year on June 30 and has five years' remaining life until maturity.

Required:

a. Give the entry for Indian Company to record the purchase of the bond on September 1, 1977.

b. Give the adjusting and closing entries for bond interest at December 31, 1977, assuming this is the end of the accounting period for Indian Company.

c. Give the entry for the first collection of interest on the bond investment.

d. Complete the following (show computations):

	1977	*1978*
Income Statement:		
Revenue from bond investment	$______	$______
Balance Sheet:		
Bond interest receivable	$______	$______
Long-term investment, bonds, Jackson Corporation	$______	$______

E14–14. On January 1, 1977, Cotton Company purchased, as a long-term investment, a $3,000 bond of Devons Company for $2,923. The bond had a stated interest rate of 7 percent, payable each January 1. The bond matures in three years. Cotton Company uses effective-interest amortization. As a consequence, the following amortization table was developed:

Date	*Cash inflow*	*Interest revenue*	*Investment change*	*Investment balance*
January 1, 1977				$2,923
End Year 1.......	$210	234	$24	2,947
End Year 2.......	210	236	26	2,973
End Year 3.......	210	237	27	3,000

Required:

Respond to the following questions:

a. What was the total cash outflow and the total cash inflow over the life of this investment? What does the difference represent? Explain.

b. How much interest revenue will be recognized on the income statement each year and in total?

c. What amounts will be shown on the balance sheet each year? Give the last year just prior to collection of the maturity amount.

d. What was the effective rate of interest per year? Show computations.

e. How were the four different amounts computed that are listed on the line "End Year 2"?

PART ONE: PROBLEM 14–1 TO 14–5

P14–1. During January, 19A, Adams Company purchased 10,000 shares of the 100,000 outstanding common stock (nopar value) of Brown Corporation at $44 per share. This block of stock was purchased as a long-term investment. Assume the accounting period for each company ends on December 31.

Subsequent to acquisition, the following data were available:

	19A	*19B*
Net income reported by Brown Corporation at December 31	$60,000	$70,000
Cash dividends paid by Brown Corporation during year	20,000	25,000
Market price per share of Brown common stock on December 31	40	43

Required:

a. What accounting method should be used? Why?

b. Give the entries required in the accounts of Adams Company for each year (use parallel columns) for the following (if none, explain why):
1. Acquisition.
2. Net income reported by Brown Corporation.
3. Dividends received.
4. Market value effects.

c. For each year show how the following amounts should be reported on the financial statements for Adams Company:
1. The long-term investment.
2. Stockholders' equity—unrealized loss.
3. Revenues.

P14–2. During January 19A, Lawson Corporation acquired the shares listed below as a long-term investment:

Corporation	Stock	Number of shares: Outstanding	Number of shares: Acquired	Cost per share
M	Common (nopar)	80,000	12,000	$10
N.......	Preferred, nonvoting (par $10)	10,000	3,000	15

Assume the accounting period for each company ends on December, 31.

Subsequent to acquisition, the following data were available:

	19A	19B
Net income reported at December 31:		
Corporation M...	$20,000	$22,000
Corporation N	30,000	31,000
Dividends paid per share during the year:		
Corporation M common stock......................	$ 1.00	$ 1.10
Corporation N preferred stock	0.20	0.20
Market value per share at December 31:		
Corporation M common stock......................	8.00	9.00
Corporation N preferred stock	16.00	15.00

Required:

a. What accounting method should be used for the M common stock? N preferred stock? Why?

b. Give the following entries for the accounts of Lawson Corporation for each year in parallel columns (if none, state why):
   1. Acquisition of the investments.
   2. Income reported by Corporations M and N.
   3. Dividends received.
   4. Market value effects.

c. For each year, show how the following amounts should be reported on the financial statements for 1977:
   1. The long-term investment.
   2. Stockholders' equity—unrealized loss.
   3. Revenues.

P14–3. Company S had outstanding 20,000 shares of common stock, par value $10 per share. On January 1, 1977, Company P purchased some of these shares at $25 per share. At the end of 1977, Company S reported the following: net income, $30,000; and cash dividends paid, $10,000. The market value of Company S stock at end of 1977 was $23 per share.

Required:

a. For each case given below, identify the method of accounting that should be used. Explain why.

b. Give the entries required in the accounts of Company P at the dates indicated below for each of the two independent cases. If no entry is required, so indicate and explain.

Items	*Case A—2,000 shares purchased*	*Case B—8,000 shares purchased*
1. Entry to record the acquisition at January 1, 1977:		
2. Entry to recognize the net income reported by Company S for 1977:		
3. Entry to recognize the dividends paid by Company S for 1977:		
4. To recognize market value effect at end of 1977:		

c. Give the separate amounts that would be reported on the financial statements of Company P, for 1977, in respect to the investment in Company S as follows:

	Dollar amounts	
	Case A	*Case B*
Balance Sheet:		
Investments and Funds:		
Stockholders' equity:		
Income Statement:		
Revenue from investments		

d. Explain why assets, stockholders' equity, and revenues are different between the two cases.

P14–4. Wilson Corporation had outstanding 150,000 shares of nopar value common stock. On January 10, 1977, Vinson Company purchased a block of these shares in the open market at $40 per share. At the end of 1977, Wilson Corporation reported net income of $90,000 and cash dividends paid $2 per share. At December 31, 1977, the Wilson stock was selling at $38.50 per share. This problem involves two separate cases:

Case A—Vinson Company purchased 22,500 shares of Wilson stock.
Case B—Vinson Company purchased 45,000 shares of Wilson stock.

Required:

a. For each case, what accounting method should be used. Explain why.

b. For each case, give, in parallel columns, entries in the accounts of Vinson Company for (if no entry is required, explain why):

1. Acquisition.
2. Revenue recognition.

3. Dividends received.
4. Market value effects.

c. For each case, show how the following should be reported on the 1977 financial statements for Vinson Company:
1. The long-term investments.
2. Any market effects.
3. Revenues.

d. Explain why the amounts reported (in Requirement [*c*]) are different as between the two cases.

P14–5. Starr Company purchased, as a long-term investment, some of the 100,000 shares of the outstanding common stock of Towns, Inc. The annual accounting period for each company ends on December 31. The following transactions occurred during 1977:

1977

Jan. 10 Purchased shares of common stock of Towns at $11 per share as follows:

Case A – 10,000 shares purchased.
Case B – 30,000 shares purchased.

Dec. 31 Received financial statements of Towns, Inc., for the year ended December 31, 1977. The reported net income was $70,000.

31 Received cash dividend of $0.30 per share from Towns, Inc.

31 Market price of Towns stock, $10.

Required:

a. For each case, what accounting method should be used? Explain why.

b. Give the entries for Starr Company for each case for the above transactions. State if no entry is required and explain why. (Hint: You can save time by using parallel columns for Case A and Case B.)

c. Give the amounts for each case that would be reported on the financial statements of Starr Corporation at December 31, 1977. Use the following format:

	Case A	*Case B*
Balance Sheet:		
Investments and Funds:		
Investment in common stock, Towns, Inc.	______	______
Owners' equity:	______	______
Income Statement		
Revenue from investments	______	______

PART TWO: PROBLEMS 14–6 TO 14–10

P14–6. On January 1, 1977, Long Company purchased $50,000, 6 percent bonds of Acme, Inc., as a long-term investment, at 100. Interest is payable annually on December 31. The bonds mature in six years from December 31, 1976. The annual accounting period for Long Company ends on December 31. In addition, on January 2, 1977, Long Company purchased in the market 5 percent of the 10,000 shares of outstanding common stock of Acme, Inc., at $30 per share.

Required:

a. Give the entry by Long Company for the purchase of the bonds on January 1, 1977.
b. Give the entry to record the purchase of the common stock on January 2, 1977.
c. Give the entry assuming a cash dividend of $2.00 per share was received on the Acme stock on December 28, 1977.
d. Give the entry for the receipt of the interest on the Acme bonds on December 31, 1977.
e. Show how the long-term investments and the related revenues would be reported on the annual financial statements of the Long Company at December 31, 1977. Market price of Acme stock, $31.

P14–7. On May 1, 1977, Stein Company purchased $20,000 maturity value, 6 percent bonds of Thomas, Inc., as a long-term investment. The interest is payable on each April 30 and October 31. The bonds mature in four years from May 1, 1977. The bonds were purchased at 96. In addition, brokerage fees of $224 were paid by Stein Company.

Required:

a. Give the entries for Stein Company on the following dates:

1977

May 1 Purchase.
Oct. 31 First interest date. Use straight-line amortization.
Dec. 31 Adjusting entry for accrued interest at the end of the annual accounting period.

b. Show how the investment, interest receivable, and related revenue would be reported on the annual financial statements of Stein Company on December 31, 1977.
c. Give the entry at the maturity date of the bonds.

P14–8. On June 1, 1977, Wallis Company purchased $30,000, 6 percent bonds of Bay Street, Inc., as a long-term investment. The interest is payable each April 30 and October 31. The bonds mature in five years from the issue date, May 1, 1977. The bonds were purchased at 103. In addition, Wallis Company paid brokerage fees of $280. The annual accounting period for Wallis Company ends on December 31.

Required:

a. Give the entries for Wallis Company on the following dates:

June 1 Purchase plus accrued interest.
Oct. 31 First interest date. Use straight-line amortization.
Dec. 31 Adjusting entry for accrued interest.

b. Show how the investment, interest receivable, and related revenue would be reported on the annual financial statements of Wallis Company on December 31, 1977.

c. Give the entry at the maturity date of the bonds, April 30, 1982.

P14–9. During 1977, Akers Company purchased the following bonds of Bounds Corporation as a long-term investment:

	Series A	*Series B*	*Series C*	*Series D*
Maturity amount	$10,000	$10,000	$10,000	$10,000
Date purchased	7/1/77	7/1/77	7/1/77	9/1/77
Interest per annum	6%	5%	7%	6%
Interest dates, annual	June 30	June 30	June 30	June 30
Maturity date	6/30/82	6/30/82	6/30/82	6/30/82
Purchase price*	100	95	106	100

* Excluding any accrued interest.

Required:

a. Record separately the purchase on the books of Akers Company for each series.

b. Give the adjusting entry required on the books of Akers Company for December 31, 1977, assuming this is the end of the accounting period. Make a separate entry for each series. Use straight-line amortization.

c. Give the entry on the books of Akers Company for each separate series that should be made on June 30, 1978, for collection of the first interest payment.

d. Compute the following amounts that should be reflected on the December 31, 1977, financial statements:

Income Statement:
Revenue from bond investments .... $________

Balance Sheet:
Long-term investment, bonds of
Bounds Corporation .... $________

P14–10. On January 1, 1977, Northern Corporation purchased, as a long-term investment, a bond of Jacks Corporation. The following table was prepared based on the investment (table captions have been omitted intentionally):

January 1, 1977				$10,339
End Year 1	$800	$724	$76	10,263
End Year 2	800	718	82	10,181
End Year 3	800	713	87	10,094
End Year 4	800	706	94	10,000

Required:

Respond to the following questions:

a. What was the maturity amount of the bond?

b. What was the purchase price of the investment?

c. What entry was made at acquisition date?
d. Was the bond acquired at a premium or discount? How much?
e. What was the stated rate of interest per year? Show computations.
f. What method of amortization apparently will be used? Explain.
g. What was the effective rate of interest?
h. What was the total cash inflow and outflow on the investment? What does the difference represent? Explain.
i. How much interest revenue will be reported each period on the income statement? How does this relate to the difference in h?
j. What amount will be reported on the balance sheet at the end of each year? (Show Year 4 just before collection of the maturity amount.)
k. How were the amounts in each of the four columns computed that are in the table? Use Year 2 and show computations.
l. Why is the method of amortization being used conceptually superior?

15

The statement of changes in financial position

PURPOSE OF THE CHAPTER

The previous chapters have emphasized that for external reporting purposes, three basic statements must be presented: (1) an income statement, (2) a balance sheet, and (3) a statement of changes in financial position.[1] In the past, the third statement, previously called a "funds-flow statement," was prepared by many companies, although it was not required.

The statement of changes in financial position now used is based on an **all-resources concept** and has been required since the issuance of APB *Opinion No. 19,* "Reporting Changes in Financial Position," dated March 1971.[2]

This chapter will focus on understanding and interpreting the statement of changes in financial position. Part One will discuss the statement prepared on a cash-flow basis. Part Two will discuss the statement prepared on a working capital–flow basis. The Appendix to this chapter

---

[1] Other supporting schedules, such as a statement of cost of goods sold, statement of retained earnings, statement of changes in capital, and a schedule of lease commitments, are essential in certain circumstances to meet the requirements of the full-disclosure principle.

[2] APB *Opinion No. 19* states: "The Board concludes that information concerning the financing and investing activities of a business enterprise and the changes in its financial position for a period is essential for financial statement users. . . . A statement summarizing changes in financial position should be presented as a basic financial statement for each period for which an income statement is presented."

discusses and illustrates the techniques used in the preparation of a statement of changes in financial position. The techniques are set out separately for the convenience of those who desire to pursue the technical aspects of preparing the statement.

CONCEPT OF THE STATEMENT OF CHANGES IN FINANCIAL POSITION

Fundamentally, the statement of changes in financial position, as prescribed in APB *Opinion No. 19,* must be based on an **all-resources concept.** This means that it must report the following:

1. The inflow of *all* resources during the period.
2. The outflow of *all* resources during the period.
3. The net increase (or decrease) in resources during the period.

APB *Opinion No. 19* also provides that, for measurement purposes, *all resources* may be measured in terms of *either* (*a*) cash or (*b*) working capital (i.e., the difference between current assets and current liabilities).

The inflow of resources (often called funds) is said to represent the **financing activities** of the business during the period (i.e., where the resources came from).[3] The outflow of resources is said to represent the **investing activities** of the business during the period (i.e., where the resources went).

The words "changes in financial position" focus on the basic concept underlying the statement. It is a "change" statement because it reports the changes in the assets, liabilities, and owners' equity amounts during the period. As indicated in the above paragraph, these changes are due to the inflow of funds (i.e., the financing activities) and the outflow of funds (i.e., the investing activities). The diagram shown in Exhibit 5–1 (page 140) should be restudied at this point. It will aid in understanding the relationships of the statement of changes in financial position to the income statement and the balance sheet. The concept of reporting the *changes* in financial position for each accounting period may be diagramed as follows:

---

[3] The word "funds" also is used in other ways by accountants. It has been used to refer to assets, generally cash, set aside for specific future use, such as a building fund or a bond sinking fund; and in governmental accounting, it has an entirely different meaning. This wide range of inconsistent usage of the term suggests the desirability of using more descriptive terms, such as "cash" and "working capital," and the use of more descriptive titles, such as "statement of changes in financial position" rather than the older title, "funds-flow statement."

Financial position at start of period		*Changes during the period*		*Financial position at end of period*
Balance Sheet, January 1, 1977	+	Statement of changes in financial position, during 1977	=	Balance Sheet, December 31, 1977
Assets Liabilities Owners' Equity		Financing activities (inflow of funds) Investing activities (outflow of funds)		Assets Liabilities Owners' Equity

The primary financing activities, or sources of funds, in most businesses are:

1. Current operations – revenue funds received from the sale of goods and services, less expense funds spent in generating those revenues.
2. Issuance of capital stock.
3. Sale of assets used in the business.
4. Borrowing (incurring debt).

The primary investing activities, or uses of funds, in most businesses are to:

1. Purchase fixed assets and to expand the business.
2. Pay cash dividends to shareholders.
3. Pay debts.

The term "funds" was used a number of times in the above paragraphs.[4] Since it is a *general* term, it must be clearly understood in the context used. When it is used in respect to the statement of changes in financial position, it means *either* cash or working capital. Both of these terms have been defined in prior chapters. In the context of the statement of changes in financial position, these two terms may be defined as follows:

1. Cash – cash plus the short-term investments (as defined in Chapter 9). Short-term investments generally are added to cash for this purpose because they are very near to cash and can be converted to cash at any time.
2. Working capital – current assets minus current liabilities. The usual current assets are cash, short-term investments, accounts receivable, and inventory. The current liabilities are short-term debts that presumably are to be paid out of the current assets. The difference between the current assets and the current liabilities is called working capital (or, sometimes, net working capital).

---

[4] Some accountants prefer to use the general term "resources" rather than "funds."

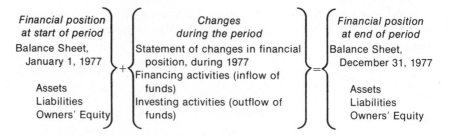

The statement of changes in financial position may present the sources (or inflows) and the uses (or outflows) of funds on *either* a cash-flow basis or a working capital basis. Each statement of changes in financial position should clearly indicate the basis on which it was prepared. We will consider each basis separately in the two parts that follow.

ILLUSTRATIVE CASE

Throughout this chapter, we will use the Fina Company, Inc., case as a basis for discussion and illustration. Assume it is December 31, 1977, the end of the annual accounting period. Fina Company, Inc., has completed all of the year-end procedures, including the preparation of the income statement and the balance sheet. The remaining reporting requirement is preparation of a **statement of changes in financial position** for 1977.

The income statement for 1977 is shown in Exhibit 15–1.

EXHIBIT 15–1

FINA COMPANY, INC.
Income Statement
For the Year Ending December 31, 1977

Sales		$100,000
Cost of goods sold		60,000
Gross margin		40,000
Less expenses:		
Expenses (not detailed)	$24,000	
Depreciation expense	6,000	
Income taxes	2,000	32,000
Net income		$ 8,000

Comparative balance sheets for the current and past year are shown in Exhibit 15–2. The prior balance sheet, at December 31, 1976, is needed for analytical purposes, as discussed later.

PART ONE: CHANGES IN FINANCIAL POSITION—CASH BASIS

CASH BASIS CONCEPT

A statement of changes in financial position prepared on a cash basis is identical in purpose and concept with one prepared on a working capital basis *except* for the definition of "funds." As explained on page 576, cash, for this purpose, is usually defined as cash plus short-term investments. The statement of changes in financial position—cash basis reports the effect of *all* transactions that increased or decreased cash during the period. It reports all cash inflows, all cash outflows, and the net increase or decrease in cash during the period. It focuses on the sources of cash and the reasons (purposes) cash was spent. Thus, it is a "change"

EXHIBIT 15–2

FINA COMPANY, INC.
Balance Sheets
At December 31, 1977, and 1976

	December 31, 1977		*December 31, 1976**	
Current Assets:				
Cash	$37,500		$30,000	
Accounts receivable (net)†	25,000		20,000	
Inventory	20,000	$ 82,500	24,000	$ 74,000
Long-term Investments:				
Common stock of X Corporation		1,000		6,000
Fixed Assets:				
Equipment (net)†		59,000		60,000
Total Assets		$142,500		$140,000
Current Liabilities:				
Accounts payable	$22,000		$20,000	
Income taxes payable	500			
Short-term notes payable (nontrade)	10,000	$ 32,500	14,000	$ 34,000
Long-Term Liabilities:				
Bonds payable		32,000		40,000
Stockholders' Equity:				
Common stock (par $10)	60,000		50,000	
Contributed capital in excess of par	6,000		5,000	
Retained earnings	12,000	78,000	11,000	66,000
Total Liabilities and Stockholders' Equity		$142,500		$140,000

* An alternate dating would be January 1, 1977, since the ending balance sheet for the past period is the beginning balance sheet for the current period.

† In analyzing and reporting changes in financial position, accounts receivable and fixed assets generally are shown *net* of the contra accounts as a matter of convenience.

statement. Since it covers a specific period of time, it is dated the same as the income statement, "For the Year Ended December 31, 19XX."

The statement of changes in financial position—cash basis is shown in Exhibit 15–3 for Fina Company for the year ended December 31, 1977, (also see Chapter 3, page 68). Fundamentally, the statement reports the

financing activities for the period on a **cash-inflow** basis under the caption "Sources of Cash," and the **investing activities** for the period on a **cash-outflow** basis under the caption "Uses of Cash."

The statement for Fina Company reports three typical sources of

EXHIBIT 15–3

FINA COMPANY, INC.
Statement of Changes in Financial Position—Cash Basis
For the Year Ended December 31, 1977*

Sources of Cash (inflows)†:		
From operations:		
Revenues	$100,000	
Add (deduct) adjustments to convert to cash basis:		
Accounts receivable increase	(5,000)	
Cash generated from revenues		$95,000
Expenses	92,000	
Add (deduct) adjustments to convert to cash basis:		
Depreciation expense	(6,000)	
Merchandise inventory decrease	(4,000)	
Accounts payable increase	(2,000)	
Income taxes payable increase	(500)	
Cash disbursed for expenses		79,500
Total cash inflow from operations		15,500
From other sources:		
Sale of unissued common stock	11,000	
Disposal of long-term investment (Note A)	5,000	
Total cash generated from other sources		16,000
Total cash generated during the period		31,500
Uses of Cash (outflows)†:		
Payment of cash dividend on common stock	7,000	
Payment on bonds payable	8,000	
Payment on notes payable, short term (nontrade)	4,000	
Acquisition of equipment (Note A)	5,000	
Total cash expended during the period		24,000
Net increase in cash during the period		$ 7,500

* Source of data, Exhibit 15–6.

† Sometimes referred to as "Cash Generated" and "Cash Applied," respectively.

Note A: Equipment was acquired in exchange for common stock of the X Corporation, which was being held as a long-term investment.

cash: (1) operations, (2) sale of unissued stock, and (3) disposal of a long-term investment. Other common sources of cash are the sales of fixed assets and borrowing. The statement reports four typical uses of cash: (1) cash dividends, (2) payment of long-term debt, (3) payment of short-term debt, and (4) purchase of fixed assets.

The total sources, $31,500, minus the total uses, $24,000, gives the increase in the cash balance of $7,500 during the period. This increase necessarily must agree with the increase in cash shown on the comparative balance sheets in Exhibit 15–2 (i.e., $37,500 − $30,000 = $7,500).[5]

SOURCES OF CASH

The typical sources of cash listed in the preceding paragraph do not need further elaboration, with one exception. Cash inflow (often called cash generated) from *operations* ($15,500) is somewhat complex because it reflects the **net cash effect** of all the revenue and expense transactions; that is, from the buying, selling, and related activities reported on the income statement. Cash inflow from operations may be thought of as the "cash inflow from the income statement."

Operations (i.e., as reflected by the income statement) generally is the primary single source of cash for all businesses over the long term. Net income reflects the effect of operations for the period on the **accrual basis.** As goods and services are sold during the period, there is an inflow of cash from *revenues* (i.e., customers); however, the cash inflow from the revenues is conditioned by the credit sales of the current and prior periods. To illustrate, assume a company sold goods during the period amounting to $100,000, of which $20,000 remained uncollected at year-end. In this case, the cash inflow would be $100,000, minus the $20,000 in accounts receivable, equals $80,000. Alternatively, if sales for the current period totaled $100,000 and, at the same time, accounts receivable decreased by $20,000, cash inflow would be $120,000 for the period.

During the period, *expenses* are incurred that cause a cash outflow; however, the cash outflow for expenses is conditioned by the amount of expenses incurred on credit in the current and prior periods. To illustrate, assume a company incurred expenses during the year of $80,000, of which $10,000 was unpaid at year-end. In this case, the cash outflow would be $80,000, minus the $10,000 increase in accounts payable, equals $70,000. Alternatively, if expenses for the current period totaled $80,000 and, at the same time, accounts payable decreased by $10,000 (because payments of old accounts exceeded new accounts), cash outflow for the current period would be $90,000.

The amount of net cash inflow (or outflow) from operations, therefore, generally will be different from net income because of the effect of **noncash revenues and noncash expenses.**

---

[5] One of several alternate reporting forms starts with "Net Income" under "From operations." Adjustments for noncash items are then reported to derive the amount "Total Cash Inflow from Operations, $15,500." The form of presentation in Exhibit 15–3 is easier to understand and better reflects the underlying events. In other respects, the alternate forms tend to be the same.

To illustrate the adjustments to net income for the period in order to derive cash inflow (or cash generated) from operations, let's return to Fina Company. The income statement shown in Exhibit 15–1 reported a net income of $8,000. On the basis of an **analysis** of the revenues on credit and the expenses on credit, including the noncash depreciation expense, the net income was converted to a **cash-inflow** basis as follows:

Revenues (as reported on the income statement; accrual basis)		$100,000
Deduct increase in accounts receivable (as between the two balance sheets)*		(5,000)
Cash inflow from revenues (revenues converted to cash basis)		95,000
Expenses (as reported on the income statement; accrual basis) $60,000 + $32,000 =	$92,000	
Deduct expense items not requiring cash during the current period (as between the two balance sheets)*:		
Depreciation expense	(6,000)	
Merchandise inventory decrease	(4,000)	
Accounts payable increase	(2,000)	
Income taxes payable increase	(500)	
Cash outflow for expenses (expenses converted to cash basis)		79,500
Net cash flow from operations (net income converted to cash basis)		$ 15,500

* Some items may be added rather than deducted. For example, an inventory increase would be added to expenses.

The above computation is reported on the statement of changes in financial position—cash basis, Exhibit 15–3.

Observe in the above computation that the net cash inflow generated by operations ($15,500) was *greater* than net income ($8,000). In some instances it will be less than net income. The adjustments to convert reported revenues and expenses (accrual basis) to a cash basis (cash flow from operations) often are quite varied. They may be grouped into 11 different items. The following tabulation is convenient for study and problem-solving purposes.[6]

[6] No useful purpose is served by memorizing this tabulation. The rationale for the "plus and minus" adjustments should be understood. At this time, it should be available for problem-solving purposes. The central purpose is to explain and illustrate the reasons for, and the nature of, the adjustments that are necessary to convert revenues and expenses (i.e., net income) from an accrual basis to a cash basis.

Nature of item	Plus and minus adjustments to derive cash basis	Illustration (Fina Company)	
Revenue (as reported on income statement, accrual basis)		$100,000	
Adjustments to cash basis:			
1. Decrease in balance of trade receivables	+		
2. Increase in balance of trade receivables	−	−5,000	
Revenue adjusted to cash basis			$95,000
Expenses (as reported on income statement, accrual basis)		92,000	
Adjustments to cash basis:			
Cost of goods sold:			
3. Decrease in merchandise inventory	−	−4,000	
4. Increase in merchandise inventory	+		
5. Increase in *trade* payables	−	−2,000	
6. Decrease in *trade* payables	+		
Expenses (other than cost of goods sold):			
7. Increase in balance of accrued (unpaid) liabilities	−	− 500	
8. Decrease in balance of accrued (unpaid) liabilities	+		
9. Decrease in balance of prepayments	−		
10. Increase in balance of prepayments	+		
11. Period's depreciation, amortization and depletion	−	−6,000	
Expenses adjusted to cash basis			79,500
Net cash flow from operations			$15,500

REPORTING DIRECT (NONCASH) EXCHANGES

Direct exchanges of noncash items for other noncash items are not uncommon. For example, a company may acquire an asset by trading another asset for it and no cash difference is paid or received; or a company may retire its bonds payable by issuing common stock to the bondholders. If there is no cash difference involved (i.e., there was no "boot"), cash will not be increased or decreased. Nevertheless, such transactions involving direct exchanges, whether there is "boot" or not, must be included on the statement of changes in financial position "as if" there were simultaneous investing and financing activities (required by APB *Opinion No. 19*). The inclusion of these direct exchanges is necessary in order for the statement to report on an **all-resources basis** (see page 575).

To illustrate, during 1977, Fina Company acquired a machine worth $5,000. Instead of paying cash for it, they traded 100 shares of stock in another corporation (designated as Corporation X) that they owned as a long-term investment. The entry made by Fina to record the transaction was:

1977:

Machinery	5,000	
Long-term investment (100 shares of Corporation X stock)		5,000

Obviously, this transaction did not increase or decrease cash. Yet, in effect, there were two economic activities:

1. A financing activity—the long-term investment was disposed of to "generate" resources (financing) amounting to $5,000.
2. An investing activity—resources amounting to $5,000 were expended (used) to acquire a fixed asset.

Such transactions, therefore, are reported under *both* sources and uses as an "in-and-out" item. For example, the trade by Fina Company is reported in Exhibit 15–3 in two places as follows:

Cash from other sources:	
Disposal of long-term investment	$5,000
Uses of cash:	
Acquisition of equipment	5,000

Thus, the new statement of changes in financial position, in contrast to the old funds statement, is said to include "all financing and investing activities" rather than a narrow report limited to the direct cash effects. This is a significant aspect of the new concept of the statement, and one of which users should be fully aware. Other examples of direct exchanges (trades) are (1) settlement of debt with capital stock, (2) exchange of land for land, (3) exchange of machinery for other machinery, and (4) exchange of tangible assets for intangible assets. It is not uncommon to see one or more direct exchanges reported on the statement of changes in financial position.

The preparation of a statement of changes in financial position is somewhat technical. A worksheet approach is almost essential. An efficient worksheet for this purpose is presented in the Appendix to this chapter.

PART TWO: CHANGES IN FINANCIAL POSITION—WORKING CAPITAL BASIS

THE CONCEPT OF WORKING CAPITAL

To understand and interpret the statement of changes in financial position prepared on a working capital basis, one must clearly understand the concept of working capital as a "fund."

Recall that working capital is a difference—current assets minus current liabilities. It is conceptual in nature since it does not represent a particular asset such as cash. For this reason, it is often not fully understood by statement users. When working capital changes, this means that one or more of the current assets or current liabilities change, but that a change in one is not offset by a change in another.

To illustrate the concept of working capital, observe in Exhibit 15–2, for Fina Company, that working capital for each year can be computed from the two balance sheets as follows:

	1977	*1976*	*Working capital increase (decrease) 1976 to 1977*
Current assets	$82,500	$74,000	$ 8,500
Less: Current liabilities	32,500	34,000	1,500
Working capital	$50,000	$40,000	$10,000

The $8,500 *increase* in current assets during the year increased working capital by that amount, and the $1,500 *decrease* in current liabilities also increased working capital. The total increase during the year in working capital, therefore, was $10,000. You should clearly understand the effect on working capital of increases and decreases in current assets and current liabilities. The statement of changes in financial position, prepared on the working capital basis, focuses on this point. That is, it measures the **inflows and outflows of funds** in terms of working capital (rather than in terms of cash). To emphasize, the statement reports where working capital came from (the sources) during the period, where working capital went (the uses), and the resultant net increase or decrease in working capital during the period.

WORKING CAPITAL BASIS ILLUSTRATED

The statement of changes in financial position—working capital basis for Fina Company for 1977 is shown in Exhibit 15–4. First, let's focus on the primary aspects of the statement. Basically, the statement includes two sections:

Section A—Sources and uses of working capital.
Section B—Changes in the internal content of working capital.

Section A reports the financing activities (i.e., the sources or inflows of working capital) and the investing activities (i.e., the uses or outflows of working capital) during the period. Section A is the basic part of the report. For Fina Company, it reports that during the period, working capital flowed in from three sources: (1) operations—net income (revenue

EXHIBIT 15-4

FINA COMPANY, INC.
Statement of Changes in Financial Position—Working Capital Basis
For the Year Ended December 31, 1977

Section A: Sources and Uses of Working Capital during the Period*

Sources of Working Capital (inflows):		
From operations:		
Net income	$ 8,000	
Add expenses not requiring working capital during the current period:		
Depreciation expense	6,000	
Total working capital generated by operations		$14,000
From other sources:		
Sale of unissued common stock	11,000	
Disposal of long-term investment (Note A)	5,000	
Total working capital generated from other sources		16,000
Total working capital generated during the period		30,000
Uses of Working Capital (outflows):		
Payment of cash dividend on common stock	7,000	
Payment on bonds payable	8,000	
Acquisition of equipment (Note A)	5,000	
Total working capital applied during the period		20,000
Net increase in working capital during the period		$10,000

Section B: Changes in the Internal Content of Working Capital during the Period*

Changes in working capital accounts	*Balances, December 31* 1977	*Balances, December 31* 1976	*Working capital increase (decrease)*
Current Assets:			
Cash	$37,500	$30,000	$ 7,500
Accounts receivable (net)	25,000	20,000	5,000
Merchandise inventory	20,000	24,000	(4,000)
Total Current Assets	82,500	74,000	
Current Liabilities:			
Accounts payable	22,000	20,000	(2,000)
Income taxes payable	500		(500)
Notes payable, short term (nontrade)	10,000	14,000	4,000
Total Current Liabilities	32,500	34,000	
Working capital	$50,000	$40,000	$10,000

* These two headings often do not appear on the statement; they are included here as an aid in the explanation of the concept. See Exhibit 15-7 for the source of the data.

Note A: Equipment was acquired in exchange for common stock of the X Corporation, which was being held as a long-term investment.

funds minus expense funds), (2) investors—funds from the sale of common stock for cash, and (3) other sources—funds from the disposal of a long-term investment. Similarly, it reports that working capital was used or applied during the period for three purposes: (1) to pay a cash dividend to stockholders, (2) to pay a long-term debt, and (3) to purchase a fixed asset (equipment). Section A concludes by reporting the **net effect** of these several changes in financial position. The net effect was a $10,000 increase in working capital during the period.

Section B of the statement is simply a listing of each current asset, each current liability, and the resultant increases and decreases in each and the net change in working capital. For example, it shows how much cash increased, how much inventory decreased, how much accounts payable increased, and so on. Observe that it also reports a $10,000 increase in working capital during the period. Obviously, this amount must agree with the net change (increase) reported in Section A. By comparing Section B with the comparative balance sheets given in Exhibit 15–2, you can see that it was copied directly from the balance sheet.[7]

It is important to understand that Sections A and B report two distinctly different aspects of working capital flows:

1. Section A—This section reports the **basic sources and uses** of working capital during the period. Thus, it focuses on the **causes** of the changes in working capital.
2. Section B—In contrast to Section A, this section reports **which working capital accounts** changed and by how much during the period. Thus, it focuses on changes in the **internal content** of working capital.

SOURCES OF WORKING CAPITAL

Transactions that increase working capital represent sources of working capital. Transactions of this type involve a debit to a current asset or current liability account and a credit to one or more nonworking capital accounts. The four primary sources of working capital are:

1. Current operations—Net income reflects the net results of operations. It is composed of *total revenue less total expense.* As goods and services are sold during the period, there is an inflow of cash and/or accounts receivable (both working capital items). Also, during the period, as expenses are incurred, usually there is a decrease in working capital occasioned by cash payments and/or the incurrence of current liabilities (both working capital items). Therefore, a reported net income generally would indicate an increase (source) of working capital. In the case of a loss, working capital generally will decrease.

[7] For this reason, some accountants consider Section B to be redundant; however, it is required by APB *Opinion No. 19.*

The increase in working capital from operations normally is somewhat more than the amount of net income for the period. This is due to the fact that the income statement usually includes some expenses that do not involve the use of working capital during the period—depreciation, depletion, and amortization of intangible assets. For example, the income statement for Fina Company, Exhibit 15–1, shows that there was an inflow of working capital of $100,000 from sales during the year. It also shows that there were outflows of working capital for cost of goods sold, $60,000; expenses, $24,000; and income taxes, $2,000 (resulting in a net inflow of $14,000). In making these computations we must recognize that there was no outflow of working capital during the period for the depreciation expense of $6,000. This latter point is evident if we recall that the entry for Depreciation Expense was:

Depreciation expense	6,000	
Accumulated depreciation		6,000

This entry neither increased nor decreased working capital, since no working capital account was debited or credited; however, net income was decreased. The working capital increase from operations, therefore, was:

Net income	$ 8,000
Add expenses that did not decrease working capital:	
Depreciation	6,000
Working capital inflow from operations	$14,000

On the statement of changes in financial position (Exhibit 15–4), operations, as a source of working capital, was reported in this way.

2. Sale of capital stock for cash or short-term receivables—A sale of capital stock causes an inflow of working capital since cash or a short-term receivable flows in for the sales price of the stock.

3. Sale of noncurrent assets—When a long-term investment, a fixed asset, or "other" asset is sold, working capital is increased by the amount of the cash and/or short-term receivable that results from its disposition.

4. Long-term borrowing—When a loan is obtained on a long-term basis, working capital (cash) is increased by the proceeds of the loan. In contrast, when a short-term loan is obtained, working capital is not increased since a working capital account (Cash) is increased and another working capital account (a current liability) is increased by the same amount. Since the two increases offset each other, working capital (current assets minus current liabilities) does not change. To illustrate, assume Fina Company borrowed $5,000 cash on a 90-day loan near the end of 1977. The working capital effect would be as follows (data from page 585):

	Before short-term loan	Effect of short term loan	After short term loan
Current assets	$82,500	+5,000	$87,000
Current liabilities	32,500	+5,000	37,500
Working capital	$50,000	-0-	$50,000*

* Effect on working capital = (+$5,000) − (+$5,000) = 0.

USES OF WORKING CAPITAL

Transactions that decrease working capital represent uses of working capital. Transactions of this type involve a credit to a working capital account and a debit to a nonworking capital account. The three primary uses of working capital are:

1. Purchase fixed assets and other noncurrent assets for cash or short-term debt—Transactions of this type generally require a payment of cash and, sometimes, the creation of a short-term debt. To the extent that cash is paid out or short-term debt is recorded, working capital is reduced.
2. Pay cash dividends—In this transaction, there is an outflow of cash; hence, working capital is reduced (used) by that amount.[8]
3. Pay a long-term liability—Payments on long-term notes, bonds, and other obligations involve an outflow of cash; hence, they represent a use of working capital. In contrast, the payment of a *current liability* does not change working capital for the same reason explained above in respect to borrowing (source) on a short-term debt basis; that is, the two working capital effects offset one another.

The above explanations should make it clear that (1) working capital is not increased or decreased by any transaction that involves debits and credits to working capital accounts *only;* and (2) working capital usually is increased or decreased by each transaction that involves debits and/or credits to working capital accounts and debits and/or credits *also* to nonworking capital accounts.

REPORTING DIRECT EXCHANGES

A business may exchange (trade) two nonworking capital items. For example, it is not unusual for a business to acquire an asset by means of a direct trade of another asset. In such cases, there may be no "working

[8] When a dividend is declared, working capital is reduced by the amount of the dividend even though payment in cash is in a later period. In this situation the dividend payable is recorded as a current liability on declaration date. The cash payment in the later period does not affect working capital at that time since equal debits and credits to working capital accounts will be made. This distinction is important only when declaration and payment dates fall in different accounting periods.

capital" paid or received. To illustrate, during 1977, recall that Fina Company acquired a machine worth $5,000. Instead of paying cash or incurring current debt for it, they traded 100 shares of stock in another corporation (designated as Corporation X) that they owned as a long-term investment. The entry made by Fina to record the transaction was:

1977:

Machinery	5,000	
Long-term investment (100 shares of Corporation X stock)		5,000

Obviously, this transaction did not increase or decrease working capital since no working capital accounts were debited or credited. Yet, in effect, there were two economic activities:

1. A financing activity—the long-term investment was disposed of to "generate" resources (financing) amounting to $5,000.
2. An investing activity—resources amounting to $5,000 were expended (used) to acquire the fixed asset.

Opinion No. 19 requires that such transactions must be included as "financing and investing activities that did not affect working capital." They are reported on the statement of changes in financial position as two activities (as if working capital actually increased and decreased by the same amount simultaneously). Such transactions, therefore, are reported under *both* sources and uses as an "in-and-out" item in a manner similar to the cash basis statement (page 582). For example, the swap by Fina Company is reported in Exhibit 15–4 in two places as follows:

Working Capital from Other Sources:	
Disposal of long-term investment	$5,000
Uses of Working Capital:	
Acquisition of equipment	5,000

The preparation of a statement of changes in financial position is best accomplished with a worksheet. An efficient worksheet for this purpose it presented in the Appendix to this chapter.

SUMMARY

The annual financial statements must include, as a minimum, an income statement, a balance sheet, and a statement of changes in financial position. The latter statement has as its central purpose the explanation of the causes of the changes in assets, liabilities, and owners' equity that occurred during the period. It accomplishes this purpose by reporting the financing activities (sources of funds for the business) and the investing activities (uses of funds) during the period.

The primary source of funds during each period generally is operations. The sale of goods and services (revenues) cause an inflow of funds to the business during the period. The incurring of expenses during the period causes an outflow of funds; therefore, net income, adjusted for the nonfund items, represents a net source of funds. In the statement of changes in financial position, net income is converted to funds generated from operations. Other common sources of funds are the sale of fixed assets, borrowing, and the sale of capital stock.

The common uses of funds are the purchase of fixed assets, payment of debts, and payment of cash dividends.

Understanding and interpreting the statement of changes in financial position is not difficult; however, preparation of the statement is somewhat technical.

IMPORTANT TERMS

All-resources concept	**Direct exchanges**
Financing activities	**Working capital flow**
Investing activities	**Cash flow**
Working capital	

APPENDIX

Procedures to develop the statement of changes in financial position

The preceding discussions should enable you to understand and interpret a statement of changes in financial position prepared on either a cash or working capital basis. You should be able to understand the basic differences between a cash basis and a working capital basis statement. The concept of funds generated (provided) by **operations** is a particularly important aspect of the statement of changes in financial position. This concept focuses on the conversion of reported net income (i.e., revenues and expenses), an accrual basis amount, to either cash generated from operations or working capital generated from operations. The statement of changes in financial position is relatively easy to understand and interpret if this basic concept is understood.

Knowledge of the technical aspects of preparing the statement is not essential to understanding and interpreting it. A worksheet designed for preparation of the statements is presented in this Appendix. Knowledge of the preparation procedures will serve to increase your level of understanding of this important statement. The statement of changes in financial position is developed primarily by analyzing the balance sheet and the income statement which are prepared from the accounts.

The complexities involved in developing a statement of changes in financial position in situations where there are numerous transactions suggest the need for the worksheet approach. Worksheets are simply a matter of convenience. They are designed for orderly grouping of essential data, for an efficient and simplified approach to the analytical processes required, and for straightforward derivation of the basic data needed for the formal statement. In Chapter 5, Exhibit 5–2, a worksheet was illustrated and explained that was evolved for developing the income statement and the balance sheet. The development of the statement of changes in financial position similarly suggests the need for an appropriately designed worksheet. A worksheet for this purpose may follow one of several mechanical approaches. Those presented in this chapter are widely used because (1) they are simple to understand; (2) they involve, in summary, repetition of certain basic accounting entries; and (3) they are capable of handling complex and voluminous data.[9] Separate worksheets will be presented for the cash basis and for the working capital basis.

Worksheet for cash basis

A facilitating worksheet to develop the statement of changes in financial position on a *cash basis* focuses on the sources and uses of cash. The worksheet is somewhat tedious because *all of the balance sheet accounts,* except the Cash account itself, must be analyzed to determine the *causes* of the inflows and outflows of cash. Simply reporting the debits and credits to the Cash account does not meet the purposes and specifications of the statement of changes in financial position. The statement must reflect the basic causes or reasons for the inflows and outflows of cash during the period, and, in addition, must include all noncash financing and investing transactions, such as the exchange of a long-term investment for machinery previously illustrated. A primary problem to be resolved on the worksheet is the conversion of revenues and expenses, as reported on the income statement on the accrual basis, to a strictly cash-flow basis (that is, to cash flow from operations). The nature of this conversion was explained on pages 581 and 582.

[9] Some worksheets are designed mechanically, so that the student is forced to *reverse* the debits and credits in the analysis, which frequently causes considerable confusion. In contrast, strictly from the pedagogical viewpoint, a T-account approach is quite useful. Although it is particularly useful for teaching purposes, it is not used in the real world of accounting because of its mechanical unsophistication and bulk. The worksheet presented in this chapter closely parallels the T-account approach since each account is analyzed in a straightforward debit and credit fashion. Also, the worksheet is so designed that the bottom portion can suffice for the formal statement in many problem situations.

We need a worksheet that will facilitate analysis of the **noncash accounts** in such a way that we can "pull out" the *sources* and *uses* of cash that occurred during the period in an orderly and efficient manner. Since the changes to be explained are between the beginning and ending balance sheets (see page 579), the worksheet should incorporate (1) the beginning balance sheet amounts, (2) the ending balance sheet amounts, and (3) provision for an *analysis* of the transactions that occurred between the beginning and ending balance sheet dates. Observe in the worksheet shown below that a column has been provided for each of these items. The *analysis* has as its purpose identification of the *sources* of cash and the *uses* of cash during the period between the two balance sheet dates. Thus, the skeleton worksheet below has five basic side captions: (1) cash, (2) a listing of the balance sheet accounts since they will be "analyzed," (3) sources of cash, (4) uses of cash, and (5) the net change in cash during the period.

Skeleton worksheet to develop the statement of changes in financial position

	(a) Beginning Balance Sheet	(b) Analysis of Interim Entries	(c) Ending Balance Sheet
1. Cash			
2. Balance sheet accounts (listed)			
3. Sources of cash			
4. Uses of cash			
5. Net change in cash			

Using the data from the beginning and ending balance sheets given in Exhibit 15–2 for Fina Company, we can set up an efficient worksheet as shown in Exhibit 15–5. Note the five column headings explained above and the five side captions.

In completing the worksheet, the first step is to enter the amounts from the two balance sheets in the first and last columns. Since we are analyzing the cash account, each account is listed separately. The second step is to complete the "Analysis of Interim Entries" in the middle column, which has been split into debit and credit columns.

The "Analysis of Interim Entries" has as its purpose the analysis (in summary fashion) of all changes during the period in each noncash account entered on the worksheet. These changes are analyzed to determine those that either (1) generated (increased) cash, (2) utilized (decreased) cash, and (3) those that did not affect cash. The analytical entries are entered directly on the worksheet in the normal debit-credit

EXHIBIT 15–5

FINA COMPANY, INC.
Worksheet to Develop Statement of Changes in Financial Position—Cash Basis
For the Year Ended December 31, 1977

	Beginning Balances, Dec. 31, 1976	Analysis of Interim Entries		Ending Balances, Dec. 31, 1977
		Debit	Credit	
Debits				
1. Cash	30,000	XXXXX	XXXXX	
2. Noncash Accounts:				
Accounts receivable (net)	20,000			
Merchandise inventory	24,000			
Investments, long term	6,000			
Equipment (net)	60,000			
	140,000			
Credits				
Accounts payable	20,000			
Income taxes payable				
Notes payable, short term (nontrade)	14,000			
Bonds payable	40,000			
Capital stock (par $10)	50,000			
Contributed capital, in excess of par	5,000			
Retained earnings	11,000			
	140,000			
3. Sources of Cash:				
From operations:				
Revenues (accrual basis)				
Expenses (accrual basis)				
From other sources:				
4. Uses of Cash				
5. Change—Increase (decrease) in Cash				

fashion; however, instead of entering amounts in the Cash account the normal debits to cash are entered in the lower section "Sources of Cash" and the credits are entered as "Uses of Cash." It is important to understand that, when the worksheet analysis is completed, the interim entries when entered on it will "account for" the changes during the period for each noncash account listed on the worksheet.

The final step in completing the worksheet is to record the *analytical entries* on the worksheet. The analytical entries are based upon data provided by the two balance sheets, the income statement, and other

EXHIBIT 15–6

FINA COMPANY, INC.
Worksheet to Develop Statement of Changes in Financial Position—Cash Basis
For the Year Ended December 31, 1977

	Beginning Balances, Dec. 31, 1976	Analysis of Interim Entries†		Ending Balances, Dec. 31, 1977
		Debit	Credit	
Debits				
1. Cash Account	30,000	7,500		37,500
2. Noncash Accounts:				
Accounts receivable (net)	20,000	(*h*) 5,000		25,000
Merchandise inventory	24,000		(*i*) 4,000	20,000
Investments, long term	6,000		(*f*-1) 5,000	1,000
Equipment (net)	60,000	(*f*-2) 5,000	(*b*) 6,000	59,000
	140,000			142,500
Credits				
Accounts payable	20,000		(*j*) 2,000	22,000
Income taxes payable			(*k*) 500	500
Notes payable, short term (nontrade)	14,000	(*g*) 4,000		10,000
Bonds payable	40,000	(*e*) 8,000		32,000
Capital stock (par $10)	50,000		(*c*) 10,000	60,000
Contributed capital in excess of par	5,000		(*c*) 1,000	6,000
Retained earnings	11,000	(*d*) 7,000	(*a*) 8,000	12,000
	140,000			142,500
3. Sources of Cash:				
From operations:				
Revenues (accrual basis)		(*a*) 100,000		
Adjustments to cash basis:				
Accounts receivable increase			(*h*) 5,000	
Expenses (accrual basis)			(*a*) 92,000	
Adjustments to cash basis:				
Depreciation expense		(*b*) 6,000		
Merchandise inventory decrease		(*i*) 4,000		
Accounts payable increase		(*j*) 2,000		
Income taxes payable increase		(*k*) 500		
From other sources:				
Sale of unissued capital stock		(*c*) 11,000		
Disposal of long-term investment*		(*f*-1) 5,000		
4. Uses of Cash:				
Payment of cash dividend			(*d*) 7,000	
Payment on bonds payable			(*e*) 8,000	
Acquisition of equipment*			(*f*-2) 5,000	
Payment on note payable, short term (nontrade)			(*g*) 4,000	
5. Change—Increase in Cash (per line 1 above)			7,500	
		128,500	128,500	

* Equipment was acquired in exchange for common stock of the X Corporation, which was being held as a long-term investment.

† These entries are keyed for ready reference to the textual discussions of the worksheet starting on page 595.

accounting records. Data, including the sources, to complete the analytical entries in Exhibit 15–6 follow for Fina Company for 1977.[10]

a. Revenues and expenses (from income statement) – The *analytical worksheet* entry, essentially the same as the closing entry, is:

Sources of cash: revenues	100,000	
Expenses		92,000
Retained earnings		8,000

This entry represents the transfer of net income of $8,000 from income summary to retained earnings. To facilitate analysis on the worksheet, total revenue and total expense amounts (that comprise net income) are entered separately.

b. Depreciation expense (from the income statement) – This expense was originally recorded as a debit to Depreciation Expense and a credit to Allowance for Depreciation. It did not increase or decrease cash; however, it did reduce net income. Since it is a noncash expense this period, an adjustment (deduction) to expense is necessary to derive cash outflow for expenses (see page 582). This is accomplished on the worksheet by essentially following the original entry; the worksheet *analytical entry* to adjust net income for depreciation would be:

Sources of cash: expenses (adjustment)	6,000	
Equipment (i.e., Allowance for depreciation)		6,000

Note: Amortization expense on intangible assets and depletion expense on natural resources would be treated the same way.

c. Sales of capital stock (from the balance sheet and other records) – The worksheet reflects a $10,000 increase in capital stock and a $1,000 increase in contributed capital in excess of par, during the period. Inspection of the records revealed that 1,000 shares of unissued capital stock were sold at $11 per share. The original entry was: debit – Cash, $11,000; and credits – Capital Stock, $10,000, and Contributed Capital in Excess of Par, $1,000. Clearly this transaction generated cash in the amount of $11,000. The original entry essentially is repeated as a worksheet *analytical entry* as shown below:

[10] In studying the worksheet, you should have observed that (1) the *analytical entries* follow very closely the debits and credits of the original entry in the accounts; and (2) there is no provision thereon for debiting and crediting the Cash account. The mechanical effect is that the original debits and credits to the Cash account are entered in the analytical entries as *debits to cash* provided and as *credits to cash* applied to the bottom portion of the worksheet. These mechanical features tend to "lead" the analyst to the correct *analytical entry* for each situation.

Observe that the Cash account is listed only for balancing purposes. It is "cleared out" in the last analytical entry as a check on the final results. Debits and credits to Cash in the original entries in the accounts are entered in the bottom position of the worksheet as *cash sources* (debits), or as *cash applied* (credits), as was done for working capital in the prior worksheet.

Sources of cash: from other sources	11,000	
Capital stock		10,000
Contributed capital in excess of par		1,000

d. Dividends declared and paid (company records)—During the year, Fina Company declared and paid a $7,000 cash dividend. The original entry to record this dividend was: debit—Retained Earnings (dividends paid), $7,000; and credit—Cash, $7,000. Clearly, cash was decreased by this transaction. The original entry essentially is repeated as a worksheet *analytical entry* as follows:

Retained earnings	7,000	
Uses of cash		7,000

At this point, you should observe on the worksheet that for the line "Retained Earnings" the beginning balance (a credit) $11,000, minus the dividend (a debit) $7,000, plus net income (a credit) $8,000, equals the ending balance of $12,000. Similarly, as subsequent analytical entries are made, the remaining change in the balance of each noncash account will be exactly accounted for, at which time the worksheet is complete.

e. Payment on bonds payable (balance sheet and other records)—The worksheet reflects a decrease of $8,000 in the balance in bonds payable. Other records reveal that, during the year, a payment of this amount was made on the bonds. The original entry was: debit—Bonds Payable, $8,000; and credit—Cash, $8,000. Clearly, cash was decreased by this transaction. Consistent with the original entry, the *analytical entry* on the worksheet is:

Bonds payable	8,000	
Uses of cash		8,000

Note that after this entry, the change in the Bonds Payable account has been explained.

f. Exchange of long-term investment for equipment (company records)—Observe that the worksheet reflects a decrease in long-term investments of $5,000. Other records revealed that the company acquired some equipment and paid for it with some common stock of the X Corporation, which was being held as a long-term investment. It was a direct swap, and no cash was disbursed or received. The original transaction was recorded as follows: debit—Equipment, $5,000; and credit—Long-Term Investments, $5,000. Clearly, this transaction completely bypasses cash since it was an outright trade.

Since *all* financing and investing activities must be included in the statement of changes in financial position, analytical entries must be made on the worksheet as if there were two transactions: one for the sale of the investments and another for the purchase of the equipment. These *two analytical entries* on the worksheet are as follows:

f–1. To record the financing activity:

Sources of cash: from other sources	5,000	
Long-term investments		5,000

f–2. To record the investing activity:

Equipment	5,000	
Uses of cash		5,000

g. Payment on current liability, short-term note payable (nontrade) (balance sheets)—During the period, Fina Company paid $4,000 on nontrade, short-term notes payable, evidenced on the worksheet by the fact that the balance of this account decreased by this amount during the year. Thus, cash was used to reduce liabilities. The original entry was: debit—Notes Payable, Short Term (nontrade), $4,000; and credit—Cash, $4,000. Therefore, the analytical entry would be:

Notes payable, short term (nontrade)	4,000	
Uses of cash		4,000

We may note that the above analytical entry reflects the net change in nontrade notes payable during the year. It is a summary entry. There may have been several debit and/or credit entries to the note account during the year; however, for analytical purposes, only the net effect is reflected. This is true in respect to all of the analytical entries. Most of them are summary entries that reflect the net effect of numerous entries of the same kind to the accounts being analyzed.

h. Accounts receivable, change in balance (balance sheets)—The worksheet reveals that the accounts receivable balance increased by $5,000. This amount reflects a difference between sales revenue on the accrual basis and cash inflow from operations. Consequently, this reflects an adjustment (reduction) to revenues to derive cash inflow from operations. The analytical entry to reflect this adjustment would be:

Accounts receivable	5,000	
Sources of cash: Revenues (adjustment)		5,000

Note that this involves a "credit" under "Sources of Cash" on the worksheet. The credit reflects the fact that this amount must be *subtracted* from revenues to derive cash inflow from operations (also see page 582).

i. Inventory of merchandise, change in balance (balance sheets)—The two balance sheets revealed that inventory decreased by $4,000 during the year. This means that $4,000 of the cost of goods sold amount of $60,000 (page 577) was represented by goods withdrawn from inventory rather than being purchased for cash this period. This amount reflects a difference in cost of goods sold between the accrual and cash basis. Therefore, since it represents a noncash expense this period, an adjustment (deduction) to expense must be made to derive cash outflow for expenses. The *analytical entry* to reflect this adjustment would be:

Sources of cash: expenses (adjustment)	4,000	
Inventory		4,000

j. Accounts payable, change in balance (balance sheets)—The worksheet indicates that accounts payable (trade) increased by $2,000 during the year. This means that expenses (including cost of goods sold) amounting to $2,000 were deducted on the income statement but are not yet paid in cash. Therefore, an adjustment (addition) to expenses must be made to derive cash outflow for expenses during the period. The *analytical entry* to reflect this adjustment would be:

Sources of cash: expenses (adjustment)	2,000	
Accounts payable		2,000

k. Income taxes payable, change in balance (balance sheet)—The worksheet indicates an increase in income taxes payable (a current liability) of $500. Since income tax expense is reported on the income statement, this amount reflects a difference between the amount accrued and the amount paid in cash. Therefore, the $500 represents an *adjustment* (addition) to expenses to derive cash outflow of this expense. The *analytical entry* on the worksheet would be:

Sources of cash: expenses (adjustments)	500	
Income taxes payable		500

After the above analytical entries are recorded on the worksheet, inspection of the worksheet will reveal that the change between the beginning and ending balances on each line (i.e., each balance sheet account) will have been accounted for exactly. This indicates that the worksheet analysis is finished. At this point the double lines should be drawn across the two middle amount columns (Analysis of Interim Entries) just above the caption "Sources of Cash." The change in cash for the period, as indicated on Line 1, should be entered at the bottom of the worksheet and the debit and credit columns in the bottom portion of the worksheet summed to test for equality. This provides a partial check on the accuracy of the results.

The data provided at the bottom of the worksheet, with appropriate captions added, were used directly in preparing the formal statement of changes in financial position—cash basis as reflected in Exhibit 15–3.

Worksheet for working capital basis

A facilitating worksheet to develop the statement of changes in financial position on a *working capital basis* is fundamentally the same as that illustrated for cash. The worksheet is somewhat less tedious since only the working capital accounts must be analyzed to determine the *causes* of the inflows and outflows of working capital. Simply reporting the debits and credits to the working capital account does not meet the purposes and specifications of the statement of changes in financial position. The statement must reflect the basic causes or reasons for the inflows and outflows of working capital during the period, and, in addition, must include all nonworking capital financing and investing transactions, such as the exchange of a long-term investment for equipment previously illustrated. A primary problem to be resolved on the worksheet is the conversion of net income, as reported on the income statement on the accrual basis, to a strictly working capital basis (that is, to working capital from operations).

The worksheet presented in Exhibit 15–6 for the cash basis, adapted slightly, will conveniently accommodate the analysis necessary to develop a statement of changes in financial position on a working capital basis. The adapted worksheet on a working capital basis, completed for Fina Company, is shown in Exhibit 15–7. It maintains all of the desirable mechanical features of the former worksheet. The analytical entries on the worksheet focus on the conversion from an accrual basis to a working capital basis. The *analytical entries* are made in a straightforward manner as before. The worksheet is set up with precisely the same three column headings as before. Likewise, the five major side captions are essentially the same. The primary difference to be observed is that only the nonworking capital accounts (and their balances) reported on the two balance sheets are captioned on the worksheet in the left column and the amounts are entered in first and last amount columns. To illustrate, compare these columns with the asset, liability, and owners' equity accounts balances given for Fina Company in Exhibit 15–2.

The final step in completing the worksheet is to record the *analytical entries* on the worksheet, similar to the approach illustrated and explained for the cash basis worksheet. The analytical entries are based upon data provided by the two balance sheets, the income statement, and other accounting records. Data, including the sources, to complete the analytical entries follow for Fina Company in 1977.

a. Net income (from the income statement)—As explained earlier, net income generates working capital. The closing entry for net income was: debit—Income Summary; and credit—Retained Earnings. We record this as an *analytical entry* on the worksheet in essentially the same manner as follows:

Sources of working capital: from operations	8,000	
Retained earnings		8,000

b. Depreciation expense (from the income statement)—This expense was originally recorded as a debit to Depreciation Expense and a credit to Accumulated Depreciation. It did not increase or decrease working capital; however, it did serve to reduce net income. Since it was a nonworking capital deduction in deriving net income, it must be added back to net income to derive "Working Capital from Operations." This is accomplished on the worksheet by essentially following the original entry; the worksheet *analytical entry* to adjust net income for depreciation would be:

Sources of working capital: from operations	6,000	
Accumulated depreciation (equipment)		6,000

(Note: Amortization expense on intangible assets and depletion expense on natural resources would be treated the same way.)

c. Sale of capital stock (from the balance sheet and other records) —The worksheet reflects a $10,000 increase in capital stock and a $1,000 increase in contributed capital in excess of par during the period. Inspection of the records revealed that 1,000 shares of unissued capital stock were sold at $11 per share. The original entry was: debit—Cash, $11,000; and credits—Capital Stock, $10,000, and Contributed Capital in Excess of Par, $1,000. Clearly, this transaction generated working capital (i.e., cash) in the amount of $11,000. The original entry essentially is repeated as a worksheet *analytical entry* as shown below:

Sources of working capital: from other sources	11,000	
Capital stock		10,000
Contributed capital in excess of par		1,000

d. Dividends declared and paid during the period (company records) —During the year, Fina Company declared and paid a $7,000 cash dividend. The original entry to record this dividend was: debit—Retained Earnings (dividends paid), $7,000; and credit—Cash, $7,000. Clearly, working capital was decreased by this transaction. The original entry essentially is repeated as a worksheet *analytical entry* as follows:

Retained earnings	7,000	
Uses of working capital		7,000

At this point observe on the worksheet that for the line "Retained earnings" the beginning balance (a credit) $11,000, minus the dividend (a debit) $7,000, plus net income (a credit) $8,000, equals the ending balance of $12,000. Similarly, as subsequent analytical entries are made, the remaining change in the balance of each nonworking capital account will be exactly accounted for, at which time the worksheet is complete.

e. Payment on bonds payable (balance sheet and other records)—The worksheet reflects a decrease of $8,000 in the balance in bonds payable. Other records reveal that during the year, a payment of this amount was made on the principal of the bonds. The original entry was: debit—Bonds Payable, $8,000; and credit—Cash, $8,000. Clearly, working capital was decreased by this transaction. Consistent with the original entry, the *analytical entry* on the worksheet is:

Bonds payable	8,000	
Uses of working capital		8,000

EXHIBIT 15–7

FINA COMPANY, INC.
Worksheet to Develop Statement of Changes in Financial Position—Working Capital Basis
For the Year Ended December 31, 1977

	Beginning Balances, Dec. 31, 1976	Analysis of Interim Entries		Ending Balances, Dec. 31, 1977
		Debit	Credit	
Debits				
1. Working Capital	40,000	10,000		50,000
2. Nonworking Capital Accounts:				
Investments, long term	6,000		(*f*–1) 5,000	1,000
Equipment (net)	60,000	(*f*–2) 5,000	(*b*) 6,000	59,000
	106,000			110,000
Credits				
Bonds payable	40,000	(*e*) 8,000		32,000
Capital stock (par $10)	50,000		(*c*) 10,000	60,000
Contributed capital in excess of par	5,000		(*c*) 1,000	6,000
Retained earnings	11,000	(*d*) 7,000	(*a*) 8,000	12,000
	106,000			110,000
3. Sources of Working Capital:				
From operations:				
Net income		(*a*)† 8,000		
Adjustments to net income: Depreciation expense		(*b*) 6,000		
From other sources:				
Sale of unissued capital stock		(*c*) 11,000		
Disposal of long-term investment*		(*f*–1) 5,000		
4. Uses of Working Capital:				
Payment of dividend on capital stock			(*d*) 7,000	
Payment on bonds payable			(*e*) 8,000	
Acquisition of equipment*			(*f*–2) 5,000	
5. Change—Increase in Working Capital (per line 1 above)			10,000	
		30,000	30,000	

* Equipment acquired in exchange for common stock of the X Corporation, which was being held as a long-term investment.

† These entries are keyed for ready reference to the textual discussions of the worksheet starting on page 599.

Note that after this entry the change in the bonds payable account has been explained.

f. Exchange of long-term investment for equipment (company records) —Observe that the worksheet reflects a decrease in long-term investments of $5,000. Other records revealed that the company acquired some equipment and paid for it with some common stock of the X Corporation, which was being held as a long-term investment. It was a direct swap, and no cash (or debt) was disbursed or received. The original transaction was recorded as follows: debit—Machinery, $5,000; and credit—Long-Term Investments, $5,000. Clearly, this transaction completely bypasses working capital since it was an outright trade.

Since *all* financing and investing activities must be included in the statement of changes in financial position, analytical entries must be made on the worksheet as if there were two transactions: one for the sale of the investment and another for the purchase of the equipment. These *two analytical entries* on the worksheet are as follows:

f-1. To record the financing activity:

Sources of working capital: from other sources	5,000	
Investments, long term		5,000

f-2. To record the investing activity:

Machinery	5,000	
Uses of working capital		5,000

Upon completion of the above analytical entries on the worksheet, observe that the amount of change from the beginning to the ending balance for *each* nonworking capital account on the worksheet has been accounted for exactly. This indicates that the analysis of the interim entries is complete. The worksheet is then completed by (1) drawing a double line under the two middle columns just above "Sources of Working Capital"; (2) determining the difference between the debits and credits in the lower portion of the worksheet ($10,000 for Fina); and (3) entering this difference to balance as the increase or decrease in working capital. Observe that in the absence of error, this difference will correspond exactly with the difference on the first line of the worksheet ($50,000 − $40,000); that is, it will agree with the change in working capital for the period. This is a valuable check on the accuracy of your analysis of the changes.

The bottom portion of the worksheet provides the detailed data for the statement of changes in financial position. The statement presented in Exhibit 15–4, with appropriate captions added, was taken directly from this portion of the worksheet.

QUESTIONS FOR DISCUSSION

1. What are the three basic statements that are now required to be included in the annual financial statements? Fundamentally, what does each report?
2. Basically, what "changes" are reported by the statement of changes in financial position?
3. What are the primary sources and uses of funds in a business?
4. What is the essential difference between a statement of changes in financial position (*a*) on a cash basis and (*b*) on a working capital basis?
5. Company X acquired a tract of land in exchange for a $10,000 bond payable. Should this noncash, nonworking capital exchange be included on the statement of changes in financial position on the working capital basis? On the cash basis?
6. Assume you are completing a statement of changes in financial position —cash basis and have the data listed below. On a separate sheet, complete the blanks to the right.

Revenues (accrual basis)		$80,000	
Increase in accounts receivable	$1,400	____	
Cash inflow from revenues			$____
Expenses (accrual basis)		70,000	
Depreciation expense	1,500	____	
Amortization of patent	200	____	
Decrease in merchandise inventory	2,200	____	
Increase in accounts payable	1,000	____	
Cash outflow for expenses			____
Cash generated from operations for the period			____

7. Define working capital.
8. What are the two basic sections on the statement of changes in financial position—working capital basis? Why is the second section considered by some to be redundant?
9. Explain the difference between (*a*) changes in the internal content of working capital and (*b*) causes of the changes in working capital.
10. Explain why net income (i.e., operations) is often the primary source of funds in a business in the long term.
11. In developing "Cash or Working Capital Generated by Operations" on the statement of changes in financial position, why are depreciation, amortization of intangible assets, and depletion added back to net income?
12. Explain why a long-term loan affects working capital but a current or short-term loan does not.
13. Why are direct exchanges reported on the statement of changes in financial position although they do not change either cash or working capital?
14. As a statement user interested in the statement of changes in financial position, would you prefer it on (*a*) the cash basis or (*b*) the working capital basis? Explain.

EXERCISES

PART ONE: EXERCISES 15–1 TO 15–4

E15–1. The accounting department of Darby Company assembled the following data at December 31, 1977, end of the accounting period, as a basis for preparing a statement of changes in financial position—cash basis:

Transactions	*Amount*	
Net income (Revenue, $200,000 – Expenses, $168,000)	$ 32,000	
Depreciation expense	7,000	
Purchase of fixed assets for cash		$ 42,000
Accrued wages payable increase	4,000	
Inventory decrease	3,000	
Accounts payable decrease		8,000
Payment of cash dividend on common stock		20,000
Amortization of patent	1,000	
Payment on short-term note payable (nontrade)		25,000
Sale of common stock for cash	15,000	
Sale of fixed assets for cash (sold at book value)	9,000	
Accounts receivable increase		6,000
Long-term borrowing during the period	50,000	
Purchase of long-term investment, stock X Co. (paid cash)		30,000
Difference—decrease in cash	10,000	
	$131,000	$131,000

Required:

Utilize the above data to prepare a statement of changes in financial position—cash basis. Assume all of the above amounts are correct. No worksheet is necessary.

E15–2. Stanley Company has completed the income statement and the balance sheet at December 31, 1977. The following data were taken from a worksheet completed as a basis for the statement of changes in financial position:

Net income (Revenues, $150,000—Expenses, $128,000)	$22,000
Depreciation expense	4,000
Purchase of fixed assets for cash	15,000
Sale of long-term investment (sold at book value for cash)	6,000
Inventory increase during the period	3,000
Paid cash dividends	8,000
Borrowed on short-term note	20,000
Accounts payable decrease	2,000

Payment of long-term note	30,000
Acquired land for future use; issued capital stock in payment	12,000

Required:

Prepare the statement of changes in financial position—cash basis. (Hint: Cash decreased by $6,000 during the year.)

E15–3. The following actual statement was taken from the annual financial statement of Collins Corporation:

COLLINS CORPORATION
Statement of Changes in Financial Position
For the Year Ended December 31, 19B

Funds Generated:		
Sales and service revenues	$85,000	
Depreciation expense	6,000	
Accounts receivable decrease	700	
Merchandise decrease	3,000	
Borrowing (short-term note payable)	20,000	
Sale of unissued stock	15,000	
Total		$129,700
Funds Used:		
Cost of goods sold	48,000	
Expenses (including depreciation and income taxes)	20,000	
Accounts payable decrease	1,000	
Income taxes payable decrease	300	
Payment on long-term mortgage	25,000	
Acquisition of fixed asset	9,000	
Dividends	7,000	
Total		110,300
Increase in cash		$ 19,400

Required:

a. Is this a cash basis or a working capital basis statement? How did you reach this conclusion?
b. Did Collins give adequate attention to the communication of financial information to shareholders?
c. Recast the above statement in good form (and terminology).
d. What was the amount of net income (or loss) reported for 19B?
e. How much did cash increase during 19B?
f. Did operations generate more or less cash than net income? Explain why.

E15–4. Use the data given below to compute (*a*) total working capital generated by operations and (*b*) total cash generated by operations.

Transactions	*(a)* *Working capital basis*	*(b)* *Cash basis*
Net income reported (accrual basis)*	$18,000	$18,000
Depreciation expense, $2,000	______	______
Increase in accrued wages payable, $1,500	______	______
Decrease in trade accounts receivable, $800	______	______
Increase in merchandise inventory, $2,300	______	______
Amortization of patents, $300	______	______
Increase in bonds payable, $10,000	______	______
Decrease in trade accounts payable, $700	______	______
Sale of unissued common stock, $5,000	______	______
Total working capital generated by operations	$______	
Total cash generated by operations		$______

* Revenues, $78,000 − Expenses, $60,000 = $18,000.

PART TWO: EXERCISES 15–5 TO 15–10

E15–5. The following statement has just been prepared by Wilson Company:

WILSON COMPANY
Statement of Changes in Financial Position—Working Capital Basis
For the Year Ended December 31, 1977

Sources of Working Capital:		
From operations:		
Net income	$ 2,000	
Add expenses not requiring working capital:		
Depreciation expense	4,000	
Patent amortization expense	1,000	
Total working capital generated by operations		$ 7,000
From other sources:		
Sale of unissued stock	10,000	
Short-term loan	33,000	
Sale of land (at cost)	5,000	
Total working capital from other sources		48,000
Total working capital generated during the period		55,000
Uses of Working Capital:		
Acquisition of machinery	22,000	
Payment of mortgage	20,000	
Cash dividend	12,000	
Total working capital applied during the period		54,000
Net increase in working capital during the period		$ 1,000

Changes in Working Capital Accounts:

	Balances at December 31		Working capital increase (decrease)
	1977	1976	
Current Assets:			
Cash	$ 1,000	$ 9,000	$ (8,000)
Accounts receivable	31,000	24,000	7,000
Inventory	38,000	21,000	17,000
Total Current Assets	70,000	54,000	
Current Liabilities:			
Accounts payable	18,000	15,000	(3,000)
Short-term notes payable	22,000	10,000	(12,000)
Total Current Liabilities	40,000	25,000	
Working capital	$30,000	$29,000	$ 1,000

Required:

a. Was there an increase or a decrease in working capital? How much?

b. What was the primary source of working capital?

c. What does your answer to (*b*) suggest as to the future potential of the company to generate working capital?

d. Can you spot a potential problem in respect to the long-term and short-term liabilities?

e. Explain how working capital of $55,000 was generated during the period when only $2,000 net income was earned.

f. Assess the soundness of the cash dividend.

g. Assess the cash-flow potentials of the company.

E15–6. The following actual statement was taken from the annual financial statement of Mason Corporation:

MASON CORPORATION
Funds Flow Statement
December 31, 1977

Funds Generated:	
Net income (plus $10,000 depreciation)	$18,000
Common stock sold	9,000
Long-term note	10,000
Total Funds Generated	$37,000
Funds Applied:	
Equipment	$15,000
Dividends	8,000
Debt	12,000
Change	2,000
	$37,000

Working Capital:	1977	Change
Cash	$ 3,200	$ 6,500
Receivables	7,500	5,000*
Inventory	30,000	13,500*
Payables	(4,800)	2,500*
Notes	(12,000)	7,500*
Total	$23,900	$ 2,000*

* Increase.

Required:

a. What was net income for 1977?

b. Is this a working capital or cash basis statement? Explain the basis for your response.

c. Did working capital increase or did it decrease? By how much?

d. Did "operations" generate more or less working capital than net income. Explain why.

e. Explain why the amount of the change in working capital was different than net income.

f. Assess the soundness of the cash dividend.

g. Can you spot any potential future problems for Mason? Explain why.

h. Did Mason give adequate attention to communication of financial information to the shareholders? Explain the basis for your response.

i. Recast the above statement in good form consistent with your comments in Requirement (*h*).

E15–7. Darby Company has never prepared a statement of changes in financial position. At the end of 1977 the company bookkeeper assembled the following data (which has been determined to be correct) for such a statement:

	Balances at Dec. 31	
	1976	1977
1. From the Balance Sheet:		
Current Assets:		
Cash	$15,000	$20,000
Accounts receivable (net)	24,000	17,000
Merchandise inventory	30,000	27,000
Current Liabilities:		
Accounts payable	(19,000)	(15,000)
Notes payable, short term	(10,000)	(12,000)
Working capital	$40,000	$37,000

	Balances at Dec. 31	
	1976	*1977*
2. From the Worksheet:		
Net income		$21,000
Depreciation expense		4,500
Amortization of patent		500
Purchase of fixed assets		(6,000)
Sale of fixed assets (at book value)		2,000
Payment of long-term note payable		(40,000)
Issuance of bonds payable		30,000
Sale of common stock		10,000
Payment of dividend on common stock		(25,000)
Difference		$ 3,000

Required:

Utilize the above data to prepare a statement of changes in financial position—working capital basis for 1977. Preparation of a worksheet is not necessary.

E15–8. White Company has completed preparation of the income statement and the balance sheet at year end, December 31, 1977. A statement of changes in financial position must be developed. The following data are available:

	Balances at Dec. 31	
	1976	*1977*
1. From Balance Sheet:		
Current Assets:		
Cash	$ 8,000	$15,000
Accounts receivable (net)	17,000	12,000
Inventory	15,000	18,000
Current Liabilities:		
Accounts payable	10,000	12,000
Notes payable, short term	18,000	13,000
2. From Income Statement:		
Net income		$20,000
Depreciation expense		6,000
3. From other records:		
Purchase of long-term investment		15,000
Payment of long-term note		5,000
Sale of unissued capital stock		10,000
Payment of cash dividend		8,000
Purchased land for future plant site, issued capital stock as payment		25,000

Required:

Prepare a statement of changes in financial position—working capital basis.

E15–9. (Based on the Appendix.) Apple Company is developing the annual financial statements at December 31, 1977. The statements are complete except for the statement of changes in financial position—cash basis. The completed balance sheet and income statement are summarized below:

	1976	*1977*
Balance Sheet at December 31:		
Cash	$ 20,000	$ 31,500
Accounts receivable (net)	26,000	25,000
Merchandise inventory	40,000	38,000
Fixed assets (net)	64,000	67,000
	$150,000	$161,500
Accounts payable	$ 24,000	$ 27,000
Accrued wages payable	500	400
Notes payable, long term	35,000	30,000
Capital stock (nopar)	70,000	80,000
Retained earnings	20,500	24,100
	$150,000	$161,500
Income Statement for 1977:		
Sales		$ 90,000
Cost of goods sold		(52,000)
Expenses (including depreciation expense, $4,000)		(32,000)
		$ 6,000

Required:

a. Set up a worksheet to develop the statement of changes in financial position—cash basis. Analytical entries should be made for the following:
   1. Net income—from income statement.
   2. Depreciation expense—from income statement.
   3. Purchased fixed assets for cash, $7,000.
   4. Paid $5,000 on the long-term note payable.
   5. Sold unissued common stock for $10,000 cash.
   6. Paid a $2,400 cash dividend on capital stock.
   7. Accounts receivable decrease—from balance sheets.
   8. Merchandise inventory decrease—from balance sheets.
   9. Accounts payable increase—from balance sheets.
   10. Accrued wages payable decrease—from balance sheets.

b. Based upon the completed worksheet, prepare the formal statement of changes in financial position—cash basis.

E15–10. (Based on the Appendix.) Fulmer Company is developing the annual financial statements at December 31, 1977. The income statement and balance sheet have been completed and the statement of changes in financial position—working capital basis is to be developed. The income statement and the balance sheet are summarized below:

	1976	1977
Balance Sheet at December 31:		
Cash	$12,800	$10,800
Accounts receivable (net)	9,000	10,500
Merchandise inventory	6,600	5,000
Fixed assets (net)	40,000	43,000
Patent	3,000	2,700
	$71,400	$72,000
Accounts payable	$11,000	$ 9,000
Income taxes payable	400	500
Notes payable, long term	10,000	5,000
Capital stock (nopar)	42,000	45,000
Retained earnings	8,000	12,500
	$71,400	$72,000

Income Statement for 1977:	
Sales	$60,000
Cost of goods sold	35,000
Gross margin	25,000
Expenses (including depreciation, $4,000, and patent amortization, $300)	18,000
Net Income	$ 7,000

Additional data for 1977:
Purchased fixed assets for cash, $7,000.
Paid $5,000 on long-term note payable.
Sold capital stock for $3,000 cash.
Declared and paid a $2,500 dividend on capital stock.

Required:

a. Based upon the above data, prepare a worksheet to develop the statement of changes in financial position—working capital basis. (Hint: Working capital decreased $200.)

b. Prepare the formal statement of changes in financial position—working capital basis.

PROBLEMS

PART ONE: PROBLEMS 15–1 TO 15–5

P15–1. The following statement has just been prepared by Baker Corporation:

BAKER CORPORATION
Statement of Changes in Financial Position—Cash Basis
For the Year Ended December 31, 1977

Sources of Cash:		
From operations:		
Revenues	$60,000	
Add (deduct) adjustments to convert to cash basis:		
Accounts receivable decrease	2,000	
Cash generated from revenues		$62,000
Expenses	70,000	
Add (deduct) adjustments to convert to cash basis:		
Depreciation expense	(3,000)	
Amortization expense	(300)	
Inventory increase	1,500	
Accounts payable decrease	1,000	
Prepaid insurance decrease	(200)	
Cash disbursed for expenses		69,000
Cash generated (used in) by operations		(7,000)
From other sources:		
Sale of capital stock	10,000	
Long-term note payable	30,000	
Land (exchanged for machinery)	7,000	
Cash from other sources		47,000
Total cash generated during the period		40,000
Uses of Cash:		
Machinery (acquired in exchange for land)	7,000	
Payment on mortgage	6,000	
Cash dividends	12,000	
Total cash expended during the period		25,000
Net increase in cash during the period		$15,000

Required:

a. What was the net income (or loss) for 1977?

b. How much did cash increase during 1977?

c. Compute the difference in dollars between (*a*) and (*b*). What does it mean?

d. Explain how management generated significantly more cash than income (or loss) during the period.

e. Did "operations" generate more or less cash than the amount of income? Explain.

f. Explain the land transaction. Why is it reported on this statement?

g. Explain why the decrease in accounts receivable increases the cash inflow from revenues.

h. Explain why the inventory increase is added to expenses.

i. Explain why the decrease in accounts payable is added to expenses.

j. Are there any reasons to question the soundness of the cash dividend payment of $12,000?

P15–2. The following statement was prepared by Dawkins Corporation:

DAWKINS CORPORATION
Statement of Changes in Financial Position
December 31, 1977

Sources of Funds:		
Operations:		
Revenues	$180,000	
Accounts receivable decrease	15,000	
	195,000	
Expenses (including depreciation and income taxes)	160,000	
Depreciation expense	(14,000)	
Inventory increase	6,000	
Accounts payable increase	(7,000)	
Income taxes payable decrease	3,000	
	148,000	$ 47,000
Sale of fixed assets (at book value)		17,000
Issuance of common stock for land		25,000
Borrowing—short-term note payable		40,000
Total		$129,000
Uses of Funds:		
Dividends	$ 20,000	
Payment on long-term mortgage	80,000	
Machinery	15,000	
Land	25,000	
Funds (decrease)	(11,000)	
Total		$129,000

Required:

a. Is this a cash basis or a working capital basis statement? Explain the basis for your answer.

b. What was the amount of net income reported for 1977?

c. Did cash increase or decrease? Explain.

d. Did the company give adequate attention to communication of financial information to the shareholders? Explain the basis for your response.

e. Recast the above statement using proper format and terminology.

f. What was the amount of the difference between net income and cash generated from operations? Why were they different?

g. Are there any potential problems for this company? Explain why.

P15–3. The following statement was prepared by Nourse Company:

NOURSE COMPANY
Statement of Funds Flow
December 31, 1977

Funds Generated:	
Sales and service revenues	$190,000
Depreciation	20,000
Amortization of deferred charges	4,000
Decrease in inventory	5,000
Decrease in accounts receivable	6,000
Increase in income taxes payable	1,000
Sale of fixed assets	15,000
Borrowing (short-term notes)	50,000
Stock issued (for land)	25,000
	$316,000
Funds Applied:	
Cost of goods sold	$110,000
Expenses (including depreciation and excluding income taxes)	70,000
Income tax expense	2,200
Decrease in accounts payable	2,000
Payment of bonds payable	70,000
Dividends	24,000
Purchase of machinery	30,000
Land acquired	25,000
Decrease in funds	(17,200)
	$316,000

Required:

a. Is this a cash basis or a working capital basis statement? How can you determine the basis?

b. What amount of net income was reported in 1977?

c. Did cash increase or decrease?

d. In your opinion, did the company give adequate attention to communication to statement users? Explain the basis for your response.

e. Recast the above statement using proper format and terminology.

f. Do you spot any potential problems for the company? Explain why.

P15–4. The following statement has just been prepared for the Amhurst Corporation:

AMHURST CORPORATION
Funds Flow Statement
Year, December 31, 1977

Funds Provided:	
Sales and other incomes	$90,000
Accounts receivable decrease	4,000
Expenses (including depreciation and income taxes)	(70,000)
Depreciation expense	2,000
Inventory increase	(3,000)
Accounts payable increase	1,000
Prepaid insurance increase	(100)
Cash from operations	23,900
Other sources:	
Capital stock	5,000
Total Sources	28,900
Funds Applied:	
Equipment	(7,000)
Bonds payable	(10,000)
Dividends	(2,000)
Total Uses	19,000
Increase in funds	$ 9,900

Required:

a. Is the above on a working capital basis or cash basis? How did you determine the basis on which the statement was prepared?

b. List the format and terminology deficiencies on the statement.

c. Recast the above statement in proper form.

P15–5. Watson Company has completed the balance sheet and the income statement at year-end, December 31, 1977. A worksheet also has been completed as a basis for the statement of changes in financial position—cash basis. Data from the worksheet follow:

Net income (Revenue, $140,000 – Expenses, $100,000)	$40,000
Depreciation expense	10,000
Paid long-term note payable	25,000
Sale of fixed assets for cash (no gain or loss on sale)	15,000
Amortization of patent	2,000
Sale of unissued capital stock for cash	20,000
Increase in accounts receivable	3,000
Purchased fixed assets for cash	34,000
Decrease in accounts payable	4,000
Decrease in merchandise inventory	6,000
Paid cash dividends	8,000
Acquired future plant site; issued bonds payable at par in full settlement	30,000

Required:

Prepare a statement of changes in financial position—cash basis. (Hint: Cash increased by $19,000 during the period.)

PART: TWO: PROBLEMS 15–6 TO 15–14

P15–6. The following statement was prepared by Ware Corporation:

WARE CORPORATION
Statement of Changes in Financial Position—Working Capital Basis
For the Year Ended December 31, 1977

Sources of Funds:			
From operations:			
Net income		$ 40,000	
Add expenses not requiring working capital:			
Depreciation expense	$12,000		
Patent amortization expense	1,000		
Goodwill amortization expense	3,000	16,000	
Total funds generated by operations			$ 56,000
From other sources:			
Bonds payable, maturity value $100,000		98,000	
Sale of land (at cost)		25,000	
Common stock (issued for plant site)		40,000	
Total funds from other sources			163,000
Total funds generated during the period			219,000
Uses of Funds:			
Pay mortgage		20,000	
Construct new plant		150,000	
Purchase plant machinery		20,000	
Plant site (for stock issued)		40,000	
Cash dividend		6,000	
Total funds used during the period			236,000
Net decrease in working capital during the period			$ 17,000

Changes in Working Capital Accounts:

	Balances at December 31		*Working capital increase (decrease)*
	1977	*1976*	
Current Assets:			
Cash	$ 6,000	$33,000	$(27,000)
Accounts receivable	13,000	9,000	4,000
Inventory	52,000	40,000	12,000
Total Current Assets	71,000	82,000	
Current Liabilities:			
Accounts payable	8,000	13,000	5,000
Short-term notes payable	16,000	5,000	(11,000)
Total Current Liabilities	24,000	18,000	
Working capital	$47,000	$64,000	$(17,000)

Required:

a. List any communication deficiencies that you observe.
b. Did working capital and cash each increase or decrease? By how much?
c. What was the primary source of working capital?
d. What was the primary use of working capital?
e. Explain the nonworking capital exchange. Did it directly affect working capital? Why should it be reported on the statement?
f. Explain why working capital decreased although there was a net income for the period.
g. Assess the soundness of the cash dividend.
h. Assess the cash position compared with the working capital position.
i. Can you spot any potential problems with respect to the future? Explain.

P15–7. The following actual statement was taken from the published annual financial statements of Laird Corporation:

LAIRD CORPORATION
Statement of Working Capital
December 31, 1977

Working Capital Generated:		
Net income	$14,000	
Add: Depreciation	15,000	
Patent amortization	1,000	
Total	30,000	
Bonds issued	50,000	
Common stock (for equipment)	15,000	
Total working capital generated		$95,000
Working Capital Applied:		
Pay mortgage	60,000	
Acquired equipment	15,000	
Dividends	10,000	
Total working capital applied		85,000
Net increase in working capital		$10,000

Working Capital Changes:

	1977	*Change*
Cash	$ 7,400	$(12,400)
Accounts receivable	9,000	6,000
Inventory	24,900	19,900
Accounts payable	(7,000)	(4,000)
Other short-term debt	(1,400)	500
Total	$32,900	$10,000

Required:

a. Did working capital and cash each change? In what direction and by how much?
b. Explain why the amount of the change in working capital was different than the amount of net income.
c. What was the largest source and use of working capital?
d. Is the working capital position sound? Explain the basis for your decision.
e. Compare the cash position with the working capital position.
f. List all of the communication deficiencies in the above format.
g. Recast the above statement to correct it for the deficiencies you listed in Requirement (*f*).

P15-8. The following actual statement was taken from the published annual financial report of the Jackson Corporation:

JACKSON CORPORATION
Statement of Funds Flow
At December 31, 1977

Funds Generated:		
Net income (plus depreciation expense, $1,500 and amortization of goodwill, $2,000)		$33,500*
Common stock issued		10,000
Funds borrowed		50,000
Total Funds Generated		$93,500
Application of Funds:		
Fixed asset acquired		$40,000
Dividends		6,000
Pay debts		20,000
Increase in funds		27,500
Total Funds Applied		$93,500
Working Capital Changes:		
Cash	($20,000)	
Receivables	14,000	
Inventory	37,500	
Payables	(4,000)	
Total	$27,500	

* During 1977, sales increased 2 percent over 1976.

Required:

a. Is this a working capital basis or a cash basis statement? How did you reach this conclusion?
b. Do you think this corporation gave adequate attention to communication of financial information to the shareholders and other parties? Explain the basis for your decision.

c. What economic strengths and weaknesses are indicated for Jackson Corporation? Explain.

d. Recast the above statement in order to enhance its communication potentials. Assume the financial statements at the end of the prior year showed: cash, $24,000; accounts receivable, $32,000; inventory, $45,500; and accounts payable, $26,000.

P15–9. Fugler Company has completed all of the adjusting and closing procedures at the end of 1977. They also have prepared the 1977 income statement and balance sheet. From these sources, the following data were developed:

	Balances at December 31	
1. Balance sheet data:	*1977*	*1976*
Current Assets:		
Cash	$20,000	$10,000
Accounts receivable (net)	15,000	16,600
Inventory	29,000	17,000
Prepaid expenses	1,500	1,400
Current Liabilities:		
Accounts payable	6,000	8,000
Accrued wages payable	500	1,000
Notes payable, short term	9,000	4,000

2. Other data for 1977:

Net income	$22,000
Depreciation expense	4,000
Purchase of fixed assets for cash – cost	24,000
Sale for cash of long-term investment (at cost)	6,000
Borrowed cash on long-term note	15,000
Sales of unissued capital stock (cash)	4,000
Payment of cash dividend	5,000
Payment on long-term note payable	4,000
Acquired land for future plant site and issued bonds payable at par (ten-year) for full purchase price	40,000

Required:

Prepare a statement of changes in financial position – working capital basis for 1977.

P15–10. Doolin Company is in the process of preparing the 1977 annual financial report. The company controller decided to prepare two statements of changes in financial position – one on the working capital basis and the other on the cash basis. A worksheet on each basis has been completed and determined to be correct. The following data were taken from the cash basis worksheet.

Items	Amounts	
Net income reported (accrual basis)	$ 44,000*	
Depreciation expense	8,000	
Purchase of long-term investment, stock Company A		$ 40,000
Sale of fixed assets for cash (no gain or loss on sale)	11,000	
Increase in income taxes payable	400	
Purchase of fixed assets for cash		11,000
Patent amortization expense	600	
Payment of cash dividend on common stock		18,000
Increase in accounts payable	4,000	
Increase in merchandise inventory		9,000
Sale of common stock for cash	20,000	
Payment on short-term notes payable (nontrade)		20,000
Decrease in accounts receivable	5,000	
Payment on long-term notes payable		30,000
Issuance of bonds payable (received cash)	50,000	
Difference—increase in cash		15,000
	$143,000	$143,000

* Revenues, $144,000 − Expenses (including depreciation and income taxes), $100,000 = $44,000.

The beginning and ending balance sheets reflected the following:

	Balances, Dec. 31	
	1977	1976
Current Assets:		
Cash	$55,000	$40,000
Inventory	39,000	30,000
Accounts receivable (net)	15,000	20,000
Current Liabilities:		
Accounts payable	(19,000)	(15,000)
Short-term notes payable (nontrade)	-0-	(20,000)
Income taxes payable	(1,400)	(1,000)
Difference—working capital	$88,600	$54,000

Required:

a. Based upon the above data, prepare in good form a statement of changes in financial position—cash basis.

b. Based upon data selected from the above, prepare in good form a statement of changes in financial position—working capital basis.

P15–11. (Based on the Appendix.) Brown Company is in the process of developing the 1977 annual reports. A statement of changes in financial position—cash basis is being developed. The following worksheet has been set up to develop the statement:

BROWN COMPANY
Worksheet to Develop Statement of Changes in Financial Position—Cash Basis
For the Year Ended December 31, 1977

	Ending Balances, Dec. 31, 1976	Analysis of Interim Entries		Ending Balances, Dec. 31, 1977
		Debit	Credit	
Debits				
Cash Account	24,000			32,200
Noncash Accounts:				
Accounts receivable (net)	26,000			30,000
Inventory	30,000			28,000
Prepaid insurance	1,200			800
Investments, long term	10,800			8,000
Fixed assets (net)	30,000			37,000
Patent (net)	3,000			2,700
	125,000			138,700
Credits				
Accounts payable	21,000			18,000
Accrued wages payable	3,000			2,000
Income taxes payable	1,000			1,200
Notes payable, long term	25,000			20,000
Capital stock (par $10)	60,000			70,000
Retained earnings	15,000			27,500
	125,000			138,700
Sources of Cash:				
From operations:				
From other sources:				
Uses of Cash				
Change in Cash Balance				

Additional data for 1977:

(*a*) Revenues, $120,000 − Expenses, $100,000 = Net income $20,000; (*b*) depreciation expense, $3,000; (*c*) amortization of patent, $300; (*d*) sale of long-term investment at cost, $2,800; (*e*) purchase of fixed assets, $10,000; (*f*) payment on long-term note payable, $5,000; (*g*) sale of unissued capital stock for $10,000 cash; (*h*) paid cash dividend, $7,500; (*i*) increase in accounts receivable balance during the period; (*j*) decrease in inventory during the period, (*k*) decrease in prepaid insurance balance during the period; (*l*) decrease in accounts payable balance during the period; (*m*) decrease in accrued wages payable balance during the period; and (*n*) increase in income taxes payable balance during the period.

Required:

Complete the above worksheet on a cash basis.

P15–12. (Based on the Appendix.) Clark Company is in the process of preparing the annual financial statements on December 31, 1977, including a statement of changes in financial position—cash basis. The balance sheet and the income statement have been completed and are summarized below:

	Balances	
	1976	1977
Balance Sheet at December 31:		
Cash	$ 10,000	$ 24,500
Accounts receivable (net)	19,000	23,000
Merchandise inventory	52,000	50,000
Prepaid insurance		2,000
Investments, long term	5,000	
Fixed assets (net)	111,000	151,000
Patent	3,000	2,000
	$200,000	$252,500
Accounts payable	$ 28,000	$ 25,000
Accrued wages payable	2,000	1,500
Income taxes payable	3,000	4,000
Notes payable, short term (nontrade)	5,000	
Notes payable, long term	25,000	60,000
Capital stock (nopar)	107,000	130,000
Retained earnings	30,000	32,000
	$200,000	$252,500
Income Statement for 1977:		
Sales		$300,000
Cost of goods sold		(170,000)
Expenses (not detailed)		(85,000)
Depreciation expense		(10,000)
Patent amortization		(1,000)
Income tax expense		(14,000)
Net Income		$ 20,000

Additional data for 1977:

From income statement: (*a*) net income, (*b*) depreciation, and, (*c*) patent amortization.

From other records: (*d*) on January 1, 1977, paid $3,000 for three-year insurance premium; (*e*) amortized one third of the insurance premium; (*f*) sold the long-term investment at cost, $5,000; (*g*) paid the short-term notes payable, $5,000; (*h*) paid $15,000 on the long-term notes payable; (*i*) sold unissued capital stock for $23,000 cash; and (*j*) declared and paid a cash dividend, $18,000.

From the balance sheets: (*k*) accounts receivable increased, (*l*) merchandise inventory decreased, (*m*) accounts payable decreased, (*n*) accrued wages payable decreased, and (*o*) income taxes payable increased.

From other records: (*p*) on December 31, 1977, acquired fixed assets and paid for them by issuing a $50,000 long-term note payable.

Required:

a. Based on the above data, set up and complete a worksheet to develop the statement of changes in financial position—cash basis. There will be an analytical entry for each of the data summarized (*a*) through (*p*).

b. Utilize the completed worksheet to develop the statement of changes in financial position—cash basis. (Hint: Cash generated by operations is $27,500.)

P15–13. (Based on the Appendix.) Kirk Company is in the process of preparing the annual financial reports at December 31, 1977; included is a statement of changes in financial position—working capital basis. In preparing the latter statement, the following work-sheet has been set up:

KIRK COMPANY
Worksheet to Develop Statement of Changes
in Financial Position—Working Capital Basis
For the Year Ended December 31, 1977

	Ending Balances, Dec. 31, 1976	Analysis of Interim Entries		Ending Balances, Dec. 31, 1977
		Debit	Credit	
Debits				
Working Capital	21,000			27,400
Nonworking Capital Accounts:				
Investments, long term	5,000			6,000
Fixed assets (net)	50,000			51,000
Patent (net).	4,000			3,600
	80,000			88,000
Credits				
Bonds payable	15,000			10,000
Capital stock	40,000			50,000
Retained earnings	25,000			28,000
	80,000			88,000
Sources of Working Capital:				
From operations:				
From other sources:				
Uses of Working Capital				
Change in Working Capital				

Additional Data:

(*a*) Net income, $7,000; (*b*) depreciation expense, $2,000; (*c*) amortization of patent, $400; (*d*) purchase of long-term investment, $1,000; (*e*) annual payment on bonds payable, $5,000; (*f*) sale of unissued common stock, $10,000; (*g*) paid cash dividend, $4,000; and (*h*) purchased fixed assets, $3,000.

Required:

Complete the above worksheet on a working capital basis.

P15–14. (Based on Appendix.) Ware Company is in the process of developing the annual financial statements, including a statement of changes in financial position—working capital basis, at December 31, 1977. The balance sheet and the income statement are already prepared as summarized below:

		Balances	
		1977	*1976*
Balance Sheet at December 31:			
Cash		$ 21,500	$ 15,000
Accounts receivable (net)		23,000	20,000
Merchandise inventory		27,000	22,000
Prepaid insurance		300	600
Investments, long term (S Corp. stock)		12,000	
Fixed assets (net)		220,000	134,000
Patent (net)		16,000	
		$319,800	$191,600
Accounts payable		$ 18,000	$ 12,000
Notes payable, short term (nontrade)		10,000	18,000
Accrued wages payable		800	1,000
Income taxes payable		1,000	600
Notes payable, long term		10,000	30,000
Bonds payable		100,000	
Capital stock (par $10)		140,000	100,000
Contributed capital in excess of par		6,000	5,000
Retained earnings		34,000	25,000
		$319,800	$191,600
Income Statement for 1977:			
Sales		$200,000	
Cost of goods sold		126,000	
Gross margin on sales		74,000	
Expenses (not detailed)	$39,000		
Depreciation expense	14,000		
Amortization of patent	1,000		
Income tax expense	7,000	61,000	
Net Income		$ 13,000	

Additional Data for 1977:

(*a*) Net income for 1977 (per above); (*b*) depreciation expense (per above); (*c*) purchased patent on January 1, 1977, for $17,000 cash; (*d*) amortize patent over 17 years; (*e*) purchased stock of S Corporation as a long-term investment for cash, $12,000; (*f*) paid $20,000 on the long-term notes payable; (*g*) sold 4,000 shares of unissued capital stock for $41,000 cash; (*h*) declared and paid a $4,000 cash dividend; (*i*) acquired a building (a fixed asset) and paid in full for it by issuing $100,000 bonds payable at par to the former owner—date of transaction was December 30, 1977.

Required:

a. Based upon the above data, prepare a worksheet to develop the statement of changes in financial position—working capital basis. (Hint: The increase in working capital was $16,000.)

b. Based upon the completed worksheet, prepare the statement of changes in financial position—working capital basis.

16

Using and interpreting financial statements

PURPOSE OF THE CHAPTER

Throughout the preceding chapters, your attention has been focused on developing an understanding of the financial reports prepared for use by external parties. The rationale and conceptual basis for the major phases of the accounting process and the resulting financial statements were presented. Throughout those discussions, we also emphasized the use and interpretation of the various items and classifications reported on the income statement, balance sheet, and statement of changes in financial position.

The broad fundamentals underlying accounting that were presented in the preceding chapters are summarized in Exhibit 16–1 for convenience in study. We have emphasized these fundamentals because an understanding of them and their impact on financial statements is essential to the statement user. The interpretation of financial reports and an appreciation of both their advantages and limitations rest basically on a knowledge of the broad fundamentals. They emphasize valuations, measurements, and the basic distinctions in the measurement and reporting processes. As a decision maker who must necessarily rely on financial statements, your understanding of these broad fundamentals should serve you to advantage.

The purpose of Part One of this chapter is to present some important uses and interpretations of external financial statements prepared in accordance with generally accepted accounting standards. Part Two of the chapter focuses on the impacts of price-level changes and replace-

EXHIBIT 16–1
Summarization of the broad fundamentals underlying accounting

Fundamental	Text Reference		Brief Explanation
	Chapter	Page	
1. Underlying Assumptions:			
a. Separate-entity assumption	1	4	Accounting is concerned with a specifically defined entity. Thus, for accounting purposes, an enterprise is assumed to be an accounting unit separate and apart from the owners, creditors, and other entities.
b. Continuity assumption	2	39	In accounting, an enterprise is assumed to be a "going-concern." That is, for accounting purposes, it is assumed that the entity will not liquidate in the foreseeable future, but will continue to carry out its business objectives in an orderly way.
c. Unit-of-measure assumption	1	3	With many diverse items and transactions to be accounted for, it is necessary that a single unit of measure be adopted. Accounting assumes the monetary unit—the dollar—as the common denominator in the measurement process.
d. Time-period assumption	5	141	Financial data must be reported for relatively short time periods: months, quarters, years. Society imposes this calendar constraint on accounting. Thus, accounting assumes that financial results must be reported for short time periods. This leads to the necessity for the accrual and deferral of revenues and expenses.
2. Underlying Principles:			
a. Cost principle..........	2	35	Cost (i.e., the resources given up in the acquisition of other goods and services) is the appropriate basis for initial recording and subsequent accounting for assets, liabilities, revenues, and expenses.
b. Revenue principle....	2	38	Revenue is the consideration received for the aggregate of goods and services transferred by an entity to its customers. Under this principle, revenue is realized when ownership to the goods sold transfers and when services are rendered.
c. Matching principle...	5	144	In conformity with the revenue principle the revenues of the period must be identified and recognized in the accounting process. Then, under the matching principle all of the costs incurred in generating that revenue, irrespec-

EXHIBIT 16–1 (*continued*)

Fundamental	*Text Reference* Chapter	Page	*Brief Explanation*
			tive of the period in which the costs were incurred, must be identified with the period in which the revenues are recognized. Thus, under this principle, the costs of generating particular revenues are matched with those revenues, period by period. This principle requires the accrual and deferral of many costs.
d. Objectivity principle	2	38	Accounting should be based on objective data and objective determinations to the fullest extent possible. It should be free from bias. The accounting data recorded and reported should be verifiable.
e. Consistency principle	8	285	The accounting process must apply all concepts, principles, standards, and measurement approaches on a consistent basis from one period to the next, in order to derive financial data that are comparable over time.
f. Full-disclosure principle	3	76	Financial reporting should be complete and understandable to the prudent user (i.e., the investor) and should include all significant information relating to the economic affairs of the entity.
g. Exception principle ..	9	323	Accounting is applied to a very diverse range of situations and transactions in the many companies and industries; therefore, a reasonable degree of flexibility is essential. As a consequence, certain exceptions to the basic concepts, standards, and procedures are necessary. There are three types of exceptions that are permitted: 1. Materiality—Amounts of small significance (i.e., relatively small amounts) need not be accorded strict theoretical treatment. 2. Conservatism—Where more than one accounting alternative (or judgment) is permissible, the one having the least favorable immediate effect on owners' equity should be selected. 3. Industry peculiarities—Unique characteristics of an industry may require the development and application of special accounting approaches in order to produce realistic financial results.

EXHIBIT 16–1 (*concluded*)

3. Accounting Practices and Procedures:		*Examples:*
a. Those related to income and asset measurement.	Illustrated and discussed throughout the chapters.	Lifo versus Fifo; straight-line versus accelerated depreciation.
b. Those related to the reporting of accounting results.		Reporting extraordinary items; terminology in financial reports.
c. Those not related to asset or income measurement or to the reporting of results.		Control and subsidiary accounts; special journals, methods of processing and recording accounting data (manual, mechanical, and electronic).

ment cost that are important in interpreting the financial statements correctly.

PART ONE: INTERPRETING FINANCIAL STATEMENTS

FINANCIAL REPORTS IN THE DECISION-MAKING PROCESS

The basic objective of financial statements is to help the users make better economic decisions. Decision makers who use financial statements constitute two broad groups. The management of the business (i.e., internal decision makers) relies on financial data in making important managerial decisions. This aspect of accounting is considered in *Fundamentals of Management Accounting.*

The second broad group that uses financial reports is frequently referred to as "external" decision makers. This group consists primarily of investors (both present and potential owners), investment analysts, creditors (both short term and long term), government, labor and the public at large. Financial accounting and the external financial reports discussed in the preceding chapters are oriented toward serving this particular group of decision makers.

Irrespective of the particular decision maker, there are three fundamental purposes for using financial data:

1. Measurement of past performance—The decision maker needs to know how the business has performed in the past. Information concerning such items as net income, sales volume, extraordinary items, cash and working capital flows, and return on the investment earned helps assess the success of the business and the effectiveness of the management. It also helps the decision maker compare one entity with others.

2. Measurement of the present condition of a business—The decision maker must have data on how the entity stands today. Relevant questions include: What types of assets are owned? How much debt does the business owe, and when is it due? What is the cash position? How much of the earnings have been retained in the business? What is the debt/equity ratio? What is the inventory position? Answers to these and similar economic questions help the decision maker assess the successes and failures of the past; but, more importantly, they provide useful information in assessing the future potentials of the business.

3. Prediction of the future potentials of the business—Statement users make decisions by selecting from several alternative courses of action. Each course of action will cause different effects *in the future* for the decision maker. Many of these future effects are financial in nature; thus, in decision making, one is faced with the problem of predicting the probable future impact. All decisions are future-oriented. They do not (and cannot) affect the past. However, in predicting the probable future impact of a decision, reliable measurements of what has happened in the recent past are valuable. This is particularly true when the decision relates to a business entity. The recent sales and profit trends of a business are good indicators of what might be reasonably expected in the future. The primary value of purposes 1 and 2 is to aid in purpose 3.

Thus, decision makers must rely substantially on the past data presented in financial reports in making assessments and predictions of probable future potentials. Generally, this is the most important use of financial statements by decision makers.

Some decisions are made intuitively and without much supporting data. In such cases there is no systematic attempt to collect measurable data such as those provided in financial reports. The decision maker does not attempt to array, measure, and evaluate the advantages and disadvantages of each alternative. There are numerous reasons for intuitive decisions of this sort. Time and cost may prevent a careful analysis. Sometimes the decision maker is unsophisticated and consequently does not understand the systematic approach to decision making and is not aware of the basic factors bearing on the decision. Unsophisticated decision makers tend to oversimplify the decision-making process, disregard basic information, and quite frequently overlook the financial impacts.

In contrast, a sophisticated decision maker will make a systematic analysis of each alternative. Information that bears on each alternative will be collected. In decisions relating to a business, the financial statements generally provide critical financial data bearing on the various alternatives. We must emphasize, however, that the financial impact is only one of several important factors that should be evaluated in most decisions.

To use financial information effectively, one must understand what it represents and how the measurements were made. With a reasonable level of understanding of the fundamentals of the accounting process, one is able to evaluate effectively the **strengths and weaknesses** (and limitations) of the financial data presented in the financial reports of a business. Your study of the preceding chapters should enable you to appreciate and evaluate these aspects. *Fundamentals of Management Accounting* will add to your level of sophistication in this respect.

USE AND INTERPRETATION OF FINANCIAL STATEMENTS

The three basic financial statements—income statement, balance sheet, and statement of changes in financial position—have evolved primarily to meet the special needs of external decision makers. Because of the varied needs of these users, special and supplementary financial data and analyses frequently are needed.

THE INVESTORS

Investors are the primary group to which external financial statements are addressed. As a group they include present owners (shareholders in the case of a corporation), potential owners (those that may become interested in purchasing shares), and investment analysts (since they advise investors). Investors include individuals, other businesses, and institutions, such as your university.

In Chapter 14, on long-term investments, we briefly discussed the concept of a controlling interest; it is discussed in more depth in Chapter 17. When purchasing shares of stock, most investors do not seek a controlling interest. Instead, they do so in the anticipation of (1) receiving revenue in the form of dividends during the investment period and (2) subsequent increases in the market value of the shares over the amount invested. Thus when making an investment of this type or in selling an investment already held, the investor is faced with the problem of predicting the future **income** and **growth** potentials of the enterprise. In making these predictions, the investor should look at several different considerations, such as the nature of the industry, the characteristics of the company, and its financial track record. The income statement provides significant data for the investor, such as revenue from products and services, extraordinary items, income tax impacts, net income, and earnings per share. Other relationships, such as gross margin, profit margin, and expense relationships, can be computed. Similarly, the balance sheet and the statement of changes in financial position, buttressed by the notes to the financial statements, provide a measurement of past profit performance, funds flow, and current financial position. These data constitute an important base from which predictions of future income and growth potentials can be made. These data are particularly valuable when available for recent past periods (see Exhibit 16–2).

The next section will elaborate on the prior discussions and present some analytical techniques commonly used in the evaluation and interpretation of financial statements.

THE CREDITORS

Financial institutions, and other parties to some extent, grant long-term and short-term credit to businesses. Those that grant credit do so in order to earn a return, that is, interest revenue. They expect to collect periodic interest during the credit period and the principal at maturity. As a consequence, in granting credit to a business, the creditor is basically concerned about (1) the profit potentials of the business, (2) its ability to generate cash, and (3) its financial position (assets owned and debts owed). Credit grantors almost always look to the financial reports for information bearing on these matters. Not infrequently the financial institution requires that it be provided with "certified" financial statements prior to making a loan and throughout the credit period.

Short-term credit grantors are particularly concerned about the cash flow and working capital position as reflected in the statement of changes in financial position and the balance sheet. Near-cash items, such as short-term investments, accounts receivable, and inventory balances, are especially relevant to their decision. Similarly, claims to cash, such as current liabilities and current installments of long-term debt, are critical to them.

In contrast, long-term credit grantors are more concerned about such factors as profit-making potentials, assets as security for loans, the ability to generate cash over long periods of time, and the overall performance of the enterprise. In addition, the notes to the financial statements and the "auditors' opinion" convey important information since they tend to disclose facts that are not quantified and certain future contingencies (such as major lawsuits pending).

This brief discussion should be sufficient to indicate the reliance that credit grantors necessarily place upon financial statements. The analytical techniques explained in the next section are widely used by credit grantors in interpreting financial statements.

ANALYSIS OF FINANCIAL STATEMENTS

Financial statements include a large volume of quantitative data supplemented by descriptive notes. The notes are intended to be particularly helpful to users in interpreting the statements; therefore, they should be viewed as an integral part of the financial statements. They elaborate on accounting policies, major financial effects and events, and certain events not directly affecting the current quantitative measurements, but which may bear on the continued success of the firm. An example of the latter situation would be a major lawsuit that is pending. The notes are intended to contribute to an understanding of the significance of such factors.

In respect to the quantitative data presented in the financial statements, there are two techniques that are widely used to assist the user in interpreting the financial statements: (1) presentation of comparative statements and long-term summaries, and (2) use of ratio and percentage analyses.

COMPARATIVE STATEMENTS

For a number of years, the accounting profession has required the presentation of **comparative financial statements** covering, as a minimum, the current year and the immediate prior year. Examples are presented on page 70 for Carborundum Company and in Exhibit 16–2.

Practically all financial statements present, side by side, the results for the current and the preceding year (similar to the statements shown in Exhibit 16–2). As published, only two amount columns generally are shown. However, two additional columns may be added for (1) the amount of change for each item and (2) the percent of change. These additional **variance** columns (amount and percent) are illustrated in Exhibit

EXHIBIT 16–2
Comparative statements illustrated

PACKARD COMPANY
Comparative Income Statement (simplified for illustration)
For the Years Ended December 31, 1977 and 1976

	Year ended Dec. 31		*Increase (decrease) 1977 over 1976*	
	1977	*1976**	*Amount*	*Percent*
Sales	$120,000	$100,000	$20,000	20.0
Cost of goods sold	72,600	60,000	12,600	21.0
Gross margin on sales	47,400	40,000	7,400	18.5
Operating expenses:				
Distribution expenses	22,630	15,000	7,630	50.9
Administrative expenses	11,870	13,300	(1,430)	(10.8)
Interest expense	1,500	1,700	(200)	(11.8)
Total Expenses	36,000	30,000	6,000	20.0
Pretax income	11,400	10,000	1,400	14.0
Income taxes	2,600	2,000	600	30.0
Net Income	$ 8,800	$ 8,000	$ 800	10.0

* Base year for computing percents.

EXHIBIT 16–2 (*continued*)

PACKARD COMPANY
Comparative Balance Sheet (simplified for illustration)
At December 31, 1977, and 1976

	At December 31		Increase (decrease) 1977 over 1976	
	1977	1976*	Amount	Percent
Assets				
Current Assets:				
Cash	$ 13,000	$ 9,000	$ 4,000	44.4
Accounts receivable (net)	8,400	7,000	1,400	20.0
Merchandise inventory	54,000	60,000	(6,000)	(10.0)
Prepaid expenses	2,000	4,000	(2,000)	(50.0)
Total Current Assets	77,400	80,000	(2,600)	3.3
Investments:				
Real estate	8,000	8,000		
Operational Assets:				
Equipment and furniture	82,500	75,000	7,500	10.0
Less accumulated depreciation	(23,250)	(15,000)	8,250	55.0
Total Operational Assets	59,250	60,000	(750)	(1.3)
Other assets	1,900	2,000	(100)	(5.0)
Total Assets	$146,550	$150,000	$ (3,450)	(2.3)
Liabilities				
Current Liabilities:				
Accounts payable	$ 13,200	$ 12,000	$ 1,200	10.0
Notes payable, short term	15,000	20,000	(5,000)	(25.0)
Accrued wages payable	7,200	8,000	(800)	(10.0)
Total Current Liabilities	35,400	40,000	(4,600)	(11.5)
Long-Term Liabilities:				
Notes payable, long term	7,150	10,000	(2,850)	(28.5)
Total Liabilities	42,550	50,000	(7,450)	(14.9)
Shareholders' Equity				
Common stock (par $10)	85,000	85,000		
Retained earnings	19,000	15,000	4,000	26.7
Total Shareholders' Equity	104,000	100,000	4,000	4.0
Total Liabilities and Shareholders' Equity	$146,550	$150,000	$ (3,450)	(2.3)

* Base year for computing percents.

16–2. The two variance columns facilitate **interpretation** by the statement user. Frequently the percent of change from the prior period is more helpful than the absolute dollar amount of change. Observe that the percents are determined independently on each line by dividing the amount of the change by the amount for the preceding year. For example, in Exhibit 16–2, the percentage on the Cash line was computed as $4,000 ÷ $9,000 = 44.4 percent. Thus the earlier year was used as the base.

In the interest of **full disclosure,** many companies also include in the annual report 5-, 10-, and even 20-year summaries of basic data, such as sales, net income, total assets, total liabilities, total owners' equity, and selected ratios. This kind of reporting is to be encouraged from the standpoint of the statement user. Data for a series of years are particularly important in interpretation of the financial statements for the current period. There is considerable likelihood of misinterpretation and unwarranted conclusions when the user limits consideration to only the last one or two periods. The vagaries of transactions, economic events, and accounting are such that the financial reports for one relatively short period of time generally do not provide a sound basis for assessing the long-term potentials of an enterprise. Sophisticated financial analysts typically use data covering a number of periods so that significant **trends** may be identified and interpreted. An excellent 15-year financial summary, presented by the Clark Equipment Company, is shown in Exhibit 16–3.

In analyzing and interpreting comparative data, the items showing significant increases and decreases should receive special attention. Care should be exercised to identify evidence of significant **turning points,** either upward or downward, in trends for important items such as net income and cash flow. The turning points often indicate significant future trends. Fundamental to the interpretation is the need to determine the **underlying causes** for significant changes in either direction (favorable or unfavorable).

RATIO AND PERCENTAGE ANALYSIS

Some amounts on financial statements, such as net income, are highly significant in and of themselves; however, the significance of many amounts is highlighted by their relationship to other amounts. These **significant relationships** can be pinpointed and isolated effectively in many instances through the use of an analytical tool known as **ratio** or **percentage analysis.** A ratio or percent simply expresses the proportionate relationship between two different amounts. A ratio or percent is computed by dividing one quantity by another quantity; the divisor is known as the *base* amount. For example, the fact that a company earned $500,000 net income assumes greater significance when that amount is compared with the stockholders' investment in the company. Assume stockholders' equity is $5,000,000 (i.e., the base amount); the relationship of earnings

EXHIBIT 16–3
Clark Equipment Company
15-Year Financial Summary

Per Share Amounts in Dollars
Other Dollar Amounts in Thousands

	1975	1974 (a)	1973	1972	1971	1970
Operating Data						
Net Sales	$1,424,580	$1,370,568	$1,127,859	$901,100	$742,172	$671,007
Other Income	36,731	50,747	27,636	20,421	19,167	12,516
Total Sales & Other Revenues	1,461,311	1,421,315	1,155,495	921,521	761,339	683,523
Wages, Salaries & Employee Benefits	388,535	407,840	352,422	284,766	229,442	196,407
Cost of Materials, Supplies & Services	895,611	842,051	646,399	523,589	438,513	386,960
Depreciation	23,502	18,652	16,676	15,958	14,749	12,383
Interest & Service Charges	77,093	73,092	43,964	26,549	24,495	20,883
Total Costs & Expenses	1,384,741	1,341,635	1,059,461	850,862	707,199	616,633
Income Before Income Taxes	76,570	79,680	96,034	70,659	54,140	66,890
Provision for Income Taxes	29,952	29,616	40,979	30,147	25,054	32,097
Net Income	46,618	50,064	55,055	40,512	29,086	34,793
Income Per Share (b)	3.43	3.68	4.06	3.01	2.37	2.88
Cash Dividends	21,757	21,753	20,419	19,431	17,112	16,935
Dividends Per Share (b)	1.60	1.60	1.51	1.45	1.40	1.40
Reinvested In The Business	24,861	28,311	34,636	21,081	11,974	17,858
Financial Data						
Current Assets	501,943	651,267	486,036	362,653	348,369	292,503
Current Liabilities	243,277	284,391	208,660	164,604	129,468	109,358
Working Capital	258,666	366,876	277,376	198,049	218,901	183,145
Current Ratio	2.1 to 1	2.3 to 1	2.3 to 1	2.2 to 1	2.7 to 1	2.7 to 1
Properties & Equipment—Net	238,827	204,263	154,164	142,951	133,888	116,390
Long-term Debt	177,568	237,182	139,111	75,776	97,548	102,955
Shareholders' Equity	408,139	383,278	354,415	317,035	291,976	231,328
Book Value Per Share (b)	30.01	28.19	26.09	23.47	21.90	19.10
Other Data						
Return on Net Sales	3.3%	3.7%	4.9%	4.5%	3.9%	5.2%
Return on Average Shareholders' Equity	11.8%	13.6%	16.4%	13.3%	11.1%	15.7%
Capital Expenditures	60,820	72,428	33,568	27,836	22,764	26,668
Shares Outstanding at Dec. 31 (b)	13,598,027	13,598,027	13,582,684	13,506,986	13,329,716	12,107,650
Number of Shareholders	13,125	13,065	12,485	12,539	12,719	13,894
Number of Employees	25,783	32,767	32,819	28,411	26,825	22,100

(a) Reflects change to the Lifo method of valuing domestic inventories.
(b) Adjusted for stock splits.

to shareholder investment would be: $500,000 ÷ $5,000,000 = 0.1, or 10 percent. Clearly, this ratio has significant informational content for the user. It enables one to compare companies more easily and meaningfully.

Fundamentally, there are two aspects of ratio analysis: (1) relationships **within one period** and (2) relationships **between periods.** In addition, ratios may be computed between amounts within one statement, such as the income statement, or between statements, such as the income statement and the balance sheet. In Exhibit 16–2, for Packard Company, the

EXHIBIT 16–3 (continued)

1969	1968	1967	1966	1965	1964	1963	1962	1961
$645,446	$529,942	$507,676	$508,622	$423,662	$347,699	$263,505	$230,075	$173,320
10,643	10,579	10,586	8,869	7,009	5,987	8,139	6,804	6,094
656,089	540,521	518,262	517,491	430,671	353,686	271,644	236,879	179,414
198,134	158,205	143,108	145,572	116,922	95,021	75,960	68,486	51,062
353,041	304,151	310,534	302,540	257,484	209,730	158,671	135,744	109,350
11,137	9,985	8,805	7,373	5,925	5,361	3,702	3,632	3,083
14,254	9,789	9,434	7,999	6,351	2,453	1,721	1,667	1,694
576,566	482,130	471,881	463,484	386,682	312,565	240,054	209,529	165,189
79,523	58,391	46,381	54,007	43,989	41,121	31,590	27,350	14,225
41,303	29,589	22,316	24,840	20,085	20,203	15,996	13,829	6,578
38,220	28,802	24,065	29,167	23,904	20,918	15,594	13,521	7,647
3.18	2.42	2.04	2.50	2.07	2.01	1.51	1.32	.79
16,446	13,623	12,939	10,871	9,226	8,064	6,921	6,140	5,793
1.40	1.20	1.15	1.00	.875	.775	.675	.60	.60
21,774	15,179	11,126	18,296	14,678	12,854	8,673	7,381	1,854
260,819	209,567	181,581	205,222	170,328	132,483	113,397	95,454	66,524
107,222	88,385	65,852	98,175	74,110	58,961	47,515	34,445	18,061
153,597	121,182	115,729	107,047	96,218	73,522	65,882	61,009	48,463
2.4 to 1	2.4 to 1	2.8 to 1	2.1 to 1	2.3 to 1	2.2 to 1	2.4 to 1	2.8 to 1	3.7 to 1
97,898	88,971	80,440	70,893	52,273	46,060	42,207	34,163	32,080
76,894	58,221	58,732	58,377	47,840	35,743	36,418	36,500	29,750
212,695	188,630	171,229	157,489	135,284	114,189	99,817	90,385	72,866
17.62	15.80	14.48	13.47	11.71	10.96	9.67	8.84	7.54
5.9%	5.4%	4.7%	5.7%	5.6%	6.0%	5.9%	5.9%	4.4%
19.1%	16.0%	14.6%	19.9%	19.2%	19.5%	16.4%	16.6%	10.7%
22,492	16,029	14,514	27,248	10,272	7,719	5,509	3,527	3,542
12,074,230	11,940,722	11,826,521	11,692,885	11,552,717	10,422,044	10,324,994	10,229,156	9,661,732
13,109	12,414	12,027	12,423	10,787	9,544	9,198	9,285	7,989
21,640	19,300	17,300	18,300	16,900	13,750	11,400	9,750	8,170

percents of change represent a percentage analysis between periods within each statement.

There is no particular list of ratios or percentages that can be identified as appropriate to all situations. Each situation usually will evidence a need for particular ratios; however, there are a number of ratios or percentages that are widely used because they are appropriate to many situations. The next paragraphs will discuss and illustrate the ratios and percentages that are commonly used.

COMPONENT PERCENTAGES

A widely used technique known as component percentages expresses each item on a particular statement as a percentage of a single base amount.[1] Exhibit 16–4 presents a component analysis for the 1977 and 1976 income statements and balance sheets for Packard Company. On the income statement, the base amount used is **net sales.** Thus, each expense is expressed as a proportional part of net sales. On the balance sheet, the base amount is **total assets.** The percents are derived by dividing the amount on each line by the base amount (total assets).

Component percentages often are quite useful in interpreting and evaluating the reported financial data. Percents have the distinct characteristic of revealing important proportional relationships. For example, on the income statement in Exhibit 16–4 we can observe that distribution expenses were 18.9 percent of sales in 1977, compared with 15 percent in 1976. On the balance sheet, for example, we may note that at the end of 1977, merchandise inventory was 36.8 percent of total assets, compared with 40 percent for 1976. These changes in important relationships often suggest the need for further inquiry because they tend to indicate future potentials and problems.

SOME WIDELY USED RATIOS

Numerous ratios can be computed from a single set of financial statements; however, only a selected number may be useful in a given situa-

EXHIBIT 16–4
Component percentages illustrated

PACKARD COMPANY
Income Statement (simplified for illustration)
For the Years Ended December 31, 1977, and 1976

	For the year ended			
	Dec. 31, 1977		*Dec. 31, 1976*	
	Amount	*Percent*	*Amount*	*Percent*
Sales*	$120,000	100.0	$100,000	100.0
Cost of goods sold	72,600	60.5	60,000	60.0
Gross margin on sales	47,400	39.5	40,000	40.0
Operating expenses:				
Distribution expenses	22,630	18.9	15,000	15.0
Administrative expenses	11,870	9.9	13,300	13.3
Interest expense	1,500	1.2	1,700	1.7
Total Expenses	36,000	30.0	30,000	30.0
Pretax income	11,400	9.5	10,000	10.0
Income taxes	2,600	2.2	2,000	2.0
Net Income	$ 8,800	7.3	$ 8,000	8.0

* Base amount.

[1] Component percentage (or ratio) analysis often is referred to as vertical analysis.

EXHIBIT 16–4 (*continued*)

PACKARD COMPANY
Balance Sheet (simplified for illustration)
At December 31, 1977, and 1976

	At			
	Dec. 31, 1977		*Dec. 31, 1976*	
	Amount	*Percent*	*Amount*	*Percent*
Assets				
Current Assets:				
Cash	$ 13,000	8.9	$ 9,000	6.0
Accounts receivable (net)	8,400	5.7	7,000	4.6
Merchandise inventory	54,000	36.8	60,000	40.0
Prepaid expenses	2,000	1.4	4,000	2.7
Total Current Assets	77,400	52.8	80,000	53.3
Investments:				
Real estate	8,000	5.5	8,000	5.3
Operational Assets:				
Equipment and furniture	82,500	56.3	75,000	50.0
Less accumulated depreciation	(23,250)	(15.9)	(15,000)	(10.0)
Total Operational Assets	59,250	40.4	60,000	40.0
Other Assets	1,900	1.3	2,000	1.4
Total Assets*	$146,550	100.0	$150,000	100.0
Liabilities				
Current Liabilities:				
Accounts payable	$ 13,200	9.0	$ 12,000	8.0
Notes payable, short term	15,000	10.2	20,000	13.3
Accrued wages payable	7,200	4.9	8,000	5.3
Total Current Liabilities	35,400	24.1	40,000	26.6
Long-Term Liabilities:				
Notes payable, long term	7,150	4.9	10,000	6.7
Total Liabilities	42,550	29.0	50,000	33.3
Shareholders' Equity				
Common stock (par $10)	85,000	58.0	85,000	56.7
Retained earnings	19,000	13.0	15,000	10.0
Total Shareholders' Equity	104,000	71.0	100,000	66.7
Total Liabilities and Shareholders' Equity*	$146,550	100.0	$150,000	100.0

* Base amount.

tion. Thus, a common procedure is to compute certain widely used ratios and then decide what additional ratios are relevant to the particular type of decisions contemplated. Since balance sheet amounts relate to one instant in time, while the income statement figures refer to transactions and events over a period of time, care must be exercised in calculating ratios that use amounts from both statements. Thus, when an income statement amount is compared with a balance sheet amount, a balance sheet **average** amount often is used to compensate for the difference in time period. In the examples to follow, the selected balance sheet average usually is computed as one half of the sum of the amounts shown on the beginning and ending balance sheets. When additional information is available, such as monthly data, an average of the monthly data is often more representative.

Commonly used financial ratios can be grouped loosely into four categories as follows:[2]

Tests of profitability:

1. Return on owners' investment.
2. Return on total investment.
3. Leverage.
4. Earnings per share (EPS).
5. Profit margin.

Tests of liquidity:

6. Working capital or current ratio.
7. Quick or "acid-test" ratio.
8. Receivable turnover ratio (or average collection period).
9. Inventory turnover ratio (or average days' supply).

Tests of solvency and equity position:

10. Debt/equity ratio.
11. Owners' equity to total equities.
12. Creditors' equity to total equities.

Market tests:

13. Price/earnings ratio (P/E ratio).
14. Dividend yield ratio.

Tests of profitability

Continuing profitability is a primary measure of the overall success of a company; it is a necessary condition for survival. Investors and others would like to be able to rely on a *single measure* of profitability that would be meaningful in all situations. Unfortunately, no single

[2] The numbers to the left are maintained in the subsequent discussions to facilitate reference.

amount has been devised to meet this comprehensive need. Tests of profitability focus on measuring the adequacy of income by comparing it with one or more primary activities or factors that are measured in the financial statements. Five different tests of profitability commonly used are explained below.

1. Return on owners' investment. This ratio is generally regarded as a fundamental test of true profitability. It relates income to the amount of investment that was committed to earning the income. To measure the profitability of any investment, whether for a company, a project, or for an individual investment, the amount of income must be gauged against the resources invested. Investors commit their funds to an enterprise because they expect to earn a return (i.e., a profit) on those funds. Fundamentally, the return on owners' investment ratio is computed as follows:

$$\text{Return on Owners' Investment} = \frac{\text{Income}}{\text{Owners' Equity}}$$

$$\text{Packard Company, 1977} = \frac{\$8{,}800^{*}}{\$102{,}000^{\dagger}} = 8.6 \text{ Percent}$$

* Income *before* extraordinary items generally should be used.

† Average owners' equity is preferable when available; that is, ($100,000 + $104,000) ÷ 2 = $102,000.

Based on Exhibit 16–4.

Thus, Packard Company can be said to have earned 8.6 percent, after income taxes, on the investment provided by the **owners.** Return on owners' investment is a particularly useful measure of profitability from the viewpoint of the owners because it relates the two fundamental factors in any investment situation—the amount of the owners' investment and the return earned for the owners' on that investment. Clearly, it focuses on the viewpoint of the investor.

2. Return on total investment. Another view of the return-on-investment concept relates income to **total assets** used (i.e., total owners' equity plus total liabilities which is total equities) rather than to owners' investment only. Under this broader concept, return on total investment would be computed as follows:

$$\text{Return on Total Investment} = \frac{\text{Net Income}^{*} + \text{Interest Expense (net of tax)}}{\text{Total Assets}^{\dagger}}$$

$$\text{Packard Company, 1977} = \frac{\$8{,}800 + (\$1{,}500 \times .77)}{\$148{,}275} = 6.7 \text{ Percent}$$

* Income before extraordinary items should be used. This assumes an average income tax rate of 23 percent.

† Average total assets should be used; that is: ($150,000 + $146,550) ÷ 2 = $148,275.

Thus, it can be said that the management of Packard Company earned 6.7 percent on **all** of the **resources** employed during the year. This concept views *investment* as the amount of resources provided by both owners and creditors. Thus it is often viewed as a fundamental measure of the management's performance in using all of the resources available.

In computing return on *total* investment, interest expense (net of tax) must be added back to income since it is the return on the creditors' investment and was deducted in deriving income. The denominator represents *total* investment; therefore, interest expense clearly must be added back in order to also raise the numerator to a *total* return basis. Interest net of tax must be used because that is the net cost to the corporation of the funds provided by creditors.

Return on total investment reflects the combined effect of both the operating and the financing activities of a company as illustrated in Exhibit 16–5.

EXHIBIT 16–5
Components of return on investment

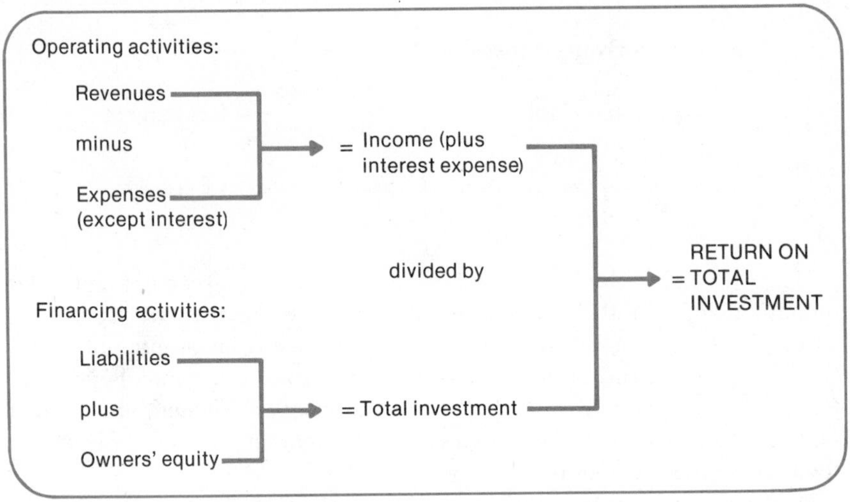

Most analysts compute return-on-investment ratios for both total investment and on owners' equity as illustrated above. Return on total investment is viewed as the preferable measure of **management performance;** that is, management performance in using all of the resources available to the company. The return on owners' equity is viewed as particularly relevant to the owners since it tends to measure the return that has accrued to them.

3. Leverage. Leverage is the advantage, or disadvantage, that derives from earning a return on total investment (total assets) that is different from the return earned on owners' equity. Most companies earn a higher rate on owners' equity than on total equity and thus enjoy a positive leverage. This is because the net interest cost of borrowed funds (debt) is less than the company's earnings rate overall (also some current liabilities have no measurable interest cost).

Leverage can be effectively measured for a company by comparing the two return-on-investment ratios discussed above. The measurement is realistic because the two rates differ only because of the effect of liabilities. The measure of leverage is as follows:

$$\text{Leverage} = \text{Return on Owners' Equity} - \text{Return on Total Assets}$$

$$\begin{aligned}\text{Packard Company, 1977} &= 8.6 \text{ Percent} - 6.7 \text{ Percent}\\ &= 1.90 \text{ Percent (positive leverage)}\end{aligned}$$

When the cost of total debt (interest expense, net of tax) is lower as an average rate than the rate of return on total investment earned by the company, the difference accrues to the benefit of the owners. Of course, this is one reason why most companies adopt a strategy of obtaining from creditors a significant amount of the resources needed.

4. Earnings per share (EPS). This ratio was illustrated in preceding chapters. This test of profitability is strictly from the common stockholders' point of view. Rather than being based on investment it is based on the number of shares of common stock outstanding. It is intended to provide a measure of profitability that can be readily adjusted for the number of shares owned. Basically, earnings per share on common stock is computed as follows:

$$\text{Earnings per Share} = \frac{\text{Income}}{\text{Average Number of Shares of Common Stock Outstanding}}$$

$$\text{Packard Company, 1977} = \frac{\$8,800}{8,500} = \$1.04 \text{ per Share}$$

As illustrated previously, EPS must be computed on (*a*) income before extraordinary items, (*b*) extraordinary items, and (*c*) net income. Of the three EPS amounts, the first one generally is considered the most relevant.

5. Profit margin. This ratio relates only to the income statement. It is computed as follows:

$$\text{Profit Margin} = \frac{\text{Income (before extraordinary items)}}{\text{Net Sales}}$$

$$\text{Packard Company, 1977} = \frac{\$8,800}{\$120,000} = 7.3 \text{ Percent}$$

This profitability test simply expressed the percent of each sales dollar, on the average, that represents profit. It may be interpreted as follows:

a. Income was 0.073 of net sales.
b. Income was 7.3 percent of net sales.
c. \$0.073 of each \$1 of sales was profit.

This ratio also is reflected in the component percentages illustrated in Exhibit 16–4. Some people appear to view this profitability test as the most important measure of overall profitability and, hence, as the fundamental indicator of managerial performance. This view is erroneous because the ratio does not take into account the amount of resources employed (i.e., total investment) to produce the income. For example, the income statements of Company A and Company B may reflect the following:

	Company A	Company B
a. Sales	$100,000	$150,000
b. Income	$ 5,000	$ 7,500
c. Profit margin (b) ÷ (a)	5%	5%
d. Total investment	$ 50,000	$125,000
e. Return on total investment* (b) ÷ (d)	10%	6%

* Assuming no interest expense.

In this example, both companies reported the same profit margin (5 percent). Company A, however, appears to be doing much better because it is earning a 10 percent return on the total investment against the 6 percent earned by Company B. The profit margin percents do not reflect the effect of the $50,000 total investment in Company A against a $125,000 total investment in Company B. The effect of the different amounts of investment in each company is reflected in the return on investment percents. Thus, the profit margin ratio omits one of the two important factors that should be used in evaluating return on the investment.

Tests of liquidity

Current liquidity refers to a company's ability to meet its currently maturing obligations; therefore, it focuses on the relationship between current assets and current liabilities. The ability of a company to meet its current liabilities is an important factor in short-term financial strength. There are two ratios that tend to reflect **current liquidity;** they are the working capital (or current) ratio and the quick (or acid-test) ratio.

6. Working capital ratio. This ratio measures the relationship between current assets and current liabilities at a specific date. It is computed as follows:

$$\text{Working Capital Ratio} = \frac{\text{Current Assets}}{\text{Current Liabilities}}$$

$$\text{Packard Company, 1977} = \frac{\$77{,}400}{\$35{,}400} = \text{2.2 Times or 2.2 to 1}$$

The working capital ratio tends to measure the adequacy of working capital as well as liquidity. It measures the cushion of working capital maintained in order to allow for the inevitable unevenness in the flow of "funds" through the working capital accounts.[3]

7. Quick ratio. This ratio is similar to the working capital ratio except that it is a much more stringent test of current liquidity. It is computed as follows:

$$\text{Quick Ratio} = \frac{\text{Quick Assets}}{\text{Current Liabilities}}$$

$$\text{Packard Company, 1977} = \frac{\$21,400}{\$35,400} = 0.60 \text{ Times or } 0.60 \text{ to } 1$$

Quick assets include cash, short-term investments held in lieu of cash, and accounts receivable (net of the allowance for doubtful accounts). Quick assets are those assets that are presumed to be readily convertible into cash at approximately their stated amounts. Inventories generally are omitted because of uncertainty and the length of the period between their acquisition and their ultimate conversion to cash. However, if they typically turn to cash very quickly, they would be included. Prepaid expenses do not "convert" to cash; rather they only "save" cash in the future, therefore, they are excluded. Thus, the quick or acid-test ratio is much more *severe* test of current liquidity than is the working capital ratio.

8. Receivable turnover. The **current liquidity position** is related to the specific items of working capital. Nearness to cash of a current asset often is measured in terms of **turnover.** There are two ratios, in addition to the two illustrated above, that help show nearness to cash: the receivable turnover and the inventory turnover.

The receivable turnover focuses on measuring the effectiveness of credit and collections. It is computed as follows:

$$\text{Receivable Turnover} = \frac{\text{Net Credit Sales*}}{\text{Average Net Receivables}}$$

$$\begin{array}{l}\text{Packard Company, 1977} \\ \text{(net credit sales assumed} \\ \text{to be \$77,000 for 1977)}\end{array} = \frac{\$77,000}{(\$7,000 + \$8,400) \div 2} = 10 \text{ Times}$$

* Where the amount of credit sales is not known, total sales may be used as a rough approximation.

This is a **turnover ratio** since it reflects how many times the receivables, on the average, were recorded, collected, then recorded again during the period. It expresses the relationship of the average balance in Trade

[3] Occasionally, "working capital" is taken to mean total current assets. This is confusing and unnecessary since "total current assets" is a perfectly good term. Sometimes the term "net working capital" is used to describe the difference between current assets and current liabilities. Throughout this book, we have followed the more general usage of working capital to mean the difference between current assets and current liabilities.

Accounts Receivable and Trade Notes Receivable to the transactions that generated those receivables—credit sales. This turnover ratio tends to measure the effectiveness of the credit-granting and collection activities of the company. The higher the turnover ratio, the better. Granting credit to poor credit risks and ineffective collection efforts will cause this ratio to be low. The receivable turnover often is converted to a time basis known as the average age of the receivables. The computation is as follows:

$$\text{Average Age of Receivables} = \frac{\text{Days in Year}}{\text{Receivable Turnover}}$$

$$\text{Packard Company, 1977} = \frac{365}{10} = 36.5 \text{ Average Days to Collect}$$

The effectiveness of credit and collection activities sometimes is judged by a "rule of thumb" that the *average days to collect* should not exceed $1\frac{1}{2}$ times the credit terms. For example, if the credit terms are 2/10, n/30, the average days to collect should not exceed 45 days (i.e., not more than 15 days past due). Like all rules of thumb, this one is rough and has many exceptions. However, an increase or decrease in the receivable turnover or average days to collect, from one period to the next, would suggest that there were changes in the implementation of credit policies and/or changes in collection efficiency. An increase in the average collection period would indicate an increasing time lag between credit sales and cash realization.

9. Inventory turnover. Inventory turnover tends to measure the liquidity (i.e., nearness to cash) of the inventory. It is the relationship of the inventory to the volume of goods sold during the period. The computation is as follows:

$$\text{Inventory Turnover} = \frac{\text{Cost of Goods Sold}}{\text{Average Inventory}}$$

$$\text{Packard Company, 1977} = \frac{\$72{,}600}{(\$60{,}000 + \$54{,}000) \div 2} = 1.3 \text{ Times}$$

The inventory may be said to have "turned over" 1.3 times on the average during the year since cost of goods sold was 1.3 times the average inventory level. Typically, this ratio is high for grocery stores and relatively low for heavy equipment dealers. Since a profit normally is realized each time the inventory is sold (i.e., turned over), an increase in the ratio is favorable, up to a point. The higher the ratio, the shorter the average "shelf span" for the items stocked. On the other hand, if the ratio is too high, sales may be lost because of items that are out of stock. The turnover ratio often is converted to a time-basis expression called the **average days' supply in inventory.** The computation would be:

$$\text{Average Days' Supply in Inventory} = \frac{\text{Days in Year}}{\text{Inventory Turnover}}$$

$$\text{Packard Company, 1977} = \frac{365}{1.3}$$

$$= 281 \text{ Average Day's Supply in Inventory}$$

(Another example: A turnover ratio of 12.0 would convert as 365 ÷ 12.0 = 30 + average days' supply in inventory.) Turnover ratios are used widely because they are easy to understand.

Tests of solvency and equity position

We noted above that current liquidity refers to the current assets and current liabilities. In contrast, **solvency** (as often used) refers to the ability of a company to meet its **long-term obligations** on a continuing basis. **Equity position** refers to the relative amount of resources provided by the two equities: creditors' equity (i.e., debt capital) and owners' equity (i.e., equity capital). Since the sum of these two equities equals total equities (i.e., total investment), certain critical relationships are significant. The three ratios discussed below are used to reflect these relationships in different ways.

10. Debt/equity ratio. This ratio expresses the direct proportion between debt and owners' equity. It is computed as follows:

$$\text{Debt/Equity Ratio} = \frac{\text{Total Liabilities (i.e., creditors' equity)}}{\text{Owners' Equity}}$$

$$\text{Packard Company, 1977} = \frac{\$42{,}550}{\$104{,}000} = 0.41 \text{ (or 41 percent)}$$

In effect, this ratio states that for each $1 of owners' equity, there is $0.41 of liabilities.

11. Owners' equity to total equity. Instead of the single ratio (debt/equity), some people prefer two ratios that in combination measure the same relationship—owners' equity to total equities and creditors' equity to total equities.

Owners' equity to total equities is computed as follows:

$$\text{Owners' Equity to Total Equities} = \frac{\text{Owners' Equity}}{\text{Total Equities (i.e., liabilities plus owners' equity)}}$$

$$\text{Packard Company, 1977} = \frac{\$104{,}000}{\$146{,}550} = 0.71 \text{ (or 71 percent)}$$

12. Creditors' equity to total equities. This ratio is computed as follows:

$$\text{Creditors' Equity to Total Equities} = \frac{\text{Creditors' Equity (i.e., liabilities)}}{\text{Total Equities}}$$

$$\text{Packard Company, 1977} = \frac{\$42{,}550}{\$146{,}550} = 0.29 \text{ (or 29 percent)}$$

Obviously, the latter two ratios are complements of each other; they will always sum to 1.00 or 100 percent. They indicate the relative amount of total resources provided by each of the two groups of suppliers of capital to the business. Debt capital is risky for the company because there are (*a*) specific maturity dates for the principal amounts and (*b*) specific interest payments that must be made. Both claims are enforceable by law and do not depend upon the earning of income by the company. In contrast, capital supplied by owners does not give rise to similar obligations; that is, it is not fixed as to amounts and dates of principal and dividend payments. Thus, equity capital generally is viewed as much less risky for the company.

In the long run, earnings rates on stockholders' equity normally must be higher than interest rates paid to creditors. Despite the element of debt risk to the company, because of leverage, it may be advantageous to the stockholders if the company derives significant amounts of capital through borrowing. For example, assume a company is earning 15 percent return on total equities (i.e., on total investment), while its borrowing rate on debt is seven percent on the average. To the extent that there is capital provided by debt, the 8 percent difference between the earnings rate on total resources (15 percent) and the interest paid to the creditors (7 percent) accrues to the benefit of the stockholders.[4] In the long run, the stockholders benefit by the 15 percent earned on the resources provided by them, plus the difference between the 15 percent return and the 7 percent interest rate paid on the resources provided by the creditors. This effect is known as leverage as discussed on page 642. A company with a high proportion of debt (such as bonds payable) is said to be **highly levered.** The debt/equity ratio or, alternatively, the two equity ratios indicate the balance that the management has attained between these two sources of capital.

Market tests

A number of ratios have been developed to measure the "market worth" of a share of stock. Basically, these market tests attempt to re-

[4] Interest expense on debt is a deductible expense on the income tax return; in contrast, payments to stockholders by means of dividends are not. Thus, in addition to the lower stated rate for debt, funds obtained by means of debt tend to be less costly because of the tax saving. The real cost of debt in the above example depends upon the income tax rate.

late the current market price of a share of stock to some indicator of the profit (or gain) that might accrue to an investor. They focus on the *current market price* of the stock because that is the amount the buyer would have to invest. There are two market test ratios that are widely quoted by analysts, stockbrokers, investors, and others. They are the price/earnings ratio and the dividend yield ratio.

13. Price/earnings ratio. This ratio measures the relationship between the current market price of the stock and its earnings per share. Assuming a current market price of \$15.60 per share for 1977, it is computed as follows:

$$\text{Price/Earnings Ratio} = \frac{\text{Current Market Price per Share}}{\text{Earnings per Share}}$$

$$\text{Packard Company, 1977} = \frac{\$15.60}{\$1.04^*} = 15 \text{ (or 15 to 1)}$$

* Page 643.

Thus, it is said that this stock was selling at 15 times the earnings per share. This ratio is frequently referred to as the multiple. The P/E ratio is widely used as an indicator of the future potentials of the stock. It changes with each change in the current market price per share and with each earnings report.

Sometimes the components of this ratio are inverted, giving what is referred to as the capitalization rate. This is said to be the rate at which the stock market apparently is capitalizing the current earnings. For example, computation of the capitalization of current earnings per share would be \$1.04 ÷ \$15.60 = 6.67 percent (called the capitalization rate).

14. Dividend yield ratio. This ratio measures the relationship between the dividends per share paid in the past and the market price of the stock. Assuming dividends paid of \$0.75 per share for 1977, it is computed as follows:

$$\text{Dividend Yield Ratio} = \frac{\text{Dividends per Share}}{\text{Market Price per Share}}$$

$$\text{Packard Company, 1977} = \frac{\$0.75}{\$15.60} = 0.0481 \text{ (or 4.81 percent)}$$

The dividend yield ratio measures the current return to the investor, based upon the dividends declared per share (which is revenue to the investor), against the cost of the investment as indicated by the market price per share. Like the P/E ratio, it is a volatile measure since the price of stock may change materially over short periods of time, and each change in market price changes the ratio. This ratio is frequently referred to simply as the "yield."

INTERPRETING RATIOS

In using ratios computed by others, one must realize that the computation of a particular ratio is not standardized. Neither the accounting profession nor security analysts have prescribed the manner in which a ratio should be computed (except for earnings per share). Thus, each user of a financial statement should compute the various ratios in accordance with the specific objectives in mind. There are no agreed-upon standards in this respect. As a consequence, before relying on a ratio or a series of ratios, the user should be informed as to the basic computational approach used. The discussions and illustrations in this section follow the approaches commonly used.

Ratio analyses, along the lines discussed in the preceding paragraphs, catch the attention of many people; however, ratios pose significant interpretative problems to the user. To evaluate a ratio, it must be compared, at least in the mind of the user, with some *standard* that represents an optimum or desirable level. For example, the return-on-investment ratio may be compared with a long-range objective expressed in this manner. Some ratios, by their characteristics, are unfavorable if they are *either* too high or too low. For example, in a certain company a working capital ratio of approximately 2:1 may be considered optimum. In this situation, a ratio of 1:1 would tend to indicate a danger of being unable to meet maturing obligations, whereas, a ratio of 3:1 may indicate that excess funds are being left idle rather than being profitably employed. Furthermore, an optimum ratio for one company frequently will not be the same as the optimum ratio for another company. Thus, comparisons of ratios between companies frequently are of questionable validity, particularly when there are important differences between companies, such as industry and nature of operations.

Another limitation is that most ratios represent *averages* and, therefore, may tend to obscure large variations in the underlying causative factors above and below the average.

Despite these difficulties there are four types of "standards" against which ratios and percents frequently are compared:

1. Comparison of the present ratios with the historical ratios of the same company, with particular attention to changes in the *trend* of each ratio over time.
2. Experience of the analyst who has a subjective feel for the right relationships in a given situation. These subjective judgments of an experienced and competent observer tend to be more reliable than purely mechanical comparisons.
3. Comparison of the present ratios with planned goals and objectives expressed as ratios. Many companies prepare, on a continuing basis, comprehensive profit plans (i.e., budgets) that incorporate realistic

plans for the future. These plans generally incorporate planned goals for significant ratios, such as profit margin and return on investment. These internally developed standards clearly have less inherent difficulties than any of the other comparisons; however, they generally are not available to external parties.

4. Comparison with external standards. These comparisons include the use of ratios and percents from other similar companies and from industry averages. Industry averages are published by many trade associations, governmental agencies, and others. For example, a variety of ratios will be found in the publications of Dun & Bradstreet, Inc., Moody's *Manual of Investments,* and Standard and Poor's *Corporation Records.*

In summary, interpretation of amounts reported on financial statements may be enhanced by expressing certain relationships as ratios or percents. Although a great many ratios can be calculated, a few usually will suffice for a given decision that is under consideration. Having selected the relevant ratios, the analyst has the central problem of evaluating them. This evaluation involves the task of selecting one or more realistic standards with which to compare them. Four types of standards are frequently used: (1) historical standards, (2) experience, (3) planned standards, and (4) external standards. Experience and competence are particularly important. The interpretation of ratios often may suggest strengths and weaknesses in the operations and/or the financial position of the company that should be accorded in-depth investigation and evaluation if significant decisions are contemplated.

Selected ratios are commonly presented in published financial statements. For example, the 15-year summary shown in Exhibit 16–3 reports the following ratios: (1) income per share, (2) dividends per share, (3) working capital ratio, (4) book value per share, (5) return on net sales (i.e., profit margin), and (6) return on average shareholders' equity. Ratios frequently are presented in graphic format. For example, Exhibit 16–6 shows a presentation by the Clark Equipment Company in its 1975 annual report.

PART TWO: EFFECTS OF PRICE-LEVEL CHANGES IN FINANCIAL STATEMENTS

In using and interpreting financial statements, the impact of significant inflationary and deflationary trends should be considered. The impact of inflation on the economy in recent years has been a major concern of government, business, economists, accountants, and others.

The impact of inflation on financial statements is difficult to assess by the user, particularly when price-level information does not appear in the statements. Many accountants and business leaders are not in agreement as to what should be done to assist the statement user in this respect. In this section we will briefly discuss the major issues and approaches that might prove helpful to the decision maker using financial statements.

THE NATURE OF PRICE-LEVEL EFFECTS

Money is the common denominator for accounting measurements. It is a unit of measure of value. That is, a dollar will command a certain amount of **real goods and services** in the marketplace at a given time. Unfortunately, the dollar, or any other monetary unit, does not maintain a stable value in terms of the real goods and services that it will command.

EXHIBIT 16–6
Clark Equipment Company

Clark Equipment Company
Average Annual Performance
Amounts in Thousands

Period	Sales	Net Income	Cash Dividends	Year-End Net Worth
1955-57	$ 139,900	$ 9,055	$ 4,791	$ 53,434
1958-60	182,524	8,531	5,292	67,056
1961-63	222,300	12,254	6,285	87,689
1964-66	426,661	24,663	9,387	135,654
1967-69	561,021	30,362	14,336	190,851
1970-72	771,426	34,797	17,826	280,113
1973-75	1,307,669	50,579	21,310	381,944

Net Sales
in millions of dollars

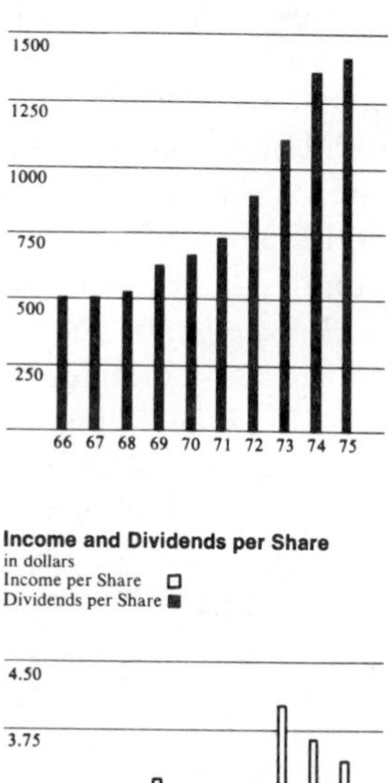

Distribution of the Income Dollar

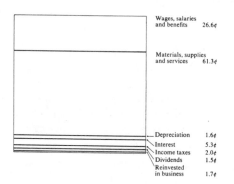

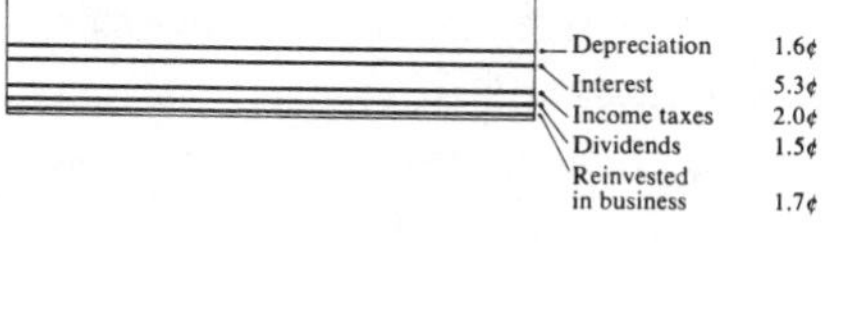

Income and Dividends per Share
in dollars
Income per Share □
Dividends per Share ■

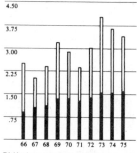

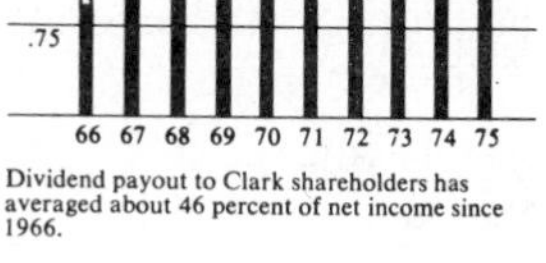

Dividend payout to Clark shareholders has averaged about 46 percent of net income since 1966.

EXHIBIT 16–6 (*continued*)

Net Income
in millions of dollars

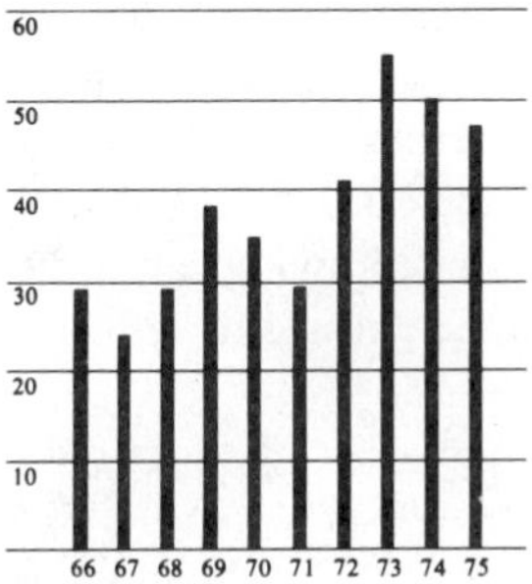

Cash Dividends
in millions of dollars

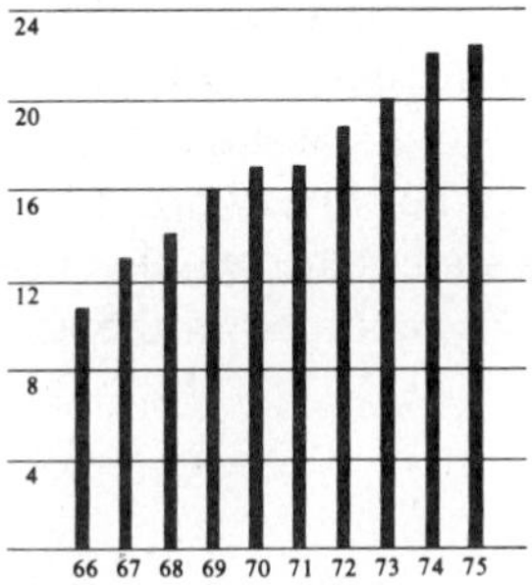

Shareholders' Equity
in millions of dollars

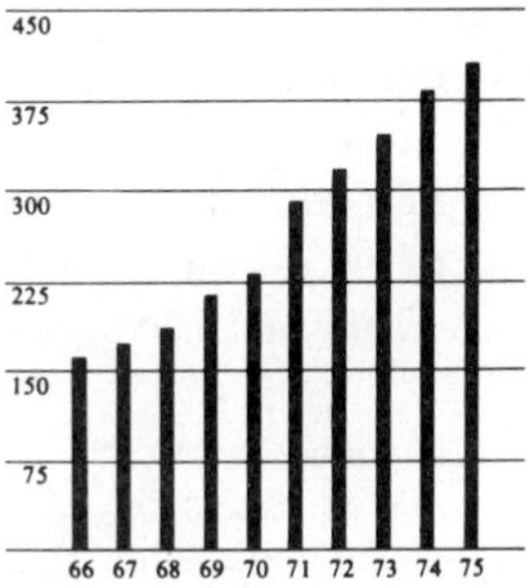

Return on Sales and Equity
in percent
Return on Sales ■
Return on Equity □

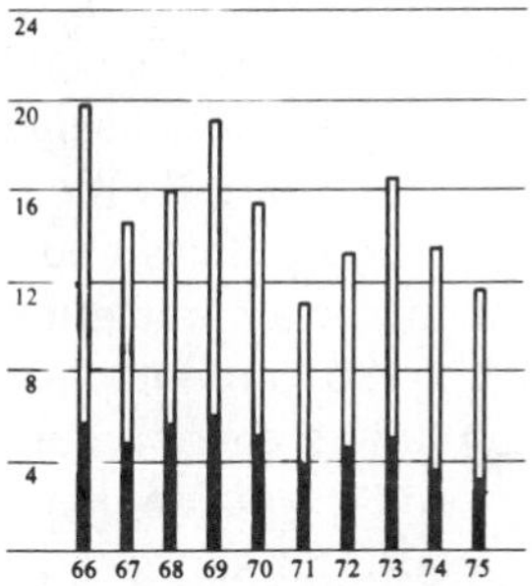

In the last ten years, Clark has shown an average return on shareholders' equity of 15.2 percent and an average return on sales of 4.7 percent.

Capital Expenditures and Depreciation
in millions of dollars
Capital Expenditures ■
Depreciation □

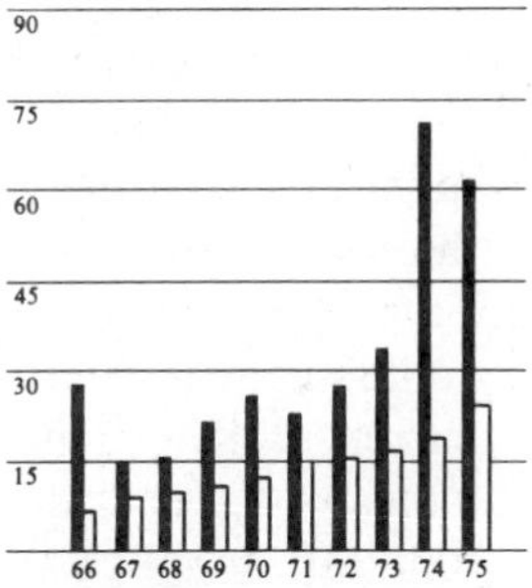

Since 1966, Clark has invested $325 million in new plant and equipment. Depreciation provisions during the period amounted to $140 million.

Clark Sales Growth
Clark Sales ■
Producers Durable Equipment □

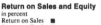

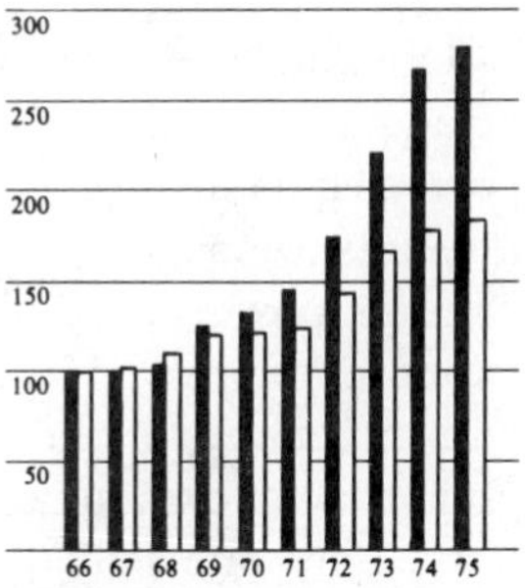

Index: 1966 = 100
*Source: The National Income & Product Accounts of the U.S.
Although subject to the capital goods cycle, Clark's sales performance has been consistently better than the general sales trend of durable goods producers.

Over time, one unit of money (e.g., one dollar) will command fewer goods and services in the case of inflation or, alternatively, more goods and services in the case of deflation; that is, its purchasing power changes. In applying the concept of historical cost (i.e., the cost principle), transactions are recorded in the accounts and subsequently reported in historical dollars. Some of those dollar amounts (such as the cost of a fixed asset) remain in the accounts and are reported in the financial statements over many years. Thus, over a period of time, the accounting system accumulates and reports dollars having different purchasing power, given inflation or deflation. Under the concept of historical cost, dollars having different real values are aggregated on the balance sheet and matched on the income statement. Thus, during periods of significant inflation or deflation, the accounting figures are apt to reflect considerable distortion because of the effects of the changing value of the monetary unit.

To illustrate, assume a company purchased a building for $200,000 when the **general price-level index** was 100.[5] Assuming straight-line depreciation, no residual value, and a 40-year life, the annual depreciation would be $5,000 per year. Let's assume that the current year is Year 30 (since acquisition) and that the current price-level index is 200. At the end of Year 30, the financial statements would show the following amounts, based on historical costs as recorded in the accounting system:

Balance Sheet:		
Fixed Assets:		
Building (at cost)	$200,000	
Accumulated depreciation	150,000	
Book value		$50,000
Income Statement:		
Depreciation expense		$ 5,000

Obviously, all the amounts shown above represent dollars "valued" at acquisition date (30 years earlier). Those dollars had a purchasing power equivalent of 100 (the index). With the current index at 200, these amounts are aggregated with other dollar amounts having a different purchasing power equivalent. On the income statement the depreciation expense, expressed in the dollars at acquisition (index 100), are matched with revenue, which is in current dollars (index 200). The current general price-level index of 200 means that each current dollar will command (buy) only one half (i.e., 100/200) as much real goods and services as when the index was 100. One could *adjust* the above amounts for the price-level change (inflation in this case). The adjustment can be accomplished by multiplying the historical cost amount by a *price-level index ratio.* Using the data given above, the price-level index ratio (often called the multiplier) would be 200/100, or 2.0. Multiplication of the historical dollar amounts by the price-level index ratio raises the cost-based amounts to the **current price-level basis.** The calculations and the resultant adjusted amounts for the data given above would be as follows:

[5] A price-level index is a statistical value that expresses the average price level of each of a series of periods in relative terms. To construct a price-level index, the prices of primary items ordinarily bought are averaged, then expressed as an index number. A base year is selected and assigned the index number of 100. Changes in the average price level then are expressed in relationship to this base. Changes in the index number, from period to period, may be viewed as a measure of inflation (cheaper dollars) and deflation (dearer dollars). For example, a change in the price level from 100 to 200 would indicate significant inflation; on the average, when the index is 200, one dollar will buy only one half as much real goods as when the index was 100.

	Historical cost basis		Price-level index ratio		Adjusted to current price-level basis
Balance Sheet Amounts:					
Fixed Assets:					
Building	$200,000	×	2.0*	=	$400,000
Accumulated depreciation	150,000	×	2.0	=	300,000
Book value	$ 50,000				$100,000
Income Statement Amount:					
Depreciation expense	$ 5,000	×	2.0	=	$ 10,000

* 200/100 = 2.0.

If all the other revenues and expenses were already expressed in current dollars, then the effect of this increase in depreciation expense would be to decrease reported net income by $5,000.

The conversion to the current price-level basis should be done each year. When reading a financial statement for 1976, one is most interested in (and thinks in terms of) 1976 dollars. In 1977, one thinks in terms of 1977 dollars. This is one rationale for restating the amounts each year in terms of the then current dollars (i.e., at the then current price level).

In recent years, the accounting profession has become particularly concerned about the distortion of accounting amounts on the financial statements as a consequence of continued inflationary trends. In periods of inflation, income, unadjusted for the effects of inflation, tends to be overstated. In June 1969, the APB issued *Statement No. 3,* "Financial Statements Restated for General Price-Level Changes," which recommended **supplementary** financial statements, in addition to the regular cost basis statements, that present the amounts restated for general price-level changes. *Statement No. 3* recommends that a business present two sets of financial statements as follows: (1) on the traditional historical cost basis and (2) on an adjusted price-level basis. However, some accountants prefer one set of financial statements with separate columns for the historical cost basis and the adjusted price-level basis. Few companies use the price-level approach since it is not mandatory.

As a basis for discussing and illustrating the basic concept of developing amounts for the financial statements adjusted for price-level changes, a simplified situation will be used. Assume Cole Company has been operating for one year only, 1977. At the start of the year, the general price-level index was 100, and at the end of the year it was 120. (A large price-level change is used to emphasize the effects.) At the end of 1977, the statements shown in Exhibit 16–7 were prepared following the usual accounting approaches (historical cost basis).

The company desires to add a column to each statement entitled "Adjusted for price-level changes to the current price-level basis." The price-

EXHIBIT 16–7

COLE COMPANY
Balance Sheet
At December 31, 1977

	Historical cost basis
Assets	
Cash	$ 34,000
Land	10,000
Building (net)	60,000
Total	$104,000
Liabilities	
Note payable, long term	$ 8,000
Stockholders' Equity	
Capital stock	80,000
Retained earnings	16,000
Total	$104,000

Income Statement
For Year Ended December 31, 1977

Revenues	$ 55,000
Expenses	(33,000)
Depreciation expense	(6,000)
Net Income	$ 16,000

Price-Level Data*

Items	*General price level when acquired or incurred*
Price level at beginning of the year – 100	
Price level at end of the year – 120	
Cash	106.25†
Land purchased	100
Building purchased	100
Note payable executed	100
Capital stock sold	100
Revenues	110†
Expenses	110†
Depreciation expense	100(same as the asset)

* The price-level data given above were developed to be used as a basis for the adjustment or restatement for the price-level changes.

† Since a number of cash, revenue, and expense transactions occurred *uniformly* throughout the year, an average index is used for each of these items for illustrative purposes.

level data given at the bottom of Exhibit 16–7 were developed to be used as a basis for the adjustment or restatement for the price-level changes.

MONETARY AND NONMONETARY ITEMS

To comprehend the restatement of amounts on the financial statements, a careful distinction must be made between two quite different types of items known as **monetary items** and **nonmonetary items.** They cause a quite different impact on the wealth of their holder when the real value of the monetary unit changes (i.e., inflation or deflation).

Monetary items have amounts stated in dollars that are **fixed** in the future by contract, such as a payable or receivable, or are otherwise fixed by their nature, such as cash. For example, the $8,000 note payable, reflected in Exhibit 16–7, requires this specific number of dollars to be paid at maturity, irrespective of inflation or deflation. Thus, the holders of monetary assets or liabilities gain or lose general purchasing power during periods of inflation or deflation simply as a result of changes in the general price level. As another example, cash held during a period of inflation incurs a loss to the holder since each dollar held progressively buys fewer real goods and services. Similarly, if one owes a debt during a period of inflation, there will be a gain for the one owing the obligation because the debt at maturity will be paid off with the specified number of dollars each of which will command fewer real goods and services than when the debt was incurred; that is, the debt will be paid off with cheaper dollars. On the other side, the one to whom the debt is owed will have a loss. In settlement of the debt, the creditor will receive dollars having less purchasing power. *Thus, the fundamental characteristic of monetary items is that the holder incurs a "general price-level gain or loss" during periods of inflation or deflation.* The gain or loss reflects command over real goods and services. The gain or loss on monetary items must be recognized in accounting for price-level changes. Restatement to a price-level adjusted basis must recognize these gains or losses on the *income statement.*

In contrast, **nonmonetary items** do not have amounts that are fixed as to future dollars; they are free to move up and down in respect to the number of dollars they will command in the marketplace. For example, a tract of land purchased for $10,000 when the price index was 100 would *tend* to move up in terms of dollars to a current cash sales price of $12,000 as the result of an increase to 120 of the general price index, assuming no change in real value (i.e., $10,000 × 120/100 = $12,000). Thus, if this happened, the holder would not incur a gain or loss on this nonmonetary asset due to the general price-level change. Under the assumption of no change in real value in this situation, the holder could sell the land that cost $10,000 for $12,000. The $12,000 then would buy at the date of sale the same quantity of real goods that the $10,000 would have bought at the earlier purchase date of the land. Of course, the land may change in "dollar value" more or less than the general price level in which case there would be a real value change. Examples of nonmonetary items are inventories, investments in common stocks, property, fixed assets, and patents. *The fundamental characteristic of nonmonetary items is that the holder does not gain or lose in real purchasing power as a result of changes in the general price level.* That is, no "general price-level gain or loss" will be recognized on nonmonetary items in accounting for price-level changes.

Restatement to a price-level basis requires adjustment of nonmonetary items on the balance sheet. Since nonmonetary items do not create gains or losses as a result of price-level changes, they do not affect the income statement upon restatement. The revenues and expenses reported on the income statement are nonmonetary because they do not have fixed dollar future amounts.

Now, let's return to our example for Cole Company and the two financial statements given in Exhibit 16–7. We will restate them in terms of the current price level. The balance sheet reflects two monetary items—cash and notes payable. As explained above, the *monetary items* are not restated on the balance sheet since they have a fixed monetary amount in the future that cannot be changed. In contrast, the *nonmonetary items* are restated on the balance sheet since their future command over dollars changes with the price level. The historical amount of each nonmonetary item is restated by multiplying each amount by the price-level index number at the end of the year divided by the price-level index number when the transaction occurred (the ratio between these two price-level index numbers often is called the price-level index ratio; see page 654). The restatement of the financial statements is reflected in Exhibit 16–8. The computations are shown in detail.

The income statement amounts are nonmonetary items; therefore they are restated by multiplying the appropriate price-level index ratio by each amount. The gain or loss on the *monetary* items is the difference between the historical cost amount and the restated amounts and must be included on the income statement. The computation of the gain or loss for Cole Company is as follows:

Monetary items	*Historical cost basis*	*Restated to price-level basis*	*Difference gain (loss)*
Cash....................	$34,000	$34,000 × 120/106.25 = $38,400*	$(4,400)
Notes payable.......	8,000	$8,000 × 120/100 = $9,600	1,600
Net price-level loss on monetary items during the period................			$(2,800)

* Rounded.

A comparison of the balance sheet items in Exhibit 16–8 shows that restatement increased total assets from $104,000 to $118,000, which is a

EXHIBIT 16–8

COLE COMPANY
Balance Sheet
At December 31, 1977

	Historical cost basis	Restatement computations	Current price-level basis
Assets			
Cash	$ 34,000	Monetary item, no restatement	$ 34,000
Land	10,000	Nonmonetary item, $10,000 × 120/100	12,000
Building (net)	60,000	Nonmonetary item, $60,000 × 120/100	72,000
Total	$104,000		$118,000
Liabilities			
Note payable, long-term	$ 8,000	Monetary item, no restatement	$ 8,000
Stockholders' Equity			
Capital stock	80,000	Nonmonetary item, $80,000 × 120/100	96,000
Retained earnings	16,000	Restatement per income statement	14,000†
Total	$104,000		$118,000

Income Statement
For Year Ended December 31, 1977

	Historical cost basis	Restatement computations	Current price-level basis
Revenues	$ 55,000	$55,000 × 120/110	$ 60,000
Expenses	(33,000)	$33,000 × 120/110	(36,000)
Depreciation expense	(6,000)	$6,000 × 120/100	(7,200)
Net Income	$ 16,000‡		$ 16,800
Price-level gains (losses) on monetary items:			
Cash		$34,000 − ($34,000 × 120/106.25 = $38,400*) =	(4,400)
Notes payable		8,000 − ($8,000 × 120/100 = $9,600) =	1,600
Net income restated			$ 14,000‡

* Rounded.

† The restated amount of retained earnings agrees with restated net income because this is Year 1. Retained earnings includes the effects of both monetary and nonmonetary items. The balance sheet can be prepared without the income statement, in which case the amount of retained earnings is a "plug figure"; that is, the amount needed to make it balance. It "plugs" correctly because all of the nonmonetary items on the balance sheet (including capital stock) have been restated. Since the monetary items have not been restated at the same time, any price-level losses or gains on them are automatically included in the "plug" amount of retained earnings.

‡ Net income on the historical cost basis ($16,000) is $2,000 higher than restated net income ($14,000) in this example because net monetary assets (which cause a price-level loss to the holder) exceeded net monetary liabilities (which cause a price-level gain to the holder). Thus, the $2,000 difference includes (1) a $800 difference ($16,800 − $16,000) because of restatement of revenues and expenses and (2) the $2,800 loss ($4,400 − $1,600) on monetary items.

13.5 percent increase. In contrast, the income statement reflected a decrease in reported income from $16,000 to $14,000, which is a 12.5 percent decrease. When there is an inflationary trend, and the relationship between monetary assets and monetary liabilities remains essentially constant, price-level adjusted net income usually will be lower than the cost basis amount.

Now that the concept and related procedures to derive price-level adjusted financial statements is understood, let's examine it in overall perspective. The historical cost basis financial statements discussed and illustrated throughout the prior chapters rests on the unit-of-measure assumption (Exhibit 2–1) that the effects of all transactions should be measured in dollars that "existed" at the date of each transaction. In the case of general price-level changes (i.e., inflation or deflation), the historical cost basis financial statements will report dollar amounts that had different purchasing power when recorded than exists at the current date. The concept of price-level adjusted statements retains the historical cost basis amounts *except* that they are restated in current dollars. That is, the historical cost amounts are adjusted for the effects of changes in the value of the monetary unit (inflation or deflation) that have occurred since each transaction was recorded. This means that all historical based dollar amounts reflected in the price-level statements have been adjusted to common (current) dollars each having the same purchasing power. The price-level adjusted income statement includes a new type of gain or loss—price-level gain or loss on monetary items. Those who support the concept of price-level adjusted statements strongly believe that two sets of financial statements should be presented: (1) one set on the traditional cost basis (unadjusted for price-level effects) and (2) another set on the price-level adjusted basis.

The primary arguments for presenting price-level adjusted financial statements are: (1) during periods of significant inflation or deflation, unadjusted statements contain serious distortions that are not revealed; (2) the price-level adjusted amounts, including the gains and losses on monetary items, are important to users of financial statements; and (3) the historical cost basis approach basically is retained with all amounts stated in terms of current dollars. In contrast, the primary arguments against price-level adjusted statements are: (1) two sets of financial statements (one unadjusted and one adjusted) would only confuse the statement user; (2) it is difficult to defend a particular price index to be used for adjustment purposes; (3) statement users would not find the adjusted amounts particularly useful; and (4) price-level effects and real-value changes are not separately revealed.

Despite recommendations included in APB *Statement No. 3* (1969) and significant inflationary trends, industry has exhibited considerable reluctance to present supplementary statements restated for price-level changes.

OTHER ACCOUNTING APPROACHES FOR VALUE CHANGES

Because of the effects on financial statements of significant price changes, consideration is being given accounting approaches, other than price-level adjusted statements, that may deal more effectively with these effects. These approaches vary from application of the Lifo concept to inventories and depreciable assets (a piecemeal approach) to comprehensive **current value accounting** (which has several variants). In considering alternative accounting approaches which may be adopted in the future to replace or supplement historical cost basis statements, we should focus on the relative income statement and balance sheet effects. In the paragraphs to follow, two alternative accounting approaches will be briefly discussed. The discussion will focus on the comparative effects on the financial statements rather than on the record keeping mechanics.

A fundamental point involved in considering price changes is the distinction between (*a*) a change in the *general* prices and (*b*) a change in *specific* prices. Changes in general prices can be measured and reported in terms of a **general price-level index** such as was illustrated in Exhibit 16–8 for the price-level adjusted statements. In contrast, changes in specific prices refer to the price change in a specific item (or group of similar items) such as a machine, an item stocked for sale, or land. Changes in **specific prices** can be measured and reported as illustrated in Exhibit 16–9.

These two distinctly different types of price changes as measured by price indexes, may be illustrated as follows:

Price change measurements

Year	*General—gross national product implicit price deflator index**	*Specific—a commodity group machine tools index†*
1953	88.33	
1958	100.00	100
1963	107.17	110
1968	122.30	128
1973	153.94	170
1975	183.63	200

* Economic Report of the President (Washington, D.C.: U.S. Government Printing Office, 1976).
† Assumed for instructional purposes.

In the above table, the specific price of machine tools increased more rapidly than the increase in the general price level; thus, it can be said that machine tools became relatively more expensive than did the general "package of goods purchased by the average consumer."

Using these two different types of price indexes, the basic concepts underlying the historical cost, general price-level, and specific price-level bases of measuring and reporting the economic effects of price changes can be illustrated.

Assume Company X acquired machine tools at the start of 1959 at a cost of $30,000. Also assume a 30-year estimated useful life and no residual value. At the end of 1975, the machine tools would be reported on the historical cost, general price level and specific price-level bases as shown in Exhibit 16–9 (using the price index amounts given above):

EXHIBIT 16–9
General and specific price changes compared, 1975

	Historical cost	*General price level adjusted**	*Specific price level adjusted†*
Balance Sheet:			
Machine tools	$30,000	$55,089	$60,000
Accumulated depreciation			
(16 years)	16,000	29,381	32,000
Carrying value	$14,000	$25,708	$28,000
Income Statement:			
Depreciation expense	$ 1,000	$ 1,836	$ 2,000

* $30,000 × 183.63/100 = $55,089; $16,000 × 183.63/100 = $29,381
† $30,000 × 200/100 = $60,000; $16,000 × 200/100 = $32,000

The data in Exhibit 16–9 reflect that each of the three alternative accounting approaches measures and reports significantly different effects on the balance sheet and income statement for 1975 (and also for each intervening year since acquisition). Because prices were rising, the asset and accumulated depreciation amounts were higher under both the general and specific price alternatives. Similarly, depreciation expense was higher. Observe that the historical cost basis disregards both the general and specific price changes; the general price-level basis measures and reports only the inflation (or deflation) effects and the specific price-level basis measures and reports the price effects on the specific items. None of them *separately* identify price level effects and real value effects.

The difference between general price-level effects (i.e., inflation or deflation) and real value effects (i.e., specific price changes) should be clearly understood. To illustrate without the complication of depreciation, assume a tract of land was acquired on January 1, 19A at a cost of $20,000 when both the *general* and *specific* price levels were 100. Now assume it is the end of 19A and the general price level is 110 and the specific price level (for this category of land) is 125. The two distinctly different effects of the price changes can be analyzed as follows:

Price-level effect ($20,000 × 110/100) − $20,000	$2,000
Real value change ($20,000 × 125/100) − ($20,000 × 110/100)	3,000
Total price change ($20,000 × 125/100) − $20,000	$5,000

Now let's return to the machine tools example and analyze the effects of the two price changes that would be reported under the historical cost, general price-level and specific price-level bases. Assume the machine tools were sold on the first day of 1976 at their then fair market value (as measured by the specific price index) of $28,000. The entry to record the disposition under each alternative method would be (data from Exhibit 16–9):

	Historical cost		*General price level*		*Specific price level*	
Cash	28,000		28,000		28,000	
Accumulated depreciation	16,000		29,381		32,000	
Machine tools		30,000		55,089		60,000
Gain (loss)		14,000		2,292		

The gain (loss) reported under the three methods are different by material amounts. These differences may be analyzed as follows:

	Computations (Exhibit 16–9)	*Gain (loss)*
Price-level effect	$25,708–$14,000	$11,708
Real value change	$28,000–$25,708	2,292
Gain reported on historical cost basis		$14,000

Observe that the historical cost basis did not recognize either general or price level changes until date of disposition at which time the cumulative effects of both changes are reflected ($14,000). In contrast, the general price-level change recognized only the general price-level change; therefore, the gain on disposal was the amount of the real value change ($2,292). Significantly, the specific price-level basis recognized no gain or loss because during each period the change in the value of the asset, as reflected by the then specific price index, was recognized in the accounts and on the financial statements. These changes are often referred to as *holding gains (or losses).*

In the above discussions, the term "specific price-level basis" was used to emphasize the distinction between general and specific price changes. However, the commonly used designation is **current value accounting.** The term, current value accounting, usually implies that the underlying measurement concept of current market value (carefully defined) will be applied to all elements in the financial statements. Current market value is variously defined (1) on an input basis, such as indexing with specific price indexes and replacement cost or (2) on an output basis, such as net realizable value and discounted value of future cash flows (i.e., net present value).

The preceding discussions and illustrations focused on the impacts of general and specific price changes on financial statements. Decision makers are in an advantageous position if they understand the fundamental nature and effects of these impacts in using and interpreting financial statements. This understanding is particularly important when (1) only historical cost basis statements are available and (2) there have been significant changes in general and specific prices. It is for these reasons that so much attention currently is being accorded such topics as reporting and/or disclosing replacement cost, current value, reproduction cost, net realizable value, or appraisal values.

IMPORTANT TERMS

Comparative statements
Ratio or percentage analysis
Component percentages
Tests of profitability
Leverage
Tests of liquidity
Turnover ratios
Tests of solvency
Equity position
Market tests
Price-level effects
Monetary items
Nonmonetary items
Price-level restatement
General price-level index
Specific price-level index
Current value accounting

QUESTIONS FOR DISCUSSION

1. What are the three fundamental uses of external financial statements by decision makers?
2. What are some of the primary items on financial statements about which creditors are concerned?
3. Explain why the notes to the financial statements are particularly important in use and interpretation.
4. What is the primary purpose of comparative financial statements?
5. Explain what is meant by ratio analysis.
6. What are component percentages?
7. Explain return on investment. Why is it considered to be the primary indicator of profitability?
8. Contrast the working capital ratio with the quick ratio.
9. What does the debt/equity ratio reflect?
10. Why are statement users especially interested in financial summaries covering a number of years?
11. What is meant by a price-level change? Explain the meaning of a general price-level index.
12. What is meant by restatement of the financial statements for price-level effects?
13. Distinguish between monetary and nonmonetary items. Explain their impacts on the business when there is inflation.

14. Explain why monetary items are not restated on the balance sheet and why nonmonetary items are restated.
15. Explain why monetary items affect the income statement but nonmonetary items do not.
16. Explain the difference between (*a*) price-level changes and (*b*) real value changes for an asset.

EXERCISES

PART ONE: EXERCISES 16–1 TO 16–4

E16–1. The comparative financial statements prepared at December 31, 1977, for Walker Company reflected the following data (summarized):

	1977	*1976*
Income Statement:		
Sales	$150,000*	$140,000
Cost of goods sold	90,000	85,000
Gross margin on sales	60,000	55,000
Operating expenses and interest expense	43,000	40,500
Pretax income	17,000	14,500
Income taxes	5,000	4,500
Net Income	$ 12,000	$ 10,000
Balance Sheet:		
Cash	$ 8,000	$ 11,000
Accounts receivable (net)	12,000	14,000
Inventory	30,000	28,000
Fixed assets (net)	50,000	43,000
	$100,000	$ 96,000
Current liabilities (no interest)	$ 15,000	$ 17,000
Long-term liabilities (6% interest)	35,000	35,000
Common stock (par $10)	40,000	40,000
Retained earnings†	10,000	4,000
	$100,000	$ 96,000

* One third were credit sales.
† During 1977, cash dividends amounting to $6,000 were declared and paid.

Required:

a. Complete the following columns for each item in the above comparative financial statements:

Increase (decrease) 1977 over 1976	
Amount	*Percent*

b. Respond to the following:
   1. What was the percentage increases in sales, net income, cash, inventory, liabilities, and owners' equity?

2. By what amount did working capital change?
3. Did the average income tax rate change? What was the percentage change in the rate?
4. What was the amount of cash inflow from revenues for 1977?
5. Did the average markup realized on goods sold change?

E16–2. Use the data given in Exercise 16–1 for Walker Company.

Required:

a. Present component percentages for 1977 only.

b. Respond to the following for 1977:
1. What was the average percentage markup on sales?
2. What was the average income tax rate?
3. What was the profit margin?
4. What percent of total resources was invested in fixed assets?
5. What was the debt/equity ratio? Does it look good or bad? Explain.
6. What was the return on owners' equity?
7. What was the return on total equities?
8. What was the leverage factor? Explain.

E16–3. Use the data given in Exercise 16–1 for Walker Company. Use a separate sheet and complete the following tabulation for 1977 only (assume a common stock price of $33 per share); compute the ratios that should be included under each category:

Name and Computation of the Ratio (show computations)	Brief Explanation and Meaning of the Ratio
A. Tests of profitability: Return on investment ratio (on total investment) Etc.	
B. Tests of liquidity: Working capital ratio Etc.	
C. Tests of solvency and equity position: Debt/equity ratio Etc.	
D. Market tests: Price/earnings ratio Etc.	

E16–4. Dodson Company has just prepared the comparative annual financial statement for 1977.

DODSON COMPANY
Income Statement
For the Years Ended December 31, 1977, and 1976

	For the year ended			
		1977		1976
Sales (one half on credit)		$100,000		$ 95,000
Cost of goods sold		48,000		46,000
Gross margin on sales		52,000		49,000
Expenses (including $2,000 interest expense each year)		34,000		33,000
Pretax income		18,000		16,000
Income taxes on operations (22%)		3,960		3,520
Income before extraordinary items		14,040		12,480
Extraordinary loss	$3,000			
Less income taxes saved	660	2,340		
Extraordinary gain			$1,000	
Applicable income tax			220	780
Net Income		$ 11,700		$ 13,260

Balance Sheet
At December 31, 1977, and 1976

	1977	1976
Assets		
Cash	$ 47,200	$ 20,000
Accounts receivable (net)	35,000	30,000
Inventory	30,000	40,000
Fixed assets (net)	90,000	100,000
Total Assets	$202,200	$190,000
Liabilities		
Accounts payable	$ 60,000	$ 50,000
Income taxes payable	1,500	1,000
Notes payable, long term	25,000	25,000
Stockholders' Equity		
Capital stock (par $10)	80,000	80,000
Retained earnings	35,700	34,000
Total Liabilities and Stockholders' Equity	$202,200	$190,000

Required:

a. Compute for 1977 the tests of (1) profitability, (2) liquidity, (3) solvency, and (4) market. Assume the quoted price of the stock to be $26.50 for 1977. Dividends paid during 1977 amounted to $10,000.

b. Respond to the following for 1977:
   1. What was the percentage change in sales, income before extraordinary items, net income, cash, inventory, and debt?
   2. Did the average income tax rate change from 1976 to 1977? By how much?

c. Identify two problems for the company suggested by your response to (*a*) and (*b*).

PART TWO: EXERCISES 16–5 TO 16–6

E16–5. The balance sheet for Wells Company, prepared on the usual historical cost basis at December 31, 1977, has been completed. Supplemental statements are to be developed on a "restated price-level basis." The following four items were selected from the balance sheet:

	Historical cost basis (when acquired)	*General price-level index (when acquired or incurred)*
Receivables	$69,000	115
Investment, stocks	42,000	105
Land, plant site	15,000	100
Payables	99,000	110

The price level at the end of 1977 was 120.

Required:

a. Indicate which are monetary and which are nonmonetary items.

b. Set up a table to derive the amount "Restated price-level basis" that should be shown on the supplementary balance sheet for each item. Show computations.

c. Compute the gain or loss resulting from price-level changes that will be shown on the price-level adjusted income statement. Show computations.

d. Explain why certain of the items were omitted from your computation in (*c*).

E16–6. In 1957, Klassen Company purchased a plant site for $23,100. Immediately thereafter, construction of a plant building was started. The building was completed in June 1958 at a cost of $336,000. The building is being depreciated on a straight-line basis assuming an estimated useful life of 30 years and no residual value.

Assume the price-level index in 1957 was 110, in 1958 it was 112, and at the end of 1977 it was 180.

Required:

a. Complete a tabulation similar to the following:

	Amount to be reported assuming:	
	Historical cost basis	*Price-level adjusted basis*
Balance Sheet at December 31, 1977:		
Fixed Assets:		
Land		
Building		
Less accumulated depreciation (20 years)		
Income Statement for 1977:		
Depreciation expense		

Show your computations.

b. Would the price-level change affect income tax expense for 1977 for the company? Explain. Do you think it should? Explain.

PROBLEMS

PART ONE: PROBLEM 16–1

P16–1. Speedy Sales Corporation had just completed the comparative statements for the year ended December 31, 1977. At this point, certain analytical and interpretative procedures are to be undertaken. The completed statements (summarized) are as follows:

	1977	*1976*
Income Statement:		
Sales	$400,000*	$390,000
Cost of goods sold	220,000	218,000
Gross margin on sales	180,000	172,000
Operating expenses (including interest on bonds)	147,000	148,000
Pretax income	33,000	24,000
Income taxes	9,000	7,000
Net income	$ 24,000	$ 17,000
Balance Sheet:		
Cash	$ 25,400	$ 2,700
Accounts receivable (net)	24,000	30,000
Merchandise inventory	30,000	24,000
Prepaid expenses	600	500
Fixed assets (net)	120,000	130,000
	$200,000	$187,200
Accounts payable	$ 19,000	$ 20,000
Income taxes payable	1,000	1,200
Bonds payable (5% interest rate)	50,000	50,000
Common stock (par $10)	100,000†	100,000
Retained earnings‡	30,000	16,000
	$200,000	$187,200

* Twenty-five percent were credit sales.

† The market price of the stock at the end of 1977 was $24 per share.

‡ During 1977 the company declared and paid a cash dividend of $10,000.

Required:

a. Prepare the "Increase (decrease)" columns for "Amount" and "Percent" for 1977 over 1976.

b. Compute the sixteen component percentages for 1977.

c. Based upon the comparative data, complete a tabulation similar to the following (show computations):

Name and Computation of the Ratio (use those illustrated in the chapter)	Ratio Amount	Brief Explanation of the Ratio
A. Tests of profitability		
B. Tests of liquidity		
C. Tests of solvency and equity position		
D. Market tests		

d. Respond to the following for 1977:

1. Did the average markup on sales change? By what percent?
2. Did the average income tax rate change? By what percent?
3. Did the change in the leverage factor look good or bad? Explain.

PART TWO: PROBLEMS 16–2 TO 16–5

P16–2. Barber Company has prepared the annual financial statements at December 31, 1977. The company is considering the development of supplemental statements on the "restated price-level basis." The following seven items were selected from the balance sheet:

Items	*Historical cost basis (when acquired)*	*General price-level index (when acquired or incurred)*
1. Cash	$ 14,800	148
2. Merchandise inventory	58,000	145
3. Accounts receivable (net)	28,800	144
4. Land	12,000	100
5. Building (net)	157,500	105
6. Accounts payable	42,000	140
7. Bonds payable	88,000	110

At the end of 1977 the price-level index was 150.

Required:

a. Group the above items into two categories: monetary and non-monetary.

b. Set up a table and compute the amount "Restated price-level basis" that should be shown on the balance sheet for each of the seven items. Show calculations. Round to even $100 in the restatement.

c. Compute the loss or gain resulting from the price-level changes that will be shown on the price-level adjusted income statement. Show calculations.

d. Explain why certain of the seven items were omitted from your computations in (*c*).

e. Assume the land had a fair-market value of $20,000 on December 31, 1977. Analyze the changes in dollar value since acquisition.

P16–3. At the end of the first year of operations, Clark Company prepared the following balance sheet and income statement:

CLARK COMPANY
Balance Sheet
At December 31, 1977

Assets	
Cash	$ 3,330
Accounts receivable (net)	5,650
Inventory	46,000
Fixed assets (net)	55,000
Total	$109,980
Liabilities	
Accounts payable	$ 3,480
Bonds payable	23,000
Stockholders' Equity	
Capital stock	66,000
Retained earnings	17,500
Total	$109,980

Income Statement
For the Year Ended December 31, 1977

Revenues	$ 69,000
Expenses (not detailed)	(46,000)
Depreciation expense	(5,500)
Net Income	$ 17,500

Price-Level Data

Items	*General price level (when acquired or incurred)*
Price level at start of year – 110	
Price level at end of year – 120	
Cash	111*
Accounts receivable	113*
Inventory	115
Fixed assets	110
Accounts payable	116
Bonds payable	115
Revenues	115*
Expenses	115*
Depreciation expense	110
Capital stock	110

* Averages.

Required:

a. Recast the income statement and balance sheet with the following headings: (1) Historical Cost Basis, (2) Restatement Computations, and (3) Current Price-Level Basis.

b. Explain why net income is different between the two statements; identify amounts.

c. Why were the nonmonetary items, but not the monetary, restated on the balance sheet?

d. Does the price-level income statement better match expenses with revenues? Explain.

e. Assume the fixed assets had a fair-market value of $75,000 on December 31, 1977. Analyze the dollar changes since acquisition. Explain.

P16–4. After operating for one year, Todd Company completed the following income statement and balance sheet:

TODD COMPANY
Balance Sheet
At December 31, 1977

Assets

Cash	$ 42,300
Accounts receivable (net)	29,580
Long-term investment, stock of Company X	7,400
Land	11,200
Plant (net)	140,000
Total	$230,480

Liabilities

Accounts payable	$ 5,880
Bonds payable	28,000

Stockholders' Equity

Capital stock	182,000
Retained earnings	14,600
Total	$230,480

Income Statement
For the Year Ended December 31, 1977

Revenues	$ 87,000
Expenses (not detailed)	(58,400)
Depreciation expense	(14,000)
Net Income	$ 14,600

Price-Level Data

Items	*General price level (when acquired or incurred)*
Price level at start of year—140	
Price level at end of year—150	
Cash	141*
Accounts receivable	141*
Long-term investment purchased	148
Land purchased	140
Plant acquired	140
Accounts payable	147*
Bonds payable sold	140
Capital stock	140
Revenues	145*
Expenses	146*
Depreciation expense	140

* Averages of a number of transactions in each instance.

Required:

a. Recast the income statement and balance sheet with the following headings: (1) Historical Cost Basis, (2) Restatement Computations, and (3) Current Price-Level Basis.

b. Explain why net income is different between the two statements; identity amounts.

c. Why were the nonmonetary items, but not the monetary, restated on the balance sheet?

d. Does the price-level income statement better match expenses with revenues? Explain.

e. Assume the land had a fair-market value of $20,000 on December 31, 1977. Analyze the dollar changes since acquisition. Explain.

P16–5. This problem pinpoints the different effects of monetary and nonmonetary items in the price-level restatement of financial statements.

On January 1, 19A, Company X acquired Asset A (monetary), $10,000, and Asset B (nonmonetary), $20,000, by incurring a liability of $12,000 and issuing common stock, $18,000.

At the end of 19A, the company prepared the following summarized financial statements:

Balance Sheet
At December 31, 19A

Asset A	$10,000
Asset B	20,000
Asset C (nonmonetary)	3,300
Total	$33,300
Liability	$12,000
Capital stock	18,000
Retained earnings	3,300
Total	$33,300

Income Statement
For Year Ended December 31, 19A

Revenues	$ 8,800
Expenses	5,500
Net Income	$ 3,300

Price-level index at January 1, 19A	100
Price-level index at December 31, 19A	120
Average price-level for Asset C, revenues, and expenses	110

Required:

a. Compute the price-level gain or loss for 19A. Show computations. Explain the nature of the amount computed.

b. Prepare a price-level adjusted income statement. Explain why price-level net income is different from net income reported by the company. Show computations.

c. Prepare a price-level adjusted balance sheet. Explain why certain items were not restated.

d. Explain why retained earnings restated is the same as net income restated.

e. Assume Asset B has a fair-market value of $25,000 at the end of 19A. Prepare an analysis, with a brief explanation, of the change in acquisition price and the fair market value at the end of the year.

17

Consolidated statements—measurement and reporting

PURPOSE OF THE CHAPTER

Chapter 14 discussed long-term investments in those situations where one company owns 50 percent or less of the outstanding voting stock of another corporation. This chapter focuses on those situations where there is a controlling interest evidenced by ownership of more than 50 percent of the outstanding voting stock of another corporation. Prior to studying this chapter you should reread Chapter 14.

A general understanding of a controlling interest, consolidation concepts, and consolidated financial statements is important at this level of your study of accounting. Those who do not plan to study accounting beyond the introductory level need this general background in order to understand and evaluate the economic and accounting implications of business combinations. In most business courses, financial statements are encountered in various situations, and most of them will be consolidated statements. Outside the classroom, you will frequently encounter consolidated statements. For those who plan to study accounting further, this background will be quite useful. An understanding of the broad issues, measurement approaches, and underlying concepts of consolidated statements is important to the statement user. This chapter has as its primary objective the presentation of these basic issues.

When an investor company owns over 50 percent of the outstanding voting stock of another corporation, a **parent** and **subsidiary** relationship is said to exist. The **investing** company is known as the **parent** company, and the **other** corporation is called a **subsidiary.** Both corporations continue as **separate legal entities,** and separate financial statements for each are prepared. However, because of their special relationship, they are viewed as a **single economic entity** for **financial measurement** and **reporting purposes.** They are generally called related or affiliated companies, and the parent company (but not the subsidiary) is required to prepare **consolidated financial statements.** To accomplish this, the individual financial statements of the parent and each of its subsidiaries are combined into one overall or consolidated set of financial statements, as if there were only one entity. The three required statements—balance sheet, income statement, and statement of changes in financial position—are consolidated by the parent company.

This chapter focuses on the interpretation and use of consolidated financial statements. Measurement approaches and reporting on a consolidated basis are accorded primary attention. The important differences that result between a pooling of interests and a combination by purchase are identified and discussed. For those who desire to gain a greater depth of understanding of the measurement and consolidation procedures involved, Appendixes A and B have been included.

THE CONCEPT OF CONSOLIDATED STATEMENTS

There are a number of operating, economic, and legal advantages to the parent-subsidiary relationship. As a consequence, most large corporations, and many medium-sized corporations, own more than 50 percent of the outstanding voting stock of one or more other corporations.

Consolidated statements are prepared in situations where two basic elements are present that relate to two or more different corporations. The two basic elements are control and economic compatibility.

Control is presumed to exist when over 50 percent of the voting stock of another entity is owned by one investor. The nonvoting stock is not included in this determination because it does not extend any avenue for control to the investor. In special circumstances, effective control may not exist, even though over 50 percent of the voting stock is owned. This situation may exist when the subsidiary is located in a foreign country where governmental restrictions are such that the parent company is powerless to exert meaningful control. In such circumstances, since control is lacking, consolidated statements would be inappropriate.

Economic compatibility means that the operations of the companies are related so that one complements the other. For example, a company manufacturing a major item and a subsidiary manufacturing a component part of the major item would have economic compatibility. On the other hand, a manufacturing company and a bank may lack economic compatability and would not be consolidated. When one company owns over 50 percent of the voting stock of another company, but for other reasons does not qualify for consolidation, the latter is reported as a long-term investment on the balance sheet as "Investment in unconsolidated subsidiary." In this case it is accounted for under the equity method as discussed in Chapter 14 and is not consolidated.

The concept of consolidated statements relates *only to reporting* by the parent company of the financial results of the parent and its subsidiaries as one economic unit. Otherwise, the accounting for each business is unaffected. The fact that another company owns a controlling interest has no affect on the accounting and reporting by a subsidiary. At the end of the accounting period, the subsidiary prepares its own financial statements. Similarly, the parent company carries out the accounting for its own operations in the normal manner and prepares its own financial statements at the end of each period.

Under the concept of consolidated statements, the financial statements of the parent and the subsidiaries, prepared in the normal manner, are combined, or aggregated, by the parent company on an **item-by-item basis** to develop the consolidated financial statements. Thus, the consolidated statement concept does not affect the recording of transactions by the parent and the subsidiaries but affects only the **reporting phase** of the combined entity represented by the parent company.

At the end of the chapter, a set of actual consolidated statements are presented for study.

ACQUIRING A CONTROLLING INTEREST

One corporation may acquire a controlling interest in another corporation either (1) by organizing a new entity and *retaining* over 50 percent of the capital stock of the new corporation; or (2) by *acquiring* over 50 percent of the outstanding stock of an existing corporation. Both approaches in acquiring a controlling interest (to establish a parent-subsidiary relationship) are widely used. Basically, the parent company may acquire over 50 percent of the voting capital stock of the other entity in one of two ways as follows:[1]

1. Exchanging shares by the parent of its own unissued capital stock (and sometimes treasury stock) for the outstanding shares of capital stock of the subsidiary (owned by the shareholders of the subsidiary)—Under certain circumstances, this is known as a combination by a **pooling of interests.** In this situation, the shareholders of the subsidiary give up their shares and become shareholders only of the parent company.

[1] This is the basic distinction between pure combination by pooling of interest and a pure purchase. However, a controlling interest may be acquired in part by a stock exchange and in part by a cash purchase. In these "nonpure" situations, a rigid list of criteria must be met to qualify as a pooling of interest (see footnote 2); otherwise, the combination must be accounted for as a combination by purchase.

EXHIBIT 17–1

COMPANY P AND COMPANY S
Separate Balance Sheets
January 1, 1977, Immediately before Acquisition

		Company P		Company S
Cash		$205,000		$ 35,000
Accounts receivable (net)*		15,000		30,000
Receivable from Company S		10,000		
Inventories		170,000		70,000
Plant and equipment (net)*		100,000		45,000
Total		$500,000		$180,000
Accounts payable		$ 60,000		$ 20,000
Payable to Company P				10,000
Stockholders' Equity:				
Common stock, Company P (par $6)	$300,000			
Common stock, Company S (par $10)			$100,000	
Retained earnings	140,000	440,000	50,000	150,000
Total		$500,000		$180,000

* Accounts receivable, less the allowance for doubtful accounts; and plant and equipment, less accumulated depreciation. The net amounts are used to simplify the example. The end results will be the same as they would have been had the separate contra accounts been used.

2. Purchasing by the parent with cash, other assets, or debt from the individual stockholders the capital stock of the subsidiary—This is known as a combination by **purchase.** In this situation, the shareholders of the subsidiary sell their shares and subsequently are not shareholders of either the parent or the subsidiary.

The different economic impacts and accounting measurements (as reflected in the consolidated financial statements) were significant factors in the merger movement that characterized the 1960s. The merger trend is continuing, although considerably diminished, in the 1970s. The next few paragraphs will discuss the major impacts, the problems of measurement, and reporting on the consolidated financial statements.

Throughout the chapter we will use a continuing example to illustrate the measurement approaches involved and the consolidated financial statements. We will use data for Company P (the parent) and Company S (the acquired subsidiary). Assume that on January 1, 1977 (just prior to the acquisition), the balance sheets for Company P and Company S reported the data shown in Exhibit 17–1.

POOLING OF INTERESTS

When one corporation acquires a controlling interest in the stock of another corporation without buying it but by *exchanging* its own shares, a purchase/sale transaction between the parties often is deemed not to have been consummated.[2] The parent company has simply issued its own stock certificates for the stock certificates of the subsidiary company. Because there was no purchase/sale transaction, the cost principle is not applied. Thus, under the consolidation concept, the exchange of stock, in many cases, is viewed as a pooling of interests rather than as a purchase. As a consequence, when the financial statements of the parent and subsidiary are combined, the **book values** of each, as shown on their respective financial statements, are added together with no consideration for the current market values of the assets of the subsidiary.

Assume that on January 2, 1977, Company P (the parent) acquired all of the outstanding stock of Company S (the subsidiary) by exchanging with the shareholders of Company S one share of Company P stock for each share of Company S stock. Thus, the shareholders of Company S turned in all of their 10,000 shares and received in return 10,000 shares of unissued Company P stock. They are now shareholders of Company P and no longer shareholders of Company S. After the exchange, Company P owns all of the outstanding shares of Company S; that is, it owns a 100 percent interest in Company S. Accordingly, Company P would make the following journal entry in its accounts:

January 2, 1977:

Investment in Company S stock (10,000 shares; 100 percent)...	150,000	
Common stock (10,000 shares par $6)		60,000
Contributed capital, from pooling of interests		90,000
Acquisition by pooling of interests.		

Observe that the long-term investment account is debited for the *book value* of the Company S stock as shown on the books of Company S ($100,000 + $50,000). This amount is used because that is the book value of the owners' equity in Company S, which Company P now controls. The Common Stock account is credited for the number of shares issued times the par value per share, and Contributed Capital, from Pooling of Interests is credited for the difference. The cost principle is not involved in the debit to the investment account (an asset) because there was no *purchase* of the stock, only a pooling of interests by exchanging "paper." The exchange of shares of stock would have no effect on the accounts of the subsidiary, Company S.

[2] APB *Opinion No. 16*, "Business Combinations," (August 1970) states precise conditions under which a business combination *must* be measured and reported as a pooling of interests. The *Opinion* states: "The combination of existing voting common stock interests by the exchange of stock is the essence of a business combination accounted for by the pooling of interests." The *Opinion* specifies a number of additional conditions that if present *require* use of the pooling-of-interests method. Because of these conditions, many stock exchanges (particularly if cash also is involved) do not qualify for the pooling-of-interests method. All combinations not meeting the specified conditions must be accounted for by the purchase method. The usual, although not exclusive, mode of combination in these latter situations is by disbursement of cash or by incurring debt for the stock.

After the above journal entry is posted to the ledger accounts of Company P, the two separate balance sheets then would be changed as shown in Exhibit 17–2.

EXHIBIT 17–2

COMPANY P AND COMPANY S
Separate Balance Sheets (pooling-of-interests basis)
January 2, 1977, Immediately after Acquisition

	Company P	*Company S*
Cash	$205,000	$ 35,000
Accounts receivable (net)	15,000	30,000
Receivable from Company S	10,000	
Inventories	170,000	70,000
Investment in Company S (100%)	150,000*	
Plant and equipment (net)	100,000	45,000
Total	$650,000	$180,000
Accounts payable	$ 60,000	$ 20,000
Payable to Company P		10,000
Common stock, Company P	360,000*	
Common stock, Company S		100,000
Contributed capital from pooling of interests	90,000*	
Retained earnings, Company P	140,000	
Retained earnings, Company S		50,000
Total	$650,000	$180,000

* Amounts changed from precombination balance sheets given in Exhibit 17–1.

Now, let's combine the two separate balance sheets shown in Exhibit 17–2 into a single **consolidated balance sheet** as if there were a single entity represented by the parent company. To combine the two, we must be careful not to double count or to include any items that are strictly between the two companies. There are two such items in this situation:

1. The balance in the investment account of $150,000 shown in the accounts of Company P will be replaced with the assets (less the liabilities) of Company S; therefore, to prevent double counting, it must be eliminated (dropped out). The balance in the common stock account of $100,000 shown in the accounts of Company S is now owned by Company P; therefore, it is an intercompany item that must be eliminated. Finally, the difference between the balances in the investment account and the common stock account of Company P ($150,000 − $100,000 = $50,000) must be offset in the account on Company P's books, Contributed Capital from Pooling of Interest. This offset is necessary because it is an intercompany amount included in the investment account balance (refer to the acquisition entry). These three eliminations or offsets of inter-

company items must be made to avoid double counting; they can be summarized as follows:[3]

	Eliminations	
	Consolidated assets	Consolidated shareholders' equity
Investment account—decrease	−$150,000	
Common stock, Company S—decrease		−$100,000
Contributed capital from pooling of interests—decrease (for the difference)		− 50,000

2. The accounts of Company P show a receivable of $10,000 from Company S, and the accounts of Company S show this as a debt to Company P. This is called an **intercompany debt.** When the two balance sheets are combined into a single consolidated balance sheet, this intercompany debt must be eliminated since there is no debt owed by the combined entity. Thus, the following elimination or offset must be made when combining the two balance sheets:

	Eliminations	
	Consolidated assets	Consolidated liabilities
Receivable from Company S—decrease	−$10,000	
Payable to Company P—decrease		−$10,000

The two separate balance sheets are restated in Exhibit 17–3 and combined (aggregated) on a line-by-line basis, after deducting the "Eliminations," to develop the **"Consolidated balance sheet"** which is shown in the last column. In an external consolidated financial statement, only the last column—the "Consolidated balance sheet" (and not the "Separate balance sheets")—would be reported by the parent company.

In the "Consolidated balance sheet" on the pooling basis, as shown in Exhibit 17–3, the following measurement procedures are evident: (1) the amounts for the combined assets, liabilities, and shareholders' equity are the combined *book values* of the parent and the subsidiary as reflected on the "Separate balance sheets"; (2) the intercompany amounts for investment, subsidiary common stock, a part of contributed

[3] This also can be viewed in the debit/credit format as follows (see Appendixes);

Common stock, Company S	100,000	
Contributed capital from pooling of interests	50,000	
Investment in Company S		150,000

EXHIBIT 17–3

COMPANY P and Its Subsidiary, COMPANY S (100 percent owned)
Consolidated Balance Sheet (pooling-of-interests basis)
At January 2, 1977, Immediately after Acquisition

	Separate balance sheets			
	*Company P**	*Company S**	*Eliminations**	*Consolidated balance sheet*
Assets				
Cash	$205,000	$ 35,000		$240,000
Accounts receivable (net)	15,000	30,000		45,000
Receivable from Company S	10,000		(*b*) − 10,000	−0−
Inventories	170,000	70,000		240,000
Investment in Company S	150,000		(*a*) − 150,000	−0−
Plant and equipment (net)	100,000	45,000		145,000
Total Assets	$650,000	$180,000		$670,000
Liabilities				
Accounts payable	$ 60,000	$ 20,000		$ 80,000
Payable to Company P		10,000	(*b*) − 10,000	−0−
Shareholders' Equity				
Common stock, Company P	360,000			360,000
Common stock, Company S		100,000	(*a*) − 100,000	−0−
Contributed capital from pooling	90,000		(*a*) − 50,000	40,000
Retained earnings, Company P	140,000			} 190,000
Retained earnings, Company S		50,000		
Total Liabilities and Shareholders' Equity	$650,000	$180,000		$670,000

* Included for instructional purposes only. A worksheet is usually used to derive the consolidated amounts. See Appendixes A and B.

capital from pooling, and the intercompany debt are eliminated; and (3) the consolidated retained earnings is the sum of the two separate amounts ($140,000 + $50,000 = $190,000).[4]

The capital stock balance reflected in the accounts of Company S is eliminated because it is an intercompany item (it is all owned by Company P). Retained earnings of Company S is not eliminated because it is not an intercompany item; the old shareholders of Company P plus the new shareholders (the former Company S shareholders) have dividend claims on the total of retained earnings for the combined unit.

In the next section, we will compare these results with those that occur when the acquisition is by purchase instead of by pooling of interests.

[4] The pooling-of-interests approach also requires that all comparative statements presented for prior years must be restated as if consolidated statements had been prepared.

COMBINATION BY PURCHASE

When one corporation acquires a controlling interest in the voting stock of another corporation by *purchase* rather than by an exchange of shares of stock, a purchase/sale transaction is deemed to have occurred.[5] This purchase/sale transaction requires that the **cost principle** be applied by the parent company in recording the long-term investment. That is, the investment account on the books of the parent company must be debited **at cost, which is the fair-market value of the shares purchased** (i.e., the cash or cash equivalent paid). The stock of the subsidiary, purchased by the parent from the subsidiary's former shareholders, may be paid for in cash or a combination of cash, other assets, and debt. The stockholders of the subsidiary are paid off and they are no longer shareholders in either the parent or the subsidiary.

At this point, the basic measurement (and reporting) distinction between a combination by pooling of interests and purchase becomes apparent. Recall that in a pooling of interests the *book value* of the subsidiary's assets are added to the book value of the parent's assets. In contrast, to prepare consolidated financial statements when the purchase method is used, the *current fair-market value* (measured at date of acquisition) is added to the book value of the parent's assets.

Since the *fair-market value* of the subsidiary's assets must be recognized in a combination by purchase and *book values* must be used in a pooling of interests (as explained above), there are significantly different economic and reporting impacts as between pooling and purchasing.

To illustrate a combination by *purchase,* we will use the example of Companies P and S as given in Exhibit 17–1. Instead of the stock exchange, we will assume that on January 2, 1977, Company P purchased 100 percent of the 10,000 shares of outstanding stock of Company S, from Company S's shareholders, at $16.50 per share (i.e., for $165,000) and paid cash. On this date, Company P would make the following journal entry in its accounts:

January 2, 1977:

Investment in stock of Company S (10,000 shares, 100 percent)	165,000	
Cash		165,000
Acquisition by purchase.		

Note that Company P paid $165,000 cash for 100 percent of the owners' equity of Company S, although the total shareholders' equity

[5] Refer to footnote 2. In some instances, stock exchanges do not qualify for the pooling approach. In these instances, the purchase approach must be used, in which case the parent company must recognize the *fair-market values* for the subsidiary assets just as if cash and/or debt were exchanged for the stock of the subsidiary. These complexities are beyond the scope of this book.

EXHIBIT 17–4

COMPANY P AND COMPANY S
Separate Balance Sheets (purchase basis)
January 2, 1977, Immediately after Acquisition

	Company P	*Company S*
Cash	$ 40,000*	$ 35,000
Accounts receivable (net)	15,000	30,000
Receivable from Company S	10,000	
Inventories	170,000	70,000
Investment in Company S (100%)	165,000*	
Plant and equipment (net)	100,000	45,000
Total	$500,000	$180,000
Accounts payable	$ 60,000	$ 20,000
Payable to Company P		10,000
Common stock, Company P	300,000	
Common stock, Company S		100,000
Retained earnings, Company P	140,000	
Retained earnings, Company S		50,000
Total	$500,000	$180,000

* Amounts changed from precombination balance sheets (given in Exhibit 17–1).

of Company S that was purchased was only $150,000. Thus, Company P paid $15,000 more than "book value." In consolidating the two balance sheets, this $15,000 difference must be taken into account as explained below. We will assume also that the plant and equipment owned by Company S at this date had a fair-market value of $50,000 (compared with the book value of $45,000).

The purchase by Company P will have no effect on the accounting and reporting by the subsidiary Company S since the stock was sold (and cash was received) by the stockholders of Company S (and not by Company S itself).

After the above entry is posted to the accounts of Company P, the two separate balance sheets then would be changed as shown in Exhibit 17–4.

The consolidated balance sheet for Company P and its subsidiary, Company S, immediately after acquisition, is shown in Exhibit 17–5 on the **purchase basis.** The two separate balance sheets, given in Exhibit 17–4, were combined in a manner similar to that previously indicated for the pooling-of-interests basis. There are two intercompany items that require eliminations similar to those illustrated for the pooling-of-interests approach; however, the first one is significantly different than before. The two eliminations or offsets are:

a. The investment account balance of $165,000, on the books of Company P, is at *fair-market value* (i.e., at cost). It is eliminated or offset

EXHIBIT 17-5

COMPANY P and Its Subsidiary, COMPANY S (100 percent owned)
Consolidated Balance Sheet (purchase basis)
At January 2, 1977, Immediately after Acquisition

	Separate balance sheet			*Consolidated*
	*Company P**	*Company S**	*Eliminations**	*balance sheet*
Assets				
Cash	$ 40,000	$ 35,000		$ 75,000
Accounts receivable (net)	15,000	30,000		45,000
Receivable from Company S	10,000		(*b*) − 10,000	-0-
Inventories	170,000	70,000		240,000
Investment in Company S	165,000		(*a*) −165,000	-0-
Plant and equipment (net)	100,000	45,000	(*a*) + 5,000	150,000
Goodwill†			(*a*) + 10,000	10,000
Total Assets	$500,000	$180,000		$520,000
Liabilities				
Accounts payable	$ 60,000	$ 20,000		$ 80,000
Payable to Company P		10,000	(*b*) − 10,000	-0-
Shareholders' Equity				
Common stock, Company P	300,000			300,000
Common stock, Company S		100,000	(*a*) −100,000	-0-
Retained earnings, Company P	140,000			140,000
Retained earnings, Company S		50,000	(*a*) − 50,000	-0-
Total Liabilities and Shareholders' Equity	$500,000	$180,000		$520,000

* Included for instructional purposes only. A worksheet usually is used to derive the consolidated amounts. See Appendixes A and B.

† A title preferred by most accountants is "Excess of Purchase Price over the Current Value of the Net Assets of the Subsidiary other than Goodwill." However, the length of this term causes the shorter term to be used extensively.

against the shareholders' equity of the subsidiary, which is at *book value*. In this case there is a difference, and it must be recognized in the consolidated statement. The difference may be analyzed as follows:

Purchase price for 100% interest in Company S	$165,000
Shareholders' equity purchased (at book value: common stock, $100,000, plus retained earnings, $50,000)	150,000
Difference—excess paid over book value of subsidiary	15,000
Analysis of the difference:	
Amount needed to write up plant and equipment to current fair-market value ($50,000 − $45,000)	5,000
Remainder—goodwill purchased	$ 10,000

Of the $15,000 paid over book value, $5,000 is attributed to the difference between the fair-market value of the plant and equipment of $50,000 over the book value of $45,000 reported by the subsidiary. The remainder is attributed to goodwill. Goodwill is the amount that Company P was willing to pay for the good reputation, customer appeal, and general acceptance of the business that Company S had developed over the years. All successful companies enjoy a measure of goodwill. Its "value" is never known except when the business is purchased, as it was in this instance.

To eliminate the investment account on the books of Company P and the owner's equity accounts on the books of Company S, the following is necessary:

1. Increase the plant and equipment to market value by $5,000.
2. Recognize the $10,000 goodwill purchased.
3. Eliminate the investment account balance of $165,000.
4. Eliminate the Company S common stock balance of $100,000.
5. Eliminate the Company S retained earnings balance of $50,000.

Recognition of these items is as follows:[6]

	Eliminations	
	Consolidated assets	*Consolidated shareholders' equity*
Plant and equipment—increase	+$ 5,000	
Goodwill—increase	+ 10,000	
Investment—decrease	− 165,000	
Common stock Company S—decrease		−$100,000
Retained earnings, Company S—decrease		− 50,000

b. The intercompany debt must be eliminated as before, viz:

	Eliminations	
	Consolidated assets	*Consolidated liabilities*
Receivable from Company S—decrease	−$10,000	
Payable to Company P—decrease		−$10,000

In contrast to pooling of interests, when purchase accounting is used, the balance of retained earnings at acquisition of the subsidiary is eliminated because it was in effect paid out to the former shareholders of

[6] This can also be viewed in the debit/credit format as follows (see Appendixes):

Plant and equipment	5,000	
Goodwill	10,000	
Common stock, Company S	100,000	
Retained earnings, Company S	50,000	
Investment, Company S		165,000

Company S when they were reimbursed in cash for the fair-market value of their shares (they are no longer shareholders of either company).

The accounts of Company S are not affected by a purchase since the transactions were between the parent company and the former shareholders of the subsidiary (and not the subsidiary itself).

The two "Separate balance sheets" are restated on Exhibit 17–5 and combined on a line-by-line basis, after the eliminations, to develop the "Consolidated balance sheet" shown in the last column. In an external consolidated financial statement, only the "Consolidated balance sheet" shown in the last column (and not the "Separate balance sheets") would be reported.

To reemphasize the measurements for consolidated purposes, observe that the *current market value* of the subsidiary's assets are added on an item-by-item basis to the book values of the parent company.

COMPARING THE EFFECTS ON THE BALANCE SHEET OF POOLING VERSUS PURCHASE

To gain some insight into the differences in measurement of balance sheet amounts that arise when the pooling-of-interests approach is used versus the purchase approach, we can compare several of consolidated amounts shown in Exhibits 17–3 and 17–5 as follows:

	Acquisition approach		
	Pooling basis	*Purchase basis*	*Difference*
Cash	$240,000	$ 75,000	$(165,000)
Plant and equipment (net)	145,000	150,000	5,000
Goodwill		10,000	10,000
Common stock, Company P	400,000	300,000	(100,000)
Retained earnings, Company P	190,000	140,000	(50,000)

We can observe that when a company elects the purchase approach, the cash position suffers; the $165,000 difference in cash was the purchase price. The $100,000 difference in the amount of common stock is due to the effect of issuing stock rather than paying cash when the pooling-of-interests approach is elected. The plant and equipment amount is higher when the purchase approach is used than when pooling of interests is used, because the former requires application of the cost principle so that *fair-market value* at date of acquisition rather than book value must be recognized for the assets of the subsidiary. Goodwill arises in purchase but does not in pooling of interests. These higher amounts for assets, of course, mean higher expenses will be reported on the income statements in the future periods when the combination is by purchase; that is, for depreciation expense and amortization expense (for goodwill).

Finally, under the pooling approach, the reported retained earnings amount is higher because the amount of retained earnings of the subsidiary is added to that of the parent. In the case of purchase, the retained earnings amount of the subsidiary is eliminated.

These constitute significant differences in the resultant consolidated financial statements of the pooling versus the purchase approach. If you consider them carefully, it should be apparent why most companies prefer the pooling to the purchase approach. The preference is not only because of the impact on the cash position but also because of the impacts on certain other reported amounts on the balance sheet and income statement in periods subsequent to the acquisition. These impacts generally are viewed as undesirable by the parent company.

EXHIBIT 17–6

COMPANY P and Its Subsidiary, COMPANY S (100% Owned)
Consolidated Financial Statements
(Pooling and Purchase Approaches Compared)
At December 31, 1977, One Year after Acquisition

	Consolidated statements	
	Pooling basis	*Purchase basis*
Income Statement (for 1977):		
Sales revenue	$510,000	$510,000
Expenses:		
Cost of goods sold	(279,000)	(279,000)
Expenses (not detailed)	(156,500)	(156,500)
Depreciation expense	(14,500)	(15,000)
Amortization expense (goodwill)		(500)
Income tax expense	(26,000)	(26,000)
Net Income (carried down to retained earnings)	$ 34,000	$ 33,000
Balance Sheet (at December 31, 1977):		
Assets		
Cash	$271,500	$106,500
Accounts receivable (net)	46,000	46,000
Inventories	250,000	250,000
Plant and equipment (net)	130,500	135,000
Goodwill		9,500
Total Assets	$698,000	$547,000
Liabilities		
Accounts payable	$ 74,000	$ 74,000
Shareholders' Equity		
Common stock	400,000	300,000
Retained earnings	190,000	140,000
Add: Net income (from above)	34,000	33,000
Total Liabilities and Shareholders' Equity	$698,000	$547,000

REPORTING CONSOLIDATED OPERATIONS AFTER ACQUISITION

The preceding discussions and illustrations focused on the impact of the pooling-of-interests approach versus the purchase approach on the balance sheet. The comparative impact of the two approaches on the income statement, for periods following the date of acquisition, are even more significant. Exhibit 17–6 presents the consolidated income statement and balance sheet for Company P and its subsidiary, Company S, after one year of operations (i.e., for 1977). The underlying data and consolidation procedures used to derive these two statements are shown in Appendix A, Exhibits 17–9 and 17-10.

The consolidation amounts, one-year after acquisition on a purchase basis, are based on the annual financial statements prepared by the parent and the subsidiary shown in Exhibit 17–8.

Recall that the fixed assets of Company S, the subsidiary, at date of acquisition, had a current market value of $5,000 in excess of their book value. These assets are being depreciated over a remaining life of ten years by Company S. Recall also that the acquisition of Company S resulted in $10,000 goodwill to be recognized in consolidation under the purchase basis. This goodwill is to be amortized over the next 20 years.

The differences in impact between the pooling basis and the purchase basis on the consolidated statements of Company P and its subsidiary, Company S, after one year of operations are as follows:

	Acquisition approach		
	Pooling basis	*Purchase basis*	*Difference*
Income Statement:			
Depreciation expense	$ 14,500	$ 15,000	$ 500
Amortization expense (goodwill)		500	500
Net Income	34,000	33,000	$ 1,000
Balance Sheet:			
Cash	271,500	106,500	$165,000
Plant and equipment (net)	130,000	135,000	(4,500)
Goodwill		9,500	(9,500)
Total	698,000	547,000	$151,000
Common stock	360,000	300,000	$ 60,000
Contributed capital from pooling of interests	40,000		40,000
Retained earnings	224,000	173,000	51,000
Total	698,000	547,000	$151,000

The above comparison shows that net income was $1,000 less under the purchase basis than under pooling of interests. This difference was due to *additional* depreciation expense and amortization expense (goodwill) that must be recognized in consolidation when the assets of the subsidiary are recognized at their fair-market values, as is done in consolidation under the purchase basis (but not under pooling of interest). The causes of the $1,000 difference may be explained as follows:

	Items	*Difference*
a. Depreciation expense on pooling-of-interests basis (on parent and subsidiary assets at book value)	$14,500	
Add depreciation on the increased asset amount of the subsidiary to fair-market value from book value ($5,000 ÷ 10 years)	500	$ 500
Depreciation expense on purchase basis (on parent assets at book value and subsidiary assets at fair-market value)	$15,000	
b. Amortization expense on the intangible asset, goodwill, recognized of $10,000, which is to be amortized over the next 20 years ($10,000 ÷ 20 years)		500
(There is no goodwill recognized under pooling of interests.)		
Total	$15,000	$1,000

The additional expenses that must be recognized on the consolidated income statement in future periods cause less net income to be reported when the purchase basis is used. Businesses generally do not like this unfavorable impact of the purchase method.

Likewise, the $151,000 difference in the balance sheet totals is an important issue. In the example, this difference in results is caused by the different way in which the stock was acquired (shares exchanged versus cash payment) and the accounting measurements implicit in each of the two methods. These differences may be restated as follows:

Cash—The $165,000 difference reflects the price paid for the stock of the subsidiary purchased under the purchase basis as opposed to the exchange of shares under pooling of interests.

Plant and equipment (net)—This difference reflects the effects of including the fixed assets of the subsidiary at book value under the pooling-of-interests basis, compared with including them at current market value under the purchase basis. The $4,500 difference in plant and equipment may be explained as follows:

Difference between fair-market value and book value of subsidiary assets at date of acquisition	$5,000
Deduct depreciation on the difference for one year ($5,000 ÷ 10 years)	500
Difference: Fixed assets (higher under purchase basis)	$4,500

Common stock—The common stock of Company P is greater by $60,000 under a pooling of interests because of the issuance of shares in exchange for the shares of Company S.

Contributed capital from pooling of interests—This value arises only under pooling of interests or as a result of the exchange of shares. In consolidation, a part or all of it is eliminated.

Retained earnings—Retained earnings is $51,000 more under the pooling-of-interests basis than under the purchase basis. This difference is due to two factors, viz:

Amount of retained earnings eliminated:		
Under pooling of interests basis	$ -0-	
Under purchase basis	50,000	$50,000
Amount of consolidated net income:		
Under pooling of interest basis	34,000	
Under purchase basis	33,000	1,000
Difference: Retained earnings (higher under pooling of interests basis)		$51,000

Now, let's return to the merger movement, mentioned briefly on page 678 and assess some of the economic and motivational impacts of pooling of interests versus combination by purchase. Primarily, these impacts are related to the differences in measurement and reporting procedures used under each of these two accounting approaches. A comparison of these impacts may make clear why the merger movement in the 1960s depended in part on the open option to use either "pooling-of-interests accounting" or "purchase accounting" in many situations. Combination by pooling of interests was popular because it (1) requires little or no disbursement of cash, other assets, or the creation of debt; (2) causes a higher net income to be reported than does purchase accounting; (3) reports higher retained earnings; and (4) is susceptible to manipulation which was evidenced by numerous abuses during the 1960s (explained below).

In the merger movement of the 1960s, the pooling-of-interests approach generally was preferred because of the economic impacts; however, in the opinion of many, the opportunities for manipulation of net income were overriding. Four fairly common practices of the 1960s may be cited and illustrated:

1. *Instant earnings*—To illustrate, assume Company P acquired Company S through an exchange of stock; that is, by a pooling of interests. At the time, Company S owned three separate plants, each of which had a relatively low book value of, say, $100,000 and a high fair-

market value of, say, $600,000. Following the pooling-of-interests approach, the $100,000 book value for each plant was reported on the subsequent consolidated balance sheet as an asset. Assume that during the next year one of the plants was sold for the $600,000 fair-market value. The result was a *gain* on the sale of fixed assets of $500,000 (disregarding income taxes), which then was reported on the income statement. This came to be referred to, in a derogatory way, as making "instant earnings." The reported gain would significantly increase *net income* and EPS and often caused the price of the shares of Company P to rise. At the higher stock prices, shares were sold to the public and/or used for another round of mergers following the same pattern and so on. Many people believe that there was no gain because the *cost* of the plant, to the acquiring company, was the fair-market value of the shares given in exchange; that is, $600,000. Under this view (i.e., the purchase concept), no gain would be reported when the plant was sold.

2. *Funny money*—This term, intended to be derogatory, refers to the use of peculiar and innovative securities that were designed to "qualify" an acquisition as a pooling of interests, when, in fact, its substance was an acquisition by purchase. These instruments were used because (1) the company wanted to use pooling-of-interests accounting, and (2) the shareholders of the acquired company (the subsidiary) wanted cash, not shares of stock of the acquiring company. Both objectives were accomplished by issuing a type of security (i.e., "funny money"). Typically, the security provided that, say, after one year, it could be turned in for either voting common stock of Company P or cash, at the option of the holder. This qualified superficially as an exchange of shares (i.e., for pooling-of-interests accounting), while at the same time it made cash available in the short run to the shareholders of the subsidiary, as would be the case in a combination by purchase. Thus, a purchase transaction was accounted for as a pooling of interests.
3. *Escalating EPS*—This term refers to what was a common practice of seeking out smaller successful companies, usually near year-end, to acquire through a pooling-of-interests exchange, so that their earnings could be added to those of the parent. Thus, by the simple expedient of year-end pooling acquisitions, at no cash cost, the acquiring company could escalate net income and EPS reported on a consolidated basis by the parent company. Many of the year-end acquisitions for this purpose were consummated *after* the end of the year but before publication of the financial statements, in which case they were allowed for inclusion in the consolidated statements of the past year. This became a favorite way to "doctor" net income and EPS at year-end.

4. *Tricky mixes*—This situation represented the ultimate in misleading and illogical accounting. It was referred to as "part-purchase, part-pooling accounting." A corporation, in acquiring another company by pooling, often found a number of shareholders of the other company who would not accept shares in exchange; they wanted cash immediately. For example, it often worked out that, say, two thirds of the shares of the subsidiary would be acquired by exchange of shares and the remaining third would be purchased for cash. In order to derive some of the "reporting benefits" of pooling-of-interests accounting, two thirds of the acquisition would be accounted for on that basis and one third on the purchase basis—thus part-purchase, part-pooling accounting. This mixture of accounting approaches not only was theoretically untenable but also was misleading and not subject to any rational explanation.

Thus, the merger movement came under considerable criticism because pooling-of-interests accounting often was used in situations that, in substance, was a purchase. In response to extensive criticism the APB issued *Opinions No. 16,* "Business Combinations," and *No. 17,* "Intangible Assets," which tended to stop the abuses cited above. *Opinion No. 16* states very specific conditions under which pooling-of-interests accounting is applicable. It is interesting to note that a number of the members of the APB strongly believed, both for conceptual and practical reasons, that pooling-of-interests accounting should be completely disallowed. The conceptual argument against pooling-of-interest reporting is that it ignores the market values on which the parties traded shares and substitutes, in violation of the cost principle, wholly irrelevant amounts—the book values carried in the accounts of the seller (i.e., the subsidiary). The practical argument against pooling-of-interests reporting is that it leads to abuses of the kinds cited above.

The primary arguments in favor of the pooling-of-interests method of reporting are (1) it avoids the problems of measuring the fair-market value of the different assets of the subsidiary at acquisition date; (2) it avoids the necessity to recognize goodwill, then having to amortize it as an expense in future periods; and (3) the exchange of shares is not a purchase/sale transaction but, rather, is a joining of common interests and risks.

DEMONSTRATION CASE FOR SELF-STUDY

This actual case, showing selected parts of the consolidated financial statements, is presented for study and discussion of the reporting of consolidated and nonconsolidated subsidiaries (see Exhibit 17–7).

EXHIBIT 17–7

Westinghouse
Consolidated
Statements of Income
and Retained Earnings

Income Statement	Year Ended December 31 1975	Year Ended December 31 1974
Income:		
Sales	$5,862,747,000	$5,798,513,000
Equity in income (loss) from non-consolidated subsidiaries and affiliated companies (Note 3)	(4,513,000)	(32,285,000)
Other income	70,374,000	71,890,000
	5,928,608,000	5,838,118,000
Costs and expenses:		
Cost of sales	4,647,161,000	4,669,745,000
Distribution, administration and general	801,283,000	727,426,000
Depreciation	128,828,000	123,518,000
Interest	76,425,000	111,261,000
Income taxes (Note 5)	93,835,000	63,970,000
Minority interest in net income of consolidated subsidiaries	2,452,000	3,261,000
	5,749,984,000	5,699,181,000
Income from continuing operations	178,624,000	138,937,000
Discontinued operations (Note 2):		
Loss from operations of discontinued businesses (net of taxes of $35,274,000)	—	(39,805,000)
Loss on disposal of discontinued businesses (net of taxes of $10,000,000 in 1975 and $42,000,000 in 1974)	(13,400,000)	(71,000,000)
Net income	$ 165,224,000	$ 28,132,000
Earnings per common share:		
Continuing operations	$2.04	$1.57
Discontinued operations:		
Loss from operations	—	(.45)
Loss on disposal	(.15)	(.81)
Net income per common share	$1.89	$ .31

Retained Earnings	Year Ended December 31 1975	Year Ended December 31 1974
Retained earnings at beginning of year	$1,162,556,000	$1,220,914,000
Plus:		
Net income	165,224,000	28,132,000
Less:		
Dividends paid on preferred stock	895,000	1,158,000
Dividends paid on common stock	84,544,000	85,332,000
Retained earnings at end of year	$1,242,341,000	$1,162,556,000

EXHIBIT 17–7 (*continued*)

Westinghouse Consolidated Balance Sheet

Assets	At December 31 1975	At December 31 1974*
Current assets:		
Cash and marketable securities (Note 7)	$ 374,584,000	$ 137,806,000
Customer receivables (Note 8)	1,142,267,000	1,247,121,000
Inventories (Note 9)	1,040,571,000	1,072,963,000
Costs of uncompleted contracts in excess of related billings (Note 10)	172,473,000	197,205,000
Prepaid and other current assets	110,729,000	184,417,000
Total current assets	2,840,624,000	2,839,512,000
Investments (Note 11)	289,188,000	226,209,000
Estimated realizable value – discontinued businesses (Note 2)	95,543,000	202,442,000
Plant and equipment, net (Note 12)	1,380,680,000	1,298,576,000
Other assets (Note 13)	260,251,000	246,879,000
Total assets	$4,866,286,000	$4,813,618,000

Liabilities and Stockholders' Equity		
Current liabilities:		
Short-term loans and current portion of long-term debt (Note 14)	$ 131,754,000	$ 236,063,000
Accounts payable – trade	361,310,000	392,835,000
Accrued payrolls and payroll deductions	201,143,000	180,473,000
Income taxes currently payable	50,248,000	47,172,000
Deferred current income taxes	53,597,000	31,146,000
Estimated future costs – discontinued businesses	32,178,000	46,394,000
Billings on uncompleted contracts in excess of related costs (Note 10)	739,480,000	511,814,000
Other current liabilities	453,711,000	382,122,000
Total current liabilities	2,023,421,000	1,828,019,000
Non-current liabilities	43,948,000	62,360,000
Deferred non-current income taxes	117,449,000	97,270,000
Revolving credit notes payable (Note 15)	—	200,000,000
Debentures and other debt (Note 17)	610,242,000	643,123,000
Minority interest	69,534,000	58,775,000
Stockholders' equity (Note 19):		
Cumulative preferred stock	16,593,000	30,482,000
Common stock	277,108,000	277,108,000
Capital in excess of par value	490,697,000	480,896,000
Retained earnings	1,242,341,000	1,162,556,000
Less: Treasury stock, at cost	(25,047,000)	(26,971,000)
Total stockholders' equity	2,001,692,000	1,924,071,000
Total liabilities and stockholders' equity	$4,866,286,000	$4,813,618,000

EXHIBIT 17–7 (*continued*)

Note 1 – Westinghouse Accounting Principles and Policies
The major accounting principles and policies followed by Westinghouse are presented to assist the reader in evaluating the consolidated financial statements and other data in this report.

Principles of Consolidation: The financial statements include the consolidation of all significant wholly and majority owned subsidiaries except Westinghouse Credit Corporation and Urban Systems Development Corporation. The equity method of accounting is followed for non-consolidated subsidiaries and for investments in significant affiliates (20 to 50 per cent owned).

Note 2 – Discontinued operations: During 1974, decisions were reached to dispose of two major business segments, the major appliance business and the mail order and record club business.

The Corporation agreed to sell the major appliance business to White Consolidated Industries, Inc. (WCI), in exchange for cash and securities, resulting in provisions for losses on disposal in 1974 of $55 million (net of income taxes of $30 million).

The initial phase of the transaction included the sale of the domestic major appliance business and the major appliance business of Westinghouse Canada Ltd., a majority owned subsidiary. The transaction for the domestic business is essentially complete. Sale of the Westinghouse Canada portion to WCI initially was denied due to a Canadian government ruling regarding non-Canadian investment. WCI has filed a second application and the Canadian government is expected to make a decision regarding this sale in early 1976. Westinghouse is continuing negotiations with WCI for sale of its major appliance operations in three other countries. No additional provisions for disposal cost are considered necessary.

During 1974, the Corporation sold the member list and inventories of the Capital Record Club. The remaining portion of the mail order and record club business was to have been phased out during 1975. A provision for disposal costs of $16 million (net of income taxes of $12 million) was charged against income in 1974. A comprehensive review and analysis of the progression of the phase-out resulted in an additional provision for losses on disposal of $13 million (net of income taxes of $10 million) against income in 1975. This additional provision was required due to extended time needed to complete successive stages of the planned phase-out, higher than anticipated costs of inventory disposal, excessive product returns and lower than anticipated collection of outstanding receivables.

Estimated Realizable Value – Discontinued Businesses includes the assets and liabilities to be disposed. These amounts consist primarily of the net assets of the major appliance manufacturing subsidiaries outside the United States.

EXHIBIT 17–7 (*concluded*)

Westinghouse
Financial Review

Note 11 – Investments include Westinghouse Credit Corporation and significant affiliates, valued at cost plus equity in undistributed earnings, and other securities at cost or less, not in excess of market value.

The partnership interest of Tenneco, the Corporation's partner in Offshore Power Systems Company (OPS), a venture formed for the purpose of manufacturing floating nuclear power plants, was retired. Tenneco will receive $15.2 million in two equal payments in 1977 and 1978. Beginning with 1975, the financial statements of OPS are consolidated.

On December 31, 1975, the Corporation acquired the capital stock of the Treasure Lake Companies (TLC) from its wholly owned subsidiary, Westinghouse Credit Corporation (WCC), for its net investment. The outstanding indebtedness of TLC to WCC was repaid. The aggregate transaction involved $26.5 million. See accompanying condensed consolidated financial statements of Westinghouse Credit Corporation.

Sale and phase-out of other businesses and investments were accomplished during 1975. These included the French and Belgian elevator subsidiaries, Econo-Car International, Inc. and a transformer manufacturing subsidiary in Greece. In addition, the Corporation disposed of its 45 per cent equity interest in Framatome, a French nuclear power plant manufacturer. Two-thirds of the shares in Framatome were delivered to the Commissariat a l'Energie Atomique. The remaining one-third of the shares will be transferred to Creusot-Loire, a French manufacturing company, in 1982 for nominal value. The effects on net income of these transactions in 1975, both individually and in the aggregate, were not material.

Note 13 – Other assets include goodwill of $80 million in 1975 and $88 million in 1974. Goodwill acquired prior to November 1, 1970, is not being amortized. Goodwill of $14.2 million at December 31, 1975, and $15.1 million at December 31, 1974, resulting from business combinations subsequent to November 1, 1970, remained to be amortized over the estimated period to be benefited, not to exceed 40 years.

SUMMARY

This chapter discussed the use of consolidated statements that must be prepared in most situations when one corporation owns over 50 percent of the outstanding voting stock of another corporation. The concept of consolidated statements is based upon the view that a parent company and its subsidiaries constitute one economic entity. Therefore, the separate income statements, balance sheets, and statements of changes in financial position should be combined each period on an item-by-item basis as a single set of financial statements.

Ownership of a controlling interest (i.e., over 50 percent of the outstanding voting stock) of another corporation may be obtained either by a pooling of interests or combination by purchase. The measurement of amounts reported on the consolidated financial statements of the parent company is influenced to a significant degree by these two quite different accounting approaches.

A pooling of interests generally occurs when the parent company exchanges shares of its own voting stock for shares of the voting stock of the subsidiary. In this situation it is usually deemed that there was no purchase/sale (exchange) transaction. Rather, there is merely a joining of interests by exchanging stock certificates and the cost principle is not applied. Therefore, in preparing consolidated statements, on a pooling-of-interests basis, the book values (i.e., those amounts reflected on the books) of each related company are added together and fair-market values are disregarded.

In a combination by purchase, the parent company usually pays cash and/or debt for the shares of the subsidiary. In these circumstances, a purchase/sale transaction has been effected and the acquisition is accounted for in conformance with the cost principle. Therefore, in preparing consolidated statements under the purchase basis, the assets of the subsidiary must be measured at their fair-market values before they are combined with the statements of the parent company.

Consolidation on a pooling-of-interests basis versus consolidation on a purchase basis causes significant differences on the consolidated financial statements. The pooling-of-interests basis in the past led to many abuses.

A large percentage of published financial statements of corporations are consolidated statements. It is important, therefore, that statement users understand the basic concept of consolidated statements and the measurement distinctions between the pooling basis and the purchase basis in reporting the results of business combinations.

The differences between pooling of interests and purchasing in measuring and reporting the results of business combinations may be generalized, for the usual case, as follows:

Item	*Pooling of interests*	*Purchasing*
1. Measurement and recording at date of acquisition.	Acquisition is accomplished by exchanging shares of stock. A purchase/sale transaction is not assumed; hence, the cost principle is not applied. The Investment account is debited for the book value of the subsidiary stock acquired.	Acquisition usually is accomplished by purchasing the shares with cash and/or debt. A purchase/sale transaction is assumed; hence, the cost principle is applied. The investment account is debited for the fair-market value of the resources acquired.
2. Goodwill	No goodwill is recognized.	Goodwill is recognized to the extent that the purchase price exceeds the fair-market value of the assets (less the liabilities) of the subsidiary.
3. Method of aggregating or combining to derive consolidated balance sheet.	Assets and liabilities of the subsidiary are added, at book value, to those of the parent.	Assets and liabilities of the subsidiary are added, at their fair-market value (as of the date of acquisition), to the book values of the assets and liabilities of the parent.
4. Method of aggregating or combining to derive income statement.	Revenues and expenses, less any eliminations, as reported by each company are aggregated.	Revenues as reported, less any eliminations are aggregated. Expenses, plus additional depreciation and amortization of goodwill, less any eliminations, are aggregated.
5. Eliminations.	Eliminate all intercompany debts, revenues, and expenses. Eliminate investment account on parent's books and owners' equity of the subsidiary, excluding retained earnings.	Eliminate all intercompany debts, revenues, and expenses. Eliminate investment account on parent's books and common stock and retained earnings of the subsidiary.
6. Usual comparative effects on the consolidated financial statements.	Expenses—lower Net income—higher EPS—higher Assets—higher cash Noncash assets—lower Liabilities—same Capital stock—higher Retained earnings—higher	Expenses—higher Net income—lower EPS—lower Assets—lower cash Noncash assets—higher Liabilities—same Capital stock—lower Retained earnings—lower

CONCLUDING NOTE

This volume focused on financial accounting and reporting to external parties, as represented by potential investors, creditors, and the public at large. We have emphasized the use and interpretation of financial statements by decision makers. The conceptual side of accounting also was emphasized in order to provide a higher level of sophistication in using and interpreting financial statements than is otherwise possible. This focus also provides the reasons underlying the various accounting concepts, measurements, and approaches. Procedures and mechanics were introduced only to the extent deemed essential to further one's study of the broad subject of accounting, particularly the important subject of management accounting.

In the next volume, attention is focused on the area of management accounting. Management accounting emphasizes the planning, controlling, and decision-making activities of management. It considers both the behavioral and quantitative implications of accounting in the management process. Throughout that volume you will find that most of the concepts and practices discussed and illustrated in this volume are applicable. However, managerial accounting is not constrained by "generally accepted accounting principles" since its primary focus is to serve **internal management** in effectively carrying out the broad functions of executive administration.

IMPORTANT TERMS

Parent company
Subsidiary company
Single economic entity
Consolidated statements
Control
Economic compatibility
Pooling of interests
Combination by purchase
Consolidated balance sheet
Consolidated income statement
Intercompany eliminations
Goodwill
Amortization of goodwill

APPENDIX A

Procedures for deriving consolidated statements—100 percent ownership

The chapter focused on the use of consolidated financial statements. This appendix discusses in more depth the measurement procedures used in preparing consolidated financial statements. To accomplish this objective, we use the typical *consolidation worksheet* because, through it, the underlying concepts and measurement procedures come into sharp focus. The worksheets should be viewed as a learning device and not something only to be mastered mechanically. At the outset we remind you that the worksheet and the entries made on it are *supplemental* to the accounts and the reports. *The worksheet entries are not recorded in the accounts under any circumstances; they are analytical devices only*. We will consider the various topics in the same order they were presented in the chapter. The example for Company P and its subsidiary, Company S, given in Exhibit 17–1, will be continued for all of the illustrations in this part.

Consolidated balance sheet immediately after acquisition

The consolidated balance sheets for Company P and its subsidiary, Company S, immediately after acquisition, were shown on the pooling-of-interests basis in Exhibit 17–3 and on the purchase basis in Exhibit 17–5. Those exhibits indicated in the first three columns the worksheet procedures essential to development of the statements. There is no need to repeat those discussions.

Developing consolidated statements for periods subsequent to acquisition

At the end of each accounting period after acquisition, a consolidated balance sheet, income statement, and statement of changes in financial position must be prepared. This section discusses the application of consolidation principles in the development of both a consolidated balance sheet and a consolidated income statement for periods subsequent to acquisition. We will illustrate a single worksheet that will meet this dual need.

To illustrate the development of a consolidation worksheet for both the balance sheet and the income statement, we will continue the situation involving the *purchase* with cash of Company S stock by Company P given in Exhibit 17–4. Recall that on January 2, 1977, Company P acquired 100 percent of the outstanding stock of Company S. To adapt the example, we will assume that it is now December 31, 1977, and, after operating for a year, each company has just prepared their separate income statements and balance sheets as shown in Exhibit 17–8.

At the end of 1977, the following data relating to intercompany eliminations were available:

a. The investment account balance of $165,000 was the same as at date of acquisition; the balance of retained earnings of Company S at acquisition was $50,000.
b. At date of purchase, January 2, 1977, the plant and equipment of Company S had a market value of $5,000 above book value and goodwill purchased amounted to $10,000 (see page 685).
c. The intercompany debt owed by Company S to Company P was $6,000 at the end of 1977.
d. The plant and equipment owned by Company S has a ten-year re-

EXHIBIT 17–8

COMPANY P AND COMPANY S
Separate Financial Statements for 1977 (unclassified)

	At December 31, 1977		
	Company P		*Company S*
	Pooling basis	*Purchase basis*	
Income Statement (for 1977):			
Sales revenue	$400,000	$400,000	$110,000
Revenue from investments (dividend from Company S)	10,000	10,000	
Cost of goods sold	(220,000)	(220,000)	(59,000)
Expenses (not detailed)	(130,000)	(130,000)	(26,500)
Depreciation expense	(10,000)	(10,000)	(4,500)
Income tax expense	(20,000)	(20,000)	(6,000)
Net Income	$ 30,000	$ 30,000	$ 14,000
Balance Sheet (at December 31, 1977):			
Cash	$226,000	$ 61,000	$ 45,500
Accounts receivable (net)	18,000	18,000	28,000
Receivable from Company S	6,000	6,000	
Inventories	185,000	185,000	65,000
Investment in Company S (by purchase, at cost)	150,000*	165,000*	
Plant and equipment (net)	90,000	90,000	40,500
	$675,000	$525,000	$179,000
Accounts payable	$ 55,000	$ 55,000	$ 19,000
Payable to Company P			6,000
Common stock (par $10)	360,000	300,000	100,000
Contributed capital in excess of par	90,000		
Beginning retained earnings*	140,000	140,000	50,000
Dividends paid during 1977			(10,000)
Net income for 1977 (per above)	30,000	30,000	14,000
	$675,000	$525,000	$179,000

* Balance at date of acquisition.

maining life from January 1, 1977, for depreciation purposes. The company uses straight-line depreciation.

e. Goodwill is to be amortized from January 1, 1977, over 20 years on a straight-line basis.

f. During December 1977, Company S declared and paid a $10,000 cash dividend to Company P. Accordingly, each company made the following entry in its accounts:

Company P			*Company S*		
Cash	10,000		Dividends Paid	10,000	
Revenue from Investments		10,000	Cash		10,000

A consolidated income statement and balance sheet are to be developed for 1977. These statements were shown in Exhibit 17–6, assuming (1) pooling-of-interests basis and (2) consolidation by purchase. A separate consolidation worksheet is shown for each: Exhibit 17–9, pooling of interests, and Exhibit 17–10, purchase. Each worksheet will be explained.

Pooling-of-interests basis—income statement and balance sheet. This worksheet (Exhibit 17–9) has side captions for each income statement and balance sheet account, and columns for the parent company, subsidiary, eliminations, and final column for the *"Consolidated Balances."* The amounts entered in the first two money columns are taken directly from the separate financial statements for 1977 prepared by the parent and the subsidiary as given above. The last column of this worksheet provided the data for the consolidated income statement and balance sheet shown in Exhibit 17–6.

The worksheet is designed so that the eliminations are entered in debit and credit format. This provides an excellent check on the accuracy of the work. We remind you, however, that the elimination entries are *worksheet entries only;* they are never entered into the accounts of either the parent or the subsidiary. This is because reporting with consolidated statements is a *reporting concept* and does not affect the accounts of either the parent or the subsidiaries.

To complete the worksheet, the elimination entries first must be developed; then each line is accumulated horizontally to derive the consolidated amount in the last column for each item to be reported on the consolidated income statement and the balance sheet. At the end of 1977, there are three elimination entries on the worksheet on the pooling-of-interests basis. They are briefly identified at the bottom of the worksheet; however, we will elaborate on them as follows:

a. Eliminate the investment account with offsets to the accounts for (1) common stock, Company S, and (2) contributed capital from pooling (see page 680). These eliminations can be accomplished by means of the following intercompany elimination entry on the worksheet:

Common stock, Company S	100,000	
Contributed capital from pooling of interests	50,000	
Investment in Company S		150,000

b. Eliminate the intercompany debt of $6,000 owed by Company S to Company P (see page 681). These two eliminations can be ac-

EXHIBIT 17–9

COMPANY P and Its Subsidiary, COMPANY S
Consolidation Worksheet (pooling of interests) for the Balance Sheet and Income Statement
December 31, 1977 (100 percent ownership)

	Statements		Intercompany Eliminations		Consolidated Balances
	Company P	Company S	Debit	Credit	
Income Statement:					
Sales revenue	400,000	110,000			510,000
Revenue from investments	10,000		(*c*) 10,000		
Cost of goods sold	(220,000)	(59,000)			(279,000)
Expenses (not detailed)	(130,000)	(26,500)			(156,500)
Depreciation expense	(10,000)	(4,500)			(14,500)
Income tax expense	(20,000)	(6,000)			(26,000)
Net Income (carried down)	30,000	14,000			34,000
Balance Sheet:					
Cash	226,000	45,500			271,500
Accounts receivable (net)	18,000	28,000			46,000
Receivable from Company S	6,000			(*b*) 6,000	
Inventories	185,000	65,000			250,000
Investment in Company S	150,000*			(*a*) 150,000	
Plant and equipment (net)	90,000	40,500			130,500
	675,000	179,000			698,000
Accounts payable	55,000	19,000			74,000
Payable to Company P		6,000	(*b*) 6,000		
Common stock, Company P	360,000*				360,000
Common stock, Company S		100,000	(*a*) 100,000		
Contributed capital from pooling	90,000*		(*a*) 50,000		40,000
Beginning retained earnings, Company P	140,000				140,000
Beginning retained earnings, Company S		50,000			50,000
Dividends paid during 1977		(10,000)		(*c*) 10,000	
Net income, 1977 (from above; not added across)	30,000	14,000			34,000
	675,000	179,000	166,000	166,000	698,000

Explanation of eliminations:

a. To eliminate investment account against common stock of subsidiary and contributed capital from pooling of interests.
b. To eliminate the intercompany debt.
c. To eliminate the intercompany revenue and dividends (paid by the subsidiary to the parent).

* These amounts are based upon the pooling-of-interests approach. The parent would have made the following entry at acquisition date:

Investment in Company S	150,000	
Common stock, Company P		100,000
Contributed capital from pooling of interests		50,000

EXHIBIT 17–10

COMPANY P and Its Subsidiary, COMPANY S
Consolidation Worksheet (by purchase) for the Balance Sheet and Income Statement
December 31, 1977 (100 percent ownership)

	Statements		Intercompany Eliminations		Consolidated Balances
	Company P	Company S	Debit	Credit	
Income Statement:					
Sales revenue	400,000	110,000			510,000
Revenue from investments	10,000		(*f*) 10,000		
Cost of goods sold	(220,000)	(59,000)			(279,000)
Expenses (not detailed)	(130,000)	(26,500)			(156,500)
Depreciation expense	(10,000)	(4,500)	(*d*) 500		(15,000)
Amortization expense (goodwill)			(*e*) 500		500
Income tax expense	(20,000)	(6,000)			(26,000)
Net Income (carried down)	30,000	14,000			33,000
Balance Sheet:					
Cash	61,000	45,500			106,500
Accounts receivable (net)	18,000	28,000			46,000
Receivable from Company S	6,000			(*c*) 6,000	
Inventories	185,000	65,000			250,000
Investment in Company S (at cost)	165,000			(*a*) 165,000	
Plant and equipment (net)	90,000	40,500	(*b*) 5,000	(*d*) 500	135,000
Goodwill			(*b*) 10,000	(*e*) 500	9,500
	525,000	179,000			547,000
Differential			(*a*) 15,000	(*b*) 15,000	
Accounts payable	55,000	19,000			74,000
Payable to Company P		6,000	(*c*) 6,000		
Common stock, Company P	300,000				300,000
Common stock, Company S		100,000	(*a*) 100,000		
Beginning retained earnings, Company P	140,000				140,000
Beginning retained earnings, Company S		50,000	(*a*) 50,000		
Dividends paid during 1977		(10,000)		(*f*) 10,000	
Net income, 1977 (from above; not added across)	30,000	14,000			33,000*
	525,000	179,000	197,000	197,000	547,000

* Carried down from above.

Explanation of eliminations:

a. To eliminate the investment account against the subsidiary stockholders' equity.
b. To allocate the difference between purchase price and book value purchased to the appropriate accounts.
c. To eliminate the intercompany debt.
d. To record additional depreciation for one year on the asset increase resulting from the acquisition.
e. To record amortization for one year on the goodwill recognized.
f. To eliminate intercompany revenue and dividends (paid by the subsidiary to the parent).

complished by means of the following intercompany elimination entry on the worksheet:

Payable to Company P	6,000	
Receivable from Company S		6,000

c. During the year, Company S paid dividends amounting to $10,000. Since Company P owned 100 percent of the outstanding stock, all of the dividends were paid to Company P. This is another intercompany item that must be eliminated. The Revenue from Investments account of Company P is debited on the worksheet and the Dividends Paid account of the subsidiary credited for $10,000. Observe that separate lines are set up on the worksheet for dividends and net income. This is simply a matter of convenience and clarity. The worksheet entry to accomplish these two eliminations is:

Revenue from investments	10,000	
Dividends paid (retained earnings, Company S)		10,000

Purchase basis—income statement and balance sheet. In this situation there will be a few more eliminations because fair-market values for the subsidiary must be recognized when the consolidation is by purchase. The intercompany eliminations on Exhibit 17–10 purchase basis, are identified at the bottom of the worksheet; however, we will elaborate on them as follows:

a. Eliminate the investment account, reported on the parent's balance sheet, against the owners' equity accounts reflected on the balance sheet of the subsidiary. This eliminating entry will be the same as at date of acquisition for each succeeding period since it is based upon the values recognized at the date of acquisition. The $15,000 differential between the purchase price and the book value can be recorded, for convenience, in the temporary clearance account "Differential." The worksheet elimination entry is:

Common stock, Company S	100,000	
Retained earnings, Company S	50,000	
Differential (clearance)	15,000	
Investment in Company S (100 percent)		165,000

b. Allocate the differential of $15,000 (set up in elimination entry a) to the fixed asset and goodwill accounts on the basis of an analysis of the purchase transaction given on page 685. The worksheet entry is:

Plant and equipment	5,000	
Goodwill	10,000	
Differential		15,000

c. Eliminate the intercompany debt of $6,000 with the following elimination entry:

Payable to Company P	6,000	
Receivable from Company S		6,000

d. Since the plant and equipment amount for Company S was increased by $5,000, for consolidation purposes we must record on the worksheet additional depreciation on that amount. The depreciation reflected on the statements of Company S does not include this $5,000 increase to market value. Accordingly, the worksheet entry must be:

Depreciation expense (Company S)	500	
Plant and equipment (Company S) (or accumulated depreciation)		500

$5,000 ÷ 10 years = $500.

e. Goodwill is an intangible asset (see Chapter 10) that must be amortized over a period not longer than 40 years (APB *Opinion No. 17*). Company P has decided to use a 20-year life. Since $10,000 goodwill was recognized in entry (*b*) above, for consolidated statement purposes it must be amortized on the worksheet in the same manner as the depreciation in entry (*d*). Therefore, the worksheet entry to accomplish this effect is:

Amortization expense (goodwill)	500	
Goodwill		500

$10,000 ÷ 20 years = $500.

f. During the year, Company S paid dividends amounting to $10,000. Since Company P owned 100 percent of the outstanding stock, all of the dividends were paid to Company P. This is an intercompany item that must be eliminated. The Revenue from Investments account of Company P must be debited on the worksheet and the Dividends Paid account of the subsidiary credited for $10,000. Observe that separate lines are set up on the worksheet for dividends and net income. This is simply for convenience and clarity. The worksheet entry to accomplish these eliminations is:

Revenue from investments	10,000	
Dividends paid (retained earnings, Company S)		10,000

All of the intercompany eliminations have been effected. The worksheet is completed for the consolidated balances by cumulating the amounts horizontally for each item. The consolidated balances taken directly from the last column of the worksheet are classified in the normal manner in preparing the consolidated income statement and balance sheet.

APPENDIX B

Consolidation measurement procedures—controlling interest less than 100 percent ownership

When the parent company owns a controlling interest that is less than 100 percent, the consolidation procedures are identical, except that certain consolidation worksheet eliminations must be based upon the *proportionate* ownership level. When there is less than 100 percent ownership, there will be a group of stockholders of the subsidiary company known as the **minority stockholders.** Their interest in the subsidiary is unaffected by the parent's interest; therefore, the minority stockholders' interest must be accorded appropriate measurement and reporting recognition. This gives rise to a new kind of owners' equity on the consolidated statements referred to as the **minority interest.** It includes their proportionate share of both the earnings and the contributed capital of the subsidiary.

Ownership interests of less than 100 percent generally are on the purchase basis since APB *Opinion No. 16* does not permit use of the pooling-of-interests basis when the ownership interest held by the parent company is less than 90 percent.

To illustrate the measurement of amounts for consolidated statements for a controlling interest of less than 100 percent, we will adapt the data for Company P and Company S given in Exhibit 17–1, page 678. Assume that on January 2, 1977, Company P purchased 80 percent of the 10,000 shares of outstanding capital stock of Company S for $132,000 cash. At that date, Company P recorded the purchase of the 8,000 shares of capital stock as follows:

January 2, 1977:

Investment, stock of Company S (80 percent ownership)........	132,000	
Cash..		132,000
Acquisition of 8,000 shares (80 percent) of the capital stock of Company S at $16.50 per share.		

On the date of purchase, the owners' equity accounts of Company S reflected the following amounts: capital stock, $100,000; and retained earnings, $50,000. Company P paid $132,000 cash for 80 percent of the owners' equity of Company S, or $150,000 × 0.80 = $120,000. Thus, they paid $12,000 more than the book value of Company S. Of this amount, $4,000 (i.e., $5,000 × 80 percent) was for the greater market value of the plant and equipment. The remaining amount, $8,000, was for *goodwill.* The analysis of the purchase transaction, at date of acquisition, follows:[7]

Purchase price for 80% interest in Company S................................	$132,000
Stockholders' equity (book value) of Company S purchased ($100,000 + $50,000) × 0.80	120,000
Difference—excess paid over book value	12,000
Analysis of the difference:	
To plant and equipment ($50,000 − $45,000) × 0.80	4,000
Remainder—goodwill purchased...	$ 8,000

[7] Some accountants believe, on the basis on conservatism, that the plant and equipment difference should be 100 percent (i.e., $5,000) rather than 80 percent (i.e., $4,000). This difference in opinion has not been resolved; however, it appears that most companies currently use the lower amount.

Assume it is now December 31, 1977, and both companies have experienced one year's operations as affiliated companies. Each company has prepared the separate 1977 financial statements as shown in Exhibit 17–11.

EXHIBIT 17–11

COMPANY P AND COMPANY S
Separate Financial Statements for 1977

	Company P	*Company S*
Income Statement (for 1977):		
Sales revenue	$400,000	$110,000
Revenue from investments (dividends from Company S)	8,000	
Cost of goods sold	(220,000)	(59,000)
Expenses (not detailed)	(130,000)	(26,500)
Depreciation expense	(10,000)	(4,500)
Income tax expense	(20,000)	(6,000)
Net Income	$ 28,000	$ 14,000
Balance Sheet (at December 31, 1977):		
Cash	$ 92,000	$ 45,500
Account receivable (net)	18,000	28,000
Receivable from Company S	6,000	
Inventories	185,000	65,000
Investment in Company S (80%, at cost)	132,000	
Plant and equipment	90,000	40,500
	$523,000	$179,000
Accounts payable	$ 55,000	$ 19,000
Payable to Company P		6,000
Common stock (par $10)	300,000	100,000
Beginning retained earnings	140,000	50,000
Dividends paid during 1977		(10,000)
Net income for 1977 (from above)	28,000	14,000
	$523,000	$179,000

Additional data developed for the consolidation worksheet:

a. Investment account balance of $132,000 to be eliminated against 80 percent of stockholders' equity of subsidiary.

b. Plant and equipment of Company S to be increased by $4,000 to fair-market value. Goodwill to be recognized, $8,000 (see analysis of purchase transaction above).

c. Company S owed Company P $6,000 on December 31, 1977.

d. The plant and equipment is being depreciated over a remaining life of ten years by Company S.

e. Goodwill will be amortized over 20 years.

f. Company S paid $10,000 cash dividends on December 15, 1977.

EXHIBIT 17–12

COMPANY P and Its Subsidiary, COMPANY S
Consolidation Worksheet (combination by purchase) for the Balance Sheet and Income Statement
December 31, 1977 (80 percent ownership)

	Statements		Intercompany Eliminations		Consolidated Balances
	Company P	Company S	Debit	Credit	
Income Statement:					
Sales revenue	400,000	110,000			510,000
Revenue from investments	8,000		(f) 8,000		
Cost of goods sold	(220,000)	(59,000)			(279,000)
Expenses (not detailed)	(130,000)	(26,500)			(156,500)
Depreciation expense	(10,000)	(4,500)	(d) 400		(14,900)
Amortization expense (goodwill)			(e) 400		(400)
Income tax expense	(20,000)	(6,000)			(26,000)
Net Income	28,000	14,000			33,200
Carried down:					
Minority interest ($14,000 × 20%)					2,800M*
Parent interest income					30,400
Balance Sheet:					
Cash	92,000	45,500			137,500
Accounts receivable (net)	18,000	28,000			46,000
Receivable from Company S	6,000			(c) 6,000	
Inventories	185,000	65,000			250,000
Investment in Company S (at cost)	132,000			(a) 132,000	
Plant and equipment (net)	90,000	40,500	(b) 4,000	(d) 400	134,100
Goodwill			(b) 8,000	(e) 400	7,600
	523,000	179,000			575,200
Differential			(a) 12,000	(b) 12,000	
Accounts payable	55,000	19,000			74,000
Payable to Company P		6,000	(c) 6,000		
Common stock, Company P	300,000				300,000
Common stock, Company S		100,000	(a) 80,000		20,000M
Beginning retained earnings, Company P	140,000				140,000
Beginning retained earnings, Company S		50,000	(a) 40,000		10,000M
Dividends paid during 1977		(10,000)		(f) 8,000	(2,000)M
Net income, 1977 (from above; not added across)	28,000	14,000			2,800M 30,400
	523,000	179,000	158,800	158,800	575,200

M—Minority interest.

* The minority interest in the earnings of the subsidiary is unaffected by the consolidation procedures of the parent company. Thus, the minority interest in the earnings is $14,000 × 20% = $2,800. This amount is subtracted from consolidated income to derive the amount of consolidated income identifiable with the controlling interest. The two separate amounts are then carried down to the balance sheet section.

Explanation of eliminations:

a. To eliminate the investment account against 80 percent of the owners' equity of the subsidiary.
b. To allocate the difference between purchase price and book value to the appropriate accounts.
c. To eliminate the intercompany debt.
d. To record depreciation for one year on the asset increase resulting from the acquisition.
e. To amortize goodwill recognized (one year).
f. To eliminate intercompany revenue arising from dividends paid by the subsidiary.

EXHIBIT 17–13

COMPANY P and Its Subsidiary, COMPANY S
Consolidated Income Statement (purchase basis)
For the Year Ended December 31, 1977

Sales revenue		$510,000
Cost of goods sold		279,000
Gross margin		231,000
Less:		
Expenses (not detailed)	$156,500	
Depreciation expense	14,900	
Amortization expense (goodwill)	400	
Income tax expense	26,000	197,800
Consolidated net income		33,200
Less: minority interest in net income		2,800
Controlling interest in net income		$ 30,400

Earnings per share of common stock ($33,200 ÷ 30,000 shares) = $1.107 (some accountants prefer to use $30,400 as the numerator).

COMPANY P and Its Subsidiary, COMPANY S
Consolidated Balance Sheet (purchase basis)
At December 31, 1977

Assets

Current Assets:		
Cash	$137,500	
Accounts receivable (net)	46,000	
Inventories	250,000	$433,500
Fixed Assets:		
Plant and equipment (net)		134,100
Intangible Assets:		
Goodwill (or excess of cost over fair value of assets of subsidiary)		7,600
		$575,200

Liabilities

Current Liabilities:		
Accounts payable		$ 74,000

Stockholders' Equity

Contributed Capital:		
Common stock, par $10, 30,000 shares outstanding	$300,000	
Retained earnings	170,400	
Total	470,400	
Minority interest	30,800*	
Total Stockholders' Interest		501,200
		$575,200

* $20,000 + $10,000 + $2,800 − $2,000 = $30,800.

The consolidation worksheet, on the purchase basis, is shown in Exhibit 17–12. It is the same as the worksheet shown in Exhibit 17–10 for 100 percent ownership, except for elimination entries (*a*), (*b*), (*d*), (*e*), and (*f*). These intercompany eliminations are the *same except for the amounts. They have been reduced to the 80 percent ownership level.*

On the worksheet the 20 percent representing the minority interest is designated with an "M." In the income statement part of the worksheet, 20 percent of the net income (i.e., $2,800) of the subsidiary is coded "M" and the remainder ($30,400) is identified with the parent. These consolidated balances, on the worksheet, are carried down to the balance sheet section. The 20 percent of subsidiary stockholders' equity was not eliminated; therefore, it is carried across as the minority interest and coded "M." Aside from these adaptations, the "Consolidated Balances" column is completed as previously explained.

The consolidated income statement and balance sheet, based on the data in the "Consolidated Balances" column of the worksheet, are shown in Exhibit 17–13. The *minority* interest share of net income is separately identified on the income statement. Similarly, the minority interest share of stockholders' equity is separately identified on the balance sheet. The minority interest share of stockholders' equity often is shown as a special caption between liabilities and stockholders' equity rather than as illustrated in the exhibit.

QUESTIONS FOR DISCUSSION

1. Explain what is meant by a parent-subsidiary relationship.
2. Explain the basic concept underlying consolidated statements.
3. What two basic elements must be present before consolidated statements are used?
4. The concept of consolidated statements relates only to reporting as opposed to entries in the accounts. Explain.
5. Explain briefly what is meant by pooling of interests.
6. Explain briefly what is meant by combination by purchase.
7. When one corporation acquires a controlling interest in another corporation, the acquiring corporation debits a long-term investment account. In the case of a pooling of interests, basically, what amount is debited to the investment account?
8. Explain what is meant by intercompany eliminations, or offsets, in consolidation procedures.
9. Explain why the investment account must be eliminated against stockholders' equity.

10. Explain why the "book values" of the parent and subsidiary are aggregated on consolidated statements when there is a pooling of interests, but fair-market values of the subsidiary assets are used when the combination was by purchase.
11. Why is goodwill not recognized in a pooling of interests? Why is it recognized in a combination by purchase?
12. Explain why additional depreciation expense generally must be recognized on consolidation when the combination was by purchase.
13. Explain what is meant by goodwill when the combination was by purchase.
14. Explain why pooling of interests has been much more popular in the merger movement than combination by purchase.
15. Explain the basis for each of the following statements:
    a. Pooling of interests, given the same situation basically, reports a higher net income than does combination by purchase.
    b. The cash position, other things being equal, is better when there is a combination by pooling than when there is a combination by purchase.
    c. Pooling of interests, other things being equal, reports a higher amount of retained earnings than does combination by purchase.

EXERCISES

E17–1. On January 2, 1977, Company P acquired all of the outstanding voting stock of Company S by exchanging, on a share-for-share basis, its own unissued stock for the stock of Company S. Immediately after the stock exchange entry was posted by Company P, the separate balance sheets showed the following:

	Balances, January 2, 1977 immediately after acquisition	
	Company P	*Company S*
Cash	$ 38,000	$12,000
Receivable from Company S	7,000	
Inventory	35,000	18,000
Investment in Company S (100%)	40,000	
Fixed assets (net of accumulated depreciation)	80,000	50,000
Total	$200,000	$80,000
Liabilities	$ 25,000	$13,000
Payable to Company P		7,000
Common stock (Company P—nopar; Company S, par $5)	140,000	40,000
Retained earnings	35,000	20,000
Total	$200,000	$80,000

Required:

a. Is this a pooling of interests or a combination by purchase? Explain why.

b. Give the entry that was made by Company P to record the acquisition. Assume pooling of interests.

c. Prepare a consolidated balance sheet immediately after the acquisition. Follow the format of Exhibit 17–3.

d. Were the assets of the subsidiary added to those of the parent, in the consolidated balance sheet, at book value or at market value? Explain why.

e. What were the balances in the accounts of Company P immediately prior to the acquisition for (1) investment and (2) common stock? Were any other accounts for either Company P or Company S different? Explain.

E17–2. On January 1, 1977, Company P acquired 100 percent of the shares of the outstanding common stock of Company S. At date of acquisition, the balance sheet of Company S reflected the following (summarized):

Total assets (fair-market value, $220,000)*	$180,000
Total liabilities	30,000
Stockholders' Equity:	
Common stock, par $10	100,000
Retained earnings	50,000

* One half subject to depreciation; 10-year remaining life.

Two separate and independent cases are given whereby Company P acquired 100 percent of the outstanding stock of Company S, viz:

Case A – Exchanged two shares of its own common stock (par $1) for each share of Company S stock.

Case B – Paid $20 per share for the stock of Company S.

Required:

For each case, answer the following:

a. Was this a combination by pooling of interests or by purchase? Explain.

b. Give the entry in the accounts of Company P to record the acquisition. If none, explain why.

c. Give the entry in the accounts of Company S to record the acquisition. If none, explain why.

d. Analyze the transaction to determine the amount of goodwill purchased. If no goodwill was purchased, explain why.

e. In preparing a consolidated balance sheet, at what amounts would the subsidiary assets be included? Explain.

f. Would there be any expenses to include on the consolidated income statement in future periods in addition to those reported by the parent and the subsidiary on their separate income statements? Explain.

E17–3. On January 1, 1977, Company P purchased 100 percent of the outstanding shares of Company S in the open market for $70,000 cash. On that date, *prior* to the acquisition, the separate balance sheets (summarized) of the two companies were as follows:

	Prior to acquisition	
	Company P	*Company S*
Cash	$ 80,000	$18,000
Receivable from Company P		2,000
Fixed assets	80,000	60,000
Total	$160,000	$80,000
Liabilities	$ 28,000	$20,000
Payable to Company S	2,000	
Common stock:		
Company P (nopar)	100,000	
Company S (par $10)		50,000
Retained earnings	30,000	10,000
Total	$160,000	$80,000

It was determined on date of acquisition that the fair-market value of the fixed assets of Company S was $6,000 in excess of their book value as reflected on the books of Company S.

Required:

a. Was this a combination by pooling of interests or by purchase? Explain why.

b. Give the entry that should be made by Company P at date of acquisition. If none is required, explain why.

c. Give the entry that should be made by Company S at date of acquisition. If none is required, explain why.

d. Analyze the acquisition to determine the amount of goodwill purchased.

e. At what value will the assets of Company S be included on the consolidated balance sheet? Explain.

f. Prepare a consolidated balance sheet immediately after acquisition. Follow the format of Exhibit 17–5.

g. Would there be any expenses to be included on the consolidated income statement in future periods in addition to those reported on the separate income statements of the parent and the subsidiary? Explain.

E17–4. On January 4, 1977, Company P acquired all of the outstanding stock of Company S for $10 per share cash. At the date of acquisition the balance sheet of Company S reflected the following:

Common stock, par $5	$50,000
Retained earnings	30,000

Immediately after the acquisition entry was posted, the balance sheets reflected the following:

	Balances, January 4, 1977, immediately after acquisition	
	Company P	*Company S*
Cash	$ 13,000	$17,000
Receivable from Company P		3,000
Investment in Company S (100%), at cost	100,000	
Fixed assets	122,000	70,000*
Total	$235,000	$90,000
Liabilities	$ 22,000	$10,000
Payable to Company S	3,000	
Common stock (par $5)	150,000	50,000
Retained earnings	60,000	30,000
Total	$235,000	$90,000

* Determined by Company P to have a fair-market value of $78,000 at date of acquisition.

Required:

a. Was this a combination by pooling of interests or by purchase? Explain why.

b. Give the entry that should be made by Company P to record the acquisition.

c. Analyze the acquisition to determine the amount of goodwill purchased.

d. At what value will the assets of Company S be included on the consolidated balance sheet? Explain.

e. Prepare a consolidated balance sheet immediately after acquisition. Follow the format of Exhibit 17–5.

f. Would there be any expenses to be included on the consolidated income statement in future periods in addition to those reported on the separate income statements of the parent and the subsidiary? Explain.

E17–5. On January 1, 1977, Company P acquired all of the outstanding stock of Company S by exchanging one share of its own stock for each share of Company S stock. At the date of the exchange, the balance sheet of Company S showed the following:

Common stock, par $10	$40,000
Retained earnings	10,000

One year after acquisition the two companies prepared their separate financial statements as shown on the following worksheet:

COMPANY P and Its Subsidiary, COMPANY S (100 percent owned)
Consolidated Balance Sheet and Income Statement (pooling basis)
December 31, 1977

	Separate Balance Sheets		Eliminations	Consolidated Statements
	Company P	Company S		
Income Statement (for 1977):				
Sales revenue	96,000	42,000		
Revenue from investments	4,000			
Cost of goods sold	(60,000)	(25,000)		
Expenses (not detailed)	(17,000)	(10,000)		
Net Income	23,000	7,000		
Balance Sheet (at December 31, 1977):				
Cash	21,000	19,000		
Receivable from Company P		2,000		
Investment in Company S (100%)	50,000			
Fixed assets	59,000	47,000		
Total	130,000	68,000		
Liabilities	17,000	15,000		
Payable to Company S	2,000			
Common stock, Company P (par $10)	50,000			
Contributed capital from pooling of interests	10,000			
Common stock, Company S (par $10)		40,000		
Beginning retained earnings, Company P	28,000			
Beginning retained earnings, Company S		10,000		
Dividend paid, 1977, Company S		(4,000)		
Net Income, 1977 (from above)	23,000	7,000		
Total	130,000	68,000		

Required:

a. Give the entry that was made by Company P to record the pooling of interests on January 1, 1977.

b. Complete the Eliminations column in the above worksheet, then combine the two sets of statements in the last column for the income statement and the balance sheet.

(Hint: In completing the two columns, follow the pattern and approaches shown in Exhibit 17–3. Eliminate the revenue from investments against the dividends paid since this represents intercompany revenue. The consolidated net income is $26,000.)

E17–6. (Based on Appendix A.) On January 1, 1977, Company P acquired 100 percent of the outstanding common stock of Company S for $106,000 cash. At that date, Company S reported the following for stockholders' equity: common stock (par $10), $60,000; and retained earnings, $30,000. It also was determined that the fair-market value of the plant and equipment was $6,000 above the book value as reflected on the accounts of Company S. One year after acquisition date, December 31, 1977, the two companies prepared their separate

COMPANY P and Its Subsidiary, COMPANY S (100 percent owned)
Consolidation Worksheet (purchase basis)
Income Statement and Balance Sheet, December 31, 1977

	Statements		Intercompany Eliminations		Consolidated Balances
	Company P	Company S	Debit	Credit	
Income Statement (for 1977):					
Sales	80,000	47,000			
Revenue from investments (*a*)	4,000				
Cost of goods sold	(45,000)	(25,000)			
Expenses (not detailed)	(15,000)	(10,000)			
Depreciation expense (*b*)	(4,000)	(2,000)			
Amortization of goodwill (*c*)					
Net Income	20,000	10,000			
Balance Sheet (at December 31, 1977):					
Cash	15,000	10,000			
Accounts receivable (net)	19,000	9,000			
Receivable from Company P		1,000			
Inventories	70,000	50,000			
Investment in Company S (at cost)	106,000				
Plant and equipment (net)	80,000	40,000			
Goodwill					
Total	290,000	110,000			
Differential:					
Accounts payable	26,000	14,000			
Payable to Company S	1,000				
Common stock, Company P (par $10)	200,000				
Common stock, Company S (par $10)		60,000			
Beginning retained earnings, Company P	50,000				
Beginning retained earnings, Company S		30,000			
Dividends paid during 1977, Company P	(7,000)				
Dividends paid during 1977, Company S		(4,000)			
Net income, 1977	20,000	10,000			
Total	290,000	110,000			

Additional data:

a. Dividends received from Company S.

b. Plant and equipment has a remaining life of 20 years.

c. Assume goodwill is amortized over a period of 20 years.

financial statements as shown on the following consolidation worksheet. You are to complete the worksheet in every respect. Show the analysis of the purchase.

E17–7. (Based on Appendix A.) On January 3, 1977, Company P purchased all of the outstanding stock of Company S at $2.50 per share. At that date the balance sheet of Company S reflected the following:

Common stock, par $1	$20,000
Retained earnings	10,000

One year after acquisition, the two companies prepared their separate financial statements as follows:

	Balances, Dec. 31, 1977	
	Company P	*Company S*
Income Statement:		
Sales	$ 99,000	$59,000
Revenue from investments	6,000	
Expenses (not detailed)	(71,000)	(40,400)
Depreciation expense	(9,000)	(3,600)
Net Income	$ 25,000	$15,000
Balance Sheet:		
Cash	$ 16,000	$ 6,000
Receivable from Company P		4,000
Investment in Company S	50,000	
Fixed assets (net)	90,000	40,000*
Total	$156,000	$50,000
Liabilities	$ 15,000	$11,000
Payable to Company S	4,000	
Common stock, Company P	80,000	
Common stock, Company S		20,000
Beginning retained earnings, Company P	32,000	
Beginning retained earnings, Company S		10,000
Dividends paid, 1977		(6,000)
Net income, 1977	25,000	15,000
Total	$156,000	$50,000

* Fair-market value of the fixed assets at date of acquisition was $12,000 more than their book value. The fixed assets have a remaining life of ten years from date of acquisition.

Required:

a. Give the entry that would be made by Company P to record the purchase on January 3, 1977.

b. Analyze the stock purchase transaction to determine the amount of goodwill purchased. Goodwill will be amortized over 20 years.

c. Prepare a consolidation worksheet (purchase basis) for the income statement and the balance sheet at December 31, 1977.

E17–8. (Based on Appendix B.) This exercise uses the data given in Exercise 17–3 for Company P and Company S, immediately prior to acquisition, and all other data given, except with respect to the number of shares purchased. Assume in this exercise that Company P purchased 70 percent of the outstanding shares of Company S in the open market for $49,000 cash. Immediately after the purchase, the balance sheets reflected the following:

	Balance sheet	
	Company P	*Company S*
Cash	$ 31,000	$18,000
Receivable from Company P		2,000
Investment in Company S (70%) at cost	49,000	
Fixed assets	80,000	60,000
Total	$160,000	$80,000
Liabilities	28,000	20,000
Payable to Company S	2,000	
Common stock (par $10)	100,000	50,000
Retained earnings	30,000	10,000
Total	$160,000	$80,000

Required:

a. Give the entry on the books of Company P to record the purchase.

b. Analyze the purchase to determine the amount of goodwill purchased.

c. Prepare a consolidation worksheet for a balance sheet immediately after acquisition.

d. What is the amount for minority interest that will be reported on the balance sheet?

PROBLEMS

P17–1. During January 1977 Company P acquired all of the outstanding voting shares of Company S by exchanging one share of its own unissued voting common stock for two shares of Company S stock. Immediately prior to the acquisition, the separate balance sheets of the two companies reflected the following:

	Balances immediately prior to acquisition	
	Company P	*Company S*
Cash	$200,000	$ 32,000
Receivable from Company P		3,000
Inventory	75,000	5,000
Fixed assets (net of accumulated depreciation)	75,000	80,000
Goodwill		
Total	$350,000	$120,000

	Balances immediately prior to acquisition	
	Company P	*Company S*
Liabilities	$ 57,000	$ 30,000
Payable to Company S	3,000	
Common stock, Company P (par $4)	180,000	
Common stock, Company S (par $5)		50,000
Contributed capital from pooling		
Retained earnings	110,000	40,000
Total	$350,000	$120,000

Additional data:

At the date of acquisition, Company P stock was quoted on the market at $16 per share; there was no established market for Company S stock.

The fixed assets of Company S were independently appraised at the date of acquisition at $130,000.

Required:

a. Is this a purchase or a pooling of interests? Explain why.
b. What account balances would be changed by the exchange of shares on each of the above balance sheets? List each account and amount.
c. Give the entry that should be made by each company to record the exchange; if no entry is required, explain why.
d. How much goodwill should be recognized? Why?
e. Prepare a consolidated balance sheet immediately after the acquisition.
f. Did you use any fair market values in solving the above requirements? Explain why.

P17–2. Assume the same facts given in Problem 17–1 except that instead of an exchange of shares of stock, Company P purchased for cash from the shareholders individually 100 percent of the outstanding shares of Company S at the market price.

Required:

a. Is this a purchase or a pooling of interests? Explain why.
b. What account balances would be changed by the purchase of the shares on each of the balance sheets? List each account and amount.
c. Give the entry that should be made by each company to record the exchange; if no entry is required, explain why.
d. How much goodwill should be recognized? Why?
e. Prepare a consolidated balance sheet immediately after acquisition.
f. Did you use any fair-market values in solving the above requirements? Explain why.

P17–3. On January 1, 1977, the separate balance sheets of two corporations showed the following:

	Balances, Jan. 1, 1977	
	Company P	*Company S*
Cash	$ 21,000	$ 9,000
Receivable from Company P		4,000
Fixed assets	99,000	32,000
Total	$120,000	$45,000
Liabilities	$ 16,000	$10,000
Payable to Company S	4,000	
Common stock (par $20)	60,000	20,000
Retained earnings	40,000	15,000
Total	$120,000	$45,000

On January 3, 1977, Company P acquired all of the outstanding shares of Company S by exchanging one share of its own stock for two shares of Company S stock.

Required:

a. Was this a combination by pooling of interests or by purchase? Explain why.

b. Company P made the following entry on its books, at date of acquisition, to record the investment:

January 3, 1977:

Investment in stock of Company S	35,000	
Common stock		10,000
Contributed capital from pooling of interests		25,000

Explain the basis for each of the three amounts in this entry.

c. Will any goodwill be recognized on the consolidated balance sheet? Explain why.

d. Prepare a consolidated balance sheet immediately after the acquisition. Follow the format shown in Exhibit 17–3.

P17–4. On January 2, 1977, Company P acquired all of the outstanding stock of Company S by exchanging its own stock for the stock of Company S. One share of Company P stock was exchanged for two shares of Company S stock. Immediately after the acquisition was recorded by Company P, the balance sheets reflected the following:

	Balances, Jan. 2, 1977 immediately after acquisition	
	Company P	*Company S*
Cash	$ 38,000	$26,000
Receivable from Company S	6,000	
Inventory	30,000	10,000
Investment in Company S (100%)	70,000	
Fixed assets (net)	90,000	50,000
Other assets	6,000	4,000
Total	$240,000	$90,000
Liabilities	$ 16,000	$14,000
Payable to Company P		6,000
Common stock (par $5)	125,000	50,000
Contributed capital from pooling of interest	45,000	
Retained earnings	54,000	20,000
Total	$240,000	$90,000

Required:

a. Was this a combination by pooling of interests or by purchase? Explain why.

b. Give the journal entry that was made by Company P to record the acquisition on January 2, 1977. Explain the basis for each amount included in the entry.

c. At what amounts will the assets of Company S be included on the consolidated balance sheet? Explain.

d. Will any goodwill be recognized on the consolidated balance sheet? Explain why.

e. Prepare a consolidated balance sheet immediately after acquisition. Follow the format illustrated in Exhibit 17–3.

P17–5. On January 5, 1977, Company P purchased all of the outstanding stock of Company S for $100,000 cash. Immediately after the acquisition the separate balance sheets of the two companies reflected the following:

	Jan. 5, 1977, immediately after acquisition	
	Company P	*Company S*
Cash	$ 22,000	$ 9,000
Accounts receivable (net)	14,000	6,000
Receivable from Company S	4,000	
Inventory	50,000	25,000
Investment in Company S (at cost)	100,000	
Fixed assets (net)	153,000	67,000
Other assets	7,000	3,000
Total	$350,000	$110,000

	Jan. 5, 1977, immediately after acquisition	
	Company P	*Company S*
Accounts payable	$ 20,000	$ 16,000
Payable to Company P		4,000
Bonds payable	90,000	
Common stock (par $5)	180,000	60,000
Contributed capital, in excess of par	8,000	
Retained earnings	52,000	30,000
Total	$350,000	$110,000

The fixed assets of Company S were estimated to have a fair-market value at date of acquisition of $71,000.

Required:

a. Was this a combination by pooling of interests or by purchase? Explain why.

b. Give the entry that would be made in the accounts of Company P at date of acquisition.

c. Analyze the acquisition to determine the amount of goodwill purchased.

d. At what amounts will the assets of Company S, the subsidiary, be included on the consolidated balance sheet immediately after acquisition? Explain.

e. Prepare a consolidated balance sheet immediately after acquisition. Follow the format illustrated in Exhibit 17–5.

f. Will there be any additional expenses to include on the income statements for future periods other than those reported on the separate income statements for the parent and the subsidiary? Explain.

P17–6. On January 4, 1977, Company P purchased 100 percent of the outstanding common stock of Company S for $240,000 cash. Immediately after the acquisition, the separate balance sheets for the two companies were prepared as shown in the worksheet below.

It was determined at date of acquisition that, on the basis of fair-market value compared with the book value, the assets as reflected on the books of Company S, should be adjusted as follows: (*a*) inventories should be reduced by $3,000; (*b*) plant and equipment should be increased to $148,000; and (*c*) land should be increased by $2,000.

Required:

a. Was this a combination by pooling of interests or by purchase? Explain why.

b. Give the entry that was made on the books of Company P to record the acquisition.

c. Analyze the acquisition transaction to determine the amount of goodwill purchased. Use data from the worksheet below if needed.

d. At what amount will the assets of Company S be included on the consolidated balance sheet? Explain.

e. Complete the "Eliminations" column in the form below and then extend the amounts for the consolidated balance sheet.

COMPANY P and Its Subsidiary, COMPANY S
Consolidated Balance Sheet
January 4, 1977, Immediately after Acquisition

	Separate balance sheets			
	Company P	*Company S*	*Eliminations*	*Consolidated balance sheet*
Assets				
Cash	80,000	40,000		
Accounts receivable (net)	26,000	19,000		
Receivable from Company P		8,000		
Inventories	170,000	80,000		
Long-term investment, bonds, Z Company	15,000			
Long-term investment, Company S	240,000			
Land	12,000	3,000		
Plant and equipment (net)	157,000	130,000		
Goodwill				
Total Assets	700,000	280,000		
Liabilities				
Accounts payable	22,000	40,000		
Payable to Company S	8,000			
Bonds payable, 5%	100,000	30,000		
Shareholders' Equity				
Common stock, Company P	500,000			
Common stock, Company S (par $10)		150,000		
Retained earnings, Company P	70,000			
Retained earnings, Company S		60,000		
Total Liabilities and Shareholders' Equity	700,000	280,000		

P17–7. This problem presents the income statement and the balance sheet on a consolidated basis for Company P and its subsidiary, Company S, one year after acquisition, under two different assumptions: Case A—pooling-of-interests basis, and Case B—purchase basis. The two different assumptions are used so that we can compare and analyze the differences.

On January 2, 1977, Company P acquired all of the outstanding common stock of Company S. At that date the shareholders' equity of Company S showed the following: common stock, par $10, $50,000; and retained earnings, $20,000. The entry made by Company P to record the acquisition under each case was as follows:

Case A—Pooling-of-Interests Basis			*Case B—Purchase Basis*		
Investment in Company S (5,000 shares, 100 percent)	70,000		Investment in Company S (5,000 shares, 100 percent)	80,000	
Common stock...		40,000	Cash.................		80,000
Contributed capital from pooling of interests.........		30,000			

On January 2, 1977, the acquisition by purchase was analyzed to determine the goodwill as follows:

Purchase price paid for 100% interest in Company S..................	$80,000
Stockholders' equity of Company S (at book value) purchased, $50,000 + $20,000	70,000
Difference—excess paid over book value.................................	10,000
Analysis of the difference:	
To fixed assets (fair-market value, $42,000—book value, $40,000 = $2,000 increase)..	2,000
Remainder—goodwill purchased	$ 8,000

For consolidated statement purposes the fixed assets are being depreciated over 10 years' remaining life and the goodwill will be amortized over 20 years.

One year after acquisition, the two companies prepared separate income statements and balance sheets. These separate statements have been consolidated under each case as reflected on page 727.

Required:

a. Prepare a schedule that shows what items are different on each statement for Case A, compared with Case B.

b. Explain the reasons why net income is different under pooling versus purchase. Use the amounts from the two statements in your explanation and tell why they are different.

c. Explain why the cash balance is different between the two cases.

d. What was the balance in the account "Investment in Company S" prior to its elimination? Explain.

e. Explain why the fixed asset amount is different between the two cases.

f. Why is there a difference in goodwill between the two cases?

g. Why does goodwill reflect a balance of $7,600, compared with the $8,000 computed above for goodwill at date of acquisition?

h. How much was eliminated for intercompany debt? Why was it eliminated?

i. What was the amount of "Common stock, Company S" that was eliminated? Why was it eliminated?

j. Why was only $20,000 of the $30,000 of contributed capital from pooling of interests eliminated?

k. Explain why the account "Contributed Capital in Excess of Par, $10,000" was not eliminated.

l. Explain why "Beginning retained earnings, Company S, $20,000," is shown under Case A (pooling) but not under Case B (purchase).

COMPANY P and Its Subsidiary, COMPANY S (100% Owned)
Consolidated Income Statement and Balance Sheet
December 31, 1977

	Consolidated statements December 31, 1977	
	Pooling basis (Case A)	*Purchase basis (Case B)*
Income Statement (for Year Ended December 31, 1977):		
Sales revenue	$236,000	$236,000
Revenue from investments ($4,000, eliminated)		
Cost of goods sold	(112,000)	(112,000)
Expenses (not detailed to simplify)	(75,500)	(75,500)
Depreciation expense	(12,500)	(12,700)
Amortization expense (goodwill)		(400)
Net Income	$ 36,000	$ 35,400
Balance Sheet (at December 31, 1977):		
Assets		
Cash	$128,000	$ 48,000
Accounts receivable (net)	53,000	53,000
Receivable from Company S ($5,000, eliminated)		
Inventory	37,000	37,000
Investment in Company S (eliminated)		
Fixed assets (net)	125,000	126,800
Goodwill		7,600
Total	$343,000	$272,400
Liabilities		
Current liabilities	$ 30,000	$ 30,000
Payable to Company P (eliminated)		
Bonds payable	50,000	50,000
Shareholders' Equity		
Common stock, Company P	140,000	100,000
Common stock, Company S (eliminated)		
Contributed capital in excess of par	10,000	10,000
Contributed capital from pooling of interests ($20,000, eliminated)	10,000	
Beginning retained earnings, Company P	47,000	47,000
Beginning retained earnings, Company S	20,000	
Dividends paid in 1977 (eliminated)		
Net income, 1977 (from income statement above)	36,000	35,400
Total	$343,000	$272,400

P17–8. (Note: This problem goes beyond the discussion in the text with respect to discontinued operations.)

Refer to Exhibit 17–7 as the basis for responding to the following questions:

General:

a. What periods are covered by the financial statements?
b. Are these comparative statements? Explain.

Income Statement:

c. Is this a multiple-step income statement? Explain.
d. Were any extraordinary items reported for either years?
e. What do you understand the part captioned "Discontinued operations" to mean? Is there evidence of intraperiod income tax allocation on the income statement? Explain.
f. Why were four EPS amounts presented in 1974?
g. What items on the 1975 income statement specifically relate to subsidiaries? Explain each.

Retained Earnings:

h. Were any prior period adjustments reported?

Balance Sheet:

i. What asset items specifically related (1) to consolidated subsidiaries and (2) to nonconsolidated subsidiaries? Explain.
j. How is the minority interest reported on the balance sheet? Explain what it means.

Notes to the Financial Statements:

k. What is the parent company's accounting policy with respect to nonconsolidated subsidiaries?
l. In your opinion, does Note 2 meet the requirements of the full-disclosure principle in respect to the discontinued operations? Why?
m. In your opinion, does Note 11 meet the requirements of the full-disclosure principle in respect to "Investments?" Why.
n. What amount of goodwill was reported in 1975? What was its source? What amortization policy is being followed?

P17–9. (Based on Appendix A.) On January 1, 1977, Company P purchased 100 percent of the outstanding capital stock of Company S for $98,000 cash. At that date the stockholders' section of the balance sheet of Company S reflected the following:

Capital stock, $10 par, 5,000 shares outstanding	$50,000
Retained earnings	30,000
	$80,000

At the date of acquisition, it was determined that the fair-market value of certain assets of Company S, in comparison with the book value of those assets as reflected on the balance sheet of Company S, should be reflected by (*a*) decreasing inventories by $2,000 and (*b*) increasing equipment by $8,000.

It is now one year after acquisition, December 31, 1977, and each company has prepared the following separate financial statements (summarized):

	Company P	*Company S*
Balance Sheet (at December 31, 1977):		
Cash	$ 52,000	$ 30,000
Accounts receivable (net)	31,000	10,000
Receivable from Company P		3,000
Inventories	60,000	70,000
Investment in Company S (at cost)	98,000	
Equipment	80,000	20,000
Other assets	9,000	17,000
	$330,000	$150,000
Accounts payable	$ 42,000	$ 30,000
Payable to Company S	3,000	
Bonds payable, 5%	70,000	30,000
Capital stock ($10 par)	140,000	50,000
Beginning retained earnings	50,000	30,000
Dividend paid during 1977	(10,000)	(5,000)
Net income for 1977 (from income statement)	35,000	15,000
	$330,000	$150,000
Income Statement (for 1977):		
Sales revenue	$360,000	$140,000
Revenue from investments	5,000	
Cost of goods sold	(220,000)	(80,000)
Expenses (not detailed)	(106,000)	(44,000)
Depreciation expense	(4,000)	(1,000)
Net Income	$ 35,000	$ 15,000

Additional data during 1977:

1. Near the end of 1977, Company S declared and paid a cash dividend amounting to $5,000.
2. The equipment is being depreciated on the basis of a 20-year remaining life.
3. Goodwill is to be amortized over a 40-year period.

Required:

a. Give the entry on the books of Company P to record the acquisition of the capital stock of Company S on January 1, 1977.

b. Analyze the acquisition of the stock to determine the purchased goodwill.

c. Prepare a consolidation worksheet (purchase basis) for the year 1977 as a basis for the 1977 income statement and balance sheet. (Hint: Consolidated net income is $44,300.)

d. Prepare a consolidated income statement and balance sheet based on the data provided by the consolidation worksheet.

P17–10. (Based on Appendix B.) On January 1, 1977, Company P purchased 90 percent of the outstanding capital stock of Company S for $100,000 cash. At the date of acquisition, the stockholders' equity accounts of Company S reflected the following: Capital Stock (par $10), $60,000; Contributed Capital in Excess of Par, $10,000; and Retained Earnings, $20,000. At that date it was determined that the book value of the fixed assets was $10,000 less than their fair-market value.

It is now December 31, 1977, and each company has independently prepared the following financial statements (summarized):

	Company P	*Company S*
Balance Sheet (at December 31, 1977):		
Cash	$ 23,000	$ 11,000
Accounts receivable (net)	57,000	13,000
Receivable from Company P		7,000
Inventories	110,000	24,000
Investment in Company S (at cost; 90% owned)	100,000	
Fixed assets (net)	120,000	50,000
Other assets	6,000	5,000
	$416,000	$110,000
Accounts payable	$ 30,000	$ 8,000
Payable to Company S	7,000	
Bonds payable, 5%	80,000	10,000
Capital stock ($10 par)	200,000	60,000
Contributed capital, in excess of par	4,000	10,000
Beginning retained earnings	80,000	20,000
Dividends paid, 1977	(15,000)	(8,000)
Net income (from income statement)	30,000	10,000
	$416,000	$110,000
Income Statement (for 1977):		
Sales revenue	$195,000	$ 75,000
Revenue from investments	7,200	
Cost of goods sold	(115,000)	(43,000)
Expenses (not detailed)	(52,200)	(19,500)
Depreciation expense	(5,000)	(2,500)
	$ 30,000	$ 10,000

Required:

a. Give the entry on the books of Company P to record the acquisition of the stock of Company S.

b. Analyze the stock purchase to determine the amount of purchased goodwill.

c. Prepare a consolidation worksheet (purchase basis) for a balance sheet and income statement for 1977. Assume the fixed assets of Company S has a 10-year remaining life and that any goodwill will be amortized over 20 years. (Hint: Consolidated net income is $31,400.)

d. Prepare a classified income statement and balance sheet based upon the data provided by the consolidation worksheet.

e. What is the minority interest claim to earnings and shareholders' equity at December 31, 1977?

Index

Q–R

This book has been set in 10 point and 9 point Times Roman, leaded 2 points. Chapter numbers are in 48 point Helvetica Medium and chapter titles are in 18 point Helvetica. The size of the type page is 27 by 46½ picas.